BORDER TEXTS

BORDER TEXTS

CULTURAL READINGS FOR CONTEMPORARY WRITERS

RANDALL BASS
GEORGETOWN UNIVERSITY

HOUGHTON MIFFLIN COMPANY BOSTON NEW YORK

Senior Sponsoring Editor: Suzanne Phelps Weir
Senior Associate Editor: Janet Edmonds
Senior Project Editor: Rosemary R. Jaffe
Production/Design Coordinator: Jennifer Meyer Dare
Senior Manufacturing Coordinator: Sally Culler
Senior Marketing Manager: Nancy Lyman

Cover Designer: Linda Manley Wade
Cover Photo Researcher: Linda Sykes
Cover Image: Dance Beneath the Diamond Sky by Cathleen Toelke

Since this page cannot legibly accommodate all the copyright notices, pages 682–686 constitute an extension of the copyright page.

Printed in the U.S.A.

Library of Congress Catalog Card Number: 98-71984

ISBN: 0-395-67728-9

2   3   4   5   6   7   8   9-DH-02   01   00   99

As part of Houghton Mifflin's ongoing
commitment to the environment, this text
has been printed on recycled paper.

CONTENTS

THRee

BORDERS OF COMMUNITY:
Belonging and Alienation

FOUR

BORDERS AS BARRIERS:
Otherness and Difference

BORDER VISIONS:

seven

THE WORLD'S NEW BORDERS:
Globalism Versus Tribalism

PREFACE TO INSTRUCTORS

Border Texts: Cultural Readings for Contemporary Writers is designed to help introductory writing students become critical writers, readers, and thinkers by exploring the borders that construct the world we live in and the texts we read and write. These borders are the spaces—physical spaces, social and cultural spaces, or written, oral, and visual communication spaces—where meaningful exchanges happen. The thematically arranged readings raise ideas related to individual and group identity; community and culture; belonging, otherness, and difference; and a sense of place—local, national, global. The connections among these ideas help students begin to think and write critically about how the ways we construct a sense of the world shape and are shaped by how we reconstruct that world in the texts we read and write.

EXPLORING A WIDE VARIETY OF TEXTS

Border Texts' readings present a wide variety of writing styles, genres, voices, and disciplinary orientations. They include literary and nonliterary texts, prose, and poetry. The prose works are chosen from various forms of fiction and storytelling, journalism, autobiography, and many other forms of the essay, as well as certain kinds of cultural documents and artifacts. Indeed, a large number of the texts included belong to the "hybrid genres" of writing that have proliferated in the last ten or twenty years: combinations of personal and political essays, of autobiography and cultural criticism. *Border Texts* also features a wide range of visual and graphic documents, treated seriously as texts for viewers to "read," which help students develop a repertoire of skills for cultural and textual analysis and that extend the definition (the borders) of the word "text."

The rich array of texts in *Border Texts* encourages students to explore relationships among individuals, groups, nations, and international communities. Throughout their exploration, three fundamental issues recur:

1. how individuals derive and express self-identity
2. how individuals connect to one another through groups of various kinds, such as cultures and communities
3. how groups define themselves, interact with other groups, and exist either in harmony or in tension in larger social units such as nations and international communities

As these issues recur, questions at the end of each selection and at the end of each chapter raise the level of inquiry from chapter to chapter. The questions ask students to think about the many shaping influences on identity, the relationship between definition of self-identity and the perception of others, and the ways that individuals and groups connect or do not connect across their differences. The recurring ideas and questions create a balance between thematic coherence and flexibility that challenges and engages students.

AN INTERCULTURAL AND INTERACTIVE BOOK

The wide range of American voices in *Border Texts* represents all the power and perils of an open and heterogeneous society. I have chosen the readings and developed the extensive apparatus with the goal of helping students become comfortable with important issues and expressive modes of American interculturalism. At the same time, I have tried to make *Border Texts* an interactive book by emphasizing active engagement at all levels of the reading and writing processes. One of the founding ideas of this book is that students learn how to read and write when they can freely cross the borders between writer and reader, student and critic, consumer and producer. Creating a classroom and course environment dedicated to this kind of boundary crossing is the most important pedagogical principle behind this book. The book itself—as well as the complementary Web site—encourages interactivity in four ways:

1. *Border Texts* encourages students to read interactively and exposes them to concepts and tools necessary to engage on a high level with texts. These concepts and tools include different kinds of reading and writing activities for re-working and interrogating the texts they read. An important part of being an interactive reader, emphasized throughout, is learning to engage critically as well as playfully with texts of all kinds at every stage of the reading process.

2. The book's pedagogical apparatus is also built around the interaction of students with other students, especially through group thinking and writing on questions at the end of the readings. The writing and group-work exercises can also be used to actively engage students in reading and critiquing each other's writing as well as encouraging them to utilize and incorporate each other's writing into their own, treating their peers' writing as "secondary sources" that they must cite and integrate. This latter activity is a further step in getting students to cross boundaries between being consumers and creators of texts, and is covered more fully in the Instructor's Resource Manual and on the Web site.

3. The apparatus and contents also encourage the interaction of texts with other texts. That is, the arrangement of selections makes it possible and productive to consider multiple texts (written, visual, or electronic) together. This "constellation" approach to reading and writing is a vital part of the book's philosophy of putting students at the center of texts and is premised on the idea that students understand individual texts better when they rigorously consider them in combination with other texts.

4. Finally, *Border Texts* encourages students to engage in interactive learning through electronic texts and spaces on the World Wide Web. Throughout the book and on its Web site, students are asked to consider how electronic writing environments and virtual communities are changing how we interact with each other and how readers and writers interact with texts.

STRUCTURE AND ORGANIZATION

Chapter 1, Approaching Borders: Critical Thinking, Reading, and Writing, provides a foundation for the thinking, reading, and writing skills developed throughout the book. The subsequent six chapters build on each other and fall into three groupings:

Chapter 2, Borders of Identity: Stories of the Self and Home, and Chapter 3, Borders of Community: Belonging and Alienation, focus on issues of self-identity, community, and how we develop a sense of place and belonging.

Chapter 4, Borders as Barriers: Otherness and Difference, and Chapter 5, Negotiating Borders: The Dynamics of Difference, are built around issues of difference and the dynamics of differences among individuals and groups.

Chapter 6, Borders and Frontiers: Imagined and Virtual Communities, and Chapter 7, The World's New Borders: Globalism Versus Tribalism, extend these issues to larger concepts of culture, geography, and the political and social implications of group identities in the context of "imagined communities," whether the nation, cyberspace, or global communities.

Border Visions: An Image Portfolio contains sixteen black-and-white images on themes that resonate with the readings throughout the book. The sixteen plates in the Image Portfolio are complemented by a framing essay on reading visual images and pedagogical notes and questions on each image.

FEATURES

I have built in pedagogical continuity among the four key structural components of each of the six thematic chapters (Chapters 2 through 7):

Critical Questions (at the beginning of each chapter)
Framing Essay (at the beginning of each chapter)
Working with the Text Questions (after each reading)
Thinking and Writing: Critical Questions Revisited (at the end of each chapter)

Altogether these components serve as springboards to all kinds of activities, ranging from fieldwork, to group work, to writing, to Web site exploration.

Critical Questions   Each chapter begins with a set of Critical Questions intended to frame students' reading and rereading of all the selections in the chapter and to provide a broad context for their writing.

Framing Essay   Each chapter opens with a seven-to-ten-page framing essay that poses the key issues of the selections. The purpose of the essay is both to clarify some key terms and concepts for the chapter and to raise more fully the key "problems" posed in the Critical Questions.

Working with the Text Questions   Each selection concludes with Working with the Text questions that ask students to focus on the writing and ideas in that selection. Students' responses may range from personal experience to a close rereading of the text looking at particular strategies employed by the author. Students' responses may be written or discussed. The Working with the Text questions also ask students to engage in fieldwork (alone or in groups) or in electronic research on the Web.

Thinking and Writing: Critical Questions Revisited   These questions for critical thinking and writing at the end of each chapter focus on particular writing topics addressed to the overall themes in each chapter. These questions revisit the Critical Questions, as well as the key points discussed in the introductory essays, and reframe the chapter's key issues as writing topics.

***Border Texts Online* World Wide Web Site**   *Border Texts* is also accompanied by an extensive World Wide Web site that is a source for critical thinking about cyberspace and the Web, as well as electronic fieldwork into issues of identity, community, place, and difference. It is also a platform for links to research and resources building on all topics in the book and a hypertext guide to the integration of concepts across the book. The Web Site address is http://www.hmco.com/hmco/college/english/bass/.

My experience has shown me that course-based materials can be a resource for critical thinking and writing if they 1) open up areas of knowledge for students by challenging them to think about big ideas that they had never considered or rethink ones they had taken for granted, 2) engage them with specific texts, activities, ideas, and resources that allow them to move in directions that they find most compelling, and 3) give them a set of pedagogical resources where complex ideas are presented in a coherent and recursive way. Achieving these goals—opening up important ideas and giving students a coherent environment in which to construct their own paths to understanding—has governed the creation of this book.

ACKNOWLEDGMENTS

I have many people to thank for their help with this book. For the time they took to review and comment extensively on drafts I am grateful to the following colleagues at other insitutions:

Peter Baker, Towson University
Diane Bogus, DeAnza College
Warren Carson, University of South Carolina–Spartanburg
Wendy Chapkis, University of California–Santa Cruz
Ashley J. Cross, Manhattan College
Juan Delgado, California State University–San Bernardino
Mary Helen Dunlop, Iowa State
Fritz Fleischmann, Babson College
John Heyda, Miami University–Middletown
Malcolm Kiniry, Rutgers University–Newark
Ted Lardner, Cleveland State University
Anne Laskaya, University of Oregon
Marie Long, University of Louisville
John Lowney, St. John's University
Sarah-Hope Parmeter, University of California–Santa Cruz
Duane H. Roen, Syracuse University
James E. Seitz, University of Pittsburgh
Leaf Seligman, University of New Hampshire
Margaret L. Shaw, Kent State University
Daphne Swabey, Eastern Michigan State University

I also want to express thanks to the students and colleagues on my own campus who helped me with the book over the past few years: Rose Saxe, Hien Nguyen, Susan Stark, Alison Schneider, Tony Krackeler, Leona Fisher, Lucy Maddox, Andrea Chiu, and Eric Hofmann.

My thanks also to my editors at Houghton Mifflin over the years, including Kristin Watts Peri (who started it all by imagining my course as a book project in the first place), George Kane and Jayne Fargnoli (who encouraged me to take some chances and be true to my original ideas), and Janet Edmonds and Rosemary Jaffe (who ruined office pools throughout Houghton Mifflin by actually bringing this book to press).

I am deeply indebted to Mark Gallaher without whom this book absolutely, positively would not have seen the light of day (and whose phone number is still taped to my wall under the name "St. Mark").

And finally, I am ever so grateful to the jewels of my life, Eli and Gail, for their patience and support, even though I'm quite sure that the past six years have slipped by without anyone around me so much as noticing that I was working on this book.

R. B.

ONE

APPROACHING BORDERS:

Critical Thinking,
Reading,
and
Writing

BORDER TEXTS AND PLACES

This is a book about the many borders that hold together the United States and its people. To say that our borders hold us together may seem a little odd. Normally, when we think of a border, we think of something that divides two places, such as the border between two states or between two countries. We usually think of borders as geographical lines—dividers that have some kind of physical presence or political meaning. And indeed, that kind of geographical and separating border is one of the many kinds of borders that this book addresses. But this book's idea of a "border" implies much more than something which merely divides two places.

A border in this text could be defined as *any place where differences come together*, whether these are national differences, cultural and social differences, differences in values or language, differences in gender, or differences in family heritage or economic status. Therefore, this book focuses on all of the many borders that shape individual identity as well as American cultural identity itself. Whether individual or cultural, our identities are constructed by borders: racial and ethnic borders, economic and class borders, borders of sexuality and gender, and borders that separate different levels of community, such as family and neighborhood. Borders even define America's sense of itself as a nation and its place in the international community. Such borders are both real and imaginary, physical and symbolic. A border can be something you can see, like the Rio Grande River that runs between the United

States and Mexico, or something you can't see, like the hidden prejudices that might keep one kind of people out of a neighborhood or away from the higher paying jobs in a company.

The idea of *borders* in this book is much like the idea of *borderlands* described by contemporary American writer Gloria Anzaldúa[1]. For Anzaldúa, who comes from Texas, the *borderlands* are, in part, the social territory on both sides of the Southwestern U.S.–Mexican border. But, she explains, other kinds of borderlands also exist, such as psychological, sexual, and spiritual borderlands. These borderlands are not particular to the Southwest, she says. In fact,

> the Borderlands are physically present wherever two or more cultures edge each other, where people of different races occupy the same territory, where under, lower, middle, and upper classes touch, where the space between two individuals shrinks with intimacy.

The flexibility of Anzaldúa's concept of *borderlands* aptly expresses the kinds of borders this book explores, borders that we all live within and cross and share every day, whether walking in the city, riding the bus, watching the news, cruising the mall, navigating the Internet, dealing with our families, or sitting in the classroom.

To say that borders are "places where differences come together" implies something beyond mere differences. Where differences come together, people or groups are rarely on equal footing. There is usually an imbalance of something: power, resources, capital, trust, understanding, or desire. No matter who you are, throughout your life you will be negotiating these borders—making transactions across boundaries and maneuvering among differences.

However, the thesis of *Border Texts* is that borders are not static dividing lines or barriers of difference but rather *places* where something happens. *Borders are never neutral.* They always convey *some* kind of difference: differences in status, resources, power, ideas, values, hopes, history, language, or culture. And the medium through which these differences find expression—whether a poem, a photograph, an essay, a story, or a billboard—is what this book calls a "border text." Border texts express the stress, creativity, tension, energy, hope, and power that exist where differences meet. Although differences may often be the source of conflict, they are not necessarily negative. What "happens" where differences meet is fundamental to social relationships, acts of communication, and the expression of one's own identity. In border texts and at "border crossings" both exciting and difficult things can happen.

In this sense border texts are a lot like border places: that is, in this book we'll look at writing as places where something happens; places where people meet across their differences, places where differences are overcome in the attempt to create meaning. There are always multiple levels of meaning in any text. All texts are formed by a perspective, and all writers and texts are embedded in cultural contexts and are thereby influenced by them. *Border Texts* encourages you to see how your own identity and perspective are shaped by cultural influences and to reflect on those influences so you can be more thoughtful about the texts you read and write. This book urges you to pay attention to how ideas travel across your cultural environment through images and media, through politics and journalism, through music and fashion, from graffiti written on freeway abutments to interactive Web

---

1. See Gloria Anzaldúa's essay "La conciencia de la mestiza," from her book *Borderlands,* in Chapter 7.

sites. Finally, looking at books as border texts is a new way of looking at certain fundamental American issues, including what it means to be an American and what it means for the United States to survive as a nation of diverse peoples. And it means thinking about the world as a whole, determining whether it is coming together or breaking down into hostile, small pieces—or perhaps doing both.

CRITICAL READING ACROSS BORDERS

As you begin to consider the concept of borders, it may be useful to start by thinking about maps, the places where traditional ideas of borders are most graphically represented. So, for starters, here is a "map" of our country. Actually, it's not a map at all, but rather a poem by Adrienne Rich about a map. Rich is one of the best-known contemporary American poets (see her essay in Chapter 4). This excerpt is part of a long poem called *An Atlas of the Difficult World*.

An Atlas of the Difficult World

Adrienne Rich

Here is a map of our country:
here is the Sea of Indifference, glazed with salt
This is the haunted river flowing from brow to groin
we dare not taste its water
This is the desert where missiles are planted like corns   5
This is the breadbasket of foreclosed farms
This is the birthplace of the rockabilly boy
This is the cemetery of the poor
who died for democracy   This is a battlefield
from a nineteenth-century war   the shrine is famous   10
This is the sea-town of myth and story   when the fishing fleets
went bankrupt   here is where the jobs were   on the pier
processing frozen fishsticks   hourly wages and no shares
These are other battlefields   Centralia   Detroit
here are the forests primeval   the copper   the silver lodes   15
These are the Suburbs of acquiescence   silence rising fumelike
          from the streets
This is the capital of money and dolor whose spires
flare up through air inversions whose bridges are crumbling
whose children are drifting blind alleys pent   20

between coiled rolls of razor wire
I promised to show you a map you say but this is a mural
then yes let it be   these are small distinctions
where do we see it from is the question

Now, there might be a number of things that are suggestive, puzzling, or elusive about Rich's poem. Let's focus first on her conclusion. What do you suppose Rich means when she maintains that her poem may be either a "map" or a "mural"? (Think of a mural that you've seen on a wall in some public place or in a book or look at the murals on the Web linked off of the *Border Texts* site. Then look at the painting *American Progress,* by John Gast, which is Plate 13 in the Image Portfolio— a painting that resembles a mural.)

> What might Rich mean when stating that the difference between a map and mural is a "small distinction"?
> And what might she mean when she declares that "where do we see it from is the question"?

By saying this, she implies that "maps" work with one set of rules, codes, and symbols, and "murals" work with another. Maps have one purpose, and murals have another, just as maps are one medium and poems another. One difference might be that maps are supposed to represent a place "objectively" while murals tell stories, perhaps from a particular point of view. However, Rich may be implying that even maps tell stories since "places" carry a certain history and certain cultural connotations. Maybe maps and murals are not all that different because places and their stories are hard to separate.

Now, let's try to put Rich's poem in perspective. One of the many ways to do this is to look at a few other maps. First, look at the two maps on pages 461 and 462 of Chapter 6. The map on page 461 is a conventional map of the world. The map on page 462 is called the "Peters' projection" map. The Peters' projection represents the countries of the world strictly according to their actual size in square miles. Traditional Western projections (such as the Mercator's projection and the more contemporary Robinson's projection) correct for the curvature of the earth by exaggerating the size of areas near and above the equator. Consequently, the United States and Western Europe appear proportionally larger than they really are. The Peters' projection de-emphasizes the United States and Western Europe. Many people feel that the Peters' projection more accurately represents underdeveloped nations. Others think that it is misleading, unscientific, and merely propaganda. (You can read more about the debate over the Peters' projection map in the selection "Maps, Projections and Ethnocentricity" in Chapter 6.)

Next look at a third map image, Plate 1 of the Image Portfolio. This map, created by Jesse Levine, is called the "Turnabout" map. Unlike the Peters' projection map, which was intended to help plan accurately for world economic development needs, the Turnabout map was made strictly for rhetorical purposes. That is, it takes the convention of putting North America at the top of the map and purposely turns it on its head. What the Turnabout map tries to show is how disorienting it can be to see something so familiar in reversed perspective. The Turnabout map tries to displace the United States from its usual "superior" location on the map for special effect. But do you think that the effect of viewing the Turnabout map would be the same for everyone? Would someone from Latin America have the same feelings about the reversal as someone from the United States?

All of the texts we have looked at so far—the three maps, the mural, and the poem—in some way *represent* the United States. None of the texts *is* the United States itself. In other words, texts are not the things they talk about, but rather *representations* of the things they talk about. And each kind of text uses its own particular symbols and language to create its representation. Each text, then, requires that you know certain things in order to make sense of it. You have to know something about a map to read a map, and you have to know something about a poem to read a poem. (Of course, in this case you have to know something about a map—and something about history and geography—to make sense of the poem, too.

Perhaps this is one way to understand the final lines of Rich's poem. She says:

I promised to show you a map you say but this is a mural
then yes let it be   these are small distinctions
where do we see it from is the question

When you consider the three maps side by side, you can see that even maps are a matter of perspective and that each map tells a story about the context from which it is drawn. Even maps are made to serve particular interests, represent certain histories, and argue certain ideas. Similarly, Rich seems to be implying that maps and murals are not that different because all acts of representation are embedded in a particular context and cannot be separated from the perspective that produces or sees it.

So what does this have to do with "critical reading"? We live in a world significantly shaped by texts: visual texts, written texts, printed texts, electronic texts, texts that tell stories, texts that try to inform, persuade, confuse, excite, or entertain you. Each of these texts operates by different rules, using different languages, strategies, symbols, and styles. In order to live wisely in a world filled with texts and images, it is important to be not just a reader but also a critical reader. Being a critical reader doesn't mean that you have to interpret, analyze, and dissect every text you encounter all day long but rather that you can if you want and need to do so. Furthermore, as much as we are shaped by texts, we can also shape ourselves through our own articulated texts. Every time we represent or express ourselves in writing, we actively exert a shaping influence on our immediate world. Becoming critical about your own expression is as important as reading critically.

Being a critical reader and writer has a lot to do with this book's central theme of borders, not only in terms of content but also in terms of its whole approach to reading and writing. Whenever you sit and examine a piece of writing or art—whether a work of fiction or poetry, a magazine article, a photograph, or another student's essay for a class assignment—you are standing at a border. To return to our original definition, if a border is a place where differences meet, then as a reader of a text, you are always at the border of someone else's meaning. On the other side of that page, on the other side of those words or images, is a whole set of ideas and experiences. To understand a writer's or artist's meaning, you have to encounter that expression on its own terms—its language, its images, its points of tension, and its manner of combining parts into a whole. The process called critical reading involves learning how to cross that border and get into the text's world of experience and meaning. It is a means to understand a text's influence or the ways that it has been shaped by a culture.

When you are critically reading a piece of writing, you're not just paying attention to what it says. You are also able to recognize and think about *how* it is saying things, able to read beyond surface meanings to understand the assumptions, arguments, and strategies behind them. Critical reading means learning about how texts work: how they express their meanings, how they appeal to your emotions and intellect, how they present arguments that are explicit and implicit, how they reason with you or try to persuade or even manipulate you.

One way to think of critical reading is to see it as the process of *slowing down* your reading. This doesn't mean you ought to read more slowly; it means that you need to read in such a way that you learn to be aware of a text's or image's various parts and processes. As you run your eye over the words on a page, for example, it is easy to think of any piece of writing as a smooth and solid object. But all writing— whether a short story by a famous writer or a paper by one of your classmates—is the result of a process and the product of a context. Both the process and the context that produce a piece of writing are reflected in various ways in a text's parts and layers. When you slow down your reading, you will see better the many components that come together during the writing process to create something that *seems* whole.

THE LANGUAGE OF BORDER TEXTS

There is a very important and basic connection in this book between what it means to think critically about texts and the formation of individual and cultural identity. If all texts are formed by a perspective, constructed through a process, and embedded in cultural contexts, then something similar is true for the individuals and cultural contexts that produce them. Individuals have perspectives that have been shaped by the complexity of the contexts in which they've lived, just as a text is shaped by *its* context. Exploring the relationship between individuals and these contexts—and their shaping power—is central to this book's purpose.

In fact, the focus of *Border Texts* is three fundamental sets of ideas: (1) how individuals derive and express a sense of self-identity; (2) how they connect to each other through groups of various kinds and affiliations, such as cultures and communities; and (3) how groups define themselves, interact with other groups, and exist in either harmony or tension within larger social units such as nations or international communities. *Individuals* and *groups, identity* and *difference, community* and *conflict:* in many ways these form this book's subject matter. For each of these key ideas, we'll basically ask the same kinds of questions, regardless of whether we're looking at individuals, groups, or something larger, like the United States:

What are the many shaping influences on identity?
What is the relationship between definition of self-identity and the perception of others?
What are the ways that individuals and groups connect and don't connect across their differences?

Let's look more closely at how these questions are raised across the chapters.

In the next two chapters of *Border Texts,* the emphasis is on the self and self-identity. How do we come to be who we are? What are the shaping influences on our identity? In what ways do the stories, expectations, and rules of our immediate culture shape us? The focus here is really on what David Sibley, in a later essay, calls the *ecological self,* the self that is constructed by the social, spatial, and cultural elements of the environment. The idea behind the ecological self is that our identity as individuals is not formed in some isolated or autonomous way. Although our sense of individuality is very much based on a feeling of freedom and autonomy, we derive all the aspects of our personality and beliefs (including our belief that we're free and autonomous) from some shaping system.

Therefore, the initial questions of this book revolve around self-identity: how we're shaped and how we make connections to others. That is, when thinking about the influences that shape our self-identity, we should consider how we connect ourselves to larger contexts. How do we develop a sense of belonging? What makes us feel at home—or *not* feel at home? What creates a sense of alienation? How do we feel and express connections to a community and a culture? How does our belonging to a culture shape who we are? There are also several layers of complexity to these questions about belonging because most of us belong to many different communities at once, and at times those communities conflict or exist in tension. In addition, there are vast differences in the ways that people feel connected to each other: sometimes through shared values, sometimes through shared physical space, and sometimes just through a sense of interdependency or a network of interrelationships. Furthermore, within social groups there is rarely equality. Within communities and cultures there are usually imbalances among members: insiders and outsiders, those closer to the center and those at the margins, even those who resist fitting in but who still play a vital role in the functioning and identity of the community.

Focusing on how individuals and groups define themselves leads inevitably to questions of how individuals and groups define *others.* How do we define insiders and outsiders? Is it possible to have a sense of community without outsiders? Whereas Chapters 2 and 3 look closely at individual identity and the ways individuals connect to each other, Chapters 4 and 5 look at how definitions of community and cultural identity depend on recognizing differences and the construction of otherness. How is "otherness" an ever-present factor in the way we construct culture? On what do we base our sense of differences?

People perceive and act on their sense of differences from others in many ways and for many reasons: out of fear, repulsion, disagreement, curiosity, fascination, attraction, indifference, habit, or ignorance. Even if constructions of otherness are based on irrational motivations (which they usually are), they can have very real, significant ramifications. In what ways do we see constructions of otherness and images of difference all around us? In what ways do our cultural values (i.e., the nature of identity within the groups to which we belong) instill and reinforce images of difference? How do differences drive us *together* as well as apart? How are differences appealing as well as the source of tension? To what extent are differences real or imagined?

The purpose of raising these questions is not to pass judgment on communities or groups that have a sense of self or of others. Human beings seem to need a sense of identity and belonging. In a heterogeneous society that means creating and maintaining borders between groups. What do vary are the different strategies for negotiating those borders and surviving what Mary Louise Pratt, in her essay in Chapter 5, calls "contact zones." A contact zone, according to Pratt, is any place where different cultures come together with some "asymmetrical relations of power." Whether this contact is at the level of cultural groups (as in the colonial situation she discusses) or at the level of individuals (for example, in a dating context that is potentially violent, as described in Mary Gaitskill's essay), a contact zone can be an important means for looking at how people communicate across their differences. What strategies do people use, either privately or publicly, to manage asymmetrical relations of power? How do people appeal to each other across differences? Do they appeal to fear, values, morality, shared destiny? When are contact zones positive and productive places?

One of the questions raised by the readings in Chapter 5 is to what extent contact zones are about imagined power and perceived differences. Indeed, this question echoes the place where the book began, with Sibley's idea of the *ecological self.* How we see ourselves, as well as how we see and interact with others, is based on a whole *ecology* of influences that are both real and imagined, physical and symbolic, simultaneously based in the world and based in language. If individual self-identity is shaped by physical and imagined forces—shaped by cultural ideas as much as by cultural places—then so too are cultures. That is, if individuals and groups are both shaped by an *ecology* of forces, they are also shaped by a *geography* that is both physical and imagined.

Chapter 6 looks at the ways that culture and communities imagine themselves as wholes existing in a particular place. Another way to think of this is to imagine that individuals as well as groups construct a whole reality for themselves that is partially based on cultural values and partially based on physical place. In other words, who you are is shaped in part by where you are. Similarly, how you perceive where you are is significantly shaped by your beliefs and values.

This brings us back to the ideas of *perspective* and *context.* Chapter 6 asks some of the book's most abstract or difficult questions: how are the perspectives of groups, cultures, communities, even nations formed by a context that could be characterized as an imagined reality—a reality based on a geographical place yet developed in the mind? How is geographical space culturally perceived? For example, how was the notion of the American frontier both a description of physical reality and a particular way of looking at cultural space—one that already had a sense of a center and an edge, of an old world and a new world, of a place where civilized peoples were settling in opposition to a wilderness? In what ways does physical environment shape cultural perceptions? Conversely, in what ways do cultural values shape our perceptions of geographical space and the physical environment?

Looking at the American notion of the frontier is useful because it is such a persistent and powerful myth in U.S. culture. The concept is also useful because it seems "natural" to people who grew up in the United States, so pervasive and ingrained are the images of frontier conquest and settlement. Yet, as more than one reading in Chapter 6 points out, thinking of a "frontier" as a dividing line between civilization and wilderness (or between culture and savagery) is not inevitable. It is possible, for example, to think of a frontier as a boundary or zone between two cultures. Along this divider there is not an inevitable sense of conquest or progress moving in a single direction (as in the movement of European civilization across the continent), but rather a more dynamic process of give-and-take across cultural boundaries. Whether one thinks of a frontier as a line or a zone brings us back to the book's most fundamental topics: the concept of borders and the human processes of self-definition and behavior that happen there. Borders, like frontiers, are places where something happens; and the construction of reality that governs what that something is has as much to do with the cultural values of the people involved as it does with the place itself.

The discussion becomes more complicated when we shift our thinking from American frontiers to "electronic" frontiers. Beginning with Columbus's discovery of the "new world, Chapter 6 concludes with a look at "cyberspace," the current new world being discovered and settled. Why do we think of cyberspace as a "space"? Why do people think of places on the World Wide Web in spatial terms as they maneuver among "home pages" and move among "sites"? Cyberspace is the ultimate expression of the conjunction of *border texts* and *border places.* After all, what are places on the Internet but texts and vice versa? And as a place built out of texts, cyberspace is nothing more than constructed realities: homemade, online communities whose structures, participants, and environments are conceived in people's minds and played out in an imagined environment with new sets of rules and limits. What can these new communities and contexts tell us about how we look at ourselves and others? How might online communication and interaction in virtual space shape the way individual or communal identity is imagined in ways face-to-face communication cannot? How do these new communities relate to the ones we already know? How will they interact? Will they compete? Will we all get bored with cyberspace? In a few years will it seem as habitual and humdrum as television? Or will we fundamentally change and not even realize it?

The compelling questions about the shape of new communities and even new geographies are what occupy the book's final chapter, which looks at the world's "new" borders. As we move into a world of interactive global technologies, is the world getting smaller and becoming more connected? Or, as seems likely with the growing number of worldwide ethnic and group conflicts, is the world becoming more fragmented? In this final chapter, the book's major questions come full circle. *Border Texts* begins by asking how individuals define themselves and connect with each other through groups. Chapter 7 looks at how groups define themselves and either connect or resist connection with some larger social identity at either the national or international level. Here we consider the issues of identity, community, and difference in terms of what Benjamin Barber calls "Jihad vs. McWorld." That is, we examine the tension between intense devotion to a group identity (symbolized in this work by the Islamic "Jihad") and the phenomenon of an increasingly homogenized global culture (symbolized by the worldwide proliferation of McDonald's and other exports—"McWorld"). Our look at borders concludes, then, with the questions of the twenty-first century: What borders and boundaries are competing for our attention? In what ways are differences increasing or decreasing among us? What will be the fate of individual self-definition and community rights as the world becomes both more coherent and more fragmented?

FROM READING TO WRITING

This book is intended to be a *resource for critical reading and writing.* No book of readings could be comprehensive or fully representative of American culture; nor can any book teach you how to write. What *Border Texts* attempts to do is to serve as a springboard for thinking and writing about these fundamental and complex issues.

If being a critical reader involves seeing how all texts are written from a perspective that has been shaped by a variety of contexts, then it is important to see yourself, as a writer, in the same way. That is, in order to read critically, you need to read actively, ask critical questions about the text, and build connections among other texts and broader ideas. To move from critical reading to writing, you need not only a critical understanding of the texts you read, but also a *context* for the ideas you're dealing with and a *perspective* from which to write about them. Just as with texts you *read,* with texts you *write,* perspective and context are very important. *Border Texts* offers a set of resources to make developing both possible.

In order to do both, *Border Texts* poses questions that continually ask you to reflect on the issues, the readings, and your own responses to them. There are three kinds of questions in *Border Texts:*

Critical Questions: Critical Questions are large, overarching questions that begin each chapter. These should help frame your reading and rereading of all the selections in the chapter as well as give you a broad context for your writing.

Reading Questions: Following each of the text selections is a set of reading questions under the title "Working with the Text." These are designed to encourage you to focus on the writing and ideas in each particular selection by engaging with them in a number of ways. The reading questions will vary from personal responses based on your own experience to a close rereading of the text that looks at particular strategies. The reading questions will ask you to engage in other kinds of activities as well, such as fieldwork you might conduct alone or in groups, or electronic research on the Web. These questions also include writing topics particular to that selection.

Writing Topics: At the end of each chapter is a set of broad writing topics addressing the overall themes in each chapter. Grouped under the heading, "Thinking and Writing: Critical Questions Revisited," these writing topics revisit the Critical Questions and reframe the chapter's key issues as topics for exploration in papers.

These three types of questions, along with the written texts and visual images, are designed to help you frame your reading and then move from reading to writing.

Let's look at how this process works with a couple of sample texts. First, consider a few Critical Questions that form the heart of this introductory chapter's discussion of the themes of *identity, perspective, language,* and *writing.*

Critical Questions

What is the relationship between language and culture? How does the language we use and feel comfortable with relate to our sense of belonging to a particular community or culture? In what ways do we use different kinds of language as a means of fitting into different contexts? How does language help us cross borders that differentiate the contexts of our lives? How does language shape our perception and identity? How does our use of language shape the ways that others perceive us?

Now, with these questions in mind, look at the following short reading by Amy Tan, a novelist and Chinese American writer who is best known for her novels *The Joy Luck Club* and *The Kitchen God's Wife.*

MOTHER TONGUE

AMY TAN

For many American students, the language spoken at home is far different from the one 1
spoken in school. For that reason, many students learn to switch back and forth between two languages, the one they use with their family and the one required for their education. Such switching, however, need not be confining or demoralizing. Rather, it can enhance one's sensitivity to language and can even be creatively enabling, as the Chinese American novelist Amy Tan suggests in this charming personal essay. "Language is the tool of my trade," Tan writes. "And I use them all—all the Englishes I grew up with."

Born into a Chinese family that had recently arrived in California, Amy Tan began 2
writing as a child and after graduation from college worked for several years as a freelance business writer. In the mid-eighties, she began writing fiction, basing much of her work on family stories. She is the author of two best-selling novels: The Joy Luck Club *(1989), which was a finalist for both the National Book Award and National Book Critics Circle Award and was made into a motion picture directed by Wayne Wang, and* The Kitchen God's Wife *(1991). In 1992 she published a popular children's book,* The Moon Lady. *She lives in San Francisco, where she is at work on a new novel. "Mother Tongue" originally appeared in* The Threepenny Review *(1990) and was selected by Joyce Carol Oates for* The Best American Essays 1991.

I am not a scholar of English or literature. I cannot give you much more than 3
personal opinions on the English language and its variations in this country or others.

I am a writer. And by that definition, I am someone who has always loved lan- 4
guage. I am fascinated by language in daily life. I spend a great deal of my time thinking about the power of language—the way it can evoke an emotion, a visual image, a complex idea, or a simple truth. Language is the tool of my trade. And I use them all—all the Englishes I grew up with.

Recently, I was made keenly aware of the different Englishes I do use. I was giv- 5
ing a talk to a large group of people, the same talk I had already given to half a dozen
other groups. The nature of the talk was about my writing, my life, and my book,
The Joy Luck Club. The talk was going along well enough, until I remembered one
major difference that made the whole talk sound wrong. My mother was in the
room. And it was perhaps the first time she had heard me give a lengthy speech,
using the kind of English I have never used with her. I was saying things like, "The
intersection of memory upon imagination" and "There is an aspect of my fiction
that relates to thus-and-thus"—a speech filled with carefully wrought grammatical
phrases, burdened, it suddenly seemed to me, with nominalized forms, past perfect
tenses, conditional phrases, all the forms of standard English that I had learned in
school and through books, the forms of English I did not use at home with my
mother.

Just last week, I was walking down the street with my mother, and I again found 6
myself conscious of the English I was using, the English I do use with her. We were
talking about the price of new and used furniture and I heard myself saying this:
"Not waste money that way." My husband was with us as well, and he didn't notice
any switch in my English. And then I realized why. It's because over the twenty years
we've been together I've often used that same kind of English with him, and sometimes he even uses it with me. It has become our language of intimacy, a different
sort of English that relates to family talk, the language I grew up with.

So you'll have some idea of what this family talk I heard sounds like, I'll quote 7
what my mother said during a recent conversation which I videotaped and then
transcribed. During this conversation, my mother was talking about a political
gangster in Shanghai who had the same last name as her family's, Du, and how the
gangster in his early years wanted to be adopted by her family, which was rich by
comparison. Later, the gangster became more powerful, far richer than my mother's
family, and one day showed up at my mother's wedding to pay his respects. Here's
what she said in part:

"Du Yusong having business like fruit stand. Like off the street kind. He is Du like 8
Du Zong—but not Tsung-ming Island people. The local people call putong, the
river east side, he belong to that side local people. That man want to ask Du Zong father take him in like become own family. Du Zong father wasn't look down on him,
but didn't take seriously, until that man big like become a mafia. Now important
person, very hard to inviting him. Chinese way, came only to show respect, don't
stay for dinner. Respect for making big celebration, he shows up. Mean gives lots of
respect. Chinese custom. Chinese social life that way. If too important won't have to
stay too long. He come to my wedding. I didn't see, I heard it. I gone to boy's side,
they have YMCA dinner. Chinese age I was nineteen."

You should know that my mother's expressive command of English belies how 9
much she actually understands. She reads the *Forbes* report, listens to *Wall Street
Week*, converses daily with her stockbroker, reads all of Shirley MacLaine's books
with ease—all kinds of things I can't begin to understand. Yet some of my friends
tell me they understand 50 percent of what my mother says. Some say they understand 80 to 90 percent. Some say they understand none of it, as if she were speaking
pure Chinese. But to me, my mother's English is perfectly clear, perfectly natural. It's
my mother tongue. Her language, as I hear it, is vivid, direct, full of observation and

imagery. That was the language that helped shape the way I saw things, expressed things, made sense of the world.

Lately, I've been giving more thought to the kind of English my mother speaks. Like others, I have described it to people as "broken" or "fractured" English. But I wince when I say that. It has always bothered me that I can think of no way to describe it other than "broken," as if it were damaged and needed to be fixed, as if it lacked a certain wholeness and soundness. I've heard other terms used, "limited English," for example. But they seem just as bad, as if everything is limited, including people's perceptions of the limited English speaker.

I know this for a fact, because when I was growing up, my mother's "limited" English limited *my* perception of her. I was ashamed of her English. I believed that her English reflected the quality of what she had to say. That is, because she expressed them imperfectly her thoughts were imperfect. And I had plenty of empirical evidence to support me: the fact that people in department stores, at banks, and at restaurants did not take her seriously, did not give her good service, pretended not to understand her, or even acted as if they did not hear her.

My mother has long realized the limitations of her English as well. When I was fifteen, she used to have me call people on the phone to pretend I was she. In this guise, I was forced to ask for information or even to complain and yell at people who had been rude to her. One time it was a call to her stockbroker in New York. She had cashed out her small portfolio and it just so happened we were going to go to New York the next week, our very first trip outside California. I had to get on the phone and say in an adolescent voice that was not very convincing, "This is Mrs. Tan."

And my mother was standing in the back whispering loudly, "Why he don't send me check, already two weeks late. So mad he lie to me, losing me money."

And then I said in perfect English, "Yes, I'm getting rather concerned. You had agreed to send the check two weeks ago, but it hasn't arrived."

Then she began to talk more loudly. "What he want, I come to New York tell him front of his boss, you cheating me?" And I was trying to calm her down, make her be quiet, while telling the stockbroker, "I can't tolerate any more excuses. If I don't receive the check immediately, I am going to have to speak to your manager when I'm in New York next week." And sure enough, the following week there we were in front of this astonished stockbroker, and I was sitting there red-faced and quiet, and my mother, the real Mrs. Tan, was shouting at his boss in her impeccable broken English.

We used a similar routine just five days ago, for a situation that was far less humorous. My mother had gone to the hospital for an appointment, to find out about a benign brain tumor a CAT scan had revealed a month ago. She said she had spoken very good English, her best English, no mistakes. Still, she said, the hospital did not apologize when they said they had lost the CAT scan and she had come for nothing. She said they did not seem to have any sympathy when she told them she was anxious to know the exact diagnosis, since her husband and son had both died of brain tumors. She said they would not give her any more information until the next time and she would have to make another appointment for that. So she said she would not leave until the doctor called her daughter. She wouldn't budge. And when the doctor finally called her daughter, me, who spoke in perfect English—lo and

behold—we had assurances the CAT scan would be found, promises that a conference call on Monday would be held, and apologies for any suffering my mother had
gone through for a most regrettable mistake.

I think my mother's English almost had an effect on limiting my possibilities in   17
life as well. Sociologists and linguists probably will tell you that a person's developing language skills are more influenced by peers. But I do think that the language
spoken in the family, especially in immigrant families which are more insular, plays
a large role in shaping the language of the child. And I believe that it affected my results on achievement tests, IQ tests, and the SAT. While my English skills were never
judged as poor, compared to math, English could not be considered my strong suit.
In grade school I did moderately well, getting perhaps B's, sometimes B-pluses, in
English and scoring perhaps in the sixtieth or seventieth percentile on achievement
tests. But those scores were not good enough to override the opinion that my true
abilities lay in math and science, because in those areas I achieved A's and scored in
the ninetieth percentile or higher.

This was understandable. Math is precise; there is only one correct answer.   18
Whereas, for me at least, the answers on English tests were always a judgment call, a
matter of opinion and personal experience. Those tests were constructed around items
like fill-in-the-blank sentence completion, such as, "Even though Tom was ———,
Mary thought he was ———." And the correct answer always seemed to be the most
bland combinations of thoughts, for example, "Even though Tom was shy, Mary
thought he was charming," with the grammatical structure "even though" limiting the correct answer to some sort of semantic opposites, so you wouldn't get answers like, "Even though Tom was foolish, Mary thought he was ridiculous." Well,
according to my mother, there were very few limitations as to what Tom could have
been and what Mary might have thought of him. So I never did well on tests like
that.

The same was true with word analogies, pairs of words in which you were sup-   19
posed to find some sort of logical, semantic relationship—for example, "*Sunset* is to
nightfall as ——— is to ———." And here you would be presented with a list of
four possible pairs, one of which showed the same kind of relationship: *red* is to
stoplight, bus is to *arrival, chills* is to *fever, yawn* is to *boring.* Well, I could never think
that way. I knew what the tests were asking, but I could not block out of my mind
the images already created by the first pair, "*sunset* is to *nightfall*"—and I would see
a burst of colors against a darkening sky, the moon rising, the lowering of a curtain
of stars. And all the other pairs of words—red, bus, stoplight, boring—just threw up
a mass of confusing images, making it impossible for me to sort out something as
logical as saying: "A sunset precedes nightfall" is the same as "a chill precedes a
fever." The only way I would have gotten that answer right would have been to imagine an associative situation, for example, my being disobedient and staying out past
sunset, catching a chill at night, which turns into feverish pneumonia as punishment, which indeed did happen to me.

I have been thinking about all this lately, about my mother's English, about achieve-   20
ment tests. Because lately I've been asked, as a writer, why there are not more Asian
Americans represented in American literature. Why are there few Asian Americans
enrolled in creative writing programs? Why do so many Chinese students go into

engineering? Well, these are broad sociological questions I can't begin to answer. But I have noticed in surveys—in fact, just last week—that Asian students, as a whole, always do significantly better on math achievement tests than in English. And this makes me think that there are other Asian-American students whose English spoken in the home might also be described as "broken" or "limited." And perhaps they also have teachers who are steering them away from writing and into math and science, which is what happened to me.

Fortunately, I happen to be rebellious in nature and enjoy the challenge of disproving assumptions made about me. I became an English major my first year in college, after being enrolled as pre-med. I started writing nonfiction as a freelancer the week after I was told by my former boss that writing was my worst skill and I should hone my talents toward account management.   21

But it wasn't until 1985 that I finally began to write fiction. And at first I wrote using what I thought to be wittily crafted sentences, sentences that would finally prove I had mastery over the English language. Here's an example from the first draft of a story that later made its way into *The Joy Luck Club,* but without this line: "That was my mental quandary in its nascent state." A terrible line, which I can barely pronounce.   22

Fortunately, for reasons I won't get into today, I later decided I should envision a reader for the stories I would write. And the reader I decided upon was my mother, because these were stories about mothers. So with this reader in mind—and in fact she did read my early drafts—I began to write stories using all the Englishes I grew up with: the English I spoke to my mother, which for lack of a better term might be described as "simple"; the English she used with me, which for lack of a better term might be described as "broken"; my translation of her Chinese, which could certainly be described as "watered down"; and what I imagined to be her translation of her Chinese if she could speak in perfect English, her internal language, and for that I sought to preserve the essence, but neither an English nor a Chinese structure. I wanted to capture what language ability tests can never reveal: her intent, her passion, her imagery, the rhythms of her speech and the nature of her thoughts.   23

Apart from what any critic had to say about my writing, I knew I had succeeded where it counted when my mother finished reading my book and gave me her verdict: "So easy to read."   24

Working with the Text

One of the most important ways to respond initially to a reading (and one that will often be posed in the questions following each reading) is to relate it to your own experience. For example, consider this reading question, one you could respond to in a journal entry or in classroom discussion:

1. Amy Tan talks about the many "Englishes" that she speaks. How many Englishes do you speak? Does the language that you use with your family differ from the language you use with friends? At school? At work? How does using different kinds of language help you survive in different contexts? If English is your second language, or if English is your parents' second language, then you probably can identify with her point about using different "Englishes." But even if that is not the case, consider the different "languages" that you speak during any given day. Surely you speak differently to different people and in different contexts.

Reflecting on a reading by considering your own experience is a good way to begin thinking about a writer's meaning. Now, let's look at her essay a little more closely in terms of its ideas. Let's consider some other reading questions that you might ask as you read the selection a second time.

2. Why does the presence of her mother make Tan "keenly aware of the different Englishes" she uses? How does the English that she uses with her mother differ from other kinds of English that she uses?

3. In what ways does Tan's short essay make connections among language, culture, and perception? How does she discuss language as a marker of cultural difference? How is language a factor in how people perceive cultural differences?

There are many ways to respond to Amy Tan's essay. It is best to read it actively the first time, writing down your own questions and comments and keeping track of questions or points that interest you. You should particularly jot down notes when you read the essay a second time and have specific analytical questions in mind.

You can take this line of response further by *acting on the reading* in different ways. One way would be to do some writing and reflecting about the language issues that Tan is raising. This kind of activity involves you in *getting writing from reading*. For example:

4. Keep a journal throughout the course of an entire day, being very conscious about the language you use with different people. How does your language vary? Does your own language change in ways that surprise you? What about the language you use to write as opposed to the language you use to speak?

Alternatively, instead of being conscious of your own language and writing a response piece about that, you might engage in a *fieldwork* experience in which you listen to other people. Here is a different kind of journal entry assignment:

5. For one day, listen very closely to how people talk. Don't just listen to what they say but also to how they say it. Listen to a number of people interact in conversation. This might be at a table in a coffeehouse, at the cash register in a store, or in an office where you work. How do people speak differently to each other? How do people react to others differently based on their language ability or tone?

That's one kind of fieldwork—research that you conduct out in the world. There is also a different kind of fieldwork that this book asks you to do on the Internet and World Wide Web—what we might call "electronic fieldwork." The Internet is filled with language: written language and visual language, public and private language, and language conveyed through colors, fonts, and pictures. It is filled with the language of commerce and intimacy, politics and entertainment.

In some ways Amy Tan's essay is really about the relationship between language (her many "Englishes") and identity. The Internet is a perfect laboratory for reflecting on the relationship between language and identity precisely because it is an environment built out of texts. After all, in electronic mail, in chat rooms, or on MUDs and MOOs, the only way people can establish their identity is through the language they choose to use.

How, then, could we use the Internet to further explore Tan's essay and its issues? How could we use the Internet to help put her essay in perspective? Here is an example of an electronic fieldwork assignment:

6. Look closely at the language that is used in some Internet setting (E-mail, a bulletin board, a chat room). As with the previous exercises, pay particularly close attention to *how* people are talking: What kind of language are they using? Is it formal language, academic language, or conversational language? Is it like talking than writing? If, for example, you think that it is more conversational or oral than formal and written language, try to explain why. You might also distinguish for yourself the differences between spoken and written language.

After you have found your examples of Internet text, you might print them out and bring them to class for another assignment, *working together in groups:*

7. Discuss each of your examples and collectively try to compile a list of language tendencies common to all of them. What kinds of generalizations or claims can you make about the way people talk on the Internet? What makes language seem oral or informal? What makes it seem formal?

These activities illustrate the kinds of things you can do using a text as a springboard for research and further exploration. Another important set of activities involves putting a work in the context of other pieces of writing. Let's compare Amy Tan's piece to the writing of Gloria Anzaldúa, who was mentioned earlier in this chapter. First, reread one particular passage from Tan's essay, although her whole essay is relevant here. She writes:

Just last week, I was walking down the street with my mother and I again found myself conscious of the English I was using, the English I do use with her. We were talking about the price of new and used furniture and I heard myself saying this: "Not waste money that way." My husband was with us as well, and he didn't notice any switch in my English. And then I realized why. It's because over the twenty years we've been together I've often used that same kind of English with him, and sometimes he even uses it with me. It has become our language of intimacy, a different sort of English that relates to family talk, the language I grew up with.

Now, here is a selection from Anzaldúa's book *Borderlands.* This chapter, "How to Tame a Wild Tongue," deals specifically with issues of language and ethnic identity. In it Anzaldúa is discussing Chicano Spanish, which she calls "a border tongue which developed naturally."

from How to Tame a Wild Tongue

GLORIA ANZALDÚA

Chicano Spanish is not incorrect, it is a living language. 1

For a people who are neither Spanish nor live in a country in which Spanish is the first language; for a people who live in a country in which English is the reigning tongue but who are not Anglo; for a people who cannot entirely identify with either standard (formal, Castilian) Spanish nor standard English, what recourse is left to them but to create their own language? A language which they can connect their identity to, one capable of communicating the realities and values true 2 to themselves—a language with terms that are neither *espanol ni ingles,* but both. We speak patois, a forked tongue, a variation of two languages.

Chicano Spanish sprang out of the Chicanos' need to identify ourselves as a dis-   3
tinct people. We needed a language with which we could communicate with ourselves, a secret language. For some of us, language is a homeland closer than the
Southwest—for many Chicanos today live in the Midwest and the East. And because
we are a complex, heterogeneous people, we speak many languages. Some of the
languages we speak are:

1. Standard English
2. Working class and slang English
3. Standard Spanish
4. Standard Mexican Spanish
5. North Mexican Spanish dialect
6. Chicano Spanish (Texas, New Mexico, Arizona and California have regional
variations)
7. Tex-Mex
8. *Pachuco* (called *calo*)

My "home" tongues are the languages I speak with my sister and brothers, with   4
my friends. They are the last five listed, with 6 and 7 being closest to my heart. From
school, the media and job situations, I've picked up standard and working class English. From Mamagrande Locha and from reading Spanish and Mexican literature,
I've picked up Standard Spanish and Standard Mexican Spanish. From *los recien lle-
gados,* Mexican immigrants, and braceros, I learned the North Mexican dialect.
With Mexicans I'll try to speak either Standard Mexican Spanish or the North Mexican dialect. From my parents and Chicanos living in the Valley, I picked up Chicano
Texas Spanish, and I speak it with my mom, younger brother (who married a Mexican and who rarely mixes Spanish with English), aunts and older relatives.

With Chicanas from *Nuevo Mexico* or *Arizona* I will speak Chicano Spanish a lit-   5
tle, but often they don't understand what I'm saying. With most California Chicanas
I speak entirely in English (unless I forget). When I first moved to San Francisco, I'd
rattle off something in Spanish, unintentionally embarrassing them. Often it is only
with another Chicana *tejana* that I can talk freely.

We raise a number of issues by putting Anzaldúa next to Tan. One possibility is to
look at the two pieces and engage in straightforward comparison and contrast:

8. How does this passage about language and identity compare to Tan's essay? What is
similar? What is different? How is Anzaldúa's approach to the reader different?

Another response is to use her essay as a way of rethinking the earlier reflective
exercises:

9. In reading Question 1 you were asked to think about the different kinds of languages that you speak every day. If you were to make a list of your different languages (one like Anzaldúa's), what would it look like?

Putting the two essays side by side helps us begin to move toward some larger issues and a broader set of critical questions:

10. One of the differences between the two essays is that Tan talks about language in relatively personal terms whereas Anzaldúa is more political. The two essays together suggest that there's a larger context in which to place the idea that language is closely tied to individual identity. How would you describe this larger context? What are some critical questions you might start asking about these issues?

> language and ethnicity
> language and power
> bilingualism
> immigration
> assimilation
> English as the official language of the United States

> Reread both essay selections carefully. Write a "critical" question about language in its social or cultural context. Use a specific passage from one of the readings as the springboard for your question.

For another approach, think about the broader context by looking at an additional reading question that points to the larger political or cultural meaning of Anzaldúa's essay:

11. Anzaldúa asserts that "Chicano Spanish is not incorrect, it is a living language." What does she mean by that statement? Why are "incorrect" and "living" opposites in this context?

Also, since this chapter began by looking at maps, we might ask whether all of this talk about language is really about borders and geography:

12. What *geographies* are implied in the essays by Tan and Anzaldúa? How is Tan's relationship to China the same as or different from Anzaldúa's relationship to Mexico or Spain, as described in their essays? How are their relationships to America the same or different?

Probably our most natural tendency is to want to read something rapidly and to "get it" as quickly as possible. All of these reading questions relate to an idea mentioned earlier about "slowing down" your reading: where the reading process consists of a variety of stages, and your experience of a text is ongoing and increasingly rich and expansive. Reading, thinking, and writing are not separate processes that take place in some kind of mechanical sequence. They are activities that overlap and cycle back and forth over each other. That is why this book has so many levels of questions asking you to think, reflect, and write at different stages during the writing process.

Ultimately, the purpose of *Border Texts* is to get you to reflect on some fundamental questions, not only about identity and culture but also about writing and communication. If reading is an act of negotiating borders, then so is writing. As a writer, you create a *place* where something happens, a text shaped by your personal and cultural identities that differs from that of any other writer. While not a border in the traditional sense of a dividing line, writing is a border in the larger sense that is the focus of this book: a space where people—writers and readers—come together more or less successfully across their differences in perspective and knowledge. To return to an idea stated at the beginning of the introduction, writing is one kind of border that holds us together—despite perhaps deep differences—because it provides a crossing point for communication.

CHAPTER

BORDERS OF IDENTITY:

Stories of the Self and Home

Critical Questions for *Borders of Identity*

Where do we get our sense of self-identity? In what ways are we shaped by the places where we grew up? By our memories, family, or community? By the stories we tell and have heard? How are stories an integral part of how we know the world? How do cultural stories or myths shape our lives? How do we know that our inner perceptions of outer reality are "true"? How does our sense of the past shape who we are in the present?

THE SHAPING POWER OF STORIES

In many ways, telling stories is a primary means of defining borders and boundaries—the borders between right and wrong, truth and fiction, ourselves and others. All forms of stories—whether folktales, literary fiction, autobiography, history, or myths—are ways to express these borders and to express cultural and social meaning.

Stories are fundamental to our identities because storytelling is basic to all cultures. We hear stories when we're children; we hear stories on the evening news; we tell stories to each other; we read stories in school and watch them on television and in movies. We attain much of our earliest and most influential knowledge through stories. Indeed, throughout our lives we are so saturated in stories that it would be impossible to separate our sense of self from the stories that have formed us. Our lives are shaped and held together by the stories that surround us. Our knowledge of family history, religion, nationality, or heritage—what are these things but stories that influence behavior and beliefs?

Individuals derive their sense of identity from their culture, and cultures are systems of belief that determine how people live their lives. Stories are a fundamental means for connecting individuals to that system of belief. The relationship among storytelling, identity, and culture is the central focus of this chapter's selections. As Stuart Hall (a writer whose essay appears in Chapter 4) puts it, "Identity is a narrative of the self; it's the story we tell about the self in order to know who we are." Exploring *the stories we tell to know who we are* is precisely what this chapter is about.

All of this chapter's selections are stories about people trying to make sense of who they are in relationship to something: their family, community, past, or multiple roles and identities. These works often invoke the idea of *cultural stories and patterns* as influences that have significantly shaped their authors' behavior and beliefs. Stories can shape our lives by giving us ideal "plots" which we would like our lives to follow or by luring us into a pattern—"locking us into a narrative," as one writer puts it—from which it is difficult to escape. At all levels, these works explore the role of stories—true stories, make-believe stories, stories that come back to us as pleasant memories, or stories that haunt us with images we try to forget or suppress.

All stories have to start somewhere, and for many of this chapter's writers, they begin at home. One persistent emphasis throughout this chapter is on the concept of "place" and "home." A home, the place we start from, has a perpetual shaping influence throughout our lives. No matter where we end up, how we change or grow, we are always the product of the place (or places) we came from. And if all people's lives are their own stories, then those stories always have a location of origin and are rooted in a particular place. For this chapter's writers that place might be as small as a grandmother's house, the neighborhood in which they grew up, or the rural region of the country they came from. The importance of a shaping place is the "imagined" borders that it creates on one's experience and how those borders define all the other patterns and influences on our lives. The idea of place also plays a powerful role in defining one's sense of self because places have very particular relationships to *change.* Places where we grew up never quite seem the same when we visit them later. Even if they seem familiar, they might seem smaller or different from the way we remembered them. Nevertheless, familiar childhood places are still important to our sense of perspective because they remain where they are while we leave, grow, and change. Whether physical, emotional, imagined, or spiritual, the images of our most formative places are closely related to our sense of ourselves and to the stories that scaffold our identity.

PAST AND PRESENT

Because stories are so important to our connections with the past, one persistent and important theme running through all of these selections is *memory*. Memories are stories that play vital roles in our lives. And although we often talk about distinguishing between a true story and a false one, memories are a kind of story where the line between truth and fiction is not always that easy to discern. It is interesting that so many of these authors reflect on memories and identity through the use of visual media: Sherman Alexie's "family portrait," Judith Ortiz Cofer's memory of old home movies, the main character in Michelle Cliff's "Screen Memory" who thinks of her past as watching herself in a film. There is something very *visual* about memories. As Alexie puts it in his story, moving back and forth between a remembered family portrait and the verbal portrait he's trying to write:

> I've been thinking about pain, how each of us constructs our past to justify what we feel now. How each successive pain distorts the preceding. Let's say I remember sunlight as a measurement of this story, how it changed the shape of the family portrait. My father shields his eyes and makes his face a shadow. He could be anyone then, but my eyes are closed in the photo. I cannot remember what I was thinking. Maybe I wanted to stand, stretch my legs, raise my arms above my head, open my mouth wide, and fill my lungs. *Breathe, breathe.* Maybe my hair is so black it collects all the available light.

Memories are in many ways images or snapshots placed in a narrative or storied context. And indeed, that is what many of these essays are about: trying to place recurrent, strong images—isolated but persistent moments—*from the past* into a larger context that makes sense to *the person's present.*

If memory is an important theme, then the idea of *time* necessarily plays a significant role in structuring these essays. As you read these works, you should be alert to the different ways that these writers represent time. Some of the authors move back and forth from past to present in complex and sometimes disorienting ways; others use a "flashback" technique to explore certain personal revelations. The manipulation of time is key to these writers because the idea of "identity" (or a sense of self) has a lot to do with time. That is, not only do we come to be who we are over time (rather than all at once), but we also become who we are by developing a certain relationship to the past—not only our personal past, but our family's and culture's pasts as well.

LIVING FICTIONS

Just as it is sometimes hard to distinguish between truth and fiction when thinking about the past, it is also true that our everyday world is structured by all kinds of "fictions" that give certain meaning and shape to our beliefs. The stories we see on television or in movies, the underlying mythology of a country or culture, or the stereotypes we have about certain kinds of people are all stories that exert power over how we act and what we believe. For example, even if we know that a television show is just a show or a TV commercial is just a commercial, its underlying stories and messages ("successful people look like this," "poor people act like that") can still help form our belief system. Many of the stories in this chapter explore the shaping power of everyday fictions and the processes people use to examine these fictions and to separate themselves from them.

For example, in Michael Nava's essay "Gardenland, Sacramento, California," a young gay man reflects on how his own identity doesn't fit into a rather narrow, ethnic neighborhood setting that prescribes a particular kind of lifestyle. Similarly, in "Cinderella," Anne Sexton's poem, a modern version of the fairy tale character resists the pattern of living "happily ever after" that characterizes the well-known original. Many of this chapter's writers realize that even if there is no clear, definitive way to separate themselves from the fictions that shaped their character, the process of trying to do so can be useful for personal development and growth. This is true whether the process involves coming to realize finally how a childhood hero was really not all that heroic or seeing how early memories that you had forgotten were really critical to forming your identity. In Leslie Marmon Silko's story "Yellow Woman," the narrator doesn't ever know if she is really herself or the embodiment of a recurring figure in Pueblo tribal stories. When describing his family, Sherman Alexie writes explicitly about the "lies" that we tell ourselves to survive. In these and other cases, the line between reality and unreality, truth and fiction, is blurred. Therefore, an important theme in these selections is the *process of writing* as a means of self-discovery.

MULTIPLE IDENTITIES

Self-discovery is the main theme of all these essays. However, sometimes it can seem that there is more than one "self" to be discovered. For many of these writers, exploring the self means exploring the multiple selves and their roles within their families and cultures. As Joy Harjo puts it in her poem "The Woman Hanging from the Thirteenth Floor Window":

> The woman hanging from the 13th floor window
> on the east side of Chicago is not alone.
> She is a woman of children, of the baby, Carlos,
> and of Margaret, and of Jimmy who is the oldest.
> She is her mother's daughter and her father's son.
> She is several pieces between the two husbands
> she has had. She is all the women of the apartment
> building who stand watching her, watching themselves.

This passage addresses the idea of multiple selves in several ways, all important to the key themes of this chapter. First, the stanza implies that the woman feels like *more* than one person because she has had to play so many different roles in her life: her children's mother, her mother's daughter, her husbands' wives. However, the passage also implies that she is *less* than one person because she is fragmented by having to play all these different roles. Indeed, this is one of the main questions that so many writers in this chapter pose: How do we combine our many selves into a single self? What stories do we tell ourselves (and others) to knit together the various pieces of our lives that are shaped by the roles we play, by the experiences we have, and by the identities we construct to survive each new situation or experience?

The Harjo passage also presents another crucial facet of self-identity: the connection between the person we think we are and the people with whom we identify. In the case of the "woman hanging from the thirteenth floor window," there is a mirroring effect between her and those watching her:

> She is all the women of the apartment
> building who stand watching her, watching themselves.

To what extent is each of us our own self as well as a reflection of someone else? How fluid is our own identity? How is it shaped by the people around us? Does it also shape others? To what degree is each of us an individual as well as a part of some collective identity—part of our families, our places of work, our group of regular friends? In most Western cultures, especially in the United States, we are used to thinking of "individuality" as a critical aspect of our identity. But in many ways the idea of an autonomous, self-created individual is a fiction of our culture. That is, the notions of "self-identity" and our sense of individuality are stories we tell ourselves to feel whole. In this way we prevent the fragmentation of the self into multiple roles and the loss of self as it merges with those around us.

For many people, the process of managing these various roles and selves is not a problem; it is not even a matter of conscious reflection. People have work identities and home identities. People act one way with their families and another with friends. But for many of the writers in this chapter, feeling whole is problematic, partly because there is conflict among their multiple sources of identity. For example, Kesaya Noda receives certain messages about being a woman, others about being Japanese, and still others about being Japanese American. In her case, messages about self-definition are also related to images and stereotypes that she encounters as a racialized minority in the United States. But the central questions she asks apply to everyone:

> How is one to know and define oneself? From the inside—within a context that is self-defined from a grounding in community and a connection with culture and history that are comfortably accepted? Or from the outside—in terms of messages received from the media and people who are often ignorant? Even as an adult I can still see two sides of my face and past. I can see from the inside out, in freedom. And I can see from the outside in, driven by the old voices of childhood and lost in anger and fear.

The question Noda poses is a poignant one. Of course, the answer has to be *both*. We are defined—and are always defining ourselves—through some interaction between "inside" feelings and "outside" influences. What is self-identity, in the end, but the boundary between the two?

THE QUIET HOUSE

MARIANNE BORUCH

■ Marianne Boruch, a poet whose collections include *Descendant* (1989) and *Moss Burning* (1993), is haunted by childhood memories, even though, as she writes in this essay, she "doesn't have a very good memory." Her work is a means of "imaginative recall, bringing up detail, making it crucial" in order to "discover something out there" beyond "mere self-expression." In this essay she particularly concerns herself with a place crucial to her childhood: the small-town home of her maternal grandparents, where she often spent holidays and summers away from her "ordinary life" in Chicago. Here she encountered mysteries of identity and self-awareness that fed her imagination in ways that affected the woman she would become. Boruch is always interested in how the notions of myth, memory, and imagination weave together to suggest the complex ways that the past shapes the present.

The closest I've ever come to myth was that favorite game in college—we called it Earliest Memory, my friends sprawled out in someone's living room. *Moonlight on the bedroom floor* we'd say or *oh god, that fall down the steep back stairs. . . .* Still, I've always been puzzled: do we carry around stories, these old images, because we remember them or because they have been told to us over and over, held up like communal treasure? That river of milk, say, pouring down the long hallway in our tiny Chicago apartment one morning when I was four, and my mother, sitting down at the end of that white expanse, suddenly crying in the most hopeless way—did I see that? Or does it haunt me because my mother herself has held up this small scene, laughing: here's our funny, luckless, cherished life.

In fact, I don't have a very good memory; everyone tells me this. But poetry is a way of imaginative recall, bringing up detail, making it crucial. More, it's making shape of these details, making them mean in a way that nearly forgets the self—that sense of the poem as mere self-expression, *I hurt* or *I love*—to discover something out there, the first large shape, the house widening to the street, the neighborhood, the world. How many women, then, in my mother's weeping that day, the hallway darkened and lit by the shattered glass, the rushing wasted milk?

If memory is a matter of *place,* then my childhood gave me two. I was born in Chicago, spent thirteen years in its Catholic schools—as odd and eloquent and unreal as any education might be—moving from neighborhood to neighborhood three or four times, finally ending those years before college at its northwest edge where the cheap suburbs begin. The fixed point in all this was my father's parents—the Boruchs—my Polish grandparents. I see them there in their Old World house on Maplewood Avenue, the continual cabbage haze in the air, the rich rise and fall of a language my brother and I never understood, the Virgin Mary on the wall with her pierced heart, the silk fringed pillows—"Greetings from Manila"—their American-born sons sent back in 1944, so thrilled to be soldiers, to be away. "Ma, these are American children," I remember my father saying sadly, inscrutably to them once, one of the few times I heard him speak English in that house. He stood in the doorway, restless, hands in his pockets.

As counterpoint, I held my mother's world: small-town central Illinois, the place   4 we went most of Christmas and Easter and much of the summer. The night train took us south three hours from the city, the wheezing diesel clouds rising as the whole thing trembled, stood still, slowed by a signal light in the railroad tower—Tuscola not a stop on the regular line. I could make out my grandparents, the Taylors, there in their old wool coats to help us down the cold metal steps.

Where does imagination begin? My ordinary life was Chicago—school and af-   5 terschool and piano lessons and the predictable noisy array of Boruch cousins, aunts, and uncles at the backyard barbecue. But Tuscola was the older, secret place. No duty there but solitude and love, and history a large part of its calm—grave-stones with our family names chiseled in, four generations back of Taylors and Gillses and Joneses. And my grandparents themselves—*old* grandparents, already in their seventies when I was born. Or perhaps, I've simply never gotten over the solemn joy of stepping down from that train into darkness, into that town, a square mile of houses and brick streets in the middle of prairie, and, of course, into those arms waiting to lift us to the ground. From the track, I could see the beat-up taxi my grandparents had hired to take us to the house, its headlights dimmed, its radio soft; though it was cold, the driver had cracked his window open so the smoke from his cigar drifted out and up and disappeared. Meanwhile we couldn't stop talking, yelling really, my grandfather even then so deaf—news of school and the people they knew from visits north, our voices the only voices in the chill night air.

It's impossible—I fear, extinct—such a catalog of riches: falling asleep later, the   6 house of chiming ticking clocks, of pipe smoke and liniment, and the line-dried sheets, stiff and rough from the wind. Outside wonders too: the train whistle again, which—from this distance—meant both routine and adventure, and in the morn-ing, walks past the drugstore with its gory pictures of nineteenth-century opera-tions set up in the window, or to Gus's for a fountain coke or outside the old hotel where my grandfather stopped to talk to the ancient men leaning back in the metal chairs—the day warm enough—among them the one gassed in the First World War, Mr. Arthur who couldn't speak, who just sat there blankly. *Mustard gas,* my mother had told me, and he had stared that way, she said, since the twenties when she was a kid.

Imagination might be tied up first—perhaps always—with mystery. I wanted, of   7 course, to walk by the old men quickly, but my grandfather, who was, after all, one of them, stood and talked happily, even sitting down for a while if there was an empty chair, while I fidgeted on the sidewalk, my eye coming back to Mr. Arthur and whatever stony secret he kept locked inside. That dark surprise, then, in the most or-dinary circumstance, the slow shock of things: is this the beginning of poetry? I kept wishing for anything else—just to be playing on the porch or in the battered side yard, to be talking endlessly in the kitchen with my grandmother about all my ur-gent nothings. Instead, it was my grandfather's usual exchange—the weather, corn prices, and as he claimed to be the town's only Democrat, certainly politics—all of it worth repeating a million times. But under their voices, Mr. Arthur loomed. Oc-casionally, he'd turn his head and look at me.

I need to be careful. It isn't some awful nostalgia that pulls me back to that look,   8
nor is it even its historical weight. I don't think I ever woke out of nightmares because of him, and it was years before I learned the gruesome facts of trench warfare.
No doubt the man dropped out of my head as soon as I could drag my grandfather
off, taking his hand to cut across Sales Street to Main and straight home. It's more,
perhaps, how Mr. Arthur's silence spoke, how his curious isolation mirrored some
underside thing in me that felt sad and true and inevitable. That this town, so won-
derfully picturesque with its band shell gazebo, its Andrew Carnegie Library, its
bright heroic WPA mural in the post office—that such a place carried inside it another place, badly lit, seemingly senseless: this was news, but only memorable because that delicate, puzzling design repeated, made a pattern.

The usual pattern of small towns, maybe: feuds, bad feeling as inherited as red   9
hair, entire streets where my grandmother refused to walk for whatever reason. But
against that, friends back to the 1880s, when my grandparents were children, one
old lady so blind, she'd stoop and feel my face—slowly, lovingly—before saying
hello. Various rituals of distress or pleasure; my brother and I were born to them,
they were clear—clear enough—meaning we largely accepted their mysteries, that
is, until that mystery came home, and filled the quiet house.

It was something my grandmother told us herself one summer: when our Uncle   10
Larry went to war—not Mr. Arthur's, but the Second World War—he went crazy.
We were on the high sleeping porch off my grandfather's bedroom, a tiny screened-
in place overlooking the backyard smelling of dust, mothballs, and faintly, almost
sweetly, of urine. My grandmother pointed to the trunk. Lawrence wrote a novel before he left, she told us, and god knows what was in it. But he locked it up, right
there. Of course, he came back; we knew that much. He'd been in North Africa,
the Italian campaign. But just raving by the time he got home, my grandmother
was saying, shouting terrible things out the back door to Mrs. Helm, and then to
the grocer, the preacher, even Tack Green, the undertaker—until he tore up the
stairs and barricaded himself right here, on the porch. My brother and I sat there;
I heard the neighbor's screen door bang, and a truck downshifting blocks away.
My grandmother was slowing up now, but it was what came next that got me, how
she found him later, standing in the cellar, feeding his novel, page by page, into the
small flaming window of the coal furnace. It was dark down there, and all so private.
She said nothing to him, turning back up the stairs, up and back into the bright
kitchen.

Pattern is tension, the weave of opposites, imaginative engagement. Mr. Arthur's   11
mute standstill among the arguing, wise-cracking old men was one thing, but my
uncle in the cellar, furious and without hope? I tried to think—still think—of this
passionate, mad flash of him against the witty, startlingly urbane uncle we knew in
Chicago who drove over from Oak Park with his cool, towering wife for an occasional Sunday afternoon. I think of the containment of that trunk, and feverish pursuit and denial of what was in it. As a kid, during those afternoons of his visits,
looking from the hallway, I kept eavesdropping as my uncle sipped his scotch, trying
to figure some grave clue from the scene's slick surface.

I'll never get to the end of these mysteries—therefore I write poems, as Descartes   12
surely meant to say. Of course, Mr. Arthur, but my uncle too, they're both dead now,

and recently, since I live only ninety miles east of Tuscola these days, I drove back to that town, first finding the place the hotel was—it burned to the ground in the mid-seventies—then parking on south Main in front of my grandparents' old house. It looked far shabbier, more desolate than I remembered. The green bamboo shades had vanished from the porch, the flowering spires uprooted from the yard. I walked around to the back where the sleeping porch still hung off the second story like a thing dreamt up later, a last good idea.

It wasn't winter but spring, though I remembered one thing more about that trunk—my uncle's wool uniforms were in it, carefully folded khaki trousers and shirts, and caps narrow as envelopes. The Christmas after we learned about the novel, my brother and I opened the trunk, and put everything on, tying up the waists with string. Outside, the alley was one long frozen slick, and we slid and fell and laughed, the pants rolled up but unrolling, the big sleeves flapping. I recall it perfectly, down to the most trivial detail. Still, I have this curious vision: I'm not playing at all, but alone in the house watching us play, looking down from the high back bedroom at these kids, reeling and breathless, their clothes way too big for them. 13

Working with the Text

1. The core of Boruch's essay is a description of the two "places" that structure her memory. As she says, "If memory is a matter of *place,* then my childhood gave me two." What is the significance of these two places for Boruch? What different feelings, values, and ideas belong to each? How did the small Illinois town and her grandparents' "quiet house" there influence her identity in ways that her "normal life" in Chicago did not? How do places structure memory and memories structure places?

2. "Where does imagination begin?" Boruch asks. Is it "tied up first—perhaps always—with mystery"? In what ways do imagination and mystery come together for her in this essay? Looking particularly at Mr. Arthur and Uncle Larry, what sorts of mysteries did Boruch perceive as a child, and how do they affect her imaginative life as an adult? What do you see as the sources of imagination?

3. What is the significance of the final image of the child Boruch and her brother playing in "clothes way too big for them" as the adult Boruch watches in her imagination? Does she finally understand the line between memory and imagination? Does it matter to her whether she can sort it out with clarity? Does it matter to you?

4. Boruch talks about the childhood game "earliest memory." What are your earliest memories? What parts are most vivid to you? Why do you happen to recall these as your earliest memories?

5. Look up several definitions of the word *myth*. Why does Boruch compare memory to myth? What meaning or meanings of *myth* make it most like memory? Do you have any early memories that have some "mythic" dimension? Do other members of your family "remember" these stories in the same

way? Do you think your identity is shaped more by what actually happened or by what and how you remember?

THE VISITOR

RUSSELL BANKS

■ A short-story writer and novelist, Russell Banks focuses in much of his fiction on working-class characters whose complex relationships are often marked by emotional conflict, even physical violence. Raised in small-town New Hampshire, Banks himself worked for several years as a plumber before achieving his first success as a writer in the late 1960s. His works include the novels *Continental Drift* (1985) and *Rule of the Bone* (1995). In the following essay he tells of returning to a childhood place where he says his family spent "the most crucial year of our shared life. It defined us: we were that family, we have remained that family." The resulting memories bring him face to face with the powerful draw that the past continues to have on our present lives.

In late April of a recent year, I drove from my home in New York City across New Jersey to deliver a lecture at East Stroudsburg University, which is located in Pennsylvania at the southern end of the Pocono Mountains, not far from the Delaware Water Gap. I arrived a few hours earlier than my hosts expected me, so that, once there, I was free to drive thirty-five miles further north to the small town of Tobyhanna, where my mother and father lived with me and my brother and sister for a single year, 1952, when I was twelve, my brother ten, and my sister six.

For the five of us, the year we lived in Tobyhanna was the most crucial year of our shared life. It defined us: we were that family, we have remained that family. The following summer, my mother and father got divorced, and from then on, although we were the same, everything else was different. Not better, just different.

Looking back, I see that both my parents were careening out of control with rage, frustration, and fear. For years, my father had been plotting ways to leave my mother, whose dependency and hysteria had imprisoned him then, as later it would me. For her part, my mother had been just as busy trying to keep him from leaving, which only made him feel more trapped today than yesterday. He was thirty-eight; his life was skidding past. And he thought he was somehow better than she, a more important person in the overall scheme of things than she, and he acted accordingly. This made my mother wild.

My father was a plumber, and he had been hired by a New England contractor as superintendent of all the plumbing, heating, and air-conditioning installation in an enormous Army shipping and storage depot then being built in Tobyhanna. It was one of the first big postwar military bases commissioned by the Eisenhower administration. My father was the company's man sent down from Hartford to run its largest out-of-state job, an extraordinary position for a young journeyman pipe fitter with no more than a high school education, a man whose biggest job up to then had been adding a wing to the Veterans' Hospital in Manchester, New Hampshire.

But he was bright, and he worked hard, and he was very good-looking and lucky. People liked him, especially men, and women flirted with him.

He was a heavy drinker, though, starting it earlier every day. And with each addi- 5 tional long night's stay at the bar in Tobyhanna, he turned increasingly nasty and sometimes violent. The job he held was, in fact, way over his head, and he was terri-fied—not of being fired, but of being found out, and not so much by other people, as by himself.

I drove my car into Tobyhanna, a poor bedraggled batch of houses and garages 6 and trailers strung along a winding two-lane road abandoned long ago for the Stroudsburg-Scranton highway, and saw at once the bar where my father used to spend his evenings after work and as much of his weekends as he could steal from the house in the woods where he had established his nervous wife and three chil-dren. It was a small depressing impoverished town, despite the presence of the Army depot—or perhaps because of it.

I drew my car up to the bar on the main street, shut off the motor, and went in- 7 side. It was dark, dirty, and damp, smelled of old beer, sweat, and pickled hard-boiled eggs, with a jukebox at the back, a U-shaped linoleum-covered bar that ran the length of the room, and several dim flickering neon beer signs in the window.

I ordered a beer from the middle-aged woman behind the bar, whose exact 8 round dun-colored double—her twin, I thought, or surely her sister—sat on a stool on the other side of the bar. She sat next to a man with a tracheotomy who was talk-ing to her in a harsh electronic moan.

A second man was perched on a stool a ways down from me—a scrawny fellow 9 in his mid-fifties whose arms were covered with badly drawn tattoos. His head was wobbling on his neck above a bottle of beer, and he seemed not to notice when I sat down.

The place had not changed a bit in the thirty-four years since I last entered it. The 10 doubling image of the round woman behind the bar and the woman sitting by the man with the hole in his throat acted like a drug or a mathematical formula or a vi-sion, instantly doubling the place itself with my memory of it, matching my arrival in Tobyhanna today with my memory of a Saturday in winter, when my father drove me and my younger brother into town with him—ostensibly to pick up a few gro-ceries or some such errand. It's no longer clear to me why we three males left the house and hearth for town that day, just as it was not clear to me why I decided to drive north from Stroudsburg, when I more easily and pleasantly could have strolled around the college campus for a few hours, killing time. There was a pow-erful need to go there, but no remembered reason.

I remember my father bringing my brother and me straight into the bar with 11 him, and I remember his cronies—soldiers and construction workers—buying my brother and me Cokes and potato chips. They teased us and praised us for our manly cleverness, our clever manliness, because we were little men, while down along the bar my father leaned over a friend's shoulder and talked intently into his ear, then smiled at a fat woman (or so she looked to me) with bright red lipstick sit-ting next to him and patted her forearm affectionately and soon switched his atten-tion completely over to her, leaving his male friend to drink alone for a while. I watched this take place.

The bartender waddled over to me, picked up my nearly empty bottle and studied it and set it back down. "Want another?" 12

I shook my head no. 13

She lit a cigarette, inhaled furiously, a large red-faced woman smoking like a steamship, and she studied my face the way she had examined my beer bottle. "You're not from around here," she stated. 14

"Last time I was in here was thirty-four years ago," I said. 15

She laughed, once, more a bark than a laugh. "It hasn't changed." 16

"Nope," I said. "It's the same." 17

The man next to me at the bar, his head wobbling like a heavy flower on a stem, was alert, more or less, and watching me now. "You ain't old enough to've been in here thirty-four years ago," he growled. 18

"I was only a kid then. With my father. My father brought me in here." 19

The man sat up straight and swept his arms around and then pointed at each of the four corners of the dingy room. "This place, it hasn't changed," he said. "Where are you from?" 20

"New York City." 21

"Hah!" he laughed. "This," he said, waving his arms again, indicating the three other people in the bar as if they were a place, "this is the way to live! You never lock your doors here. It's safe," he proclaimed. "Not like, not like your goddamned New York City." 22

I nodded in agreement, got off my stool, and made for the door. 23

He called after me, "Hey, buddy! You're welcome!" He grinned through loose red lips and broken teeth and started to cackle at his joke on me and then cough and finally wheeze and whoop with joy, as I hurried out the front door to my car. 24

On our way home from the bar, me in front in the passenger's seat, my brother in back, my father had said, "Listen, boys, let's just say we spent the time at the depot. In the office. I should've gone over some drawings there anyhow, so we might's well say that's what we did, right?" He looked over at me intently. "Right?" 25

"Sure," I said. "I don't care." 26

I peered out the window at the gauze curtains of snow falling, the houses that occasionally flashed past, the dark shadows of trees and of the Poconos closing off the sky. I didn't care. 27

My brother didn't say anything, but my father never asked him to. I was the one he worried about: I was the one my mother would interrogate. 28

The house itself had not changed. Except for the coat of blue-gray paint, it was still the same two-story farmhouse with the long shed attached at the rear and the weatherbeaten, unpainted barn across the circular drive. The two stone chimneys at the ends of the house were matched by the pair of huge maple trees next to the road. Hanging from one of the trees was a small wooden sign. RETTSTADT'S RESTAURANT, it said. SERVING DINNERS FRI. TO SAT., 5 PM TO 9 PM. I could not imagine who would drive all the way out from Tobyhanna—five miles through the woods on a narrow winding hilly road, passing barely a dozen other houses on the way, broken-down and half-finished bungalows and trailers set on cinderblocks among car chassis and old refrigerators and tires—for dinner at Rettstadt's. 29

I looked at my watch, 4:45, and drew my car off the road, pulled into the drive- 30 way, and parked by the back porch, facing the door that, when we lived there, opened into the kitchen. By now my limbs felt weak and awash with blood and my heart was pounding furiously, as if I were at the entrance to a cave.

By the time my father and brother and I arrived home, the snow was coming 31 down heavily, and my father told my mother that the snow had slowed him up, he had got stuck twice, and besides, he had to spend quite a while at the office at the depot working on some drawings for Monday. That was why we were so late getting home from town.

My mother looked at him wearily. It was the same old story, the same old chal- 32 lenge tossed down, the dare for her to take him on one more time: either believe the liar or enrage him by forcing him to tell the truth.

I know from photographs that my mother was a pretty woman—small, blond, 33 precisely featured, with lively hazel eyes and a sensitive mouth. "Petite," she liked to say of herself. People said she looked like beautiful women—Claudette Colbert, Ann Blyth, Bette Davis—and she did. Not like any one of them, but she belonged to that particular caste of beauty. I remember her that afternoon as standing before the stove, a ladle in hand, a steaming pot before her—but that, too, is a generic image, like her beauty. It was a Saturday afternoon, it was snowing.

My brother dodged around her and disappeared like a mouse through the living 34 room, toward the stairs and the unused bedroom on the second floor, a kind of attic in the back where we had set up our electric trains. My sister—I have no idea where she was, possibly in the kitchen, possibly with a friend for the afternoon: country children often visited each other on weekends; it made the driving back and forth easier for the parents. I hung around by the kitchen door, as if waiting for orders from one or the other of my parents. They were looking angrily at one another, however, and did not seem to know that I existed.

My mother said, "I know where you've been. I can smell it on you. I can smell her, 35 too."

My father's face reddened, and he glowered down at her from his full height, 36 which, because my mother was small and I was only twelve years old, seemed a con- siderable height, though he was never any taller than six feet, which turned out to be my height as well. He began to shout at her. It was at first a welling up and then an overflow of anger, wordless—or no words that I can recall—a kind of sustained roar, which she answered by letting loose with shrieks, cries, calls, wails—again, with no words that I can recall now and surely could not hear then, for the tone was all one needed in order to understand the sad rage this man and woman felt toward each other, like a pair of beasts caught side by side, each with a limb in the jaws of the same cruel trap, and at first they scream and bite at each other's face, and then they begin to gnaw on the flesh and bone of their own trapped limb.

What in 1952 had been the kitchen was now a restaurant dining room, the floor 37 covered with bright green indoor-outdoor carpeting, the walls paneled over in imi- tation pine with five-and-dime framed pictures of a trout stream with a deer bend- ing its head to drink, a barn and silo and waves of grain, a covered bridge with throngs of fall foliage behind it. I smelled food cooking, and I walked through the door that had once led to the woodshed behind the kitchen and discovered that it led now to a large open room filled with stainless steel counters, dishwashers, sinks, and stoves. I saw in the far corner of the room a small man in white pants and

T-shirt scrubbing utensils in a sink. He saw me and waved, as if he'd been expecting me. He was in his late fifties, I guessed, square faced, short, thick bodied.

I said, "I'm not here to eat, don't worry." 38

He smiled and nodded. "We're not set up yet, anyhow. Too early, friend." 39

"Yes, well, I'm not here to eat," I repeated. "I used to live here." 40

He squinted across the room at me. Then he pursed his lips and pronounced my last name. My very name. 41

"Yes!" I said, astonished. "That's right!" I did not know this man, I had never seen him before. I felt my father loom up beside me, huge and red and full of heat, and I looked automatically to my left, where I felt his presence most, and leaned away from him, then recovered and stood straight and regarded the small man in white before me. 42

He put down the spoon he'd been scrubbing and took a step closer. He said my father's first name and his last. "The plumber. Right? The plumber?" 43

"Well, yes. My father. I'm not him, though. I'm his son." 44

He examined my face for a few seconds, as if he did not believe me. He was looking at a gray-haired man in his late forties, a man nearly a decade older than my father had been in 1952. I was, however, more likely my father than my father's son. 45

I told him that my father had died five years ago. 46

He was sad to hear that and asked what he died of. 47

"Liver," I said. "He pretty much drank himself to death." 48

He nodded. "Yeah, well, those construction guys. They all hit the booze pretty hard. I ran the food concession for the job your dad was on, down there at the depot," he said. "I was a kid then, just out of the service. I knew your dad, what a guy he was! Memorable. He had what you call real personality, your dad." He wiped his hands with a towel and stuck one out to shake. "George Rettstadt," he said. "I bought this place a few years after your dad lived here. He rented it, right? Brought your mom and the kids out from someplace in New England for a while, right? C'mon and look around, if you want. I've made loads of changes, as you can see," he said, waving his arms at the four corners of the room, just like the drunk at the bar. 49

I agreed. There had been a lot of changes. But even so, it was the same house, and it smelled the same to me, the light fell at familiar angles through the maple trees and tall narrow windows, rooms opened into rooms where they always had. Rettstadt had turned woodshed into kitchen and kitchen into dining room, he had covered walls and floors and he had lowered ceilings, hung brass lamps and tacky pictures. He had altered the whole function of the house—though he still lived in it, he assured me, upstairs. The living room was now a large second dining room that was for private parties, which he said was most of his business. "You know, Lions Club, Boy Scouts, stuff like that. Reunions, weddings, like that." 50

Rettstadt walked ahead of me, pointing out the changes, while I saw only the house that lay hidden beneath this one, the white house under the blue one, the drab decaying farmhouse in the woods where a young man had stuck his unhappy wife and bewildered children while he drove into town to work every day and to drink every night and tried to invent a man he could never become. 51

On that snowy Saturday long ago, while my mother shrieked at my father and he bellowed back, barking like an angry dog at her small spitting face, I finally darted past them and fled the kitchen for the bedroom upstairs that I shared with my 52 brother. It was a corner room with a pair of long windows on one side and our twin beds on the other. I remember lying on my bed, the one nearer the windows, reading a comic book, probably, with my wet feet on the clean bedspread, my arm crooked back to support my head, when suddenly the door flew open, and my mother was hovering over me like a great bird, clutching my shirt and yanking me up beside her on the bed.

"Tell me!" she cried. "Tell me where you went! Don't you lie to me, too!" She 53 raised her hand and held it, palm out, a few inches from my face, as if she wanted me to read it, and she said, "Don't *you* lie to me, too, or I swear, I'll go crazy. Tell me where you went all afternoon. I know he took you to the bar in town. He did, didn't he? He didn't get stuck in the snow, and he didn't go to the depot. He just went to the bar. And there was a woman there, I know it. Tell me the truth."

I did not protest, I did not hesitate. I nodded my head up and down, and said, 54 "We went to the bar in town. Nowhere else."

She smiled, wiped the tears from her cheeks and stood. "Good boy," she said. 55 "Good boy." She turned and left the room. I lay back down trembling, and in a few seconds the buzz of the electric trains from the attic room in back replaced the buzz in my head, and I believe I fell asleep.

When George Rettstadt asked me if I wanted to see how he'd changed the rooms 56 upstairs, where he said he had fixed up a large apartment for himself and his wife, I felt my chest tighten. "No," I said very quickly, as if he had invited me to look steadily at a gruesome object. "No, that's okay, I'm in kind of a hurry, anyhow," I said, easing toward the door. "I wanted to walk around the yard a minute. I wanted to see where my brother and sister and I used to play. You know."

Rettstadt said, "Sure, take all the time you want. Look at whatever you want to 57 look at, everything's unlocked. We never lock our doors out here, you know." He opened the door, we shook hands, and I stepped out, breathing rapidly.

I did poke into the barn, but there was nothing about it that spoke to me. I stood 58 inside the dark cluttered building and it was as if I were resting, idling, conserving energy for a more strenuous enterprise to come.

A moment later I had walked around the back of the house, crossed through the 59 tangled brush and crumbling stone walls in the gathering dusk and had come to stand next to the house on the far side, just below my old bedroom window.

My father's heavy footsteps on the stairs had wakened me. He swung open the 60 bedroom door, and I knew instantly, as if I had been standing downstairs in the kitchen between my mother and father, what had happened between them when she had returned from my room armed with betrayal, and with utter clarity and an almost welcoming acceptance, I knew what would happen now between him and me.

Violence produces white light and heat inside the head, and it happens both to 61 the person who administers the beating and to the person who is beaten. It is never dark and cold. It happens at the instant of violent contact, before pain is felt, or fear, even, or guilt, so that pain, fear, and guilt come to be seen as merely the price one pays afterward for this extraordinary immolation. It's as if violence were a gift worth any price. Beyond the light and the heat, it's a gift that engenders gorgeous dreams of retribution that last for tens of generations of fathers and children, husbands and wives—it shapes and drives fantasies of becoming huge as a glacier and hard as iron, fast as light and sudden, like a volcano.

When you are hit in the head or slammed in the ribs and thrown to the floor by   62
a powerful man, you find instantly that you are already halfway into a narrative that
portrays your return to that moment, a narrative whose primary function is to provide reversal: to make the child into the man, the weak into the strong, the bad into
the good. Listen to me: you are locked into that narrative, and no other terms, except those present at its inception, at the very opening of the drama, are available for
the reversal—and, oh! when that happens, I have risen up from my narrow bed in
the upstairs corner room I shared with my brother in Tobyhanna in 1952, and I
overwhelm my dead father's rage with an awful crippling rage of my own.

I eventually moved away from that spot beneath the window of the bedroom and   63
got into my car and drove back to Tobyhanna and then on down to East Stroudsburg University, where that evening I gave my lecture to a small gathering of students and teachers, who seemed appreciative and expressed it with good-natured
gentle applause. Afterwards, we ate and drank a little wine in a local restaurant, and
I drove home to New York.

I will not go back to the house in Tobyhanna or to the bar in town, just as—after   64
having been there once—I have not returned to any of the other houses we lived in
when I was growing up, or to the apartments and barrooms in Florida and Boston
and New Hampshire, where I first learned the need to protect other people from
myself, people who loved me, male and female, and utter strangers, male and female. I go back to each, one time only, and I stand silently outside a window or a
door, and I deliberately play back the horrible events that took place there. Then I
move on.

I have traveled a lot in recent years, and consequently I have completed almost all   65
my journeys now. When I have returned to every place where someone beat me or I
beat someone, when there is no place left to go back to, then for the rest of my life I
will have only my memories, these stories, to go to—for the heat, for the light, for
the awful endlessly recurring end of it.

Working with the Text

1. Banks's story falls into two interwoven parts: one is set in the recent past as
the narrator returns to the town and the house where his troubled family lived
for "the most crucial year of our shared life"; the other recounts his memories
of a specific traumatic incident played out in that setting some forty years earlier. What sort of interplay among place, memory, and story does Banks establish? How, for example, are memories triggered by the places the narrator
visits—the bar, the different rooms of the house? Why does the narrator
choose not to go upstairs? What memory is he afraid of confronting?

2. At one point the bartender tells the narrator that in this small town, "you
never lock your doors here. It's safe." How does that turn out to be an ironic
comment? What roles do the ideas—or myths—of safety and security play in
the story?

3. Near the end of the story, the narrator comments, "When you are hit in the
head or slammed in the ribs and thrown to the floor by a powerful man, you
find instantly that you are already halfway into a narrative that portrays your

return to that moment, a narrative whose primary function is to provide reversal: to make the child into the man, the weak into the strong, the bad into the good. Listen to me: you are locked into that narrative. . . ." What does he mean? Can you think of other ways that our experiences lock us into "narratives" that we replay throughout our lives? What about the role of "class" in the story? Can class determine a certain narrative? Does it in this story? What other dimensions of people's lives lock them into narratives?

4. The narrator ends by recalling his return to other places "where I first learned the need to protect other people from myself," "where someone beat me or I beat someone." What is the point of his revisiting—only once—each of these places? What is your response to the final line, where he says that once he's returned to each of the places, "I will have only my memories, these stories, to go to—for the heat, for the light, for the awful endlessly recurring end of it"?

 5. There are many resources on the World Wide Web related to domestic violence. There are also newsgroups and bulletin boards devoted to discussions of domestic violence. As you look at some of these sources, think about the ways that Banks describes the emotions he feels as the victim of child abuse and domestic violence. Can you find a discussion about violence on any of these Internet sources that voices anything like Banks's emotions? Or contrasts with them?

GROWING UP ASIAN IN AMERICA

KESAYA NODA

■ Born in the United States to second generation Japanese American parents who had been forced into internment camps during World War II, Kesaya Noda grew up in New Hampshire with few other Japanese neighbors or friends. Before attending college, she studied in Japan for a year and a half, then returned to her birthplace, California, to research the history of Japanese American settlement prior to World War II for her book *The Yamamoto Colony*. She later entered divinity school and has devoted much of her time to studying Shinto, the native religion of Japan. In the following essay, written for a collection of works by Asian American women entitled *Making Waves*, Noda reflects on what she sees as the three central pieces of her identity: "racially Japanese," "Japanese-American," "Japanese-American woman." The result is a multilayered meditation on self-definition.

Sometimes when I was growing up, my identity seemed to hurtle toward me and paste itself right to my face. I felt that way, encountering the stereotypes of my race perpetuated by non-Japanese people (primarily white) who may or may not have had contact with other Japanese in America. "You don't like cheese, do you?" someone would ask. "I know your people don't like cheese." Sometimes questions came making allusions to history. That was another aspect of the identity. Events that had happened quite apart from the me who stood silent in that moment connected my face with an incomprehensible past. "Your parents were in California? Were they in those camps during the war?" And sometimes there were phrases or nicknames: "Lotus Blossom." I was sometimes addressed or referred to as racially Japanese, sometimes as Japanese-American, and sometimes as an Asian woman. Confusions and distortions abounded.

How is one to know and define oneself? From the inside—within a context that is self-defined from a grounding in community and a connection with culture and history that are comfortably accepted? Or from the outside—in terms of messages received from the media and people who are often ignorant? Even as an adult I can still see two sides of my face and past. I can see from the inside out, in freedom. And I can see from the outside in, driven by the old voices of childhood and lost in anger and fear.

I AM RACIALLY JAPANESE

A voice from my childhood says: "You are other. You are less than. You are unalterably alien." This voice has its own history. We have indeed been seen as other and alien since the early years of our arrival in the United States. The very first immigrants were welcomed and sought as laborers to replace the dwindling numbers of Chinese, whose influx had been cut off by the Chinese Exclusion Act of 1882. The Japanese fell natural heir to the same anti-Asian prejudice that had arisen against the Chinese. As soon as they began striking for better wages, they were no longer welcomed.

I can see myself today as a person historically defined by law and custom as being forever alien. Being neither "free white," nor "African," our people in California were deemed "aliens, ineligible for citizenship," no matter how long they intended to stay here. Aliens ineligible for citizenship were prohibited from owning, buying, or leasing land. They did not and could not belong here. The voice in me remembers that I am always a *Japanese*-American in the eyes of many. A third-generation German-American is an American. A third-generation Japanese-American is a Japanese-American. Being Japanese means being a danger to the country during the war and knowing how to use chopsticks. I wear this history on my face.

I move to the other side. I see a different light and claim a different context. My race is a line that stretches across ocean and time to link me to the shrine where my grandmother was raised. Two high, white banners lift in the wind at the top of the stone steps leading to the shrine. It is time for the summer festival. Black characters are written against the sky as boldly as the clouds, as lightly as kites, as sharply as the big black crows I used to see above the fields in New Hampshire. At festival time there is liquor and food, ritual, discipline, and abandonment. There is music and drunkenness and invocation. There is hope. Another season has come. Another season has gone.

I am racially Japanese. I have a certain claim to this crazy place where the prayers intoned by a neighboring Shinto priest (standing in for my grandmother's nephew who is sick) are drowned out by the rehearsals for the pop singing contest in which most of the villagers will compete later that night. The village elders, the priest, and I stand respectfully upon the immaculate, shining wooden floor of the outer shrine, bowing our heads before the hidden powers. During the patchy intervals when I can hear him, I notice the priest has a stutter. His voice flutters up to my ears only occasionally because two men and a woman are singing gustily into a microphone in the compound, testing the sound system. A prerecorded tape of guitars, samisens, and drums accompanies them. Rock music and Shinto prayers. That night, to loud applause and cheers, a young man is given the award for the most *netsuretsu*—passionate, burning—rendition of a song. We roar our approval of the reward. Never mind that his voice had wandered and slid, now slightly above, now slightly below the given line of the melody. Netsuretsu. Netsuretsu.

In the morning, my grandmother's sister kneels at the foot of the stone stairs to offer her morning prayers. She is too crippled to climb the stairs, so each morning she kneels here upon the path. She shuts her eyes for a few seconds, her motions as matter of fact as when she washes rice. I linger longer than she does, so reluctant to leave, savoring the connection I feel with my grandmother in America, the past, and the power that lives and shines in the morning sun. 7

Our family has served this shrine for generations. The family's need to protect this claim to identity and place outweighs any individual claim to any individual hope. I am Japanese. 8

I AM A JAPANESE-AMERICAN

"Weak." I hear the voice from my childhood years. "Passive," I hear. Our parents and grandparents were the ones who were put into those camps. They went without resistance; they offered cooperation as proof of loyalty to America. "Victim," I hear. And, "Silent." 9

Our parents are painted as hard workers who were socially uncomfortable and had difficulty expressing even the smallest opinion. Clean, quiet, motivated, and determined to match the American way; that is us, and that is the story of our time here. 10

"Why did you go into those camps?" I raged at my parents, frightened by my own inner silence and timidity. "Why didn't you do anything to resist? Why didn't you name it the injustice it was?" Couldn't our parents even think? Couldn't they? Why were we so passive? 11

I shift my vision and my stance. I am in California. My uncle is in the midst of the sweet potato harvest. He is pressed, trying to get the harvesting crews onto the field as quickly as possible, worried about the flow of equipment and people. His big pickup is pulled off to the side, motor running, door ajar. I see two tractors in the yard in front of an old shed; the flatbed harvesting platform on which the workers will stand has already been brought over from the other field. It's early morning. The workers stand loosely grouped and at ease, but my uncle looks as harried and tense as a police officer trying to unsnarl a New York City traffic jam. Driving toward the shed, I pull my car off the road to make way for an approaching tractor. The front wheels of the car sink luxuriously into the soft, white sand by the roadside and the car slides to a dreamy halt, tail still on the road. I try to move forward. I try to move back. The front bites contentedly into the sand, the back lifts itself at a jaunty angle. My uncle sees me and storms down the road, running. He is shouting before he is even near me. 12

"What's the matter with you?" he screams. "What the hell are you doing?" In his   13
frenzy, he grabs his hat off his head and slashes it through the air across his knee. He
is beside himself. "Don't you know how to drive in sand? What's the matter with
you? You've blocked the whole roadway. How am I supposed to get my tractors out
of here? Can't you use your head? You've cut off the whole roadway, and we've got to
get out of here."

I stand on the road before him helplessly thinking, "No, I don't know how to   14
drive in sand. I've never driven in sand."

"I'm sorry, uncle," I say, burying a smile beneath a look of sincere apology. I no-   15
tice my deep amusement and my affection for him with great curiosity. I am usually
devastated by anger. Not this time.

During the several years that follow I learn about the people and the place, and   16
much more about what has happened in this California village where my parents
grew up. The issei, our grandparents, made this settlement in the desert. Their first
crops were eaten by rabbits and ravaged by insects. The land was so barren that men
walking from house to house sometimes got lost. Women came here too. They bore
children in 114-degree heat, then carried the babies with them into the fields to
nurse when they reached the end of each row of grapes or other truck-farm crops.

I had had no idea what it meant to buy this kind of land and make it grow green.   17
Or how, when the war came, there was no space at all for the subtlety of being who
we were—Japanese-Americans. Either/or was the way. I hadn't understood that
people were literally afraid for their lives then, that their money had been frozen in
banks; that there was a five-mile travel limit; that when the early evening curfew
came and they were inside their houses, some of them watched helplessly as people
they knew went into their barns to steal their belongings. The police were patrolling
the road, interested only in violators of curfew. There was no help for them in the
face of thievery. I had not been able to imagine before what it must have felt like to
be an American—to know absolutely that one is an American—and yet to have almost everyone else deny it. Not only deny it, but challenge that identity with machine guns and troops of white American soldiers. In those circumstances it was
difficult to say, "I'm a Japanese-American." "American" had to do.

But now I can say that I am a Japanese-American. It means I have a place here in   18
this country, too. I have a place here on the East Coast, where our neighbor is so
much a part of our family that my mother never passes her house at night without
glancing at the lights to see if she is home and safe; where my parents have hauled
hundreds of pounds of rocks from fields and arduously planted Christmas trees and
blueberries, lilacs, asparagus, and crab apples, where my father still dreams of an-
gling a stream to a new bed so that he can dig a pond in the field and fill it with water
and fish. "The neighbors already came for their Christmas tree?" he asks in December. "Did they like it? Did they like it?"

I have a place on the West Coast where my relatives still farm, where I heard the   19
stories of feuds and backbiting, and where I saw that people survived and flourished
because fundamentally they trusted and relied upon one another. A death in the
family is not just a death in a family; it is a death in the community. I saw people
help each other with money, materials, labor, attention, and time. I saw men gather
once a year, without fail, to clean the grounds of a ninety-year-old woman who had

helped the community before, during, and after the war. I saw her remembering them with birthday cards sent to each of their children.

I come from a people with a long memory and a distinctive grace. We live our   20
thanks. And we are Americans. Japanese-Americans.

I AM A JAPANESE-AMERICAN WOMAN

Woman. The last piece of my identity. It has been easier by far for me to know my-   21
self in Japan and to see my place in America than it has been to accept my line of connection with my own mother. She was my dark self, a figure in whom I thought I saw all that I feared most in myself. Growing into womanhood and looking for some model of strength, I turned away from her. Of course, I could not find what I sought. I was looking for a black feminist or a white feminist. My mother is neither white nor black.

My mother is a woman who speaks with her life as much as with her tongue. I   22
think of her with her own mother. Grandmother had Parkinson's disease and it had frozen her gait and set her fingers, tongue, and feet jerking and trembling in a terrible dance. My aunts and uncles wanted her to be able to live in her own home. They fed her, bathed her, dressed her, awoke at midnight to take her for one last trip to the bathroom. My aunts (her daughters-in-law) did most of the care, but my mother went from New Hampshire to California each summer to spend a month living with Grandmother, because she wanted to and because she wanted to give my aunts at least a small rest. During those hot summer days, mother lay on the couch watching the television or reading, cooking foods that Grandmother liked, and speaking little. Grandmother thrived under her care.

The time finally came when it was too dangerous for Grandmother to live alone.   23
My relatives kept finding her on the floor beside her bed when they went to wake her in the mornings. My mother flew to California to help clean the house and make arrangements for Grandmother to enter a local nursing home. On her last day at home, while Grandmother was sitting in her big, overstuffed armchair, hair combed and wearing a green summer dress, my mother went to her and knelt at her feet. "Here, Mamma," she said. "I've polished your shoes." She lifted Grandmother's legs and helped her into the shiny black shoes. My Grandmother looked down and smiled slightly. She left her house walking, supported by her children, carrying her pocket book, and wearing her polished black shoes. "Look, Mamma," my mom had said, kneeling. "I've polished your shoes."

Just the other day, my mother came to Boston to visit. She had recently lost a lot   24
of weight and was pleased with her new shape and her feeling of good health. "Look at me, Kes," she exclaimed, turning toward me, front and back, as naked as the day she was born. I saw her small breasts and the wide, brown scar, belly button to pubic hair, that marked her because my brother and I were both born by Caesarean section. Her hips were small. I was not a large baby, but there was so little room for me in her that when she was carrying me she could not even begin to bend over toward the floor. She hated it, she said.

"Don't I look good? Don't you think I look good?"   25

I looked at my mother, smiling and as happy as she, thinking of all the times I 26
have seen her naked. I have seen both my parents naked throughout my life, as they
have seen me. From childhood through adulthood we've had our naked moments,
sharing baths, idle conversations picked up as we moved between showers and closets, hurried moments at the beginning of days, quiet moments at the end of days.

I know this to be Japanese, this ease with the physical, and it makes me think of 27
an old Japanese folk song. A young nursemaid, a fifteen-year-old girl, is singing a
lullaby to a baby who is strapped to her back. The nursemaid has been sent as a servant to a place far from her own home. "We're the beggars," she says, "and they are
the nice people. Nice people wear fine sashes. Nice clothes."

> If I should drop dead,
> bury me by the roadside!
> I'll give a flower
> to everyone who passes.
>
> What kind of flower?
> The cam-cam-camellia [*tsun-tsun-tsubaki*]
> watered by Heaven:
> alms water.

The nursemaid is the intersection of heaven and earth, the intersection of the 28
human, the natural world, the body, and the soul. In this song, with clear eyes, she
looks steadily at life, which is sometimes so very terrible and sad. I think of her while
looking at my mother, who is standing on the red and purple carpet before me,
laughing, without any clothes.

> I am my mother's daughter. And I am myself.
> I am a Japanese-American woman.

EPILOGUE

I recently heard a man from West Africa share some memories of his childhood. He 29
was raised Muslim, but when he was a young man, he found himself deeply drawn
to Christianity. He struggled against his inner impulse for years, trying to avoid the
church yet feeling pushed to return to it again and again. "I would have done *anything* to avoid the change," he said. At last, he became Christian. Afterwards he was
afraid to go home, fearing that he would not be accepted. The fear was groundless,
he discovered, when at last he returned—he had separated himself, but his family
and friends (all Muslim) had not separated themselves from him.

The man, who is now a professor of religion, said that in the Africa he knew as a 30
child and a young man, pluralism was embraced rather than feared. There was "a
kind of tolerance that did not deny your particularity," he said. He alluded to zest-
ful, spontaneous debates that would sometimes loudly erupt between Muslims and
Christians in the village's public spaces. His memories of an atheist who harangued
the villagers when he came to visit them once a week moved me deeply. Perhaps the
man was an agricultural advisor or inspector. He harassed the women. He would
say: "Don't go to the fields! Don't even bother to go to the fields. Let God take care

of you. He'll send you the food. If you believe in God, why do you need to work? You don't need to work! Let God put the seeds in the ground. Stay home."

The professor said, "The women laughed, you know? They just laughed. Their at-   31
titude was, 'Here is a child of God. When will he come home?'"

The storyteller, the professor of religion, smiled a most fantastic tender smile as   32
he told this story. "In my country, there is a deep affirmation of the oneness of God," he said. "The atheist and the women were having quite different experiences in their encounter, though the atheist did not know this. He saw himself as quite separate from the women. But the women did not see themselves as being separate from him. 'Here is a child of God,' they said. 'When will he come home?'"

Working with the Text

1. Noda begins by posing a question that is central to the themes of this chapter: "How is one to know and define oneself? From the inside—within a context that is self-defined, from a grounding in community and a connection with culture and history that are comfortably accepted? Or from the outside—in terms of messages received from the media and people who are often ignorant?" To what extent do you think that the realities of "community and culture" can be influenced by external images, by stereotypes and media myths? Is this a particular problem for "hyphenated" Americans, as Noda suggests, or do most people struggle with such "received" messages?

2. Of the shrine she visits with her grandmother's sister in Japan, Noda writes, "The family's need to protect this claim to identity and place outweighs any individual claim to any individual hope." Do you agree that some "family needs" outweigh any "individual claims"? What sorts of specific family needs may seem to have this pull?

3. Of the Japanese internment during the Second World War, Noda writes that she "had not been able to imagine before what it must have felt like to be an American—to know absolutely that one is an American—and yet to have almost everyone else deny it." How do you think "imagining" this feeling might contribute to her sense of being Japanese American? Can you imagine yourself receiving some unjust treatment that others have been subjected to but that you haven't literally experienced? Does your attempt to do so change your perception of that injustice?

4. In looking for a woman who is a model of strength, Noda states that she first turned away from her mother, in whom, she tells us, "I thought I saw all that I feared most in myself." What is it that she feared? In what ways does the adult Noda writing this essay seem both like and unlike her mother? How do you think Noda would define "Japanese-American woman"?

5. Do you think that all people have multiple aspects to their identity, as Noda illustrates by breaking down her identity in this essay? Do these change over the course of one's life? Using yourself as an example—perhaps along with close family members or friends—consider the extent to which identity can be divided in terms of race, national affiliation, gender, sexual orientation,

and other aspects of the self. Are these ever in conflict? If so, how might the conflict be resolved?

FAMILY PORTRAIT

SHERMAN ALEXIE

■ Of native Spokane/Coeur d'Alene heritage, Sherman Alexie grew up in the 1970s and 1980s on the Spokane Reservation near Wellpint, Washington. He began writing while in college and is currently one of the country's most well-regarded young novelists and short-story authors. Among his highly praised books are *The Business of Fancydancing* (1992), *Reservation Blues,* and *Indian Killer* (1996). You may find the following story, from *The Lone Ranger and Tonto Fistfight in Heaven* (1993), a bit of a challenge. Instead of conventional narrative, what Alexie offers here is a series of impressionistic, sometimes fantastic, and even surreal images and scenes of family life on the reservation. As you read, consider what the discontinuities and surreal images suggest about the identity of the son telling the story.

The television was always loud, too loud, until every conversation was distorted, fragmented.   1

"Dinner" sounded like "Leave me alone."   2

"I love you" sounded like "Inertia."   3

"Please" sounded like "Sacrifice."   4

Believe me, the television was always too loud. At three in the morning I woke   5
from ordinary nightmares to hear the television pounding the ceiling above my bed. Sometimes it was just white noise, the end of another broadcasting day. Other times it was a bad movie made worse by the late hour and interrupted sleep.

"Drop your weapons and come out with your hands above your head" sounded   6
too much like "Trust me, the world is yours."

"The aliens are coming! The aliens are coming!" sounded too much like "Just one   7
more beer, sweetheart, and then we'll go home."

"Junior, I lost the money" sounded too much like "You'll never have a dream   8
come true."

I don't know where all the years went. I remember only the television in detail.   9
All the other moments worth remembering became stories that changed with each telling, until nothing was aboriginal or recognizable.

For instance, in the summer of 1972 or 1973 or only in our minds, the reserva-   10
tion disappeared. I remember standing on the front porch of our HUD house, practicing on my plastic saxophone, when the reservation disappeared.

Finally, I remember thinking, but I was six years old, or seven. I don't know for   11
sure how old; I was Indian.

Just like that, there was nothing there beyond the bottom step. My older brother   12
told me he'd give me a quarter if I jumped into the unknown. My twin sisters cried equal tears; their bicycles had been parked out by the pine trees, all of it vanished.

My mother came out to investigate the noise. She stared out past the bottom step 13 for a long time, but there was no expression on her face when she went back to wash the potatoes.

My father was happily drunk and he stumbled off the bottom step before any of 14 us could stop him. He came back years later with diabetes and a pocketful of quarters. The seeds in the cuffs of his pants dropped to the floor of our house and grew into orange trees.

"Nothing is possible without Vitamin C," my mother told us, but I knew she 15 meant to say, "Don't want everything so much."

Often the stories contain people who never existed before our collective imagi- 16 nations created them.

My brother and I remember our sisters scraped all the food that dropped off our 17 plates during dinner into a pile in the center of the table. Then they placed their teeth against the edge of the table and scraped all the food into their open mouths.

Our parents don't remember that happening, and our sisters cry out, "No, no, we 18 were never that hungry!"

Still, my brother and I cannot deny the truth of our story. We were there. Maybe 19 hunger informs our lives.

My family tells me stories of myself, small events and catastrophic diseases I don't 20 remember but accept as the beginning of my story.

After surgery to relieve fluid pressure on my brain, I started to dance. 21

"No," my mother tells me. "You had epileptic seizures." 22

"No," my father tells her. "He was dancing." 23

During "The Tonight Show" I pretended sleep on the couch while my father sat 24 in his chair and watched the television.

"It was Doc's trumpet that made you dance," my father told me. 25

"No, it was grand mal seizures punctuated by moments of extreme perception," 26 my mother told him.

She wanted to believe I could see the future. She secretly knew the doctors had 27 inserted another organ into my skull, transplanted a twentieth-century vision.

One winter she threw me outside in my underwear and refused to let me back 28 into the house until I answered her questions.

"Will my children love me when I'm old?" she asked, but I knew she wanted to 29 ask me, "Will I regret my life?"

Then there was music, scratched 45's and eight-track tapes. We turned the vol- 30 ume too high for the speakers, until the music was tinny and distorted. But we danced, until my oldest sister tore her only pair of nylons and wept violently. But we danced, until we shook dust down from the ceiling and chased bats out of the attic into the daylight. But we danced, in our mismatched clothes and broken shoes. I wrote my name in Magic Marker on my shoes, my first name on the left toe and my last name on the right toe, with my true name somewhere in between. But we danced, with empty stomachs and nothing for dinner except sleep. All night we lay awake with sweat on our backs and blisters on our soles. All night we fought waking nightmares until sleep came with nightmares of its own. I remember the nightmare about the thin man in a big hat who took the Indian children away from their parents. He came with scissors to cut hair and a locked box to hide all the amputated braids. But we danced, under wigs and between unfinished walls, through broken promises and around empty cupboards.

It was a dance.   31

Still, we can be surprised.   32

My sister told me she could recognize me by the smell of my clothes. She said she   33
could close her eyes and pick me out of a crowd by just the smell of my shirt.

I knew she meant to say *I love you.*   34

With all the systems of measurements we had available, I remember the degree of   35
sunlight most. It was there continuously, winter or summer. The cold came by accident, the sun by design.

Then there was the summer of sniffing gas. My sisters bent their heads at impos-   36
sible angles to reach the gas tanks of BIA vehicles. Everything so bright and precise, it hurt the brain. Eardrums pounded by the slightest noise; a dog barking could change the shape of the earth.

I remember my brother stretched out over the lawnmower, his mouth pressed   37
tightly to the mouth of the gas tank. It was a strange kiss, his first kiss, his lips burnt and clothes flammable. He tried to dance away, he named every blade of grass he crushed when he fell on his ass. Everything under water, like walking across the bottom of Benjamin Lake, past dead horses and abandoned tires. Legs tangled in seaweed, dance, dance again, kick the feet until you break free. Stare up at the surface, sunlight filtered through water like fingers, like a hand filled with the promise of love and oxygen.

WARNING: *Intentional misuse by deliberately concentrating and inhaling the con-*   38
tents can be harmful or fatal.

How much do we remember of what hurts us most? I've been thinking about   39
pain, how each of us constructs our past to justify what we feel now. How each successive pain distorts the preceding. Let's say I remember sunlight as a measurement of this story, how it changed the shape of the family portrait. My father shields his eyes and makes his face a shadow. He could be anyone then, but my eyes are closed in the photo. I cannot remember what I was thinking. Maybe I wanted to stand, stretch my legs, raise my arms above my head, open my mouth wide, and fill my lungs. *Breathe, breathe.* Maybe my hair is so black it collects all the available light.

Suddenly it is winter and I'm trying to start the car.   40

"Give it more gas," my father shouts from the house.   41

I put my foot to the fire wall, feel the engine shudder in response. My hands grip   42
the steering wheel tightly. They are not mine this morning. These hands are too strong, too necessary for even the smallest gestures. I can make fists and throw my anger into walls and plasterboard. I can pick up a toothbrush or a pistol, touch the face of a woman I love. Years ago, these hands might have held the spear that held the salmon that held the dream of the tribe. Years ago, these hands might have touched the hands of the dark-skinned men who touched medicine and the magic of ordinary gods. Now, I put my hand to gearshift, my heart to the cold wind.

"Give it more gas," my father yells.   43

I put the car into Drive and then I am gone, down the road, carefully, touching   44
the brake like I touch my dreams. Once, my father and I drove this same road and
he told the story of the first television he ever saw.

"The television was in the window of a store in Coeur d'Alene. Me and all the   45
guys would walk down there and watch it. Just one channel and all it showed was a
woman sitting on top of a television that showed the same woman sitting on top of
the same television. Over and over until it hurt your eyes and head. That's the way I
remember it. And she was always singing some song. I think it was 'A Girl on Top of
the World.'"

This is how we find our history, how we sketch our family portrait, how we snap   46
the photograph at the precise moment when someone's mouth is open and ready to
ask a question. *How?*

There is a girl on top of the world. She is owldancing with my father. That is the   47
story by which we measure all our stories, until we understand that one story can
never be all.

There is a girl on top of the world. She is singing the blues. That is the story by   48
which we measure heartbreak. Maybe she is my sister or my other sister or my oldest sister dead in the house fire. Maybe she is my mother with her hands in the fry
bread. Maybe she is my brother.

There is a girl on top of the world. She is telling us her story. That is the story by   49
which we measure the beginning of all of our lives. *Listen, listen, what can be calling?*
She is why we hold each other tight; she is why our fear refuses naming. She is the
fancydancer; she is forgiveness.

The television was always loud, too loud, until every emotion was measured by   50
the half hour. We hid our faces behind masks that suggested other histories; we
touched hands accidentally and our skin sparked like a personal revolution. We
stared across the room at each other, waited for the conversation and the conversion, watched wasps and flies battering against the windows. We were children; we
were open mouths. Open in hunger, in anger, in laughter, in prayer.

Jesus, we all want to survive.   51

Working with the Text

1. Alexie's language and narrative style in this story are often surprising and
unconventional. Sometimes he uses unexpected sentences or parts of sentences that repeat what he has said before. One of the purposes of this style, it
seems, is to draw attention to his "jumps" between thoughts. Evaluate Alexie's
technique. What do all these quickly described scenes and impressions add up
to? (One way to analyze Alexie's technique would be to pick a passage from
the story and then write something about your own life while imitating his
style. You might share your imitations in class or post them on a discussion
list.)

2. At one point Alexie writes, "How much do we remember of what hurts us
most? . . . Each of us constructs our past to justify what we feel now." In what

other ways does he describe the relation among memory, identity, and story-telling? How does he portray the relationship among storytelling (our personal histories), imagination, memory, and a sense of self-identity? Begin to address this question by looking at a single passage and talking specifically about it, then moving out more broadly to discuss the whole story.

3. Alexie raises some interesting issues about language and communication when he repeats conversational exchanges in terms of what the words spoken "sounded like" or "really meant." What is the connection between "words" and "understood meaning" in these exchanges? Can you relate them in any way to communication within your own family?

4. Note Alexie's references to traditional imagery and myths of Native American culture as well as to some of the social problems associated with contemporary reservation life. How does he seem to suggest these are involved in shaping his individual and family identity?

5. Alexie calls his story "Family Portrait." How is his story a portrait? Look through the images in the portfolio and elsewhere in this book, several of which are "portraits" of one kind or another—for example, Plate 4, *Familiar Names and Not-so-Familiar Faces,* and Plate 3, *Studio City.* How do people look in portraits? What kind of image or persona do people project in that kind of photograph? Which picture in this book do you think best relates to Alexie's story? Do you have a picture of your own family that embodies Alexie's style?

 6. In paragraph 20, Alexie notes, "My family tells me stories of myself, small events and catastrophic diseases I don't remember but accept as the beginning of my story." How does Alexie's story explore the shaping power of stories we receive about ourselves? How is identity, as explored in his story, the product of the gap between realities—between what we hear and what people mean, between what we remember and what we are told, between what we desire and what actually is? Is reality entirely defined by perception and perspective?

SILENT DANCING

JUDITH ORTIZ COFER

■ Born in Puerto Rico, Judith Ortiz Cofer spent much of her childhood in Paterson, New Jersey, during the late 1950s and 1960s. The author of poetry, fiction, and several collections of autobiographical essays, including *Silent Dancing* (1990) and *The Latin Deli* (1993), Ortiz Cofer currently teaches at the University of Georgia. In the following essay, she explores the conflict between assimilating into mainstream U.S. culture and maintaining the values and customs of one's cultural heritage. She does so by interspersing incidents from the life of her family with images from a home movie of a party attended by various uncles, aunts,

and cousins whose differing feelings about their new home reflect conflicts that
would shape Ortiz Cofer's own identity.

*We have a home movie of this party. Several times my mother and I have watched it to-
gether, and I have asked questions about the silent revelers coming in and out of focus.
It is grainy and of short duration, but it's a great visual aid to my memory of life at that
time. And it is in color—the only complete scene in color I can recall from those years.*

1

We lived in Puerto Rico until my brother was born in 1954. Soon after, be-
cause of economic pressures on our growing family, my father joined the
United States Navy. He was assigned to duty on a ship in Brooklyn
Yard—a place of cement and steel that was to be his home base in the States until his
retirement more than twenty years later. He left the Island first, alone, going to New
York City and tracking down his uncle who lived with his family across the Hudson
River in Paterson, New Jersey. There my father found a tiny apartment in a huge tenement that had once housed Jewish families but was just being taken over and transformed by Puerto Ricans, overflowing from New York City. In 1955 he sent for us.
My mother was only twenty years old, I was not quite three, and my brother was a
toddler when we arrived at El Building, as the place had been christened by its
newest residents.

2

My memories of life in Paterson during those first few years are all in shades of
gray. Maybe I was too young to absorb vivid colors and details, or to discriminate
between the slate blue of the winter sky and the darker hues of the snow-bearing
clouds, but that single color washes over the whole period. The building we lived in
was gray, as were the streets, filled with slush the first few months of my life there.
The coat my father had bought for me was similar in color and too big; it sat heavily on my thin frame.

3

I do remember the way the heater pipes banged and rattled, startling all of us out
of sleep until we got so used to the sound that we automatically shut it out or raised
our voices above the racket. The hiss from the valve punctuated my sleep (which has
always been fitful) like a nonhuman presence in the room—a dragon sleeping at the
entrance of my childhood. But the pipes were also a connection to all the other lives
being lived around us. Having come from a house designed for a single family back
in Puerto Rico—my mother's extended-family home—it was curious to know that
strangers lived under our floor and above our heads, and that the heater pipe went
through everyone's apartment. (My first spanking in Paterson came as a result of
playing tunes on the pipes in my room to see if there would be an answer.) My
mother was as new to this concept of beehive life as I was, but she had been given
strict orders by my father to keep the doors locked, the noise down, ourselves to
ourselves.

4

It seems that Father had learned some painful lessons about prejudice while
searching for an apartment in Paterson. Not until years later did I hear how much
resistance he had encountered with landlords who were panicking at the influx of
Latinos into a neighborhood that had been Jewish for a couple of generations. It
made no difference that it was the American phenomenon of ethnic turnover which

5

was changing the urban core of Paterson, and that the human flood could not be held back with an accusing finger.

"You Cuban?" one man had asked my father, pointing at his name tag on the navy uniform—even though my father had the fair skin and light brown hair of his northern Spanish background, and the name Ortiz is as common in Puerto Rico as Johnson is in the United States.   6

"No," my father had answered, looking past the finger into his adversary's angry eyes. "I'm Puerto Rican."   7

"Same shit." And the door closed.   8

My father could have passed as European, but we couldn't. My brother and I both have our mother's black hair and olive skin, and so we lived in El Building and visited our great-uncle and his fair children on the next block. It was their private joke that they were the German branch of the family. Not many years later that area too would be mainly Puerto Rican. It was as if the heart of the city map were being gradually colored brown—*café con leche* brown. Our color.   9

The movie opens with a sweep of the living room. It is "typical" immigrant Puerto Rican decor for the time: the sofa and chairs are square and hard-looking, upholstered in bright colors (blue and yellow in this instance) and covered with the transparent plastic that furniture salesmen then were so adept at convincing women to buy. The linoleum on the floor is light blue; where it had been subjected to spike heels, as it was in most places, there were dime-size indentations all over it that cannot be seen in this movie. The room is full of people dressed up: dark suits for the men, red dresses for the women. When I have asked my mother why most of the women are in red that night, she has shrugged and said, "I don't remember. Just a coincidence." She doesn't have my obsession for assigning symbolism to everything.   10

The three women in red sitting on the couch are my mother, my eighteen-year-old cousin, and her brother's girlfriend. The novia is just up from the Island, which is apparent in her body language. She sits up formally, her dress pulled over her knees. She is a pretty girl, but her posture makes her look insecure, lost in her full-skirted dress, which she has carefully tucked around her to make room for my gorgeous cousin, her future sister-in-law. My cousin has grown up in Paterson and is in her last year of high school. She doesn't have a trace of what Puerto Ricans call la mancha *(literally, the stain: the mark of the new immigrant—something about the posture, the voice, or the humble demeanor that makes it obvious to everyone the person has just arrived on the mainland). My cousin is wearing a tight, sequined, cocktail dress. Her brown hair has been lightened with peroxide around the bangs, and she is holding a cigarette expertly between her fingers, bringing it up to her mouth in a sensuous arc of her arm as she talks animatedly. My mother, who has come up to sit between the two women, both only a few years younger than herself, is somewhere between the poles they represent in our culture.*   11

It became my father's obsession to get out of the barrio, and thus we were never permitted to form bonds with the place or with the people who lived there. Yet El Building was a comfort to my mother, who never got over yearning for *la isla*. She felt surrounded by her language: the walls were thin, and voices speaking and arguing in   12

Spanish could be heard all day. *Salsas* blasted out of radios, turned on early in the morning and left on for company. Women seemed to cook rice and beans perpetually—the strong aroma of boiling red kidney beans permeated the hallways.

Though Father preferred that we do our grocery shopping at the supermarket 13 when he came home on weekend leaves, my mother insisted that she could cook only with products whose labels she could read. Consequently, during the week I accompanied her and my little brother to La Bodega—a hole-in-the-wall grocery store across the street from El Building. There we squeezed down three narrow aisles jammed with various products. Goya and Libby's—those were the trademarks that were trusted by her *mamá*, so my mother bought many cans of Goya beans, soups, and condiments, as well as little cans of Libby's fruit juices for us. And she also bought Colgate toothpaste and Palmolive soap. (The final *e* is pronounced in both these products in Spanish, so for many years I believed that they were manufactured on the Island. I remember my surprise at first hearing a commercial on television in which "Colgate" rhymed with "ate.") We always lingered at La Bodega, for it was there that Mother breathed best, taking in the familiar aromas of the foods she knew from Mamá's kitchen. It was also there that she got to speak to the other women of El Building without violating outright Father's dictates against fraternizing with our neighbors.

Yet Father did his best to make our "assimilation" painless. I can still see him car- 14 rying a real Christmas tree up several flights of stairs to our apartment, leaving a trail of aromatic pine. He carried it formally, as if it were a flag in a parade. We were the only ones in El Building that I knew of who got presents on both Christmas and *día de Reyes*, the day when the Three Kings brought gifts to Christ and to Hispanic children.

Our supreme luxury in El Building was having our own television set. It must 15 have been a result of Father's guilt feelings over the isolation he had imposed on us, but we were among the first in the barrio to have one. My brother quickly became an avid watcher of Captain Kangaroo and Jungle Jim, while I loved all the series showing families. By the time I started first grade, I could have drawn a map of Middle America as exemplified by the lives of characters in *Father Knows Best, The Donna Reed Show, Leave It to Beaver, My Three Sons*, and (my favorite) *Bachelor Father*, where John Forsythe treated his adopted teenage daughter like a princess because he was rich and had a Chinese houseboy to do everything for him. In truth, compared to our neighbors in El Building, *we* were rich. My father's navy check provided us with financial security and a standard of living that the factory workers envied. The only thing his money could not buy us was a place to live away from the barrio—his greatest wish, Mother's greatest fear.

In the home movie the men are shown next, sitting around a card table set up in one 16 *corner of the living room, playing dominoes. The clack of the ivory pieces was a familiar sound. I heard it in many houses on the Island and in many apartments in Paterson. In* Leave It to Beaver, *the Cleavers played bridge in every other episode; in my childhood, the men started every social occasion with a hotly debated round of dominoes. The women would sit around and watch, but they never participated in the games.*

Here and there you can see a small child. Children were always brought to parties   17
and, whenever they got sleepy, were put to bed in the host's bedroom. Babysitting was a
concept unrecognized by the Puerto Rican women I knew: a responsible mother did not
leave her children with any stranger. And in a culture where children are not considered
intrusive, there was no need to leave the children at home. We went where our mother
went.

Of my preschool years I have only impressions: the sharp bite of the wind in De-   18
cember as we walked with our parents toward the brightly lit stores downtown; how
I felt like a stuffed doll in my heavy coat, boots, and mittens; how good it was to walk
into the five-and-dime and sit at the counter drinking hot chocolate. On Saturdays
our whole family would walk downtown to shop at the big department stores on
Broadway. Mother bought all our clothes at Penney's and Sears, and she liked to buy
her dresses at the women's specialty shops like Lerner's and Diana's. At some point
we'd go into Woolworth's and sit at the soda fountain to eat.

We never ran into other Latinos at these stores or when eating out, and it became   19
clear to me only years later that the women from El Building shopped mainly in
other places—stores owned by other Puerto Ricans or by Jewish merchants who had
philosophically accepted our presence in the city and decided to make us their good
customers, if not real neighbors and friends. These establishments were located not
downtown but in the blocks around our street, and they were referred to generically
as La Tienda, El Bazar, La Bodega, La Botánica. Everyone knew what was meant.
These were the stores where your face did not turn a clerk to stone, where your
money was as green as anyone else's.

One New Year's Eve we were dressed up like child models in the Sears catalogue: my   20
brother in a miniature man's suit and bow tie, and I in black patent-leather shoes
and a frilly dress with several layers of crinoline underneath. My mother wore a
bright red dress that night, I remember, and spike heels; her long black hair hung to
her waist. Father, who usually wore his navy uniform during his short visits home,
had put on a dark civilian suit for the occasion: we had been invited to his uncle's
house for a big celebration. Everyone was excited because my mother's brother Hernan—a bachelor who could indulge himself with luxuries—had bought a home
movie camera, which he would be trying out that night.

Even the home movie cannot fill in the sensory details such a gathering left im-   21
printed in a child's brain. The thick sweetness of women's perfumes mixing with the
ever-present smells of food cooking in the kitchen: meat and plantain *pasteles,* as
well as the ubiquitous rice dish made special with pigeon peas—*gandules*—and sea-
soned with precious *sofrito* sent up from the Island by somebody's mother or smuggled in by a recent traveler. *Sofrito* was one of the items that women hoarded, since
it was hardly ever in stock at La Bodega. It was the flavor of Puerto Rico.

The men drank Palo Viejo rum, and some of the younger ones got weepy. The   22
first time I saw a grown man cry was at a New Year's Eve party: he had been reminded of his mother by the smells in the kitchen. But what I remember most were
the boiled *pasteles,* plantain or yucca rectangles stuffed with corned beef or other
meats, olives, and many other savory ingredients, all wrapped in banana leaves.

Everybody had to fish one out with a fork. There was always a "trick" *pastel*—one without stuffing—and whoever got that one was the "New Year's Fool."

There was also the music. Long-playing albums were treated like precious china 23 in these homes. Mexican recordings were popular, but the songs that brought tears to my mother's eyes were sung by the melancholy Daniel Santos, whose life as a drug addict was the stuff of legend. Felipe Rodríguez was a particular favorite of couples, since he sang about faithless women and brokenhearted men. There is a snatch of one lyric that has stuck in my mind like a needle on a worn groove: *De piedra ha de ser mi cama, de piedra la cabezera . . . la mujer que a mi me quiera . . . ha de quererme de veras. Ay, Ay, Ay, corazón, porque no amas . . .* I must have heard it a thousand times since the idea of a bed made of stone, and its connection to love, first troubled me with its disturbing images.

The five-minute home movie ends with people dancing in a circle—the creative 24 filmmaker must have set it up, so that all of them could file past him. It is both comical and sad to watch silent dancing. Since there is no justification for the absurd movements that music provides for some of us, people appear frantic, their faces embarrassingly intense. It's as if you were watching sex. Yet for years, I've had dreams in the form of this home movie. In a recurring scene, familiar faces push themselves forward into my mind's eye, plastering their features into distorted close-ups. And I'm asking them: "Who is *she?* Who is the old woman I don't recognize? Is she an aunt? Somebody's wife? Tell me who she is."

> "See the beauty mark on her cheek as big as a hill on the lunar landscape of her face—well, that runs in the family. The women on your father's side of the family wrinkle early; it's the price they pay for that fair skin. The young girl with the green stain on her wedding dress is *la novia*—just up from the Island. See, she lowers her eyes when she approaches the camera, as she's supposed to. Decent girls never look at you directly in the face. *Humilde,* humble, a girl should express humility in all her actions. She will make a good wife for your cousin. He should consider himself lucky to have met her only weeks after she arrived here. If he marries her quickly, she will make him a good Puerto Rican–style wife; but if he waits too long, she will be corrupted by the city, just like your cousin there."

> "She means me. I do what I want. This is not some primitive island I live on. Do they expect me to wear a black mantilla on my head and go to mass every day? Not me. I'm an American woman, and I will do as I please. I can type faster than anyone in my senior class at Central High, and I'm going to be a secretary to a lawyer when I graduate. I can pass for an American girl anywhere—I've tried it. At least for Italian, anyway—I never speak Spanish in public. I hate these parties, but I wanted the dress. I look better than any of these *humildes* here. *My* life is going to be different. I have an American boyfriend. He is older and has a car. My parents don't know it, but I sneak out of the house late at night sometimes to be with him. If I marry him, even my name will be American. I hate rice and beans—that's what makes these women fat."

"Your *prima* is pregnant by that man she's been sneaking around with. Would I lie to you? I'm your *tía política,* your great-uncle's common-law wife—the one he abandoned on the Island to go marry your cousin's mother. *I* was not invited to this party, of course, but I came anyway. I came to tell you that story about your cousin that you've always wanted to hear. Do you remember the comment your mother made to a neighbor that has always haunted you? The only thing you heard was your cousin's name, and then you saw your mother pick up your doll from the couch and say: 'It was as big as this doll when they flushed it down the toilet.' This image has bothered you for years, hasn't it? You had nightmares about babies being flushed down the toilet, and you wondered why anyone would do such a horrible thing. You didn't dare ask your mother about it. She would only tell you that you had not heard her right, and yell at you for listening to adult conversations. But later, when you were old enough to know about abortions, you suspected.

"I am here to tell you that you were right. Your cousin was growing an *americanito* in her belly when this movie was made. Soon after, she put something long and pointy into her pretty self, thinking maybe she could get rid of the problem before breakfast and still make it to her first class at the high school. Well, *niña,* her screams could be heard downtown. Your aunt, her *mamá,* who had been a midwife on the Island, managed to pull the little thing out. Yes, they probably flushed it down the toilet. What else could they do with it—give it a Christian burial in a little white casket with blue bows and ribbons? Nobody wanted that baby—least of all the father, a teacher at her school with a house in West Paterson that he was filling with real children, and a wife who was a natural blonde.

"Girl, the scandal sent your uncle back to the bottle. And guess where your cousin ended up? Irony of ironies. She was sent to a village in Puerto Rico to live with a relative on her mother's side: a place so far away from civilization that you have to ride a mule to reach it. A real change in scenery. She found a man there—women like that cannot live without male company—but believe me, the men in Puerto Rico know how to put a saddle on a woman like her. *La gringa,* they call her. Ha, ha, ha. *La gringa* is what she always wanted to be . . ."

The old woman's mouth becomes a cavernous black hole I fall into. And as I fall, I can feel the reverberations of her laughter. I hear the echoes of her last mocking words: *la gringa, la gringa!* And the conga line keeps moving silently past me. There is no music in my dream for the dancers.   25

When Odysseus visits Hades to see the spirit of his mother, he makes an offering of sacrificial blood, but since all the souls crave an audience with the living, he has to listen to many of them before he can ask questions. I, too, have to hear the dead and the forgotten speak in my dream. Those who are still part of my life remain silent, going around and around in their dance. The others keep pressing their faces forward to say things about the past.   26

My father's uncle is last in line. He is dying of alcoholism, shrunken and shriveled like a monkey, his face a mass of wrinkles and broken arteries. As he comes closer I realize that in his features I can see my whole family. If you were to stretch that rub-   27 bery flesh, you could find my father's face, and deep within *that* face—my own. I don't want to look into those eyes ringed in purple. In a few years he will retreat into silence, and take a long, long time to die. *Move back, Tío, I tell him. I don't want to hear what you have to say. Give the dancers room to move. Soon it will be midnight. Who is the New Year's Fool this time?*

Working with the Text

1. Ortiz Cofer uses two levels to tell her story: descriptions of the home movie and memories of incidents, places, and activities from her childhood. Reread the essay and think carefully about the relationship between the home movie and her other memories. How do they play off each other? What details of the movie are echoed or extended in the main part of the narrative? In what sense does the movie become important to Ortiz Cofer in terms of her understanding of her own identity?

2. How do Cofer's memories of her childhood and her parents—as well as those of her relatives, particularly the older cousin who gets pregnant by her "American boyfriend" (paragraph 24)—suggest about the process of assimilation and identity? Do you think that the issues today differ from those suggested by Cofer's memories of some thirty-five years ago?

3. Do you have any childhood images that you recall in a way similar to Ortiz Cofer's "home movie," whether actual film or video recordings or simply scenic memories that play themselves out in your mind or in your dreams? Why do such images linger? What do they suggest about the interplay between memory and self-awareness?

4. Compare Cofer's essay with Sherman Alexie's "Family Portrait." Both pieces of writing invoke a medium other than writing to render *in writing* a representation of a memory (Alexie uses the "portrait," as in a series of snapshots, and Cofer the "home movie"). What is the different effect of each technique? Are there any similarities? How might you recall childhood memories by filtering them imaginatively through "filmed" imagery?

5. How is Cofer's story illustrative of a "border" experience? What are some of the kinds of borderlands that Cofer and her family negotiate? What tensions and conflicts exist between the two worlds of Puerto Rico and the United States? What other borderlands are important in the story? How might the story be typical of many immigrant experiences? How might it differ?

THE GRAVITY OF PINK (STUDENT ESSAY)

EDEN ABIGAIL TROOBOFF

■ Eden Abigail Trooboff was a sophomore at Columbia University, in New York City, when she wrote this essay. In the essay, she tries to reconcile messages she receives from others about her sense of femininity and identity as a woman with her own feelings and memories. In the piece she tries to model how a personal essay might also make use of academic material.

> But if I wish to define myself, I must first of all say: "I am a woman"; on this truth must be based all further discussion (de Beauvoir xv).

n Hebrew School we were asked to decide whether we would fight for the Americans or the Israelis if the U.S. and Israel ever went to war. We were choosing our identities and loyalties, examining those parts of ourselves that the school considered most complex in the context of faith and religion. They needed us to decide how our Americanism and Judaism would mesh, to deal with questions of assimilation at a young age. I didn't get too involved in this question, partly because my father said such a war would never happen, but also because the notions of religious and national self-definition seemed so distant and open; there were lots of choices to be made, and none of them had to be made anytime soon.

I wonder why we never addressed questions that now seem so much more urgent and problematic; why we didn't deal particularly with the given identities, especially sexual identity, which may not be a directly religious issue, but which becomes problematic in the context of Biblical gender roles and particularly Eve in the Garden of Eden. Perhaps we didn't discuss these problems because we had no choice about who ate the apple. When I considered the fall out of Eden spurred by Eve, being female and feminine seemed horrifyingly up-in-the-air, in that I was born into this role of temptress and scapegoat without any say. I negotiated early on, if not in so many words, how my moral weight would be taken from me.

Some parts of the self are up for grabs. Others are identities that we cannot transcend, regardless of our choices and of the questions well-intentioned teachers ask us to ponder. Who am I before all else? Jewish? American? female? Can I form my identity like a grocery list, putting certain items first as the staples in the refrigerator of myself?

Aristotle believed that "the female is a female by virtue of a certain lack of qualities" (De Beauvoir xvi). If traditionally I am an emptiness to be filled, life formed as an addendum rather than as an initial creative idea, identifying myself means adding parts of myself to a void. It means encountering the body that I am born in, and considering it perhaps not just as a passive, unavoidable identity, but as a vital dwelling place. How will I come to understand this home?

> Anatomy is a woman's destiny, say the theorists of femininity; the identity of woman is determined by her biology (Friedan 79).

I don't know if this strange man with gray in his hair wanted me to feel flirted   5
with. Really he was coming on to our leggy, blonde Dutch houseguest who was traveling with my family through New England for the summer. But I was wearing a
pink dress with a big V in back and I felt too female to be a child. He danced extrav-
agantly with all three of us, my sister, Anna, and me, maybe just to cross that line
which exists in every wedding reception between the adults and the children. I was
twelve, flattered and amused to be feeling the silly tingles of flirtation. With him
leaning over to put his arm around my back, I felt my body for the first time in relation to a man's. At the end of the song, he scooped up my legs and twirled me
around. With the myopic vision one adopts of childhood memories, I remember
everyone turning around to watch this little pink girl get picked up so easily by this
charming man. I was unable or unwilling to show my anger at being lifted without
being asked. I smiled a little uncontrollably, conscious that any other response
would betray the sensitivity that my parents reminded me I had far too much of.

I have become protective of my gravity. I feel sick to my stomach when I wear   6
pink, as though my insides had lost the weight that keeps them together. When
friends try to lift me up, I sit down, keeping my weight as earth-bound as I can. I
keep my back covered. I try to be more mind than body. I've swallowed the pink in
me. I am thrown off kilter when I am made aware that I have a body at times when
I have nearly forgotten.

Gravity is taken from women. My friends have told me slowly of their weight-   7
lessness, not saying the R-word that they know applies to their loss of themselves.
How can I form an allegiance to a group that is victimized? Why would I want to belong? How can I think about my female consciousness when I am forced to feel it
every time girl friends get together and talk about mistrust, loss of power, and violence? The process of finding identity becomes emotional rather than intellectual
when the loss of control means abuse.

Women are bound together psychologically by a fear of the dark, by the impulse   8
to check the backseat before driving off, by the inability to walk through an unlit
place alone, by the subtle suggestions of how small you are compared to him, how
easily he could lift you or hold you down. Maybe the real fear is of floating, feeling
your body out of your own control, fearing it is less your own than that of those who
may take it from you. I wonder if there is an experience of fear or loss of self that
bonds men together. Or are they connected by an awareness of their gravity? I find
my femininity wrapped in vulnerability. I wonder if masculinity is wrapped in
strength.

I seek to see my body as my own, as the place that I dwell in which remains mine   9
even if it is victimized. The fear of our weightlessness causes me to hunker down
with other women, to keep each other from floating away.

> The closest I've ever come to myth was that favorite game in college—we
> called it Earliest Memory, my friends sprawled out in someone's living room.
> *Moonlight on the bedroom floor* we'd say or *oh god, that fall down the steep back*
> *stairs* . . . (Boruch, "The Quiet House").

Physical memories seem the oldest to me; I can't remember when pain seemed   10
unfamiliar. My mom tells me the most interesting time to watch infants is when
they first discover their body parts, seizing at their toes and fingers, developing the

strange physical habits that stay with us for life, establishing the bodies that won't feel quite so new again. And since this joyful time which my mom remembers for me, physical realization is what brings me down to earth, what gives me weight when sleep or distraction has all but removed me from my body: falling out of bed the night my sister did too and broke her collar bone; tripping on an acorn and scarring my knee; the tingly feeling of a fever. When I realize my sexuality, I am replaying that physical discovery that began with belly buttons and wrists.

Bodily weight can become symbolic and spiritual. In an Eastern Religions class, I learned how Buddhist writings merge the idea of physical temporality with *nirvana*. They embrace the body in its ability to experience pleasure, but also believe that pleasure to be far from the enlightenment experience that can be reached only by divorcing the self from the body. In *The Unbearable Lightness of Being*, Milan Kundera discusses the relationship of body and soul through his character Tereza, who stares at herself in the mirror in the hopes of seeing her soul show itself in her body. Her body becomes a way to keep anonymity at bay. The physical is what keeps us near the ground and nearer to ourselves. 11

Coming to terms with my body and my relationship to it means considering my hands. I try to see myself in them. I am a heavily left-handed lefty, and my left hand has very dry skin that cracks in the winter and gets red in the summer. I am very self-conscious about my hands, but also very proud of how used and unkempt my left hand looks—the leathery writer's bump, the guitar calluses, the nails cut below the quick. 12

As a feminist and inheritor of Betty Friedan's philosophy of womanhood, I wonder if her ideology dictates that I should separate my mind from my body, believe that my anatomy is neither my destiny nor an essential part of my identity. But I need to know my body to understand where exactly I live, to consider it the basis of my identity for no other reason than that the physical is the first and last thing I will know. 13

In elementary school, I was often asked what my favorite place in the world is. We don't associate our bodies as a place because it is the ultimate mobile home, the place we cannot leave. But when we have nowhere else to go, the body is our being's only shelter. I seek to understand that body enough to know that it has enough spiritual weight and pulsation not to float away. 14

WORKS CITED

de Beauvoir, Simone. *The Second Sex.* New York: Alfred A. Knopf, 1953.
Friedan, Betty. *The Feminine Mystique.* New York: Bantam Doubleday Dell Publishing Group, 1983.
Kundera, Milan. *The Unbearable Lightness of Being.* New York: Harper & Row, 1984.

Working with the Text

1. In "The Gravity of Pink," Trooboff plays with the term "gravity" in several ways and uses the idea of weight and weightlessness metaphorically as well as literally. How does her use of gravity and weight contribute to her meaning about her sense of self? How does she link the idea of weight and weightlessness to a feeling of control?

2. Trooboff says that "physical memories seem the oldest to me." But are her memories strictly physical? Can you clearly separate the border between the physical and the emotional in her essay?

3. How do you respond to her depiction of her body as a place, or even a home? In what ways do you think of your body as a place you inhabit?

4. Explore the ways that a sense of control or loss of control is tied to gender roles in this essay. How are boundaries of personal space, touch, and control scripted into our environments as matters of social convention? To what extent, for example, is identity constructed in part by a sense of one's "weightlessness," or conventions of interaction?

GARDENLAND, SACRAMENTO, CALIFORNIA

MICHAEL NAVA

■ A graduate of Stanford University Law School, Michael Nava worked briefly as an attorney for the city of Los Angeles before beginning a full-time career as a writer. He is best known for his series of mystery novels, the hero of which is a gay Mexican American detective still trying to resolve the influences of an isolated, sometimes painful childhood—much like Nava's own childhood which he presents in the following essay. Written for a collection entitled *Hometowns: Gay Men Write About Where They Belong,* "Gardenland, Sacramento, California" describes the poor neighborhood where Nava grew up, which he encourages readers to think of "not as an American suburb at all, but rather as a Mexican village, transported perhaps from Guanajuato. . . ." For Nava, ultimately, Gardenland was a place from which he had to escape in order to achieve an identity of his own.

I grew up in a neighborhood of Sacramento called Gardenland, a poor community, almost entirely Mexican, where my maternal family, the Acunas, had lived since the 1920s. Sacramento's only distinction used to be that it was the state capital. Today, because it frequently appears on lists of the country's most livable cities, weary big-town urbanites have turned it into a boomtown rapidly becoming unlivable. But when I was a child, in the late fifties and early sixties, the only people who lived in Sacramento were the people who'd been born there.

Downtown the wide residential neighborhoods were lined with oaks shading turreted, run-down Victorian mansions, some partitioned into apartments, others still of a piece, but all of them exuding a shadowy small-town melancholy. The commercial district was block after block of shabby brick buildings housing small businesses. The city's skyline was dominated by the gold-domed capitol, a confectioner's spun-sugar dream of a building. It was set in a shady park whose grass seemed always to glisten magically, as if hidden under each blade of grass were an Easter egg.

Sacramento's only other landmarks of note were its two rivers, the American and the Sacramento. They came together in muddy confluence beneath the slender iron joints of railroad bridges. Broad and shallow, the rivers passed as slowly as thought between the thick and tumble of their banks.

A system of levees fed into the rivers. One of these tributaries was called the Bannon Slough. Gardenland was a series of streets carved out of farmland backed up against the slough. It flowed south, curving east behind a street called Columbus Avenue, creating Gardenland's southern and eastern boundaries. The northern boundary was a street called El Camino. Beyond El Camino was middle-class tract housing. To the west, beyond Bowman Street, were fields and then another neighborhood that may just as well have existed on another planet for all I knew of it.

What I knew were the nine streets of Gardenland: Columbus, Jefferson, Harding, Cleveland, El Camino, Peralta, Wilson, Haggin, and Bowman; an explorer, an odd lot of presidents, an unimaginative Spanish phrase, and three inexplicable proper names, one in Spanish, two in English. It was as if the streets had been named out of a haphazard perusal of a child's history text. There were two other significant facts about the streets in Gardenland; they all dead-ended into the levee and their names were not continued across El Camino Boulevard into the Anglo suburb, called Northgate. Gardenland's streets led, literally, nowhere.

Unlike El Camino, where little square houses sat on little square lots, Gardenland had not been subdivided to maximum utility. Broad uncultivated fields stretched between and behind the ramshackle houses. Someone's "front yard" might consist of a quarter acre of tall grass and the remnants of an almond orchard. The fields were littered with abandoned farming implements and the foundations of long-gone houses. For a dreamy boy like me, these artifacts were magical. Finding my own world often harsh, I could imagine from these rusted pieces of metal and fragments of walls a world in which I would have been a prince.

But princes were hard to come by in Gardenland. Almost everyone was poor, and most residents continued to farm after a fashion, keeping vegetable gardens and flocks of chickens. There were neither sidewalks nor streetlights, and the roads, cheaply paved, were always crumbling and narrow as country lanes. At night, the streets and fields were lit by moonlight and the stars burned with millennial intensity above the low roofs of our houses.

The best way to think of Gardenland is not as an American suburb at all, but rather as a Mexican village, transported perhaps from Guanajuato, where my grandmother's family originated, and set down lock, stock, and chicken coop in the middle of California.

My cousin Josephine Robles had divided her tiny house in half and ran a beauty shop from one side. Above her porch was a wooden sign that said in big blue letters GARDENLAND and, in smaller print below, BEAUTY SALON. Over the years the weather took its toll and the bottom half faded completely, leaving only the word GARDENLAND in that celestial blue, like a road sign to a cut-rate Eden.

By the time I was born, in 1954, my family had lived in Gardenland for at least twenty-five years. Virtually all I know of my grandfather's family, the Acunas, was that they were Yaqui Indians living in northern Mexico near the American border at Yuma, Arizona. My grandmother's family, the Trujillos, had come out of central Mexico in 1920, escaping the displacements caused by the Mexican

Revolution of 1910. I have dim memories of my great-grandparents, Ygnacio and Phillipa Trujillo, doll-like, white-haired figures living in a big, dark two-story house in east Sacramento.

My grandparents settled on Haggin Avenue in a house they built themselves. My cousins, the Robles, lived two doors down. My family also eventually lived on Haggin Avenue, next door to my grandparents. Our house was the pastel plaster box that became standard suburban architecture in California in the fifties and sixties but it was the exception in Gardenland. [11]

Most houses seemed to have begun as shacks to which rooms were added to accommodate expanding families. They were not built with privacy in mind but simply as shelter. We lived in a series of such houses until our final move to Haggin Avenue. In one of them, the living room was separated from the kitchen by the narrow rectangular bedroom in which my brothers and sisters and I slept. Adults were always walking through it while we were trying to sleep. This made for jittery children, but no one had patience for our complaints. It was enough that we had a place to live. [12]

By the standards of these places, my grandparents' house was luxurious. It was a four-bedroom, L-shaped building that they had built themselves. My grandmother put up the original three rooms while my grandfather was in the navy during World War II. My aunt Socorro told me that my grandmother measured the rooms by having her children lie head to toe across a plot of ground. She bought the cement for the foundations, mixed and troweled it, and even installed pipes for plumbing. Later, when my grandfather returned, they added a series of long, narrow rooms paneled in slats of dark-stained pine, solid and thick walled. [13]

Massive, dusty couches upholstered in a heavy maroon fabric, oversize beds soft as sponges, and a leather-topped dining room table furnished the house. Like the rusted combines in the field, these things seemed magical in their antiquity. I would slip into the house while my grandparents were both at work and wander through it, opening drawers and inspecting whatever presented itself to my attention. It was in this fashion that I opened a little-used closet and found it full of men's clothes that obviously were not my grandfather's. Later I learned that they had belonged to my uncle Raymond who had been killed in a car accident. In a subsequent exploration I found pictures of his funeral, including a picture taken of him in his casket, a smooth-faced, dark-skinned, pretty boy of fifteen. [14]

Another time, I found a voluminous red petticoat in a cedar chest. Without much hesitation, I put it on and went into my grandmother's bedroom where I took out her face powder and lipstick. I applied these in the careful manner of my grandmother, transforming myself in the dressing mirror beneath the grim gaze of a crucified Christ. Looking back, I don't think I was trying to transform myself into a girl, but only emulating the one adult in my family who loved me without condition. Because she was the soul of kindness, it never occurred to me, as a child, that my grandmother might be unhappy. Only looking back do I see it. [15]

She and my grandfather slept in separate rooms at opposite ends of their house. In the evening, my grandfather would sit on a couch in front of the television quietly drinking himself into a stupor while my grandmother did needlework at the kitchen table. They barely spoke. I would sit with my grandmother, looking at pic- [16]

tures in the *Encyclopedia Americana,* comfortable with the silence, which, to her, must have been a deafening indictment of a failed marriage.

In my parents' house, the marriage of my mother and stepfather was as noisily 17 unhappy as my grandparents' was quietly miserable. In each shabby house where we lived I would be awakened by their fights. I learned to turn myself into a stone, or become part of the bed or the walls so as to abate the terror I felt. No one ever spoke of it. There was only one house in which my family lived together peaceably but it only existed as a blueprint that had come somehow into my stepfather's possession.

In the evening, he would take it down from a shelf and unroll it on the kitchen 18 table. Together we would study it, laying claim to rooms, planning alterations. At the time, we lived in a tiny one-bedroom cinder-block house. My brother and I slept on a bunk bed in an alcove off the kitchen. At night, I could hear mice scampering across the cement floor, terrifying me when I woke up having to pee and pick my way through the darkness to the bathroom.

When we finally moved from the cinder-block house, it was to another, bigger 19 version of that house rather than to the dream house of the blueprint. One night, my mother's screaming woke me. I hurried into the bedroom she and my stepfather occupied and found him beating her. When I tried to stop him, he threw me across the room. The next morning my mother told me he was sorry, but it was too late. Where I lived no longer mattered to me because I learned to live completely within myself in rooms of rage and grief. Now I think these rooms were not so different from the rooms we all occupied, my unhappy family and I.

Although not literally cut off from the outside world, Gardenland was little touched 20 by it. We were tribal in our outlook and our practices. Anglos were generically called "paddies," whether or not they were Irish. All fair-skinned people were mysterious but also alike. Even TV, that great equalizer, only emphasized our isolation since we never saw anyone who looked remotely like us, or lived as we did, on any of the popular shows of the day. At school, the same homogeneity prevailed. Until I was nine I attended a neighborhood grade school where virtually every other child was like me, dark eyed and dark skinned, answering to names like Juarez, Delgadillo, Robles, Martinez. My own name, Michael Angel, was but an Anglicized version of Miguel Angel, a name I shared with at least three other of my classmates.

I had a remarkable amount of freedom as a child. As I said, we eventually lived 21 on the same street as other members of my maternal family and I roamed their houses as unself-consciously as a Bedouin child might move among the tents of his people. I ate in whatever house I found myself at mealtime and the meals were the same in each of my relatives' houses—rice, beans, lettuce and tomato salad, stewed or fried meat, tortillas, salsa. My grandparents did not lock their doors at night—who did? what was there to steal?—so that I could slip into their house quietly and make my bed on their sofa when my parents were fighting.

But most of the time I spent outdoors, alone or with my friends. In spring, the 22 field behind my house was overrun with thistles. We neighborhood kids put in long days cutting trails through them and hacking out clearings that became our forts. Tiring of the fields, we'd lurk in abandoned houses, empty barns, and chicken coops. When all other amusements failed, there was always Bannon Slough, a muddy brown creek that flowed between thickly wooded banks. It was too filthy to swim in. Instead, in the steep shadows of bridges and railroad trestles we taught each other how to smoke and to swear.

Just as often I would be off by myself. Early on, I looked for ways to escape my family. I found it in the stillness of the grass and the slap of the slough's brown water against the shore. There I discovered my own capacity for stillness. Lying on the slope of the levee, I could hear my own breath in the wind and feel my skin in the warm blades of grass that pressed against my neck. In those moments, Gardenland *was* Eden, and I felt the wonder and loneliness of the first being. 23

For, like Adam, I was lonely. Being everyone's child, I was no one's child. I could disappear in the morning and stay out until dusk and my absence went unnoticed. Children barely counted as humans in our tribe. We were more like livestock and our parents' main concern was that the head count at night matched the head count in the morning. 24

My loneliness became as much a part of me as my brown hair and the mole above my lip, something unremarkable. When I came out, I missed that sense of joining a community of others like me that so many of my friends describe. My habits of secrecy and loneliness were too deeply ingrained. I had become like my grandfather, who, in a rare moment of self-revelation, told me he was a "lone wolf"; the most unsociable of an unsociable tribe. Though I've changed as I've grown older, I still sometimes wonder if one reason I write is because I am filled with all the words I never spoke as a child. 25

Two things opened up for me the narrow passage through which I finally escaped Gardenland for good. The first was books. I learned to read early and, once started, could not get enough of books. In this affinity, I was neither encouraged nor discouraged by my family. Education beyond its most basic functions, learning how to read and write, to do sums, had absolutely no interest for them. My love of reading became simply another secret part of me. 26

There wasn't a library in Gardenland. Instead, a big white van pulled up to the corner of Wilson and El Camino, the city Bookmobile. Inside, patrons squeezed into a narrow passageway between tall shelves of books. The children's books occupied the bottom shelves. At the exit, a woman checked out books from a standing desk. The Bookmobile came once a week and I was a regular customer, always taking my limit of books. 27

Everything about the process pleased me. I was proud of my library card, a yellow piece of cardboard with my name typed on it, which I carried in a cowhide wallet that was otherwise empty. I liked taking books from the shelves, noting their heft and volume, the kind of type, whether they were illustrated, and I studied the record of their circulation, the checkout dates stamped in blue on stiff white cards in paper pockets on the inside covers. I loved the books as much as I loved reading. To me, they were organic things, as alive in their way as I was. 28

Like so many other bright children growing up in the inarticulate world of the poor, books fueled my imagination, answered my questions, led me to new ones, and helped me conceive of a world in which I would not feel so set apart. Yet I do not believe that my brains alone, even aided by my bookish fantasies, would have 29 been enough to escape Gardenland. For this, I needed the kind of courage that arises out of desperation.

I found this courage in my homosexuality. Early on, I acquired a taste for reading   30
history, particularly ancient history. I suppose that pictures of ruined Greek cities reminded me of the crumbling, abandoned houses in the fields of Gardenland. But I was also fascinated by pictures of the nude male statues. There was something about the smooth, headless torsos, the irisless eyes of ephebes that made me stop my idle flipping through pages and touch the paper where these things were depicted. By the time I was twelve I understood that my fascination was rooted in my sexual nature. One day, walking to school, clutching my books to my chest, girl-style, I heard myself say, "I'm a queer."

It was absolutely clear to me that Gardenland could not accommodate this reve-   31
lation. Gardenland provided the barest of existences for its people. What made it palatable was the knowledge that everyone was about the same, united in ethnicity and poverty and passivity. The only rituals were the rituals of family, and family was everything there. But I knew that I was not the same as everyone else. And I was certain that my family, already puzzled by my silent devotion to books, would reject me entirely if it became known exactly what thoughts occupied my silence.

Had I been a different child I would have run away from home. Instead, I ran   32
away without leaving home. I escaped to books, to sexual fantasy, to painful, unrequited crushes on male classmates. No one ever knew. I turned myself into an outsider, someone at the margins of a community that was itself outcast. Paradoxically, by doing this, I learned the peasant virtues of my hometown, endurance and survival. As a member of yet another embattled community, those virtues I absorbed as a child continue to serve me.

Working with the Text

1. In paragraph 6 Nava refers to himself as a "dreamy boy," and throughout the essay he pictures himself as a quiet loner lost in imagination and books. His realization at the age of twelve that he was "queer" grew in large part out of his previous sense of isolation and difference. How do you think these issues—Nava's "secrecy and loneliness" as a child and his ultimate realization that he was gay—are related? Would you expect that most gay men and lesbians would experience a similar sense of isolation as children even before they knew they were gay? Or did other cultural and family issues contribute more to Nava's sense of isolation?

2. When he dresses up in his grandmother's petticoat and makeup, Nava writes that he wasn't trying "to transform myself into a girl, but only emulating the one adult in my family who loved me without condition." Recall childhood occasions when you "dressed up" in adult clothes or other costumes of your own device, or think about children you have observed playing dress-up. To what extent do you think childhood games of dress-up and play-acting are ways of "emulating" that which children admire or aspire to be? Does such fantasy playing serve an important role in the development of a child's iden-

tity? To what extent do the adults around children provide "scripts" or models for them to follow?

3. At one point Nava wonders "if one reason I write is because I am filled with all the words I never spoke as a child." Consider any of the other childhood reminiscences in this chapter—those by Boruch, Noda, Ortiz Cofer, or William Kittredge—along with your own experience and the work of other writers with whom you're familiar. Do you think that people who become writers were often quiet, inward observers as children? How do you think a person comes to identify himself or herself as "a writer"? In what ways does the personal/public writing in this chapter grow from attempts to fill in silences and speak what was not spoken?

4. Nava says that despite his intelligence and his "bookish fantasies," he doesn't believe he could have escaped Gardenland if he hadn't found "the kind of courage that arises out of desperation" when he recognized his homosexuality. What made Gardenland "palatable," he writes, was that "everyone was about the same, united in ethnicity and poverty and passivity," but he knew that he "was not the same as everyone else." Do you think that many young homosexuals today face the same kind of desperation? Are there any communities that "accommodate" homosexuality in ways that Gardenland could not?

5. Imagine that you were a counselor to whom Nava had come as a young teenager to explain his predicament and to ask for advice. What would you have told him?

Yellow Woman

Storytelling

LESLIE MARMON SILKO

■ The tradition of "Yellow Woman" stories is widespread among Native American tribes throughout the Southwest and Southern plains. This "genre" of Native American stories depicts the capture or seduction of the symbolically feminine figure "Yellow Woman" by some masculine force or spirit, one sometimes portrayed as a natural force and sometimes as a transitional figure between animal and human. Even if the woman is depicted as going willingly, "Yellow Woman" stories often serve to blur the boundaries between seduction and rape and between conscious knowledge and unconscious desires. The two selections included here are modern reworkings of the Yellow Woman tradition by the contemporary poet and fiction writer Leslie Marmon Silko, who draws on her Laguna Pueblo heritage in much of her work. In the story "Yellow Woman," the narrator self-consciously recalls the Yellow Woman stories she heard growing up and even wonders if she is Yellow Woman herself. The selection "Storytelling" is more experimental in form, telling the fragments of several stories, all having to do with married women who either "run off with" or are "stolen by" other men. As these works suggest, Silko blends traditional and modern meanings of Native American stories while always attending to "storytelling" itself as a basic cultural act.

What Whirlwind Man Told Kochininako, Yellow Woman
    I myself belong to the wind
    and so it is we will travel swiftly
    this whole world
    with dust and with windstorms.

YELLOW WOMAN

My thigh clung to his with dampness, and I watched the sun rising up through the tamaracks and willows. The small brown water birds came to the river and hopped across the mud, leaving brown scratches in the alkali-white crust. They bathed in the river silently. I could hear the water, almost at our feet where the narrow fast channel bubbled and washed green ragged moss and fern leaves. I looked at him beside me, rolled in the red blanket on the white river sand. I cleaned the sand out of the cracks between my toes, squinting because the sun was above the willow trees. I looked at him for the last time, sleeping on the white river sand.

I felt hungry and followed the river south the way we had come the afternoon before, following our footprints that were already blurred by lizard tracks and bug trails. The horses were still lying down, and the black one whinnied when he saw me but he did not get up—maybe it was because the corral was made out of thick cedar branches and the horses had not yet felt the sun like I had. I tried to look beyond the pale red mesas to the pueblo. I knew it was there, even if I could not see it, on the sandrock hill above the river, the same river that moved past me now and had reflected the moon last night.

The horse felt warm underneath me. He shook his head and pawed the sand. The bay whinnied and leaned against the gate trying to follow, and I remembered him asleep in the red blanket beside the river. I slid off the horse and tied him close to the other horse, I walked north with the river again, and the white sand broke loose in footprints over footprints.

"Wake up."

He moved in the blanket and turned his face to me with his eyes still closed. I knelt down to touch him.

"I'm leaving."

He smiled now, eyes still closed. "You are coming with me, remember?" He sat up now with his bare dark chest and belly in the sun.

"Where?"

"To my place."

"And will I come back?"

He pulled his pants on. I walked away from him, feeling him behind me and smelling the willows.

"Yellow Woman," he said. 12

I turned to face him. "Who are you?" I asked. 13

He laughed and knelt on the low, sandy bank, washing his face in the river. "Last 14
night you guessed my name, and you knew why I had come."

I stared past him at the shallow moving water and tried to remember the night, 15
but I could only see the moon in the water and remember his warmth around me.

"But I only said that you were him and that I was Yellow Woman—I'm not really 16
her—I have my own name and I come from the pueblo on the other side of the
mesa. Your name is Silva and you are a stranger I met by the river yesterday afternoon."

He laughed softly. "What happened yesterday has nothing to do with what you 17
will do today, Yellow Woman."

"I know—that's what I'm saying—the old stories about the ka'tsina spirit and 18
Yellow Woman can't mean us."

My old grandpa liked to tell those stories best. There is one about Badger and 19
Coyote who went hunting and were gone all day, and when the sun was going down
they found a house. There was a girl living there alone, and she had light hair and
eyes and she told them that they could sleep with her. Coyote wanted to be with her
all night so he sent Badger into a prairie-dog hole, telling him he thought he saw
something in it. As soon as Badger crawled in, Coyote blocked up the entrance with
rocks and hurried back to Yellow Woman.

"Come here," he said gently. 20

He touched my neck and I moved close to him to feel his breathing and to hear 21
his heart. I was wondering if Yellow Woman had known who she was—if she knew
that she would become part of the stories. Maybe she'd had another name that her
husband and relatives called her so that only the ka'tsina from the north and the storytellers would know her as Yellow Woman. But I didn't go on; I felt him all around
me, pushing me down into the white river sand.

Yellow Woman went away with the spirit from the north and lived with him and 22
his relatives. She was gone for a long time, but then one day she came back and she
brought twin boys.

"Do you know the story?" 23

"What story?" He smiled and pulled me close to him as he said this. I was afraid 24
lying there on the red blanket. All I could know was the way he felt, warm, damp, his
body beside me. This is the way it happens in the stories, I was thinking, with no
thought beyond the moment she meets the ka'tsina spirit and they go.

"I don't have to go. What they tell in stories was real only then, back in time im- 25
memorial, like they say."

He stood up and pointed at my clothes tangled in the blanket. "Let's go," he said. 26

I walked beside him, breathing hard because he walked fast, his hand around my 27
wrist. I had stopped trying to pull away from him, because his hand felt cool and the
sun was high, drying the river bed into alkali. I will see someone, eventually I will see
someone, and then I will be certain that he is only a man—some man from
nearby—and I will be sure that I am not Yellow Woman. Because she is from out of
time past and I live now and I've been to school and there are highways and pickup
trucks that Yellow Woman never saw.

It was an easy ride north on horseback. I watched the change from the cotton- 28 wood trees along the river to the junipers that brushed past us in the foothills, and finally there were only piñons, and when I looked up at the rim of the mountain plateau I could see pine trees growing on the edge. Once I stopped to look down, but the pale sandstone had disappeared and the river was gone and the dark lava hills were all around. He touched my hand, not speaking, but always singing softly a mountain song and looking into my eyes.

I felt hungry and wondered what they were doing at home now—my mother, my   29
grandmother, my husband, and the baby. Cooking breakfast, saying, "Where did she go?—maybe kidnapped." And Al going to the tribal police with the details: "She went walking along the river."

The house was made with black lava rock and red mud. It was high above the   30
spreading miles of arroyos and long mesas. I smelled a mountain smell of pitch and buck brush. I stood there beside the black horse, looking down on the small, dim country we had passed, and I shivered.

"Yellow Woman, come inside where it's warm."   31

He lit a fire in the stove. It was an old stove with a round belly and an enamel cof-   32
feepot on top. There was only the stove, some faded Navajo blankets, and a bedroll and cardboard box. The floor was made of smooth adobe plaster, and there was one small window facing east. He pointed at the box.

"There's some potatoes and the frying pan." He sat on the floor with his arms   33
around his knees pulling them close to his chest and he watched me fry the potatoes. I didn't mind him watching me because he was always watching me—he had been watching me since I came upon him sitting on the river bank trimming leaves from a willow twig with his knife. We ate from the pan and he wiped the grease from his fingers on his Levi's.

"Have you brought women here before?" He smiled and kept chewing, so I said,   34
"Do you always use the same tricks?"

"What tricks?" He looked at me like he didn't understand.   35

"The story about being a ka'tsina from the mountains. The story about Yellow   36
Woman."

Silva was silent; his face was calm.   37

"I don't believe it. Those stories couldn't happen now," I said.   38

He shook his head and said softly, "But someday they will talk about us, and they   39
will say, 'Those two lived long ago when things like that happened.'"

He stood up and went out. I ate the rest of the potatoes and thought about   40
things—about the noise the stove was making and the sound of the mountain wind outside. I remembered yesterday and the day before, and then I went outside.

I walked past the corral to the edge where the narrow trail cut through the black   41
rim rock. I was standing in the sky with nothing around me but the wind that came down from the blue mountain peak behind me. I could see faint mountain images in the distance miles across the vast spread of mesas and valleys and plains. I wondered who was over there to feel the mountain wind on those sheer blue edges—who walks on the pine needles in those blue mountains.

"Can you see the pueblo?" Silva was standing behind me.   42

I shook my head. "We're too far away."   43

"From here I can see the world." He stepped out on the edge. "The Navajo reser-   44 vation begins over there." He pointed to the east. "The Pueblo boundaries are over here." He looked below us to the south, where the narrow trail seemed to come from. "The Texans have their ranches over there, starting with that valley, the Concho Valley. The Mexicans run some cattle over there too."

"Do you ever work for them?"   45

"I steal from them," Silva answered. The sun was dropping behind us and the   46
shadows were filling the land below. I turned away from the edge that dropped forever into the valleys below.

"I'm cold," I said. "I'm going inside." I started wondering about this man who   47
could speak the Pueblo language so well but who lived on a mountain and rustled cattle. I decided that this man Silva must be Navajo, because Pueblo men didn't do things like that.

"You must be a Navajo."   48

Silva shook his head gently. "Little Yellow Woman," he said, "you never give up,   49
do you? I have told you who I am. The Navajo people know me, too." He knelt down and unrolled the bedroll and spread the extra blankets out on a piece of canvas. The sun was down, and the only light in the house came from outside—the dim orange light from sundown.

I stood there and waited for him to crawl under the blankets.   50

"What are you waiting for?" he said, and I lay down beside him. He undressed me   51
slowly like the night before beside the river—kissing my face gently and running his hands up and down my belly and legs. He took off my pants and then he laughed.

"Why are you laughing?"   52

"You are breathing so hard."   53

I pulled away from him and turned my back to him.   54

He pulled me around and pinned me down with his arms and chest. "You don't   55
understand, do you, little Yellow Woman? You will do what I want."

And again he was all around me with his skin slippery against mine, and I was   56
afraid because I understood that his strength could hurt me. I lay underneath him and I knew that he could destroy me. But later, while he slept beside me, I touched his face and I had a feeling—the kind of feeling for him that overcame me that morning along the river. I kissed him on the forehead and he reached out for me.

When I woke up in the morning he was gone. It gave me a strange feeling because   57
for a long time I sat there on the blankets and looked around the little house for some object of his—some proof that he had been there or maybe that he was coming back. Only the blankets and the cardboard box remained. The .30–30 that had been leaning in the corner was gone, and so was the knife I had used the night before. He was gone, and I had my chance to go now. But first I had to eat, because I knew it would be a long walk home.

I found some dried apricots in the cardboard box, and I sat down on a rock at the   58
edge of the plateau rim. There was no wind and the sun warmed me. I was surrounded by silence. I drowsed with apricots in my mouth, and I didn't believe that there were highways or railroads or cattle to steal.

When I woke up, I stared down at my feet in the black mountain dirt. Little black   59
ants were swarming over the pine needles around my foot. They must have smelled the apricots. I thought about my family far below me. They would be wondering

about me, because this had never happened to me before. The tribal police would file a report. But if old Grandpa weren't dead he would tell them what happened—he would laugh and say, "Stolen by a ka'tsina, a mountain spirit. She'll come home—they usually do." There are enough of them to handle things. My mother and grandmother will raise the baby like they raised me. Al will find someone else, and they will go on like before, except that there will be a story about the day I disappeared while I was walking along the river. Silva had come for me; he said he had. I did not decide to go. I just went. Moonflowers blossom in the sand hills before dawn, just as I followed him. That's what I was thinking as I wandered along the trail through the pine trees.

It was noon when I got back. When I saw the stone house I remembered that I 60
had meant to go home. But that didn't seem important any more, maybe because there were little blue flowers growing in the meadow behind the stone house and the gray squirrels were playing in the pines next to the house. The horses were standing in the corral, and there was a beef carcass hanging on the shady side of a big pine in front of the house. Flies buzzed around the clotted blood that hung from the carcass. Silva was washing his hands in a bucket full of water. He must have heard me coming because he spoke to me without turning to face me.

"I've been waiting for you."   61

"I went walking in the big pine trees."   62

I looked into the bucket full of bloody water with brown-and-white animal hairs   63
floating in it. Silva stood there letting his hand drip, examining me intently.

"Are you coming with me?"   64

"Where?" I asked him.   65

"To sell the meat in Marquez."   66

"If you're sure it's O.K."   67

"I wouldn't ask you if it wasn't," he answered.   68

He sloshed the water around in the bucket before he dumped it out and set the   69
bucket upside down near the door. I followed him to the corral and watched him saddle the horses. Even beside the horses he looked tall, and I asked him again if he wasn't Navajo. He didn't say anything; he just shook his head and kept cinching up the saddle.

"But Navajos are tall."   70

"Get on the horse," he said, "and let's go."   71

The last thing he did before we started down the steep trail was to grab the .30–30   72
from the corner. He slid the rifle into the scabbard that hung from his saddle.

"Do they ever try to catch you?" I asked.   73

"They don't know who I am."   74

"Then why did you bring the rifle?"   75

"Because we are going to Marquez where the Mexicans live."   76

The trail leveled out on a narrow ridge that was steep on both sides like an animal   77
spine. On one side I could see where the trail went around the rocky gray hills and disappeared into the southeast where the pale sandrock mesas stood in the distance near my home. On the other side was a trail that went west, and as I looked far into the distance I thought I saw the little town. But Silva said no, that I was looking in

the wrong place, that I just thought I saw houses. After that I quit looking off into the distance; it was hot and the wildflowers were closing up their deep-yellow petals. Only the waxy cactus flowers bloomed in the bright sun, and I saw every color that a cactus blossom can be; the white ones and the red ones were still buds, but the purple and the yellow were blossoms, open full and the most beautiful of all.

Silva saw him before I did. The white man was riding a big gray horse, coming up   78
the trail towards us. He was traveling fast and the gray horse's feet sent rocks rolling off the trail into the dry tumbleweeds. Silva motioned for me to stop and we watched the white man. He didn't see us right away, but finally his horse whinnied at our horses and he stopped. He looked at us briefly before he lapped the gray horse across the three hundred yards that separated us. He stopped his horse in front of Silva, and his young fat face was shadowed by the brim of his hat. He didn't look mad, but his small, pale eyes moved from the blood-soaked gunny sacks hanging from my saddle to Silva's face and then back to my face.

"Where did you get the fresh meat?" the white man asked.   79

"I've been hunting," Silva said, and when he shifted his weight in the saddle the   80
leather creaked.

"The hell you have, Indian. You've been rustling cattle. We've been looking for   81
the thief for a long time."

The rancher was fat, and sweat began to soak through his white cowboy shirt and   82
the wet cloth stuck to the thick rolls of belly fat. He almost seemed to be panting from the exertion of talking, and he smelled rancid, maybe because Silva scared him.

Silva turned to me and smiled. "Go back up the mountain, Yellow Woman."   83

The white man got angry when he heard Silva speak in a language he couldn't   84
understand. "Don't try anything, Indian. Just keep riding to Marquez. We'll call the state police from there."

The rancher must have been unarmed because he was very frightened and if he   85
had a gun he would have pulled it out then. I turned my horse around and the rancher yelled, "Stop!" I looked at Silva for an instant and there was something ancient and dark—something I could feel in my stomach—in his eyes, and when I glanced at his hand I saw his finger on the trigger of the .30–30 that was still in the saddle scabbard. I slapped my horse across the flank and the sacks of raw meat swung against my knees as the horse leaped up the trail. It was hard to keep my balance, and once I thought I felt the saddle slipping backward; it was because of this that I could not look back.

I didn't stop until I reached the ridge where the trail forked. The horse was   86
breathing deep gasps and there was a dark film of sweat on its neck. I looked down in the direction I had come from, but I couldn't see the place. I waited. The wind came up and pushed warm air past me. I looked up at the sky, pale blue and full of thin clouds and fading vapor trails left by jets.

I think four shots were fired—I remember hearing four hollow explosions that   87
reminded me of deer hunting. There could have been more shots after that, but I couldn't have heard them because my horse was running again and the loose rocks were making too much noise as they scattered around his feet.

Horses have a hard time running downhill, but I went that way instead of uphill   88 to the mountain because I thought it was safer. I felt better with the horse running southeast past the round gray hills that were covered with cedar trees and black lava rock. When I got to the plain in the distance I could see the dark green patches of tamaracks that grew along the river; and beyond the river I could see the beginning of the pale sandrock mesas. I stopped the horse and looked back to see if anyone was coming; then I got off the horse and turned the horse around, wondering if it would go back to its corral under the pines on the mountain. It looked back at me for a moment and then plucked a mouthful of green tumbleweeds before it trotted back up the trail with its ears pointed forward, carrying its head daintily to one side to avoid stepping on the dragging reins. When the horse disappeared over the last hill, the gunny sacks full of meat were still swinging and bouncing.

I walked toward the river on a wood-hauler's road that I knew would eventually lead   89
to the paved road. I was thinking about waiting beside the road for someone to drive by, but by the time I got to the pavement I had decided it wasn't very far to walk if I followed the river back the way Silva and I had come.

The river water tasted good, and I sat in the shade under a cluster of silvery wil-   90
lows. I thought about Silva, and I felt sad at leaving him; still, there was something strange about him, and I tried to figure it out all the way back home.

I came back to the place on the river bank where he had been sitting the first time   91
I saw him. The green willow leaves that he had trimmed from the branch were still lying there, wilted in the sand. I saw the leaves and I wanted to go back to him—to kiss him and to touch him—but the mountains were too far away now. And I told myself, because I believe it, he will come back sometime and be waiting again by the river.

I followed the path up from the river into the village. The sun was getting low, and I   92
could smell supper cooking when I got to the screen door of my house. I could hear their voices inside—my mother was telling my grandmother how to fix the Jell-O and my husband, Al, was playing with the baby. I decided to tell them that some Navajo had kidnaped me, but I was sorry that old Grandpa wasn't alive to hear my story because it was the Yellow Woman stories he liked to tell best.

STORYTELLING

> You should understand
> the way it was
> back then,
> because it is the same
> even now.   5
>
> Long ago it happened
> that her husband left

to hunt deer
before dawn
And then she got up   10
and went to get water.
Early in the morning
she walked to the river
when the sun came over
the long red mesa.   15

He was waiting for her
that morning
in the tamarack and willow
beside the river.

Buffalo Man   20
in buffalo leggings.
"Are you here already?"
"Yes," he said.
He was smiling.
"Because I came for you."   25
She looked into the
shallow clear water.
"But where shall I put my water jar?"
"Upside down, right here," he told her,
"on the river bank."   30

"You better have a damn good story,"
her husband said,
"about where you been for the past
ten months and how you explain these
twin baby boys."   35

"No! That gossip isn't true.
She didn't elope
She was *kidnapped* by
that Mexican
at Seama feast.   40

You know
my daughter
isn't
that kind of girl."

It was   45
in the summer
of 1967.
T.V. news reported
a kidnapping.
Four Laguna women   50
and three Navajo men
headed north along
the Rio Puerco river
in a red '56 Ford
and the F.B.I. and   55
state police were
hot on their trail
of wine bottles and
size 42 panties
hanging in bushes and trees   60
all along the road.

"We couldn't escape them," he told police later.
"We tried, but there were four of them and
only three of us."

Seems like   65
it's always happening to me.
Outside the dance hall door
late Friday night
in the summertime,
and those   70
brown-eyed men from Cubero,
smiling.
They usually ask me
"Have you seen the way stars shine

up there in the sand hills?"   75
And I usually say "No. Will you show me?"

It was
that Navajo
from Alamo,
you know,   80
the tall
good-looking
one.

He told me
he'd kill me   85
if I didn't
go with him
And then it
rained so much
and the roads   90
got muddy,
That's why
it took me
so long
to get back home.   95

My husband
left
after he heard the story
and moved back in with his mother.
It was my fault and   100
I don't blame him either.
I could have told
the story
better than I did.

Working with the Text

1. Compare the structure and styles of the two Silko selections. Clearly they
are linked by theme (they appear together in one of her books). How are they

alike and different? How do their respective forms affect the way you read them? Is one clearer and less ambiguous than the other?

2. In part, "Yellow Woman" is a story about the borders of identity. How is Silko playing with those borders in the two works? Can you think of contemporary situations or analogies to this tale of confused identity?

3. Look closely at "Storytelling" and explore how many different "stories" are being told. Go through the text of the poem and mark between the "paragraphs" where you think each story starts and stops. Pick one of the stories and expand it to a full page or so. Fill in or make up details that are suggested by the story fragment.

4. Look at the portfolio Plate 15, *Biblical Times,* and Plate 16, *Biblical Times, New York City, 1987/93* [annotated], and then at the description of the making of *Biblical Times* included in the Notes on the Images section. Consider how Meyer's image and Silko's story are alike in their manipulation of what is real and what is not. Where is the line of "truth" in each text? Is it identifiable?

5. In an essay called "Language and Literature from a Pueblo Indian Perspective," Silko says this about Pueblo stories:

> I think what is essential is this sense of story, and story within story, and the idea that one story is only the beginning of many stories, and the sense that stories never truly end.

Keeping this passage in mind, explore how Silko's two works seem to be expressions of Pueblo ideas about storytelling. How might the fluid nature of stories be related to Silko's treatment of identity?

6. How are Silko's stories like other alternative storytelling forms, such as hypertext fiction and digital storytelling, found on the World Wide Web? Use the links on the Storytelling Platform on the *Border Texts* Web site as a starting point for exploring these other forms.

CINDERELLA

ANNE SEXTON

■ Anne Sexton was a Massachusetts housewife when she suffered a nervous breakdown, leading her therapist to suggest that she channel some of her feelings into writing. The result was a series of lyrical, intensely personal poems exploring a complicated emotional landscape. Her eight collections of poetry were well received by critics and readers alike, and she won the Pulitzer Prize in 1967. Still, she spent much of her life fighting a host of personal demons, and she committed suicide in 1974. Her 1971 collection *Transformations,* which includes the following poem, was something of a departure for Sexton. Each of these poems retold a classic fairy tale from a modern perspective, ironically suggesting that what lies below the surface of the story often goes far beyond the traditional "happily–ever–after" ending. As you read "Cinderella," notice how Sexton uses abrupt shifts of diction and tone to jar her readers' expectations.

You always read about it:
the plumber with twelve children
who wins the Irish Sweepstakes.
From toilets to riches.
That story.   5

Or the nursemaid,
some luscious sweet from Denmark
who captures the oldest son's heart.
From diapers to Dior.
That story.   10

Or a milkman who serves the wealthy,
eggs, cream, butter, yogurt, milk,
the white truck like an ambulance
who goes into real estate
and makes a pile.   15
From homogenized to martinis at lunch.

Or the charwoman
who is on the bus when it cracks up
and collects enough from the insurance.
From mops to Bonwit Teller.   20
That story.

Once
the wife of a rich man was on her deathbed
and she said to her daughter Cinderella:
Be devout. Be good. Then I will smile   25
down from heaven in the seam of a cloud.
The man took another wife who had
two daughters, pretty enough

but with hearts like blackjacks.
Cinderella was their maid.   30
She slept on the sooty hearth each night
and walked around looking like Al Jolson.
Her father brought presents home from town,
jewels and gowns for the other women
but the twig of a tree for Cinderella.   35
She planted that twig on her mother's grave
and it grew to a tree where a white dove sat.
Whenever she wished for anything the dove
would drop it like an egg upon the ground.
The bird is important, my dears, so heed him.   40

Next came the ball, as you all know.
It was a marriage market.
The prince was looking for a wife.
All but Cinderella were preparing
and gussying up for the big event.   45
Cinderella begged to go too.
Her stepmother threw a dish of lentils
into the cinders and said: Pick them
up in an hour and you shall go.
The white dove brought all his friends;   50
all the warm wings of the fatherland came,
and picked up the lentils in a jiffy.
No, Cinderella, said the stepmother,
you have no clothes and cannot dance.
That's the way with stepmothers.   55

Cinderella went to the tree at the grave
and cried forth like a gospel singer:
Mama! Mama! My turtledove,
send me to the prince's ball!
The bird dropped down a golden dress   60
and delicate little gold slippers.
Rather a large package for a simple bird.
So she went. Which is no surprise.

Her stepmother and sisters didn't
recognize her without her cinder face   65
and the prince took her hand on the spot
and danced with no other the whole day.

As nightfall came she thought she'd better
get home. The prince walked her home
and she disappeared into the pigeon house   70
and although the prince took an axe and broke
it open she was gone. Back to her cinders.
These events repeated themselves for three days.
However on the third day the prince
covered the palace steps with cobbler's wax   75
and Cinderella's gold shoe stuck upon it.

Now he would find whom the shoe fit
and find his strange dancing girl for keeps.
He went to their house and the two sisters
were delighted because they had lovely feet.   80
The eldest went into a room to try the slipper on
but her big toe got in the way so she simply
sliced it off and put on the slipper.
The prince rode away with her until the white dove
told him to look at the blood pouring forth.   85
That is the way with amputations.
They don't just heal up like a wish.
The other sister cut off her heel
but the blood told as blood will.
The prince was getting tired.   90
He began to feel like a shoe salesman.
But he gave it one last try.
This time Cinderella fit into the shoe
like a love letter into its envelope.

At the wedding ceremony   95
the two sisters came to curry favor
and the white dove pecked their eyes out.

Two hollow spots were left
like soup spoons.

Cinderella and the prince   100
lived, they say, happily ever after,
like two dolls in a museum case
never bothered by diapers or dust,
never arguing over the timing of an egg,
never telling the same story twice,   105
never getting a middle-aged spread,
their darling smiles pasted on for eternity.
Regular Bobbsey Twins.
That story.

Working with the Text

1. Stanzas 1, 2, and 4, as well as the final stanza of the poem, end with the phrase "That story." In what sense are these all the same story? Can you think of other versions, either fictional—such as in books or films—or true? What is the appeal of stories such as these?

2. What aspects of the traditional Cinderella tale does Sexton treat ironically? What comment is she making on the original story? How does she transform its values and meaning?

3. In "Yellow Woman" and "Storytelling," Leslie Marmon Silko also retells traditional stories, giving them a more modern perspective. How do her motives and approach seem different from Sexton's? Are they similar in any way? Think about the "Yellow Woman" stories and other traditional Native American stories you may know. Do these seem to play a role in Native American culture that is more similar to or more different from the role fairy tales play in Western culture?

4. What were some of your favorite childhood stories? Why do you think they appealed to you? What lessons did they teach you about the world? Do you think they had any influence in shaping your values or sense of self?

5. Looking particularly at several stories that are especially familiar or widely told, consider the role fairy tales, folktales, myths, and other traditional stories play in shaping children's perceptions and values within your culture. Are there any that you think children might be better off *not* being told?

6. In what ways do fairy tales always contain both explicit and implicit messages? How does Sexton's version of Cinderella reveal the unspoken or smoothed over in fairy tales? How might fairy tales be condensations or "shorthand" for certain cultural messages?

THE WOMAN HANGING FROM THE THIRTEENTH FLOOR WINDOW

JOY HARJO

■ Poet Joy Harjo was born in Tulsa, Oklahoma, of Creek and Cherokee descent. Author of *In Mad Love and War* (1990) and *Woman Who Fell from the Sky* (1994), among other books, she often focuses on issues of ethnicity and gender in her poetry. The following poem demonstrates another set of issues important to Harjo: the problems of staying whole and mentally healthy in the modern urban world. Here Harjo portrays a woman who is literally—and figuratively—hanging on by her fingernails. Many of the poem's images are indirect and metaphorical. The narrative voice is somewhat complicated because it is cast in the third person (looking from the outside at the central figure), yet much of the action seems to occur within the woman's mind. Is it characteristic of Harjo's style to switch seamlessly between sentences and phrases that seem to be externally descriptive and those that seem to be internal and personal?

She is the woman hanging from the 13th floor
window. Her hands are pressed white against the
concrete moulding of the tenement building. She
hangs from the 13th floor window in east Chicago,
with a swirl of birds over her head. They could   5
be a halo, or a storm of glass waiting to crush her.

She thinks she will be set free.

The woman hanging from the 13th floor window
on the east side of Chicago is not alone.
She is a woman of children, of the baby, Carlos,   10
and of Margaret, and of Jimmy who is the oldest.
She is her mother's daughter and her father's son.
She is several pieces between the two husbands
she has had. She is all the women of the apartment
building who stand watching her, watching themselves.   15

When she was young she ate wild rice on scraped down
plates in warm wood rooms. It was in the farther
north and she was the baby then. They rocked her.

She sees Lake Michigan lapping at the shores of
herself. It is a dizzy hole of water and the rich   20
live in tall glass houses at the edge of it. In some
places Lake Michigan speaks softly, here, it just sputters
and butts itself against the asphalt. She sees
other buildings just like hers. She sees other
women hanging from many-floored windows   25
counting their lives in the palms of their hands
and in the palms of their children's hands.

She is the woman hanging from the 13th floor window
on the Indian side of town. Her belly is soft from
her children's births, her worn levis swing down below   30
her waist, and then her feet, and then her heart.
She is dangling.

The woman hanging from the 13th floor hears voices.
They come to her in the night when the lights have gone
dim. Sometimes they are little cats mewing and scratching   35
at the door, sometimes they are her grandmother's voice,
and sometimes they are gigantic men of light whispering
to her to get up, to get up, to get up. That's when she wants
to have another child to hold onto in the night, to be able
to fall back into dreams.   40

And the woman hanging from the 13th floor window
hears other voices. Some of them scream out from below
for her to jump, they would push her over. Others cry softly
from the sidewalks, pull their children up like flowers and gather
them into their arms. They would help her, like themselves.   45

But she is the woman hanging from the 13th floor window,
and she knows she is hanging by her own fingers, her
own skin, her own thread of indecision.

She thinks of Carlos, of Margaret, of Jimmy.
She thinks of her father, and of her mother.   50

She thinks of all the women she has been, of all
the men. She thinks of the color of her skin, and
of Chicago streets, and of waterfalls and pines.
She thinks of moonlight nights, and of cool spring storms.
Her mind chatters like neon and northside bars.   55
She thinks of the 4 a.m. lonelinesses that have folded
her up like death, discordant, without logical and
beautiful conclusion. Her teeth break off at the edges.
She would speak.

The woman hangs from the 13th floor window crying for   60
the lost beauty of her own life. She sees the
sun falling west over the grey plane of Chicago.
She thinks she remembers listening to her own life
break loose, as she falls from the 13th floor
window on the east side of Chicago, or as she   65
climbs back up to claim herself again.

Working with the Text

1. How has the identity of the woman hanging from the thirteenth floor window been shaped? What kinds of stories does she recall as she dangles? What does the poem have to say about the woman's sense of self? Based only on what you can tell from the poem, does the woman's perception of herself differ from others' perceptions of her? How might the poem be taken in a broader context about gender, identity, and self-hood?

2. How do you interpret the ending? Is it positive or negative? What lines or images would you use to support a position one way or the other?

3. Rewrite the poem as if it were a news story on the front page of the Chicago daily newspaper. Imagine that the article you are writing follows the headline "Woman Hangs from the Thirteenth Floor Window!!" Or, alternatively, rewrite the poem as if it were a diary entry you were writing to yourself. The first line of your diary entry for this day begins, "I was hanging from the thirteenth floor window today. . . ."

HOME

WILLIAM KITTREDGE

■ William Kittredge was born in Portland, Oregon, in 1932 and grew up on his family's ranch in a remote portion of southeastern Oregon. He didn't begin writing seriously until he was in his mid-thirties and since then has produced a collection of stories, *We Are Not in This Together* (1984); a collection of essays, *Owning It All* (1987); and a memoir, *Hole in the Sky* (1992). He has also coauthored a number of Western adventure novels under the pseudonym Owen Rountree. Kittredge is a professor at the University of Montana. The following essay is a richly complex meditation on the nature of storytelling and memory, the relationship of place to personal and cultural identity, and the influences of youth that shape who we become. In the essay, Kittredge weaves several different stories, telling about the distant war, the ranch hands, the early pioneers, his grandfather, his own boyhood experiences, and his observations of the Paiute native people. Seemingly unconnected, all of those stories contribute to his notion of "home."

In the long-ago land of my childhood we clearly understood the high desert country of southeastern Oregon as the actual world. The rest of creation was distant as news on the radio. 1

In 1945, the summer I turned thirteen, my grandfather sentenced his chuck-wagon cow outfit to a month of haying on the IXL, a little ranch he had leased from the Sheldon Antelope Refuge in Nevada. Along in August we came in to lunch one noontime, and found the cook, a woman named Hannah, flabbergasted by news that some bomb had just blown up a whole city in Japan. Everybody figured she had been into the vanilla extract, a frailty of cooks in those days. As we know, it was no joke. Nagasaki and then V-J Day. We all listened to that radio. Great changes and possibilities floated and cut in the air. But such far-off strange events remained the concern of people who lived in cities. We might get drunk and celebrate, but we knew such news really had nothing to do with us. Not in the far outback of southeastern Oregon. 2

When I came home from the Air Force in 1958, I found our backland country rich with television from the Great World. But that old attitude from my childhood, the notion that my people live in a separate kingdom where they own it all, secure from the world, is still powerful and troublesome. When people ask where I'm from I still say southeastern Oregon, expecting them to understand my obvious pride. 3

Jack Ray was one of the heroes of my boyhood. A slope-shouldered balding little man, Jack dominated the late roughhouse craziness at our mid-July country dances. The Harvest Moon Ball. 4

"He can hit like a mule kicking," my father used to say after those dances, winking at us kids and grinning at my mother's back while she served up a very late Sunday breakfast of steak and fried mush and biscuits and thick sausage gravy. 5

At that time I was maybe five or six years old, and I would have been asleep in the 6 back seat of our car for a couple of hours when the shouting and fighting started around midnight. So I recall those scenes with a newly awakened child's kind of strobe-light clarity, a flash here and there, all illuminated in the headlights of 1930s automobiles. The ranch women would be crowded outside on the porch where they could see, some wife weeping, the men out closer to the battle in the parking lot, passing bottles.

But what I see mainly is Jack Ray getting up off the ground, wiping a little trickle   7
of blood from the corner of his mouth, glancing down at the smear on his hand, his eyes gone hard while some sweating farm boy moved at him again; and torn shirts, the little puffs of dust their feet kicked there in the headlights. At that point my memory goes fragile. There is some quick slippery violence, and the farm boy is on his knees. Jack Ray is standing above him, waiting, wheezing as he breathes.

It's over, everybody knows, and soon it is. Two more grunting punches, and the   8
farm boy is down again, and Jack Ray steps back, his eyes gone soft and almost bewildered in the light as a little shudder moves through the crowd, and someone shouts, and the bottles pass again. I see Jack Ray, there in those headlights, smiling like a child now that it's finished, the farm boy up on his knees, shaking his head.

No harm done, the air clear. I see it over and over, summer dance after summer   9
dance. I see the kind of heroism my boyhood educated me to understand and respect.

And I hate the part that comes next. I grew up and ran the haying and combine   10
crews on our ranch, and there eventually came a time when I hired Jack Ray to work for me. He had worked a lot of seasons for my father, and such men always had a job with us. Jack was maybe fifty by that time, and crippled by his life, the magic gone, a peaceable man who seemed to have turned a little simple. He did what he could, chores around the cook house, and once in a while he drank. After a bout in town which earned him some time in the county jail, he would show up grinning in the bunk house. "Well, hell, Jack," I would say, "it's a new day."

"Kid," he would say, "she's a new world every morning."   11

Looking backward is one of our main hobbies here in the American West, as we   12
age. And we are aging, which could mean we are growing up. Or not. It's a difficult process for a culture which has always been so insistently boyish. Jack Ray has been dead a long time now. As my father said, he drank his liver right into the ground. "But, by God," my father said, "he was something once."

Possibility is the oldest American story. Head west for freedom and the chance of   13
inventing a spanking new life for yourself. Our citizens are always leaping the traces when their territory gets too small and cramped.

Back in the late fifties, living with my wife and our small children in our little cat-   14
tle-ranch house, when things would get too tight on a rainy Sunday afternoon in November I always had the excuse of work. "I got to go out," I would say, and I would duck away to the peacefulness of driving the muddy fields and levee banks in my old Ford pickup. Or, if the roads were too bad, I would go down to the blacksmith shop and bang on some damned thing.

Whenever I find myself growing grim about the mouth; whenever it is damp, driz-   15
zly November in my soul; whenever I find myself involuntarily pausing before coffin

warehouses, and bringing up the rear of every funeral I meet . . . Then he runs away to sea. *Ishmael.*

". . . lighting out for territory," says Huckleberry Finn, with his broken-hearted optimism, right at the end of his getaway down the Mississippi.   16

And it wasn't just the runaway boys in books. John Colter left Ohio at the age of thirty, to head up the Missouri with Lewis and Clark in 1804. He stayed west another five years, earning his keep as a fur trapper in pursuit of the beaver. One fearsome Montana winter he took a legendary walk from Fort Lisa on the Yellowstone, traveling through what is Yellowstone Park to circumnavigate the Tetons—about a thousand miles on snowshoes through country where no white man had ever been before. A thing both wondrous and powerful drove him. Maybe it was a need so simple as being out, away.   17

Imagine those shining snowy mountains burning against the sheltering endless bowl of clean sky, and Colter alone there in Jackson Hole. We will not see such things again, not any of us, ever. It's gone. We know it is. Only one man ever got to be Colter. Not even Bridger or Joe Meek or Jedediah Smith had a world so absolutely to themselves. Except for some natives, who maybe never thought they were alone.   18

In 1836 Narcissa and Marcus Whitman came west with Eliza and Henry Spalding. The first white women had crossed the Rockies. Along the way they witnessed one of the last fur-trapper rendezvous, on the Green River in Wyoming. Think of those Presbyterian women among the inhabitants of wilderness. Less than ten years later Marcus Whitman was leading one of the first wagon trains west from St. Louis to the Oregon country.   19

The New York newspaper editor Horace Greeley worried about the exodus, wondering what those families could be seeking, leaving behind the best of climates and agricultural lands, schools and churches and markets: "For what, then, do they brave the desert, the wilderness, the savage, the snowy precipices of the Rocky Mountains, the early summer march, the storm-drenched bivouac, and the gnawings of famine? Only to fulfill their destiny! There is probably not one among them whose outward circumstances will be improved by this perilous pilgrimage."   20

Anybody sensible, Greeley suggested, would stop "this side of the jumping-off place." The only practice stupider than such migration, he said, was suicide.   21

It's easy to understand his puzzlement. The wagon trains were predominantly middle-class ventures. Poor folks couldn't afford a wagon, much less provisions. The basic outfitting cost up toward a thousand dollars. And in those long-gone days that was some real money. But seemingly sensible people persisted in selling their good farms and heading west.   22

Imagine half the population of Ohio picking up sticks, selling out, and heading for one of our latter-day mythological frontiers, Alaska or Australia. Greeley was right, it was crazy, it was a mania.   23

What was pushing them? Lots of things. Among them a quite legitimate fear of mortal corruption and death. Cholera. By the spring of 1849 an epidemic had reached St. Louis. Ten percent of the population died of the disease. The road west from Independence was likened to traveling through a graveyard.   24

But mostly, we have to believe, they were lured west by promises. Promises of paradise for the taking. Free land, crystalline water, great herds of game roaming the   25 natural meadowlands, good fishing, gold, all in unfettered abundance, a new world every morning.

What compelled men to believe promises of paradise on earth with such simple-   26
minded devotion? Well, for openers, a gut yearning for the chance of becoming someone else, and freedom from the terrible weight of responsibilities, freedom too often equaling free, without cost.

My own great-grandfather on my father's side left Michigan in 1849 to travel   27
down the Mississippi and across to Panama, where he hiked west through the jungles on the route Balboa had blazed, and caught a ship north to California and the gold camps. After a long and bootless career of chasing mineral trace in the mountain streams, first in the central Sierra and then up around the foothills of Mount Shasta, he gave it up and turned to ranching and school teaching in one place after another around the Northwest, until in 1897 he died white-trash poor in the sagebrush backlands near Silver Lake, Oregon, leaving a family determined to shake his suicidal despair.

It wasn't just the gold that he never found—such instant boomer riches were to   28
have been only the beginning. The green and easy dreamland fields of some home place were to have been the ultimate reward for his searching, the grape arbor beside the white house he would own outright, where he could rest out some last serene years while the hordes of grandchildren played down across the lawns by the sod-banked pond where the tame ducks swam and fed and squawked in their happy, idiot way. The pastoral heaven on this earth—some particular secret and heart's-desire version of it—has time and again proved to be the absolute heart in American dreams. All this we promise you.

II

Childhood, it has been said, is always partly a lie of poetry. When I was maybe eight   29
years old, in the fall of the year, I would have to go out in the garden after school with damp burlap sacks and cover the long rows of cucumber and tomato plants, so they wouldn't freeze.

It was a hated, cold-handed job which had to be done every evening. I day-   30
dreamed along in a halfhearted, distracted way, flopping the sacks onto the plants, sorry for myself and angry because I was alone at my boring work. No doubt my younger brother and sister were in the house and warm. Eating cookies.

But then a great strutting bird appeared out from the dry remnants of our corn,   31
black tail feathers flaring and a monstrous yellow-orange air sac pulsating from its white breast, its throat croaking with popping sounds like rust in a joint.

The bird looked to be stalking me with grave slow intensity, coming after me   32
from a place I could not understand as real, and yet quite recognizable, the sort of terrifying creature which would sometimes spawn in the incoherent world of my night dreams. In my story, now, I say it looked like death, come to say hello. Then, it was simply an apparition.

The moment demanded all my boyish courage, but I stood my ground, holding   33
one of those wet sacks out before me like a shield, stepping slowly backwards, listening as the terrible creature croaked, its bright preposterous throat pulsating—and

then the great bird flapped its wings in an angry way, raising a little commonplace dust.

It was the dust, I think, that did it, convincing me that this could not be a dream. 34 My fear collapsed, and I felt foolish as I understood this was a creature I had heard my father talk about, a courting sage grouse, we called them prairie chickens. This was only a bird, and not much interested in me at all. But for an instant it had been both phantom and real, the thing I deserved, come to punish me for my anger.

For that childhood moment I believed the world to be absolutely inhabited by an 35 otherness which was utterly demonic and natural, not of my own making. But soon as that bird was enclosed in a story which defined it as a commonplace prairie chicken, I was no longer frightened. It is a skill we learn early, the art of inventing stories to explain away the fearful sacred strangeness of the world. Storytelling and make-believe, like war and agriculture, are among the arts of self-defense, and all of them are ways of enclosing otherness and claiming ownership.

Such emblematic memories continue to surface, as I grow older and find ways to 36 accept them into the fiction of myself. One of the earliest, from a time before I ever went to school, is of studying the worn oiled softwood flooring in the Warner Valley store where my mother took me when she picked up the mail three times a week. I have no idea how many years that floor had been tromped and dirtied and swept, but by the time I recall it was worn into a topography of swales and buttes, traffic patterns and hard knots, much like the land, if you will, under the wear of a glacier. For a child, as his mother gossiped with the postmistress, it was a place, high ground and valleys, prospects and sanctuaries, and I in my boredom could invent stories about it—finding a coherency I loved, a place which was mine. They tore up that floor somewhere around the time I started school, and I had the sense to grieve.

The coherency I found worn into those floorboards was mirrored a few years 37 later, just before the war began, when I was seven or eight, in the summertime play of my brother and sister and cousins and myself, as we laid out roads to drive and rectangular fields to work with our toy trucks in the dirt under the huge old box elder which also functioned as a swing tree near the kitchen door to our house. It was a little play world we made for ourselves, and it was, we believed, just like the vast world beyond. In it we imitated the kind of ordering we watched each spring while our father laid out the garden with such measured precision, and the kind of planning we could not help but sense while riding with him along the levee banks in his dusty Chevrolet pickup truck. All the world we knew was visible from the front porch of our house, inside the valley, and all the work he did was directed toward making it orderly, functional, and productive—and of course that work seemed sacred.

Our play ended when a small rattlesnake showed up in our midst, undulating in 38 sweeping little curving lines across our dusty make-believe fields. A young woman who cooked for my mother killed the snake in a matter-of-fact way with a shovel. But the next spring my mother insisted, and my father hauled in topsoil and planted the packed dirt, where we had played at our toylike world of fields, into a lawn where rattlesnakes would never come. We hated him for it.

These stories suggest reasons why, during childhood winters through the Second 39 World War, such an important segment of my imagination lived amid maps of Europe and the Pacific. Maps delineated the dimensions of that dream which was the war for me, maps and traced drawings of aircraft camouflaged for combat. I collected them like peacetime city boys collect baseball cards, and I colored them in with crayons, my far South Pacific and Europe invaded and shaped by dreams and invisible forces I could not hope to make sense of in any other way.

In the spring of 1942, just before I turned ten years old, we opened every first-   40
period class in our one-room Warner Valley schoolhouse singing "Praise the Lord and Pass the Ammunition." We embraced the war. We heard it every morning on the Zenith Trans-Oceanic radio while we got ready for school, and during recess we ran endless games of gunfighter pursuit and justifiably merciless death in the playgrounds. Mostly we killed Hitler and Mister Tojo.

Fall down, you're dead.   41

When it came your turn to play Nazi, you were honor bound eventually to fall   42
killed through the long adult agony, twisting and staggering to heedless collapse in the dirt. Out in our landlocked, end-of-the-road, rancher valley, the air was bright and clean with purpose.

Always, at least in memory, those running battles involve my cousins and my   43
younger brother and my even younger sister, and a black-and-white dog named Victory. Out back of the house in the summer of 1942 we circled and shot our ways through groves of wild plum in heavy fruit, and we swung to ambush from gnarled limbs in the apple orchard where the blue flies and the yellowjackets were mostly interested in having their way with the rotting fallen fruit: yellowjackets flitting to a hive in the hollow trunk of a Lombardy poplar along the irrigation ditch, burning the air with their going, and near to the secret, stinging, irreligious heart of *my* paradise.

In late September our dog named Victory was crushed under the rear duals of a   44
semi truck flatbed hauling one-hundred-pound burlap sacks of my father's newly combined oats across forty twisting miles of gravel road over the Warner Mountains to town and the railroad. My sister ran shrieking to the kitchen door, and my mother came to the roadside in her apron, and I was stoic and tough-minded as that poor animal panted and died. *Beyond the crystal sea, undreamed shores, precious angels.*

This was a time when our national life was gone to war against U-boats and   45
Bataan and the death march, betrayal reeking everywhere. The death of that dog with cockleburrs matted into his coat must have shimmered with significance past heartbreak. We were American and proud, and we were steeled to deal with these matters.

So we unearthed a shallow grave in the good loam soil at the upper end of the   46
huge rancher garden my father laid out each spring in those days, before it became cheaper to feed our crews from truckloads of canned goods bought wholesale in the cities. We gathered late-blooming flowers from the border beneath my mother's bedroom window, we loaded the stiffening carcass of that dead dog on a red wagon, and we staged a funeral with full symbolic honors.

My older cousin blew taps through his fist, my brother hid his face, and my six-   47
year-old sister wept openly, which was all right since she was a little child. I waved a

leafy bough of willow over the slope-sided grave while my other cousins shoveled the loose dry soil down on the corpse.

It is impossible to know what the child who was myself felt, gazing east across the valley which I can still envision so clearly—the ordered garden and the sage-covered slope running down to the slough-cut meadows of the Thompson Field, willows there concealing secret hideaway places where I would burrow away from the world for hours, imagining I was some animal, hidden and watching the stock cows graze the open islands of meadow grass. [48]

On the far side of the valley lay the great level distances of the plow-ground fields which had so recently been tule swamps, reaching to the rise of barren eastern ridges. That enclosed valley is the home I imagine walking when someday I fall into the dream which is my death. My real, particular, vivid and populated solace for that irrevocable moment of utter loss when the mind stops forever. The chill of that remembered September evening feels right as I imagine that heartbreakingly distant boy. [49]

It's hard for me to know where I got the notion of waving that willow branch over our burial of that poor dog unless I find it in this other memory, from about the same time. A Paiute girl of roughly my own age died of measles in the ramshackle encampment her people maintained alongside the irrigation ditch which eventually led to our vast garden. A dozen or so people lived there, and true or not, I keep thinking of them as in touch with some remnant memories of hunting and gathering forebears who summered so many generations in the valley we had so recently come to own. [50]

In the fall of 1890 a man named James Mooney went west under the auspices of the Bureau of Ethnology to investigate the rise of Native American religious fervor which culminated in the massacre at Wounded Knee on December 29. In Mooney's report, *The Ghost Dance Religion and the Sioux Outbreak of 1890*, there is a statement delivered by a Paiute man named Captain Dick at Fort Bidwell in Surprise Valley—right in the home territory I am talking about, at the junction on maps where California and Nevada come together at the Oregon border. [51]

> All Indians must dance, everywhere, keep on dancing. Pretty soon in the next spring Big Man come. He bring back game of every kind. The game be thick everywhere. All dead Indians come back and live again. They all be strong just like young men, be young again. Old blind Indians see again and get young and have fine time. When the Old Man comes this way, then all the Indians go to the mountains, high up away from the whites. Whites can't hurt the Indians then. Then while Indians way up high, big flood comes like water and all white people die, get drowned. After that water go away and then nobody but Indians everywhere game all kinds thick. Then medicine-man tell Indians to send word to all Indians to keep up dancing and the good time will come. Indians who don't dance, who don't believe in this word, will grow little, just about a foot high, and stay that way. Some of them will turn into wood and will be burned in the fire.

In the 1950s and '60s a Paiute named Conlan Dick lived in a cabin on our ranch in Warner Valley, and helped to look after the irrigation and fences. Conlan was re- [52]

puted to be a kind of medicine man in our local mythology, related to the man who delivered that statement. His wife, whose name I cannot recall, did ironing for women in the valley. And there was a son, a young man named Virgil Dick, who sometimes came to Warner for a few weeks and helped his father with the field work.

In the early 1960s my cousin, the one who blew taps through his fist in 1942, was   53
riding horseback across the swampy spring meadows alongside Conlan. He asked if Virgil was Conlan's only child.

Conlan grinned. "Naw," he said. "But you know, those kids, they play outside, and   54
they get sick and they die."

Story after story. Is it possible to claim that proceeding through some incidents   55
in this free-associative manner is in fact a technique, a way of discovery? Probably. One of our model narrators these days is the patient spinning and respinning the past and trying to resolve it into a story that makes sense.

". . . they get sick and they die." Once I had the romance in me to think that this   56
was the mature comment of a man who had grown up healed into wholeness and connection with the ways of nature to a degree I would never understand. Now I think it was more likely the statement of a man trying to forget his wounds—so many of which were inflicted by schoolyard warriors like us. A healthy culture could never have taught him to forgo sorrow.

In any event, Captain Dick's magic was dead.   57

All these stories are part of my own story about a place called Home, and a time   58
in which I imagined we owned it all. The girl who died was named Pearl. I recall her name with that particular exactness which occasionally hovers in memories. She was of enormous interest to us because she so obviously disdained our foolish play with make-believe weapons and miniature trucks. Or so it seemed. Maybe she was only shy, or had been warned away from us. But to our minds she lived with adults and shared in the realities of adult lives in ways we did not, and now she was being paid the attention of burial.

Try to imagine their singing that spring morning. I cannot. I like to think our   59
running brigade of warrior children might have been touched by dim sorrow-filled wailing in the crystalline brightness of her morning, but the memory is silent.

Maybe it's enough to recall the sight of people she loved, carrying her elaborately   60
clothed body in an open home-built casket. Not that we saw it up close, or that we ever really saw a body, clothed or unclothed.

They were making their slow parade up a sandy path through the sagebrush to   61
her burial in the brushy plot, loosely fenced with barbed wire, which we knew as the "Indian Graveyard." I see them high on the banking sand-hill behind our house, and beyond them the abrupt two-thousand-foot lift of rimrock which forms the great western lip of our Warner Valley. That rim is always there, the table of lava flow at the top breaking so abruptly, dropping through long scree slopes clustered with juniper. As I grow older it is always at my back. The sun sets there, summer and winter. I can turn and squint my eyes, and see it.

From the flowering trees in the homesteader's orchard behind our house we   62
watched that astonishing processional through my father's binoculars, and then we ran out through the brush beyond the garden, tasting the perfect spring morning

and leaping along the small animal trails, filled with thrilling purpose, and silent and urgent. We had to be closer.

The procession was just above us on the sandy trail when we halted, those people paying us no mind but frightening us anyway, mourning men and women in their dark castaway clothing and bright blankets and strange robes made of animal skins, clutching at spring blossoms and sweeping at the air with thick sheaves of willow in new leaf. It is now that I would like to hear the faint singsong of their chanting. I would like to think we studied them through the dancing waves of oncoming heat, and found in them the only models we had ever had for such primal ceremonies. 63

But this keeps becoming fiction. Ours was a rising class of agricultural people, new to that part of the world, too preoccupied with an endless ambition toward perfection in their work to care at all for any tradition of religion. No one in our immediate families had ever died, and no one ever would so far as we knew. None of us, in those days, had any interest in religion or ritual. 64

So I have this story of those shrouded people proceeding through my imagination. I feel them celebrating as that young girl entered into the ripe fruit of another paradise, lamenting the dole-food exigencies of their own lives, some of them likely thinking she was lucky to have escaped. 65

But I don't really have much idea what was going on behind the story I've made of that morning. It was as if those people were trailing along that sandy path toward tomorrow-morrow land themselves. Some of them, somewhere, are likely still alive. 66

In a book called *Shoshone,* the poet Ed Dorn tells of interviewing an ancient man and woman in a trailer house on the Duck Valley Reservation, a couple of hundred miles east of us but still deep in the high basin and range desert, along the border between Idaho and Nevada. They were both more than one hundred years old, and told Dorn they had never heard of white men until past the age of thirty. Which is possible. 67

It's easy to imagine those ancient people grinning in what looks to be a toothless old way in their aluminum-sided trailer house, with screens on the windows, on the Duck Valley Reservation. They must have understood the value of stories. Dorn says they demanded cartons of cigarettes before they allowed themselves to be photographed. The point is, they were willing to be part of any make-believe anybody could invent for them, willing to tell their stories and let us make of them what we could. But not for nothing. Stories are valuable precisely to the degree that they are for the moment useful in our ongoing task of finding coherency in the world, and those old people must have known that whatever story Dorn was imagining was worth at least the price of some smokes. 68

My father's catskinners bulldozed the shacktown Indian camp with its willow-roofed ramada into a pile of old posts and lumber, and burned it, after the last of those people had gone to wherever they went. Our children? In the fall of 1942, the same year that girl named Pearl was buried, they learned something about the emotional thrust of a warrior code as the news from the Zenith Trans-Oceanic radio was translated into singing in first-period music class, and they loaded that dead dog named Victory in a red wagon, and trailed him toward burial at the upper end of the garden. And I waved sweeps of willow over the ceremony while my cousin blew taps through his fist. 69

Working with the Text

1. Kittredge says that "storytelling and make-believe, like war and agriculture, are among the arts of self-defense, and all of them are ways of enclosing otherness and claiming ownership" (paragraph 35). How do you interpret that statement? How does this statement relate to his own essay? In what other contexts might storytelling be "an art of self-defense"?

2. Some readers find the structure and style of this essay a little frustrating. Kittredge himself refers to the "free-associative manner" of the piece. How does the essay function through a kind of free association"? Read through the essay, marking each transition or shift from one story or subject to the next. How do the different parts—the stories of working at the ranch during the Second World War, the pioneers and his grandfather, his simple boyhood experiences, and the native Paiutes—work together? How do all these different strands come together in the final image of the young Kittredge waving the willow for his dead dog as his cousin played taps? What is he implying about the notion of storytelling?

3. What is Kittredge's point in writing so extensively here about the settlement of the American West? How does all that talk about the West relate to his discussion of his childhood? To the subject of "home"? Think about Kittredge's essay in the context of Patricia Nelson Limerick's essay "The Adventures of the Frontier in the Twentieth Century" in Chapter 6. How does Limerick's notion of "innocence" shed light on Kittredge's discussion of his childhood? Does reading Limerick's discussion help clarify why Kittredge includes passages about the American movement westward?

4. In paragraph 68 Kittredge writes that stories "are valuable precisely to the degree that they are for the moment useful in our ongoing task of finding coherency in the world." What kinds of stories do you find most valuable for interpreting the world or for finding coherency?

5. Look at the John Gast painting *American Progress* (Plate 13 in the Image Portfolio). How does the painting relate to Kittredge's discussion? Pick one paragraph of Kittredge's essay that could be a caption for the painting.

6. What does Kittredge's essay suggest about how we define a sense of community and self-identity based, at least in part, on notions of "otherness"? Discuss this idea in general using examples from Kittredge's essay.

SCREEN MEMORY

MICHELLE CLIFF

■ Michelle Cliff was born in Jamaica but has spent much of her adult life in the United States and England. Known primarily as a poet, she has also written short stories, including the collection *Bodies of Water* (1990), and served as the editor of several volumes of literature by women and people of color. Her latest book is *Free Enterprise* (1993). Of her work she has said, "I have spent most of my life exploring my identity as a light-skinned Jamaican, the privilege and damage that comes from that identity." The following story explores questions of identity concerning a light-skinned black girl who finds that her sense of difference keeps her from developing any true sense of community.

T he sound of a jump rope came around in her head, softly, steadily marking time. Steadily slapping ground packed hard by the feet of girls.   1

Franklin's in the White House. Jump/Slap. *Talking to the ladies.* Jump/Slap.   2
Eleanor's in the outhouse. Jump/Slap. *Eating chocolate babies.* Jump/Slap.

Noises of a long-drawn-out summer's evening years ago. But painted in such rich tones she could touch it.   3

A line of girls wait their turn. Gathered skirts, sleeveless blouses, shorts, bright, flowered—peach, pink, aquamarine. She spies a tomboy in a striped polo shirt and cuffed blue jeans.   4

A girl slides from the middle of the line. The woman recognizes her previous self. The girl is dressed in a pale blue starched pinafore, stiff and white in places, bleached and starched almost to death. She edges away from the other girls; the rope, their song, which jars her and makes her sad. And this is inside her head.   5

She senses there is more to come. She rests her spine against a wineglass elm. No one seems to notice her absence.   6

The rope keeps up its slapping, the voices speed their chanting. As the chant speeds up, so does the rope. The tomboy rushes in, challenging the others to trip her, burn her legs where she has rolled her jeans. Excitement is at a pitch. Franklin! Ladies! Eleanor! Babies! The tomboy's feet pound the ground. They are out for her. A voice sings out, above the others, and a word, strange and harsh to the observer's ears, sounds over the pound of feet, over the slap of rope. *Bulldagger! Bulldagger! Bulldagger! Bulldagger!* The rope sings past the tomboy's ears. She feels its heat against her skin. She knows the word. Salt burns the corners of her eyes. The rope-turners dare, singing it closer and closer. Sting!   7

The girl in the pinafore hangs back. The girl in the pinafore who is bright-skinned, ladylike, whose veins are visible, as the ladies of the church have commented so many times, hangs back. The tomboy, who is darker, who could not pass the paper bag test, trips and stumbles out. Rubbing her leg where the rope has singed her. The word stops.   8

Where does she begin and the tomboy end?   9

Fireflies prepare to loft themselves. Mason jars with pricked lids are lined on the ground waiting to trap them. Boys swing their legs, scratched and bruised from adventure or fury, from the first rung of a live oak tree. Oblivious to the girls, their singing—nemesis. The boys are swinging, talking, over the heads of the girls. Mostly of the War, their fathers, brothers, uncles, whoever represents them on air or land or sea.   10

The woman in the bed can barely make out their voices, though they speak inside her head.   11

Sudden lightning. A crack of thunder behind a hill. Wooden handles hit the dirt as the rope is dropped. Drops as big as an elephant's tears fall. The wind picks up the pace. Girls scatter to beat the band. Someone carefully coils the rope. Boys dare each other to stay in the tree.   12

The girl in the blue pinafore flies across the landscape. She flies into a window. To   13
the feet of her grandmother.

Slow fade to black.   14

The woman in the bed wakes briefly, notes her pain, the dark outside.   15

Her head is splitting.   16

She and her grandmother have settled in a small town at the end of the line. At   17
the edge of town where there are no sidewalks and houses are made from plain
board, appearing ancient, beaten into smoothness, the two grow dahlias and peonies and azaleas. A rambling rose, pruned mercilessly by the grandmother, refuses
to be restrained, climbing across the railings of the porch, masking the iron of the
drainpipe, threatening to rampage across the roof and escape in a cloud of
pink—she is wild. As wild as the girl's mother, whom the girl cannot remember, and
the grandmother cannot forget.

The grandmother declares that roses are "too showy" and therefore she dislikes   18
them. (As if dahlias and peonies and azaleas in their cultivated brightness are not.)
But the stubborn vine is not for her to kill—nothing, no living thing, is, and that is
the first lesson—only to train.

While the rose may evoke her daughter, there is something else. She does not tell   19
her granddaughter about the thing embedded in her thigh, souvenir of being chased
into a bank of roses. Surely the thing must have worked its way out by now—or she
would have gotten gangrene, lost her leg clear up to the hip—but she swears she can
feel it. A small sharp thorn living inside her muscle. All because of a band of fools to
whom she was nothing but a thing to chase.

The grandmother's prized possession sits against the wall in the front room, sou-   20
venir of a happier time: when her husband was alive and her daughter held promise.
An upright piano, decorated in gilt, chosen by the King of Bohemia and the Knights
of the Rosy Cross, so says it. The grandmother rubs the mahogany and ebony with
lemon oil, cleans the ivory with rubbing alcohol, scrubbing hard, then takes a
chamois to the entire instrument, slower now, soothing it after each fierce cleaning.

The ebony and the ivory and the mahogany come from Africa—the birthplace of   21
civilization. That is another of the grandmother's lessons. From the forests of the
Congo and the elephants of the Great Rift Valley, where fossils are there for the taking and you have but to pull a bone from the great stack to find the first woman or
the first man.

The girl, under the eye of the grandmother, practices the piano each afternoon.   22
The sharp ear of the grandmother catches missed notes, passages played too fast, articulation, passion lost sliding across the keys. The grandmother speaks to her of
passion, of the right kind. "Hastiness, carelessness, will never lead you to any real
feeling, or"—she pauses—"any lasting accomplishment. You have to go deep inside
yourself—to the best part." The black part, she thinks, for if anything can cloud your
senses, it's that white blood. "The best part," she repeats to her granddaughter seated
beside her on the piano bench, as she is atilt, favoring one hip.

The granddaughter, practicing the piano, remembers them leaving the last place,   23
on the run, begging an old man and his son to transport the precious African
thing—for to the grandmother the piano is African, civilized, the sum of its
parts—on the back of a pickup truck.

A flock of white ladies had descended on the grandmother, declaring she had no   24
right to raise a white child and they would take the girl and place her with a "decent"
family. She explained that the girl was her granddaughter—sometimes it's like that.
They did not hear. They took the girl by the hand, down the street, across the town,
into the home of a man and a woman bereft of their only child by diphtheria. They
led the girl into a pink room with roses rampant on the wall, a starched canopy
hanging above the bed. They left her in the room and told her to remove her clothes,
put on the robe they gave her, and take the bath they would draw for her. She did
this.

Then, under cover of night, she let herself out the back door off the kitchen and   25
made her way back, leaving the bed of a dead girl behind her. The sky pounded and
the rain soaked her.

When the grandmother explained to the old man the circumstances of their leav-   26
ing he agreed to help. To her granddaughter she said little except she hoped the
piano would not be damaged in their flight.

There is a woman lying in a bed. She has flown through a storm to the feet of her   27
grandmother, who is seated atilt at the upright, on a bench which holds browned
sheets of music. The girl's hair is glistening from the wet but not a strand is out of
place. It is braided with care, tied with grosgrain. Her mind's eye brings the ribbon
into closer focus; its elegant dullness, no cheap satin shine.

Fifty cents a yard at the general store on Main Street.   28

"And don't you go flinging it at me like that. I've lived too long for your rudeness.   29
I don't think the good Lord put me on this earth to teach each generation of you politeness." The grandmother is ramrod straight, black straw hat shiny, white gloves
bright, hair restrained by a black net. The thing in her thigh throbs, as it always does
in such situations, as it did in front of the white ladies, as it did on the back of the
old man's truck.

The granddaughter chafes under the silence, scrutiny of the boy who is being ad-   30
dressed, a smirk creasing his face. She looks to the ceiling where a fan stirs up dust.
She looks to the bolts of cotton behind his head. To her reflection in the glass-
fronted cabinet. To the sunlight blaring through the huge windows in front, fading
everything in sight: except the grandmother, who seems to become blacker with
every word. And this is good. And the girl is frightened.

She looks anywhere but at the boy. She has heard their "white nigger" hisses often   31
enough, as if her skin, her hair signify only shame, a crime against nature.

The grandmother picks up the length of ribbon where it has fallen, holds   32
the cloth against her spectacles, examining it, folding the ribbon inside her
handkerchief.

The boy behind the counter is motionless, waiting for his father's money, waiting   33
to wait on the other people watching him, as this old woman takes all the time in the
world. Finally: "Thank you, kindly," she tells him, and counts fifty cents onto the
marble surface, slowly, laying the copper in lines of ten; and the girl, in her imagination, desperate to be anywhere but here, sees lines of Cherokee in canoes skim-
ming an ice-bound river, or walking to Oklahoma, stories her grandmother told her.
"They'd stopped listening to their Beloved Woman. Don't get me started, child."

The transaction complete, they leave—leaving the boy, two dots of pink sparking   34
each plump cheek, incongruous against his smirk.

The woman in the bed opens her eyes. It is still, dark. She looks to the window. A   35
tall, pale girl flies in the window to the feet of her grandmother. Seated at the piano,
she turns her head and the grandmother's spectacles catch the lightning.

"I want to stay here with you forever, Grandma."   36

"I won't be here forever. You will have to make your own way."   37

"Yes, ma'am."   38

"We are born alone and we die alone and in the meanwhile we have to learn to   39
live alone."

"Yes, Grandma."   40

"Good."   41

They speak their set-piece like two shadow puppets against a white wall in a   42
darkened room. They are shades, drawn behind the eye of a woman, full-grown,
alive, in withdrawal.

"Did something happen tonight?"   43

"Nothing, Grandma; just the storm."   44

"That's what made you take flight?"   45

"Yes, ma'am."   46

"Are you sure?"   47

"Yes, ma'am."   48

She could not tell her about the song, nor the word they had thrown at the other   49
girl, to which the song was nothing.

She could not tell her about the pink room, the women examining her in the   50
bath, her heart pounding as she escaped in a dead girl's clothes. They had burned
hers.

Two childish flights. In each the grace which was rain, the fury which was storm   51
chased her, saved her.

In the morning the sky was clear.   52

"Grandma?"   53

"Yes?"   54

"If I pay for it, can we get a radio?"   55

"Isn't a piano, aren't books enough for you?"   56

Silence.   57

"Where would you get that kind of money?"   58

"Mrs. Baker has asked me to help her after school. She has a new baby."   59

"Do I know this Mrs. Baker?"   60

"She was a teacher at the school before we came here. She left to get married and   61
have a baby."

"Oh." The grandmother paused. "Then she is a colored woman?" As if she would   62
even consider having her granddaughter toil for the other ilk.

"Yes. And she has a college education." Surely this detail would get the seal of ap-   63
proval, and with it the chance of the radio.

"What a fool."   64

"Grandma?"   65

"I say what a foolish woman. To go through all that—all that she must have done,   66
and her people too—to get a college education and become a teacher and then to
throw it all away to become another breeder. What a shame!"

With the last she was not expressing sympathy for a life changed by fate, or   67
circumstances beyond an individual's control; she meant disgrace, of the Eve-
covering-her-nakedness sort.

"Yes, Grandma." The girl could but assent.   68

The woman in the bed is watching as these shadows traverse the wall.   69

"Too many breeders, not enough readers. Yes—indeed."   70

"She seems like a very nice woman."   71

"And what, may I ask, does that count for? When there are children who de-   72
pended on her? Why didn't she consider her responsibilities to her students, eh?
Running off like that."

Watching the shadows engage and disengage.   73

"She didn't run off, Grandma."   74

No, Grandmother. Your daughter, my mother, ran off, or away. My mother who   75
quit Spelman after one year because she didn't like the smell of her own hair burning—so you said. Am I to believe you? Went north and came back with me, and then
ran off, away—again.

"You know what I mean. Selfish woman. Selfish and foolish. Lord have mercy,   76
what a combination. The kind that do as they please and please no one but
themselves."

The grandmother turned away to regard the dirt street and the stubborn rose.   77

The granddaughter didn't dare offer that a selfish and foolish woman would not   78
make much of a teacher. Nor that Miss Elliston—whose pointer seemed an extension of her right index finger, and whose blue rayon skirt bore an equator of chalk
dust—was a more than permanent replacement. The bitterness went far too deep
for mitigation or comfort.

"Grandma, if I work for her, may I get a radio?"   79

"Tell me, why do you want this infernal thing?"   80

"Teacher says it's educational." Escape. I want to know about the outside.   81

"Nonsense. Don't speak nonsense to me."   82

"No, ma'am."   83

"And just how much do you think this woman is willing to pay you?"   84

"I'm not sure."   85

"What does her husband do, anyway?"   86

"He's in the navy, overseas."   87

"Of course." Her tone was resigned.   88

"Grandma?"   89

"Serving them coffee, cooking their meals, washing their drawers. Just another   90
servant in uniform, a house slave, for that is all the use the United States Navy has
for the Negro man."

She followed the War religiously, *Crisis* upon *Crisis*.   91

"Why didn't he sign up at Tuskegee, eh? Instead of being a Pullman porter on the   92
high seas, or worse."

"I don't know," her granddaughter admitted quietly, she who was half-them.   93

"Yellow in more ways than one, that's why. Playing it safe, following a family tra-   94
dition. Cooking and cleaning and yassuh, yassuh, yassuh. They are yellow, am I right?"

"Yes, ma'am."   95

"Well, those two deserve each other."   96

It was no use. No use at all to mention Dorie Miller—about whom the grand-   97
mother had taught the granddaughter—seizing the guns on the *Arizona* and blasting the enemy from the sky. No use at all. She who was part-them felt on trembling
ground.

Suddenly—   98

"As long as you realize who, what these people are, then you may work for the   99
woman. But only until you have enough money for that blasted radio. Maybe
Madame Foolish-Selfish can lend you some books. Unless," her voice held an extraordinary coldness, "she's sold them to buy diapers."

"Yes, ma'am."   100

"You will listen to the radio only at certain times, and you must promise me to   101
abide by my choice of those times, and to exercise discretion."

"I promise," the girl said.   102

Poor Mrs. Baker was in for one last volley. "Maybe as you watch the woman de-   103
teriorate, you will decide her life will not be yours. Your brain is too good, child. And
can be damaged by the likes of her, the trash of the radio."

Not even when Mr. Baker's ship was sunk in the Pacific and he was lost, did she   104
relent. "Far better to go down in flames than be sent to a watery grave. He died no
hero's death, not he."

> *"Full fathom five thy father lies;*
> *Of his bones are coral made;*
> *Those are pearls that were his eyes:"*

The baby with the black pearl eyes was folded into her chest as she spoke to him.   105

> *"Nothing of him that doth fade,*
> *But doth suffer a sea-change*
> *Into something rich and strange."*

She imagined a deep and enduring blackness. Salt stripping him to bone, coral   106
grafting, encrusted with other sea-creatures. She thought suddenly it was the wrong
ocean that had claimed him—his company was at the bottom of the other.

> *"Sea nymphs hourly ring his knell:*
> *Ding-dong.*
> *Hark! now I hear them—ding-dong, bell."*

She heard nothing. The silence would be as deep and enduring as the blackness.   107

The girl didn't dare tell her grandmother that she held Mrs. Baker's hand when   108
she got the news about her husband, brought her a glass of water, wiped her face.
Lay beside her until she fell asleep. Gave the baby a sugar tit so his mother would not
be waked.

The girl was learning about secrecy.   109

The girl tunes the radio in. Her head and the box are under a heavy crazy quilt,   110
one of the last remnants of her mother; pieced like her mother's skin in the tent
show where, as her grandmother said, "she exhibits herself." As a savage. A woman
with wild hair. A freak.

That was a while ago; nothing has been heard from her since.   111

It is late. The grandmother is asleep on the back porch on a roll-away cot. Such is   112
the heat she sleeps in the open air covered only by a thin muslin sheet.

The misery, heaviness of the quilt, smelling of her mother's handiwork, are more than compensated for by *The Shadow*. Who knows what evil lurks in the hearts of men?

The radio paid for, her visits to Mrs. Baker are meant to stop—that was the agreement. But she will not quit. Her visits to Mrs. Baker—like her hiding under her mother's covers with the radio late at night, terrified the hot tubes will catch the bed afire—are surreptitious and fill her with a warmth she is sure is wrong. She loves this woman, who is soft, who drops the lace front of her camisole to feed her baby, who tunes in to the opera from New York on Saturday afternoons and explains each heated plot as she moves around the small neat house. 113

The girl sees the woman in her dreams. 114

On a hot afternoon in August Mrs. Baker took her to a swimming hole a mile or two out in the country, beyond the town. They wrapped the baby and set him by the side of the water, "Like the baby Moses," Mrs. Baker said. Birdsong was over them and the silver shadows of fish glanced off their legs. 115

"Come on, there's no one else around," Mrs. Baker told her, assuring her when she hesitated, "There's nothing to be ashamed of." And the girl slipped out of her clothes, folding them carefully on the grassy bank. Shamed nonetheless by her paleness. 116

Memory struck her like a water moccasin sliding through the muddy water. The women who would save her had her stand, turn around, open her legs—just to make sure. 117

She pulls herself up and comes to in her hospital bed. The piano in the corner of the room, the old lady, the girl, the jump rope, the white ladies, recede and fade from her sight. Now there is a stark white chest which holds bedclothes. In another corner a woman in a lace camisole, baby-blue ribbon threaded through the lace, smiles and waves and rises to the ceiling, where she slides into a crack in the plaster. 118

The woman in the bed reaches for the knob on the box beside her head and tunes it in; Ferrante and Teicher play the theme from *Exodus* on their twin pianos. 119

Her brain vibrates in a contrecoup. She is in a brilliantly lit white room in Boston, Massachusetts. Outside is frozen solid. It is the dead of winter in the dead of night. She could use a drink. 120

What happened, happened quickly. The radio announced a contest. She told Mrs. Baker about it. Mrs. Baker convinced her to send her picture in to the contest: "Do you really want to spend the rest of your days here? Especially now that your grandmother's passed on?" Her heart stopped. Just like that. 121

The picture was taken by Miss Velma Jackson, Mrs. Baker's friend, who advertised herself as V. JACKSON, PORTRAIT PHOTOGRAPHY, US ARMY RET. Miss Jackson came to town a few years after the War was over, set up shop, and rented a room in Mrs. Baker's small house. In her crisp khakis, with her deep brown skin, she contrasted well with the light-brown pasteled Mrs. Baker. She also loved the opera, and together they sang the duet from *Norma*. 122

When she moved in talk began. "There must be something about that woman and uniforms," the grandmother said in one of her final judgments. 123

Miss Jackson, who preferred "Jack" to "Velma," performed a vital service to the community, like the hairdresser and the undertaker. Poor people took care to keep a record of themselves, their kin. They needed Jack, and so the talk died down. Died 124 down until another photographer came along—a traveling man who decided to settle down.

Jack's portrait of the girl, now a young woman, came out well. She stared back in 125
her green-eyed, part-them glory against a plain white backdrop, no fussy ferns or
winged armchairs. The picture was sent in to the contest, a wire returned, and she
was summoned.

She took the plain name they offered her—eleven letters, to fit best on a mar- 126
quee—and took off. A few papers were passed.

"Will you come with me?" 127

"No." 128

"Why not?" 129

"I can't." 130

"Why not?" 131

"Jack and I have made plans. She has some friends in Philadelphia. It will be eas- 132
ier for us there."

"And Elijah?" 133

"Oh, we'll take him along, of course. Good schools there. And one of her friends 134
has a boy his age."

"I'm going to miss you." 135

"You'll be fine. We'll keep in touch. This town isn't the world, you know." 136

"No." 137

Now there was nothing on the papers they sent—that is, no space for RACE? 138

Jack said, "And what do you propose to do? Say, hey, Mr. Producer, by the way, al- 139
though I have half-moons on my fingernails, a-hem, a-hem?"

She was helped to her berth by a Pullman porter more green-eyed than she. In his 140
silver-buttoned epauleted blue coat he reminded her of a medieval knight, on an
iron horse, his chivalric code—RULES FOR PULLMAN PORTERS—stuck in his breast
pocket. He serenaded her.

> "De white gal ride in de parlor car.
> De yaller gal try to do de same.
> De black gal ride in de Jim Crow car.
> But she get dar jes' de same."

He looked at her as he stowed her bag. "Remember that old song, Miss?" 141

"No." 142

Daughter of the Mother Lode. The reader might recall that one. It's on late-night 143
TV and also on video by now. She was the half-breed daughter of a Forty-Niner. At
first, dirty and monosyllabic, then taken up by a kindly rancher's wife, only to be
kidnapped by some crazy Apaches.

Polysyllabic and clean and calicoed when the Apaches seize her, dirty and mono- 144
syllabic and buck-skinned when she breaks away—and violated, dear Lord, violated
out of her head, for which the rancher wreaks considerable havoc on the Apaches.
You may remember that she is baptized and goes on to teach school in town and becomes a sort of mother confessor to the dance-hall girls.

As she gains speed, she ascends to become one of the more-stars-than-there-are- 145 in-the-heavens, and her parts become lighter, brighter than before. Parts where "gay" and "grand" are staples of her dialogue. As in, "Isn't she gay!" "Isn't he grand!" She wears black velvet that droops at the neckline, a veiled pillbox, long white gloves.

She turns out the light next to the bed, shuts off the radio, looks out the window. 146 Ice. Snow. Moon. The moon thin, with fat Venus beside it.

The door to the room suddenly whooshes open and a dark woman dressed in 147 white approaches the bed.

"Mother?" 148

"Don't mind me, honey. I'm just here to clean up." 149

"Oh." 150

"I hope you feel better soon, honey. It takes time, you know." 151

"Yes." 152

The woman has dragged her mop and pail into the room and is now bent under 153 the bed, so her voice is muffled beyond the whispers she speaks in—considerate of the drying-out process.

"Can I ask you something?" This soft-spoken question comes to the actress from 154 underneath.

"Sure." 155

"Would you sign a piece of paper for my daughter?" 156

"I'd be glad to." 157

If I can remember my name. 158

The woman has emerged from under the bed and is standing next to her, look- 159 ing down at her—bedpan in her right hand, disinfectant in her left.

The actress finds a piece of paper on the bedside table, asks the girl's name, signs 160 *With every good wish for your future.*

"Thank you kindly." 161

She lies back. Behind her eyelids is a pond. Tables laden with food are in the 162 background. In the scum of the pond are tadpoles, swimming spiders. Darning nee-dles dart over the water's surface threatening to sew up the eyes of children.

A child is gulping pond water. 163

Fried chicken, potato salad, coleslaw, pans of ice with pop bottles sweating from 164 the cold against the heat.

The child has lost her footing. 165

A woman is turning the handle of an ice-cream bucket, a bushel basket of ripe 166 peaches sits on the grass beside her. Three-legged races, sack races, races with an un-cooked egg in a spoon, all the races known to man, form the landscape beyond the pond, the woman with the ice-cream bucket, the tables laden with food.

Finally—the child cries out. 167

People stop. 168

She is dragged from the water, filthy. She is pumped back to life. She throws up in 169 the soft grass.

The woman wakes, the white of the pillow case is stained. 170

She pulls herself up in the bed. 171

The other children said she would turn green—from the scum, the pond water, 172 the baby frogs they told her she had swallowed. No one will love you when you are green and ugly.

She gets up, goes to the bathroom, gets a towel to put over the pillow case.   173
"Hello. Information?"   174
"This is Philadelphia Information."   175
"I would like the number of Velma Jackson, please."   176
"One moment please."   177
"I'll wait."   178
"The number is—"   179
She hangs up. It's too late.   180

"She did run away from them, Mama. She came back to you. I don't think you   181
ever gave her credit for that."
"And look where she is now, Rebekah."   182
"She ran away from them, left a room with pink roses. Sorry, Mama, I know how   183
you hate roses."
"Who is speaking, please?" The woman sits up again, looks around. Nothing.   184

What will become of her?   185
Let's see. This is February 1963.   186
She might find herself in Washington, D.C., in August. A shrouded marcher in   187
the heat, dark-glassed, high-heeled.
That is unlikely.   188

Go back? To what? This ain't *Pinky*.   189
Europe? A small place somewhere. Costa Brava or Paris—who cares? Do cameos   190
for Fellini; worse come to worse, get a part in a spaghetti western.
She does her time. Fills a suitcase with her dietary needs: Milky Ways, cartons of   191
Winston's, golden tequila, boards a plane at Idlewild.
Below the plane is a storm, a burst behind a cloud, streak lightning splits the sky,   192
she rests her head against the window; she finds the cold comforting.

Working with the Text

1. We realize at the end of the story that the central character is a movie actress apparently recovering from some sort of nervous collapse, perhaps related to the revelation that she is actually a black woman. How do the various
events and impressions that she recalls during the course of the story affect
her? What does she seem to be trying to get in touch with through the haze of
memories that she experiences during her hospital stay? How do the story's
various layers work together?

2. Why is it significant that the young woman became a movie actress, playing apparently superficial roles in light comedies and romances? What does
this suggest about her identity? In what ways is the title of the story, "Screen
Memory," ambiguous or ironic?

3. How do the events related through the story serve to shape the central
character's identity? Does she seem to have made many choices of her own?

Do you think the fact that she looks white can be seen as one of the greatest influences on the person she becomes?

4. Consider the character of the grandmother. Does she seem to care for her granddaughter? What lessons does she attempt to teach the girl? How does the girl respond?

5. The story ends in early 1963, just a few months before a huge political demonstration occurred in Washington, D.C. It was organized by Martin Luther King Jr., and during it he delivered his famous "I Have a Dream" speech. What does this plot element contribute to the meanings of the story?

Thinking and Writing: *Critical Questions Revisited*

1. Sources of Self-identity

How do the authors in this chapter address the concept of self-identity? Which forces and influences seem to weigh most heavily on different authors? What are the various ways that we derive our sense of self-identity? What are some examples of how these authors sort through the competing influences of innate, community, or cultural identity on the one hand and received messages or the influence of perceptions on the other? How do different authors approach the idea of a fractured or multiple self? You might pick two authors to discuss together or use one or more authors as a springboard for a discussion about the multiple roles or selves that make up one's self-identity. Do some authors treat this fracturing as normal or abnormal? Do you think that the multiple nature of self-identity is normal, or is it something that people have to work through, fight through, to understand their place in the world?

2. The Shaping Power of Place

Marianne Boruch begins her essay in this chapter, "If memory is a matter of *place,* then my childhood gave me two." For many of the authors in this chapter, memory and identity are grounded in a particular place. The idea of a "home place" functions very differently in the selections. Sometimes that place is the source of comfort, and at other times it causes great confusion or pain. Consider how the notions of "home" and "place" function for Kittredge, Boruch, and Banks. Or consider the roles of "home" and "place" in your own life. How has the place (or places) where you've grown up helped define your perspective and identity? How does it limit you? How is your sense of home or place bound to your family and community?

3. The Shaping Power of Stories

Consider these three passages on the shaping power of stories:

> Storytelling and make-believe, like war and agriculture, are among the arts of self-defense. . . . (William Kittredge, "Home")

> When you are hit in the head or slammed in the ribs and thrown to the floor by a powerful man, you find instantly that you are already halfway into a narrative that portrays your return to that moment, a narrative whose primary function is to provide reversal: to make the child into the man, the weak into the strong, the bad into the good. Listen to me: you are locked into that narrative, and no other terms, except those present at its inception, at the very opening of the drama, are available for the reversal—and, oh! when that happens, I have risen up from my narrow bed in the upstairs corner room I shared with my brother in Tobyhanna in 1952, and I overwhelm my dead father's rage with an awful crippling rage of my own. (Russell Banks, "The Visitor")

> You always read about it:
> the plumber with twelve children
> who wins the Irish Sweepstakes.
> From toilets to riches.
> That story. (Anne Sexton, "Cinderella")

Each of these three passages (and many others from the chapter) points to the complicated way that stories shape our lives and our sense of who we are. On one hand, we use stories to connect ourselves to our past; on the other hand, stories shape our beliefs, sometimes beyond our control. At the most extreme, as Banks puts it, we "get locked into a narrative" from which it is difficult or impossible to escape. What kinds of influence do stories exert on your life? How do these writers explore the role stories play in shaping our lives and in determining how we deal with the world? How do people "live out" certain stories despite their efforts to free themselves from their grip?

4. Truths and Fictions

Many of the authors in this chapter explore the sometimes fuzzy line between truth and fiction. This is true not only in the selections of fiction (such as those by Silko and Cliff) but also in some of the nonfiction writing (such as that by Kittredge and Cofer). In all of these works is the theme that sometimes, when we look closely, we can't always tell the difference between what is real and what is not, what is true and what is make-believe. What are some of the ways that the line between truth and make-believe can blur? How do these writers make that line an important part of their explorations of memory and self-identity?

5. Past and Present

In Sherman Alexie's short story "Family Portrait," he says:

> How much do we remember of what hurts us most? I've been thinking about pain, how each of us constructs our past to justify what we feel now. How each successive pain distorts the preceding. Let's say I remember sunlight as a measurement of this story, how it changed the shape of the family portrait. My father shields his eyes and makes his face a shadow. He could be anyone then, but my eyes are closed in the photo. I cannot remember what I was thinking. Maybe I wanted to stand, stretch my legs, raise my arms above my head, open my mouth wide, and fill my lungs. *Breathe, breathe.* Maybe my hair is so black it collects all the available light.

What is the relationship between the past and the present? How does the past make its way to the present? How is what we remember about the past filtered and shaped by the present? These are important questions that run throughout the chapter. They are made particularly poignant in the selections of writers who are dealing with pain and violence. In many of these readings, the past is a place of violence or painful memories that have a very particular relationship to the present. In some stories violence coexists with the desire to inhabit a fairy-tale or make-believe world or to substitute romance and idealism for a painful reality. What are some examples where violence and romance—or pain and idealism—exist together? How do they sometimes function in people's memories? What about the stories that we see around us in popular culture? How, for example, does Sexton's jarring use of violent images fit into her retelling of the Cinderella story? Or how do Alexie's surprising turns of phrase and sometimes too honest and revealing painful details disappear into other kinds of language, words characterized by his desire to idealize and make rosy his family situation? How do past and present shape each other?

6. Writing Your Own Story

Write your own autobiographical essay about some of the influences that shaped your sense of your self. Using the writers in this chapter as examples, think about what you might emphasize in your essay. On what influences will you focus? How will you represent time and the relationship between past and present? Is there a particular place that serves to ground a memory? Or certain details of a memory that ground an emotion? How can your essay have meaning for the reader who didn't undergo your experiences?

CHAPTER

BORDERS OF COMMUNITY:

Belonging and Alienation

Critical Questions for *Borders of Community*

How do people develop a sense of belonging? How is it expressed? What makes a community? Is it sameness or the overcoming of differences? What does it mean to feel like you belong to a community? To what extent is a community defined by the physical space its members occupy? How do communities shape and maintain their own identity? Under what circumstances do people feel a sense of alienation, sometimes from contexts that feel most familiar? How are the ideas of community and culture related? How is culture personal? What are the roles of individuals in a culture? What role does individuality play in the functioning of communities? Can you have a community based on difference?

WHERE DO YOU BELONG?

In his essay later in this chapter, Leonard Kriegel remembers the graffiti that was written on the surface of a tunnel leading to an abandoned reservoir in the North Bronx where he and his friends used to play when he was young. The tunnel was threatening enough, he recalls, but it was made more so by the "rage and fury" of the graffiti written on the walls in such phrases as "Unite Unite/Keep America White!" and "Kill all Jews!" "The graffiti on that tunnel wall mobilized my rage," he writes,

> nurturing my need for vengeance in the midst of isolation. It wasn't simply the anti-Semitism I wanted vengeance upon; it was my own solitary passage through that entrance tunnel. As I moved through it alone, the tunnel was transformed into everything my budding sense of myself as embryonic American hated. Walking through it became an act of daring for graffiti had converted its emptiness into a threat that could only be taken the way it was offered—a threat that was distinctly personal.

That Kriegel sees the threat of the anti-Semitic graffiti as "distinctly personal" is poignant. His emotional response is not as a Jewish boy in behalf of all Jews, but as an individual whose place and sense of belonging in America seem challenged. He says, "Even the anti-Semitic graffiti of that tunnel remains in my memory as less the product of hatred than an expression of the distance existing between groups struggling to claim a portion of the American past." The racist writing on the wall poses a struggle for Kriegel between a sense of belonging and alienation. And it is that struggle, however overt or subtle it may be for any of us, that organizes the readings in this chapter.

In the previous chapter, the readings focused on the idea of identity—how we come to be who we are. That chapter in many ways was about how outside forces—stories, beliefs, customs, or the environment—form the individual. In other words, Chapter 2 asks, what *shapes* us? This chapter changes the question somewhat to ask, what *connects* us? What connects us to the place, the community, or the culture that surrounds us? What gives or withholds a sense of belonging for us? In what ways do we feel the strengths of that connection? What challenges or threatens that sense of connection?

Throughout these readings, the idea of belonging means different things. The first and most obvious is the kind of belonging that is rooted in a physical place. In an essay later in this book, Joel Garreau tells the story of a newspaper reporter who, having given up "the prestige of being a Washington correspondent in order to return to the quieter life of the medium-sized western paper," is driving across the country to the place in the Western United States where he grew up. As the reporter headed west, Garreau explains, he "hardly noticed his surroundings, wondering whether the choice he had made was right." Garreau goes on to relate:

> He told me he remembered with great clarity finally losing his indecision on Interstate 80, not far from Cheyenne, Wyoming, as the flatlands gave way to the mountains and their small towns.
>
> It was there, he said, that suddenly a knot disappeared from his stomach, a knot he hadn't known was there. It was there that he discovered a feeling of familiarity with the colors, the horizon, the names of the towns.
>
> Every North American knows a place like that, a place where on your way back from your wandering, surroundings stop feeling threatening, confusing, or strange.

Garreau claims that everyone has a place like this. When you're in it, "you know you're home." But what is it that makes a place feel like home? Returning to a place where we grew up that feels familiar is surely one kind of belonging. But it is only one, and the feeling of belonging that each of us needs and looks for is usually more complicated than simply being in a place or returning to our origins.

What about, for example, people who migrate from one part of the country to another? Or even more pointedly, people who emigrate from another country? Can you ever have a sense of belonging not only in a place but also in a culture that differs from the one in which you were born and raised? In one of this chapter's essays, the fiction writer Bharati Mukherjee discusses the two very different kinds of connection that she and her sister—both residents of the United States for more than thirty years—feel for America. Mukherjee, who is Indian, married a non-Indian, Canadian citizen and hence adopted a new citizenship outside of India. Her sister married an Indian, and although she has worked in this country for thirty-six years, she dreams of retiring in India. About the differences in orientation, Mukherjee asks:

> In one family, from two sisters alike as peas in a pod, there could not be a wider divergence of immigrant experience. America spoke to me—I married it—I embraced the demotion from expatriate aristocrat to immigrant nobody, surrendering those thousands of years of "pure culture," the saris, the delightfully accented English. She retained them all. Which of us is the freak?

The similarities and differences between the story Garreau tells and the situation Mukherjee describes are telling ones. In the story of the reporter who left Washington, D.C., to head back west, his return to a comfortable place was a matter of choice. He decided to return to a "home-place" waiting for him that made him feel as if he belonged. In contrast, Mukherjee's immigrant situation is very different. She, unlike her sister, was even willing to give up the "purity" of her home culture to adopt a new one—a culture that she connected with through a marriage across ethnic groups, a new citizenship, and a new cross-cultural identity. The reporter's sense of belonging to a place was entirely in his own hands. For Mukherjee, her sister, and all immigrants (and to some extent for minorities in any situation), belonging depends *both* on individual choice and attitude and on the capacity of the surrounding culture to accept them. The struggle between belonging and alienation, in other words, can result from the interplay between internal attitude and external circumstances. The balance between those two forces depends a lot on who you are—majority, minority, native, immigrant—in any given situation.

This all points to one major set of questions posed in this chapter. A sense of belonging always comes at a price. That is, to feel part of something, to feel at home, you always have to give something up. What are the costs of belonging? What are the privileges? What does it mean to belong to a community or a culture? What is it about a sense of community or culture that gives people a feeling of belonging or alienation? What holds a community or a culture together, and how do individuals fit into them?

BELONGING TO A CULTURE

Probably the single most important concept related to belonging is *culture*. How is our sense of belonging dependent on culture? What does it mean to "belong" to a culture? Is it possible to belong to more than one culture? Do individuals belong to cultures, or are cultures the creations of individuals?

Culture is a complicated word that has many different usages. Also, there are differing opinions about how culture should be defined. Most people would generally agree that culture is a set of customs, beliefs, rules, behaviors, and identities that constitute a "system" or "way of living" for a particular people. Although we might refine that definition, the common view is that "culture" is a system of living that connects people to their surrounding world.

When people use a term like "American culture" to refer to the culture of the United States, they usually are implying two things simultaneously. On the one hand, they mean a national culture, one which is generated by a combination of media, economics, and the dominant political and social ideals. On the other hand, American "culture" often refers to the network of cultures that are somehow knit together, but not blended, within American society. Certainly, individuals can live within both of these notions of culture, and many people feel the *doubleness* of cultural belonging very strongly. For others, there is only a sense of being "an American." Nonetheless, all of us in one way or another in the United States belong to both a national culture and at least one cultural orientation that is defined by our class, "race," social status, gender or sexuality, or other influences. Whether or not one's own personal cultural orientation has affinity or friction with the national culture varies from group to group and from person to person.

Although culture is a complex idea used in the most sweeping and abstract ways, each of us can feel and experience our own culture every day in the smallest, most familiar, and most intimate things: in the food we eat, the clothes we wear, the holidays we celebrate, the songs we sing, and the rituals we practice. We can see culture in the most important values, or history, or heritage, but we can also feel it in the small things, in the personal details. One of those personal things—one which has broad implications—is language. As Victor Cruz, who immigrated from Puerto Rico to the United States, says of his bilingual nature:

> Because language represents a world, we can see the contradictions that besiege the users of the Spanish language in the United States; the world it is from is not in their presence. Words have lives of their own, it is what we fit into, were they not here before us. Experience is the word that passes through the things that we do. Language is a cultural attitude accumulated over the centuries.

Language, like other aspects of our lives, often serves as an invisible link to our culture. If you happen to be bilingual or an immigrant, then language might be very visible. But many aspects of culture are invisible to us in the sense that they are habitual. Regardless of its precise definition, culture helps constitute our way of seeing the world. And oftentimes, we think of that way as the natural way and of other ways as different. This, then, is one of the links between culture and belonging. One way to think of "belonging" is as the way we feel when we're at home with the language, beliefs, rituals, and practices of a particular culture.

WHAT IS A COMMUNITY?

Surely, though, we can feel a sense of belonging at more than one level at a time. A connection to a culture is just one level. Another critical level of personal connection is the idea of community. Like culture, the term "community" is used in many different ways and contexts. For simplicity, we can make two initial distinctions in the types of communities: *physical* communities and communities of *interest*. Physical communities are those where people are connected by their physical proximity, as in a part of a city, a rural area, a small town, or a neighborhood. Many uses of the concept of community have this idea as their premise, even if the implications of community consciousness go beyond mere geographical bonding.

Probably the most comprehensive description of a physical community in this chapter is in Kai Erikson's exploration of the meaning of community in Buffalo Creek, an area of Appalachia that was destroyed in a disastrous flood in 1972. His analysis of the community—by way of the residents' self-description of what was "lost" in the flood—leads him to describe something special and extraordinary in the social and emotional ties that form around physical proximity. These emotional ties are so important that Erikson distinguishes between a "community," which is based simply on physical proximity, and "communality," which is something else. He explains: "I use the term 'communality' here rather than 'community' in order to underscore the point that people are not referring to particular village territories when they lament the loss of community but to the network of relationships that make up their general human surround." For the people of Buffalo Creek, community is like a culture (and inseparable from it) because their sense of communality defines the web of living conditions that connects people to their world. As Erikson says, "The closeness of communal ties is experienced on Buffalo Creek as part of the natural order of things, and residents can no more describe that presence than fish are aware of the water they swim in. It is just there, the envelope in which they live, and it is taken entirely for granted."

This comparison leads to one useful way to think about the relationship between culture and community. A *culture* is a network of beliefs, customs, practices, behaviors, and values. A *community* is a network of human relationships. The two together—culture and community—go a long way toward defining how and when we feel a sense of belonging and connection to our surroundings.

Regardless of what kind of community we're talking about, often implicit is the idea that people *need* to have a sense of community and that if it is lacking, people yearn for it. In the modern world we have many ways to find community other than just being in a physical location. As Scott Walker puts it (in his introduction to the *Greywolf Anthology* volume about "community"):

> We are no longer able to define community simply as "these people in this place." We're faced with a complex set of options. We can find community through geographic location, geologic affinity (people who love the mountains), ethnic or racial cultures, peer and interest groups, regional and bioregional associations, sexual preference, linguistic and religious affiliations, etc. At the same time that the mass market works to blur the distinctions between us and we are faced with enormous pressure to homogenize, we must struggle to satisfy our basic need for community.

It is interesting to consider that our modern need for community might spring from both a reaction to media and commercial culture trying to make us all the same, on the one hand, and the incredible diversity and politics of the world making us seem irreconcilably different, on the other. One dimension of both community and culture is the border where sameness and difference come together.

WHAT MAKES INSIDERS AND OUTSIDERS?

If a culture is about shared practices and customs, and if a community is about interdependence of people who share resources or values, then what about people in those contexts who do not share in those practices or values? Do concepts like community and culture necessarily imply the existence of "insiders" and therefore also "outsiders"? Does some people's feeling of belonging imply a sense of alienation for others? What if people feel alienated from the cultures that are supposedly their own?

The sense of alienation or "outsiderness" is expressed in many ways in this chapter. For example, many of this chapter's writers live in more than one place and spread their consciousness beyond more than one "home." Whether they have a double identification with the United States and India, Puerto Rico, Mexico, Canada, or China, many of these writers live with a double consciousness, their spirit and sensibilities existing in two cultures. In all cases of biculturalism, there is a distinct contrast—and occasional conflict—between the two geographies of identification. When Ivette Chavarria, one of the writers in this chapter, heads with her family from her residence in the United States to visit her relatives in Mexico, at first she feels at home. She says:

> We were a handful of Mexicans headed down to Mexico from California. I felt at home with what surrounded me when we crossed the border from Douglas, Arizona, into Agua Prieta, Mexico. Many if not all the aspects of Mexican living were integrated into our family's way of living in Los Angeles. The language, music, food, morals, religion, and beliefs were all part of my upbringing.

And yet after she arrives, her emotions are mixed—she feels like both an insider and an outsider—in part because of the reaction of some of her relatives: "The boys on the street had called me blond. They meant American. They meant different. They saw me as a tourist and a stranger. I ignored it and now it haunted me." Her ambivalence plays out during the remainder of her visit when the family's rituals of food preparation and eating both attract and repulse her.

By contrast, in "Borders," a story by Thomas King, a young boy tries to make sense of his mother's behavior at the Canadian border. The mother is "Blackfoot" Indian, but when she crosses the border, the law requires that she declare her citizenship as either American or Canadian. The mother refuses to choose, insisting that she is only "Blackfoot," so considerable trouble ensues. The story invokes some of the critical questions raised earlier: What do you give up for a sense of belonging? What are the costs of belonging? What are the costs of refusing? King's story reminds us of the personal dimensions of cultural belonging. As with Leonard Kriegel's response to the hate-speech graffiti in the tunnel of his youth, these are not big, sweeping, abstract questions but rather are personal ones. What connects you, personally, to the people, institutions, and values around you?

COOKING CULTURE: THE TAMALE

IVETTE CHAVARRIA

■ Ivette Chavarria was a student at Georgetown University when she wrote the following essay for an English composition course. Raised in Los Angeles by immigrant parents, Chavarria continues to feel close ties to family members still living in Mexico. In "Cooking Culture: The Tamale," she remembers a Christmas trip to visit her grandmother in Chihuahua and the family rituals that helped her feel connected to her family, that made her—in many ways a visiting outsider—feel "part of the whole."

We were on a road trip, and my stomach twirled with excitement. My brothers jumped up and down inside the van singing, "No school . . . No school." We were on a special trip to Mexico. "It'll be the first time in years that my entire family gathers for Christmas. Thank God because your grandmother is getting old. Funny how that woman keeps trucking—I just hope she doesn't snap like a rubber band one of these days," Mom said. On the way there, my dad kept pointing out old roads and rest areas we had been to in the past. My brother asked, "We have been here?" Mom said, "You were too young, silly."

"Just nine-hundred-and-ninety-nine miles until we get to Chihuahua, Mexico," my dad yelled out.

I stared at the highway which stretched before us. It was a gray carpet with a bright yellow stripe running through it. It was rolled out to guide us across the cactus-filled landscape. The distance was clearly emphasized but with every revolution of the tires, we were propelled closer. This feeling allowed the rush of energy in me to continue.

We were a handful of Mexicans headed down to Mexico from California. I felt at home with what surrounded me when we crossed the border from Douglas, Arizona, into Agua Prieta, Mexico. Many if not all the aspects of Mexican living were integrated into our family's way of living in Los Angeles. The language, music, food, morals, religion, and beliefs were all part of my upbringing.

We finally entered the tiny town my mother grew up in. My father honked the horn as we approached my grandmother's house. Neighbors peeped their heads out their windows, probably wondering who the hell was in town. They simply saw a big, white van with bundles tied to the roof, partly obscured by the thick clouds of dirt it lifted as it bumped down the crooked road. In a split second, my crazy aunt Cipriana ran out the door. She looked like a chicken who is in desperate panic, trying to outrun a fox. She opened the gates to the corral as she yelled out, "Tina is here . . . Tina and her family!" We were received with hugs, kisses, and tears as we stepped off the van.

I was soon running around town with my cousins. We delivered candy, coffee, and clothes to several of our family members. These were bought in the U.S. It was not much, but it made them happy. On the way back to grandma's house, a bunch of guys whistled. From the crowd someone asked my cousin, "Martin, who is that cute blond you've got with you?" I was very embarrassed. As we walked away, I said to my cousin, "Blond? Take a closer look!" He laughed and said, "Well, you know—you're from the other side, and heck, you're not as tanned as we are. You can be though. How about working out on the field with us?"

It was Christmas Eve, and my grandmother's house was in a state of chaos. We were making tamales, which are traditionally made every Christmas. We do this only once a year because this task requires a group effort. The leader of our effort, grandma, paced in and out the door instructing people. My aunt Cipriana was sent to the mill with a couple of my cousins. They carried pails full of corn kernels that had been soaked overnight. Dad went to a neighbor's house to ask for dried corn leaves which were saved after the harvest, especially for this season. Mom hauled a tin tub to the front porch and filled it with water. I dumped the corn leaves into the tub. Soaking the leaves would prevent them from cracking. As I finished, my aunt Cipriana returned with three pails full of corn dough. These were simply the preliminaries. 7

My uncles, aunts, and their families began to arrive. Tico, my eldest uncle, walked in with a sharp pick, several knives, and a rope in his hands. He went to the refrigerator for a beer and asked, "Are you going to help?" I cringed and answered, "I don't think I can." He laughed and headed out the door. My dad whispered, "Come on, let's go to the store while the pig gets slaughtered." He understood, and I thanked him with a smile. 8

When we returned, about a half hour later, some of my aunts and uncles were outside laughing and drinking. I decided to join them out in the back of the house. Their hands and aprons were stained with blood. The pig's body parts were laid on a table. When I intently observed my uncle who was cutting the skins off in perfect sheets, I was disgusted. This bothered only me. This was a normal part of their lives not mine. I managed to slowly drift away, unnoticed. 9

I sat alone thinking. The boys on the street had called me blond. They meant American. They meant different. They saw me as a tourist or a stranger. I ignored it, and now it haunted me. I was unable to witness the slaughter or help clean the bloody pieces. I was not connected to the true Mexican's soil or to the reality of their everyday lives. Sure, my parents were born and raised in Mexico, but I was not. My silence was interrupted by my mother who called me from inside the house. 10

Mother wanted me to watch my grandmother prepare the masa (dough). Grandma knelt on the floor by a huge tin tub full of masa. She added chili, baking powder, lard, hot water, salt, and spices. She began to fold the dough several times. Then she moved her arm in a circular motion which swirled everything together and softened the dough into a thick spread. Grandma's arm looked old and wrinkled, but every revolution hurled the dough around the tub with greater force. It was as if time had only affected the outside of her arm—the energy it exerted was equal to a young man's. 11

Once the meat and masa were ready, the actual tamales were made. A caso (huge copper pot used for cooking over an open flame) was carried in by two men. It contained the meat which had been cut and cooked in a thick chili sauce. All the women gathered in a circle. Spoons were used to spread the dough onto the corn leaves. Meat was put in the center, and the leaf was folded. These were stacked neatly in 12 huge pots where they would be steamed until the dough peeled neatly from the leaves. We did this at home, and I was happy to help.

"Well, you're a mighty fine spreader—maybe you should do it for a living," grandma   13
told me and smiled.
"That would be torture mom!" my mother said, almost choking.   14
"Don't you be lazy, don't you forget!"   15
"Oh . . . mother, you know things have gotten easier. It is you who insists on doing   16
things the hard way. You know we'll always dream about the stubborn woman bending
over a tub of dough, forever," mom said.
"Yea . . . yea . . . you young people," grandma mumbled.   17

Mother was right. Making tamales was much easier at home. The masa is pre-   18
pared by machines and is ready to spread. The meat is always packaged neatly in Styrofoam dishes which are wrapped in plastic. The rest of the process is basically the same. It is the dirty work which has been filtered out, and is no longer dealt with. It could be easier than this dough. We can go to the store and buy them made. My mother opposes the idea of doing so. She says that merely making them brings her satisfaction and allows her to savor them.

Later that night the celebration began. We dressed nicely and went to church.   19
Upon arriving, grandma served dinner. We sat at the table and anywhere near it where there was room. Grace was led by my father. As soon as he finished, we all ate heartily. I stopped eating and observed the family as they continued eating, drink-ing, and conversing. I began to understand what my mother meant when she said making the tamales allowed her to savor them. It was not savoring with my mouth but with my eyes and through my understanding. It was sharing in a common task that she focused on. It was my aunt who carried the pails. It was my mother who hauled the tub, father who went next door, and the neighbor who gave him the leaves. It was my aunts and uncles who prepared the meat. It was my grandmother who not only instructed but knelt to prepare the masa. Most important, it was the bringing of all these people together to make the meal before us. This was the magic in the tamale.

After dinner everyone gathered outside around a small fire. We were drinking   20
hot champurrado (a thick chocolate drink) and listening to the men who were singing and playing their guitars. After a few minutes everyone joined the chorus. These songs connected us and so did the tamales. I was part of the whole. I helped make the tamales.

Working with the Text

1. Chavarria says that she felt at home "when we crossed the border from Douglas, Arizona, to Agua Prieta, Mexico." How does she continue to talk about that border? What aspects of being in Mexico do you think make her feel at home?

2. Later in the essay Chavarria describes her feelings as a combination of "belonging" and "distance." What accounts for her feelings of distance? Can you recall a situation when you similarly felt "distant" within a group you

"belong" to? Were you able to resolve these contradictory feelings? Does Chavarria?

3. The grandmother makes tamales the traditional way. Chavarria suggests that at home her family takes shortcuts by using already prepared masa and meat filling ("the dirty work has been filtered out") but still going through the process of assembling the tamales. She also writes that even this step could be skipped, that tamales can be purchased already made. What is the value of maintaining cultural and family traditions in "modern" life? For example, is there something about making tamales from scratch that is "better" than making them by using prepared ingredients or buying them ready-made?

4. What does the grandmother's suggestion that her granddaughter might spread tamales for a living say about differences "across the border"?

TWO WAYS TO BELONG IN AMERICA

BHARATI MUKHERJEE

■ Novelist Bharati Mukherjee was born in Calcutta, India, and immigrated to the United States more than thirty-five years ago, when she was twenty-one. After marrying a Canadian husband, she lived in Canada for some time, but she is now a naturalized U.S. citizen and teaches at Skidmore College. In explaining her decision to become an American citizen, Mukherjee has noted that, unlike other places where she has lived, the United States "*includes* you and is curious about other people . . . allows you to think of yourself as American. . . ." Much of her fiction—including her most recent novel, *The Holder of the World* (1993), and the prize-winning collection *Middleman and Other Stories* (1988)—centers on immigrants, often women from India, and the pains and pleasures they face in experiencing and adapting to a new culture. The following editorial was written for the *New York Times* after Congress passed legislation cutting off most social services and benefits to all legal immigrants who are not citizens—that is, resident aliens—even those who have worked in the United States and paid taxes for many years. Using her sister as a point of contrast, Mukherjee explores the differing mindsets of immigrants like herself who choose to become citizens and those like her sister who choose to remain citizens of their birth country.

T his is a tale of two sisters from Calcutta, Mira and Bharati, who have lived in the United States for some 35 years, but who find themselves on different sides in the current debate over the status of immigrants. I am an American citizen and she is not. I am moved that thousands of long-term residents are finally taking the oath of citizenship. She is not.

Mira arrived in Detroit in 1960 to study child psychology and pre-school educa- 2 tion. I followed her a year later to study creative writing at the University of Iowa. When we left India, we were almost identical in appearance and attitude. We dressed alike, in saris; we expressed identical views on politics, social issues, love and marriage in the same Calcutta convent-school accent. We would endure our two years in America, secure our degrees, then return to India to marry the grooms of our father's choosing.

Instead, Mira married an Indian student in 1962 who was getting his business administration degree at Wayne State University. They soon acquired the labor certifications necessary for the green card of hassle-free residence and employment.   3

Mira still lives in Detroit, works in the Southfield, Mich., school system, and has become nationally recognized for her contributions in the fields of pre-school education and parent-teacher relationships. After 36 years as a legal immigrant in this country, she clings passionately to her Indian citizenship and hopes to go home to India when she retires.   4

In Iowa City in 1963, I married a fellow student, an American of Canadian parentage. Because of the accident of his North Dakota birth, I bypassed labor-certification requirements and the race-related "quota" system that favored the applicant's country of origin over his or her merit. I was prepared for (and even welcomed) the emotional strain that came with marrying outside my ethnic community. In 33 years of marriage, we have lived in every part of North America. By choosing a husband who was not my father's selection, I was opting for fluidity, self-invention, blue jeans and T-shirts, and renouncing 3,000 years (at least) of caste-observant, "pure culture" marriage in the Mukherjee family. My books have often been read as unapologetic (and in some quarters overenthusiastic) texts for cultural and psychological "mongrelization." It's a word I celebrate.   5

Mira and I have stayed sisterly close by phone. In our regular Sunday morning conversations, we are unguardedly affectionate. I am her only blood relative on this continent. We expect to see each other through the looming crises of aging and ill health without being asked. Long before Vice President Gore's "Citizenship U.S.A." drive, we'd had our polite arguments over the ethics of retaining an overseas citizenship while expecting the permanent protection and economic benefits that come with living and working in America.   6

Like well-raised sisters, we never said what was really on our minds, but we probably pitied one another. She, for the lack of structure in my life, the erasure of Indianness, the absence of an unvarying daily core. I, for the narrowness of her perspective, her uninvolvement with the mythic depths or the superficial pop culture of this society. But, now, with the scapegoating of "aliens" (documented or illegal) on the increase, and the targeting of long-term legal immigrants like Mira for new scrutiny and new self-consciousness, she and I find ourselves unable to maintain the same polite discretion. We were always unacknowledged adversaries, and we are now, more than ever, sisters.   7

"I feel used," Mira raged on the phone the other night. "I feel manipulated and discarded. This is such an unfair way to treat a person who was invited to stay and work here because of her talent. My employer went to the I.N.S. and petitioned for the labor certification. For over 30 years, I've invested my creativity and professional skills into the improvement of *this* country's pre-school system. I've obeyed all the   8 rules, I've paid my taxes, I love my work, I love my students, I love the friends I've made. How dare America now change its rules in midstream? If America wants to make new rules curtailing benefits of legal immigrants, they should apply only to immigrants who arrive after those rules are already in place."

To my ears, it sounded like the description of a long-enduring, comfortable yet loveless marriage, without risk or recklessness. Have we the right to demand, and to expect, that we be loved? (That, to me, is the subtext of the arguments by immigration advocates.) My sister is an expatriate, professionally generous and creative, socially courteous and gracious, and that's as far as her Americanization can go. She is here to maintain an identity, not to transform it.

I asked her if she would follow the example of others who have decided to become citizens because of the anti-immigration bills in Congress. And here, she surprised me. "If America wants to play the manipulative game, I'll play it too," she snapped. "I'll become a U.S. citizen for now, then change back to Indian when I'm ready to go home. I feel some kind of irrational attachment to India that I don't to America. Until all this hysteria against legal immigrants, I was totally happy. Having my green card meant I could visit any place in the world I wanted to and then come back to a job that's satisfying and that I do very well."

In one family, from two sisters alike as peas in a pod, there could not be a wider divergence of immigrant experience. America spoke to me—I married it—I embraced the demotion from expatriate aristocrat to immigrant nobody, surrendering those thousands of years of "pure culture," the saris, the delightfully accented English. She retained them all. Which of us is the freak?

Mira's voice, I realize, is the voice not just of the immigrant South Asian community but of an immigrant community of the millions who have stayed rooted in one job, one city, one house, one ancestral culture, one cuisine, for the entirety of their productive years. She speaks for greater numbers than I possibly can. Only the fluency of her English and the anger, rather than fear, born of confidence from her education, differentiate her from the seamstresses, the domestics, the technicians, the shop owners, the millions of hard-working but effectively silenced documented immigrants as well as their less fortunate "illegal" brothers and sisters.

Nearly 20 years ago, when I was living in my husband's ancestral homeland of Canada, I was always well-employed but never allowed to feel part of the local Quebec or larger Canadian society. Then, through a Green Paper that invited a national referendum on the unwanted side effects of "nontraditional" immigration, the Government officially turned against its immigrant communities, particularly those from South Asia.

I felt then the same sense of betrayal that Mira feels now. I will never forget the pain of that sudden turning, and the casual racist outbursts the Green Paper elicited. That sense of betrayal had its desired effect and drove me, and thousands like me, from the country.

Mira and I differ, however, in the ways in which we hope to interact with the country that we have chosen to live in. She is happier to live in America as expatriate Indian than as an immigrant American. I need to feel like a part of the community I have adopted (as I tried to feel in Canada as well). I need to put roots down, to vote and make the difference that I can. The price that the immigrant willingly pays, and that the exile avoids, is the trauma of self-transformation.

Working with the Text

1. What are the two kinds of immigrants that Mukherjee describes? How would you characterize each? Are your sympathies more with the writer or with her sister Mira? Or do you find value in both positions?

2. In explaining her reluctance to become an American citizen, Mira refers to her "irrational attachment to India." Do you understand such an attachment continuing after her more than thirty years of living abroad? Under similar circumstances do you think you would continue to feel such an attachment to your home country?

3. What does Mukherjee mean at the end when she talks about the "trauma of self-transformation"? In what ways can you see the act of assuming a new culture as "traumatic"? How much of his or her "home" culture can an immigrant maintain and still find a sense of belonging in the United States?

4. What do you think about the issue at the heart of Mukherjee's essay? Do both sisters belong equally in the United States, sharing the same benefits? Should an expatriate like Mira who has been immersed in the community for many years be forced to renounce her "home" citizenship to be fully accepted in this country? What do you think of her argument that any new rules "should apply only to immigrants who arrive after those rules are already in place"?

BORDERS

THOMAS KING

■ Born in California, novelist Thomas King has spent most of his life teaching and writing in Canada and the Upper Midwest. He is currently on the faculty at the University of Minnesota. Of Cherokee as well as German and Irish descent, King has used much of his work to explore the diversity of Native American life today. Feeling no strong tie to any particular native culture, King has said that he feels "free to ask some of the really nasty questions that other writers may not want to ask. . . . One of the questions that's important to ask is, 'Who is an Indian? How do we get this idea of Indianness?' " King's recent work includes the novels *Medicine River* (1990) and *Green Grass, Running Water* (1993). The latter offers a complex rendering of the conflicts among environmentalism, development, and the roots of Native American culture in the natural world. "Borders," the following short story, raises interesting questions about citizenship, community, and identity as a Blackfoot woman refuses to claim Canadian citizenship in order to cross the border into the United States.

When I was twelve, maybe thirteen, my mother announced that we were going to go to Salt Lake City to visit my sister who had left the reserve, moved across the line, and found a job. Laetitia had not left home with my mother's blessing, but over time my mother had come to be proud of the fact that Laetitia had done all of this on her own.

"She did real good," my mother would say.

Then there were the fine points of Laetitia's going. She had not, as my mother liked to tell Mrs. Manyfingers, gone floating after some man like a balloon on a string. She hadn't snuck out of the house, either, and gone to Vancouver or Edmonton or Toronto to chase rainbows down alleys. And she hadn't been pregnant.

"She did real good."

I was seven or eight when Laetitia left home. She was seventeen. Our father was from Rocky Boy on the American side.

"Dad's American," Laetitia told my mother, "so I can go and come as I please."

"Send us a postcard."

Laetitia packed her things, and we headed for the border. Just outside of Milk River, Laetitia told us to watch for the water tower.

"Over the next rise. It's the first thing you see."

"We got a water tower on the reserve," my mother said. "There's a big one in Lethbridge, too."

"You'll be able to see the tops of the flagpoles, too. That's where the border is."

When we got to Coutts, my mother stopped at the convenience store and bought her and Laetitia a cup of coffee. I got an Orange Crush.

"This is real lousy coffee."

"You're just angry because I want to see the world."

"It's the water. From here on down, they got lousy water."

"I can catch the bus from Sweetgrass. You don't have to lift a finger."

"You're going to have to buy your water in bottles if you want good coffee."

There was an old wooden building about a block away, with a tall sign in the yard that said "Museum." Most of the roof had been blown away. Mom told me to go and see when the place was open. There were boards over the windows and doors. You could tell that the place was closed, and I told Mom so, but she said to go and check anyway. Mom and Laetitia stayed by the car. Neither one of them moved. I sat down on the steps of the museum and watched them, and I don't know that they ever said anything to each other. Finally, Laetitia got her bag out of the trunk and gave Mom a hug.

I wandered back to the car. The wind had come up, and it blew Laetitia's hair across her face. Mom reached out and pulled the strands out of Laetitia's eyes, and Laetitia let her.

"You can still see the mountain from here," my mother told Laetitia in Blackfoot.

"Lots of mountains in Salt Lake," Laetitia told her in English.

"The place is closed," I said. "Just like I told you."

Laetitia tucked her hair into her jacket and dragged her bag down the road to the brick building with the American flag flapping on a pole. When she got to where the guards were waiting, she turned, put the bag down, and waved to us. We waved back. Then my mother turned the car around, and we came home.

We got postcards from Laetitia regular, and, if she wasn't spreading jelly on the 24 truth, she was happy. She found a good job and rented an apartment with a pool.

"And she can't even swim," my mother told Mrs. Manyfingers. 25

Most of the postcards said we should come down and see the city, but whenever 26 I mentioned this, my mother would stiffen up.

So I was surprised when she bought two new tires for the car and put on her blue 27 dress with the green and yellow flowers. I had to dress up, too, for my mother did not want us crossing the border looking like Americans. We made sandwiches and put them in a big box with pop and potato chips and some apples and bananas and a big jar of water.

"But we can stop at one of those restaurants, too, right?" 28

The border was actually two towns, though neither one was big enough to 29 amount to anything. Coutts was on the Canadian side and consisted of the convenience store and gas station, the museum that was closed and boarded up, and a motel. Sweetgrass was on the American side, but all you could see was an overpass that arched across the highway and disappeared into the prairies. Just hearing the names of these towns, you would expect that Sweetgrass, which is a nice name and sounds like it is related to other places such as Medicine Hat and Moose Jaw and Kicking Horse Pass, would be on the Canadian side, and that Coutts, which sounds abrupt and rude, would be on the American side. But this was not the case.

Between the two borders was a duty-free shop where you could buy cigarettes 30 and liquor and flags. Stuff like that.

We left the reserve in the morning and drove until we got to Coutts. 31

"Last time we stopped here," my mother said, "you had an Orange Crush. You re- 32 member that?"

"Sure," I said. "That was when Laetitia took off." 33

"You want another Orange Crush?" 34

"That means we're not going to stop at a restaurant, right?" 35

My mother got coffee at the convenience store, and we stood around and 36 watched the prairies move in the sunlight. Then we climbed back in the car. My mother straightened the dress across her thighs, leaned against the wheel, and drove all the way to the border in first gear, slowly, as if she were trying to see through a bad storm or riding high on black ice.

The border guard was an old guy. As he walked to the car, he swayed from side to 37 side, his feet set wide apart, the holster on his hip pitching up and down. He leaned into the window, looked into the back seat, and looked at my mother and me.

"Morning, ma'am." 38

"Good morning." 39

"Where you heading?" 40

"Salt Lake City." 41

"Purpose of your visit?" 42

"Visit my daughter." 43

"Citizenship?" 44

"Blackfoot," my mother told him. 45

"Ma'am?"   46

"Blackfoot," my mother repeated.   47

"Canadian?"   48

"Blackfoot."   49

It would have been easier if my mother had just said "Canadian" and been   50
done with it, but I could see she wasn't going to do that. The guard wasn't angry or
anything. He smiled and looked towards the building. Then he turned back and
nodded.

"Morning, ma'am."   51

"Good morning."   52

"Any firearms or tobacco?"   53

"No."   54

"Citizenship?"   55

"Blackfoot."   56

He told us to sit in the car and wait, and we did. In about five minutes, another   57
guard came out with the first man. They were talking as they came, both men sway-
ing back and forth like two cowboys headed for a bar or a gunfight.

"Morning, ma'am."   58

"Good morning."   59

"Cecil tells me you and the boy are Blackfoot."   60

"That's right."   61

"Now, I know that we got Blackfeet on the American side and the Canadians got   62
Blackfeet on their side. Just so we can keep our records straight, what side do you
come from?"

I knew exactly what my mother was going to say, and I could have told them if   63
they had asked me.

"Canadian side or American side?" asked the guard.   64

"Blackfoot side," she said.   65

It didn't take them long to lose their sense of humor, I can tell you that. The one   66
guard stopped smiling altogether and told us to park our car at the side of the building and come in.

We sat on a wood bench for about an hour before anyone came over to talk to us.   67
This time it was a woman. She had a gun, too.

"Hi," she said. "I'm Inspector Pratt. I understand there is a little misunderstanding."   68

"I'm going to visit my daughter in Salt Lake City," my mother told her. "We don't   69
have any guns or beer."

"It's a legal technicality, that's all."   70

"My daughter's Blackfoot, too."   71

The woman opened a briefcase and took out a couple of forms and began to   72
write on one of them. "Everyone who crosses our border has to declare their citizenship. Even Americans. It helps us keep track of the visitors we get from the various countries."

She went on like that for maybe fifteen minutes, and a lot of the stuff she told us   73
was interesting.

"I can understand how you feel about having to tell us your citizenship, and here's   74
what I'll do. You tell me, and I won't put it down on the form. No one will know but
you and me."

Her gun was silver. There were several chips in the wood handle and the name   75
"Stella" was scratched into the metal butt.

We were in the border office for about four hours, and we talked to almost   76
everyone there. One of the men bought me a Coke. My mother brought a couple of
sandwiches in from the car. I offered part of mine to Stella, but she said she wasn't
hungry.

I told Stella that we were Blackfoot and Canadian, but she said that that didn't   77
count because I was a minor. In the end, she told us that if my mother didn't declare
her citizenship, we would have to go back to where we came from. My mother stood
up and thanked Stella for her time. Then we got back in the car and drove to the
Canadian border, which was only about a hundred yards away.

I was disappointed. I hadn't seen Laetitia for a long time, and I had never been to   78
Salt Lake City. When she was still at home, Laetitia would go on and on about Salt
Lake City. She had never been there, but her boyfriend Lester Tallbull had spent a
year in Salt Lake at a technical school.

"It's a great place," Lester would say. "Nothing but blondes in the whole state."   79

Whenever he said that, Laetitia would slug him on his shoulder hard enough to   80
make him flinch. He had some brochures on Salt Lake and some maps, and every so
often the two of them would spread them out on the table.

"That's the temple. It's right downtown. You got to have a pass to get in."   81

"Charlotte says anyone can go in and look around."   82

"When was Charlotte in Salt Lake? Just when the hell was Charlotte in Salt Lake?"   83

"Last year."   84

"This is Liberty Park. It's got a zoo. There's good skiing in the mountains."   85

"Got all the skiing we can use," my mother would say. "People come from all over   86
the world to ski at Banff. Cardston's got a temple, if you like those kinds of things."

"Oh, this one is real big," Lester would say. "They got armed guards and   87
everything."

"Not what Charlotte says."   88

"What does she know?"   89

Lester and Laetitia broke up, but I guess the idea of Salt Lake stuck in her mind.   90

The Canadian border guard was a young woman, and she seemed happy to see us.   91
"Hi," she said. "You folks sure have a great day for a trip. Where are you coming from?"

"Standoff."   92

"Is that in Montana?"   93

"No."   94

"Where are you going?"   95

"Standoff."   96

The woman's name was Carol and I don't guess she was any older than Laetitia.   97
"Wow, you both Canadians?"

"Blackfoot."   98

"Really? I have a friend I went to school with who is Blackfoot. Do you know   99
Mike Harley?"

"No."   100

"He went to school in Lethbridge, but he's really from Browning."   101

It was a nice conversation and there were no cars behind us, so there was no rush.   102

"You're not bringing any liquor back, are you?" 103

"No." 104

"Any cigarettes or plants or stuff like that?" 105

"No." 106

"Citizenship?" 107

"Blackfoot." 108

"I know," said the woman, "and I'd be proud of being Blackfoot if I were Black- 109
foot. But you have to be American or Canadian."

When Laetitia and Lester broke up, Lester took his brochures and maps with him, so 110
Laetitia wrote to someone in Salt Lake City, and, about a month later, she got a big
envelope of stuff. We sat at the table and opened up all the brochures, and Laetitia
read each one out loud.

"Salt Lake City is the gateway to some of the world's most magnificent skiing. 111

"Salt Lake City is the home of one of the newest professional basketball fran- 112
chises, the Utah Jazz.

"The Great Salt Lake is one of the natural wonders of the world." 113

It was kind of exciting seeing all those color brochures on the table and listening 114
to Laetitia read all about how Salt Lake City was one of the best places in the entire
world.

"That Salt Lake City place sounds too good to be true," my mother told her. 115

"It has everything." 116

"We got everything right here." 117

"It's boring here." 118

"People in Salt Lake City are probably sending away for brochures of Calgary and 119
Lethbridge and Pincher Creek right now."

In the end, my mother would say that maybe Laetitia should go to Salt Lake City, 120
and Laetitia would say that maybe she would.

We parked the car to the side of the building and Carol led us into a small room on 121
the second floor. I found a comfortable spot on the couch and flipped through some
back issues of *Saturday Night* and *Alberta Report*.

When I woke up, my mother was just coming out of another office. She didn't say 122
a word to me. I followed her down the stairs and out to the car. I thought we were
going home, but she turned the car around and drove back towards the American
border, which made me think we were going to visit Laetitia in Salt Lake City after
all. Instead she pulled into the parking lot of the duty-free store and stopped.

"We going to see Laetitia?" 123

"No." 124

"We going home?" 125

Pride is a good thing to have, you know. Laetitia had a lot of pride, and so did my 126
mother. I figured that someday, I'd have it, too.

"So where are we going?" 127

Most of that day, we wandered around the duty-free store, which wasn't very 128
large. The manager had a name tag with a tiny American flag on one side and a tiny
Canadian flag on the other. His name was Mel. Towards evening, he began suggesting that we should be on our way. I told him we had nowhere to go, that neither the

Americans nor the Canadians would let us in. He laughed at that and told us that we should buy something or leave.

The car was not very comfortable, but we did have all that food and it was April, so even if it did snow as it sometimes does on the prairies, we wouldn't freeze. The next morning my mother drove to the American border.   129

It was a different guard this time, but the questions were the same. We didn't spend as much time in the office as we had the day before. By noon, we were back at the Canadian border. By two we were back in the duty-free shop parking lot.   130

The second night in the car was not as much fun as the first, but my mother seemed in good spirits, and, all in all, it was as much an adventure as an inconvenience. There wasn't much food left and that was a problem, but we had lots of water as there was a faucet at the side of the duty-free shop.   131

One Sunday, Laetitia and I were watching television. Mom was over at Mrs. Manyfingers's. Right in the middle of the program, Laetitia turned off the set and said she was going to Salt Lake City, that life around here was too boring. I had wanted to see the rest of the program and really didn't care if Laetitia went to Salt Lake City or not. When Mom got home, I told her what Laetitia had said.   132

What surprised me was how angry Laetitia got when she found out that I had told Mom.   133

"You got a big mouth."   134

"That's what you said."   135

"What I said is none of your business."   136

"I didn't say anything."   137

"Well, I'm going for sure, now."   138

That weekend, Laetitia packed her bags, and we drove her to the border.   139

Mel turned out to be friendly. When he closed up for the night and found us still parked in the lot, he came over and asked us if our car was broken down or something. My mother thanked him for his concern and told him that we were fine, that things would get straightened out in the morning.   140

"You're kidding," said Mel. "You'd think they could handle the simple things."   141

"We got some apples and a banana," I said, "but we're all out of ham sandwiches."   142

"You know, you read about these things, but you just don't believe it. You just don't believe it."   143

"Hamburgers would be even better because they got more stuff for energy."   144

My mother slept in the back seat. I slept in the front because I was smaller and could lie under the steering wheel. Late that night, I heard my mother open the car door. I found her sitting on her blanket leaning against the bumper of the car.   145

"You see all those stars," she said. "When I was a little girl, my grandmother used to take me and my sisters out on the prairies and tell us stories about all the stars."   146

"Do you think Mel is going to bring us any hamburgers?"   147

"Every one of those stars has a story. You see that bunch of stars over there that look like a fish?"   148

"He didn't say no."   149

"Coyote went fishing, one day. That's how it all started." We sat out under the stars that night, and my mother told me all sorts of stories. She was serious about it,   150

too. She'd tell them slow, repeating parts as she went, as if she expected me to remember each one.

Early the next morning, the television vans began to arrive, and guys in suits and   151
women in dresses came trotting over to us, dragging microphones and cameras and
lights behind them. One of the vans had a table set up with orange juice and sandwiches and fruit. It was for the crew, but when I told them we hadn't eaten for a
while, a really skinny blonde woman told us we could eat as much as we wanted.

They mostly talked to my mother. Every so often one of the reporters would   152
come over and ask me questions about how it felt to be an Indian without a country. I told them we had a nice house on the reserve and that my cousins had a couple
of horses we rode when we went fishing. Some of the television people went over to
the American border, and then they went to the Canadian border.

Around noon, a good-looking guy in a dark blue suit and an orange tie with lit-   153
tle ducks on it drove up in a fancy car. He talked to my mother for a while, and, after
they were done talking, my mother called me over, and we got into our car. Just as
my mother started the engine, Mel came over and gave us a bag of peanut brittle and
told us that justice was a damn hard thing to get, but that we shouldn't give up.

I would have preferred lemon drops, but it was nice of Mel anyway.   154

"Where are we going now?"   155

"Going to visit Laetitia."   156

The guard who came out to our car was all smiles. The television lights were so   157
bright they hurt my eyes, and, if you tried to look through the windshield in certain
directions, you couldn't see a thing.

"Morning, Ma'am."   158

"Good morning."   159

"Where you heading?"   160

"Salt Lake City."   161

"Purpose of your visit?"   162

"Visit my daughter."   163

"Any tobacco, liquor, or firearms?"   164

"Don't smoke."   165

"Any plants or fruit?"   166

"Not any more."   167

"Citizenship?"   168

"Blackfoot."   169

The guard rocked back on his heels and jammed his thumbs into his gun belt.   170
"Thank you," he said, his fingers patting the butt of the revolver. "Have a pleasant
trip."

My mother rolled the car forward, and the television people had to scramble out   171
of the way. They ran alongside the car as we pulled away from the border, and, when
they couldn't run any farther, they stood in the middle of the highway and waved
and waved and waved.

We got to Salt Lake City the next day. Laetitia was happy to see us, and, that first   172
night, she took us out to a restaurant that made really good soups. The list of pies
took up a whole page. I had cherry. Mom had chocolate. Laetitia said that she saw us
on television the night before and, during the meal, she had us tell her the story over
and over again.

Laetitia took us everywhere. We went to a fancy ski resort. We went to the tem-   173
ple. We got to go shopping in a couple of large malls, but they weren't as large as the
one in Edmonton, and Mom said so.

After a week or so, I got bored and wasn't all sad when my mother said we should   174
be heading back home. Laetitia wanted us to stay longer, but Mom said no, that she
had things to do back home and that, next time, Laetitia should come up and visit.
Laetitia said she was thinking about moving back, and Mom told her to do as she
pleased, and Laetitia said that she would.

On the way home, we stopped at the duty-free shop, and my mother gave Mel a   175
green hat that said "Salt Lake" across the front. Mel was a funny guy. He took the hat
and blew his nose and told my mother that she was an inspiration to us all. He gave
us some more peanut brittle and came out into the parking lot and waved at us all
the way to the Canadian border.

It was almost evening when we left Coutts. I watched the border through the rear   176
window until all you could see were the tops of the flagpoles and the blue water
tower, and then they rolled over a hill and disappeared.

Working with the Text

1. The narrator says that he and his mother dress up for the trip because his
mother doesn't want them "crossing the border looking like Americans."
What does this suggest about the mother's view of American culture?

2. In refusing to identify herself as Canadian, do you think the mother is
making a political statement, intending to become a "cause"? Or is she following her heart? Or is she simply being stubborn? Do you agree with Mel
that she is "an inspiration to us all"?

3. This whole incident is related from the perspective of the young boy. How
does this narrative voice contribute to the effect of the story? How does the
fact that the boy is willing to tell the authorities that he and his mother are
"Blackfoot and Canadian" color the issue?

4. There are three "places" in this story: Canada, the United States, and the
space in between. To whom does this middle space belong? How does it relate
to the mother's identity as Blackfoot? What does it suggest about the nature of
borders generally? Do borders always force choices? Can you think of other
examples where people are asked to make an either/or choice where an alternative or more complicated response is appropriate or desirable?

5. Look at the Web exercise at the *Border Texts* site called "How many sides
does a border have?" Are there other examples linked there of border situations where identity is not simply a matter of one thing or the other?

EVERYDAY USE

ALICE WALKER

■ Born into a poor Georgia sharecropping family in the 1940s, Alice Walker went on to become one of the premier writers of her generation, praised both for her poetry and for such early works of fiction as the novel *Meridian* (1976) and the short-story collection *You Can't Keep a Good Woman Down* (1981). Her best-selling novel *The Color Purple* (1982) brought her wide public attention and was adapted into a highly popular film. She is also known for her essays, published in the collections *In Search of Our Mothers' Gardens: Womanist Prose* (1983) and *Living by the Word* (1988). Her work, often overtly political in its viewpoint, explores issues of class, race, and gender inequality and seeks to give voice to the powerless and the forgotten. The following short story, first published in the early 1970s, is told from the perspective of an elderly sharecropping woman, one of whose daughters has left this poor rural life for an education and an urban career. It presents an interesting view of what it means to shape a sense of belonging from one's relationship to one's cultural heritage.

For Your Grandmama

I will wait for her in the yard that Maggie and I made so clean and wavy yesterday afternoon. A yard like this is more comfortable than most people know. It is not just a yard. It is like an extended living room. When the hard clay is swept clean as a floor and the fine sand around the edges lined with tiny, irregular grooves anyone can come and sit and look up into the elm tree and wait for the breezes that never come inside the house. 1

Maggie will be nervous until after her sister goes: she will stand hopelessly in corners homely and ashamed of the burn scars down her arms and legs, eyeing her sister with a mixture of envy and awe. She thinks her sister has held life always in the palm of one hand, that "no" is a word the world never learned to say to her. 2

You've no doubt seen those TV shows where the child who has "made it" is confronted, as a surprise, by her own mother and father, tottering in weakly from backstage. (A pleasant surprise, of course: What would they do if parent and child came on the show only to curse out and insult each other?) On TV mother and child embrace and smile into each other's faces. Sometimes the mother and father weep, the child wraps them in her arms and leans across the table to tell how she would not have made it without their help. I have seen these programs. 3

Sometimes I dream a dream in which Dee and I are suddenly brought together on a TV program of this sort. Out of a dark and soft-seated limousine I am ushered into a bright room filled with many people. There I meet a smiling, gray, sporty man like Johnny Carson who shakes my hand and tells me what a fine girl I have. Then we are on the stage and Dee is embracing me with tears in her eyes. She pins 4 on my dress a large orchid, even though she has told me once that she thinks orchids are tacky flowers.

In real life I am a large, big-boned woman with rough, man-working hands. In the winter I wear flannel nightgowns to bed and overalls during the day. I can kill and clean a hog as mercilessly as a man. My fat keeps me hot in zero weather. I can work outside all day, breaking ice to get water for washing; I can eat pork liver cooked over the open fire minutes after it comes steaming from the hog. One winter I knocked a bull calf straight in the brain between the eyes with a sledge hammer and had the meat hung up to chill before nightfall. But of course all this does not show on television. I am the way my daughter would want me to be: a hundred pounds lighter, my skin like an uncooked barley pancake. My hair glistens in the hot bright lights. Johnny Carson has much to do to keep up with my quick and witty tongue.

But that is a mistake. I know even before I wake up. Who ever knew a Johnson with a quick tongue? Who can even imagine me looking a strange white man in the eye? It seems to me I have talked to them always with one foot raised in flight, with my head turned in whichever way is farthest from them. Dee, though. She would always look anyone in the eye. Hesitation was no part of her nature.

"How do I look, Mama?" Maggie says, showing just enough of her thin body enveloped in pink skirt and red blouse for me to know she's there, almost hidden by the door.

"Come out into the yard," I say.

Have you ever seen a lame animal, perhaps a dog run over by some careless person rich enough to own a car, sidle up to someone who is ignorant enough to be kind to him? That is the way my Maggie walks. She has been like this, chin on chest, eyes on ground, feet in shuffle, ever since the fire that burned the other house to the ground.

Dee is lighter than Maggie, with nicer hair and a fuller figure. She's a woman now, though sometimes I forget. How long ago was it that the other house burned? Ten, twelve years? Sometimes I can still hear the flames and feel Maggie's arms sticking to me, her hair smoking and her dress falling off her in little black papery flakes. Her eyes seemed stretched open, blazed open by the flames reflected in them. And Dee. I see her standing off under the sweet gum tree she used to dig gum out of; a look of concentration on her face as she watched the last dingy gray board of the house fall in toward the red-hot brick chimney. Why don't you do a dance around the ashes? I'd wanted to ask her. She had hated the house that much.

I used to think she hated Maggie, too. But that was before we raised the money, the church and me, to send her to Augusta to school. She used to read to us without pity; forcing words, lies, other folks' habits, whole lives upon us two, sitting trapped and ignorant underneath her voice. She washed us in a river of make-believe, burned us with a lot of knowledge we didn't necessarily need to know. Pressed us to her with the serious way she read, to shove us away at just the moment, like dimwits, we seemed about to understand.

Dee wanted nice things. A yellow organdy dress to wear to her graduation from high school; black pumps to match a green suit she'd made from an old suit somebody gave me. She was determined to stare down any disaster in her efforts. Her eye-lids would not flicker for minutes at a time. Often I fought off the temptation to shake her. At sixteen she had a style of her own: and knew what style was.

I never had an education myself. After second grade the school was closed down. 13 Don't ask me why: in 1927 colored asked fewer questions than they do now. Some-times Maggie reads to me. She stumbles along good-naturedly but can't see well. She knows she is not bright. Like good looks and money, quickness passed her by. She will marry John Thomas (who has mossy teeth in an earnest face) and then I'll be free to sit here and I guess just sing church songs to myself. Although I never was a good singer. Never could carry a tune. I was always better at a man's job. I used to love to milk till I was hooked in the side in '49. Cows are soothing and slow and don't bother you, unless you try to milk them the wrong way.

I have deliberately turned my back on the house. It is three rooms, just like the 14 one that burned, except the roof is tin; they don't make shingle roofs any more. There are no real windows, just some holes cut in the sides, like the portholes in a ship, but not round and not square, with rawhide holding the shutters up on the outside. This house is in a pasture, too, like the other one. No doubt when Dee sees it she will want to tear it down. She wrote me once that no matter where we "choose" to live, she will manage to come see us. But she will never bring her friends. Maggie and I thought about this and Maggie asked me, "Mama, when did Dee ever *have* any friends?"

She had a few. Furtive boys in pink shirts hanging about on washday after school. 15 Nervous girls who never laughed. Impressed with her they worshiped the well-turned phrase, the cute shape, the scalding humor that erupted like bubbles in lye. She read to them.

When she was courting Jimmy T she didn't have much time to pay to us, but 16 turned all her faultfinding power on him. He *flew* to marry a cheap gal from a fam-ily of ignorant flashy people. She hardly had time to recompose herself.

When she comes I will meet—but there they are! 17

Maggie attempts to make a dash for the house, in her shuffling way, but I stay her 18 with my hand. "Come back here," I say. And she stops and tries to dig a well in the sand with her toe.

It is hard to see them clearly through the strong sun. But even the first glimpse of 19 leg out of the car tells me it is Dee. Her feet were always neat-looking, as if God him-self had shaped them with a certain style. From the other side of the car comes a short, stocky man. Hair is all over his head a foot long and hanging from his chin like a kinky mule tail. I hear Maggie suck in her breath. "Uhnnnh," is what it sounds like. Like when you see the wriggling end of a snake just in front of your foot on the road. "Uhnnnh."

Dee next. A dress down to the ground, in this hot weather. A dress so loud it hurts 20 my eyes. There are yellows and oranges enough to throw back the light of the sun. I feel my whole face warming from the heat waves it throws out. Earrings gold, too, and hanging down to her shoulders. Bracelets dangling and making noises when she moves her arm up to shake the folds of the dress out of her armpits. The dress is loose and flows, and as she walks closer, I like it. I hear Maggie go "Uhnnnh" again.

It is her sister's hair. It stands straight up like the wool on a sheep. It is black as night and around the edges are two long pigtails that rope about like small lizards disappearing behind her ears.

"Wa-su-zo-Tean-o!" she says, coming on in that gliding way the dress makes her move. The short stocky fellow with the hair to his navel is all grinning and he follows up with "Asalamalakim, my mother and sister!" He moves to hug Maggie but she falls back, right up against the back of my chair. I feel her trembling there and when I look up I see the perspiration falling off her chin.   21

"Don't get up," says Dee. Since I am stout it takes something of a push. You can see me trying to move a second or two before I make it. She turns, showing white heels through her sandals, and goes back to the car. Out she peeks next with a Polaroid. She stoops down quickly and lines up picture after picture of me sitting there in front of the house with Maggie cowering behind me. She never takes a shot without making sure the house is included. When a cow comes nibbling around the edge of the yard she snaps it and me and Maggie *and* the house. Then she puts the Polaroid in the back seat of the car, and comes up and kisses me on the forehead.   22

Meanwhile Asalamalakim is going through the motions with Maggie's hand. Maggie's hand is as limp as a fish, and probably as cold, despite the sweat, and she keeps trying to pull it back. It looks like Asalamalakim wants to shake hands but wants to do it fancy. Or maybe he don't know how people shake hands. Anyhow, he soon gives up on Maggie.   23

"Well," I say. "Dee."   24

"No, Mama," she says. "Not 'Dee,' Wangero Leewanika Kemanjo!"   25

"What happened to 'Dee'?" I wanted to know.   26

"She's dead," Wangero said. "I couldn't bear it any longer being named after the people who oppress me."   27

"You know as well as me you was named after your aunt Dicie," I said. Dicie is my sister. She named Dee. We called her "Big Dee" after Dee was born.   28

"But who was *she* named after?" asked Wangero.   29

"I guess after Grandma Dee," I said.   30

"And who was she named after?" asked Wangero.   31

"Her mother," I said, and saw Wangero was getting tired. "That's about as far back as I can trace it," I said. Though, in fact, I probably could have carried it back beyond the Civil War through the branches.   32

"Well," said Asalamalakim, "there you are."   33

"Uhnnnh," I heard Maggie say.   34

"There I was not," I said, "before 'Dicie' cropped up in our family, so why should I try to trace it that far back?"   35

He just stood there grinning, looking down on me like somebody inspecting a Model A car. Every once in a while he and Wangero sent eye signals over my head.   36

"How do you pronounce this name?" I asked.   37

"You don't have to call me by it if you don't want to," said Wangero.   38

"Why shouldn't I?" I asked. "If that's what you want us to call you, we'll call you."   39

"I know it might sound awkward at first," said Wangero.   40

"I'll get used to it," I said. "Ream it out again."   41

Well, soon we got the name out of the way. Asalamalakim had a name twice as long and three times as hard. After I tripped over it two or three times he told me to   42 just call him Hakim-a-barber. I wanted to ask him was he a barber, but I didn't really think he was, so I didn't ask.

"You must belong to those beef-cattle peoples down the road," I said. They said "Asalamalakim" when they met you, too, but they didn't shake hands. Always too busy: feeding the cattle, fixing the fences, putting up salt-lick shelters, throwing down hay. When the white folks poisoned some of the herd the men stayed up all night with rifles in their hands. I walked a mile and a half just to see the sight. 43

Hakim-a-barber said, "I accept some of their doctrines, but farming and raising cattle is not my style." (They didn't tell me, and I didn't ask, whether Wangero [Dee] had really gone and married him.) 44

We sat down to eat and right away he said he didn't eat collards and pork was un-clean. Wangero, though, went on through the chitlins and corn bread, the greens and everything else. She talked a blue streak over the sweet potatoes. Everything de-lighted her. Even the fact that we still used the benches her daddy made for the table when we couldn't afford to buy chairs. 45

"Oh, Mama!" she cried. Then turned to Hakim-a-barber. "I never knew how lovely these benches are. You can feel the rump prints," she said, running her hands underneath her and along the bench. Then she gave a sigh and her hand closed over Grandma Dee's butter dish. "That's it!" she said. "I knew there was something I wanted to ask you if I could have." She jumped up from the table and went over in the corner where the churn stood, the milk in it clabber by now. She looked at the churn and looked at it. 46

"This churn top is what I need," she said. "Didn't Uncle Buddy whittle it out of a tree you all used to have?" 47

"Yes," I said. 48

"Uh huh," she said happily. "And I want the dasher, too." 49

"Uncle Buddy whittle that, too?" asked the barber. 50

Dee (Wangero) looked up at me. 51

"Aunt Dee's first husband whittled the dash," said Maggie so low you almost couldn't hear her. "His name was Henry, but they called him Stash." 52

"Maggie's brain is like an elephant's," Wangero said, laughing. "I can use the churn top as a centerpiece for the alcove table," she said, sliding a plate over the churn, "and I'll think of something artistic to do with the dasher." 53

When she finished wrapping the dasher the handle stuck out. I took it for a mo-ment in my hands. You didn't even have to look close to see where hands pushing the dasher up and down to make butter had left a kind of sink in the wood. In fact, there were a lot of small sinks; you could see where thumbs and fingers had sunk into the wood. It was beautiful light yellow wood, from a tree that grew in the yard where Big Dee and Stash had lived. 54

After dinner Dee (Wangero) went to the trunk at the foot of my bed and started rifling through it. Maggie hung back in the kitchen over the dishpan. Out came Wangero with two quilts. They had been pieced by Grandma Dee and then Big Dee and me had hung them on the quilt frames on the front porch and quilted them. One was in the Lone Star pattern. The other was Walk Around the Mountain. In both of them were scraps of dresses Grandma Dee had worn fifty and more years ago. Bits and pieces of Grandpa Jarrell's paisley shirts. And one teeny faded blue 55 piece, about the size of a penny matchbox, that was from Great Grandpa Ezra's uniform that he wore in the Civil War.

"Mama," Wangero said sweet as a bird. "Can I have these old quilts?"   56

I heard something fall in the kitchen, and a minute later the kitchen door   57
slammed.

"Why don't you take one or two of the others?" I asked. "These old things was just   58
done by me and Big Dee from some tops your grandma pieced before she died."

"No," said Wangero. "I don't want those. They are stitched around the borders by   59
machine."

"That'll make them last better," I said.   60

"That's not the point," said Wangero. "These are all pieces of dresses Grandma   61
used to wear. She did all this stitching by hand. Imagine!" She held the quilts securely in her arms, stroking them.

"Some of the pieces, like those lavender ones, come from old clothes her mother   62
handed down to her," I said, moving up to touch the quilts. Dee (Wangero) moved
back just enough so that I couldn't reach the quilts. They already belonged to her.

"Imagine!" she breathed again, clutching them closely to her bosom.   63

"The truth is," I said, "I promised to give them quilts to Maggie, for when she   64
marries John Thomas."

She gasped like a bee had stung her.   65

"Maggie can't appreciate these quilts!" she said. "She'd probably be backward   66
enough to put them to everyday use."

"I reckon she would," I said. "God knows I been saving 'em for long enough with   67
nobody using 'em. I hope she will!" I didn't want to bring up how I had offered Dee
(Wangero) a quilt when she went away to college. Then she had told me they were
old-fashioned, out of style.

"But they're *priceless!*" she was saying now, furiously; for she has a temper. "Mag-   68
gie would put them on the bed and in five years they'd be in rags. Less than that!"

"She can always make some more," I said. "Maggie knows how to quilt."   69

Dee (Wangero) looked at me with hatred. "You just will not understand. The   70
point is these quilts, *these* quilts!"

"Well," I said, stumped. "What would *you* do with them?"   71

"Hang them," she said. As if that was the only thing you *could* do with quilts.   72

Maggie by now was standing in the door. I could almost hear the sound her feet   73
made as they scraped over each other.

"She can have them, Mama," she said, like somebody used to never winning any-   74
thing, or having anything reserved for her. "I can 'member Grandma Dee without
the quilts."

I looked at her hard. She had filled her bottom lip with checkerberry snuff and it   75
gave her face a kind of dopey, hangdog look. It was Grandma Dee and Big Dee who
taught her how to quilt herself. She stood there with her scarred hands hidden in the
folds of her skirt. She looked at her sister with something like fear but she wasn't
mad at her. This was Maggie's portion. This was the way she knew God to work.

When I looked at her like that something hit me in the top of my head and ran   76
down to the soles of my feet. Just like when I'm in church and the spirit of God
touches me and I get happy and shout. I did something I never had done before:

hugged Maggie to me, then dragged her on into the room, snatched the quilts out of Miss Wangero's hands and dumped them into Maggie's lap. Maggie just sat there on my bed with her mouth open.

"Take one or two of the others," I said to Dee.   77

But she turned without a word and went out to Hakim-a-barber.   78

"You just don't understand," she said, as Maggie and I came out to the car.   79

"What don't I understand?" I wanted to know.   80

"Your heritage," she said. And then she turned to Maggie, kissed her, and said,   81
"You ought to try to make something of yourself, too, Maggie. It's really a new day for us. But from the way you and Mama still live you'd never know it."

She put on some sunglasses that hid everything above the tip of her nose and her   82
chin.

Maggie smiled; maybe at the sunglasses. But a real smile, not scared. After we   83
watched the car dust settle I asked Maggie to bring me a dip of snuff. And then the two of us sat there just enjoying, until it was time to go in the house and go to bed.

Working with the Text

1. This story was originally published in 1973 when many African Americans were asserting their African heritage as a way of fighting the heritage of slavery and discrimination. Why do you think Walker chose to treat the representatives of this movement in the story, Dee/Wangero and her friend, less sympathetically than she does the mother and Maggie?

2. Dee/Wangero and her mother and sister have come to represent very different cultures. Why do you think Dee/Wangero has been so alienated from the culture of her mother and sister? Does her desire to have the parts of the churn and the quilts suggest that she now wishes to be more closely related to their culture? Do you feel she is at all sincere?

3. What do you think of Dee/Wangero's accusation that her mother doesn't understand her "heritage" and her assertion to Maggie that "it's really a new day for us. But from the way you and Mama still live you'd never know it"? What point is Walker making about how African Americans are connected to—and alienated from—their U.S. heritage?

4. Why do you think the story's dedication is "For Your Grandmama"? How can this story apply to any reader's relationship to his or her "grandmama"?

HOME IS WHERE THE MUSIC IS

VICTOR HERNANDEZ CRUZ

■ Born in Puerto Rico, Victor Hernandez Cruz grew up in New York City in the 1950s and 1960s. A poet, he published his first collection in 1966 and since then has published ten more collections, including *Rhythm, Content, and Flavor* (1989). Of his poetry he has said, "My work is on the border of a new language, because I create out of a consciousness steeped in two of the important world languages, Spanish and English." In the following essay, Hernandez Cruz recalls his childhood home in Puerto Rico as well as his family's adopted home in New York City, where he found a way of adapting his rural Hispanic identity to the harsher tempos of urban life: "A pendulum swinging between the heat and the cold. The Spanish and English coming together, giving a multiple choice of sounds to select from for objects, experience, emotion, sensation." Feeling that one belongs, he suggests, can mean creating an inner space to accommodate an individual sense of belonging.

I was born in a barrio with the name of a Taino fruit: El Guanabano. Located in the central or urban area of the town of Aguas Buenas, Puerto Rico, some 35 minutes from San Juan. The streets of El Guanabano were not yet paved. When it rained everything became a mess, the downpour created a small river flowing down to the town plaza, the red dirt making the stream appear to be guava juice. Kids would jump outside to play in the torrential tropical showers.

The humidity, the mountain entanglement of lucid bush, spontaneity of trees, and the improvisation of the foliage invented creatures berserk through mating calls of nocturnal *coquis*—a kind of toad chirping in choral concerto. The native inhabitants of the island were certain that trees were the home of spirits, so they sang poetry to them, asked them in what direction were they walking. To walk the mountains was to encounter the trees as individuals. You could hide from the rain under a Palo de Guayacan; to see from a distant mountain curve a Palo de Roble is to recognize its almost whiteness separating it from the bold green. The fruit of Aguas Buenas is the mamey, a native fruit tree; it has been ripened into ice cream and melted into malt. A tall Palo de Maga points into the clouds while inviting its liquid down. A scattered Palo de Almacigo brushes up arboresque into a Palo de Maria, assisting in the process of fertilization. A Palo de Hiquera hangs round gourds, oval and festive mobiles, worked into bowls by Arawak-speaking hands or into *cacique*-size maracas to mark the meters of a poem within the *arieto*. Encountering a Palo de Ceiba is like first communion, sacred to the Tainos; some are hundreds of years old, a huge trunk and roots can take over a region. Lizards fleeting like electrical charges or suspended motionless for hours awaiting the trajectory of a predestined singular fly. Iguanas, mini crocodiles by the rivers. At night under the mosquito nets the world was a kaleidoscope of sounds, insects, dogs, the dance of trees like layers in the wind. The *cucubanos* (fire flies) sparkling in the dark, we kids would run after them and palm them right out of the air, put them in clear glass jars, and watch them light up in unison as if we were holding a star in our hands.

All the houses were made of wood; if there was any cement, it was down by the structures that surrounded the plaza where the middle class supposedly dwelled. The windows were small doors that swung open. Many of the houses were elevated off the earth creating a space underneath, a place where chickens and roosters roamed wild in their persistent flirtation that ended up being the eggs on your plate.

Skinny brown legs accompanied packs of mothers heading towards the river to wash clothes. The women used to bang the clothes against the river rocks, hitting the dirt out with pieces of boards as they sang and gossiped, talking, laughing, exchanging information, saying things no man could imagine. We children disappeared into the flora, playing by the eternal contemplation of the cows. Jumping into the river, all of us boys and girls butt naked, with a giggling and mirth that was recorded by the trees.

The fertile land around us was full of coffee and tobacco, which were the two prominent agricultural crops. We had our own coffee label, "El Jibarito." Coffee was always conducive to conversation, its aroma was the melody of the morning. The *campesino* custom of the three o'clock cup still maintains its fanatics, like court in session with jury and all. Unlike the custom of *la siesta,* the afternoon repose, which is fading in these regions. A rest during the day is bad for production; you can't fall asleep on the machine. If they found you horizontal in bed at one-thirty in the afternoon in the northern longitudes, urbanites might christen you lazy, or worse, useless to the economy.

The center of town was full of tobacco workshops known as "*chin-chales*" in the island vernacular. My grandfather, Julio El Bohemio, was a well known *tabaquero.* He was a picturesque character who created a legend for himself as a singer; men were always looking for him to render serenades to the sleeping women of their fancy. In the dark of night the silence was broken by guitar strings and harmonic voices in bolero; those songs' lyrics have stayed with me through all metamorphoses of regions and climates. My grandfather used to sing ". . . I want the love of a dark skin woman, those bronze ladies of my native earth . . ." to the ears in the heart of the night. They sang Cuban, Mexican, Argentinian, Chilean songs written by composers who were popular poets.

The *chin-chals* were active places, for the *tabaqueros* in the Caribbean were notorious for their socialist and anarchist politics, philosophers of the masses, dramatic declaimers of poetry, and, as in the case of my grandfather, singers of the love-romance songs sometimes known as *tragedia.* Many *tabaqueros* were rebels and *independentistas* (those who wanted freedom from Spanish, and then North American, possession of the island). Within the context of Caribbean agricultural workers, *tabacconists* had a much more leisurely work process, freeing their minds for contemplation and aesthetic flight. Coffee pickers, by comparison, had to battle bees all day long, and cane cutters had to chop vigorously under the Caribbean sun. A significant number of *tabaqueros* went on to become great labor leaders, writers, and historians.

It was within the *chin-chals* of Aguas Buenas that my imagination first heard poetry declaimed, thrown outloud in coordination with head and hands weaving. I was only a child amidst the tobacco leaves, taken there by my grandfather or my uncle Carlos who used to go and recite poetic standards like "El Brindis Del Bohemio." My uncle continued this tradition of declaiming into the frozen zones of New York's lower East Side tenements.

Tobacco production employed a good proportion of the town. There were farmers who cultivated the plants in the mountain ranchos, taking meticulous care of them, watching out for tobacco worms and other harmful insects. There was a period allowed for the tobacco leaves to age and dry so that they could acquire their deep aromatic *cafe con leche* color; the timing had to be perfect, for while they wanted a drying of the leaves, they did not want to lose all the moisture. Some men dedicated themselves to hauling stacks of bundled tobacco down to the *despalilladoras. Despalillar*—to remove the center stem from the tobacco leaf—was a task that was accomplished by women; old and young worked side by side, telling stories, reviewing every shadow of public and private life. Nothing escaped their scrutiny, the narratives making the passage of time painless. Once the leaves were done, they were bundled again and sent to all the local *chin-chales* where the men rolled them into various styles of cigars. The finished cigars were picked up and taken to these massive *fábricas* for packaging; some of the workers specialized in putting on the ring or little gold wrapper that identified the company and the cigar type. All day they put those little wedding bands on the tips of cigars, keeping an eye out for those that appeared to be damaged. It was also within these cigar terminals where they were arranged into their handsome boxes. The whole process took some six months after which the town went into a slumber.

It is recounted by those who lived this epoch that the *tabaqueros* were paid well. 10 They had their golden age. They dressed well: white linen *guayaberas,* two-tone shoes with white on the top, pra-pra sombreros. The area around the plaza was full of places to dance and hear the best orchestras of the day. *Cafetin* rumor has it that once Ramito, Puerto Rico's best-known *trovador,* spinner of mountain music, came to hang out with the *tabaqueros* of El Guanabano. They went into such a jubilance and frolic of singing and scratching *quiro,* stomping and dancing that through beat and vibration they caused an abandoned and ageing wooden house next door to collapse. My grandfather filled the air on Fridays with a white suit and a white Panama sombrero. I remember him walking off towards town gleaming clean like white chalk under the pretext of going to the *colmado* to buy a pound of *café,* and vanishing through the hole of a *cuatro* guitar for two days.

My grandmother Tina must've known him well; when he sculptured that bo- 11 hemian mischievous grin on his Jibaro face, his features were such that he could have been a *campesino* from the Rio Plata region of Argentina where the tangos that he sang so well were born. Tina Velasquez Ortiz had Africa inside of her, a dark, tall, heavy-set woman whose family hailed from the mountain, Jagueyes, which is seen from the center of town like a towering wall. Situated as we are not far from the coast, we have a substantial amount of African blood, which in one way or another runs through the community. We are truly *criollos* and a visual festival. The term *criollo* has meant many different things through different historical periods and re- gions of Latin America; in some areas it designates a Spaniard born in the New World. To us in Puerto Rico, it has come to mean the mixing of the cultural ele- ments of the Indian, the Spanish, the African—a tripolarity that we recognize in music, dance, physical looks, and cuisine.

My grandmother fell ill with cancer at 46. In the interior of a small wooden 12 house, I could see her laying in a hammock swinging and singing the pain away, a singing that scaled into a humming that went through the house like a humid vapor. The air had an odor of rubbing alcohol mixed with medicinal plants, a kerosene lantern flickering in her room making shadows dance on a wooden cross. She had eight children, one right after the other plus one that died at birth. My mother's tribe would have been nine, but eight was enough. She was slowly being eaten by time, dissolving like chocolate in the sun.

Through a rewind of archived pictures, a Caribbean *mulata* fries *alcapurrias* in 13 the combustion of barrio life, green bananas, *yautia*—part African, part Indian. How did she walk when she was nineteen at the instant my grandfather, Julio El Bohemio, saw her in the Maria-go-round of plaza coquetry? Did his voice swell in the balada producing spacious gardens of flowers? She drops a handkerchief, they take a stroll into the night, the scent of a mamey tree, within a glance my mother was born.

My mother was the oldest of the eight children and she spent her teenage years helping rear her brothers and sisters. She had her father's gift of singing, and into the despair of the necessities of materialism and the limitations imposed on the female by a strong rural machismo, she sang her transcendental boleros. She married young and stayed in the local area where the extended family was in forceful practice. 14

In the rural communities women used to give birth within their own homes with the assistance of a midwife, *comadrona.* Into the scenario of my mother's advanced stages of labor, Dona Lola, the *comadrona* who brought me into the world, came in smoking a cigar and flinging herbs towards the sinistral and dextral of the ambiance, as if fishing spirits with hooks so that they can come forward to assist, to align the celestial with the biological process at hand. I was born on a Sunday between five and six in the morning. My mother remembers that Dona Lola made it to seven o'clock mass at the local Catholic church, Los Tres Santos Reyes. 15

The wooden house where I was born was painted a passion-fruit yellow, adding to the rainbow formed by all the houses on the street. You throw brush with what you got, a blue home next to an orange kiosk, natural wood made gray by age. Gauguin could have come here before going to Tahiti. The color spectrum exhausting itself as the Guanabano housing drops down the sloped street. Time slowly transformed the street into other hues, other textures. 16

Through a series of chance circumstances, my old house has now been converted into a *cafetin*—a small community bar and grocery store, a place where men gather to drink, cultivate the art of conversation, tell jokes. Through a further set of coincidences, the *cafetin* came under the ownership of a cousin of my mother's, Julio Hernández Hernández, who was what I would designate as a popular poet of our town. Not a poet of text or literature but a versifier, his poems written in the traditional Spanish forms of *coplas* and *decimas.* His compositions approximate the limericks of boleros, the same sentimental, emotional sphere in a language of preconceived formula. Like all popular poets, he had the ability to declaim his verses from memory; going into his *cafetin* always meant the possibility of a spontaneous outburst of recitation. 17

The tobaeco workshop where my grandfather rolled was directly across the street from where we lived. He worked next to his lifelong friend, Alegria, spicing the rolling of cigars by singing in duo. In the mornings the *tabaqueros* would put a little money together and hire a reader to come in and read the newspaper, *El Imparcial;* other times the *tabaqueros* would hire a reader to come read them a chapter of a book a day. It seems that all the *tabacconists* in Aguas Buenas were Socialist. It was the party of my grandfather, Julio El Bohemio, and that's how my grandmother voted too; my mother tells me that when she became eligible to vote, she also voted for the socialist party. They were all that way through some kind of popular spirit and not as intellectuals inspired by some economic ideals which penetrated them through readership. Melodies and people's anarchy rose from the salt of the earth, from a sector where the only things affordable sometimes were pride and emotion. 18

Songs entered the leaves to be heard on some future plane within the eventual aroma of smoke.

In the late '40s and the early '50s, people were speaking of a place called Nujol; it caused a lot of agitation in all sectors of the town. Relatives already up in the northern ledge were sending letters inflating and inflaming imaginations and hopes. There was trouble in paradise. How did that happen in a place so fertile? The greater portion of the rural population was still feeling the effects of many years of Spanish exploitation by remote control, shipping medieval economic plans in coffins to the Americas. The conquest still bubbling in the veins. Even objects felt the despair. The pineapple was turning sour in the mountains of sweet music. Where the coffee grew, where the cane was tall, where aboriginal cigar was grown and rolled—they say that they saw the devil run, being chased by necessity from the inferno, his very home. [19]

The Puerto Rican tribal-social network helped ease the scarcity of food. Many families heard the call of the yonder, the whispers of the north. People in knots started to untangle and maneuver. Children were left with relatives while the adults were flying Eastern Airline propeller planes to the Bronx. Once up there, stumble around the English looking for employment, set up a home, and send for their children. [20]

New York City has been a center for Caribbean immigrants since the late eighteen hundreds. Exiled Cuban and Puerto Rican revolutionaries established la Sociedad Republicana de Cuba y Puerto Rico in the 1860s to assist in the cause of those on the islands fighting against Spanish colonialism. [21]

Most of the new arrivals from the Antilles moved into the lower West Side, an area with an established Spanish community; there were Spanish and Argentinian restaurants, book stores, and a Spanish Cultural Center that continues to exist today. Perhaps many of these Spaniards were Andalus merchant seamen who came on work visits through the Brooklyn Navy Yard docks, near the areas of Red Hook and Williamsberg, which was also where the first Puerto Rican families settled into sometime after the 1900s. Later, after the 1920s, the Puerto Rican community started to *sofrito* spice the East Harlem area around 100th street. *Tabaqueros* constituted a strong force in this first wave of migration. [22]

In El Guanabano, the commotion of cement trucks mixed with the whirlwind of families who were organizing themselves to jump off the edge of the world. It was not the upper classes that had to leave; the bourgeois never leave where they are milking. In proportion to the population of the island, it was one of the most dimensional cases of human exodus. People were tying boxes like *pasteles* with banana leaves and heading for the iron bird. My mother wanted to know why people kept borrowing that antique heavy iron we had that had to be fed charcoal, when they were going to fold the clothes after ironing and place them in the suitcases to wrinkle again. Puerto Ricans were obsessed with ironing apparel in those days, and they used a homemade starch to get a crease on a pair of pants that could have cut you; women used to complain that they even had to iron their husbands' underwear. This anti-wrinkle mania is something that could be studied. El Guanabano was in a ruckus with public cars taking people to the airport in the mornings and afternoons: tears, hugs, farewells. My grandfather walked through the chaos with a fine grip on his guitar. [23]

My own family jumped on one of those massive waves of island evacuation. The   24
decision was beyond anything I could comprehend. I was busy trying to split "*alao-
rrobas*" seeds in half in a boys' game known as "*gallitos.*" It was our time to go forward
into the regions beyond the mountains, from the comforts and hardships of Aguas
Buenas to industry and entertainment, to the jungle of concrete and lights in the hy-
perborean windows of Manhattan.

I have always been haunted by the strong impression that the first gulps of cold   25
winter air registered in my childhood nostrils. We migrated from the tropics in the
middle of winter. What did we know coming from one extreme to another, like
putting the sun in the freezer. In New York it was snowing; those who love contrast
could satisfy themselves here. We went to the traditional immigrant neighborhood
of New York—the lower East Side where the tenement buildings towered like magic
over us. Had someone poured cement on the mountains, I wondered, recalling all
those cement trucks back home. A cold metallic incense permeated the ether, the ol-
fact of steel, iron, cement, and glass.

English was just a scattering of noise coming out of people's mouths—who   26
could arrange that strange new furniture, where would one sit? Walking slowly, I
picked up neighborhood jargon, stoop yap, hallway vocabulary; out on the streets
children exchanged information. Puerto Rican kids had apparently arrived before
we did, for I encountered many that were already speaking English, hanging it like
fragmented and distorted Cubist paintings. The lower East Side was full of accents.
English waved, leaned, flew, got squashed, shredded, sautéed, made into puree. Italian, Polish, Jewish thoughts danced their own angles into Shakespeare.

On the street where we lived, there was still a Jewish synagogue lingering from   27
the past life of the neighborhood that was erasing right before our eyes. The local
stores were full of things I'd never seen. Jars of sauerkraut, pickles, knishes, winter
hats with ear flaps that made people look like sputniks, a new empire of gadgetry
like that which opened up the eyes of Pinzon, the Spanish explorer. Bubbling it was,
flashing, dashing, darting, a new vertical comprehension—cars, buses, subways.

The encounter between rural and urban landscape, a debate released through   28
migration, a discussion of spacial tempos, city versus tropical paths are steeped in
my consciousness and echo through my poetic creation. This for me is the center of
metaphor, sharp contrast that keeps one in northern metros aware of profound
elsewhere. El Guanabano—view of the mountains; the lower East Side—view of the
Empire State Building. A pendulum swinging between the heat and the cold. The
Spanish and English coming together, giving a multiple choice of sounds to select
from for objects, experience, emotion, sensation. For me, writing in straight English
or Spanish is always a process of translation—it is a duality that opens up a third dimension beyond the actual semantics. What comes first in Spanish could come last
in English. This same polarization can create problems; it is to the advantage of a
writer to be bilingual, but for the general speaker it would be best to be anchored in
a native tongue before venturing off into another language. The great Spanish poet
Migual Unamuno said something to the effect that, "Language is the blood of the
spirit." Consequently it is through words that we fulfill our personality. Without a
strong linguistic spine, you could fold into a mush of blah-blah. Because language
represents a world, we can see the contradictions that besiege the users of the Spanish language in the United States; the world it is from is not in their presence. Words

have lives of their own, it is what we fit into, were they not here before us. Experience is the word that passes through the things that we do. Language is a cultural attitude accumulated over the centuries; when I write in Puerto Rican Spanish—the first sounds that my body heard and felt when I played in El Guanabano was the ambit of fruits in harmony with boiling manioc—I am writing in a language which has Taino, Arabic-Gypsy-Berber Desert Wind, African words. In addition, many new vocals were created by the collision of all that energy and diction in the Caribbean.

The Spanish radio programs kept us warm. Flowing from an Emerson radio was 29
Puerto Rican, Cuban, Santo Domingo, Argentinian, Chilean, Mexican music. Being Latin American mestizo is a condition supplied by the criss-crossing of multi-nations. The cultures go one into another as through the common root language, an extended nationalism that includes the entire continent. We danced to the guarachas of Cuba, beat our feet to the rancheras of Mexico, became sad and nostalgic to the boleros of Trio San Juan.

My father, who had gone to New York and was already settled and working when 30
we arrived, found our railroad flat on the lower East Side. It was on the third floor facing the backyard, a steel fire escape hung immediately outside one of the windows. It offered a view uptown towards 14th street, a Con Edison electrical plant with pipes systematically dispensing smoke into the sky. Looking to the right, your eyes focused upon the long stretch of brick mountains that made up the edifices of the Avenue D housing projects. We could hear the fog horns of ships on the East River in the mornings as we drank Cafe Bustelo, getting ready to go out and wrestle with the streets.

In our household there was a constant dialogue, debate, discussion, argument, 31
chaos, fights between my mother and father as to when we would get back to Aguas Buenas. Originally the plan was that they would be in New York to work for a period, gather some money, and eventually work our way back home. Every year we would make plans to leave that never got beyond the motions of my mother starting to pack the luggage. Puerto Ricans perfected the art of packaging. They used to encase clothes, personal knickknacks, and even tree bark like sardines into cans. Rumor has it that back in the '50s, when transportation was bad, Puerto Ricans knew how to get to the airports on public trains.

In the public schools the teachers prohibited the use of Spanish among the island 32
children who were recent arrivals. They would come and say, "Shisssh-hush, speak in English, it's what's going to get you ahead" or they'd say, "You're in America now." Looking out the window, we knew we were on the East Side, an aspect of America. A group of us once got in trouble because we used to have to sing the National Anthem at the beginning of each day. Every time it came to the part "Oh say can you see," most of the students in the class—we were all still learning English—heard "Oh Jose can you see." So we always sang it this way while we all mumbled something to the two Joses in the room. The teacher—I think her name was Mrs. Straus—was old and had a crooked finger. When she said "Hey you" and pointed, the person sitting next to who she meant would always stand up. When she hooked an ear into how we were singing, she separated a group of us—maybe because we had the highest pitch—and made us stay after class. She told us we had to bring our parents in, which was the most embarrassing thing. So we did, but what was that for? Our par-

ents spoke no English and there was no one around to translate. So there was Mrs. Straus talking with our island mothers; our mothers just kept saying, "Yeah-yeah-yeah." One of them knew how to say the word Right, going, "Rye-rye." They figured another way to get out of it was by shaking their heads up and down because this would give the impression that they were absorbing information.

As the bricks aged we entered the age of flowers—walking molasses, cha-cha   33 boots, bolero blouses. Mothers found places to make white dresses for their daughters. The youth had inherited the Caribbean spirit of fiesta and carnival and used any excuse to have a party. Over in the Avenue D projects, we'd borrow an apartment, and walked the neighborhood to the fringes inviting every girl we saw. With our portable record players, we formed a bembe anywhere—in the school yard, up on the roof. There we were, sons and daughters of the Antilles throwing pachanga steps, dancing slow to the doo-wop of "The Paragons Meet The Jesters."

The years washed the red mountain dirt from our shoes, but the abyss created by   34 the migration remained like a root-canal cavity in the wisdom molars, hungry for excavation and filling. Puerto Rican musicians and writers made the journey up north for reasons of economy and because of the traditional restlessness of artists. It was an opportunity for the writers to get a bird's eye view of island politics and culture and their extension in the diaspora.

The music and the songs would go back to the island to become part of the cul-   35 tural panoramas of a Caribbean nation. Culture produced in the streets of New York would take the airplanes with the people who are in continuous reverse migration—there is something like an on-going back and forward shaft keeping those in the North resupplied with tropical resistance.

Cuban and Puerto Rican musicians met in the clubs and large ballrooms of Man-   36 hattan, discussing with each other new levels of rhythms and poly-rhythms. On 110th street there was the now defunct Park Palace Ballroom where the music was on fire way before it traveled downtown to the famous Palladium. I was too young in the early '50s to make it to these dramas of island life in the states. It was like *fiestas patronales* indoors. I watched my Uncle Juan and my Aunt Chela get glazed up with those shoes that used to look like glass to go to these Mambo groves. With their friends they would form balls to take the subway together to 53rd where the Palladium was. They would all get back late, couples kissing all over the hallways, leaning against brass mailboxes, then taking off their shoes to walk up the marble stairs. In the mornings when I was sent out to get bread for the coffee, I could sense the lingering scent of gardenia perfume throughout the hallway.

The music of the guitar and the music of the drum came together in the ears and   37 hearts of a generation that was bilingual and bred in the States. Everything was jumping with Symphony Sid in the City; he had a late night radio program playing the New York based Cuban and Puerto Rican music (it wasn't called Salsa then, that came later). A dance called la pachanga, which featured some vicious foot stomping, was knocking buildings down. My generation developed a boogaloo with Latin rhythms and English lyrics; dancers started jumping all around the floor. Buildings roofs were stretched with conga drum hide and something was playing them.

On a clear, warm summer night of my youth I was trying to search for some   38 sleep, staring from a third floor window at the moon, which seemed to be falling into one of the pipes of the Con Edison plant; there was too much energy elevating up. Out on the street a group was drumming an African beat through which they were weaving a deep Gypsy *canto hondo* that sang of Spain, Goya and Velazquez paintings melting onto Bantu shrines, someone shaking native maracas into the brick Bohíos. As I looked down towards the sound, they appeared like a gathering of agricultural tribes in a fertility fest—Hindu Gypsies, Andaluces, Asturians, Arabs, Congolese, nomadic Berber shepherds. It was such a kaleidoscope that I decided to paint the fire escape gold. By morning it was dry and the drums had turned to strings. The troubadours were praising a lady, studying her walk they measured the meter of the verse. The morning light brought images out of haze.

I remembered then, sitting in the sunshine out on the fire escape, the songs of my grandfather, Julio El Bohemio, the proclaimer of poems around the old *chin-chal* of tobacco in the town of my childhood. The mountain, Jagueyes, blocked out the projects. Sitting upon the golden mineral, I got the urge to write, to tell a story as if from a balcony, use the juices of a guanabana for ink. I knew I would some day go back with words, searching for the past in the future. I knew my body was right, right where it was. With Hugh Masekela, I second the emotion when he put out the album, "Home Is Where The Music Is."[1]

Working with the Text

1. There is a saying that "culture is in the details." Cruz's essay is full of descriptive details that contrast two cultural spaces, a town in rural Puerto Rico and the tenement neighborhoods of Manhattan's Lower East Side. What details does Cruz emphasize in each environment? In what ways are they different and in what ways similar? Does Cruz seem to be more at home in one than in the other, or do his descriptions seem equally affirmative?

2. Cruz says that the "encounter between rural and urban landscape . . . city versus tropical paths [is] steeped in my consciousness and [echoes] through my poetic creation." How is this reflected in his attitude toward the English language versus his native "Puerto Rican Spanish"? Where does English fit in with other elements of his cultural environment? How does bilingualism relate to a sense of belonging? What gets lost through assimilation or through accommodating to a new culture?

3. Why did so many Puerto Rican natives immigrate to New York when Cruz's family did? Why do you think the family made plans every year to return to Puerto Rico, but the plans "never got beyond the motions of [Cruz's] mother starting to pack the luggage"? To what extent does Cruz suggest his ambivalent feelings about living in New York?

4. What do you think is the significance of Cruz's painting the fire escape gold? In what sense can this final image be seen as summarizing Cruz's sense of where he belongs?

5. The title of this essay, "Home Is Where the Music Is," plays off the expression "home is where the heart is." In what ways does Cruz suggest that his

1. Title of a Hugh Masekela album.

sense of culture is defined by music? Do you think that this connection is particularly true of Latin culture? How are other cultures defined by the music indigenous to them?

A LONG LINE OF VENDIDAS

CHERRIE MORAGA

■ Cherrie Moraga grew up during the 1950s and 1960s in Whittier, California, the light-skinned daughter of a dark-skinned Chicana mother and an emotionally distant Anglo American father. She was one of the first members of her family to attend college and later received a master's degree from San Francisco State University. She currently teaches at the University of California, Berkeley, in the Division of Chicano Studies. A poet, playwright, and essayist, Moraga writes from a strongly feminist perspective and often focuses on the disjunction between her family's traditional Mexican American values and her identity as an outspoken lesbian. At the same time, she strongly identifies herself as a Chicana writer, often switching from English to Spanish in her work and drawing on themes from Mexican history and myth. Her collections include *Loving in the War Years: Lo Que Nunce Paso Por Sus Labios* and *Giving Up the Ghost.* She was coeditor with Gloria Anzaldúa of *This Bridge Called My Back: Writings by Radical Women of Color*, one of the first anthologies to give voice to a number of important female writers outside the mainstream. In "A Long Line of Vendidas," Moraga attempts to situate herself within a number of contradictory cultures, none to which she feels she can truly belong.

para Gloria Anzaldúa, in gratitude

MY BROTHER'S SEX WAS WHITE. MINE, BROWN

If somebody would have asked me when I was a teenager what it means to be Chicana, I would probably have listed the grievances done me. When my sister and I were fifteen and fourteen, respectively, and my brother a few years older, we were still waiting on him. I write "were" as if now, nearly two decades later, it were over. But that would be a lie. To this day in my mother's home, my brother and father are waited on, including by me. I do this now out of respect for my mother and her wishes. In those early years, however, it was mainly in relation to my brother that I resented providing such service. For unlike my father, who sometimes worked as much as seventy hours a week to feed my face every day, the only thing that earned my brother my servitude was his maleness.

It was Saturday afternoon. My brother, then seventeen-years-old, came into the house with a pile of friends. I remember Fernie, the two Steves, and Roberto. They were hot, sweaty, and exhausted from an afternoon's basketball and plopped themselves down in the front room, my brother demanding, "Girls, bring us something to drink."

"Get it yourself, pig," I thought, but held those words from ever forming inside my mouth. My brother had the disgusting habit on these occasions of collapsing my sister, JoAnn's and my name when referring to us as a unit: his sisters. "Cher'ann," he would say. "We're really thirsty." I'm sure it took everything in his power *not* to snap his fingers. But my mother was out in the yard working and to refuse him would have brought her into the house with a scene before these boys' eyes which would have made it impossible for us to show our faces at school that following Monday. We had been through that before.

When my mother had been our age, over forty years earlier, she had waited on her brothers and their friends. And it was no mere lemonade. They'd come in from work or a day's drinking. And las mujeres, often just in from the fields themselves, would already be in the kitchen making tortillas, warming frijoles or pigs feet, albondigas soup, what-have-you. And the men would get a clean white tablecloth and a spread of food laid out before their eyes and not a word of resentment from the women.

The men watched the women—my aunts and mother moving with the grace and speed of girls who were cooking before they could barely see over the top of the stove. Elvira, my mother, knew she was being watched by the men and loved it. Her slim hips moved patiently beneath the apron. Her deep thick-lidded eyes never caught theirs as she was swept back into the kitchen by my abuelita's call of "Elvirita," her brown hands deepening in color as they dropped back into the pan of flour.

I suppose my mother imagined that Joe's friends watched us like that, too. But we knew different. We were not blonde or particularly long-legged or "available" because we were "Joe's sisters." This meant no boy could "make" us, which meant no boy would bother asking us out. Roberto, the Guatemalan, was the only one among my brother's friends who seemed at all sensitive to how awkward JoAnn and I felt in our role. He would smile at us nervously, taking the lemonade, feeling embarrassed being waited on by people he considered peers. He knew the anglo girls they visited would never have succumbed to such a task. Roberto was the only recompense.

As I stopped to wait on their yearning throats, "jock itch" was all that came to my mind. Their cocks became animated in my head, for that was all that seemed to arbitrarily set us apart from each other and put me in the position of the servant and they, the served.

I wanted to machine-gun them all down, but swallowed that fantasy as I swallowed making the boy's bed every day, cleaning his room each week, shining his shoes and ironing his shirts before dates with girls, some of whom *I* had crushes on. I would lend him the money I had earned house-cleaning for twelve hours, so he could blow it on one night with a girl because he seldom had enough money because he seldom had a job because there was always some kind of ball practice to go to. As I pressed the bills into his hand, the car honking outside in the driveway, his double-date waiting, I knew I would never see that money again.

Years later, after I began to make political the fact of my being a Chicana, I remember my brother saying to me, "*I've* never felt 'culturally deprived'," which I guess is the term "white" people use to describe Third World people being denied access to *their* culture. At the time, I wasn't exactly sure what he meant, but I re-member in re-telling the story to my sister, she responded, "Of course, he didn't. He grew up male in our house. He got the best of both worlds." And yes, I can see now that that's true. *Male in a man's world. Light-skinned in a white world. Why change?*

The pull to identify with the oppressor was never as great in me as it was in my brother. For unlike him, I could never have *become* the white man, only the white man's *woman.*

The first time I began to recognize clearly my alliances on the basis of race and sex was when my mother was in the hospital, extremely ill. I was eight years old. During my mother's stay in the hospital, my tía Eva took my sister and me into her care; my brother stayed with my abuela; and my father stayed by himself in our home. During this time, my father came to visit me and my sister only once. (I don't know if he ever visited my brother.) The strange thing was I didn't really miss his visits, although I sometimes fantasized some imaginary father, dark and benevolent, who might come and remind us that we still *were* a family.

I have always had a talent for seeing things I don't particularly want to see and the one day my father did come to visit us with his wife/our mother physically dying in a hospital some ten miles away, I saw that he couldn't love us—not in the way we so desperately needed. I saw that he didn't know how and he came into my tía's house like a large lumbering child—awkward and embarrassed out of his league—trying to play a parent when he needed our mother back as much as we did just to keep him eating and protected. I hated and pitied him that day. I knew how he was letting us all down, visiting my mother daily, like a dead man, unable to say, "The children, honey, I held them. They love you. They think of you." Giving my mother *something.*

Years later, my mother spoke of his visits to the hospital. How from behind the bars of her bed and through the tubes in her nose, she watched this timid man come and go daily—going through the "motions" of being a husband. "I knew I had to live," she told us. "I knew he could never take care of you."

In contrast to the seeming lack of feeling I held for my father, my longings for my mother and fear of her dying were the most passionate feelings that had ever lived inside my young heart.

We are riding the elevator. My sister and I pressed up against one wall, holding hands. After months of separation, we are going to visit my mamá in the hospital. Mi tía me dice, "Whatever you do, no llores Cherrie. It's too hard on your mother when you cry." I nod, taking long deep breaths, trying to control my quivering lip.

As we travel up floor by floor, all I can think about is not crying, breathing, holding my breath. "¿Me prometes?" she asks. I nod again, afraid to speak fearing my voice will crack into tears. My sister's nervous hand around mine, sweating too. We are going to see my mamá, mamá, after so long. She didn't die after all. She didn't die.

The elevator doors open. We walk down the corridor, my heart pounding. My eyes are darting in and out of each room as we pass them, fearing/anticipating my mamá's face. Then as we turn around the corner into a kind of lobby, I hear my tía say to an older woman—skin and bones. An Indian, I think, straight black and grey hair pulled back. I hear my tía say, "Elvira."

I don't recognize her. This is not the woman I knew, so round and made-up with her

10

11

12

13

14

15

16

17

18

hair always a wavy jet black! I stay back until she opens her arms to me—this strange and familiar woman—her voice hoarse, "¡Ay mi'jita!" Instinctively, I run into her arms, still holding back my insides—"Don't cry. Don't cry." I remember. "Whatever you do, no llores." But my tía had not warned me about the smell, the unmistakable smell of the woman, mi mama—el olor de aceite y jabón and comfort and home. "Mi mamá." And when I catch the smell I am lost in tears, deep long tears that come when you have held your breath for centuries.

There was something I knew at that eight-year-old moment that I vowed never to forget—the smell of a woman who is life and home to me at once. The woman in whose arms I am uplifted, sustained. Since then, it is as if I have spent the rest of my years driven by this scent toward la mujer.

19

> *when her india makes love*
> *it is with the greatest reverence*
> *to color, texture, smell*
>
> *by now she knew the scent of earth*
> *could call it up*
> *even between the cracks*
> *in sidewalks*
> *steaming dry*
> *from midday summer*
> *rain*

With this knowledge so deeply emblazed upon my heart, how then was I supposed to turn away from La Madre, La Chicana? If I were to build my womanhood on this self-evident truth, it is the love of the Chicana, the love of myself as a Chicana I had to embrace, no white man. Maybe this ultimately was the cutting difference between my brother and me. To be a woman fully necessitated my claiming the race of my mother. My brother's sex was white. Mine, brown.

20

LIKE A WHITE SHEEP I FOLLOWED

Sueño: 3 de julio

I am having my face made up, especially my eyes by a very beautiful Chicana. The make-up artist changes me entirely for only five dollars. I think this is a very low price for how deep and dark she makes me look.

21

When I was growing up, I looked forward to the days when I hoped my skin would toast to match my cousins, their skin turning pure black in the creases. I never could catch up, but my skin did turn smooth like theirs, oily brown—like my mamá's, holding depth, density, the possibility of infinite provision. Mi abuela raised the darkest cousins herself, she never wanting us the way she molded and managed them.

22

To write as a Chicana feminist lesbian, I am afraid of being mistaken, of being made an outsider again—having to fight the kids at school to get them to believe

23

Teresita and I were cousins. "You don't *look* like cousins!" I feel at times I am trying to bulldoze my way back into a people who forced me to leave them in the first place, who taught me to take my whiteness and run with it. Run with it. Who want nothing to do with me, the likes of me, the white of me—in them.

When was I forced to choose? When Vivian Molina after two years of the deepest,   24
richest friendship, two years of me helping her through "new math," helping her not flunk once more—once was enough—and her so big already, fat, and dark-skinned. When Vivian left me flat, I didn't know what happened, except I knew she was beginning to smell like a woman and once, just before our split-up, the neighbor-kid talked of Vivian growing hair "down there." I didn't get it, except I knew that none of these changes were settling right in Vivian. And I was small and thin, still, and light-skinned and I loved Vivian which didn't seem to matter in the way teachers were wondering if Vivian was going to make it through the year. So, one day that year Vivian came to school and never spoke to me again. Nothing happened between us. I swear nothing happened.

I would call her and plead, "Vivian, what did I do?" "Vivian, ¿por que?" I would   25
have asked in Spanish if they had let me." "¿Qué pasó? No entiendo ¿Qué pasó?" But she never let on, except once when she nearly started to cry near the water fountain in the school corridor when I asked her for the last time and her eyes met mine finally and she said, I think or I'd like to remember, "I'm sorry." And even if she didn't say that, exactly, I know she said something that told me we were in different leagues now. And it couldn't be helped. It was out of our control. Something she, a year and a half older and much darker, knew before I knew and like a white sheep I followed the path paved for me.

Rocky Hernandez was brilliant and tough. Got mostly A's in school, like Carmen   26
Luna who was her second cousin in the same grade. They were both wizards, but Rocky was sharper and mean in her sharpness. "Antagonistic," the nuns would say and she'd prove it in her handwriting which slanted way off to the left which I admired greatly, which the nuns found incorrigible. When it came time for the Catholic high school entrance exams, we learned in May what track we would be in for the coming freshman year. To my amazement, I got into the "A" group—college prep. To my equal amazement, Rocky and her cousin were tracked into the "C" group—business and general education where they teach you home economics and typing. Rocky could talk and write and compute circles around me, which didn't seem to compute on our entrance exams.

After we got into high school, the Irish and Italian girls became my friends. And   27
Rocky and I seldom, if ever, spoke.

It was my mother, not my father, who fixed me on this idea of getting an educa-   28
tion. "Without an education, you're nothing," she would say. "Look at me. If only I could write better, I could get a different kind of job, I wouldn't have to do the kind of work I do." She was constantly criticizing this or that younger aunt or uncle or in-law who had what she did not—basic reading and writing skills—who still worked factory. It never occurred to her, or if it did, she never let on to us children, that *color* was any factor in reducing one's chances for success.

And in terms of rearing her three light-skinned brown-haired children, we in fact 29 did not have to fear, like my cousins, racial discrimination. On the surface of things we could pass as long as we made no point of our Chicano heritage. As long as we moved my father's name through our lives like a badge of membership to the white open-door policy club.

In fact, I had never fully realized until this year when I went back to California 30 and the words tumbled out of my mouth to my sister, that color had anything to do with the reason my sister and brother and I were *the* success stories of the family. Within our sex, we have received the most education and work in recognized professions. I had acknowledged this inequity between myself and my mother's generation, but not within my own.

I remember my friend Tavo's words only two years ago, "You get to choose." He 31 told me he didn't trust güeros, that we had to prove ourselves to him in some way. And you see I felt that challenge for proof laid out flat on the table between us.

So, I say, "Well, I understand that because it's awfully hard to be in this position 32 under suspicion from so many." This constant self-scrutiny, digging deeper, digging deeper.

Then Tavo says to me, "You see at any time, if they (meaning me) decide to use 33 their light skin privilege they can." I say, "Uh huh. Uh huh." He says, "You can decide you're suddenly no Chicano."

That I can't say, but once my light skin and good English saved me and my lover 34 from arrest. And I'd use it again. I'd use it to the hilt over and over to save our skins.

"You get to choose." Now I want to shove those words right back into his face. 35 You call this a choice! To constantly push up against a wall of resistance from your own people or to fall away nameless into the mainstream of this country, running with our common blood?

But I *have* betrayed my people. 36

Rita Villareal and I used to go to the roller rink together. I never noticed how dark 37 she was until my mother pointed this out to me, warning me against her. How her jet black straight hair and coffee bean skin marked her as a different grade of Mexicana. Una india, de clase baja. It was the first fight about race I ever had with my mother. When I protested, she said to me, "It isn't her color and I never tell you about your friends, but *this* girl is going to get you in trouble. She's no good for you." Our friendship soon broke off, me keeping a distance from Rita. Later, she got into boys and booze. *Was my mother right?*

Maybe this was what Vivian had feared/expected in me. My turning my back on 38 her, like I had on Rocky.

Many years later when I was already in college, I had come home for the weekend 39 and went on a short run to the supermarket for my mom. There, for the first time in at least three years, I ran into Rocky. She was pushing a shopping cart and inside it was one of the most beautiful baby boys I had ever laid eyes on, jabbering and wide-eyed.

Rocky and I talked. It was clear we both still felt some affection for each other 40 from those early grade school days. I touched the kid's cheek, complimenting her on him. When she turned to enter the check-out line, I wanted to stop her, invite her to dinner, not let her out of my sight again. But I hesitated, wondering what we would have to say to each other after so many years. I let her go.

Driving home, I remembered that there had been rumors that Rocky was preg-   41
nant at graduation.

TRAITOR BEGETS TRAITOR

What looks like betrayal between women on the basis of race originates, I believe, in   42
sexism/heterosexism. Chicanas begin to turn our backs on each other either to gain male approval or to avoid being sexually stigmatized by them under the name of puta, vendida, jota. This phenomenon is as old as the day is long, and first learned in the school yard, long before it is played out with a vengeance within political communities.

In the seventh grade, I fell in love with Manuel Poblano. A small-boned boy. Hair   43
always perfectly combed and oiled. Uniform shirt pressed neatly over shoulder blades jutting out. At twelve, Manual was growing in his identity—sexually, racially—and Patsy Juárez, my one-time fifth-grade friend wanted him too. Manuel was pals with Leticia and Connie. I remember how they flaunted a school picture of his in front of my face, proving how *they* could get one from him, although I had asked first. The two girls were conspiring to get him to "go" with Patsy, which in the end, he finally did. I, knowing all along I didn't have a chance. Not brown enough. And the wrong last name.

At puberty, it seemed identity alliances were beginning to be made along rigid   44
and immovable lines of race, as it combined with sex. And everyone—boy, girl, anglo, and Chicano—fell into place. Where did *I* stand?

I did not move away from other Chicanos because I did not love my people. I   45
gradually became anglocized because I thought it was the only option available to me toward gaining autonomy as a person without being sexually stigmatized. I can't say that I was conscious of all this at the time, only that at each juncture in my development, I instinctively made choices which I thought would allow me greater freedom of movement in the future. This primarily meant resisting sex roles as much as I could safely manage and this was far easier in an anglo context than in a Chicano one. That is not to say that anglo culture does not stigmatize its women for "gender-transgressions"—only that its stigmatizing did not hold the personal power over me which Chicano culture did.

Chicanas' negative perceptions of ourselves as sexual persons and our conse-   46
quential betrayal of each other finds its roots in a four-hundred-year-long Mexican history and mythology. It is further entrenched by a system of anglo imperialism which long ago put Mexicanos and Chicanos in a defensive posture against the dominant culture.

The sexual legacy passed down to the Mexicana/Chicana is the legacy of betrayal,   47
pivoting around the historical/mythical female figure of Malintzin Tenepal. As translator and strategic advisor and mistress to the Spanish conqueror of México, Hernan Cortez, Malintzin is considered the mother of the mestizo people. But unlike La Virgen de Guadalupe, she is not revered as the Virgin Mother, but rather

slandered as La Chingada, meaning the "fucked one," or La Vendida, sell-out to the white race.

Upon her shoulders rests the full blame for the "bastardization" of the indigenous people of México. To put it in its most base terms: Malintzin, also called Malinche, fucked the white man who conquered the Indian peoples of México and destroyed their culture. Ever since, brown men have been accusing her of betraying her race, and over the centuries continue to blame her entire sex for this "transgression." 48

As a Chicana and a feminist, I must, like other Chicanas before me, examine the effects this myth has on my/our racial/sexual identity and my relationship with other Chicanas. There is hardly a Chicana growing up today who does not suffer under her name even if she never hears directly of the one-time Aztec princess. 49

The Aztecs had recorded that Quetzalcoatl, the feathered serpent god, would return from the east to redeem his people in the year One Reed according to the Aztec calendar. Destiny would have it that on this very day, April 21, 1519 (as translated to the Western calendar), Cortez and his men, fitting the description of Quetzalcoatl, light-haired and bearded, landed in Vera Cruz. 50

At the time of Cortez's arrival in México, the Aztecs had subjugated much of the rest of the Indian population, including the Mayans and Tabascans, who were much less powerful militarily. War was a necessity for the Aztecs in order to take prisoners to be used for sacrificial offerings to the warrior-god, Huitzilopochtli. As slaves and potential sacrificial victims to the Aztecs, then, these other Indian nations, after their own negotiations and sometimes bloody exchanges with the Spanish, were eager to join forces with the Spanish to overthrow the Aztec empire. The Aztecs, through their systematic subjugation of much of the Mexican Indian population, decreed their own self-destruction. 51

Aleida Del Castillo, Chicana feminist theorist, contends that as a woman of deep spiritual commitment, Malinche aided Cortez because she understood him to be Quetzalcoatl returned in a different form to save the peoples of México from total extinction. She writes, "The destruction of the Aztec empire, the conquest of México, and as such, the termination of her indigenous world," was, in Malinche's eyes, "inevitable" in order to make way for the new spiritual age that was imminent. 52

Del Castillo and other Chicana feminists who are researching and re-interpreting Malinche's role in the conquest of México are not trying to justify the imperialism of the Spanish. Rather, they are attempting to create a more realistic context for, and therefore a more sympathetic view of, Malinche's actions. 53

The root of the fear of betrayal by a woman is not at all specific to the Mexican or Chicano. The resemblance between Malinche and the Eve image is all too obvious. In chronicling the conquest of México and founding the Catholic Church there, the Spanish passed on to the mestizo people as legacy their own European-Catholic interpretation of Mexican events. Much of this early interpretation originated from Bernal del Castillo's eye-witness account of the conquest. As the primary source of much contemporary analysis as well, the picture we have of Mexican Indian civilization during that period often contains a strong Catholic and Spanish bias. 54

In his writings, Bernal Diaz del Castillo notes that upon the death of Malinche's father, the young Aztec princess was in line to inherit his estate. Malinche's mother wanted her son from her second marriage to inherit the wealth instead. She therefore sold her own daughter into slavery. 55

According to Gloria Anzaldúa, there are writings in México to refute this account. But it was nevertheless recorded—or commonly believed—that Malinche was betrayed by her own mother. It is this myth of the inherent unreliability of women, our natural propensity for treachery, which has been carved into the very bone of Mexican/Chicano collective psychology. 56

Traitor begets traitor. 57

Little is made of this early betrayal, whether or not it actually occurred, probably because no man was immediately affected. In a way, Malinche's mother would only have been doing her Mexican wifely duty: *putting the male first.* 58

There is none so beautiful as the Latino male. I have never met any kind of Latino who, although he may have claimed his family was very woman-dominated ("mi mamá made all the real decisions"), who did not subscribe to the basic belief that men are better. It is so ordinary a statement as to sound simplistic and I am nearly embarrassed to write it, but that's the truth in its kernel. 59

Ask, for example, any Chicana mother about her children and she is quick to tell you she loves them all the same, but she doesn't. *The boys are different.* Sometimes I sense that she feels this way because she wants to believe that through her mothering, she can develop the kind of man she would have liked to have married, or even have been. That through her son she can get a small taste of male privilege, since without race or class privilege that's all there is to be had. The daughter can never offer the mother such hope, straddled by the same forces that confine the mother. As a result, the daughter must constantly earn the mother's love, prove her fidelity to her. The son—he gets her love for free. 60

After ten years of feminist consciousness and activism, why does this seem so significant to me—to write of the Mexican mother favoring the son? I think because I had never quite gone back to the source. Never said in my own tongue, *the boys, they are men, they can do what they want . . . after all, he's a man.* 61

Journal Entry: April 1980

Three days ago, my mother called me long distance full of tears, loving me, wanting me back in her life after such a long period of separation. My mother's tears succeed in getting me to break down the edge in my voice, the protective distance. My mother's pleading "mi'jita, I love you, I hate to feel so far away from you." succeed in opening my heart again to her. 62

I don't remember exactly why my heart had been shut, only that it had been very necessary to keep my distance, that in a way we had agreed to that. But, it only took her crying to pry my heart open again. 63

I feel myself unriveting. The feelings begin to flood my chest. Yes, this is why I love women. This woman is my mother. There is no love as strong as this, refusing my separation, never settling for a secret that would split us off, always at the last minute, like now, pushing me to brink of revelation, speaking the truth. 64

I am as big as a mountain! I want to say, "Watch out, Mamá! I love you and I am as 65
big as a mountain!" And it is on the brink of this precipice where I feel my body de-
scending into the places where we have not spoken, the times I did not fight back. I am
descending, ready to speak the truth, finally.

And then suddenly, over the phone, I hear another ring. My mother tells me to 66
wait. There is a call on my father's work phone. Moments later, "It is your brother," she
says. My knees lock under me, bracing myself for the fall . . . Her voice lightens up.
"Okay, mi'jita. I love you. I'll talk to you later," cutting off the line in the middle of the
connection.

I am relieved when I hang up that I did not have the chance to say more. The grace- 67
ful reminder. This man doesn't have to earn her love. My brother has always come first.

Seduction and betrayal. Since I've grown up, no woman cares for me for free. There 68
is always a price. My love.

What I wanted from my mother was impossible. It would have meant her going 69
against Mexican/Chicano tradition in a very fundamental way. You are a traitor to
your race if you do not put the man first. The potential accusation of "traitor" or
"vendida" is what hangs above the heads and beats in the hearts of most Chicanas
seeking to develop our own autonomous sense of ourselves, particularly through
sexuality. Even if a Chicana knew no Mexican history, the concept of betraying one's
race through sex and sexual politics is as common as corn. As cultural myths reflect
the economics, mores, and social structures of a society, every Chicana suffers from
their effects. And we project the fear onto each other. We suspect betrayal in one another—first to other men, but ultimately and more insidiously, to the white man.

Journal Entry: noviembre 1980
. . . this white man coming up over and over again. There's something about him 70
that feels like such a suck to me. And so I ask myself, is it only that my Chicana mother
fed my white father all the days of her life? Is it this model I am struck with/stuck with?
The white man getting the attention that should go to the Chicana daughters, that
should be shared between women?

I don't sense within our culture the same fear of a man betraying our race. It is 71
the woman who is the object of our contempt. We can't ultimately hold onto her,
not in the cosmic sense. She who could provide us with the greatest sense of belonging is never truly ours; for she is always potential chattel for the white man. As
with so many of our mothers, my mother's relationship with white men made survival of her and her family possible.

It was Mr. Bowman who saved the day. Saved the day in Tijuana. Big white busi- 72
nessman Mr. Bowman. Not very good-looking, but did he need to be? Had money. A
very good dresser, mi mamá would say. The second wife, a mexicana—or was that his
mistress? No recuerdo, pero this was a man to be counted on.

Cuando se murió mi abuelo, he gave mamá the bucks for the funeral. Mi abuela 73
never asking where it came from. Mi mamá said to me, "She didn't care how I got it.
How did she think I got it. I was only a girl, hija, a girl."

'Bout the time she got to the Foreign Club, they were both older. He was no spring   74
chicken, never, even in the early years, but by now she was close to eighteen and he
thought, after all, it's about time.

The chauffeur, a Mexicano, put them into the back seat of the big blue sedan and   75
they all began their way down the coast toward Rosarita Beach. Mi mamá prayin the
entire way, prayin "santo niño madre de dios san antonio" . . . you name it, she brought
out every saint and holy person she could think of, but focusing, of course, on her pa-
tron, San Antonio. Running the rosary beads through her mind, she prayed, "san anto-
nio, por favor, ayúdeme."

She had seen the chauffeur fill the tank with gas. They had all gone to the station to-   76
gether. She remembered that. She had seen him fill it up. But there they were, her prayin
between snatches of conversation, Big Bowman sitting next to her, pleased with himself,
and the car starts sputtering and jerking to a stop. They were out of gas. Smack in the
desert.

It was a day's journey back to town.   77

No gas. No hotel. No Rosarita. No sex with Mr. Bowman.   78

That time the saints saved her.   79

"He never laid a hand on me. It wasn't that he didn't want to," she said, "but I was   80
very lucky. If he would of wanted me, what could I do? But I was very lucky."

So little has been documented as to the actual suffering Chicanas have experi-   81
enced resisting or succumbing to the sexual demands of white men. The ways we
have internalized the sexual hatred and exploitation they have displayed against us
are probably too numerous and too ingrained to even identify. If the Chicana, like
her brother, suspects other women of betrayal, then she must, in the most profound
sense, suspect herself. How deep her suspicions run will measure how ardently she
defends her commitment, above all, to the Chicano male. As obedient sister/daugh-
ter/lover she is the committed heterosexual, the socially acceptable Chicana. Even if
she's politically radical, sex remains the bottom line on which she proves her commitment to her race.

WE FIGHT BACK WITH OUR FAMILIES

. . . The one aspect of our identity which has been uniformly ignored by every exist-   82
ing political movement in this country is sexuality, both as a source of oppression
and a means of liberation. Although other movements have dealt with this issue,
sexual oppression and desire have never been considered specifically in relation to
the lives of women of color. Sexuality, race, and sex have usually been presented in
contradiction to each other, rather than as part and parcel of a complex web of personal and political identity and oppression.

Female sexuality must be controlled, whether it be through the Church or the   83
State. The institutions of marriage and family, and necessarily, heterosexuality, prevail and thrive under capitalism as well as socialism. Patriarchal systems of whatever
ilk must be able to determine how and when women reproduce. For even "after the
revolution," babies must be made, and until they find a way of making them without us (which is not that far off into the future), we're here for the duration. In
China, for example, married couples are now being mandated by the State to limit

their children to one. Abortions are not only available, but women are sometimes forced by family and friends to undergo an abortion or meet with severe economic recriminations from the State. In the U.S., the New Right's response to a weakening economic system, which they attribute in part to women's changing position in the family, is to institute legislation to ensure governmental control of women's reproductive rights. Unlike in China, however, the New Right is "morally" opposed to abortion. The form their misogyny takes is the dissolution of government-assisted abortions for the poor, bills to limit teenage girls' right to birth control, and the advocacy of the Human Rights Amendment, which allows the fetus greater right to life than the mother. These backward political moves hurt all women, but most especially the poor and "colored."

The white man's so-called "benevolent protection" of the family and the role of 84 women within it has never extended to the woman of color. She is most often the victim of enforced pregnancy and sterilization. She is always the last to "choose."

Unlike most white people, with the exception of the Jews, Third World people 85 have suffered the threat of genocide to our races since the coming of the first European expansionists. The family, then, becomes all the more ardently protected by oppressed peoples, and the sanctity of this institution is infused like blood into the veins of the Chicano. At all costs, la familia must be preserved: for when they kill our boys in their own imperialist wars to gain greater profits for American corporations; when they keep us in ghettos, reservations, and barrios which ensure that our own people will be the recipients of our frustrated acts of violence; when they sterilize our women without our consent because we are unable to read the document we sign; when they prevent our families from getting decent housing, adequate child care, sufficient fuel, regular medical care; then we have reason to believe—although they may no longer technically be lynching us in Texas or our sisters and brothers in Georgia, Alabama, Mississippi—they intend to see us dead.

So we fight back, we think, with our families—with our women pregnant, and 86 our men, the indisputable heads. We believe the more severely we protect the sex roles within the family, the stronger we will be as a unit in opposition to the anglo threat. And yet, our refusal to examine *all* the roots of the lovelessness in our families is our weakest link and softest spot.

Our resistance as a people to looking at the relationships within our fami- 87 lies—between husband and wife, lovers, sister and brother, father, son, and daughter, etc.—leads me to believe that the Chicano male does not hold fast to the family unit merely to safeguard it from the death-dealings of the anglo. Living under Capitalist Patriarchy, what is true for "the man" in terms of misogyny is, to a great extent, true for the Chicano. He, too, like any other man, wants to be able to determine how, when, and with whom his women—mother, wife, and daughter—are sexual. For without male imposed social and legal control of our reproductive function, reinforced by the Catholic Church, and the social institutionalization of our roles as sexual and domestic servants to men, Chicanas might very freely "choose" to do otherwise, including being sexually independent *from* and/or *with* men. In fact, the forced "choice" of the gender of our sexual/love partner seems to precede the forced "choice" of the form (marriage and family) that partnership might take. The control of women begins through the institution of heterosexuality.

Homosexuality does not, in and of itself, pose a great threat to society. Male ho- 88 mosexuality has always been a "tolerated" aspect of Mexican/Chicano society, as long as it remains "fringe." A case can even be made that male homosexuality stems from our indigenous Aztec roots. But lesbianism, in any form, and male homosexuality which openly avows both the sexual and emotional elements of the bond, challenges the very foundation of la familia.[1]

The question remains. Is the foundation as it stands now sturdy enough to meet the face of the oppressor? I think not. There is a deeper love between and amongst our people that lies buried between the lines of the roles we play with each other. It is the earth beneath the floor boards of our homes. We must split wood, dig bare-fisted into the packed ground to find out what we really have to hold in our hands as muscle.

Family is *not* by definition the man in a dominant position over women and children. Familia is cross-generational bonding, deep emotional ties between opposite sexes, and within our sex. It is sexuality, which involves, but is not limited to, intercourse or orgasm. It springs forth from touch, constant and daily. The ritual of kissing and the sign of the cross with every coming and going from the home. It is finding familia among friends where blood ties are formed through suffering and celebration shared.

The strength of our families never came from domination. It has only endured in spite of it—like our women.

LA MALINCHISTA

Chicanos' refusal to look at our weaknesses as a people and a movement is, in the most profound sense, an act of self-betrayal. The Chicana lesbian bears the brunt of this betrayal, for it is she, the most visible manifestation of a woman taking control of her own sexual identity and destiny, who so severely challenges the anti-feminist Chicano/a. What other reason is there than that for the virtual dead silence among Chicanos about lesbianism? When the subject *is* raised, the word is used pejoratively.

For example, Sonia A. López writes about the anti-feminism in El Movimiento of the late 60s:

> The Chicanas who voiced their discontent with the organizations and with
> male leadership were often labeled "women's libbers," and "lesbians." This
> served to isolate and discredit them, a method practiced both covertly and
> overtly.

This statement appears without qualification. López makes no value judgment on the inherent homophobia in such a divisive tactic. Without comment, her statement reinforces the idea that lesbianism is not only a white thing, but an insult to be avoided at all costs.

Such attempts by Chicana feminists to bend over backwards to prove criticism of their people is love (which, in fact, it is) severely undermines the potential radicalism of the ideology they are trying to create. Not quite believing in their love, suspecting their own anger, and fearing ostracism from Chicano males (being

---

1. The "faggot" is the object of the Chicano/Mexicano's contempt because he is consciously choosing a role his culture tells him to despise. That of a woman.

symbolically "kicked out of bed" with the bait of "lesbian" hanging over their work), the Chicana's imagination often stops before it has a chance to consider some of the most difficult, and therefore, some of the most important, questions.

It is no wonder that the Chicanas I know who *are* asking "taboo" questions are often forced into outsiderhood long before they begin to question el carnal in print. Maybe like me they now feel they have little to lose.   96

It is important to say that fearing recriminations from my father never functioned for me as an obstacle in my political work. Had I been born of a Chicano father, I sometimes think I never would have been able to write a line or participate in a demonstration, having to repress all questioning in order that the ultimate question of my sexuality would never emerge. Possibly, even some of my compañeras whose fathers died or left in their early years would never have had the courage to speak out as Third World lesbians the way they do now, had their fathers been a living part of their daily lives. The Chicana lesbians I know whose fathers are very much a part of their lives are seldom "out" to their families.   97

During the late 60s and early 70s, I was not an active part of la causa. I never managed to get myself to walk in the marches in East Los Angeles (I merely watched from the sidelines); I never went to one meeting of MECHA on campus. No soy tonta. I would have been murdered in El Movimiento—light-skinned, unable to speak Spanish well enough to hang; miserably attracted to women and fighting it; and constantly questioning all authority, including men's. I felt I did not belong there. Maybe I had really come to believe that "Chicanos" were "different," not "like us," as my mother would say. But I fully knew that there was a part of me that was a part of that movement, but it seemed that part would have to go unexpressed until the time I could be a Chicano and the woman I had to be, too.   98

The woman who defies her role as subservient to her husband, father, brother, or son by taking control of her own sexual destiny is purported to be a "traitor to her race" by contributing to the "genocide" of her people—whether or not she has children. In short, even if the defiant woman is *not* a lesbian, she is purported to be one; for, like the lesbian in the Chicano imagination, she is una *Malinchista.* Like the Malinche of Mexican history, she is corrupted by foreign influences which threaten to destroy her people. Norma Alarcón elaborates on this theme of sex as a determinant of loyalty when she states: 99

> The myth of Malinche contains the following sexual possibilities: woman is
> sexually passive, and hence at all times open to potential use by men whether
> it be seduction or rape. The possible use is double-edged: that is, the use of her
> as pawn may be intracultural —"amongst us guys" or intercultural, which
> means if we are not using her then "they" must be using her. Since woman is
> highly pawnable, nothing she does is perceived as choice.

Lesbianism can be construed by the race then as the Chicana being used by the white man, even if the man never lays a hand on her. *The choice is never seen as her own.* Homosexuality is *his* disease with which he sinisterly infects Third World people, men and women alike. (Because Malinche is female, Chicano gay men rebelling against their prescribed sex roles, although still considered diseased, do not suffer the same stigma of traitor.) Further, the Chicana lesbian who has relationships with white women may feel especially susceptible to such accusations, since   100 the white lesbian is seen as the white man's agent. The fact that the white woman may be challenging the authority of her white father, and thereby could be looked upon as a potential ally, has no bearing on a case closed before it was ever opened.

The first dyke I remember in school was Sally Frankel, whom everyone called   101
"Frank," the way she liked it. She could play the meanest game of four-square of them all—built lean and solid as an eighth-grade boy, and smart too. And very, very clearly white. *Were all lesbians white?* I remember thinking that I had never quite met a girl like Frank before—so bold, somehow freer than the rest of us. She was an "army brat" and so had lived many places, even in Europe. While all my Chicana friends were leaving me high and dry for the guys, this girl—although not particularly interested in me—represented a life beyond the tight group discussions of girls, locked arm-in-arm, where the word "chinga" was dropped like a slug in my throat. (Even at fourteen, I was still to wonder if I could get pregnant slow-dancing with a boy, picking up my knowledge of sex from these cryptic conversations.) The desire I felt for women had nothing and everything to do with the vulgarity of intercourse; had nothing and everything to do with the dreams that wracked my bed at night. Somehow Frank connected with all this—as did the "funny couple" I had encountered surreptitiously one hot afternoon a few years before.

At the time we were living in the Kenwood Hotel, a kind of "drifter" hang-out,   102
down on Main Street in Huntington Beach, long before there was any development there. Just a few bars, a little drugstore, "The Paddock" restaurant, and a surfboard shop. My mom was managing the place.

One day I was making my way down the long hallway to go play out on the big   103
sundeck when I suddenly stopped short of the screen door. Some "new" people were out there who were not the "regulars." Hiding behind the screen door, I decided to observe.

One woman looked like a Marilyn Monroe type—50s style. Her hair was brassy   104
blonde and in a kind of permanent wave. Her yellow sundress was very tight around her waist and low-cut. The other person next to her I knew was really a woman, although she looked mostly like a man: white dress shirt with sleeves rolled up, pack of cigs in her front breast pocket, black men's trousers. She was a pretty big woman, about twice the size of Marilyn, except her head was small—dark haired and greased back.

Marilyn had her dress hiked up above her knees and between her thighs she had   105
put an open jar of Skippy peanut butter. I watched the two women as she dipped the knife into the jar, pulled out a thick glob of the brown mass, then ran her tongue along it luxuriously like she had all day to eat the stuff. She then gave it to the other one to lick in the same place. All I could think about were the germs that were being passed back and forth.

The next day, I learned that the "funny" women in room six had sneaked out in   106
the middle of the night without paying. They had stolen the alarm clock too. My momma said she had tried to give them the benefit of the doubt, but "never again." *Were all lesbians white? And decent ladies, Mexican? Who was I in this?*

But it was the Mexican women I had loved first.   107

Sandra García and I used to make out after school. I think we mostly put a pillow 108
between our faces so our lips wouldn't touch, but our bodies would get all en-
wrapped with each other. At eleven, Sandra was already "stacked" and, very innocently, we would take the role of movie stars—she playing Deborah Walley and me,
James Darren, lusting after each other. Sandra's young body seemed a miracle of
womanhood to me, the bow of her pink brassiere always cropping up out between
the opening of her too-small white uniform blouse.

I wanted Sandra and as long as she was interested, I'd throw myself up on the 109
couch with her and make out until my cheeks were sore.

My cousin Teresa and I made out too; and this was for real. Making up stories 110
about shipwrecks and sailor/saviors of young French women, we would shut ourselves up in our abuelita's bedroom and press our lips long and hard against each
other. One time we touched tongues which I remember so delighted us that we even
demonstrated this to my mom who happened into the bedroom. "Mira, tía," Teresita said, and we touched tongues tip-to-tip and giggled uproariously. My mother,
of course, reprimanded us immediately and it was only then that I realized that the
strange sensation running through me had something to do with "down there." Our
games soon came to an end, my feeling guilty for taking advantage of my cousin
three years younger than me.

But I can see now that these experiences with Sandra and Teresa were brief mo- 111
ments of sexual connection with other Chicanas that were to be systematically denied me for the next twenty years of my life.

The Mexican women in my life, a pain I don't want to get to. 112

It seems my life has always been a kind of Catch 22. For any way you look at it, 113
Chicanas are denied one another's fidelity. If women betray one another through
heterosexism, then lesbianism is a kind of visible statement of our faithfulness to
one another. But if lesbianism is white, then the women I am faithful to can never
be my own. And we are forced to move away from our people. As Gloria Anzaldúa
once said to me, "If I stayed in Hargill, I would never have been able to be myself. I
had to leave to come out as the person I really was." And if I had stayed in the San
Gabriel Valley, I would have been found for dead, at least the walking dead.

I have always known too much. It was too clear to me—too tangible—too alive 114
in the breath of my nose, the pulse in my thighs, the deep exhales that flowed from
my chest when I moved into a woman's arms.

Journal Entry: primavera 1980
I don't know what happened to make me this way. I do fear for my life sometimes. 115
Not that a bullet would hit my brain, but that I will forget to be afraid of the enemy. I
dreamed last night of a hostility in me so great that on the job I put a pen through the
skull of a white man. I have felt like an outcast on my job lately. The new manager
wants to fire me for my "politics." I am a lesbian. I love women to the point of killing for
us all.

An old friend came to visit me yesterday. She is leaving her good husband for the 116
wild love of a woman. We were both very sad together. Not for the separation from her
husband but for so many years of separation from women.

Some people try to convince me that the secrets I hold about loving women do not 117 *put me in a position of threat to my life. You see, you can't see this condition—this pos-ture of mind and heart and body—in the movement of my joints or on the surface of my skin. And then again, sometimes you can. But I know they are wrong.*

I feel very threatened and very threatening . . . 118

My mother does not worry about me; she fears me. She fears the power of the life she 119 *helped to breathe into me. She fears the lessons she taught me will move into action. She fears I might be willing to die rather than settle for less than the best of loving.*

The line of reasoning goes: 120

Malinche sold out her indio people by acting as courtesan and translator for 121 Cortez, whose offspring symbolically represent the birth of the bastardized mestizo/Mexicano people. My mother then is the modern-day Chicana, Malinche marrying a white man, my father, to produce the bastards my sister, my brother, and I are. Finally, I—a half-breed Chicana—further betray my race by *choosing* my sexuality which excludes all men, and therefore most dangerously, Chicano men.

I come from a long line of Vendidas. 122

I am a Chicana lesbian. My own particular relationship to being a sexual person; 123 and a radical stand in direct contradiction to, and in violation of, the women I was raised to be.

Working with the Text

1. The first section of Moraga's essay focuses on her family—particularly on her mother, her brother, her father, and herself—and the roles they played within the family structure. How is the family she describes different from and/or similar to the way you define family roles? To what extent do you think such definitions are culturally determined?

2. The second section of Moraga's essay focuses on skin color and racism. In what ways has being a light-skinned Chicana led Moraga to feel doubly alienated?

3. The third section focuses on the concept of the Chicana woman as "traitor" (or *vendida*). What different manifestations of "traitor" in this sense does Moraga discuss? How are these related to the historical/mythical figure of Malinche? What does Moraga mean when she writes that "sex remains the bottom line on which [the Chicana] proves her commitment to her race"?

4. Go to the *Border Texts* Web site and explore some of the links to resources on La Malinche. What are some of the associations she has in Chicana culture? How is she like and unlike the figure of Eve?

5. Of Chicanos Moraga writes, "We believe the more severely we protect the sex roles within the family, the stronger we will be as a unit in opposition to the anglo threat." How would Moraga define "strong family"? How do you feel about her definition?

6. Write an essay in which you compare Moraga's experiences with those of Michael Nava, a gay Chicano male whose essay "Gardenland, Sacramento,

California" appears in Chapter 2. What important differences and similarities
do these two writers reveal?

PERSIMMONS

LI-YOUNG LEE

■ Born in Jakarta, Indonesia, in 1957, poet Li-Young Lee later came with his family to the United States, where he received degrees from the University of Pittsburgh, the University of Arizona, and the State University of New York. He is
now a U.S. citizen and was awarded National Endowment for the Arts fellow-
ships in 1986 and 1995. Lee often writes from the perspective of a Chinese
American who grew up in an immigrant home. His poetry collections include
Rose (1986), *The City in Which I Love You* (1990), and *The Winged Seed* (1995). In
the following poem, the image of persimmons suggests both the speaker's sense
of belonging and his childhood feelings of alienation in a new environment in a
new country.

In sixth grade Mrs. Walker
slapped the back of my head
and made me stand in the corner
for not knowing the difference
between *persimmon* and *precision*.   5
How to choose

persimmons. This is precision.
Ripe ones are soft and brown-spotted.
Sniff the bottoms. The sweet one
will be fragrant. How to eat: 10
put the knife away, lay down newspaper.
Peel the skin tenderly, not to tear the meat.
Chew the skin, suck it,
and swallow. Now, eat
the meat of the fruit,   15
so sweet,
all of it, to the heart.

Donna undresses, her stomach is white.
In the yard, dewy and shivering

with crickets, we lie naked,   20
face-up, face-down.
I teach her Chinese.
Crickets: *chiu chiu.* Dew: I've forgotten.
Naked: I've forgotten.
Ni, wo: you and me.   25
I part her legs,
remember to tell her
she is beautiful as the moon.

Other words
that got me into trouble were   30
fight and *fright, wren* and *yarn.*
Fight was what I did when I was frightened,
fright was what I felt when I was fighting.
Wrens are small, plain birds,
yarn is what one knits with.   35
Wrens are soft as yarn.
My mother made birds out of yarn.
I loved to watch her tie the stuff;
a bird, a rabbit, a wee man.

Mrs. Walker brought a persimmon to class   40
and cut it up
so everyone could taste
a *Chinese apple.* Knowing
it wasn't ripe or sweet. I didn't eat
but watched the other faces.   45

My mother said every persimmon has a sun
inside, something golden, glowing,
warm as my face.

Once, in the cellar, I found two wrapped in newspaper,
forgotten and not yet ripe.   50
I took them and set both on my bedroom windowsill,

where each morning a cardinal
sang, *The sun, the sun.*

Finally understanding
he was going blind,   55
my father sat up all one night
waiting for a song, a ghost.
I gave him the persimmons,
swelled, heavy as sadness,
and sweet as love.   60

This year, in the muddy lighting
of my parents' cellar, I rummage, looking
for something I lost.
My father sits on the tired, wooden stairs,
black cane between his knees,   65
hand over hand, gripping the handle.

He's so happy that I've come home.
I ask how his eyes are, a stupid question.
All gone, he answers.

Under some blankets, I find a box.   70
Inside the box I find three scrolls.
I sit beside him and untie
three paintings by my father:
Hibiscus leaf and a white flower.
Two cats preening.   75
Two persimmons, so full they want to drop from the cloth.

He raises both hands to touch the cloth,
asks, *Which is this?*

This is persimmons, Father.

Oh, the feel of the wolftail on the silk,   80
the strength, the tense

precision in the wrist.
I painted them hundreds of times
eyes closed. These I painted blind.
Some things never leave a person:
scent of the hair of one you love,
the texture of persimmons,
in your palm, the ripe weight.

85

Working with the Text

1. What different meanings are suggested by the images of persimmons presented throughout the poem? What do you make of the contrast between the unripe "Chinese apple" Mrs. Walker brings to class and the other persimmons described in the poem?

2. The speaker tells about English words that he found confusing and that "got [him] into trouble": *persimmon* and *precision, fight* and *fright, wren* and *yarn.* How were these pairs connected in his mind? What do these connections suggest about differences between the poet's native Chinese language and the English he was trying to learn?

3. At first, the third stanza doesn't seem directly related to the rest of the poem. What do you see as the movement from the second stanza to the third? In what ways does the speaker's seduction of Donna by using Chinese words resonate in the poem? What is suggested by the speaker's having "forgotten" some words?

4. Interpret the last six stanzas of the poem in terms of what they suggest about culture and heritage. What might be the "something" that the speaker has "lost" (line 63)? What does he find? How does the linkage of *persimmon* and *precision* at the conclusion relate to the same images at the beginning?

GOING UP IN L.A.

RUBEN MARTINEZ

■ A native of Los Angeles, Ruben Martinez is an Emmy-award-winning journalist as well as a poet and performance artist. A writer and editor at *LA Weekly* from 1986 to 1992, he currently serves as the U.S.-Mexico correspondent for the Pacific News Service, cohosts the PBS cultural and political series *Life and Times,* and acts as a guest commentator on NPR's *All Things Considered.* His 1992 book, *The Other Side: Notes from the New L.A., Mexico City, and Beyond,* includes a number of personal reports focusing on Hispanic American life and identity. The following chapter from that book looks at the thriving culture of graffiti artists in Los Angeles and its relation to adolescent solidarity, gang warfare, individual expression, and possible escape from a life of poverty and crime.

Los Angeles, April 1989

The stain on the old couch that sits in the empty lot has already turned brown, a dark flower spread out upon the grimy fabric. Although it's a school day and only 10:30 in the morning, about a dozen teenagers stand about, passing around a quart of Colt 45 Malt Liquor. Some of the faces show fear; others are hardened into stony stares. "We know who did it, but we're not going to tell you," says one of the younger boys. His hair is cropped stubby short, and he wears dark jeans and a plain T-shirt. "We're not going to spell it out, but you can pretty much guess what's going to happen tonight."

At approximately seven o'clock the previous evening, these kids had been seated on or standing around the couch. Among the group was Prime, a seventeen-year-old homeboy. They'd all been "kickin' it"—drinking and talking to the accompaniment of a ghettoblaster alternately pumping out hip-hop and oldies—when a car pulled up to the curb below, and two figures climbed up the hill in the darkness. "Where you from?" one of them yelled from a distance of about ten feet. A moment later, several rounds exploded from a shotgun and a .45. Prime and another boy fell in the hail of bullets, and lay bleeding on the couch.

We walk around to the side of one of the dilapidated stucco bungalows that crown the hill. A wall displays the local gang's roster—hundreds of names spray-painted in furious, spidery lettering. Someone points to the "R.I.P." section: more than a dozen names. "Rest In Power," mumbles one of the boys. Nobody is sure whether the next name to go up on the wall will be Prime's.

A few days earlier, Prime was sitting in his family's living room, which doubles as a bedroom, in a neighborhood not far from the empty lot. It is a crime-ridden area to be sure, dominated by one of the city's oldest Latino gangs. This is where Prime grew up, and where his two unemployed parents try to scrape by on welfare.

Although Prime admitted that he'd been "in the wrong place at the wrong time" on more than one occasion, he saw himself less as a gangster, more as a "writer" (as graffiti artists call themselves), one of the best-known among the city's thousands of young, spraycan-wielding "bombers."

Prime shook hands gingerly that day. His right hand still bore the chalky plaster stains from a cast that had been removed the day before, the bones in his right—and writing—hand having been broken in a fist fight.

As soon as I entered the room, he began to show off his canvases. After years of doing complex, colorful works on walls across the city, Prime had begun experimenting with acrylics, airbrush, oils, washes. It was Valentine's Day, and he'd done a piece for his girlfriend—a brightly colored Cupid surrounded by soft pink roses, with a dedication that read, "José and Nery, *por vida*." He pointed to a larger work dominated by grays, blacks and silvers, titled *Dazed and Confused,* an ambitious circular composition centered on a pair of dice that become a large syringe, then a huddled, shadowy figure and, finally, a large, wicked-looking skull.

Prime sat down on the sagging bed, the plaster wall behind him bulging with cracked paint. At the age of eight, he tells me, he snatched his sister's goldfleck hairspray and wrote "Little Joe, 18 Street" in the back yard. Soon afterward his initials were "up" in the neighborhood alleys.

PRIME

"I never got really crazy," he told me. But as gang violence in the inner city in-   9
creased dramatically in the mid-1980s, he was busted for various misdemeanors, including "vandalism" (i.e., spraypainting), and he once almost did time for armed
robbery. It wasn't until about 1984 that Prime graduated from gang-writing to more
original and complex forms of graffiti. He developed a style that set him apart
from other graffiti artists, working closely with several colleagues in the K2S—STN
("Kill To Succeed—Second To None") crew, one of the first to appear on the city's
Eastside.

By last Valentine's Day, 10Prime could look back on it all and vow that it was the   10
art that really mattered in his life. And, as he brought out photo albums stuffed with
color photographs of graffiti works he'd done over the years, he told me he'd enrolled in art classes at the East L.A. Occupational Center. He spoke to me of a future
without drive-by shootings, overdoses or girls pregnant at fifteen. "I want to have a
big lot when I grow older," he said, leaning forward, a small gold crucifix swinging
in front of his dark blue sweatshirt. "It'll have big, long, movable walls. I'll put canvases up, and have kids and artists there, have it be like a big maze of art. Then, with
the money I make in one day, I'll buy some more canvas and change the maze . . ."

By 1984, movies like *Wild Style, Beat Street* and *Breakin'* had apprised L.A. teenagers   11
of the graffiti writing explosion that had taken place in the Bronx, where a complex,
multicolored graffiti known as "wildstyle" had evolved in the late 1970s and early
1980s. Behind its New York counterparts by several years, L.A. created its own distinct scene. In New York, most of the work had been painted onto the sides of subway cars. L.A.'s answer was to "bomb" the freeways.

L.A. writers had a rich history to draw upon. Graffiti had been around since the   12
World War Two era Pachucos (the first style-conscious Latino gangs, who incorporated Old English lettering into their "tags," or nicknames); the East L.A. mural
artists of the sixties, with their close ties to Mexican muralism, were a local artistic
and political institution. The city was ripe for a new public-art explosion.

The city's first graffiti "crew" was the L.A. Bomb Squad, whose membership con-   13
sisted almost exclusively of Latino youths from the *barrios* of Pico-Union and East

THE BELMONT TUNNEL

L.A. Soon, however, the movement spread west, south and north, to include teens from other impoverished neighborhoods and from the middle-class suburbs as well.

And so the L.A. version of hip-hop graffiti was born. Many of the more aesthetically developed works (known as "pieces," short for "masterpieces") were done in hidden-away places like the Belmont Tunnel, an old, fenced-off trolley stop near Belmont High School. There were also more daring exploits. Simple tags and "throw-ups" (two-color tags) went up on buses, benches, sidewalks, street lights, stop signs, anywhere that was highly visible to the public. Competition as to who could top whom in originality and quantity was intense.

The glory days of the nascent L.A. scene came in 1984, when a youth club named Radio-Tron opened its doors. "It was a cultural center where people could go practice breaking and drawing," recalls Moda (the tag is Spanish for "fashion"), a founding member of the Bomb Squad. Housed in a building in the Westlake *barrio* near MacArthur Park, Radio-Tron was akin to an established artist's studio, a haven from the streets where writers always ran the risk of a bust. Soon, every inch of the site was covered with tags and pieces. "All the guys I knew were being thrown in jail or getting killed," says Primo D, also of the Bomb Squad. "Radio-Tron was an alternative."

The center's curriculum, according to founder and director Carmelo Alvarez, a longtime inner-city youth activist, included deejaying, scratch and rap, and "advanced graffiti." "I just took what they had and structured it." But the experiment didn't last long. Wrangles with the city (Alvarez balked when the Department of Parks and Recreation made a move to take over the center), as well as a Fire Marshall's citation (for storage of "hazardous chemicals"—aerosol cans), led to its being closed. "When Radio-Tron shut down, everybody started getting into the gang thing," says Primo D. "There was nothing else to do."

Not long after the Bomb Squad's tags and cartoonlike "characters" first appeared in the downtown area, a group of mostly middle-class Anglo Westside teens took note and founded WCA (West Coast Artists), soon the biggest crew in the city with an active membership of about thirty-five, plus a subsidiary crew (BC, or Beyond Control) of a dozen or so. Today, on any given weekend morning, you can see WCA at work, along with other Westside crews like KSN (Kings Stop at Nothing), at one of their favorite spots, the Motor Yard in West Lost Angeles.

Everything in the yard, including the rails, the ties, the torched wrecks of cars, has been tagged, pieced, bombed—as the writers say, "terrorized." The thousands of discarded spraycans testify to the countless generations of pieces that have gone up, one on top of another, on the half-mile stretch of concrete retaining wall that flanks the railroad tracks.

Carrying in dozens of Krylon spraycans in backpacks or milk crates, the crews usually arrive early in the day and work alongside the railroad tracks that run parallel to the Santa Monica freeway near National Boulevard. A box will invariably be blasting Eazy E's "Boys-N-the-Hood" or Boogie Down Production's "My Philosophy" as the writers, ranging in age from six to their early twenties, fish sketches out of their back pockets, [open] the cans, press down customized nozzles ("fat tips"

14

15

16

17

18

19

NBC—NEVER BEEN CAUGHT

culled from small Testor's spraycans, which allow for a thicker, smoother line) and begin the sweeping rhythmic motions that trace the skeleton of a new piece.

Phoe of BC, a wiry, clean-cut teenager of Hawaiian–Filipino ancestry, is there 20 one weekend, wearing a dark blue baseball cap embroidered with the name of his crew. His tag, he tells me, is an intentional misspelling of "foe," which, according to him, means "society's enemy." He works on a three-dimensional wildstyle piece that is typical of Westside work. The edges of the letters are sharp as shards of glass, but serif-like cuts and arrows make the composition virtually unreadable to the un-trained eye.

"Writing is, like, a different community," says Phoe, yelling to be heard over the 21 freeway roar that almost drowns out his high-pitched voice. "It's communication with other writers throughout the city." Wherever he goes ("even when I go out to dinner with my parents"), the tools of the trade—markers or spraycans—are at his disposal.

As with many Westside writers, Phoe's response to the city's anti-graffiti forces, 22 or to those sympathetic adults who encourage him to professionalize his talent, is lackadaisical. "Yeah, yeah, yeah. They're telling me to go out and sign up for schol-arships and art classes, and get paid for writing, and I'm, like, well, I don't really need the money because I work." Yet some WCA writers do take "legal" jobs now and then, pounding the streets in search of sympathetic business owners who'll pay them to paint storefront signs and the like. Risk, one of WCA's premier writers, re-cently did backgrounds for a Michael Jackson video.

Still, there's an allure to the "illegal" work. And, since most writers lack studio 23
space, sites like the Motor Yard are indispensable. "They just don't understand," says
Ash, another respected WCA writer. "We need this place to paint, or else we're going
to bomb the streets more, straight up."

Although a few Westside writers are friendly with their Eastside counterparts, inter- 24
action between the two groups is limited. Indeed, the rivalry between WCA and
K2S—STN dates back to the origins of the L.A. writing scene. Like breakdancers,
writers "battle" each other. The spoils of victory may include several dozen spraycans, or the appropriation of a writer's tag.

As soon as WCA and K2S—STN each became aware of the other, the stage was 25
set for the East–West battle, which took place at the Belmont Tunnel in 1985. WCA
went up with the bigger production in their trademark flashy style, featuring a pas-
tel-yellow/clover-green/pastel-aqua, black-outlined, white-highlighted, hot-pink-
and-avocado-bordered piece by Risk. Next to it was a character by fellow writer
Cooz, of a Japanese-animation-style buxom woman wearing shiny wraparound
shield glasses, a cascade of auburn hair spilling over her shoulders.

K2S—STN countered with a shocker from Prime. Employing an abstract, futuris- 26
tic style, he wrote his tag with an altered color scheme and composition: triangles
and squares of hot pink, white, true blue and baby blue produced a new kind of three-
dimensional effect. Next to it he drew a robot character he'd found in a comix mag.

Some West Coast writers congratulated Prime afterward in an apparent admis- 27

K2S—STN
Kill To Succeed—Second To None

sion of defeat. By the next morning, however, all of the WCA productions, as well as a substantial part of Prime's, had been "dissed" (painted over) by unknown writers, and the bad blood began. To this day, some WCA writers maintain that Prime was the culprit, although he always denied the allegation.

There are substantial stylistic differences between East and West Los Angeles writers. WCA writers are sensitive to the charge that they are "biting" (the writer's term for plagiarism) New York styles. "We took the New York styles and made them into our own style," says Wisk, the crew's most prolific writer, a little defensively. Using thin letters with stylized swirls and blends of color accented with arrows and sparkles, West Coast's work often achieves a slick magazine look—the New York stamp is unmistakable. K2S—STN, on the other hand, while sometimes drawing on the same influences, produces more readable block- or bubblelike letters that echo old gang-writing styles updated with the wildstyle. The result is aesthetically analogous to the split between the Anglo and ethnic art worlds of the 1960s and 1970s—playful abstraction on the one hand, Socialist Realism-flavored work on the other. 28

But the stylistic differences between the two groups hide deeper tensions. The Eastside writers, who lay claim to being the original Los Angeles bombers, feel that WCA has received a disproportionate share of media attention, including articles in the *Los Angeles Times* that have largely ignored the Eastside writers in favor of Westsiders. 29

"It was only when white people started doing graffiti that they said it was art," Prime once said bitterly. "We were doing it before them, but [the media] were blaming us for vandalism." These sentiments are echoed by most Eastside writers, and their resentment is obviously both class- and race-based. 30

"Most of the West Coast writers are from middle-class families," says Moda of the original L.A. Bomb Squad. "On this side of town, you're faced with the gang problem and graffiti at the same time. It affects the writers from poor neighborhoods: because they have the distraction of gangs, they might not be able to pursue it all the way. Like Prime—he's stuck between gangs and graffiti." 31

Prime's father approaches the bed slowly. An oxygen mask all but hides the son's incipient beard and mustache. Dried blood is still encrusted on his forehead and temples. The father takes his son's bloody hand into his own, leans down and whispers something into his ear. Prime tries to speak, but the words are mumbled, delirious. His father lifts back the white sheet and peers at Prime's right arm, swathed in bandages. After two major operations, the doctors are finally willing to predict that Prime is going to make it. 32

Over the next few days, Prime's fellow writers will visit his bedside in an endless procession. Among them is Duke, twenty years old, a native of Guatemala and a seven-year writing veteran of K2S—STN. Like Prime, Duke has been involved in gangsterism. When he heard the news about the shooting, his first impulse was "to go out and take care of shit," but he checked himself. "The art took me out of the trip," says Duke, who is dressed in his trademark smoke-gray jeans, his boyish face showing a spotty beard. "It helped me to look at this world in a more positive sense." 33

Initiated into gangs at an early age, Duke says his first spraycan escapade involved simple tagging. But after some heavy violence on the streets—he was once tied to a 34

KINGS STOP AT NOTHING

car bumper by rival gang members and dragged for two blocks—he decided to try to "clean up his act." When the first wave of graffiti art hit L.A., he began devoting more and more of his time to piecing.

"I wanted to kick back," Duke says of the early days of graffiti. At that time, when he was in tenth grade, "jungle football" clubs were sprouting up all over the inner city. The emphasis at first was on sports, but soon fights were breaking out between the rival groups. Then guns were brandished, and the club Duke had helped to or-

35

ganize quickly became one of the largest gangs in the Pico-Union area, a *barrio* that is home to over a quarter of a million central Americans.

Early one morning in October 1985, a shotgun blast tore Duke's stomach open as he was walking to school. The doctors later told him it was a miracle that he had survived. Then came family problems and a difficult separation from his girlfriend. He gave up writing for months and found himself at a crossroads, uncertain as to which path to follow. But today he's back in the writing scene, and serious about moving up from the streets to a "legal" career by painting storefront signs and doing everything he can to set up his own art studio at home. 36

Prime, like Duke, had begun to distance himself from the gang world before he was shot. "He wasn't the kind to go out and say, 'Let's take care of these dudes,'" says Duke after visiting Prime one day. "Thank God he's not gone. And I hope he never goes." Like Geo, who was shot for yelling out the wrong gang name when they asked him, "Where you from?" Or Sine, who was stabbed when he tried to defend a younger kid from a gangster wielding a switchblade. Or Risko, who died in a car that tumbled off a Harbor Freeway overpass as he and another friend fled from the police after a gang outing. All were writers associated with K2S—STN. 37

Veterans of the writing scene estimate that at any given time there are probably several hundred full-fledged writers at work in Los Angeles. But one must add to this figure the hundreds, perhaps thousands of teens who are bombing the city with single-color tags, the bane of the Rapid Transit District and other city agencies. "There are so many people into tagging, and that's what's messing it up for the people who do art," says Cash, a K2S—STN veteran. "Tags, all they do is destroy, make the city look ugly. The art beautifies the walls that have been tagged up." 38

On the other hand, there is no doubt that straight-out vandalism is part of the appeal, especially for the younger, or "toy," writers. On a recent Friday ("Ditching Day") morning, the Panic Zone, East L.A.'s best-known writing yard, was crawling with up-and-coming writers, most of them of junior high school age, and their crew names alone—KCC (Kids Committing Crime) and CIA (Criminals In Action)—tell the story. With a ravenous hunger for recognition, they announce their names: POSES, KORE, MICRO, MIST, ERGER, SED, SOEWHAT, DEVO, SKOE, DEES, STINGER, BEAST, DE-FEAT, KINE, SETO. The selection of a tag is the all-important first step in establishing the writer's originality (hence the purposeful misspellings). Most of the tags deliberately cultivate either a dark, brooding image—DOOM, DREAD, DYE—or conjure a notion of hip-hop "badness"—REGENT, PRIME, SLICK. 39

The young writers at the Panic Zone are rabid taggers. "We all write on 'em all," proclaims one writer whose voice hasn't changed yet, pointing at the buses lined up at the Rapid Transit District maintenance yard, which lies only about fifty yards from the northernmost end of the Panic Zone. Why? "To get up, be known!" he says, and all the other writers nod eagerly. 40

Government agencies in Los Angeles County spend some $150 million annually in the war against graffiti. Sandblasters are available for heavy-duty "buffing" across the city, and a city-run warehouse doles out free paint to any citizen who asks for it. (30,000 gallons, enough to cover 6 million square feet of graffiti, have been given 41 away since 1986.) A legal offensive is also in the works. Daniel Ramos, a.k.a. Chaka, probably the most prolific writer in the history of graffiti (some 10,000 tags up and down the state), was busted by the LAPD and the City Attorney threw the proverbial book at him. He languished in jail for months and was recently assigned to a special reformatory "boot camp." Anti-graffiti forces, springing from well-to-do and generally conservative home-owners' associations nationwide, have lobbied for special anti-graffiti legislation—a ban on the sale of spraycans, for example.

"We're really deterring them," says LAPD spokesperson William Medina, who   42
coordinates a neighborhood cleanup effort in the Rampart *barrio* area of L.A. For the LAPD, even the elaborate pieces that have gone up at the various "yards" around town are considered illegal. "We view it as graffiti," says Medina. "The only things we don't consider illegal are [city-] organized and approved murals."

Community meetings focusing on graffiti typically draw standing-room-only   43
audiences. Responding to an increasingly vociferous public, Mayor Tom Bradley formed the Mayor's Committee for Graffiti Removal and Prevention. The chairman of the committee, Stuart Haines, is the owner of Textured Coatings of America, a profitable paint manufacturing company. "It's like a guy who works in a weapons manufacturing plant being named head of a task force to stop a war," said one supporter of graffiti art.

The adult response, then, has placed top priority on eradication and enforce-   44
ment of anti-vandalism statutes. Only a pittance has been funnelled into public mural programs, which gave youngsters the opportunity to refine their talents under the tutelage of established artists. "The real answer is to pass tougher laws to punish the graffiti artists who deface public property, along with the gang members who are identifying their turf," says Stuart Haines.

Among the adults searching for alternatives to this deadlock is Adolfo V. Nodal,   45
the general manager of the city's Cultural Affairs Department and a longtime supporter of public arts, via endeavors like the MacArthur Arts Project, which featured art by local writers on the park's amphitheater. "Arresting kids and abatement through paint-outs is not the only way to do it," says Nodal. "It has to be an issue of implementing cultural programs for kids. We've been fighting a losing battle on this issue."

"We haven't looked at *why* they're painting," says Mary Trotter of the Vernon   46
Central Merchants Association, which is sponsoring a graffiti art contest that offers a cash prize of $1,200, plus wall space donated by neighborhood businesses. "They want to communicate something to us, and we're not listening."

"Hollywood should understand," says independent filmmaker Gary Glaser, who   47
produced a documentary on the L.A. writing scene called *Bombing L.A.* "This is hype town Number One. The kids can't get on television, so they tag."

Beneath the visor of a baseball cap that barely contains his shock of bushy red hair,   48
the sea of parking lights is reflected in Wisk's glasses. It's about nine in the evening, and we are driving east on the Santa Monica Freeway.

One of the most famous taggers in town, Wisk is a founding member of WCA.   49
His simple but undeniably attractive tag consists of a butterfly-like *W.* He numbers every one of them, as would an artist producing a limited edition of serigraphs. The *W*s are visible as far west as Venice Beach, north to the San Fernando Valley, south

to Watts and east to Pomona. After two years of almost nightly "bombing" runs, Wisk broke the 2,000 mark this week.

Blowing bubbles and snapping his wad of chewing gum, Wisk directs me to exit the Santa Monica Freeway at Crenshaw Avenue, and we park near an overpass. He opens the door a crack and shakes each of his cans, pressing the nozzles a touch to make sure they're in working order.   50

"Ready?" asks Wisk. He pushes his glasses back up on his nose.   51

We walk, real cool and slow, across the overpass to a spot of fence already bent from previous bombing raids. We slow down, even walk in place until no more cars are passing by. After a glance left and right to make sure nobody's around, Wisk says, "Go!" and we hop over the fence.   52

Like soldiers on maneuvers, we run low alongside the freeway wall, Wisk shaking his can all the way. We zip past sooty ivy and sickly palm trees, the roar of traffic all around us. Wisk stops about two hundred yards down from the overpass, before a spot of wall clear of bushes and trees. "Stay low, dude! Look out for 5–0s and if you see one, yell out, 'Cops!'"   53

The can hisses as Wisk moves up and down, arcs around, outlining his throw-up in black. Then comes the fill-in, rapid back-and-forth motions with white or silver. *W*s number 2021, 2022, 2023 are up in a matter of minutes.   54

"Everybody takes the freeways," says Wisk, pausing before beginning *W* number 2024. "Everybody, *everybody* and their mother sees this! This is like the subways in New York, except you move past it instead of having it move past you."   55

Wisk, getting greedy and perhaps a bit reckless, risks a bust by going up with *W* number 2025. He's already covered fifty yards. Whatever aerosol mist doesn't make it onto the wall rises up in a cloud that is gilded by the amber street lamp above us. Wisk notices me looking at the sight. "I love it!" he exclaims, satisfaction sweeping over his freckled face.   56

Later, driving back down the freeway, westbound, Wisk tells me, "Look at that shit that we did the other night," pointing excitedly to his and a fellow WCA writer's tags. "Look! *W, W, W, W, J-A, J-A, J-A!* Look at all them *W*s lined up, bro'! Boom! Boom! Boom! Boom! Boom!"   57

"We were just kickin' it up there, drinking beer," says Skept, his freckled face and light green eyes showing the strain of the days since Prime was shot. His usual gregarious demeanor is subdued. "We were sitting down on the couch. Then, *chk, chk, BOOM! BOOM! BOOM!*"   58

Skept (short for "Skeptical"), a Japanese-American who grew up in a mostly Latino *barrio,* is another veteran of K2S—STN. Like Duke and Prime, he's been leading a double life for years now, although he's long since left the old 'hood and now lives in a comfortable downtown loft with his father, a well-known abstract expressionist. We walk into the ample, brightly lit studio. His father sits near the southernmost wall, smoking a pipe, poring over papers. Skept's room is at the northern end. We enter and he closes the door behind him, revealing a poster of the heavy metal group Iron Maiden.   59

He pops a Jungle Brothers rap tape into the player and brings out some photo albums. There's a piece by Prime, in his trademark color-patch style. And there's a photo of Geo standing before a piece, a shot taken not long before he died. He was   60 a good-looking, slightly overweight Latino kid with a bright, adolescent smile. "Lots of friends have passed away in the last couple of years," says Skept, staring at the photo.

Then he shows me his recent work, "psychedelic" paintings on small art boards, 61 pieces that "even my dad was surprised by." Multicolored circles, squares and bubbles appear to float in a primordial miasma. He plans on doing such a piece soon, up on a wall, perhaps here, downtown.

The question that is running through my mind as we kick back and talk about 62 writing is, Why did Skept have to go back to the neighborhood the night the shooting took place, knowing that there was a possibility of yet another drive-by killing?

Instead I ask, "You know what adults would tell you about all this, don't you?" 63

"'You shouldn't go, this and that.' My dad doesn't even know I was there when 64 they shot him. I haven't even told anybody in my family about Prime. I didn't want to hear it. I already know what they'll say."

Skept will sometimes ensconce himself in the studio, drawing for days on end. Or 65 he'll go out piecing at the yards. Then there'll be the urge to do a daring, illegal piece on the streets. Then he'll go back and "kick it" in the old gang neighborhood. "But the shooting," I remind him.

"It's happened so many times already, I'm getting used to it," he says, then pauses. 66 "But—I don't know why—this time it seems so different. Maybe because I was there, I was so close . . ."

"You'll go back even though you know this might happen again?" I ask. 67

"Probably." 68

A few days earlier, I had accompanied Skept, who was unshaven and had sleepless 69 circles under his eyes, on a writing excursion to the Belmont Tunnel. Several writers were out that day, but Skept wandered off by himself to an out-of-the-way spot in the shadow of the old trolleycar station. There, he did a quick throw-up. With a baby-blue outline and a dark gray fill-in, he wrote his crew's name. The fat, block-like letters seemed to collapse upon each other, as though plummeting through the air. In gold he wrote the names of Geo and Sine. He knelt before the piece in silence for several minutes.

Prime is sitting up in bed, flanked by two *cholos* in dark glasses. He offers his left 70 hand in greeting. The doctors, he says, have told him that he's doing all right, "so far." He's kind of worried about their emphasis on the "so far," but says he's already going stir-crazy. He wants to go home.

He reminisces about the writing binges of the early days, when he and Skept and 71 Geo would "walk from the Beverly Center Mall all the way downtown, tagging up all the way." They'd go all night sometimes, catching a wink wherever they could rather than go home. At dawn, they'd search for an apartment building with a swimming pool for a makeshift bath, then warm up at a local laundromat.

Prime stops suddenly. A grimace of pain crosses his face, and his right shoulder 72 twitches involuntarily. I ask him about his arm. "I don't know, ey. I don't know," he says, looking away.

On my way out of Prime's room, I run into Duke and Radio-Tron founder 73 Carmelo Alvarez, who continues to work closely with many of the K2S—STN writers. Duke stays with me in the hallway, leaning against the yellow wall under the bad fluorescent lights. He's working on a storefront for a neighborhood residents' association, he tells me. And he's recently been talking with Frank Romero, the famous Chicano artist. "I tripped out when he said that I could work with him on a project," says Duke, flashing a quick grin. For now, everything's "fresh."

I recall a photo Duke once showed me of Prime. It was taken on the day they worked together on a big piece near Belmont High, not far from where Prime was shot. The photo was taken looking down from the top of the wall, showing Prime frozen in mid-stroke—his right arm raised, a look of tremendous concentration on his face.   *74*

The piece they worked on that day is the one Duke is proudest of. He drew his "Dream Lady," with a soft, sensuous aqua face and windborne orange hair. Prime contributed a Cerebus-like character, K2S—STN's mascot, in baby blue, with touches of clover green and turquoise. The piece is long gone, but has been immortalized in Duke's photo album.   *75*

"If Prime comes out not being able to draw with his right hand, he'll do it with his left," Duke says with almost desperate conviction. "And if he comes out not being able to move his left hand, he'll do it with his feet."   *76*

It is difficult not to be impressed by Duke's determination. At the same time, I find myself doubting. Graffiti art is temporal, fragile. It has a lifespan of only a week or two before another writer goes over a piece, or the city buffs it out. How far can the kids really go with it? The New York gallery scene's fascination with street art only directly affected a few writers in the short time it lasted. And even if some do make it into the L.A. galleries, will their work lose its power in that context?   *77*

And what of the inner-city black hole that threatens to swallow all the colors and deny every escape route? One well-known Eastside writer was awarded a scholarship to a prestigious local art school, which he attended for three years. He's now doing time for murder. Art doesn't always save, but here's Duke before me, all enthusiasm and faith, and who's to say that he and Prime and Skept can't realize their dreams?   *78*

Later, Prime's visitors are walking out of County together, past the emergency entrance, where two paramedic trucks and a sheriff's patrol car are parked. The sun has just set and high, dark gray clouds streak across the sky, creating a dark canvas. Duke stops and stares. He has caught something we hadn't noticed: a small, baby-blue aperture in the gray.   *79*

"It's like a gateway to a new world," he says.   *80*

Working with the Text

1. In paragraph 21 Martinez quotes the graffiti artist Phoe as saying, "Writing is, like, a different community. . . . It's communication with other writers throughout the city." In what ways are the graffiti artists depicted in this article a community? Does graffiti writing seem to be more an expression of belonging or of alienation? What are the graffiti writers alienated from?

2. In paragraph 47 documentary filmmaker Gary Glaser is quoted as saying that graffiti in Los Angeles couldn't be more natural: "This is hype town Number One. The kids can't get on television, so they tag." What are the implications of Glaser's statement in terms of how individuals in the United States

derive a sense of importance and belonging? Do you agree with Glaser's assessment?

3. What is the relationship between graffiti and gangs or between graffiti and violence? To what extent is graffiti an alternative to violence? From the attitudes expressed in this article, can the attraction of writing graffiti be separated from its illegality and the lure of gangs and violence? Or can such art "save" in some cases as Martinez suggests?

4. What are your feelings about graffiti? How do you respond when you see it? Can you "read" most of the graffiti you see? If not, how does this fact affect your response? If you live in a place where graffiti is prevalent, do you even notice it most of the time?

5. The Internet offers several important sites on graffiti, the most extensive of which is ART CRIMES. Starting at the *Border Texts* Web site, look at some of the examples of graffiti from cities around the world contained there. How are these similar to or different from the graffiti discussed in "Going Up in L.A."? Look closely at one section and consider how the examples there express violence, anger, alienation, and specific political statements. Does graffiti writing look the same on the street as it does on the Web?

GRAFFITI: TUNNEL NOTES OF A NEW YORKER

LEONARD KRIEGEL

■ A life-long resident of New York City, Leonard Kriegel taught English for many years at City College of the City University of New York, a school known for its large percentage of immigrant students. He is the author of a study of the contemporary American urban university, an analysis of masculine images in modern society, a novel, and most recently, a collection of autobiographical essays, *Falling into Life*. The following essay originally appeared in the *American Scholar*, a publication of the Phi Beta Kappa Society. In it, Kriegel argues that the kind of graffiti one finds in urban environments today expresses a savage sense of alienation, "an urban statement whose ultimate end is nothing less than the destruction of urban life" and community.

When I was eight, I loved to run with my friends through the tunnel leading into Reservoir Oval in the North Central Bronx. The Oval occupied the site of a former city reservoir dredged by the WPA and then landscaped with playgrounds, wading pools, softball fields, a quarter-mile dirt track, and some of the finest tennis courts in the city—all ringed by attractive bush- and tree-lined walks that provided a natural shield for the sexual probings of early adolescence. Nothing else that bordered our neighborhood—not the wilds of Bronx Park or the chestnut trees of Van Cortlandt Park or the small camel-humped rock hill in

Mosholu Parkway down which we went belly-whopping on American Flyer sleds in winter—fed us so incontrovertible a sense that America's promise now included us as did the long green and gray sweep of Reservoir Oval.

We would run through that entrance tunnel like a pack of Hollywood Indians on the warpath, our whoops echoing off the walls until we emerged from its shadows into the lush green lawns and brick walks and playing fields. Our portion of the Bronx was an ethnically mixed stew of immigrant families and their children, many of whom had fled Manhattan's crowded Lower East Side tenements for the spacious, park-rich green borough where Jonas Bronck had followed his cow across the Harlem River three hundred years earlier. The Bronx was still the city's "new" borough in 1941. Sparsely settled until after World War I, our neighborhood contained typical New York working- and lower-middle-class families on the rise in an America emerging from the Depression.

We children had already been assimilated into the wider American world. All of us—Irish and Italian Catholic as well as Eastern European Jew—believed we could ride the dream of success to a singular destiny. We were not yet of an age where we could physically journey into that wider America the books we read and the movies we saw told us was ours for the taking. The Oval was where we played together. It was also where we sometimes fought each other over myths that grew increasingly foreign and more raggedly European with each passing day. (Not that we were unaware of our parents' cultural baggage: marriage between Italian and Irish Catholics was still considered "mixed" in 1941.)

Occasionally, I would chance the Oval alone, in search of more solitary adventure. A curious metamorphosis would envelop me at such times: the entrance tunnel seemed darker and more threatening, the shadows warning me to move cautiously past walls peppered with graffiti. Alone, I let loose no war whoops to echo through that emptiness. Instead, I picked my way carefully through that dark half-moon of enclosed space, as if the graffiti scrawled on its surface held the clue to my future. There was something menacing about words scrawled on walls. Like an archaeologist probing ruins, I might turn in terror at any moment and run back to the security of my apartment three blocks south of the Oval.

Most of the graffiti was of the "John loves Mary!" kind, no different from the scribbled notes we passed one another in the P.S. 80 school yard down the hill. But it was also on that tunnel's walls that I first read the rage and fury of those who stained the world with conspiratorial fantasies. As rage exploded like bullets, words burrowed into my consciousness. "Roosevelt Jew Bastard!" "Unite Unite / Keep America White!" "Father Coughlin Speaks Truth!" "Kill All Jews!" In the raw grasp of age-old hatreds, politics was plot and plot was history and that reality seemed as impregnable as it was inescapable.

Like adults, children learn to shape anger through the words they confront. The graffiti on that tunnel wall mobilized my rage, nurturing my need for vengeance in the midst of isolation. It wasn't simply the anti-Semitism I wanted vengeance upon; it was my own solitary passage through that entrance tunnel. As I moved through it alone, the tunnel was transformed into everything my budding sense of myself as embryonic American hated. Walking through it became an act of daring, for graffiti had converted its emptiness into a threat that could only be taken the way it was offered—a threat that was distinctly personal.

In no other part of that huge complex of fields and walks was graffiti in great evidence. Other than the occasional heart-linked initials carved into the green-painted slats of wooden benches, I remember nothing else defacing the Oval. One emerged from that tunnel and the graffiti disappeared—all of it, "John loves Mary!" as well as "Kill All Jews!" It was as if an unwritten compact had been silently agreed upon, allowing the tunnel leading to the Oval to be scrawled over (despite occasional whitewashing, the tunnel was dark and poorly lit) while the rest of that huge recreation complex remained free of the presence of graffiti. Running that tunnel alone was an act of purgation, rewarded when one was safely home with the illusion (and occasionally the reality) of ethnic harmony.

Other than that tunnel, the presence of graffiti was localized to a few alleys and [8] subway stations and public urinals in the New York I remember from the forties and fifties. Until the sixties, even chalk and paint adhered to the unwritten laws of proportion in neighborhoods like mine. Buildings had not yet been crusted over with curlicued shapes and exploding slashes, zigzagging to a visual anarchy that testified to a love of color and line overwhelmed by hatred of the idea that color and line do not dictate the needs of community. Even the anti-Semitic graffiti of that tunnel remains in my memory as less the product of hatred than an expression of the distance existing between groups struggling to claim a portion of the American past.

In an essay published in 1973, Norman Mailer labeled graffiti a "faith," a word [9] that struck me even back then as an odd use of language when applied to what a graffiti writer does. From the perspective of that eight-year-old child moving through that tunnel entrance, graffiti was the very antithesis of faith. It embodied a poetics of rage and hatred, a syntax in which anyone could claim the right, if he possessed the will, to impose his needs on others. But rage is not faith, as even an eight-year-old knew. It is simply rage.

In today's New York—and in today's London and Paris and Amsterdam and Los [10] Angeles—the spread of graffiti is as accurate a barometer of the decline of urban civility as anything else one can think of. Paradoxically, even as it spread, graffiti was hailed as one of the few successful attempts the voiceless in our nation's cities made to impose their presence on urban culture. If graffiti is now the most obvious form of visual pollution city landscapes are forced to endure (even more polluting than those paste-up false windows with flower pots that grow like urban ivy on the deserted apartment houses fronting the Major Deegan Parkway in the East Bronx), it has assumed for New Yorkers the shape and frame of this city's prospects. Where expectation is confused with coherence, those savage slashes on brick and sidewalk embody our idea of all that city life is and all that we can now expect it to be.

In books and photographic essays, graffiti is heralded as the art structuring the [11] real urban landscape that the poor confront in their daily lives. "Graffiti makes a statement!" is the rallying cry of those who defend its presence. True enough—even if one believes that the statement graffiti makes chokes the very idea of what a city can be. One can argue that it is not what the statement says but the style the statement employs that lends graffiti its insistent singularity. But the evidence of the streets insists that graffiti is an urban statement whose ultimate end is nothing less than the destruction of urban life. Regardless of whether it is considered art or public nuisance, graffiti denies the possibility of an urban community by insisting that individual style is a more natural right than the communitarian demands of city life.

Defenders of graffiti may insist that its importance lies in the voice it gives to   12
anger and that its triumph resides in the alternative it offers to rage. Perhaps so. But
anyone who walks through the streets of today's New York understands that the
price graffiti demands is an emotional exhaustion in which we find ourselves the
victims of that same rage and anger supposedly given voice—*vented* is today's fashionable word—by these indiscriminate slashes of color plastered against brick and
wall and doorway and telephone booth.

Contemporary graffiti is not particularly political—at least not in New York. On   13
those few times when one spots graffiti that does seek to embrace a message, the
politics seem prepubescent sloganeering. Few openly political sayings are lettered
onto these buildings and walls. Even the huge graffiti-like wall mural of a small
Trotskyite press that one sees driving north on West Street in lower Manhattan
speaks not of politics but of a peculiar Third World clubbiness more characteristic
of the early 1970s than of our time. Malcolm X, Che Guevara—originally offered as
a pantheon of Third World liberators, the faces over the years have taken on the likeness of the comic-book superheroes in whose image one suspects they were originally conceived and drawn. The future they appeal to is curiously apolitical, as if the
revolution they promise lies frozen in a nineteenth-century photograph in which
reality assumes the proportions of myth. One has the impression that these are
icons that have been hung on the wall for good luck, like a rabbit's foot or one of
those plastic Jesuses one sees hanging from the rear-view mirrors of battered old
Chevys.

The single most effective political graffito I have seen over the past few years was   14
not in New York. Last summer, as I drove through streets filled with the spacious
walled-in homes and immaculate concrete driveways of a wealthy Phoenix suburb,
on my way to visit Frank Lloyd Wright's Taliesin West, I came across "Save Our
Desert" slashed in large dripping red letters across a brown sun-drenched adobe
wall surrounding one of the huge sun palaces that root like cacti in the nouveau
riche wilds of Goldwater Country. Here was a graffito in which politics was central,
a gauntlet thrown at the feet of developers for whom the Arizona desert is mere
space to be acquired and used and disposed of for profit.

Perhaps because it is more traditional, political graffiti seems more understand-   15
able than these explosions of line and color and ectoplasmic scrawl now plastered
like dried mucus against New York's brick and concrete. "Save Our Desert!" may be
simplistic, but at least it expresses a desire to right a balance deemed unjust and un-
necessary. Political graffiti intrudes on privacy by voicing a specific protest. This
alone serves to distinguish it from the public stains New Yorkers now assume are as
natural as blades of grass growing between the cracks in a sidewalk.

In 1972, I lived with my family in London. What little graffiti I saw in an England   16
that had discovered the mod was still an expression of class and caste. It did not yet
encrust London like a multi-colored scab. I remember no initials or words slashed
across public monuments or statue pedestals.

On weekend afternoons, my wife and I and our two young sons would wander   17
from stall to stall at the Portobello Road flea market. On one of those Saturdays, as
my sons hopped from one seller hawking medals and military insignia to another, I
walked off alone and found myself staring up at huge white letters spray-painted

across a large gray Dickensian wall: "BOGSIDE OR CLYDESIDE," the letters read, "Support the Angry Side!"

A bitter strike was in progress at the Clyde River Ship Works in Scotland, while   18
the struggle between Catholic and Protestant in the Bogside of Derry had already turned as murderous and self-righteous as, invariably, religious wars do. As my sons searched for military treasures, I stood transfixed before that rage of identity shaped by men unwilling to suffer indignities without trying to right the balance and even the score.

In 1972, I still thought of myself as in good part a product of my social class. The   19
anger of Clydeside was easy enough for me to identify with. An allegiance to trade unionism—at times, a blind allegiance—was as much political religion as I could muster back then. But during the four months I had spent in London, I watched in bewilderment as the events in Northern Ireland were regurgitated on the nightly television news. The cool English accents of the BBC announcer served to make the Bogside more politically confusing than I could afford to acknowledge. I wanted a politics simple enough to fit the cut of ideology. Yet even after trips to Southampton to seek out dockworkers with whom I could discuss what was taking place in Ulster, I couldn't figure out which side I should be on: If anger and rage were the criteria, both sides seemed eminently worthy of support.

A few weeks later I, along with the rest of the world, would witness the murder of   20
Israeli athletes at the Munich Olympics. That was an easier religious war for me to understand, one that echoed and re-echoed with the tremors of the tunnel graffiti of my childhood. Birth and history told me very clearly which side I was on in the struggle between Arab and Jew. But between Ulster Protestant and Ulster Catholic, I knew nothing other than the boundaries of my ignorance. Not even that BBC voice calmly reciting the day's casualties made the struggle in Derry anything other than a free-fall of demands and counterdemands.

Why do these two images—the shadowy entrance tunnel to the playing fields of   21
my childhood and the gray Dickensian wall in London—spring from the sheath of memory when I think about graffiti today? And I think about graffiti a great deal. For to live in my New York and not think about graffiti is to make oneself either purposefully blind or oblivious. Why is it that I find both "Death for Christ Killers!" and "Support the Angry Side!" somehow preferable to the curlicued shapes and exploding stars and slashing initials slapped like overturned garbage cans at curbside against the walls and trucks, the steel gates and red brick, the subway entrances and superb nineteenth-century cast-iron architecture of a city that grows more and more fragile with each passing day? Why does today's New York graffiti seem even more ominous than that 1941 scrawl "Kill All Jews!"? And why does the current state of this city seem to me more accurately captured by these wordless dispatches from rootless souls than by all the statistics about street crime and drug abuse and white flight to the suburbs in the New York Times?

Until about five years ago, I used to go back to my old neighborhood in the Bronx.   22
Occasionally, I would drift through the decaying tunnel entrance to the Oval. The smells had grown more sour than when I was eight, and the faces of the children in the playground had grown darker. But those darker faces merely indicated that the ethnic successions that had been taking place in this city for the past hundred and fifty years were still taking place. Far more striking was how the graffiti had changed.

No longer did the words echo with pent-up hatreds or speak of adolescent romance. Instead, the tunnel walls, along with the playing fields and playgrounds, were crusted over with color and line. In a city seething with the raucous claims of victimization hurled against counter-victimization, few privileges were demanded by that graffiti. As if in some huge art gallery, the focus was on color, line, ubiquitous form and curlicued signal. Like an avalanche, line and color moved toward an ultimate disintegration that would not violate the demands of those who had created these graffiti waves. In this New York, art now rode even the artists, while the new beckoned to the bored Columbus in each American soul.

We live in a culture in which the cartoon explosions of the graffiti artist Basquiat are heralded as the work of a Renoir or a Van Gogh. An Andy Warhol toy, taken up and then discarded by the whims of fashion. Basquiat's death by a heroin overdose is transmogrified into a mirror image of city life. Like Van Gogh's ear, it is the artist's physical presence, not the work, on which we are expected to concentrate. Even as art rides the artists, artists are transformed into what our conception of what city life should be demands. 23

On the surface, style has never been in greater demand than in today's New York. From an art in which performance is defined as a nude body covered by chocolate and music is the sound of silence, the culture reverberates to the beat of the contemporary. Curlicues and initials and slashes against conventional surfaces scream to be noticed. Claim is splashed against counter-claim. It is not talent but defiance that is sold as a commodity. From doorway and mailbox, from truck and metal store guards, from telephone booth and statue pedestal, Kilroy is here, there, and everywhere. Only this Kilroy is no mere democratic signature. This Kilroy is not a name anchored to an idea of a country. This Kilroy stands before us in spasms of color, initialed explosions of red on white, black on red. And what, we ask as we listen to a boom box in some passing car in the street below, is more attractive than style in a city so intent on creating itself anew? 24

Over and over, voices insist that graffiti proves that behind the rage of urban poverty there remains an endurance of aspiration. Perhaps. But why should rage become so prevalent at a moment in history when style has been deemed so ubiquitous? That question speaks tellingly of the true politics of this "tough" city as it spins like a gyroscope out of control through our fashion-conscious age. Lured by myths celebrating their endemic toughness ("If you can make it here," Sinatra sings—and we New Yorkers echo him, even as we nervously glance over our shoulders to see how or what is coming up behind us—"you'll make it anywhere"), New Yorkers crave absolution through symbols: Bella Abzug's hats, Felix Rohatyn's suits, Al Sharpton's hairdo, the electric signs blinking through the cash-and-carry hustler's moment in Times Square, the graffiti scrawls on our streets. 25

The truth, of course, is that people in this city are anything but tough. New Yorkers endure conditions that would be unacceptable in most Third World cities. Even the city's millionaires live with a fatalism one might logically expect to find in illiterate Latin American peasants or Bosnian Muslims shunted from place to place to the horrible music of "ethnic cleansing." The real truth is that we New Yorkers more and more sound like people so used to being beaten over the head that our primary instinct is to hunker down and ride out any storm, burdened by the knowledge that another catastrophe is just around the corner. And so we try to turn a blind eye to 26 these graffiti initials jumbled together like alphabet soup, plastered against wall and kiosk, public telephone and public urinal, staining our aspirations and our lives.

In 1973, when he wrote "The Faith of Graffiti," Mailer was able to view those wall stains as an urban stamp of vitality, the shifting emblems of a New York underclass alive and vibrant with the tremor of its inability to rest. But Mailer should have known better. Mailer was, after all, raised in Brooklyn. And he must have known that, in this chameleon of a city, the new quickly becomes the old, the lived-with, the used-by. Lacking substance, the new grows boring. And we begin to remember the not-new with a nostalgia that breeds a breakdown of confidence in what it is we actually do see. How long can one love the idea of New York at the cost of the actual city's reality? Not a question to be asked lightly in the physical and intellectual squalor in which we New Yorkers live now. 27

How unusually clear New York seems in black-and-white newsreels from the forties and fifties. Not that the streets were so much cleaner than they are today (they were somewhat cleaner, but New Yorkers have always been slobs and garbage has long since been among the city's badges). Not that one longs for the kitsch of double-decker buses on Fifth Avenue. But how solid and enduring the stone buildings appear in black and white, how singularly they command our affection. Yes, empty paper cups were discarded in the streets back then, too, and traffic bottlenecked into impregnable jams. But where are those savage strokes of line and color demanding recognition of rage as actuality? Why are the walls quiet with the grain of brick and granite instead of explosive with the desecration of graffiti? Did no one in that New York belong to the angry side? Did no one see his function in life as spray-painting red and black and orange initials on any surface that had the temerity to remain ignorant of his singular presence? 28

To deny this city's painful decline over the past three decades is to deny the obvious. One can measure that decline through the spread of graffiti. The process began with the insistence that these mindless blotches and savage strokes embodied a legitimate, if admittedly different, sense of fashion, that they could be viewed—indeed, they had to be viewed—as a "natural" expression of the new and daring. This is the gist of the argument Mailer makes, and it is not an argument we can afford to ignore even today. We certainly could not afford to ignore it back in 1973, as we witnessed graffiti's spectacular rise as a New York growth industry. Only today the vision has rubbed down, like overwatered brick that soon chips and crumbles, and these savage slashes of color fill us with a weary disgust at their seeming omnipresence. An ocean of painted initials laps in growing waves against brick and concrete, even as we pretend it isn't there. 29

Like everything else in this city, graffiti demands an emotional investment from those who defend it. One can only vindicate these slashes and blobs of color because their presence is so overwhelming. What choice do we have but to demand that the world recognize the "art" in these urban voices? Anything else forces us to examine the consequences of what we have allowed through the intimidating fear of not being in fashion. Even as acceptance is demanded, graffiti continues to pound against the city, having grown as mechanical and fixed as the sound of the boom boxes in the streets below our windows. We label graffiti "real," we label it "authen- 30

tic," we label it "powerful." Like true pedants, we discuss the nuances of these different voices. We create graffiti martyrs from Keith Haring, dead of AIDS, and from
Basquiat, dead of a drug overdose. In their deaths, we tell ourselves, our city lives.
For their art is "urban." And urban counts. Urban must count. If not, why have we
permitted what has been done to this city we claim to love?

If the graffiti plastered first on subway cars and then on billboard and doorway   31
and brick truly constitutes an art form, then it is an art that seeks to rip out the root
idea of what supposedly created it—the idea that a specifically urban culture exists.
Defended as a creative act in which the city itself becomes the artist's canvas, the
paradox of graffiti is the extent to which its existence connotes an implicit hatred of
what a city is and what it can offer its citizens. At the core of graffiti's spread lurks
the dangerously romantic notion that the city is a place of such overwhelming evil
that it must be torn apart, savaged into its own death, its residents given a "voice" in
the irrational hope that in this way its more urbane voices will be stilled. Graffiti
slashes at the heart of New York, the heart of urbanity, by attacking the city's splendid nineteenth-century monuments of cast-iron architecture in the resurrected
Soho neighborhood of lower Manhattan as indifferently as it attacks the playful
1930s art deco apartment house façades that once made the now-dingy Grand Con-
course in the Bronx so singularly playful an example of urban aspiration.

New Yorkers stand like helpless mannequins before the onslaught. Graffiti does   32
not, after all, destroy lives. It is not like the scourge of crack, or the horrendous
spread of AIDS, or the rising tension in our neighborhoods between blacks and Jews
and between blacks and Asians. Graffiti is no more than a background for the
homeless who cage themselves in makeshift cardboard boxes or laundry baskets at
night or the crazies who walk the streets engaged in heated dialogues with Jesus or
Lenin or Mary Baker Eddy or George Steinbrenner or the dead yet still-celebrated
Basquiat. Graffiti is innocent, or so we continue to tell ourselves even in the face of
powerful evidence to the contrary. "No one ever died from graffiti!" a friend impa-
tiently snaps, as I point out a deserted bank on the northwest corner of Fourteenth
Street and Eighth Avenue, its once-attractive façade gouged and stabbed by slashes
of black spray paint. "There are more important problems in this city."

Of course, there *are* more important problems in this city. Yet none speak more   33
directly to the true state of affairs in this New York than the mushrooming graffiti in
our streets. And nothing traces the actual state of those streets better than the insistence graffiti makes that there are neither rules nor obligations for the survival of
urban hope and aspiration. The prospect of a voice for the voiceless illuminates
every dark alley in the New Yorker's mind, like the reflection of one of those stars already extinguished millions and millions of light years away. But is that to be all
those of us who claim to love this city are finally left with, these dead light gleanings
of one false revolution after another, beneath whose costly illusions—in the name of
fashion—we have bent this great and wounded metropolis out of time and out of
function and perhaps even out of its future?

Working with the Text

1. How does Kriegel describe his and his childhood friends' feelings of belonging in America? What is his background? How does he interpret the anti-

Semitic and other racist graffiti he remembers encountering during his child-hood in the Bronx? What does he mean when he suggests that it was "less the product of hatred than an expression of the distance existing between groups struggling to claim a portion of the American past"? How does graffiti reflect on a sense of belonging in urban spaces?

2. What distinctions does Kriegel make between racist or political graffiti and the kind of contemporary graffiti he criticizes: "curlicued shapes and explod-ing stars and slashing initials . . . these wordless dispatches from rootless souls" (¶ 21), "savage strokes of line and color demanding recognition of rage as actuality" (¶ 28)? He uses the word *savage* several times in relation to the new graffiti. What do you think of his characterization of graffiti writers as "savage"? Why does he think this kind of graffiti is different from statements like "Death to the Christ Killers," which he finds "somehow preferable"? Why do you think he finds the new graffiti so alienating?

3. In paragraph 11 Kriegel writes that "graffiti is an urban statement whose ultimate end is nothing less than the destruction of urban life. Regardless of whether it is considered art or public nuisance, graffiti denies the possibility of an urban community by insisting that individual style is a more natural right than the communitarian demands of city life." What assumptions is Kriegel making about the values that should prevail in urban communities? What do you think are the "communitarian demands" of the place where you live?

4. Compare Kriegel's assertions with what the graffiti writers say about them-selves in Ruben Martinez's "Going Up in L.A." How accurate are his charac-terizations? Do you think the two sides could ever find common ground? You might try writing a dialogue between, say, Prime from Martinez's article and Kriegel, exploring some areas of disagreement and possible agreement.

COLLECTIVE TRAUMA: LOSS OF COMMUNALITY

KAI ERIKSON

■ The work of Kai Erikson, a renowned sociologist and professor at Yale Uni-versity, has been widely applauded as among the most innovative and influential in his field. The following essay is a chapter from his groundbreaking 1976 book, *Everything in Its Path: Destruction of Community in the Buffalo Creek Disaster*. In the aftermath of a devastating flood that killed 125 people in a rural West Virginia community and left as many as 5,000 people homeless, Erikson painstakingly in-terviewed survivors to assess the impact of such a disaster on individuals and their sense of community. The result was called "not only a comprehensive study of the tragedy . . . but a document that may well serve as a model of what a so-ciological investigation can yield." Here Erikson suggests that within so tightly

knit a community as Buffalo Creek, where most residents spent their lives without ever leaving, the sense of self was so closely tied to a sense of belonging
to the community as a whole that loss of community meant loss of personal
identity.

The disaster stretched human nerves to their outer edge. Those of us who
did not experience it can never really comprehend the full horror of that
day, but we can at least appreciate why it should cause such misery and
why it should leave so deep a scar on the minds of those who lived through it. Our
imagination can reach across the gulf of personal experience and begin to re-create
those parts of the scene that touch the senses. Our eyes can almost see a burning
black wave lashing down the hollow and taking everything in its path. The ears can
almost hear a roar like thunder, pierced by screams and explosions and the crack of
breaking timbers. The nostrils can almost smell the searing stench of mine wastes
and the sour odor of smoke and death and decay. All this we can begin to picture because the mind is good at imagery.

But the people of Buffalo Creek suffered a good deal more that day, for they were
wrenched out of their communities, torn from the human surround in which they
had been so deeply enmeshed. Much of the drama drains away when we begin to
talk about such things, partly because the loss of communality seems a step removed from the vivid terror of the event itself and partly because the people of the
hollow, so richly articulate when describing the flood and their reaction to it, do not
really know how to express what their separation from the familiar tissues of home
has meant to them. The closeness of communal ties is experienced on Buffalo Creek
as a part of the natural order of things, and residents can no more describe that
presence than fish are aware of the water they swim in. It is just there, the envelope
in which they live, and it is taken entirely for granted. In this chapter, then, . . . I will
use quotations freely, but one must now listen even more carefully for the feelings
behind the words as well as registering the content of the words themselves.

I use the term "communality" here rather than "community" in order to underscore the point that people are not referring to particular village territories when
they lament the loss of community but to the network of relationships that make up
their general human surround. The persons who constitute the center of that network are usually called "neighbors," the word being used in its Biblical sense to identify those with whom one shares bonds of intimacy and a feeling of mutual concern.
The people of Buffalo Creek are "neighbor people," which is a local way of referring
to a style of relationship long familiar among social scientists. Toennies called it
"gemeinschaft," Cooley called it "primary," Durkheim called it "mechanical," Red-
field called it "folk," and every generation of social scientists since has found other
ways to express the same thought, one of the most recent being Herbert Gans's concept of "person orientation."

What is a neighbor? When you ask people on Buffalo Creek what the term
means, they try to remember that you come from the city and they illustrate their
answer with the kind of concrete detail that makes mountain speech so clear and
direct.

What's a neighbor? Well, when I went to my neighbor's house on Saturday or Sun- 5
day, if I wanted a cup of coffee I never waited until the lady of the house asked me. I just
went into the dish cabinet and got me a cup of coffee or a glass of juice just like it was
my own home. They come to my house, they done the same. See?

We was like one big family. Like when somebody was hurt, everybody was hurt. You 6
know. I guess it was because it was the same people all the time. I don't know how to ex-
plain it. It's a good feeling. It's more than friends. If someone was hurt, everybody
was concerned, everybody. If somebody lost a member of their family, they was always
there. Everybody was around bringing you something to eat, trying to help. It's a deeper
feeling.

Here, if you have a neighbor, it's somebody you know, it's somebody that maybe you 7
take them to the store. I mean, to us neighbors are people that we have. We just know
each other, that's all.

Neighbor? It means relationship. It means kin. It means friends you could depend 8
on. You never went to a neighbor with a complaint that they didn't listen to or some-
body didn't try to help you with. That's a neighbor. When you wanted a baby-sitter you
went next door and they'd baby-sit. Or you did something for them. They'd either need
something or we'd need something, you know. When you see somebody going down the
road, it's "Where are you going?" "To the store." "Well, bring me back such and such."

A neighbor, then, is someone you can relate to without pretense, a familiar and 9
reliable part of your everyday environment; a neighbor is someone you treat as if he
or she were a member of your immediate family. A good deal has been said in the
literature on Appalachia about the clannishness of mountain life, but on Buffalo
Creek, as in many coal camps, this sense of tribal attachment reaches beyond link-
ages of kin to include a wider circle, and the obligations one feels toward the people
within that circle are not unlike the obligations one normally feels toward one's own
family.

In good times, then, every person on Buffalo Creek looks out at the larger com- 10
munity from a fairly intimate neighborhood niche. If we were to devise a map representing the average person's social world, we would capture at least the main
contours by drawing a number of concentric circles radiating out from the individual center—the inner ring encompassing one's immediate family, the next ring encompassing one's closest neighbors, the third encompassing the familiar people
with whom one relates on a regular basis, and the fourth encompassing the other
people whom one recognizes as a part of the Buffalo Creek community even though
one does not really know them well. Beyond the outermost of those rings is the rest
of the world, the terrain populated by what an older generation called "foreigners."
Given the size of Buffalo Creek, it is obvious that the community contained people
who were relative strangers to one another. Yet there was a clear sense of kinship
linking even those relative strangers together—although, as we shall see shortly, that
sense of kinship turned out to depend to a greater degree than people realized on
the security of one's neighborhood niche.

Communality on Buffalo Creek can best be described as a state of mind shared   11
among a particular gathering of people, and this state of mind, by definition, does
not lend itself to sociological abstraction. It does not have a name or a cluster of distinguishing properties. It is a quiet set of understandings that become absorbed into
the atmosphere and are thus a part of the natural order. The remarks below, for example, are separate attempts by a husband and wife to explain the nature of those
"understandings."

Braeholm was more like a family. We had a sort of understanding. If someone was   12
away, then we sort of looked after each other's property. We didn't do a lot of visiting,
but we had a general understanding. If we cooked something, we would exchange
dishes. It was sort of a close-knit type of thing.

Before the disaster, the neighbors, we could look out and tell when one another   13
needed help or when one was sick or something was disturbing that person. We could
tell from the lights. If the lights was on late at night, we knew that something unusual
was going on and we would go over. Sometimes I'd come in from work on a cold day and
my neighbor would have a pot of soup for me. There was just things you wouldn't think
about. I would look forward to going to the post office. If my car wouldn't start, all
I'd have to do is call my neighbors and they would take me to work. If I was there by
myself or something, if my husband was out late, the neighbors would come over and
check if everything was okay. So it was just a rare thing. It was just a certain type of re-
lationship that you just knew from people growing up together and sharing the same
experiences.

And the key to that network of understandings was a constant readiness to look   14
after one's neighbors, or, rather, to know without being asked what needed to be
done.

If you had problems, you wouldn't even have to mention it. People would just know   15
what to do. They'd just pitch in and help. Everyone was concerned about everyone else.

I don't think there was a better place in the world to live. People was there when you   16
needed them. You got sick, they helped you. If you needed help of any kind, you got it.
You didn't even have to ask for it. Now I'm a person that didn't make friends easy. I
wasn't hard to get along with, I just didn't mix. But I knew everybody, and—Well, I just
don't know no way to explain it to you, to make you see it.

You'd just have to experience it, I guess, to really know. It was wonderful. Like when   17
my father died. My neighbors all came in and they cleaned my house, they washed my
clothes, they cooked. I didn't do nothing. They knew what to do. I mean it's just like
teamwork, you know. If one of the kids was sick, they'd drop every what they were
doing, take the kid to the hospital or sit up all night with him. It was just good. How did
they know when you needed help? I don't know how to explain it, really. The morning
my daddy died—he died in Logan—my aunt called me and told me on the phone at
about ten o'clock in the morning, and I had just got time to get off the phone and go set

on the bed and in come three of my neighbors. They knew it that quick. I don't know how. They just knew.

The difficulty is that when you invest so much of yourself in that kind of social arrangement you become absorbed by it, almost captive to it, and the larger collectivity around you becomes an extension of your own personality, an extension of your own flesh. This means that not only are you diminished as a person when that surrounding tissue is stripped away, but that you are no longer able to reclaim as your own the emotional resources you invested in it. To "be neighborly" is not a quality you can carry with you into a new situation like negotiable emotional currency; the old community was your niche in the classic ecological sense, and your ability to relate to that niche is not a skill easily transferred to another setting. This is true whether you move into another community, as was the case with the first speaker [who follows], or whether a new set of neighbors moves in around your old home, as was the case with the second.

Well, I have lost all my friends. The people I was raised up and lived with, they're scattered. I don't know where they're at. I've got to make new friends, and that's a hard thing to do. You don't make new friends and feel towards them like you did the people you lived with. See, I raised my family there. We moved there in '35 and stayed there. I knew everybody in the camp and practically everybody on Buffalo, as far as that is concerned. But down here, there ain't but a few people I know, and you don't feel secure around people you don't know.

Neighbors. We used to have our children at home, we didn't go to hospitals to have children. The one on this side of me, them two in back of me, this one in front of me—they all lived there and we all had our children together. Now I've got all new neighbors. I even asked my husband to put our home up for sale, and he said, "What do you think we're going to do? We're old people, we can't take to buy another home." And I said, "I don't care what you do with it. I'm not staying here. I can't tell you in words what's the matter." I said, "I don't care if we go to the moon, let's just get out of here. I'm just not interested enough anymore. You go out the back door here and there's a new neighbor. In front of me is a new neighbor and on the other side of me is a new neighbor. It's just not the same home that I've been living in for thirty-five years. It's just not the same to me."

A community of the sort we are talking about here derives from and depends on an almost perfect democracy of the spirit, where people are not only assumed to be equal in status but virtually identical in temperament and outlook. Classes of people may be differentiated for certain purposes—women from men, adults from children, whites from blacks, and so on—but individual persons are not distinguished from one another on the basis of rank, occupation, style of life, or even recreational habits. This is not hard to understand as a practical matter. The men all work at the same jobs; the women all command domestic territories of roughly the same original size and quality; the children all attend the same schools as an apprenticeship for the same futures; and everybody buys the same goods at the same stores from equivalent paychecks. Yet the leveling tendency goes even beyond that, for the people of the hollow, like the people of Appalachia generally, do not like to feel different from their fellows and tend to see status distinctions of any kind as fissures in the smooth surface of the community. Good fences may make good neighbors in places like New Hampshire, where relationships depend on cleanly marked parcels of individual space, but they are seen as lines of division in places like Buffalo Creek.

In most of the urban areas of America, each individual is seen as a separate being,   22
with careful boundaries drawn around the space he or she occupies as a discrete personage. Everyone is presumed to have an individual name, an individual mind, an individual voice, and, above all, an individual sense of self—so much so that persons found deficient in any of those qualities are urged to take some kind of remedial action such as undergoing psychotherapy, participating in a consciousness-raising group, or reading one of a hundred different manuals on self-actualization. This way of looking at things, however, has hardly any meaning at all in most of Appalachia. There, boundaries are drawn around whole groups of people, not around separate individuals with egos to protect and potentialities to realize; and a person's mental health is measured less by his capacity to express his inner self than by his capacity to submerge that self into a larger communal whole.

It was once fashionable in the social sciences generally to compare human com-   23
munities to living organisms. Scholars anxious to make the kind of distinction I am wrestling with now would argue that persons who belong to traditional communities relate to one another in much the same fashion as the cells of a body: they are dependent on one another for definition, they do not have any real function or identity apart from the contribution they make to the whole organization, and they suffer a form of death when separated from that larger tissue. Science may have gained something when this analogy was abandoned, but it may have lost something, too, for a community of the kind being discussed here *does* bear at least a figurative resemblance to an organism. In places like Buffalo Creek, the community in general can be described as the locus for activities that are normally regarded as the exclusive property of individuals. It is the *community* that cushions pain, the *community* that provides a context for intimacy, the *community* that represents morality and serves as the repository for old traditions.

Now one has to realize when talking like this that one is in danger of drifting off   24
into a realm of metaphor. Communities do not have hearts or sinews or ganglia; they do not suffer or rationalize or experience joy. But the analogy does help suggest that a cluster of people acting in concert and moving to the same collective rhythms can allocate their personal resources in such a way that the whole comes to have more humanity than its constituent parts. In effect, people put their own individual resources at the disposal of the group—placing them in the communal store, as it were—and then draw on that reserve supply for the demands of everyday life. And if the whole community more or less disappears, as happened on Buffalo Creek, people find that they cannot take advantage of the energies they once invested in the communal store. They find that they are almost empty of feeling, empty of affection, empty of confidence and assurance. It is as if the individual cells had supplied raw energy to the whole body but did not have the means to convert that energy back into a usable personal form once the body was no longer there to process it. When an elderly woman on Buffalo Creek said softly, "I just don't take no interest in

nothing like I used to, I don't have no feeling for nothing, I feel like I'm drained of life," she was reflecting a spirit still numbed by the disaster, but she was also reflecting a spirit unable to recover for its own use all the life it had signed over to the community.

I am going to propose, then, that most of the traumatic symptoms experienced   25
by the Buffalo Creek survivors are a reaction to the loss of communality as well as a reaction to the disaster itself, that the fear and apathy and demoralization one encounters along the entire length of the hollow are derived from the shock of being ripped out of a meaningful community setting as well as the shock of meeting that cruel black water. The line between the two is difficult to draw, as one survivor suggested:

We can't seem to put it all together. We try, but it just isn't there. It may be the shock   26
of the disaster or the aftermath of it all. I don't know. It's hard to separate the two. . . .

LOSS OF CONNECTION

It would be stretching a point to imply that the neighborhoods strung out along   27
Buffalo Creek were secure nests in which people had found a full measure of satisfaction and warmth, but it is wholly reasonable to insist that those neighborhoods were like the air people breathed—sometimes harsh, sometimes chilly, but always a basic fact of life. For better or worse, the people of the hollow were enmeshed in the fabric of their community; they drew their being from it. When that fabric was torn away by the disaster, people found themselves exposed and alone, suddenly dependent on their own personal resources.

And the cruel fact of the matter is that many survivors, when left to their own   28
mettle, proved to have meager resources, not because they lacked the heart or the competence, certainly, but because they had always put their abilities in the service of the larger community and did not know how to recall them for their own individual purposes. A good part of their personal strength turned out to be the reflected strength of the collectivity—on loan from the communal store—and they discovered that they were not very good at making decisions, not very good at getting along with others, not very good at maintaining themselves as separate persons in the absence of neighborly support.

Words like "lonely" and "lonesome" appear again and again in local conversations.   29

I can't get used to the way it is. It is very lonesome and sad. I'm disgusted. I'm mov-   30
ing out of this valley.

A lot has changed. Nothing is the same. It is just a big lonesome hollow to me, and I   31
hope I don't ever have to go back up there.

People are "lonely" in the sense that old and trusted neighbors have moved away,   32
leaving them isolated; but the word "lonesome" means something else as well. The people of the hollow are lone some-ones, left to themselves, out of touch even with those they see every day. Despite the obvious fact that most of them are surrounded

by other people, they feel as if they have been cast on a distant beach, drenched and bruised and frightened beyond measure, but suffering mainly from the feeling that they are in a land of strangers, with no one to talk to about the past, no one to share what is left of the future, and no one from whom to draw a sense of who they are. One elderly woman who moved several miles from Buffalo Creek into a nearby town crowded with people has already been quoted: "It is like being all alone in the middle of a desert." And a man of about the same age who continued to live in his damaged home after the flood put it:

Well, there is a difference in my condition. Like somebody being in a strange world 33
with nobody around. You don't know nobody. You walk the floor or look for somebody
you know to talk to, and you don't have anybody.

Many survivors fear that they are beginning to suffer the kind of disorientation 34
and even madness that can come from prolonged stretches of isolation.

I just stay mad. Sometimes I think they have brighter people in the nut house than I 35
am. I haven't had a real good night's sleep in nine months. Sometimes I wake up and
have a big fear inside of me. It feels like something has chased me for miles. I feel numb,
my heart feels like it is jumping out of me. My mind is just a blank.

One result of this fear is that people tend to draw farther and farther into them- 36
selves and to become even more isolated. This is the behavior of wounded animals that crawl off to nurse their hurts. It is also the behavior of people who string rough coils of barbed wire around their lonely outposts because they feel they have nothing to offer those who draw near.

I don't know. I'm a different person since the disaster. People get on my nerves. They 37
irritate me. People that I always liked prior to the flood, I've alienated myself from them
now. I like to be in seclusion. I seldom have a civil word for people now. I'm rather sar
castic and sometimes I'm a bit too smart. It's mostly because I don't want to fool with
anyone.

I took nervous fits all the time. I went crazy. I got real upset and started shaking all 38
over, and I would just forget about everybody. I couldn't remember nobody. I didn't
want nobody around me. I didn't want nobody to speak to me or even to look at me. I
wanted nobody even ten miles around me to call my name, I got like that. I just wanted
to hit them and make them leave me alone.

Seems like everything in you just curls up in knots and you want to explode. I've al 39
ways been an easygoing man all my life and good to everybody. But here lately I'm as ill
as a copperhead. I'm just ready to explode on anybody right there.

Well, I can't hold a conversation like I once could, I can't give people a good word. I 40
was always a quiet-termed man, you know, but I could always hold a conversation with
any man I met. But I ain't been able to do that since this thing has happened. I'm just
a different man. I don't have the same attitude towards people that I had. It used to be

that I cared for all people, but anymore I just keep myself alive. That's the only thing I study about.

So the lonesomeness increases and is reinforced. People have heavy loads of grief   41
to deal with, strong feelings of inadequacy to overcome, blighted lives to restore, and
they must do all this without very much in the way of personal self-confidence.
Solving problems and making decisions, those are the hard parts.

Yes, I think the whole society of Buffalo Creek has changed. The people are more de-   42
pressed and despondent. Uncertainty seems to rule their lives. They aren't sure of how
to make decisions. If they make a decision, they aren't sure they have done the right
thing. My parents can't decide whether they want to move somewhere else, whether
they want to build on their lot. They don't know what to do. They don't know what is
going to happen. And I know my in-laws have already purchased one house and sold it
because they didn't like it. They are in the process of buying another, which they aren't
sure they want to buy. That's the type of thing. People don't know where to go.

Well, I'm disorganized. It's like I lost my life and I've never been able to find it again.   43
That's the way I feel. I want to find it. I try to find it, but I don't know how. In a way, I
gave my life up in the flood, and it's like I'm not repented. Since then, everything has
been disorganized. I can't organize anything anymore. If I pound a nail, I'll scar myself
all up. Anything I do, I do it wrong. I wanted to get away from people, so I thought I'll
get me some animals or something to raise. So I got me some dogs to take care of and
chickens to take care of and the damned dogs killed my chickens. It's all simple, but I
can't seem to solve the problems. I mean there are so many problems I've got to look at
and try to solve, but I can't seem to solve any of them. I used not to make mistakes in de-
cisions, and I do today on about everything. . . .

One result of all this is that the community, what remains of it, seems to have lost   44
its most significant quality—the power it generated in people to care for one
another in times of need, to console one another in times of distress, to protect one
another in times of danger. Looking back, it does seem that the general community
was stronger than the sum of its parts. When the people of the hollow were sheltered
together in the embrace of a secure community, they were capable of extraordinary
acts of generosity; but when they tried to relate to one another as individuals, separate entities, they found that they could no longer mobilize whatever resources are
required for caring and nurturing. This story is certainly not a new one. Daniel
Defoe wrote of the London plague:

> Indeed the distress of the people at this seafaring end of the town was very
> deplorable, and deserved the greatest commiseration: but alas! this was a time
> when every one's private safety lay so near them, that they had no room to pity
> the distresses of others; for every one had death, as it were, at his door, and
> many even in their families, and knew not what to do, or whither to fly. . . . It
> is not indeed to be wondered at; for the danger of immediate death to our-
> selves took away all bowels of love, all concern for one another.

And that is what happened on Buffalo Creek—a loss of concern, a loss of human   45
trust. "It seems like the caring part of our lives is over," one elderly woman said, and

this thought was echoed over and over again by persons of all ages. The following speakers are, in order, a teen-age boy, a woman in her middle years, and a man in his seventies.

It used to be that everyone knew everyone. When you were hitchhiking, you just put out your thumb and the first car along would pick you up. But it's not like that now. They just don't care about you now. They got problems of their own, I guess.   46

The changes I see are in the people. They seem to be so indifferent toward their fellow man. I guess it's because they had to watch a whole lifetime go down the drain.   47

I'm getting old, too, and I can't get no help. Nobody'll help you do nothing. You have to pay somebody, and they'll come and start a project for you, but then they'll walk off and leave you. It's just too much.   48

Behind this inability to care is a wholly new emotional tone on the creek—a distrust even of old neighbors, a fear, in fact, of those very persons on whom one once staked one's life. A disaster like the one that visited Buffalo Creek makes everything in the world seem unreliable, even other survivors, and that is a very fragile base on which to build a new community.   49

I've just learned that you don't trust nobody. I just feel that way. You don't put no confidence in nobody. You believe nothing you're told. I don't know, you could have come along before the flood and told me you was going to give me the moon, and I'd have believed you.   50

That's it. Nobody trusts anybody anymore. You know, when we moved back home I was so scared I went out and bought a pistol. I don't know whether it was the place or the house or the people or what I was so scared of. And I'm still scared. I don't know what of, either. Why, my husband and I used to go to bed at night and leave our front door open, but now, of a day, those doors are locked. I'm scared to death.   51

This emptiness of concern, although he did not say so directly, may have been what a young miner had in mind when he said: 52

Well, it seems like everything just don't go right no more. There's a part of you gone and you can't find it. You don't know what part it is. It's just a part that's gone.   53

Working with the Text

1. What are the characteristics of *communality,* according to Erikson? How do the quotations from the people of Buffalo Creek help define *communality*? Have you ever been part of a "network of relationships" like this, sharing "bonds of intimacy and a feeling of mutual concern"? How do you think such communities develop?

www 2. Explore some of the links to Buffalo Creek and Appalachia on the *Border Texts* Web site. How have matters changed since 1972? Is the physical environment the same? Is the cultural environment the same?

3. In paragraph 21 Erikson discusses the role of "democracy" and the role of "leveling" in maintaining the kind of community he describes. Must all communities be based on relative equality and similarity? Can a community be built on diversity, difference, or inequality in status? How would you describe such a community, and how would it differ from the community Erikson describes? How, for example, would individual members of such a community respond if a disaster of some sort essentially destroyed the community?

4. In paragraph 22 Erikson draws a distinction between most of urban America, where "each individual is seen as a separate being" with "an individual sense of self," and Appalachian communities, where "boundaries are drawn around whole groups of people." What seems to happen when the people of Buffalo Creek lose their community and have only their individuality to fall back on? Do you think the beneficial aspects of such communities outweigh the apparent loss of individuality?

5. Based on your own experiences and on your reading in this chapter, how would you define a community? Would you say that you live in a community now? What are the common concerns of your community? What are the differences within your community? What gives it a sense of identity as a *community*?

THE LAST BEST PLACE: HOW HARDSHIP AND LIMITS BUILD COMMUNITY

DANIEL KEMMIS

■ Born in Fairview, Montana, Daniel Kemmis has spent most of his life in the state, leaving only to attend law school. A long-term Montana state representative, Kemmis is now the Democratic mayor of the city of Missoula. His books include *Community and the Politics of Place* (1990) and *The Good City and the Good Life* (1995). In the following selection, which was originally delivered as a speech, Kemmis ponders how we will define the idea of belonging to a "community" in the United States in the future. He thinks the definition will be strongly influenced by whether or not we can agree on shared goals concerning the rights of individual property owners versus the right of the government to serve what it considers the interests of the citizenry as a whole.

While the spirit of democracy sweeps eastward across Europe, over the Urals, whistling through the cracks in the Great Wall, America stands bemused, with no hint of any awareness, at least in official policy, of what all this might mean. Schiller's words and Beethoven's music resound in Berlin and will again, I believe, in Beijing. But in Boston or Boise a self-satisfied smugness resembling a hypnotic slumber holds the world spirit at bay.

Watching all of this, I can't help but recall certain words of Hegel, whose articulation of the idea of a spirit of history seems indispensable to capturing what is happening to the world. In 1820 Hegel set out to write his *Philosophy of History,* seeking to identify those forces that had made and would make real human history. Hegel paused for a moment at the starting gate to dispose of one nagging question, namely whether America had any prospect of contributing anything worthwhile to the history of human civilization. His answer, delivered without hesitation, was "no." His reason speaks still to America, and especially to the American West.

In a nutshell, Hegel predicted that America would not begin to contribute to civilization until it had confronted its own limits. Specifically, he argued that the safety valve of the frontier had prevented and would continue to prevent the development of a truly civil society. In making his case, Hegel took a position diametrically the opposite of Jefferson's. Jefferson had argued that civic culture was essentially rooted in agriculture and threatened by the growth of cities. He therefore assigned to the Western frontier a crucial and at the same time foredoomed role, which he repeated over and over in a standard Jeffersonian formula that went like this: Civic culture would remain strong in America as long as agriculture expanded faster than cities grew, which would happen as long as there was "vacant" Western land into which agriculture could expand. That this pattern could not recur indefinitely—that there had to be an end, sometime, to the filling in of what white Americans called vacant land—was a reality that Jefferson chose to suppress. In doing so, he contributed very substantially to the Myth of the West—specifically, to the myth that it was somehow a place without limits.

Hegel, as I have said, argued that civic culture, far from depending on the existence of the frontier, could only be achieved once the frontier was closed. More specifically, he turned Jefferson on his head by assuming that civic culture was an essentially urban phenomenon—something that really only occurred when significant numbers of people were forced to stop farming and to gather in cities. He agreed with Jefferson that the Western frontier allowed agriculture to outpace urbanization. His conclusion was simply the exact opposite of Jefferson's; he wrote that until Americans began facing each other in cities, they would not become a truly civil society and would not make a substantial contribution to the history of civilization.

Now, one hundred years after the 1890 census, which led the Census Bureau and then Frederick Jackson Turner to declare the frontier closed, we stand, here in the West, at a cross-wiring of historical currents that almost forces us to ask who we are and where we are going. We mark the centennial of the closing of the frontier just as world history turns Karl Marx on his head, which presumably might mean that Hegel has again landed on his feet. If Hegel were here at this conference, along with Thomas Jefferson, what would he say now about the West and about the possibility of its contributing to the history of civilization?

I'm going to use the challenge of this occasion to propose an answer to that question. I believe the world spirit is alive in Western valleys and to the leeward side of Western cutbanks where people claimed by this landscape have gathered to carry out the business of living well in hard country. I believe that there is, native to this soil, a politics of truly human proportions. It is a politics that we have not yet been bold enough to propose to ourselves. But the hour of its being proposed is drawing near. When that proposition is articulated in a genuinely Western voice, the West will respond, and its response will make its mark on the course of history.

Now, predictions like these deserve to be subjected to a variety of tests, the chief one being, of course, the test of time. Beyond that, anyone making such predictions might be asked to warrant in some way his or her standing to make predictions. In America, we can always make the grand claim of citizenship; we can remind our listeners that it is, after all, a free country, and I can predict anything I want to. Since I hope to deal with a more meaningful form of citizenship, I had better pass up that way of backing my claim. Others can warrant predictions by their training in the discipline of history, but while I deeply admire the discipline, I am certainly not trained in it. It is, rather, as a politician that I make my predictions about the near future of the West. And I think that is fitting enough, since my predictions are about the political future of the region.

I have long believed that places select people. Portland selects people who like   8
rain. Having grown up in Montana in a pioneer family that settled four generations ago in eastern Montana, I have observed over the years how frequently recurring the pattern of my own ancestors was in the settlement of the high plains of the state. My great-grandparents tried Oregon in the early 1880s, but the rain and the over-crowding finally drove them away, and they moved east, back across the Rockies, to the open country that could be cursed in an almost infinite variety of ways but could never be accused of being too wet. Over time, the place of my upbringing came to be peopled by folks whose words were as sparse as rain and whose humor was as dry as the hills out of which they eked a living.

The shaping of a people by the land they inhabit takes time, and in America it has   9
taken longer, simply because we have never been quite sure that we were here to stay. Wendell Berry begins his book *The Unsettling of America* by observing that Americans have never quite intended to be where they were—that they have always thought more in terms of where they would go, rather than of where they actually were. But Berry also identifies a second strain in the pattern of settlement—what he calls a tendency to stay put, to say, "No further—this is the place." One peculiarity of the settlement of the West is that it attracted—it selected—people who were more given than others to escape settlement. Only they would be willing to put up with the harshness, the inhospitality of the land, which grew more inhospitable the nearer they came to inhabiting the last of the frontier.

So the West drew to itself more than its share of unsettlers, of people whose es-   10
sential relation to place was the denial of place. And yet the places that they came to, being the last place to go, finally took hold of them, drew them down into their flinty soil, rooted them, claimed them, shaped them the way they shaped sagebrush. Over the generations, these people increasingly came to recognize themselves and to recognize their neighbors in the forms the land produced. And the selection process did not stop at some point; it goes on still. People still are drawn here not just in spite of but because of the hardness of the land.

Gradually, a culture grew out of the land, a group of storytellers and imagemak-   11
ers capable of holding this people up to itself. In Montana we relied on people like Joseph Kinsey Howard and K. Ross Toole to show us who we were, and in each locality there were similar voices. But there have been regional voices as well, not least that of Wallace Stegner, and now a new generation including voices like Bill Kittredge's. Bill and Annick Smith have proven, dramatically, how deep and powerful the common culture of place is by producing for Montana's centennial an exceptional and exceptionally popular collection of voices entitled *The Last Best Place.*

Let me touch now for just a moment on democracy—about what, at least from   12
the perspective of a practicing politician, democracy is or might be. There is an unsettling premonition, as we watch East Berliners pouring through the breached wall
to go shopping in West Berlin, that democracy may in the end not reach very far beyond some notion of equal access to all good things, especially blue jeans and
cheeseburgers. As a politician, I have had my fair share of exposure to the behavior,
and the fundamental insatiability, of the citizen as consumer. I am convinced that
democracy is steadily diminished, just as the earth's capital is steadily diminished, by
this version of democracy. It is a democracy that cannot endure, and all true democrats must warn against its dangers.

In the age of fast food and pervasive fingertip convenience, we have come to be-   13
lieve that democracy is a birthright that is as easy to practice as a precooked
microwave dinner is to heat and serve. But it has never been so, and it will not be so
for the coming generation of world democrats. Here, at least, Frederick Jackson
Turner still speaks in a voice of Jeffersonian democracy to which we need to attend
if we are to understand what makes democracy possible. Turner speaks of how the
frontier created democrats; he writes that the rigors of the frontier instilled (and I
would argue selected for) what Turner called a "competency"—a capacity to get
done what needed doing—which translated into a truly democratic confidence.
Hard country breeds capable people—capable, among other things, of genuine
democracy.

But let's take a little closer look at this competence. It is, has always been, and   14
must necessarily be the competence, not simply of individuals, but of a *demos,* of a
people. To have this kind of competence, a people must be bound together in ways
that enable them to work together. What the project of inhabiting hard country
does, above all, is to create these bonds. And when I speak of bonds here, I do not
mean to evoke anything particularly soft or mushy. These are practical bonds, although they do often lead to a kind of affection among those so bonded. But they
are in the first instance practical. They are the kinds of bonds that made of barn-
building and similar acts of cooperation something that must be understood as a
culture. It is a culture bred of hard places, nurtured by the practice of inhabiting
those places.

I want to draw attention to two words I have just used. The first is "practice" (and   15
its derivative "practical"). The second is "inhabitation." These words are
rooted—quite literally rooted—in the same quite literal soil. Inhabitation depends
upon habits; to inhabit is to dwell in a place in an habituated way. To do this requires
practice. This practice revolves around certain practical necessities of living in hard
country, necessities like a good barn. But to say a "good barn" is not to speak lightly,
for not just any barn will do, and this is true of [a] great range of such practical necessities. What was done must be done well or it would not survive—it would not
enable survival. Thus, the practices that lie at the root of all true inhabitation—especially of the inhabitation of hard country—are always practices that carry within
themselves demanding standards of excellence.

It is these standards of excellence, arising out of the soil itself, bodied forth in cer-   16
tain habituated and deeply shared patterns of behavior—it is these lived standards
of excellence that alone give meaning to the concept of "value." Over the past decade
or so, more and more people have engaged in a vague recognition of the fact that

"values" are somehow an important political factor. This has been a rather astonishing realization for liberals, instructed as we all have been in the liberal dogma that values are private concerns, and no business of the state. But as politics has increasingly become a game of "values, values, who's got the values?" even liberals have had to pay lip service to this new political icon.

But we have not yet understood that values are not something that simply come out of a black box in the individual soul, as the liberal dogma would have it, or from a deep voice on a mountaintop, as the fundamentalists think. What makes values shared and what makes them politically powerful is that they arise out of the challenge of living well together in hard country. When people do that long enough to develop a pattern of shared values, those values acquire a political potency. 17

It is here that the West has the capacity to contribute something deep and important and lasting to the history of politics and civilization. Simply because we have for so many generations worked on the project of living together in hard country, we have, although we don't recognize it, developed among ourselves certain patterns of behavior, which amount to shared values. The question is whether we will recognize this Western fact of life. The question is whether those of us who call ourselves liberals and those of us who call ourselves conservatives, all of whom are inhabitants of the West, can begin to turn to each other and begin to recognize what it is we have built together in terms of shared patterns of inhabitation and therefore of shared values. That is the challenge of the West. If we can begin to understand how we have been shaped by this country, shaped in similar ways, not so that we think alike all the time, not so that we believe alike, but so that we in fact have developed some shared values that give us the capacity to do difficult and important work together, then on this basis we can begin to contribute to democracy and to the history of civilization. 18

I say this as a politician who is willing to bet his career on the fact that this is a possibility. I am absolutely convinced that people will respond to being appealed to as inhabitants of a common place. They are willing to respond to anyone who will speak to their weariness with the kind of deadlock that our politics all too often creates. They will respond to a politics that speaks directly to their deep desire to be respected and to be treated as people—people who are capable of treating other people with respect. They will respond to a politics that speaks to their commonly shaped patterns of doing good work, to a politics that says to people on the right and on the left, "You are one people; you understand each other better than you think you do and you are capable of treating each other as if you do understand each other." And finally, they will respond to a politics that addresses their sense of what a good city or a good community might be, and how we would have to treat each other if we were going to go about the task of creating it. 19

It is said of Athens that in spite of its deep social divisions, it sustained its experiment in democracy and developed an outstanding culture because, in the end, each of the contestants in each divisive issue cared more about Athens than they cared about winning. I am convinced that in communities across the West, a majority of the people care more about their communities than they care about winning. But they have not been given a politics that encourages them to behave in that way. They have been given a politics that only encourages them to care about winning. 20

Are we capable of real politics in the West? I believe we are if we are willing to face 21 ourselves and our neighbors in a way that we have never done. We need to be willing in the first instance to face the implications of our historical unwillingness to face ourselves. Jefferson, democrat that he was, believer that he was in the idea that democracy could only exist when it was practiced on a small scale, was yet willing through the Louisiana Purchase to engage in the building of an empire. He did that because in the long run he believed that democracy could only survive if it was rooted on the farm and that it could be rooted on the farm only if agriculture could expand endlessly. So he bought into an empire, and our ancestors bought into an empire, and we, by inheritance, bought into an empire. Part of the reason for this is because we, like Jefferson, have been unwilling to image the possibility of a good city. Jefferson could not image a city being good. All too often, I think, we are guilty of the same way of thinking. Robinson Jeffers, in his poem "Shine Perishing Republic," talks about the republic "heavily thickening into empire," and he ends the poem by writing:

> But for the children, I would have them keep their distance
>   from the thickening center; corruption
> Never has been compulsory, when the cities lie at the
>   monster's feet, there are left the mountains.

That has been too much the Western attitude. We believed—we still believe—that we can somehow escape ourselves by slipping into the mountains, avoiding the hard task of facing up to ourselves in cities. Our mistake has always been that we have let empire shape our cities, rather than letting cities shape themselves and, above all, demanding of people that they shape their cities. 22

But the complicity goes beyond that. Once Thomas Jefferson bought the Louisiana Purchase, we had no choice but to buy both the military and the bureaucratic superstructure that went with it. We can take the attitude of saying all of that has been forced on the West. Or we can say that we have been complicit in it and that we have the capacity to do something about it. The way we will do something about it is to claim our homeland—to say this is our home, and to be able to say "our" and mean it, not only of the people that think and dress and behave like us, but of the other inhabitants of the region who are equally rooted here. When the West is ready to do that, then it will be ready for a real politics of inhabitation. 23

I will make one final prediction: that when that time comes, we will understand that, like every other region of the country, we are going to have to be in control of our homeland. That means that 90 percent of it can't be owned someplace else. The imperial presence would have to be removed from the ownership of Western lands. The West will not be ready for its own politics until it is ready to claim its own land. The real test of that will be whether we ever understand that the U.S. Senate was created in order that land-dominated regions like the West might assert their own land-based ways of life. When the time comes, when we are ready to develop a history and politics of the West, we will begin to elect a cadre of U.S. senators who will go to Washington to assert sovereignty over this country that we inhabit. Will we do it? Are we serious? Or are we just playing games? 24

In 1636 John Winthrop, soon to become governor of the Massachusetts Bay Colony, sailed with a shipload of Pilgrims from England toward the land to the west. As they sailed, he prepared for his shipmates a sermon on how they should expect 25 to go about the task of inhabiting the fiercely inhospitable land that they hoped to make their home. He knew how hard it would be. And he knew how, out of that hardship, they might create what he called "the city on a hill." This is what he said to them: "We must delight in each other. We must labor together, suffer together, rejoice and mourn together, keeping always before our eyes our condition as members of one body."

In our time, Wendell Berry, in a poem called "Work Song," sought to capture   26
once again the essence of the enterprise of winning a good living from a hard piece of land. "This is no paradisal dream," he wrote. But in a land-rooted voice of hope that is the true voice of the West, he concluded, "Its hardship is its possibility."

Working with the Text

1. How does Kemmis describe the American West as a place? He refers to the "myth of the West as being a place without limits." How does his discussion of the American West differ from that myth? What do you think accounts for the difference? He cites the philosopher Hegel who said that America could never contribute to civilization unless it confronted its own limits. How might that notion apply to the concept of a community? According to Kemmis, could you have a community in a place without limits? Do you think a sense of limits is traditionally a part of an American self-identity? Do you think that is changing?

2. In his essay Kemmis puts a number of key concepts together: words like *place, community, citizenship, democracy,* and *values.* How does he tie these various concepts together? What do democracy, citizenship, and a sense of community have to do with place? What are at least two different meanings of *citizenship* and *democracy* that he describes or implies?

3. Early in the essay, Kemmis says that he believes environments have a way of "selecting" people rather than the other way around. Do you agree with that statement? Are there circumstances when that notion might be true?

4. In paragraph 17 Kemmis says: "What makes values shared and what makes them politically powerful is that they arise out of the challenge of living well together in hard country. When people do that long enough to develop a pattern of shared values, those values acquire a political potency." Naturally, he is speaking here of the American West. Do you think that he could make the same argument for an urban environment? That is, if the "hard country" were a city, would you agree that people would develop shared values arising from the challenge of "living well" in that environment?

5. Think about Kemmis's essay in relation to some of the images in the Image Portfolio, in particular John Gast's *American Progress.* How does this image speak to a perspective about limits in America? How do you reconcile this with Kemmis's ideas? Are there other communities built on limits in America?

Thinking and Writing: *Critical Questions Revisited*

1. A Sense of Belonging

What feels like "home" to you? What defines your home? Is it your family? Is it familiarity with the environment? Are there places that feel like home to you that are not necessarily your home? What makes a new environment feel like home? How does the feeling of home extend to one's country or nation? Think about the essays in this chapter by writers such as Bharati Mukherjee and Victor Hernandez Cruz. How does one feel at home in a new country? Can one feel at home in more than one country? Have you ever travelled or lived in another country? (Or perhaps the United States is your second country.) What made it feel like home? What made it feel different from home?

2. The Creation of Community

How would you define a community? Think about and describe a community that you know well. What makes it a community? Why do its members feel a part of that community? What holds it together—shared values, background, goals? Is it shared physical space? Is the community held together in any way by "limits," as Daniel Kemmis discusses? Or, as Kai Erikson suggests, is it bound together by "a network of relationships" and "bonds of intimacy and a feeling of mutual concern"? Or is it something else? Do communities have to be defined *against* something? Or can they be defined in and of themselves? Are there different kinds of communities?

3. Place and Community

A number of this chapter's selections address the relationship between place or environment and the shaping of a sense of community. The nature of this relationship varies widely among the writers in this chapter. Kai Erikson talks about how the Appalachian residents' sense of community is tied to their regional "niche." In a similar way, but in a different setting, Victor Hernandez Cruz ties his sense of belonging and community to both his local neighborhood in the United States and his local village in Puerto Rico. He then uses the contrast between the two as the central metaphor for his whole migration experience. On the negative side, Leonard Kriegel and Ruben Martinez suggest something else about the impact of the physical environment (in these cases, urban spaces) on the creation of community. What role does the nature of a place play in shaping a community? How is a rural community different from an urban one? What aspects of a place affect the kind of community that can develop there? In what ways does a community based on physical or "ecological" influences differ from a community based on values, heritage, goals, or activity (such as a virtual online community)?

4. Belonging and Alienation

There are many ways that the writers express their sense of alienation or belonging in this chapter's selections. One level of belonging is a matter of national belonging, as regards a national culture or citizenship, which we saw in the works by Mukherjee, King, and Hernandez Cruz. In fact, in Mukherjee's descriptions of the difference between her own and her sister's relationship to America, she describes how her sister, after thirty years, still resists the feeling of belonging in America. By contrast, in the poem by Li-Young Lee, the boy tries to use language as a bridge between cultures, but his mistakes with words that sound alike serve further to heighten his sense of difference and alienation. Language also serves as a marker of alienation in the essays about graffiti, but in a different way. For Martinez, graffiti writing is an expression of alienation from an urban environment but also is a means to create a community among graffiti artists. By contrast, Kriegel finds that seeing graffiti everywhere that he "cannot read" makes him feel supremely alienated from his once familiar and comfortable urban environment.

As you think about these themes and issues, write an essay about what factors make people feel like insiders or outsiders. What are the ways that belonging and alienation get constructed, communicated, and expressed? Are all communities based to some degree on people's sense of being insiders or outsiders? Is that what attracts people to join clubs or to move to particular neighborhoods? Can you have a community that does not construct a sense of outsiderness to go along with its sense of insiderness? What about competing feelings of belonging, such as those expressed in Cherrie Moraga's essay, in which she says her gender makes her feel one way, her skin color another, and her sexuality altogether another? Have you ever been in a situation in which you felt a sense of being inside and outside of a community simultaneously?

5. Community, Culture, and the Personal

How is culture personal? What is the relationship among senses of culture, belonging, and alienation? What gives us a feeling of cultural belonging? How is culture present or exhibited in the places in which we live? In the objects in our house or in our behavior? In the food we eat and in the smells we're used to? Many of the writers in this chapter "live" in more than one place, splitting their consciousness and sense of belonging—for example, living both in India and in the United States, or in Puerto Rico and in the Lower East Side of New York. In all of these cases, there are elements of culture associated with national and political boundaries, but ultimately the meaning of culture is very personal. Consider, for example, Alice Walker's story "Everyday Use." In that story, the characters have completely different senses of their own culture and past, each expressed through different relationships to particular objects. Write an essay in which you consider how culture is both felt and expressed personally. Is it experienced and expressed through ritual and tradition (such as the proper way to make tamales by hand) or aesthetically and symbolically (such as Dee/Wangero's wanting the quilt as an art object in Walker's story)?

How do you feel connected to your culture? How does your family express or practice its cultural roots? Are there tangible signs? Are there things that your family does or possesses simply to maintain a personal and visible connection or sense of cultural belonging?

6. Community, Equality, and Difference

In his essay on communality in Appalachia Kai Erikson says, "A community of the sort we are talking about here derives from and depends on an almost perfect democracy of the spirit, where people are not only assumed to be equal in status but virtually identical in temperament and outlook." He talks about there being "classes of people" marked by some differences (men/women, white/black), but these individuals are not differentiated on bases of rank, status, outlook, and so forth. His statement raises a critical question: can you have a community that is based on difference, or must there be some kind of fundamental sameness or equality to make it communal? Or must all communities find an equilibrium where what people have in common outweighs what differences exist among them?

The question of difference and equality extends to the idea of *individuality*. In Kriegel's essay about urban graffiti, he complains that "graffiti denies the possibility of an urban community by insisting that individual style is a more natural right than the communitarian demands of city life." Can you think of an example of a community where "individual style" and "communitarian demands" are in tension and have to be balanced? How is this balance expressed in communities with which you have been involved?

CHAPTER FOUR

BORDERS AS BARRIERS:

Otherness and Difference

Elizabeth Bishop: *In the Waiting Room* [poem]
Tara L. Masih: *Exotic, or "What Beach Do You Hang Out on?"* [essay]
Jacob Riis: from *How the Other Half Lives* [essay]
Toni Cade Bambara: *The Lesson* [story]
Peter Marin: *Helping and Hating the Homeless* [essay]
Nathan McCall: *Makes Me Wanna Holler* [essay]
David Sibley: *Feelings About Difference* [essay]
Robert Berkhofer Jr.: *The White Man's Indian* [essay]
Martin Espada: *The Other Alamo* [poem]
Adrienne Rich: *Split at the Root: An Essay on Jewish Identity* [essay]
Art Spiegelman: from *MAUS: A Survivor's Tale* [graphic story]
Stuart Hall: *Ethnicity: Identity and Difference* [essay]

Critical Questions for *Borders as Barriers*

How do we think about and express differences between ourselves and others? What does it mean to create a sense of otherness? In what ways are differences manifested and expressed through language or through images? How do representations of otherness and difference contribute to individual, communal, or cultural identity? Are societal dichotomies—the sense of an "us" versus a "them"—inevitable? Can we come together with a mutual sense of difference? How do irrational and rational notions of difference get expressed? To what extent is a sense of otherness created through misplaced fear? What happens when marginalized groups resist the categories to which they are "assigned"? Is anger a legitimate act of resistance? How are differences and ways to overcome them positive and productive social influences?

"NATIONAL GEOGRAPHIC NUDITY"

Once while reading a local newspaper in Louisville, Kentucky, I came across a review for a movie I had already seen called *Medicine Man,* which stars Sean Connery as a doctor conducting research in the Brazilian rain forest and Lorraine Bracco as his assistant. At the end of each review, the paper listed factors that made the movie appropriate for various audiences. The warning for *Medicine Man* read:

> Some strong language;
> moderate violence;
> national geographic nudity.

"National geographic nudity" apparently referred to the many more or less naked indigenous people who were constantly in the background of the film. But what did the phrase "national geographic nudity" communicate to the Louisville moviegoer? Did it mean that although the movie contained nudity, *only* the native people were nude? Was "national geographic nudity" meant as a warning or as an assurance? What if Sean Connery's costar, Lorraine Bracco, had been as scantily clad as the natives were throughout the film? What might the warning have said then? Is nudity not really considered nudity when it is the customary "attire" of rain forest natives? Or is it not really nudity because those people are a natural part of the film's location, like the trees and animals, and thus not the same as the British or American actors? Somehow the phrase "national geographic nudity" implies that the natives were not as present or as *visible* as the other people in the movie.

In her poem that opens this chapter, Elizabeth Bishop recounts a childhood experience of sitting in a dentist's office waiting room and passing the time by thumbing through a *National Geographic* magazine.

> My Aunt was inside
> what seemed like a long time
> and while I waited I read
> the *National Geographic*
> (I could read) and carefully
> studied the photographs . . .
>
> A dead man slung on a pole
> —"Long Pig," the caption said.
> Babies with pointed heads
> wound round and round with string;
> black, naked women with necks
> wound round and round with wire
> like the necks of light bulbs.
> Their breasts were horrifying.
> I read it straight through.
> I was too shy to stop.

Bishop's memory of seeing the women in the *National Geographic* is punctuated by her memory of hearing her Aunt Consuelo's brief "*oh!* of pain" from the dentist's chair. The voice of her aunt, the strangers in the waiting room, and the pictures of the women in the magazine all combine, despite her shyness, to create a mysterious connection across the globe:

What similarities—
boots, hands, the family voice
I felt in my throat, or even
the *National Geographic*
and those awful hanging breasts—
held us all together
or made us all just one?

Bishop's poem and the newspaper warning about *Medicine Man* raise the central question of this chapter: what do we *see* when we encounter people different from ourselves? What do we see, and how do we respond, when confronted with otherness and difference? In Chapters 2 and 3, the selections considered how we come to be who we are—the forces that shape the self and the community and culture to which we feel we belong. This chapter is the first of two in which we will look at the other side of who we are—that is, who we are *not*. In fact, the two ideas are connected because there is a complementary relationship between who we are and who we are not. Our attempts to know and define ourselves inevitably involve defining others. In many cases, defining others means viewing them through the prejudice of a framework that casts them as the opposite or the antithesis of the defining perspective. When people rigidly define others as separate from or the opposite of a particular cultural identity, they are engaging in the construction of *otherness.*

Not only is identity, as we saw earlier, shaped by all kinds of cultural influences (such as stories, family, and customs), but it is also shaped by how others perceive us. Although we experience such reactions in very personal terms, in a larger sense we also construct our sense of self partly on the messages we receive from our culture about other people who are different. As Stuart Hall puts it in his essay in this chapter:

Thus, another critical thing about identity is that it is partly the relationship between you and the Other. Only when there is an Other can you know who you are. To discover that fact is to discover and unblock the whole enormous history of nationalism and of racism. Racism is a structure of discourse and representation that tries to expel the Other symbolically—blot it out, put it over there . . . at the margin.

By calling "racism" a structure of "discourse and representation," Hall notes that when we speak of constructions of "otherness," we mean not only an attitude or belief, but also the embodiment of that belief in language and images that make up the cultural environment.

This chapter looks at how the idea of "otherness" is depicted in American culture in explicit, implicit, and sometimes very subtle ways. We will explore such images of otherness and difference and ask what force they have in our culture. How are they expressed? What have they to do with creating and maintaining individual, communal, and cultural identity?

WHAT IS NORMAL?

In his documentary exposé of conditions on the Lower East Side of Manhattan in the 1890s, investigative journalist Jacob Riis writes that in Lower New York

[o]ne may find for the asking an Italian, a German, a French, African, Spanish, Bohemian, Russian, Scandinavian, Jewish, and Chinese colony. Even the Arab, who peddles "holy earth" from the Battery as a direct importation from Jerusalem, has his exclusive preserves at the lower end of Washington Street. The one thing you shall vainly ask for in the chief city of America is a distinctively American community.

What, we might ask, in a nation of immigrants, is a distinctively American community? What kind of people is Riis looking for?

Riis's quest for a "distinctively American community" was recently echoed in a comment made by television personality Pat O'Brien. He complained jokingly that most of the Americans had been eliminated from the 1997 U.S. Open tennis tournament competition, saying, "I mean, this is the U.S. Open and there is only one player from the U.S. left in the tournament—and *his* name is Chang."

Examining the two comments together is a useful way to raise the idea of "normative" assumptions that often underlie the construction of otherness. What is the operative definition in either Riis's or O'Brien's mind that makes an American an American? Why did Pat O'Brien not consider Chang an American name—while he probably thought that O'Brien was—even though both the Changs and O'Briens had no doubt come to America as immigrants at some point. Jacob Riis himself had come from Denmark fewer than twenty years before his remark. One implication, to use a key word from the previous chapter, is that some people *belong* in America and others don't. Another implication is that if everyone does belong in America, some people belong to the core of American society while others belong in some other way—perhaps as guests, as aliens, or as residents on the periphery—but forever *outside* the center.

Implicit definitions of national identity are just one of the many often unspoken notions of what is normal that operate in the public rhetoric of our society. There are, of course, many other applications of normative behavior and appearance that also operate in our culture. Naturally, there are common ways of living in any culture that form the center of that culture; this is the way of most of the world's cultures and societies. All cultures have certain norms, even if different cultures vary in their capacity to accommodate differences. This chapter examines the question of how difference is constructed as otherness in the United States. More specifically, it focuses on those aspects of American expression and thinking in which the dominant culture is used as the standard for labeling, judging, and treating people.

We can find one of the longest-standing examples of this kind of thinking in American culture in the encounter between European explorers and the original inhabitants of the New World, particularly in the application of the "general term Indian" to all native peoples despite their differences. As Robert Berkhofer Jr. points out in his essay later in this chapter, no matter how much the Europeans learned about the differences among various tribes, the differences between "Indians" and "Europeans" were considered the most important. He notes that the general category of "Indian"—and all that the term implied about native peoples being the very *opposite* or *negative* of Europeans—persisted well into the twentieth century. "Americans and Africans appeared naked, and the former usually wore a feathered headdress and carried a bow and arrow. Europe, in brief, represented civilization and Christianity and learning confronting nature in America. The general terms *heathen, barbarian, pagan, savage,* and even *Indian* revealed these criteria of judgment at the same time that they validated the use of collective terms for the peoples of other continents." Berkhofer further argues:

> Another persistent theme in White imagery is the tendency to describe Indian life in terms of its lack of White ways rather than being described positively from within the framework of the specific culture under construction. Therefore, tribal Americans were usually described not as they were in their own eyes but from the viewpoint of outsiders, who often failed to understand their ideas and customs. Images of the Indian, accordingly, were (and are) usually what he was not or had not in White terms, rather than in terms of individual tribal cultures and social systems as modern anthropologists aim to do.

Ever since the "discovery" of the so-called "New World," America has been defined by shifting sets of dichotomies between white/dark, civilized/savage, and cultured/primitive. During the nineteenth and twentieth centuries, as Native Americans were considered less of a threat, the dominant construction of otherness was projected onto African Americans, darker European immigrants, Asian Americans, Mexican Americans, and Latin American immigrants. Whichever racialized minorities were seen as somehow "outside" the core of American society—either as an overt threat or as a necessary but marginalized underclass—varied according to region and period. But what is consistent in the worst of these instances is not just a sense of *difference*, but also a sense of *otherness*.

When the construction of otherness occurs on top of a sense of difference, a seemingly impassable gulf between cultures will often also occur. In his essay titled "Makes Me Wanna Holler," Nathan McCall recounts his early childhood perceptions of the way racial difference structured his stepfather's dealings with his "white" employers:

> It is difficult sometimes to pinpoint defining moments in a life. But I'm certain that that period marked my realization of something it seemed white folks had been trying to get across to me for most of my young life—that there were two distinct worlds in America, and a different set of rules for each: The white one was full of possibilities of life. The dark one was just that—dark and limited.

Although McCall strongly remembers getting a distinct message about "two worlds," sometimes the construction of otherness is not so clearly dichotomized or overtly negative. In part, this is Tara L. Masih's point in her essay on the term *exotic*, which she says can mean a whole range of things in our language. When someone is told he or she looks *exotic*, or that some product is said to have a taste or appearance that is *exotic*, the word can mean, Masih says, anything from "foreign" to "strange" to "unusual" to "different." Even if such uses of *exotic* are meant as a compliment (and she implies that when she is told by men, for example, that they love her "exotic looks," they are giving a compliment), the implication is still that she is *outside* some cultural norm. And, in fact, as she points out, the word *exotic* comes from a Greek word meaning "outside."

One of the questions raised in this chapter and throughout the book focuses on the relationship between otherness and difference. Is it possible to think of people as being different without thinking of them as being *outside* some cultural norm? Is it possible to have a culture with a sense of identity yet without a sense of cultural outsiders or others? Is it possible to recognize difference as diversity and not as oth-erness? At the end of her essay, Masih argues that it is necessary to move beyond di-chotomies. She suggests, "Perhaps the real definition of *exotic* should be '[a] recognition of that which is especially unique to each culture.'" Such a suggestion seems reasonable enough, but what prevents people from looking at others as merely different?

FEAR AND DIFFERENCE

The answer to that question, which is both complex and sensitive, surely has much to do with a network of irrational beliefs and fears that are tied to a host of social, economic, and emotional factors. David Sibley puts it this way:

> Who is felt to belong and not to belong contributes in an important way to the shap-ing of social space. It is often the case that this kind of hostility to others is articulated as a concern about property values but certain kinds of difference, as they are cultur-ally constructed, trigger anxieties and a wish on the part of those who feel threatened to distance themselves from others. This may, of course, have economic consequences.
>
> Feelings about others, people marked as different, may also be associated with places. Nervousness about walking down a street in a district which has been labelled as dangerous, nauseousness associated with particular smells, or conversely, excite-ment, exhilaration or a feeling of calm may be the kinds of sensations engendered by other environments. Repulsion and desire, fear and attraction, attach both to people and to places in complex ways.

Peter Marin echoes Sibley's ideas when he discusses some residents' reactions to homeless people in his neighborhood. He claims that what affects our relation to homeless people is not a sense of *danger* per se, but rather a set of anxieties he labels the "Family of bourgeois fears." "Our response to the homeless," he says, "is fed by a complex set of cultural attitudes, habits of thought, and fantasies and fears so fa-miliar to us, so common, that they have become a *second* nature and might as well be instinctive, for all the control we have over them. And it is by no means easy to untangle this snarl of responses. What does seem clear is that the homeless embody all that bourgeois culture has for centuries tried to eradicate and destroy."

We can apply Marin's observations about mainstream responses to the homeless to most attitudes about "otherness." People are considered "others" when they are perceived to be (through some "snarl of responses") in competition with or threat-ening to the very core of a culture's sense of self-identity. What results, as several of the authors in this chapter imply, is a self-perpetuating cycle of positive cultural self-definition and negative representations of the "other." Whether examining the clear, racialized divisions drawn by Nathan McCall in his memories of growing up black in "white America," Art Spiegelman's depiction of the strict dichotomies of Ger-mans and Jews in Nazi Germany (by drawing the Jews as mice and the Germans as cats), or the more complicated and subtle conflicts of identity Adrienne Rich feels when rediscovering her family's abandoned Judaism in the South, this chapter is about the representation of the border between people as a seemingly impassable barrier of otherness.

In the Waiting Room

ELIZABETH BISHOP

■ Born in Worcester, Massachusetts, in 1911, Elizabeth Bishop (who died in 1979) is among the most widely admired of American poets. She published her first volume of poetry in 1946 and won the Pulitzer Prize in 1955 for *North and South—A Gold Spring*. She lived for a number of years in Brazil, later returning to Massachusetts, where she taught at Harvard University. Her volume *Complete Poems* was published in 1979. Bishop's work often focuses on seemingly unremarkable incidents and objects through which she communicates a special insight. Her language is characterized by a unique clarity and precision. In the following poem, a young girl's mundane visit to a doctor's waiting room is transformed by a revelation, a moment in which "nothing stranger / had ever happened."

In Worcester, Massachusetts,
I went with Aunt Consuelo
to keep her dentist's appointment
and sat and waited for her
in the dentist's waiting room.   5
It was winter. It got dark
early. The waiting room
was full of grown-up people,
arctics and overcoats,
lamps and magazines.   10
My aunt was inside
what seemed like a long time
and while I waited I read
the *National Geographic*
(I could read) and carefully   15
studied the photographs:
the inside of a volcano,
black, and full of ashes;
then it was spilling over
in rivulets of fire.   20
Osa and Martin Johnson
dressed in riding breeches,
laced boots, and pith helmets.
A dead man slung on a pole

—"Long Pig," the caption said.   25
Babies with pointed heads
wound round and round with string;
black, naked women with necks
wound round and round with wire
like the necks of light bulbs.   30
Their breasts were horrifying.
I read it right straight through.
I was too shy to stop.
And then I looked at the cover:
the yellow margins, the date.   35

Suddenly, from inside,
came an *oh!* of pain
—Aunt Consuelo's voice—
not very loud or long.
I wasn't at all surprised;   40
even then I knew she was
a foolish, timid woman.
I might have been embarrassed,
but wasn't. What took me
completely by surprise   45
was that it was *me:*
my voice, in my mouth.
Without thinking at all
I was my foolish aunt,
I—we—were falling, falling,   50
our eyes glued to the cover
of the *National Geographic,*
February, 1918.

I said to myself: three days
and you'll be seven years old.   55
I was saying it to stop
the sensation of falling off
the round, turning world
into cold, blue-black space.
But I felt: you are an *I,*   60

you are an *Elizabeth,*
you are one of *them.*
Why should you be one, too?
I scarcely dared to look
to see what it was I was.   65
I gave a sidelong glance
—I couldn't look any higher—
at shadowy gray knees,
trousers and skirts and boots
and different pairs of hands   70
lying under the lamps.
I knew that nothing stranger
had ever happened, that nothing
stranger could ever happen.
Why should I be my aunt,   75
or me, or anyone?
What similarities—
boots, hands, the family voice
I felt in my throat, or even
the *National Geographic*   80
and those awful hanging breasts—
held us all together
or made us all just one?
How—I didn't know any
word for it—how "unlikely" . . .   85
How had I come to be here,
like them, and overhear
a cry of pain that could have
got loud and worse but hadn't?

The waiting room was bright   90
and too hot. It was sliding
beneath a big black wave,
another, and another.

Then I was back in it.
The War was on. Outside,   95
in Worcester, Massachusetts,

were night and slush and cold,
and it was still the fifth
of February, 1918.

Working with the Text

1. This poem describes a sudden revelation or insight, the epiphany of a child who suddenly sees herself as both "an *I*" and "one of *them.*" What specifically leads the speaker to this realization? Why is she so stunned? What does she find so "unlikely"?

2. What is the significance of the *National Geographic* at the beginning of the poem? In what sense does this magazine present images of "otherness"? Why do you think the speaker "read it right straight through . . . too shy to stop"? Do you recall your own early responses to images of other kinds of people in *National Geographic,* or other magazines or media?

3. How does the setting—a dentist's office on a late winter afternoon—contribute to the poem's meanings? What is the effect of the speaker's noting in the final stanza that World War I was in progress?

4. How would you define the central theme of this poem? Is it primarily about difference or about similarities? Or is Bishop getting at something more complex than these polarities? Explore some of the ways that people form connections to others across the globe or in seemingly distant places. Do we connect rationally, irrationally, emotionally, morally?

EXOTIC, OR "WHAT BEACH DO YOU HANG OUT ON?"

TARA L. MASIH

■ In the following essay, Tara L. Masih reflects on what it means to be called "exotic." A woman of mixed-race parentage, Masih suggests that the label, while perhaps intended positively, has several not-so-positive connotations. Part of Masih's point is also that words like "exotic" can have multiple meanings simultaneously, and that sometimes it is the complex of all those meanings that conveys the total sense of a term, even if the user has a narrower intention in mind. This essay is from *Two Worlds Walking,* edited by Diane Glancy and C. W. Truesdale (New Rivers Press, 1994).

When you are of mixed parentage—one parent dark-skinned, one light—you come out looking like café au lait, something people struggle with—their compulsion to categorize you, label you, and place you neatly on the shelf in a safe spot, safe because the species is one that has already been identified. Yet while humans have always feared the unfamiliar and foreign, times are forcing us to change.

"Your look is in," I'm told by friends. "I like exotic-looking women," I'm told by   2
men. I still have not learned how to react to these well-meaning comments. I bite my
lip, smile, and nod vaguely, hoping they'll take my expression as a thank you.

What that expression really reflects is a reaction to my own struggle, a reluctance   3
to be placed in any category to satisfy the comfort of others. Now I am labeled, and
they can rest easy. Everything's safe.

Fear of the stranger goes back centuries. In her essay, Susan Sontag uses this   4
metaphor to explain the fear of AIDS victims: "The fact that illness is associated
with the poor—who are, from the perspective of the privileged, aliens in one's
midst—reinforces the association of illness with the foreign: with an *exotic* place"
[my italics].

There is no doubt that words have power, or rather, we imbue them with power.   5
As the Bible proclaims, the word is flesh and dwells among us. Like humans, words
are either accepted or rejected, synthesized into culture or banished. For instance,
during the McCarthy era, the term *communist,* like the person it labeled, was
claimed to be evil and therefore every effort was made to eradicate it from the
American vocabulary.

What many people may not realize is that the word *exotic* is derived from the   6
Greek word *exō,* meaning "outside." "Exotic" itself carries several meanings in modern times, and as cultural and collective views change terms and phrases,
chameleon-like, are made to reflect and adapt. (*Communism* is no longer an evil
word, communists no longer exist in an "evil empire.") According to *Webster's Ninth
Collegiate,* there are four modern definitions of *exotic.*

1. *Introduced from another country: not native to the place where found*

It is amazing what a short-term memory we Americans have. Our history begins   7
with the discovery, by Italian explorer Cristofero Colombo, of this land and its exotic American Indians (and we all know he was looking for a quicker trade route to
my ancestors, those other exotics in India proper). But by definition it was Colombo
and his followers, religious refugees and convicts, who were the exotics. In essence,
all Americans are exotic. Our history, riddled with convenient lapses in memory,
takes a great leap to the American Revolution, discounting the fact that the non-
native Europeans, with "savage-like" enthusiasm, slaughtered the natives (now
rightly referred to as Native Americans). Our fear of foreigners is no doubt a projection of our fear of ourselves.

2. *archaic: outlandish, alien*

By this definition, *exotic* is hardly a compliment. The word again addresses the   8
fear of the unfamiliar. (The *Oxford English Dictionary* uses the words *barbarous,
strange, uncouth* as synonymous with foreigners.) It's why we seek to erase differences in this culture. By covering our bodily smells with the same scents, by following the current trends in hair styles (now that Di and Fergie are old hat, who will
women follow? Hillary and Tipper?), by spending all our energy/time/money to
wear the same clothes during the same season, and by keeping up with the latest
profanity, we are saying to our compatriots: "Hey, I'm just like you, therefore I'm
safe and *familiar.*" (Note how these two adjectives are often paired.) It is no accident
that most of the women and men accused of witchcraft during the hysteria of the

seventeenth and eighteenth centuries were citizens who lived by themselves, outside of the community—social lepers. In our own century, Michael Jackson is the epitome of one who has tried, literally, to erase his exotic features, even going so far as to erase his gender—he is generic in every sense, and therefore can be marketed to a broader audience. His attempts, nevertheless, backfired. In erasing all differences he has become that which he tried to avoid. A true alien, living a solitary life away from society, he is like the witches of old—a target for outlandish rumors and supernatural speculation.

3. Strikingly or excitingly different or unusual

The word's own definitions contradict each other. While the unfamiliar can be frightening, it can also be exciting. As psychologists have discovered, love and lust are heightened in the presence of fear. Now we know how to make someone fall in love with us—take them on a walk over a shaky bridge. And as fear and excitement appear to be in opposition, so do different cultures' concepts of beauty. In the States it is considered an asset to be tan, though the tan shouldn't be natural. It should be achieved through leisurely hours of sunning on tropical beaches or through the assistance of artificial means. Americans brave melanoma, carcinoma, early aging for this brief stain of color. I enjoy being the barometer every summer for my friends to measure their tan by. With what glee some of them greet their achieved goal—to be darker than I am. But only in the summer, when it's acceptable. Or if they've been to Florida. I went to the beach once with a friend. "Look how everyone's staring at me," she said. "Black people aren't supposed to go to the beach, it's only for whites trying to look black." 9

I find it ironic that meanwhile, on the other side of the earth, people are doing their best to appear light-skinned. Hindu gods are rendered by artists with a blue tint to their skin, and Indian movie stars are lighter than many Europeans. I was appalled to find my own cousin, in preparation for her wedding, spreading hair bleach all over her amber-tinted face and neck. "I'm too dark," she said. "It's not pretty." 10

If we go beyond the outward schizophrenia of these opposing ideals, we find a sad explanation—it is class related. In the States, a tan is a sign of wealth. It takes money and leisure time to be able to noticeably tan—not burn, but tan, like the model in the Bain de Soleil advertisements. 11

But in equatorial countries such as India, a tan is a sign of the lower caste. The wealthy stay indoors, cooling themselves under rotating ceiling fans, while the rest of society works beneath a branding sun. 12

4. of or relating to striptease

This meaning is so repugnant it's comical. Is an exotic woman expected to dance her version of the seven veils for the edification (or destruction) of men? Visions of Salome arise, and again that fear of what is different, or man's fear of woman. As Jung noted, we give women all the characteristics that "swarm in the male Eros." Because of the sexual connotations, it has become de rigueur for a man to be seen with a foreign-looking woman. The advertising community, taking note of this, has littered their ads with exotic women, the cosmetics industry is cashing in on their 13 growing number, and the film industry is giving more roles to women who don't look like Christie Brinkley, beautiful as she is.

Which brings me to the real definition of *exotic*. 14

A growing segment of the U.S. population being targeted for consumerism

As the discussions of the previous definitions reveal, in our society industry and 15 consumerism build the foundation from which change evolves. The foundation for consumerism began with the colonists' revolt against taxation. A growing consumerism held our country together, forcing a civil war: according to some social historians, the North didn't want to lose the South's textile or agricultural contributions, which fed the Northern industries. It met the demands of the civil rights and the women's movement during the sixties, when the work force was in dire need of replenishment. Today, consumerism is behind the efforts to manufacture environmentally safe products, fake fur, and to provide dolphin-safe nets.

And it now causes publishers to compete against each other so that they may 16 proudly announce that thirty-five percent of their authors are minorities; it causes politicians to include minority policies in their political platforms; it's behind the slight darkening of the skin and rearranging of models' features; and it drives fashion designers to steal other cultures' traditional attire, reproduce it, and sell it for a criminal price. Are women aware that they're wearing a mini sarong from Africa? Or *shalwars* from India? These pants cost as much as $200 in the States, but in India, depending on how well you can bargain, you can get them for $5. Westerners don't see the women sitting cross-legged in dark rooms and on thin mats, a useless protection from damp floors, embroidering or weaving their own fallen hair into the materials. And they never haggle with a street vendor for 5 rupees (the equivalent of about 25¢), until the boy says earnestly, with that tilt of the head peculiar to Indians, "Look, miss, to you 5 rupees is nothing—to me it is everything." True.

The melting pot is recognized as an anachronistic term. The new buzz-word for 17 the nineties is *multicultural* or *multinational*, because we know that soon minorities will be the majority. They are gaining economic independence and buying their way into acceptance. So out of fear, our culture is adopting their clothing and jewelry, eating their foods in restaurants with purple decors, and taking up their causes to the point where we will forget who it all really belongs to. But I hope that we will fight the desire to have these groups assimilate, and that the prefix *multi* will begin to take power, allowing this country to exist as many rather than as one generic, incestuous mass. May the words of *M*A*S*H*'s Frank Burns be banished to an unenlightened past: "Individuality is fine. As long as we do it together."

No one should be labeled and shelved. I hope that we open our minds to learn 18 from other cultures, accept what each has to offer, not because we can make a profit from them but because it will enrich our own culture. As Richard Rodriguez writes, "Diversity which is not shared is no virtue. Diversity which is not shared is a parody nation."

Perhaps the real definition of *exotic* should be "A recognition of that which is es- 19 pecially unique to each culture." For if someone calling me exotic meant a recognition of a proud people who persevere in the face of terrible poverty and disease, if they saw in me even a spark of Paul, a disfigured leper who, every evening, sits on the leprosarium stairs to take in the beauty of the Himalayan foothills during sunset, with no bitterness at his lot, then I would smile widely and say, "Thank you."

Working with the Text

1. What are some examples in the media (television, advertising) that express the mix of meanings that Masih discusses for the term *exotic*? Can you think of examples where some type or group of people are treated as exotic in a way that—while not being overtly negative—does cast them as marginal or outside of the mainstream? Bring an example to class.

2. Why do you think Masih gives so much attention to the word *exotic* itself? What does she think about the power or importance of words? What are some ways that language both reflects social attitudes about difference and perpetuates them?

3. What are some of the larger contexts for her essay? Discuss one or two social concepts that are related to the term *exotic*. What are some terms related to *exotic* that might not seem so harmless?

4. What kind of commentary does her examination of the term *exotic* make on the concept of "multiculturalism"? Why does she talk at the end about "shared diversity"? Is there an implicit conflict between the "exoticization of the other" and the concept of "shared diversity," or are they compatible?

5. Explore the linked resources related to images of otherness online on the *Border Texts* Web site. Do you see some of the range of meanings that Masih associates with the "exotic" represented there? Can you bookmark a link to a Web site that similarly constructs the "exotic" or the "other"?

FROM **HOW THE OTHER HALF LIVES**

JACOB RIIS

■ Journalist and social reformer Jacob Riis was born in Denmark in 1849. After immigrating to the United States in 1870, he worked for several different New York City newspapers, often reporting on the living conditions within slums and on the exploitation of the lower classes. Later in life, he was a major force in the movement to improve housing and education for the poor and to create public parks and other amenities to improve urban life. He died in 1914. His most famous book, *How the Other Half Lives* (1890), was among the first publications to reveal the squalor of the tenement dwellings which housed New York City's poorest and least powerful residents. In the following excerpt from that book, Riis looks unsparingly at tenement life and urges reform.

nough of them [tenements] everywhere. Suppose we look into one? No.—Cherry Street. Be a little careful, please! The hall is dark and you might stumble over the children pitching pennies back there. Not that it would hurt them; kicks and cuffs are their daily diet. They have little else. Here where the hall turns and dives into utter darkness is a step, and another, another. A flight of stairs. You can feel your way, if you cannot see it. Close? Yes! What would you have? All the fresh air that ever enters these stairs comes from the hall door that is forever slamming, and from the windows of dark bedrooms that in turn receive from the stairs their sole supply of the elements God meant to be free, but man deals out with such niggardly hand. That was a woman filling her pail by the hydrant you just bumped against. The sinks are in the hallway, that all the tenants may have access—and all be poisoned alike by their summer stenches. Hear the pump squeak! It is the lullaby of tenement house babes. In summer, when a thousand thirsty throats pant for a cooling drink in this block, it is worked in vain. But the saloon, whose open door you passed in the hall, is always there. The smell of it has followed you up. Here is a door. Listen! That short hacking cough, that tiny, helpless wail—what do they mean? They mean that the soiled bow of white you saw on the door downstairs will have another story to tell—Oh! a sadly familiar story—before the day is at an end. The child is dying with measles. With half a chance it might have lived; but it had none. That dark bedroom killed it.

"It was took all of a suddint," says the mother, smoothing the throbbing little body with trembling hands. There is no unkindness in the rough voice of the man in the jumper, who sits by the window grimly smoking a clay pipe, with the little life ebbing out in his sight, bitter as his words sound: "Hush, Mary! If we cannot keep the baby, need we complain—such as we?"

Such as we! What if the words ring in your ears as we grope our way up the stairs and down from floor to floor, listening to the sounds behind the closed doors— some of quarrelling, some of coarse songs, more of profanity. They are true. When the summer heats come with their suffering they have meaning more terrible than words can tell. Come over here. Step carefully over this baby—it is a baby, [in] spite of its rags and dirt—under these iron bridges called fire escapes, but loaded down, despite the incessant watchfulness of the firemen, with broken household goods, with washtubs and barrels, over which no man could climb from a fire. This gap between dingy brick walls is the yard. That strip of smoke-colored sky up there is the heaven of these people. Do you wonder the name does not attract them to the churches? That baby's parents live in the rear tenement here. She is at least as clean as the steps we are now climbing. There are plenty of houses with half a hundred such in. The tenement is much like the one in front we just left, only fouler, closer, darker—we will not say more cheerless. The word is a mockery. A hundred thousand people lived in rear tenements in New York last year. Here is a room neater than the rest. The woman, a stout matron with hard lines of care in her face, is at the washtub. "I try to keep the childer clean," she says, apologetically, but with a hopeless glance around. The spice of hot soapsuds is added to the air already tainted with the smell of boiling cabbage, of rags and uncleanliness all about. It makes an overpowering compound. It is Thursday, but patched linen is hung upon the pulley line from the window. There is no Monday cleaning in the tenements. It is washday all the week round, for a change of clothing is scarce among the poor. They are poverty's honest badge, these perennial lines of rags hung out to dry, those that are not the washerwoman's professional shingle. The true line to be drawn between pauperism and honest poverty is the clothesline. With it begins the effort to be clean that is the first and the best evidence of a desire to be honest.

What sort of an answer, think you, would come from these tenements to the question "Is life worth living?" were they heard at all in the discussion? It may be that this, cut from the last report but one of the Association for the Improvement of the Condition of the Poor, a long name for a weary task, has a suggestion of it: "In the depth of winter the attention of the Association was called to a Protestant family living in a garret in a miserable tenement in Cherry Street. The family's condition was most deplorable. The man, his wife, and three small children shivering in one room through the roof of which the pitiless winds of winter whistled. The room was almost barren of furniture; the parents slept on the floor, the elder children in boxes, and the baby was swung in an old shawl attached to the rafters by cords by way of a hammock. The father, a seaman, had been obliged to give up that calling because he was in consumption, and was unable to provide either bread or fire for his little ones."[1]

Perhaps this may be put down as an exceptional case, but one that came to my notice some months ago in a Seventh Ward tenement was typical enough to escape that reproach. There were nine in the family: husband, wife, an aged grandmother, and six children; honest, hard-working Germans, scrupulously neat, but poor. All nine lived in two rooms, one about ten feet square that served as parlor, bedroom, and eating room, the other, a small half room made into a kitchen. The rent was seven dollars and a half a month, more than a week's wages for the husband and father, who was the only breadwinner in the family. That day the mother had thrown herself out of the window, and was carried up from the street dead. She was "discouraged," said some of the other women from the tenement, who had come in to look after the children while a messenger carried the news to the father at the shop. They went stolidly about their task, although they were evidently not without feeling for the dead woman. No doubt she was wrong in not taking life philosophically, as did the four families a city missionary found housekeeping in the four corners of one room. They got along well enough together until one of the families took a boarder and made trouble. Philosophy, according to my optimistic friend, naturally inhabits the tenements. The people who live there come to look upon death in a different way from the rest of us—do not take it as hard. He has never found time to explain how the fact fits into his general theory that life is not unbearable in the tenements. Unhappily for the philosophy of the slums, it is too apt to be of the kind that readily recognizes the saloon, always handy, as the refuge from every trouble, and shapes its practice according to the discovery. . . .

1. Riis trimmed this quotation and slightly altered its ending thereby omitting some interesting material on the resources of New York's poor. After the word "consumption" the original text continues "and was earning a precarious living by gathering roots and flowers in the woods and selling them on the streets. But the inclement weather had kept him from going out, and a sick child claimed the mother's attention, so that these parents though willing were unable to provide either bread or fire for their little ones." The report goes on to say that the family was aided by the society, moved to better quarters, and that the father was better now owing to the help and care of his friends. The Board of Health was notified, and steps were taken to repair the tenement. N.Y.A.I.C.P., *Forty-fifth Annual Report, 1888* (New York, 1888), pp. 56–57.

Today, what is a tenement? The law defines it as a house "occupied by three or more   6
families, living independently and doing their cooking on the premises; or by more
than two families on a floor, so living and cooking and having a common right in
the halls, stairways, yards, etc." That is the legal meaning, and includes flats and
apartment houses, with which we have nothing to do.[2] In its narrower sense the typical tenement was thus described when last arraigned before the bar of public justice: "It is generally a brick building from four to six stories high on the street,
frequently with a store on the first floor which, when used for the sale of liquor, has
a side opening for the benefit of the inmates and to evade the Sunday law; four families occupy each floor, and a set of rooms consists of one or two dark closets, used
as bedrooms, with a living room twelve feet by ten. The staircase is too often a dark
well in the center of the house, and no direct through ventilation is possible, each
family being separated from the other by partitions. Frequently the rear of the lot is
occupied by another building of three stories high with two families on a floor." The
picture is nearly as true today as ten years ago, and will be for a long time to come.
The dim light admitted by the air shaft shines upon greater crowds than ever. Tenements are still "good property," and the poverty of the poor man his destruction. A
barrack downtown where he *has to live* because he is poor brings in a third more
rent than a decent flat house in Harlem. The statement once made a sensation that
between seventy and eighty children had been found in one tenement. It no longer
excites even passing attention, when the sanitary police report counting 101 adults
and 91 children in a Crosby Street house, one of twins, built together. The children
in the other, if I am not mistaken, numbered 89, a total of 180 for two tenements! Or
when a midnight inspection in Mulberry Street unearths a hundred and fifty
"lodgers" sleeping on filthy floors in two buildings. Spite of brownstone trimmings,
plate glass and mosaic vestibule floors, the water does not rise in summer to the second story, while the beer flows unchecked to the all-night picnics on the roof. The
saloon with the side door and the landlord divide the prosperity of the place between them, and the tenant, in sullen submission, foots the bills.

Where are the tenements of today? Say rather: where are they not? In fifty years   7
they have crept up from the Fourth Ward slums and the Five Points the whole length
of the island, and have polluted the Annexed District to the Westchester line.
Crowding all the lower wards, wherever business leaves a foot of ground unclaimed;
strung along both rivers, like ball and chain tied to the foot of every street, and filling up Harlem with their restless, pent-up multitudes, they hold within their clutch
the wealth and business of New York, hold them at their mercy in the day of mob
rule and wrath. The bulletproof shutters, the stacks of hand grenades, and the
Gatling guns of the Subtreasury are tacit admissions of the fact and of the quality of
the mercy expected. The tenements today are New York, harboring three-fourths of
its population. When another generation shall have doubled the census of our city,
and to that vast army of workers, held captive by poverty, the very name of home
shall be as a bitter mockery, what will the harvest be?

---

2. This definition of a tenement was the one established by the 1867 New York statute.

Working with the Text

1. Reread the selection and think specifically about Riis's narrating style. At the time, Riis was seen as a pioneering journalist. In what ways is his writing journalistic? In what ways does it seem sensational or subjective? Analyze how he appeals to readers and manipulates them. How does he mix factual and emotional appeals?

2. In what ways does Riis seem ambivalent in his feelings toward the "other half"? When does he seem most sympathetic? What fears does he express about the "restless, pent-up multitudes" in tenement housing? What alarm does he sound about "another generation [doubling] the census of our city"? What, ultimately, do you think motivated him to write about the living conditions of the poor? Look closely at his language and style. What does his manner in writing about the poor reveal about his mixed attitudes about the poor?

3. Riis notes of tenements that "[t]he saloon with the side door and the landlord divide the prosperity of the place between them, and the tenant, in sullen submission, foots the bills." Do you see this as exploitation or as legitimate business practice? Are there similar connections today?

4. Compare Riis's essay to the relevant photographs in the Image Portfolio: His photograph of the *Street Arabs* (Plate 9); the selections from *Shooting Back* (Plates 8 and 10). Then look at some of the resources on the Web site related to "otherness". What does Riis express in writing that is similar and different from the images that you find?

5. How would you compare the situation Riis described more than a hundred years ago with issues revolving around poverty and substandard living conditions today? Note, for example, that Riis suggests (elsewhere, not in this selection) that tenement dwellers "touch the family file with deadly moral contagion," which is their "worst crime." How is this related to today's debates over "family values"? Are there still people today who connect morality and poverty?

[handwritten: Identify again. To do better can come out of hole. Math lesson on surface, inside to do better.]

THE LESSON

TONI CADE BAMBARA

■ A native of New York City, Toni Cade Bambara grew up in Harlem and Brooklyn's Bedford-Stuyvesant neighborhood. A graduate of the City University system, she also studied dance and mime in Italy and France. She began writing fiction in the 1960s. Bambara's first collection of stories, *Gorilla, My Love,* was published in 1972 when she was thirty-three. Her other works include *The Sea Birds Are Still Alive* (1977), a second story collection, and *The Salt Eaters* (1980), a novel, as well as several screenplays. Bambara also taught college and worked with a variety of social welfare programs. She died in 1997. The following story, included in *Gorilla, My Love*, focuses on a group of street-smart Harlem kids who get a hint of "how the other half lives."

Back in the days when everyone was old and stupid or young and foolish and me and Sugar were the only ones just right, this lady moved on our block with nappy hair and proper speech and no makeup. And quite naturally we laughed at her, laughed the way we did at the junk man who went about his business like he was some big-time president and his sorry-ass horse his secretary. And we kinda hated her too, hated the way we did the winos who cluttered up our parks and pissed on our handball walls and stank up our hallways and stairs so you couldn't halfway play hide-and-seek without a goddamn gas mask. Miss Moore was her name. The only woman on the block with no first name. And she was black as hell, cept for her feet, which were fish-white and spooky. And she was always planning these boring-ass things for us to do, us being my cousin, mostly, who lived on the block cause we all moved North the same time and to the same apartment then spread out gradual to breathe. And our parents would yank our heads into some kinda shape and crisp up our clothes so we'd be presentable for travel with Miss Moore, who always looked like she was going to church, though she never did. Which is just one of the things the grownups talked about when they talked behind her back like a dog. But when she came calling with some sachet she'd sewed up or some gingerbread she'd made or some book, why then they'd all be too embarrassed to turn her down and we'd get handed over all spruced up. She'd been to college and said it was only right that she should take responsibility for the young ones' education, and she not even related by marriage or blood. So they'd go for it. Specially Aunt Gretchen. She was the main gofer in the family. You got some ole dumb shit foolishness you want somebody to go for, you send for Aunt Gretchen. She been screwed into the go-along for so long, it's a blood-deep natural thing with her. Which is how she got saddled with me and Sugar and Junior in the first place while our mothers were in a la-de-da apartment up the block having a good ole time.

So this one day Miss Moore rounds us all up at the mailbox and it's pure-dee hot and she's knockin herself out about arithmetic. And school suppose to let up in summer I heard, but she don't never let up. And the starch in my pinafore scratching the shit outta me and I'm really hating this nappy-head bitch and her goddamn college degree. I'd much rather go to the pool or to the show where it's cool. So me and Sugar leaning on the mailbox being surly, which is a Miss Moore word. And Flyboy checking out what everybody brought for lunch. And Fat Butt already wasting his peanut-butter-and-jelly sandwich like the pig he is. And Junebug punchin on Q.T.'s arm for potato chips. And Rosie Giraffe shifting from one hip to the other waiting for somebody to step on her foot or ask her if she from Georgia so she can kick ass, preferably Mercedes'. And Miss Moore asking us do we know what money is, like we a bunch of retards. I mean real money, she say, like it's only poker chips or monopoly papers we lay on the grocer. So right away I'm tired of this and say so. And would much rather snatch Sugar and go to the Sunset and terrorize the West Indian kids and take their hair ribbons and their money too. And Miss Moore files that remark away for next week's lesson on brotherhood. I can tell. And finally I say we oughta get to the subway cause it's cooler and besides we might meet some cute boys. Sugar done swiped her mama's lipstick, so we ready.

So we heading down the street and she's boring us silly about what things cost   3 and what our parents make and how much goes for rent and how money ain't divided up right in this country. And then she gets to the part about we all poor and live in the slums, which I don't feature. And I'm ready to speak on that, but she steps out in the street and hails two cabs just like that. Then she hustles half the crew in with her and hands me a five-dollar bill and tells me to calculate 10 percent tip for the driver. And we're off. Me and Sugar and Junebug and Flyboy hangin out the window and hollering to everybody, putting lipstick on each other cause Flyboy a faggot anyway, and making farts with our sweaty armpits. But I'm mostly trying to figure how to spend this money. But they all fascinated with the meter ticking and Junebug starts laying bets as to how much it'll read when Flyboy can't hold his breath no more. Then Sugar lays bets as to how much it'll be when we get there. So I'm stuck. Don't nobody want to go for my plan, which is to jump out at the next light and run off to the first bar-b-que we can find. Then the driver tells us to get the hell out cause we there already. And the meter reads eighty-five cents. And I'm stalling to figure out the tip and Sugar say give him a dime. And I decide he don't need it bad as I do, so later for him. But then he tries to take off with Junebug foot still in the door so we talk about his mama something ferocious. Then we check out that we on Fifth Avenue and everybody dressed up in stockings. One lady in a fur coat, hot as it is. White folks crazy.

"This is the place," Miss Moore say, presenting it to us in the voice she uses at the   4 museum. "Let's look in the windows before we go in."

"Can we steal?" Sugar asks very serious like she's getting the ground rules   5 squared away before she plays. "I beg your pardon," says Miss Moore, and we fall out. So she leads us around the windows of the toy store and me and Sugar screamin, "This is mine, that's mine, I gotta have that, that was made for me, I was born for that," till Big Butt drowns us out.

"Hey, I'm goin to buy that there."   6

"That there? You don't even know what it is, stupid."   7

"I do so," he say punchin on Rosie Giraffe. "It's a microscope."   8

"Whatcha gonna do with a microscope, fool?"   9

"Look at things."   10

"Like what, Ronald?" ask Miss Moore. And Big Butt ain't got the first notion. So   11 here go Miss Moore gabbing about the thousands of bacteria in a drop of water and the somethinorother in a speck of blood and the million and one living things in the air around us is invisible to the naked eye. And what she say that for? Junebug go to town on that "naked" and we rolling. Then Miss Moore ask what it cost. So we all jam into the window smudgin it up and the price tag say $300. So then she ask how long'd take for Big Butt and Junebug to save up their allowances. "Too long," I say. "Yeh," adds Sugar, "outgrown it by that time." And Miss Moore say no, you never outgrow learning instruments. "Why, even medical students and interns and," blah, blah, blah. And we ready to choke Big Butt for bringing it up in the first damn place.

"This here costs four hundred eighty dollars," says Rosie Giraffe. So we pile up all   12 over her to see what she pointin out. My eyes tell me it's a chunk of glass cracked with something heavy, and different-color inks dripped into the splits, then the whole thing put into a oven or something. But for $480 it don't make sense.

"That's a paperweight made of semi-precious stones fused together under   13
tremendous pressure," she explains slowly, with her hands doing the mining and all the factory work.

"So what's a paperweight?" asks Rosie Giraffe.   14

"To weigh paper with, dumbbell," say Flyboy, the wise man from the East.   15

"Not exactly," say Miss Moore, which is what she say when you warm or way off   16
too. "It's to weigh paper down so it won't scatter and make your desk untidy." So right away me and Sugar curtsy to each other and then to Mercedes who is more the tidy type.

"We don't keep paper on top of the desk in my class," say Junebug, figuring Miss   17
Moore crazy or lyin one.

"At home, then," she say. "Don't you have a calendar and pencil case and a blot-   18
ter and a letter-opener on your desk at home where you do your homework?" And she know damn well what our homes look like cause she nosys around in them every chance she gets.

"I don't even have a desk," say Junebug. "Do we?"   19

"No. And I don't get no homework neither," says Big Butt.   20

"And I don't even have a home," say Flyboy like he do at school to keep the white   21
folks off his back and sorry for him. Send this poor kid to camp posters, is his specialty.

"I do," says Mercedes. "I have a box of stationery on my desk and a picture of my   22
cat. My godmother bought the stationery and the desk. There's a big rose on each sheet and the envelopes smell like roses."

"Who wants to know about your smelly-ass stationery," say Rosie Giraffe fore I   23
can get my two cents in.

"It's important to have a work area all your own so that . . ."   24

"Will you look at this sailboat, please," say Flyboy, cuttin her off and pointin to   25
the thing like it was his. So once again we tumble all over each other to gaze at this magnificent thing in the toy store which is just big enough to maybe sail two kittens across the pond if you strap them to the posts tight. We all start reciting the price tag like we in assembly. "Handcrafted sailboat of fiberglass at one thousand one hun- dred ninety-five dollars."

"Unbelievable," I hear myself say and am really stunned. I read it again for myself   26
just in case the group recitation put me in a trance. Same thing. For some reason this pisses me off. We look at Miss Moore and she lookin at us, waiting for I dunno what.

"Who'd pay all that when you can buy a sailboat set for a quarter at Pop's, a tube   27
of glue for a dime, and a ball of string for eight cents? It must have a motor and a whole lot else besides," I say. "My sailboat cost me about fifty cents."

"But will it take water?" say Mercedes with her smart ass.   28

"Took mine to Alley Pond Park once," say Flyboy. "String broke. Lost it. Pity."   29

"Sailed mine in Central Park and it keeled over and sank. Had to ask my father   30
for another dollar."

"And you got the strap," laugh Big Butt. "The jerk didn't even have a string on it.   31
My old man wailed on his behind."

Little Q.T. was staring hard at the sailboat and you could see he wanted it bad.   32

But he too little and somebody'd just take it from him. So what the hell. "This boat for kids, Miss Moore?"

"Parents silly to buy something like that just to get all broke up," say Rosie Giraffe.   33

"That much money it should last forever," I figure.   34

"My father'd buy it for me if I wanted it."   35

"Your father, my ass," say Rosie Giraffe getting a chance to finally push Mercedes. 36

"Must be rich people shop here," say Q.T.   37

"You are a very bright boy," say Flyboy. "What was your first clue?" And he rap   38
him on the head with the back of his knuckles, since Q.T. the only one he could get away with. Though Q.T. liable to come up behind you years later and get his licks in when you half expect it.

"What I want to know is," I says to Miss Moore though I never talk to her, I   39
wouldn't give the bitch that satisfaction, "is how much a real boat costs? I figure a thousand'd get you a yacht any day."

"Why don't you check that out," she says, "and report back to the group?" Which   40
really pains my ass. If you gonna mess up a perfectly good swim day least you could do is have some answers. "Let's go in," she say like she got something up her sleeve. Only she don't lead the way. So me and Sugar turn the corner to where the entrance is, but when we get there I kinda hang back. Not that I'm scared, what's there to be afraid of, just a toy store. But I feel funny, shame. But what I got to be shamed about? Got as much right to go in as anybody. But somehow I can't seem to get hold of the door, so I step away from Sugar to lead. But she hangs back too. And I look at her and she looks at me and this is ridiculous. I mean, damn, I have never ever been shy about doing nothing or going nowhere. But when Mercedes steps up and then Rosie Giraffe and Big Butt crowd in behind and shove, and next thing we all stuffed into the doorway with only Mercedes squeezing past us, smoothing out her jumper and walking right down the aisle. Then the rest of us tumble in like a glued-together jig-saw done all wrong. And people lookin at us. And it's like the time me and Sugar crashed into the Catholic church on a dare. But once we got in there and everything so hushed and holy and the candles and the bowin and the handkerchiefs on all the drooping heads, I just couldn't go through with the plan. Which was for me to run up to the altar and do a tap dance while Sugar played the nose flute and messed around in the holy water. And Sugar kept givin me the elbow. Then later teased me so bad I tied her up in the shower and turned it on and locked her in. And she'd be there till this day if Aunt Gretchen hadn't finally figured I was lyin about the boarder takin a shower.

Same thing in the store. We all walkin on tiptoe and hardly touchin the games   41
and puzzles and things. And I watched Miss Moore who is steady watchin us like she waitin for a sign. Like Mama Drewery watches the sky and sniffs the air and takes note of just how much slant is in the bird formation. Then me and Sugar bump smack into each other, so busy gazing at the toys, specially the sailboat. But we don't laugh and go into our fat-lady bump-stomach routine. We just stare at that price tag. Then Sugar run a finger over the whole boat. And I'm jealous and want to hit her. Maybe not her, but I sure want to punch somebody in the mouth.

"Watcha bring us here for, Miss Moore?"   42

"You sound angry, Sylvia. Are you mad about something?" Givin me one of them   43 grins like she tellin a grown-up joke that never turns out to be funny. And she's lookin very closely at me like maybe she planning to do my portrait from memory. I'm mad, but I won't give her that satisfaction. So I slouch around the store bein very bored and say, "Let's go."

Me and Sugar at the back of the train watchin the tracks whizzin by large then small then getting gobbled up in the dark. I'm thinkin about this tricky toy I saw in the store. A clown that somersaults on a bar then does chin-ups just cause you yank lightly at his leg. Cost $35. I could see me askin my mother for a $35 birthday clown. "You wanna who that costs what?" she'd say, cocking her head to the side to get a better view of the hole in my head. Thirty-five dollars could buy new bunk beds for Junior and Gretchen's boy. Thirty-five dollars and the whole household could go visit Granddaddy Nelson in the country. Thirty-five dollars would pay for the rent and the piano bill too. Who are these people that spend that much for performing clowns and $1000 for toy sailboats? What kinda work they do and how they live and how come we ain't in on it? Where we are is who we are, Miss Moore always pointin out. But it don't necessarily have to be that way, she always adds then waits for somebody to say that poor people have to wake up and demand their share of the pie and don't none of us know what kind of pie she talking about in the first damn place. But she ain't so smart cause I still got her four dollars from the taxi and she sure ain't gettin it. Messin up my day with this shit. Sugar nudges me in my pocket and winks. 44

Miss Moore lines us up in front of the mailbox where we started from, seem like years ago, and I got a headache for thinkin so hard. And we lean all over each other so we can hold up under the draggy-ass lecture she always finishes us off with at the end before we thank her for borin us to tears. But she just looks at us like she readin tea leaves. Finally she say, "Well, what did you think of F. A. O. Schwarz?" 45

Rosie Giraffe mumbles, "White folks crazy." 46

"I'd like to go there again when I get my birthday money," says Mercedes, and we shove her out the pack so she has to lean on the mailbox by herself. 47

"I'd like a shower. Tiring day," say Flyboy. 48

Then Sugar surprises me by sayin, "You know, Miss Moore, I don't think all of us here put together eat in a year what that sailboat costs." And Miss Moore lights up like somebody goosed her. "And?" she say, urging Sugar on. Only I'm standin on her foot so she don't continue. 49

"Imagine for a minute what kind of society it is in which some people can spend on a toy what it would cost to feed a family of six or seven. What do you think?" 50

"I think," say Sugar pushing me off her feet like she never done before, cause I whip her ass in a minute, "that this is not much of a democracy if you ask me. Equal chance to pursue happiness means an equal crack at the dough, don't it?" Miss Moore is besides herself and I am disgusted with Sugar's treachery. So I stand on her foot one more time to see if she'll shove me. She shuts up, and Miss Moore looks at me, sorrowfully I'm thinkin. And somethin weird is goin on, I can feel it in my chest. 51

"Anybody else learn anything today?" lookin dead at me. I walk away and Sugar has to run to catch up and don't even seem to notice when I shrug her arm off my shoulder. 52

"Well, we got four dollars anyway," she says. 53

"Uh hunh." 54

"We could go to Hascombs and get half a chocolate layer and then go to the Sun- 55
set and still have plenty money for potato chips and ice cream sodas."

"Un hunh." 56

"Race you to Hascombs," she say. 57

We start down the block and she gets ahead which is O.K. by me cause I'm going 58
to the West End and then over to the Drive to think this day through. She can run if
she want to and even run faster. But ain't nobody gonna beat me at nuthin.

Working with the Text

1. What do you learn from this story about life in New York City's Harlem in
the early 1960s? Why do you think the parents let Miss Moore take their children under her wing?

2. The children in the story seem to have had little awareness of the economic
inequities of American life before being educated by Miss Moore's "lesson."
Why do you think this might have been the case? Would poor children today
be similarly unaware?

3. Why do the children hang back before going into the store? How would
you describe the narrator's response to the events of the day, particularly at
the conclusion of the story?

4. If you have read Jacob Riis's *How the Other Half Lives* (a selection in this
chapter) consider the extent to which "The Lesson" offers support for and
criticism of Riis's view of the urban poor, the condition of their lives, and ways
that these conditions could be improved.

5. Keeping in mind the sassy and quite funny tone of the narrative, what
would you say is the theme of this story? Is it simply an indictment of economic inequity? Or does it suggest something larger about how a sense of inclusion or exclusion develops?

HELPING AND HATING THE HOMELESS

PETER MARIN

■ Freelance writer Peter Marin studied literature at Swarthmore College and
received his master's degree from Columbia University in 1958. Awarded fellow-
ships by both the Guggenheim Foundation and the National Endowment for the
Arts, Marin has published fiction and poetry, as well as several works of nonfiction including *The World of the Homeless* (1986) and *Freedom and Its Discontents:
Reflections on Four Decades of American Moral Experience* (1995). He has written
for a variety of publications and has been a contributing editor to *Harper's* magazine since 1982. In the following 1987 essay written for *Harper's,* Marin looks at
mainstream America's often contradictory and irrational response to the homeless, arguing that "the homeless embody all that bourgeois culture has for centuries tried to eradicate and destroy."

When I was a child, I had a recurring vision of how I would end as an old man: alone, in a sparsely furnished second-story room I could picture quite precisely, in a walk-up on Fourth Avenue in New York, where the secondhand bookstores then were. It was not a picture which frightened me. I liked it. The idea of anonymity and solitude and marginality must have seemed to me, back then, for reasons I do not care to remember, both inviting and inevitable. Later, out of college, I took to the road, hitchhiking and traveling on freights, doing odd jobs here and there, crisscrossing the country. I liked that too: the anonymity and the absence of constraint and the rough community I sometimes found. I felt at home on the road, perhaps because I felt at home nowhere else, and periodically, for years, I would return to that world, always with a sense of relief and release.

I have been thinking a lot about that these days, now that transience and homelessness have made their way into the national consciousness, and especially since the town I live in, Santa Barbara, has become well known because of the recent successful campaign to do away with the meanest aspects of its "sleeping ordinances"—a set of foolish laws making it illegal for the homeless to sleep at night in public places. During that campaign I got to know many of the homeless men and women in Santa Barbara, who tend to gather, night and day, in a small park at the lower end of town, not far from the tracks and the harbor, under the rooflike, overarching branches of a gigantic fig tree, said to be the oldest on the continent. There one enters much the same world I thought, as a child, I would die in, and the one in which I traveled as a young man: a "marginal" world inhabited by all those unable to find a place in "our" world. Sometimes, standing on the tracks close to the park, you can sense in the wind, or in the smell of tar and ties, the presence and age of that marginal world: the way it stretches backward and inevitably forward in time, parallel to our own world, always present, always close, and yet separated from us—at least in the mind—by a gulf few of us are interested in crossing.

Late last summer, at a city council meeting here in Santa Barbara, I saw, close up, the consequences of that strange combination of proximity and distance. The council was meeting to vote on the repeal of the sleeping ordinances, though not out of any sudden sense of compassion or justice. Council members had been pressured into it by the threat of massive demonstrations—"The Selma of the Eighties" was the slogan one heard among the homeless. But this threat that frightened the council enraged the town's citizens. Hundreds of them turned out for the meeting. One by one they filed to the microphone to curse the council and castigate the homeless. Drinking, doping, loitering, panhandling, defecating, urinating, molesting, stealing—the litany went on and on, was repeated over and over, accompanied by fantasies of disaster: the barbarian hordes at the gates, civilization ended.

What astonished me about the meeting was not what was said; one could have predicted that. It was the power and depth of the emotion revealed: the mindlessness of the fear, the vengefulness of the fury. Also, almost none of what was said had anything to do with the homeless people I know—not the ones I once traveled with, not the ones in town. They, the actual homeless men and women, might not have existed at all.

If I write about Santa Barbara, it is not because I think the attitudes at work here are unique. They are not. You find them everywhere in America. In the last few months I have visited several cities around the country, and in each of them I have found the same thing: more and more people in the streets, more and more suffering. (There are at least 350,000 homeless people in the country, perhaps as many as 3 million.) And, in talking to the good citizens of these cities, I found, almost always, the same thing: confusion and ignorance, or simple indifference, but anger too, and fear.

What follows here is an attempt to explain at least some of that anger and fear, to clear up some of the confusion, to chip away at the indifference. It is not meant to be definitive; how could it be? The point is to try to illuminate some of the darker corners of homelessness, those we ordinarily ignore, and those in which the keys to much that is now going on may be hidden.   6

The trouble begins with the word "homeless." It has become such an abstraction, and is applied to so many different kinds of people, with so many different histories and problems, that it is almost meaningless.   7

Homelessness, in itself, is nothing more than a condition visited upon men and women (and, increasingly, children) as the final stage of a variety of problems about which the word "homelessness" tells us almost nothing. Or, to put it another way, it is a catch basin into which pour all of the people disenfranchised or marginalized or scared off by processes beyond their control, those which lie close to the heart of American life. Here are the groups packed into the single category of "the homeless":   8

- Veterans, mainly from the war in Vietnam. In many American cities, vets make up close to 50 percent of all homeless males.
- The mentally ill. In some parts of the country, roughly a quarter of the homeless would, a couple of decades ago, have been institutionalized.
- The physically disabled or chronically ill, who do not receive any benefits or whose benefits do not enable them to afford permanent shelter.
- The elderly on fixed incomes whose funds are no longer sufficient for their needs.
- Men, women, and whole families pauperized by the loss of a job.
- Single parents, usually women, without the resources or skills to establish new lives.
- Runaway children, many of whom have been abused.
- Alcoholics and those in trouble with drugs (whose troubles often begin with one of the other conditions listed here).
- Immigrants, both legal and illegal, who often are not counted among the homeless because they constitute a "problem" in their own right.
- Traditional tramps, hobos, and transients, who have taken to the road or the streets for a variety of reasons and who prefer to be there.

You can quickly learn two things about the homeless from this list. First, you can learn that many of the homeless, before they were homeless, were people more or less like ourselves: members of the working or middle class. And you can learn that the world of the homeless has its roots in various policies, events, and ways of life for which some of us are responsible and from which some of us actually prosper.   9

We decide, as a people, to go to war, we ask our children to kill and to die, and the   10
result, years later, is grown men homeless on the street.

We change, with the best intentions, the laws pertaining to the mentally ill, and   11
then, without intention, neglect to provide them with services; and the result, in our
streets, drives some of us crazy with rage.

We cut taxes and prune budgets, we modernize industry and shift the balance of   12
trade, and the result of all these actions and errors can be read, sleeping form by
sleeping form, on our city streets.

The liberals cannot blame the conservatives. The conservatives cannot blame the   13
liberals. Homelessness is the *sum total* of our dreams, policies, intentions, errors,
omissions, cruelties, kindnesses, all of it recorded, in flesh, in the life of the streets.

You can also learn from this list one of the most important things there is to   14
know about the homeless—that they can be roughly divided into two groups: those
who have had homelessness forced upon them and want nothing more than to escape it; and those who have at least in part *chosen* it for themselves, and now accept,
or in some cases, embrace it.

I understand how dangerous it is to introduce the idea of choice into a discussion   15
of homelessness. It can all too easily be used to justify indifference or brutality
toward the homeless, or to argue that they are only getting what they "deserve." And
yet it seems to me that it is only by taking choice into account, in all of the intricacies of its various forms and expressions, that one can really understand certain
kinds of homelessness.

The fact is, many of the homeless are not only hapless victims but voluntary ex-   16
iles, "domestic refugees," people who have turned not against life itself but against
us, our life, American life. Look for a moment at the vets. The price of returning to
America was to forget what they had seen or learned in Vietnam, to "put it behind
them." But some could not do that, and the stress of trying showed up as alcoholism,
broken marriages, drug addiction, crime. And it showed up too as life on the street,
which was for some vets a desperate choice made in the name of life—the best they
could manage. It was a way of avoiding what might have occurred had they stayed
where they were: suicide, or violence done to others.

We must learn to accept that there may indeed be people, and not only vets, who   17
have seen so much of our world, or seen it so clearly, that to live in it becomes impossible. Here, for example, is the story of Alice, a homeless middle-aged woman in
Los Angeles, where there are, perhaps, 50,000 homeless people. It was set down a few
months ago by one of my students at the University of California, Santa Barbara,
where I taught for a semester. I had encouraged them to go find the homeless and
listen to their stories. And so, one day, when this student saw Alice foraging in a
dumpster outside a McDonald's, he stopped and talked to her:

> She told me she had led a pretty normal life as she grew up and eventually
> went to college. From there she went on to Chicago to teach school. She was
> single and lived in a small apartment.
>
> One night, after she got off the train after school, a man began to follow
> her to her apartment building. When she got to her door she saw a knife and
> the man hovering behind her. She had no choice but to let him in. The man
> raped her.

After that, things got steadily worse. She had a nervous breakdown. She went to a mental institution for three months, and when she went back to her apartment she found her belongings gone. The landlord had sold them to cover the rent she hadn't paid.

She had no place to go and no job because the school had terminated her employment. She slipped into depression. She lived with friends until she could muster enough money for a ticket to Los Angeles. She said she no longer wanted to burden her friends, and that if she had to live outside, at least Los Angeles was warmer than Chicago.

It is as if she began back then to take on the mentality of a street person. She resolved herself to homelessness. She's been out West since 1980, without a home or job. She seems happy, with her best friend being her cat. But the scars of memories still haunt her, and she is running from them, or should I say *him.*

This is, in essence, the same story one hears over and over again on the street. You begin with an ordinary life; then an event occurs—traumatic, catastrophic; smaller events follow, each one deepening the original wound; finally, homelessness becomes inevitable, or begins to *seem* inevitable to the person involved—the only way out of an intolerable situation. You are struck continually, hearing these stories, by something seemingly unique in American life, the absolute isolation involved. In what other culture would there be such an absence or failure of support from familial, social, or institutional sources? Even more disturbing is the fact that it is often our supposed sources of support—family, friends, government organizations—that have caused the problem in the first place. [18]

Everything that happened to Alice—the rape, the loss of job and apartment, the breakdown—was part and parcel of a world gone radically wrong, a world, for Alice, no longer to be counted on, no longer worth living in. Her homelessness can be seen as flight, as failure of will or nerve, even, perhaps, as *disease.* But it can also be seen as a mute, furious refusal, a self-imposed exile far less appealing to the rest of us than ordinary life, but *better,* in Alice's terms. [19]

We like to think, in America, that everything is redeemable, that everything broken can be magically made whole again, and that what has been "dirtied" can be cleansed. Recently I saw on television that one of the soaps had introduced the character of a homeless old woman. A woman in her thirties discovers that her long-lost mother has appeared in town, on the streets. After much searching the mother is located and identified and embraced; and then she is scrubbed and dressed in style, restored in a matter of days to her former upper-class habits and role. [20]

A triumph—but one more likely to occur on television than in real life. Yes, many of those on the streets could be transformed, rehabilitated. But there are others whose lives have been irrevocably changed, damaged beyond repair, and who no longer want help, who no longer recognize the *need* for help, and whose experience in our world has made them want only to be left alone. How, for instance, would one restore Alice's life, or reshape it in a way that would satisfy *our* notion of what a life should be? What would it take to return her to the fold? How to erase the four years of homelessness, which have become as familiar to her, and as much a home, as her "normal" life once was? Whatever we think of the way in which she has resolved her difficulties, it constitutes a sad peace made with the world. Intruding ourselves upon [21] it in the name of redemption is by no means as simple a task—or as justifiable a task—as one might think.

It is important to understand too that however disorderly and dirty and unman- 22 ageable the world of homeless men and women like Alice appears to us, it is not without its significance, and its rules and rituals. The homeless in our cities mark out for themselves particular neighborhoods, blocks, buildings, doorways. They impose on themselves often obsessively strict routines. They reduce their world to a small area, and thereby protect themselves from a world that might otherwise be too much to bear.

Daily the city eddies around the homeless. The crowds flowing past leave a few 23 feet, a gap. We do not touch the homeless world. Perhaps we cannot touch it. It remains separate even as the city surrounds it.

The homeless, simply because they are homeless, are strangers, alien—and there- 24 fore a threat. Their presence, in itself, comes to constitute a kind of violence; it deprives us of our sense of safety. Let me use myself as an example. I know, and respect, many of those now homeless on the streets of Santa Barbara. Twenty years ago, some of them would have been my companions and friends. And yet, these days, if I walk through the park near my home and see strangers bedding down for the night, my first reaction, if not fear, is a sense of annoyance and intrusion, of worry and alarm. I think of my teenage daughter, who often walks through the park, and then of my house, a hundred yards away, and I am tempted—only tempted, but tempted, still—to call the "proper" authorities to have the strangers moved on. Out of sight, out of mind.

Notice: I do not bring them food. I do not offer them shelter or a shower in the 25 morning. I do not even stop to talk. Instead, I think: my daughter, my house, my privacy. What moves me is not the threat of *danger*—nothing as animal as that. Instead there pops up inside of me, neatly in a row, a set of anxieties, ones you might arrange in a dollhouse living room and label: Family of bourgeois fears. The point is this: Our response to the homeless is fed by a complex set of cultural attitudes, habits of thought, and fantasies and fears so familiar to us, so common, that they have become a *second* nature and might as well be instinctive, for all the control we have over them. And it is by no means easy to untangle this snarl of responses. What does seem clear is that the homeless embody all that bourgeois culture has for centuries tried to eradicate and destroy.

If you look to the history of Europe you find that homelessness first appeared (or 26 is first acknowledged) at the very same moment that bourgeois culture begins to appear. The same processes produced them both: the breakup of feudalism, the rise of commerce and cities, the combined triumphs of capitalism, industrialism, and individualism. The historian Fernand Braudel, in *The Wheels of Commerce,* describes, for instance, the armies of impoverished men and women who began to haunt Europe as far back as the eleventh century. And the makeup of these masses? Essentially the same then as it is now: the unfortunates, the throwaways, the misfits, the deviants.

> In the eighteenth century, all sorts and conditions were to be found in this
> human dross . . . widows, orphans, cripples, . . . journeymen who had broken
> their contracts, out-of-work labourers, homeless priests with no living, old

men, fire victims, . . . war victims, deserters, discharged soldiers, would-be
vendors of useless articles, vagrant preachers with or without licenses, "pregnant servant-girls and unmarried mothers driven from home," children sent
out "to find bread or to maraud."

Then, as now, distinctions were made between the "homeless" and the suppos-   27
edly "deserving" poor, those who knew their place and willingly sustained, with
their labors, the emergent bourgeois world.

> The good paupers were accepted, lined up and registered on the official list;
> they had a right to public charity and were sometimes allowed to solicit it
> outside churches in prosperous districts, when the congregation came out, or
> in market places. . . .
>   When it comes to beggars and vagrants, it is a very different story, and
> different pictures meet the eye: crowds, mobs, processions, sometimes mass
> emigrations, "along the country highways or the streets of the Towns and
> Villages," by beggars "whom hunger and nakedness has driven from
> home." . . . The towns dreaded these alarming visitors and drove them out as
> soon as they appeared on the horizon.

And just as the distinctions made about these masses were the same then as they   28
are now, so too was the way society saw them. They seemed to bourgeois eyes (as
they still do) the one segment of society that remained resistant to progress, unas-
similable and incorrigible, inimical to all order.

It is in the nineteenth century, in the Victorian era, that you can find the begin-   29
nings of our modern strategies for dealing with the homeless: the notion that they
should be controlled and perhaps eliminated through "help." With the Victorians
we begin to see the entangling of self-protection with social obligation, the strategy
of masking self-interest and the urge to control as *moral duty.* Michel Foucault has
spelled this out in his books on madness and punishment: the zeal with which the
overseers of early bourgeois culture tried to purge, improve, and purify all of urban
civilization—whether through schools and prisons, or, quite literally, with public
baths and massive new water and sewage systems. Order, ordure—this is, in essence,
the tension at the heart of bourgeois culture, and it was the singular genius of the
Victorians to make it the main component of their medical, aesthetic, *and* moral
systems. It was not a sense of justice or even empathy which called for charity or
new attitudes toward the poor; it was *hygiene.* The very same attitudes appear in
nineteenth-century America. Charles Loring Brace, in an essay on homeless and
vagrant children written in 1876, described the treatment of delinquents in this
way: "Many of their vices drop from them like the old and verminous clothing they
left behind. . . . The entire change of circumstances seems to cleanse them of bad
habits." Here you have it all: *vices, verminous clothing, cleansing them of bad
habits*—the triple association of poverty with vice with dirt, an equation in which
each term comes to stand for all of them.

These attitudes are with us still; that is the point. In our own century the person   30
who has written most revealingly about such things is George Orwell, who tried to
analyze his own middle-class attitudes toward the poor. In 1933, in *Down and Out
in Paris and London,* he wrote about tramps:

> In childhood we are taught that tramps are blackguards, . . . a repulsive, rather
> dangerous creature, who would rather die than work or wash, and wants noth-
> ing but to beg, drink or rob hen-houses. The tramp monster is no truer to life
> than the sinister Chinaman of the magazines, but he is very hard to get rid of.
> The very word "tramp" evokes his image.

All of this is still true in America, though now it is not the word "tramp" but the   31
word "homeless" that evokes the images we fear. It is the homeless who smell. Here,
for instance, is part of a paper a student of mine wrote about her first visit to a Rescue Mission on skid row.

> The sermon began. The room was stuffy and smelly. The mixture of body
> odors and cooking was nauseating. I remember thinking: How can these
> people share this facility? They must be repulsed by each other. They had
> strange habits and dispositions. They were a group of dirty, dishonored, weird
> people to me.
>   When it was over I ran to my car, went home, and took a shower. I felt
> extremely dirty. Through the day I would get flashes of that disgusting smell.

To put it as bluntly as I can, for many of us the homeless are *shit*. And our poli-   32
cies toward them, our spontaneous sense of disgust and horror, our wish to be rid
of them—all of this has hidden in it, close to its heart, our feelings about excrement.
Even Marx, that most bourgeois of revolutionaries, described the deviant *lumpen* in
The Eighteenth Brumaire of Louis Bonaparte as "scum, offal, refuse of all classes."
These days, in puritanical Marxist nations, they are called "parasites"—a word, perhaps not incidentally, one also associates with human waste.

What I am getting at here is the *nature* of the desire to help the homeless—what   33
is hidden behind it and why it so often does harm. Every government program, almost every private project, is geared as much to the needs of those giving help as it
is to the needs of the homeless. Go to any government agency, or, for that matter, to
most private charities, and you will find yourself enmeshed, at once, in a bureaucracy so tangled and oppressive, or confronted with so much moral arrogance and
contempt, that you will be driven back out into the streets for relief.

Santa Barbara, where I live, is as good an example as any. There are three main   34
shelters in the city—all of them private. Between them they provide fewer than a
hundred beds a night for the homeless. Two of the three shelters are religious in nature: the Rescue Mission and the Salvation Army. In the mission, as in most places
in the country, there are elaborate and stringent rules. Beds go first to those who
have not been there for two months, and you can stay for only two nights in any
two-month period. No shelter is given to those who are not sober. Even if you go to
the mission only for a meal, you are required to listen to sermons and participate in
prayer, and you are regularly proselytized—sometimes overtly, sometimes subtly.
There are obligatory, regimented showers. You go to bed precisely at ten: lights out,
no reading, no talking. After the lights go out you will find fifteen men in a room
with double-decker bunks. As the night progresses the room grows stuffier and hot-
ter. Men toss, turn, cough, and moan. In the morning you are awakened precisely at
five forty-five. Then breakfast. At seven-thirty you are back on the street.

The town's newest shelter was opened almost a year ago by a consortium of local   35 churches. Families and those who are employed have first call on the beds—a policy which excludes the congenitally homeless. Alcohol is not simply forbidden *in* the shelter; those with a history of alcoholism must sign a "contract" pledging to remain sober and chemical-free. Finally, in a paroxysm of therapeutic bullying, the shelter has added a new wrinkle: If you stay more than two days you are required to fill out and then discuss with a social worker a complex form listing what you perceive as your personal failings, goals, and strategies—all of this for men and women who simply want a place to lie down out of the rain!

It is these attitudes, in various forms and permutations, that you find repeated endlessly in America. We are moved either to "redeem" the homeless or to punish them. Perhaps there is nothing consciously hostile about it. Perhaps it is simply that as the machinery of bureaucracy cranks itself up to deal with these problems, attitudes assert themselves automatically. But whatever the case, the fact remains that almost every one of our strategies for helping the homeless is simply an attempt to rearrange the world *cosmetically,* in terms of how it looks and smells to *us.* Compassion is little more than the passion for control. 36

The central question emerging from all this is, What does a society owe to its members in trouble, and *how* is that debt to be paid? It is a question which must be answered in two parts: first, in relation to the men and women who have been marginalized against their will, and then, in a slightly different way, in relation to those who have chosen (or accept or even prize) their marginality. 37

As for those who have been marginalized against their wills, I think the general answer is obvious: A society owes its members whatever it takes for them to regain their places in the social order. And when it comes to specific remedies, one need only read backward the various processes which have created homelessness and then figure out where help is likely to do the most good. But the real point here is not the specific remedies required—affordable housing, say—but the basis upon which they must be offered, the necessary underlying ethical notion we seem in this nation unable to grasp: that those who are the inevitable casualties of modern industrial capitalism and the free-market system are entitled, *by right,* and by the simple virtue of their participation in that system, to whatever help they need. They are entitled to help to find and hold their places in the society whose social contract they have, in effect, signed and observed. 38

Look at that for just a moment: the notion of a contract. The majority of homeless Americans have kept, insofar as they could, to the terms of that contract. In any shelter these days you can find men and women who have worked ten, twenty, forty years, and whose lives have nonetheless come to nothing. These are people who cannot afford a place in the world they helped create. And in return? Is it life on the street they have earned? Or the cruel charity we so grudgingly grant them? 39

But those marginalized against their will are only half the problem. There remains, still, the question of whether we owe anything to those who are voluntarily marginal. What about them: the street people, the rebels, and the recalcitrants, those who have torn up their social contracts or returned them unsigned? 40

I was in Las Vegas last fall, and I went out to the Rescue Mission at the lower end of town, on the edge of the black ghetto, where I first stayed years ago on my way 41 west. It was twilight, still hot; in the vacant lot next-door to the mission 200 men were lining up for supper. A warm wind blew along the street lined with small houses and salvage yards, and in the distance I could see the desert's edge and the smudge of low hills in the fading light. There were elderly alcoholics in line, and derelicts, but mainly the men were the same sort I had seen here years ago: youngish, out of work, restless and talkative, the drifters and wanderers for whom the word "wanderlust" was invented.

At supper—long communal tables, thin gruel, stale sweet rolls, ice water—a huge   42
black man in his twenties, fierce and muscular, sat across from me. "I'm from the Coast, man," he said. "Never been away from home before. Ain't sure I like it. Sure don't like *this* place. But I lost my job back home a couple of weeks ago and figured, why wait around for another. I thought I'd come out here, see me something of the world."

After supper, a squat Portuguese man in his mid-thirties, hunkered down against   43
the mission wall, offered me a smoke and told me: "Been sleeping in my car, up the street, for a week. Had my own business back in Omaha. But I got bored, man. Sold everything, got a little dough, came out here. Thought I'd work construction. Let me tell you, this is one tough town."

In a world better than ours, I suppose, men (or women) like this might not exist.   44
Conservatives seem to have no trouble imagining a society so well disciplined and moral that deviance of this kind would disappear. And leftists envision a world so just, so generous, that deviance would vanish along with inequity. But I suspect that there will always be something at work in some men and women to make them restless with the systems others devise for them, and to move them outward toward the edges of the world, where life is always riskier, less organized, and easier going.

Do we owe anything to these men and women, who reject our company and what   45
we offer and yet nonetheless seem to demand *something* from us?

We owe them, I think, at least a place to exist, a way to exist. That may not be a   46
moral obligation, in the sense that our obligation to the involuntarily marginal is clearly a moral one, but it is an obligation nevertheless, one you might call an existential obligation.

Of course, it may be that I think we owe these men something because I have   47
liked men like them, and because I want their world to be there always, as a place to hide or rest. But there is more to it than that. I think we as a society need men like these. A society needs its margins as much as it needs art and literature. It needs holes and gaps, *breathing spaces,* let us say, into which men and women can escape and live, when necessary, in ways otherwise denied them. Margins guarantee to society a flexibility, an elasticity, and allow it to accommodate itself to the natures and needs of its members. When margins vanish, society becomes too rigid, too oppressive by far, and therefore inimical to life.

It is for such reasons that, in cultures like our own, marginal men and women   48
take on a special significance. They are all we have left to remind us of the narrowness of the received truths we take for granted. "Beyond the pale," they somehow redefine the pale, or remind us, at least, that *something* is still out there, beyond the pale. They preserve, perhaps unconsciously, a dream that would otherwise cease to exist, the dream of having a place in the world, and of being *left alone.*

Quixotic? Infantile? Perhaps. But remember. . . . [w]hat we are talking about here is *freedom,* and with it, perhaps, an echo of the dream men brought, long ago, to wilderness America. I use the word "freedom" gingerly, in relation to lives like these: skewed, crippled, emptied of everything we associate with a full, or realized, freedom. But perhaps this is the condition into which freedom has fallen among us. Art has been "appreciated" out of existence; literature has become an extension of the university, replete with tenure and pensions; and as for politics, the ideologies which ring us round seem too silly or shrill by far to speak for life. What is left, then, is this mute and intransigent independence, this "waste" of life which refuses even interpretation, and which cannot be assimilated to any ideology, and which therefore can be put to no one's use. In its crippled innocence and the perfection of its superfluity it amounts, almost, to a rebellion against history, and that is no small thing. 49

Let me put it as simply as I can: What we see on the streets of our cities are two dramas, both of which cut to the troubled heart of the culture and demand from us a response we may not be able to make. There is the drama of those struggling to survive by regaining their place in the social order. And there is the drama of those struggling to survive outside of it. 50

The resolution of both struggles depends on a third drama occurring at the heart of the culture: the tension and contention between the magnanimity we owe to life and the darker tendings of the human psyche: our fear of strangeness, our hatred of deviance, our love of order and control. How we mediate by default or design between those contrary forces will determine not only the destinies of the homeless, but also something crucial about the nation, and perhaps—let me say it—about our own souls. 51

Working with the Text

1. In paragraph 3 Marin records the litany of complaints leveled at the homeless during a Santa Barbara town meeting: "Drinking, doping, loitering, panhandling, defecating, urinating, molesting, stealing." He goes on to suggest that "almost none of what was said had anything to do with the homeless people I know." How does he account for these images? How do you?

2. When Marin maintains that some people are homeless by choice, why does he go on to note "how dangerous it is to introduce the idea of choice into a discussion of homelessness"? What is he suggesting about feelings of difference when he says that these "voluntary exiles" "have turned not against life itself but against us, our life, American life"? What is your response to such an attitude toward "American life"?

3. In what ways does Marin suggest that the world of the homeless is a community?

4. What does Marin mean when he refers to the "set of anxieties" (¶ 25) he calls "bourgeois fears"? How do these fears underlie "the *nature* of the desire to help the homeless" that "often does harm" (¶ 33)?

5. Analyze what Marin considers society's obligation to those who have been "marginalized against their wills." Why does he believe society bears this obligation? Do you agree with his assessment?

6. In arguing that we owe those who are marginalized by choice "a place to exist, a way to exist" (¶ 46), Marin makes a complex point about the need for margins in a society. What is he getting at here? Do you agree with him?

MAKES ME WANNA HOLLER

NATHAN McCALL

■ Nathan McCall grew up in a working-class household in Portsmouth, Virginia, during the 1960s and 1970s. During and after high school, he had several brushes with the law—including serving a three-year prison term for armed robbery—before finishing his education and receiving a degree in journalism. He is now a reporter for the *Washington Post*. In 1994 he published the autobiographical *Makes Me Wanna Holler: A Young Black Man in America,* which chronicles his transformation from an angry, self-destructive criminal to a successful journalist. He has said, "Sometimes I feel suspended in a sort of netherworld, belonging fully neither to the streets nor to the establishment." In the following chapter from *Makes Me Wanna Holler,* McCall recounts some of the events of his childhood and early teens that shaped him into the angry young man he would have to tame.

The folks in my neighborhood were resolute about trying to protect our physical safety, but seemed confused when confronted with more subtle racial hazards, such as our fixation on color. I was a product of that confusion.

My enchantment with whiteness dated at least as far back as Key West, where our family got our first television set. I'd spend hours in front of that black-and-white set, gazing spellbound at whites on TV, drinking in the beauty of their ivory skin, which seemed purer, cleaner, than my own. I was no more than seven or eight years old, but I still recall the Clairol hair-coloring commercial where they zoomed the camera in for a close-up on some saucy white broad who sensually tossed her blond mane backward and forward all over her face. Near the end of the commercial, a throaty voice chimed in and asked, "Is it true blondes have more fun?"

I thought of that ad every time I saw a blonde in real life or on TV. It also came to mind one day when I noticed a group of young whites riding down the street in a convertible ahead of our family car. The convertible's top was down, and the white people's long hair fluttered in the wind, like the TV blonde's. I thought, *White people have more fun.*

One sunny afternoon around that time, I was playing at the beach with my brothers when a little white girl standing nearby began covering her body with the pale, paste-like clay that blankets the Key West ocean floor. I imitated her, rubbing clay on my upper body. The girl looked at me and said, kindly, "If you let the clay dry, maybe you'll be white like me." For a moment, I considered that it might just work. It seemed a grand idea to let the clay dry on my body and turn me chalky white: After all, *White people have more fun.*

It's funny how the memory works. You can forget the name of someone you were introduced to yesterday, yet recall minor details of incidents that took place in your life years ago. For some reason, I always remembered that exchange. When I reflected on it years later, it occurred to me that even at that young age a little black boy and a little white girl had already begun to learn their place in this race-obsessed country. The girl knew she was a member of the favored race, and I understood that my color would be a burden to me.

In Cavalier Manor, I sensed that other blacks struggled with variations of my racial affliction (though I didn't recognize it as such). Even some of the grown-ups who set out to arm their young with racial pride seemed haunted by contradictions, which their children absorbed. Whenever we were going to restaurants or other public places where a lot of white folks would be around, my mother insisted that we get meticulously groomed and pressed beforehand, and when we got there she reminded us (it was more of a threat) to sit, stiff as soldiers, and be quiet. Every now and then, if one of us dared to cut up in public, Mama would yank him firmly by one arm, pull him to within an inch of her face, and whisper through clenched teeth, "Stop showing your color. Stop acting like a *nigger!*"

My brothers and I would sit solemnly and watch as rowdy white kids entered those same public places, shirtless, barefoot, and grimy. Their parents gave them the run of the joint, allowing them to stomp, shout, scream, do virtually anything they wanted, including tear up the place. I envied their freedom and craved the specialness that excluded them from our self-defeating burden: It seemed we were niggers by birthright and destined to spend our entire lives striving in vain to shed that rap. But white people could never be niggers, even when they acted like niggers with a capital *N.*

Without knowing what they were doing, a lot of adults in black families passed along notions to their young about white folks' superiority. Even Bampoose, my grandmother, did her part to condition us. Her husband—my grandfather—died of mysterious causes before I was born. Bampoose lived with our family for most of the time after that and worked as a domestic for white folks, cleaning their homes, cooking their meals, and raising their children. When we moved to Cavalier Manor, Bampoose began working for an affluent Jewish family, the Diamondsteins, who lived in Norfolk. Every morning, she rose before daybreak and caught several city buses to get to their house, ten miles away.

The daily trips to the Diamondsteins provided Bampoose her only diversion away from our home. She was shy and never socialized outside the family. About the most exciting thing going in Bampoose's life was the fierce games of checkers she played with my brothers and me; during those games, Bampoose often told us what the Diamondsteins' children had done that day.

The two Diamondstein children, Richard and Jamie, were about my age. Bampoose told us every detail about them—their habits, their likes and dislikes, and how well they were doing in school. She also told us about the fine dinner parties their parents threw and the elaborate vacations the family took. It was our first glimpse into the world of white people beyond *My Three Sons* and *Leave It to Beaver* on TV.

To me, Richard and Jamie took on the flawless, larger-than-life quality of story- 11 book characters. I decided I wanted to be just like them. When Bampoose brought us clothes that Richard and Jamie's parents were throwing away, I relished those threads like they were store-bought, and nourished a secret pride that they made me look like their former owners. Once, when Bampoose was helping me get dressed, she said, "Richard and Jamie tuck their T-shirts inside their underwear." I began tucking my T-shirt inside my Fruit of the Loom briefs, just like them.

Bampoose saw how much I admired Richard and Jamie, and used it to gain ad- 12 vantage when she was unable to catch me to lay on a spanking for some misdeed of mine. All she needed to do to regain control of me was mention my white child idols. "Boy, why don't you stop actin' up like that! I don't have to tell Richard and Jamie more than once to stop doin' something. They are *nice* boys. They do everything I tell them to." It worked, too. I'd straighten up and try to behave like the gentlemen I imagined Richard and Jamie to be.

I had often tried to imagine how that family looked. One evening, when my 13 brothers and I were sitting in the den, watching TV, Bampoose brought home a picture of herself taken at the Diamondsteins' home. When she handed me the picture, I studied long and hard the faces of the white people I'd heard so much about. In the picture, Bampoose, dressed in a maid's uniform, stood in the Diamondsteins' kitchen with an apron tied around her waist. Jamie, the younger boy, stood directly in front of her, clasping her wrinkled, caramel-colored hands. Richard stood beside his brother, in front of Bampoose. The boys had a scrubbed, well-attended look about them. They were dressed in fine clothes, and their hair was neatly combed. Bampoose, a short, petite woman who usually maintained a poker face, stood there smiling, like she was the proud mother of those two white boys. Looking at that picture, I couldn't help but feel jealous. It seemed Richard and Jamie had laid claim to attentions and affections from my grandmother that should have been reserved for me.

I also noticed in the picture that Jamie had dark, straight hair, which he parted 14 and combed sideways on top, like Beaver Cleaver's. I wondered why my thick, unyielding naps couldn't be straight and supple so I could jerk my head back to sling my hair out of my eyes the way white folks constantly did. One day, I got a can of my stepfather's pomade and set out to change my steel wool into "good" hair. I packed the thick, heavy grease into my hair and brushed it until the naps began to unfurl and lie down on my head in perfect submission, just like Jamie's. Minutes later, my hair started to shrivel. It went from straight, to curly, and back to nappy. Nappy and greasy.

My parents were preparing to take us to church that morning. Just as I was about 15 to climb into the car, my mother took one look at my glistening head and got mad as hell. "Boy, *what* did you do to your hair?!"

"I only put some grease in it, Mama!" 16

Mama yanked me away from the car and slapped me in the back of the head. 17 *Whack!* "Get your butt back in that house and wash that mess outta your head, boy!"

I went inside, wailing, grabbed a bar of soap, and began scouring my greasy head 18 in the bathroom sink, like dirty clothes on a washboard. I nearly scalded my scalp trying to rinse out that gummy pomade. Worse than the blistering water was the painful realization that no matter how hard I tried I could never make my hair straight like white people's hair.

After retiring from the Navy in 1966, my stepfather held two jobs to make ends meet. He worked in the shipyard, and on weekends he went to do gardening work for white people in a neighborhood called Sterling Point. 19

Initially, my parents decided I was too young to go to Sterling Point, but Billy, Dwight, and Junnie went almost from the start. They hated it and bitched all the time. It wasn't clear to me what they were so annoyed about. Our stepfather paid them by the hour for working with him, so I figured they should feel grateful. My brothers used the money they earned to buy school clothes. They always had spending change in their pockets. What more did they want? I had big-time dreams of what I'd do with the money I made when I got old enough to go to Sterling Point. Finally, when I turned thirteen, I got my chance. 20

Sterling Point was the most affluent neighborhood in Portsmouth. Not only were its white residents set apart from everybody else in the city by their wealth and status, they were physically separated from the rest by the James River and the Churchland Bridge. I remember that when we cruised down High Street toward the bridge, my stepfather slowed the car at the incline to avoid rattling the garden tools sticking out from the back of the opened trunk. I sat in the backseat, sandwiched between Dwight and Billy, who were staring quietly out their windows. We reached the top of the high-arcing bridge and I looked over into the river and saw hordes of colorful sailboats drifting lazily along in the water. I nudged Billy. "Look at all those sailboats in the river!" 21

He yanked his elbow away from my hand, gritted his teeth, and growled in a whisper, "Leave me alone, boy!" 22

Dwight, likewise, and Junnie, who was sitting up front, ignored the dazzling sight of the boats with their brilliantly colored sails. I didn't know specifically why my brothers had an attitude that Saturday morning, but it was clear that our destination had a lot to do with it. 23

When we reached the other side of the bridge, Dad turned left into the elegant neighborhood and I saw shady streets and sprawling, two-story brick estates with antebellum-style columns, expansive yards, and wrought-iron fences. Despite its elegance, the neighborhood had a ghostly, antiseptic air about it. People didn't socialize outdoors or walk down the streets like they did in Cavalier Manor. The only people visible in the placid streets were groups of black women who trudged slowly up the curbless lanes into winding driveways and stately mansions. I nudged Dwight and asked, "Who are they?" 24

"They work for white people out here. They do the same kind of work Bampoose does for the Diamondsteins." 25

In those first few weekends, I learned to mow the grounds of the large estates, trim the hedges, prune the shrubs, and tend the flower beds. We gave the places the manicured look the you see in *House and Garden* magazine. It seemed just like working at home—until, that is, three white boys about my age reminded me one 26 day where I was. My stepfather and I were down on our knees, pulling up crabgrass, when they bolted out the front door of the house we were tending to and began bouncing a ball in the spiraling driveway, a few feet away from where we were working. Every now and then, I looked up and waited for them to acknowledge my stepfather's presence in the way that my parents had taught my brothers and me to speak to grown-ups when entering their company. But the boys never said a word. They didn't even look his way. They kept on bouncing the ball and ran around us as if we were trees, shrubs, or some other inanimate part of the scenery. Any other time, my stepfather would've gotten on the children's cases for forgetting their manners. But this day, he looked up whenever the ball bounced close by, flashed the three boys a fixed smile, and kept working.

Those kids' arrogance made me self-conscious. It occurred to me how docile my [27] stepfather and I must have looked there on our knees, working on their yard while they played, carefreely, about. They were as self-assured about their exalted place in the world as my stepfather was certain of how contained his life was. To them, he was no more than a fucking utility, a faceless gardener. To him, they were important people, children of some of the most powerful white folks in Portsmouth.

One of these powerful white folks—and one of my father's best clients—was [28] Richard Davis, who eventually became mayor of Portsmouth. We saw him occasionally, buttoned down in suit and tie, rushing to his car. Always, he dashed out, waved, then hurriedly drove off. I saw more of his wife, an attractive young blonde who busied herself supervising domestic matters. One hot day, she came outside to talk with my stepfather. "Bonnie, I brought you and your boys some lemonade to help cool you off. It sure is hot out here!"

"Yeah, it really is hot," he said, straining to make small talk. [29]

We took a break and gulped down the lemonade. Mrs. Davis looked at us and [30] smiled a contented smile, then issued more instructions for the day. "Bonnie, I want you to do the flower beds for me today, and pull up the grass around the back of the house. I don't want it to build up too much because it might attract snakes."

When she had finished, Mrs. Davis pranced back into her spacious, air- [31] conditioned house and closed the door. My stepfather glanced uneasily at me. I turned away, embarrassed that I had seen the humiliating exchange. I set down my unfinished drink, returned to work, and thought about what I'd just heard. *Bonnie?* That was the first time I'd heard anybody, including my mother, call my stepfather by his first name. He disliked the name anyway because it was a girl's name, but most important was the issue of respect. He addressed Mrs. Davis by her last name, but she called him *Bonnie.* The sound of the name rolling so casually off that white woman's lips stabbed me like a knife in the chest. It sounded like she was talking to a child. A boy.

At school, it was commonly understood that white folks considered grown black [32] men to be boys. "Boy" was a fighting word, one of the most detested, disrespectful things somebody could call someone else. More fights started over one person calling another "boy" than over anything else. To counter that indignity, we addressed each other respectfully as "man," even though we were not adults:

"Hey, man, you goin' to play basketball today?" [33]

"Naw, man, I got too much homework to do." [34]

In the following weeks, I began to pay close attention to other racial nuances in   35
my stepfather's interactions with people in Sterling Point. I didn't like what I saw. I
didn't like the way he humbled himself and smiled when white folks were around. I
grew to hate the sight of his big six-foot two-inch frame kneeling, with a wide-
brimmed straw hat on his head, pulling up crabgrass while one of those privileged
white people stood over him, supervising the menial work. It looked too much like
pictures of downtrodden sharecroppers and field slaves I'd seen in books.

It is difficult sometimes to pinpoint defining moments in a life. But I'm certain   36
that that period marked my realization of something it seemed white folks had been
trying to get across to me for most of my young life—that there were two distinct
worlds in America, and a different set of rules for each: The white one was full of the
possibilities of life. The dark one was just that—dark and limited.

Over time, I shared my brothers' resentment when my stepfather made us go   37
with him to Sterling Point, even though I knew our family badly needed the extra
money. When we drove through Cavalier Manor during our rides to Sterling Point,
I slumped down in the seat so my friends wouldn't see me riding in a car with a lawn
mower and gardening tools sticking out of the trunk. I joined my brothers' silent
brooding during the rides back home and, like them, became sullen, even when we
crossed the scenic Churchland Bridge overlooking the colorful sailboats below.

My harshest introduction to the world of white folks came in September 1966, when   38
my parents sent me to Alford J. Mapp, a white school across town. It was the beginning of my sixth-grade school year, and I was walking down the hall, searching for
my new class, when a white boy timed my steps, extended his foot, and tripped me.
The boy and his friends nudged each other and laughed as I stumbled into a locker,
spilling books and papers everywhere. "Hey, nigger," the boy said. "You dropped
something."

The word sounded vile coming from his white mouth. When I regained my foot-   39
ing, I tore into that cat and tried to take his head off. Pinning him against a locker, I
punched him in the face and kept on punching him until his two buddies jumped
in to help him out. While other white students crowded around and cheered them
on, we scuffled there in the hall until the bell rang, signaling the start of the next
class period. Like combatants in a prizefight, we automatically stopped throwing
punches and separated at the sound of the bell. The white boys went their way down
the hall, calling me names along the way and threatening to retaliate. I gathered my
papers, straightened my clothes, and reeled toward my next class, dazed, trying to
figure out what had just happened to me.

My parents sent me to Mapp in 1966 because that was the first year that blacks in   40
Portsmouth were able to attend school wherever they wanted. The U.S. Supreme
Court had long before ruled against the notion of separate but equal schools; still,
Virginia, one of the states that had resisted desegregation, was slow in putting together a busing plan. Without a plan to ship black students to schools across town,
over the years blacks and whites in Portsmouth had simply remained in separate
schools. I could have gone to W. E. Waters, a junior high school that had just been
built in our neighborhood, but, like many blacks then, my parents figured I could
get a better education at the white school across town.

I was proud of their decision and held it out teasingly to my brothers as proof   41
that I was the smart one in the family, that I held more academic promise than
them. Billy had flunked the second grade, and Dwight and Junnie never showed
much interest in books. My less studious brothers would attend their regular, all-
black high school, but I was going to a *white* school, which made me feel special.

My parents didn't talk with me beforehand about the challenge I would face as   42
one in the first wave of blacks to integrate Mapp. We had all seen TV news footage
of police in riot gear escorting black students through hostile, jeering crowds to en-
roll in all-white high schools and colleges across the country, but for various reasons
my parents saw no cause for alarm at Mapp. It was only a junior high school, which
seemed far less menacing than the racially torn high schools and college campuses
we heard about. Besides, there were no warning signals in Portsmouth to tip off my
parents, no public protests by white citizens or high-profile white supremacist
politicians like Alabama governor George Wallace threatening to buck the school
integration plan.

At Mapp, I was the only African American in most of my classes. When I walked   43
into one room and sat down, the students near me would get up and move away, as
if my dark skin were dirty and hideous to them. Nobody talked directly to me. Instead, they shot daggers to each other that were intended for me. "You know, I hate
niggers," they would say. "I don't understand why they're always following white
people everywhere. We can't seem to get away from them. Why don't they just stay
in their own schools?"

It wasn't much better dealing with white teachers. They avoided eye contact with   44
me as much as possible and pretended not to see or hear white student hecklers. It
was too much for an eleven-year-old to challenge, and I didn't try. Instead, I tried to
become invisible. I kept to myself, remained quiet during class discussions, and
never asked questions in or after class. I kept my eyes glued to my desk or looked
straight ahead to avoid drawing attention to myself. I staggered, numb and withdrawn, through each school day and hurried from my last class, gym, without show-
ering so that I wouldn't miss the only bus headed home. Students who missed the
first school bus had to walk through the white neighborhood to the main street to
catch the city bus. Mapp was located in a middle-class section of town called Crad-
dock, where the whites were as hateful as the poor whites in Academy Park.

The daily bus ride home brought its own set of fears. A group of white boys got   45
on our bus regularly for the sole purpose, it seemed, of picking fights. I was scared
to death of them. With older brothers to fight at home, I was confident I could whip
any white boy my age and size, but many of the white guys who got on that bus were
eighth graders, and they looked like giants to me. Others were older, white, leather-
jacket-wearing hoods who I was certain were high school dropouts.

When we boarded the bus, blacks automatically moved to the rear, as if Jim Crow   46
laws were still in effect. The white boys would board last, crowd into the aisles, and
start making racial slurs when the bus pulled away from school. "I hate the smell of
niggers. They sure do stink. Don't you think niggers stink, Larry?"

"They sure do, man. They smell bad."   47

Before long, fists flew, girls screamed, and people tussled in the aisles. Few of the   48
black guys on the bus were big and bad enough to beat the tough white boys, who

outnumbered us seven to one. I never joined in to help the black guys out. I huddled in the far corner at the rear of the bus, tense, scared as hell, hoping the fighting wouldn't reach that far before the driver broke it up.

Children have an enormous capacity to adapt to insanity. I took my lumps in   49
school and tried as much as possible to shrug it off when I went home. Billy, Dwight, and Junnie came home most days full of stories about the fun they were having at pep rallies and football games at their all-black high school. I envied them because I couldn't match their stories with tales of my own about fun times at Mapp. I savored every minute of my weeknights at home and used weekends to gather the heart to face Mapp again. Monday mornings, I rose and dutifully caught the school bus back to hell.

The harassment never let up. Once, when my English teacher left the room, a girl   50
sitting near me drew a picture of a stickman on a piece of paper, colored it black, scribbled my name below it, and passed it around the classroom for others to see. I lost my temper, snatched it from her, and ripped it up. She hit me. I hit her back, then the whole class jumped in. When the teacher returned, I was standing up, punching one guy while another one was riding my back and hitting me in the head. The teacher demanded, "What's going on here?"

The white kids cried out in unison, "That *black* boy started a fight with us!"   51

Without another word, the teacher sent me to the principal's office and I was dis-   52
missed from school. The weeklong suspension alerted my parents that something was wrong. Mama sat me down and tried to talk to me about it. "Why were you fighting in school?"

"It wasn't my fault, Mama. That girl drew a picture of me and colored it black."   53

"That's no reason to fight. What's the matter with you? Your grades are falling   54
and now you get into a fight. Don't you like your school?"

I tried to explain, then choked up and broke down in tears. Seeing that, my   55
parents sought and got approval to transfer me to the neighborhood school, W. E. Waters.

But it wasn't over yet. One day, before the transfer went through, I was sitting on   56
the gym floor with the rest of the student body, watching a school assembly program, when a group of rowdy white upperclassmen began plucking my head and ridiculing me. I got confused. *What should I do?* To turn around and say something to them would start another fight. To get up and leave would require me to wade through a sea of hostile white students to reach the nearest exit. With nowhere to go, I sat there and took the humiliation until I broke. Tears welled in my eyes and started running, uncontrollably, down my face. I sat silently through the remainder of the assembly program with my vision blurred and my spirit broken. That was the only time, then or since, that I've been crushed so completely. When it was over, I collected myself, went to the boys' bathroom, and boohooed some more.

There was no greater joy than that last bus ride home from Mapp. I sat near a win-   57
dow and stared out, trying to make sense of those past few months. Everything that had happened to me was so contrary to all I'd been taught about right and wrong. Before Mapp, every grudge I had ever held against a person could be traced to some specific deed. I couldn't understand someone hating me simply for being black and alive. I wondered, *Where did those white people learn to hate so deeply at such a young*

age? I didn't know. But, over time, I learned to hate as blindly and viciously as any of them.

Working with the Text

1. In his opening McCall relates his exchange in the early 1960s with the little white girl on a Key West beach, noting that "a little black boy and a little white girl had already begun to learn their place in this race-obsessed country." When you were a young child, what did you see as your place in American society in terms of relative power and social standing? What were the sources of that perception? Do you see yourself in the same position now or see yourself differently?

2. When McCall writes that "white people could never be niggers, even when they acted like niggers with a capital *N*," how do you think he is defining "nigger"?

3. Consider the relationship between McCall's grandmother and the Diamondstein boys and the one between Mrs. Davis and his stepfather. How were these relationships different from the hatred and abuse McCall encountered at the mostly white junior high school? What accounts for these differences? Consider some of the ironies inherent in the fact that blacks were considered by many whites to be "dirty" ("They sure do stink"), yet they were entrusted with the care of white children and households. Explore some of the ways that power relations across racial and ethnic experiences get expressed through social interactions.

4. "Children," McCall writes, "have an enormous capacity to adapt to insanity." Why didn't he complain to his parents about his treatment at school? Did the reason have anything to do with his perception of his "place" in American society?

5. Imagine (or remember) a time when you were in a group where racial slurs were being made or when someone was being picked on because of his or her "otherness." How would you (or did you) respond? What does this reaction suggest about your attitude toward difference and fitting in? How would you respond if, like McCall, you were being singled out for abuse?

FEELINGS ABOUT DIFFERENCE

DAVID SIBLEY

■ David Sibley is a British sociologist and currently senior lecturer at the University of Hull in England. His first major work was *Outsiders of Urban Societies* (1981), which looked at the economic and social situations of transient populations in established capitalist countries—"gypsies" and other "traveling people" who move about nomadically with no fixed address or home. He is also the author of *Geographies of Exclusion: Society and Difference in the West* (revised 1995)

and coauthor of *Adolescent Drinking and Family Life* (1993). His teaching and research focus on human geography and issues of how communities develop in
terms of the physical space that they occupy. In the following essay Sibley considers some ways in which notions of difference (or deviation from the "norm") are
created through images of cleanliness and dirt, "white" and "black."

The senior partner of a well-known professional firm around here put his
home on the market with us and said: "You sent me a Mr. Shah and you sent
me a Mr. Patel and you sent me a Mr. Whatever-it-was." He said: "I recognize
that a lot of the big money comes from several thousand miles east of Dover
nowadays, and I don't want you to think that I've got any prejudice at all, but
would you be able to send me an Englishman one day?"   (Suburban London
estate agent)[1]

There are several possible routes into the problem of social and spatial exclusion. I want to start by considering people's feelings about others because of the importance of feelings in their effect on social interaction,
particularly in instances of racism and related forms of oppression. If, for example,
we consider the question of residential segregation, which is one of the most widely
investigated issues in urban geography, it could be argued that the resistance to a
different sort of person moving into a neighbourhood stems from feelings of anxiety, nervousness or fear. Who is felt to belong and not to belong contributes in an
important way to the shaping of social space. It is often the case that this kind of
hostility to others is articulated as a concern about property values but certain kinds
of difference, as they are culturally constructed, trigger anxieties and a wish on the
part of those who feel threatened to distance themselves from others. This may, of
course, have economic consequences.

Feelings about others, people marked as different, may also be associated with
places. Nervousness about walking down a street in a district which has been la-
belled as dangerous, nauseousness associated with particular smells or, conversely,
excitement, exhilaration or a feeling of calm may be the kinds of sensations engen-
dered by other environments. Repulsion and desire, fear and attraction, attach both
to people and to places in complex ways. Central to this question is the construction
of the self, the way in which individual identity relates to social, cultural and spatial
contexts. In this chapter, I will suggest some of the connections between the self and
material and social worlds, moving towards a conception of the "ecological self."[2]

ALTERNATIVE PERSPECTIVES ON THE SELF

Central to early visions of the self was the idea of human individuality.[3] Rationalist
philosophers recognized that only human beings were consciously aware of their
own life, which gave them the capacity to act autonomously. Nineteenth-century
romanticism similarly encouraged a view of the free spirit, and this notion of the
self was reinforced by capitalist forms of social organization according to which
people are highly individuated and assumed to have control of their own destinies.
The subject was thus detached from his or her social milieu.

A shift in conceptions of the self was signalled by Freudian psychoanalysis. Freud   4
situated the self in society and argued for connections between the developing self
and the material world. Central to his thesis was the unconscious, that "aspect of
psychoanalysis that directly challenges the emphasis in Western thought on the
power of reason and rationality, of reflective and conscious control over the self." Although Freud suggested that on one level the unconscious was detached from reality, on another level "it is deeply entwined with the needs of the human body, the
nature of external reality, and actual social relations."[4] The importance of external
reality for the psyche was outlined in *Civilization and its Discontents,* published in
1929. In this book, Freud wrote about the repression of libidinal desires specifically
in relation to the materialism of capitalist societies. He claimed that one form of repression was an excessive concern with cleanliness and order.[5] Personal hygiene, for
example, is widely accepted as desirable on medical and social grounds, but it removes bodily smell as a source of sexual stimulation. Washing and deodorizing the
body has assumed a ritual quality and in some people can become obsessive and
compulsive. This kind of observation raises issues about the role of dominant social
and political structures in the sublimation of desire and the shaping of the self.
What are the sanctions against a group or an individual represented as dirty or disorderly? In *Civilization and its Discontents* Freud brackets cleanliness and order,
both distancing the subject from the uncertainties and fears of the urban-industrial
environment. However, as Smith observes, "order is a part of the tragedy of modern
urban culture: it brings frustration but it cannot be done without."[6] . . .

THE GENERALIZED OTHER

The concept of "the generalized other" provides a means of spatializing the problem   5
and producing what we might describe as an ecological account of the self, one
which situates the self in a full social and cultural context. The term "generalized
other" was first used by George Herbert Mead, who noted the elision of people and
objects to whom the child relates in developing a sense of self. He argued that:

> It is possible for inanimate objects, no less than for other human organisms, to
> form parts of the generalized and organized—the completely socialized—
> other for any given individual . . . Any thing—any object or set of objects,
> whether animate or inanimate, human or animal, or merely physical—to-
> wards which he acts, or to which he responds socially, is an element in what
> for him is the generalized other.[7]

Mead's interpretation of the relationship between self and other has fundamental   6
implications for geographical studies of social interaction because it locates the individual in the social and material world. Ian Burkitt gives prominence to Mead's
object relations theory for similar reasons.[8] He argues that:

> Mead's conception of the self and the psychical apparatus is more useful than
> Derrida's or Freud's in studying *the body in action.* That is because Mead rec-
> ognized the practical nature of the psyche, *that it is always connected to social
> practice* and does not exist in some separate textual or mental domain.
> Whereas Derrida and Freud struggled with the metaphor of the mystic writing
> pad [for Derrida, a cultural and historical text written into the unconscious,

positioning the subject in a textual world], Mead conceptualized that which remains open to new experiences and information as the active person *in their various social locations and settings* (the "I"). It is the embeddedness in social contexts that allows the individual to be constantly receptive to new stimuli, while at the same time the body carries the forms of history in terms of the cultural image of the self and the disciplines involved in social interaction (the "me"). So the "I" and the "me" are not just psychical but also bodily [my italics].

The social positioning of the self means that the boundary between self and other is formed through a series of cultural representations of people and things which frequently elide so that the non-human world also provides a context for selfhood. To give one example of this kind of cultural representation, in racist discourse animals represented as transgressive and therefore threatening unsullied categories of things and social groups, like rats which come out of the sewers and spread disease, have in turn been used to represent threatening minority groups, like Jews and Gypsies, who are thus constructed as bad objects to which the self relates. To animalize or de-humanize a minority group in this way, of course, legitimates persecution. Interestingly from a geographical perspective, one of the few applications of Mead's generalized other has been in studies of the organization of domestic space by Csikszentmihalyi and Rochberg-Halton,[9] where things in the home which are both positively valued and rejected are seen to have a defining role in relation to the self. They note, in particular, that

> the impact of inanimate objects in this self-awareness process is much more important than one would infer from its neglect. Things tell us who we are, not in words but by embodying our intentions. In our everyday traffic of existence, we can also learn about ourselves from objects, almost as much as from people.[10]

People and things come to stand for each other, Csikszentmihalyi and Rochberg-Halton suggest, so that object relations can include relating to others through the material environment. Thus, for one woman,

> her home environment reflects an expanded boundary of the self, one that includes a number of past and present relationships. The meanings of the objects she is surrounded by are signs of her ties to this larger system of which she is a part.[11]

This seemed to me to be a promising but little-developed direction for research, one in which the signing of spaces could be examined specifically in relation to the social self. It had considerable implications for studies of inclusion and exclusion in other spaces.

CONCLUSION

. . . In subsequent chapters, the geographies of exclusion, the literal mappings of power relations and rejection, are informed by the generalized other. Apart from the collapse of categories like the public and the private which I see as a necessary feature of these geographies, the generalized other of object relations theory gives an invitation to open up debates about otherness, to examine the interconnections of people and things as they constitute and are constituted by places, what I take to be the ecological self (and the ecological other). This has to be taken one step at a time, however. I first look at social boundaries, filling in some details about the people who erect the boundaries and those who are excluded by them, and I then consider the issue of exclusionary landscapes as they have developed in different times and places.

NOTES

1. Daniel Meadows, *Nattering in Paradise: A word from the suburbs,* Simon and Schuster, London, 1988, p. 40.

2. This term comes from Ulric Neisser, "Five kinds of self-knowledge," *Philosophical Psychology,* 1 (1), 1988, 35–59. Neisser makes a number of interesting points about the ways in which the self relates to the environment, although he does not say what the environment is. He suggests (1) that we perceive ourselves as embedded within the environment, and acting with respect to it; (2) that the self and the environment exist objectively; information about the self allows us to perceive not only the location of the ecological self but also the nature of its interaction with the environment; (3) that much of the relevant information is kinetic, i.e., relating to movement. Optical structure is particularly important, but self-specifying information is often available to several perceptual modalities at once; and (4) the ecological self is veridically perceived from earliest infancy, but self perception develops with increasing age and skill. I use the term "ecological self" in a more inclusive sense, to refer to the self defined in relation to people, things and places, as they relate to each other.

3. Ian Burkitt provides an excellent account of the western self in an historical context in I. Burkitt, "The shifting concept of the self," *History of the Human Sciences,* 7 (2), 1994, 7–28.

4. Anthony Elliott, *Social Theory and Psychoanalysis in Transition,* Basil Blackwell, Oxford, 1992, pp. 16–17.

5. Michael Smith, *The City and Social Theory,* Basil Blackwell, Oxford, 1980, pp. 57–58.

6. ibid., p. 58.

7. George Herbert Mead, *Mind, Self and Society,* Chicago University Press, Chicago, 1934.

8. Burkitt, op. cit., p. 23.

9. Mihalyi Csikszentmihalyi and Eugene Rochberg-Halton, *The Meaning of Things: Domestic symbols and the self,* Cambridge University Press, Cambridge, 1981.

10. ibid., p. 91.

11. ibid., p. 104. In a later essay, Eugene Rochberg-Halton suggested that "the meaning of things one values is not limited just to the individual object itself but also includes the spatial context in which the object is placed, forming a domain of personal territoriality. In other words, the background context or gestalt of the thing also reveals something and results show how different rooms reveal different conceptions of the self" (Eugene Rochberg-Halton, "Object relations, role models and the cultivation of the self," *Environment and Behavior,* 16 (3), 1984, 335–368).

IMAGES OF DIFFERENCE

The determination of a border between the inside and the outside according to "the simple logic of excluding filth," as Kristeva puts it, or the imperative of "distancing from disgust" (Constance Perin) translates into several different corporeal or social images which signal imperfection or a low ranking in a hierarchy of being. Exclu-

sionary discourse draws particularly on colour, disease, animals, sexuality and nature, but they all come back to the idea of dirt as a signifier of imperfection and inferiority, the reference point being the white, often male, physically and mentally
able person. In this chapter, I will discuss ways in which psychoanalytical theory has
been used in the deconstruction of stereotypes, those "others" from which the subject is distanced, and I will then examine some of the particular cultural sources of
stereotyping in western societies. Stereotypes play an important part in the config-
uration of social space because of the importance of distanciation in the behaviour
of social groups, that is, distancing from others who are represented negatively, and
because of the way in which group images and place images combine to create landscapes of exclusion. The issues I examine concern oppression and denial. I try to
show how difference is harnessed in the exercise of power and the subordination of
minorities.[1]

STEREOTYPES

The reception and acceptance of stereotypes, "images of things we fear and glorify,"   10
as Sander Gilman puts it,[2] is a necessary part of coming to terms with the world. In
the following passage from his psychoanalytical account of the deep structure of
stereotypes, Gilman assigns a central role to stereotyping in the structuring or
bounding of the self:

> The child's sense of self splits into a "good" self which, as the self mirroring the
> earlier stage of the complete control of the world [the stage of pre-Oedipal
> unity with the mother] is free from anxiety, and the "bad" self which is unable
> to control the environment and is thus exposed to anxieties. The split is but a
> single stage in the development of the normal personality. In it lies, however,
> the root of all stereotypical perceptions. For, in the normal course of develop-
> ment, the child's understanding of the world becomes seemingly ever more
> sophisticated. The child is able to distinguish even finer gradations of "good-
> ness" and "badness" so that by the later Oedipal stage an illusion of versimili-
> tude is cast over the inherent (and irrational) distinction between the "good"
> and "bad" world and self, between control and loss of control, between acqui-
> escence and denial.[3]

Both the self and the world are split into good and bad objects, and the bad self,   11
the self associated with fear and anxiety over the loss of control, is projected onto
bad objects. Fear precedes the construction of the bad object, the negative stereotype, but the stereotype—simplified, distorted and at a distance—perpetuates that
fear. Most personalities draw on a range of stereotypes, not necessarily wholly good,
not necessarily wholly bad, as a means of coping with the instabilities which arise in
our perceptions of the world. They make the world seem secure and stable. While
both good and bad stereotypes serve to maintain the boundaries of the self, to protect the self from transgressions when it appears to be threatened, most people have
a large and sophisticated array of objects to draw on. As Gilman reminds us:

> Our Manichean perception of the world as "good" and "bad" is triggered by
> the recurrence of the type of insecurity which induced our initial division of

the world into "good" and "bad." For the pathological individual, every confrontation sets up this echo . . . for the non-pathological individual, the stereotype is a momentary coping mechanism, one that can be used and then discarded once anxiety is overcome.[4]

It is evident that good and bad both resonate in stereotypical representations of others. As Zygmunt Bauman commented on taboos, which is what many stereotypes are, "the human attitude is an intricate mixture of interest and fear, reverence and abhorrence, impulsion and repulsion."[5] Thus, the stereotype may capture something that has been lost, an emotional lack, a desire, at the same time that it represents fear or anxiety. The good stereotype may represent an unattainable fantasy whereas the bad stereotype may be perceived as a real, malign presence from which people want to distance themselves. A common good stereotype of Gypsies, for example, locates them in the past or in a distant country where they are seen through a romantic mist. This is convenient because the good stereotype does not then contradict the bad stereotype. The Gypsy as a "good object," an association of Gypsies with desire, is conveyed nicely in Hermann Hesse's poem *Glorious World:*

> Sultry wind in the tree at night, dark Gypsy woman
> World full of foolish yearning and the poet's breath.

Compare this with a characterization of Gypsies by Gina Ferrero, the daughter of the racist anthropologist Cesare Lombroso, in a commentary on her father's writing:[6]

> an entire race of criminals, with all the passions and vices common to delinquent types: idleness, ignorance, impetuous fury, vanity, love of orgies and ferocity.

Both a fear for the boundaries of the self and a desire to merge are intimated in these representations, but in fact both dehumanize and contribute to a deviant image because both are, by definition, distortions. As Homi Bhabha suggests,[7] the stereotype is a simplification because it is an arrested, fixated form of representation which denies the play of difference. "Others" disturb the observer's world-view, but the stereotype removes them from the scene in the sense that they are distinct from the world of everyday experience. Because there is little or no interaction with "others," the stereotyped image, whether "good" or "bad," is not challenged.

Obviously, it is negative stereotypes which are of greatest consequence in understanding instances of social and spatial exclusion. Here, Julia Kristeva's conception of abjection, that unattainable desire to expel those things which threaten the boundary, and the abject, that list of threatening things and threatening others, seems to me to be fundamental. The earliest experience of abjection in the child is a reaction to excrement as the infant is socialized into adult categorizations of the pure and the defiled, and this then becomes a metaphor for other sources of defilement which are embodied in stereotypes. The sources of bodily defilement are projected onto others, whose world is *epidermalized.* As Iris Young argues:

> When the dominant culture defines some groups as different, as the Other, the members of these groups are imprisoned in their bodies. Dominant discourse defines them in terms of bodily characteristics and constructs those bodies as ugly, dirty, defiled, impure, contaminated or sick.[8]

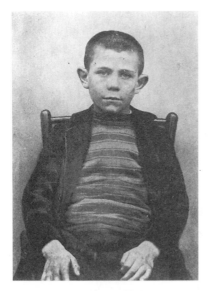

Boy Morally Insane

Boy Morally Insane

Head of Criminal

Head of Criminal

"Criminal types" from Cesare Lombroso's collection. Lombroso's use of photographic portraits in his work on criminality and madness demonstrates the historical importance of physical categorization in the cultural construction of normality and deviance (source: Ferrero 1911).

Or, as Stallybrass and White put it succinctly: "Differentiation depends upon disgust."[9] Verbal and visual images which have their source in the idea of defilement shade into those which represent the body as less than perfect. Thus, the photographs [on page 254], which come from Cesare Lombroso's catalogue of the other,[10] point to a connection between visual images of physical imperfection, according to his scale of being which differentiates the normal and the deviant, and mental illness or disability, conditions which threaten the boundaries of the self. An obsession with scaling and measurement of physical characteristics in order to determine moral boundaries and marginalize the other was particularly characteristic of nineteenth-century and early twentieth-century science, but the association of appearances and moral characteristics is an enduring one.

I suggested in the last chapter that the social self could also be seen as a place-related self, and this applies also to stereotypes of the other which assume negative or positive qualities according to whether the stereotyped individual or group is "in place" or "out of place." The cases that I discuss later in the book demonstrate how this condition of being discrepant or, conversely, of belonging, is identified. The issue concerns the extension of the "generalized other" to things, material objects and places. Thus, a place stereotype might be a romantic representation of a landscape to which a social group are seen to belong or not, depending on the consistency or incongruity of the group and place stereotypes. For the moment, I will focus on some of the main signifiers of otherness in western cultures as a prelude to an integration of the social and spatial dimensions of the problem. The key areas that I examine are those of colour, disease and nature.

BLACK AND WHITE

The use of colour to signify positive/negative, life/death, superior/inferior, safe/dangerous, and so on, is evident in all cultures. Here, I will refer only to the use of colour in white European cultures, and then only black and white, because a cross-cultural account of the use of a wide palette of colours would be long-winded and not particularly relevant. The justification for considering these two colours is, first, that European nations are implicated in most accounts of racism and colonialism and rules expressed in terms of black and white have been important in the process of regulating and dominating the colonized and, second, that they are readily associated with defilement and purity.

Black is used routinely to describe dirt which, in turn, is associated with shame and disease. In other words, it has both practical and moral associations, which make it a potent marker of social difference. In the common usage of white Europeans, it is a negative signifier of class, race, ethnicity. The way in which black has been used to indicate class difference is suggested by the illustrations [on pages 256 and 257], which come from a teachers' guide to health and cleanliness (published by the Health and Cleanliness Council in London in the 1920s and written by two Ph.D.s, one of whom was also the author of *Psychoanalysis in the Classroom*!). Black is also the colour of death, a source of defilement, a state which threatens life, and of the corpse, which signifies decay and contagion: "If dung signifies the other side of the border, the place where I am not and permits me to be, the corpse, the most sickening of all wastes, is a border that has encroached upon everything."[11] It is notable that organizations that have been devoted in a big way to death, the extreme rejec-

Dirt brings Flies
Flies bring Disease

Cleanliness means Health
Dirt means Suffering

The result of Cleanliness is Happiness

The result of Dirt is Misery

Where there's Dirt there's Danger

Dirt and blackness as signifiers in a white society. Moral instruction by the Health and Cleanliness Council, London (probably 1920s).

tion of difference, like the Nazis and other fascists, have adopted black for their collective identity.

Black, then, has been used in white societies to signal fear. A clear example of the use of black and associated images to convey a threatening otherness appears in Emily Brontë's *Wuthering Heights,* in which, as Rosemary Jackson notes,

> The family excludes everything foreign to itself as being unnatural. It guarantees ontological stability through limitation and closure. By the end of *Wuthering Heights,* the threat represented by Cathy and Heathcliff has been exorcised by confining it to their own vampiric relationship: they are merely restless spirits drifting around the abandoned closure of the Heights.[12]

Children Know Well Their Teacher's Attitude Towards Dirt.

The fear instilled in the family by Heathcliff depended on his portrayal from the beginning as other, as an outsider. Thus, as he came into the family (chapter 4):

> We crowded round, and over Miss Cathy's head I had a peep at the dirty,
> ragged, black haired child . . . I was frightened, and Mrs. Earnshaw was ready
> to fling it out of doors. She did fly up, asking how he could fashion to bring

that gipsy brat into the house, when they had their own bairns to feed and
fend for?

Black-haired, dirty, Gypsy combine to suggest a threatening difference, drawing on
an ethnic stereotype well established in British culture.

Black and white as racial signifiers have deep significance. In white, former colo-   19
nial societies, as Dyer observes,

> there are inevitable associations of white with light, and therefore safety, and
> black with dark and therefore danger, and . . . this explains racism (whereas
> one might well argue about the safety of the cover of darkness and the danger
> of exposure to light).[13]

In a colonial context, black and white represent a whole set of social characteristics
and power relations. Dyer's conclusion about three films portraying the white presence in colonial Africa—*Jezebel* (USA, 1938), *Simba* (Britain, 1955) and *Night of the
Living Dead* (USA, 1969)—is that "they all associate whiteness with order, rationality, rigidity, qualities brought out by contrast with black disorder, irrationality and
looseness."

This use of white and black is clearly intended to make white social behaviour   20
virtuous and to legitimate white rule. However, white people should consider the
question also from a black perspective. bell hooks argues that whites have a deep
emotional investment in the myth of "sameness" even as their actions reflect the primacy of whiteness as "the sign informing who they are and how they think."[14] In
other words, whites do not think about themselves as white but only about others as
not-white and other, which was the point of Dyer's examination of whiteness in
films about colonialism. It is useful then to compare the dominant white view of
blackness with black experience, like bell hooks's observations on the meaning of
whiteness in her own childhood:

> Returning to memories of growing up in the social circumstances created by
> racial apartheid, to all black spaces on the edge of town, I reinhabit a location
> where black folks associated whiteness with the terrible, the terrifying, the ter-
> rorizing. White people were regarded as terrorists, especially those who dared
> to enter the segregated space of blackness.[15]

An-other voice? White has been normalized in Europe, North America and Aus-
tralasia and, in order to recognize that what seems normal is also a symbol of domination, it is important to listen to and to appreciate black perspectives rather than,
as bell hooks suggests white people do, "[travel] around the world in pursuit of the
other and otherness"—a sobering comment on academic enthusiasm for difference.

Returning to the wider associations of blackness in white societies, the associa-   21
tion between black and dirt, between dirt and disease, emphasizes the threatening
quality of blackness. Removing blackness, injecting light, removes fear, but this fear
may be a fear of others as much as a fear of darkness. Thus, Corbin maintained that
Haussmann's plans for Paris in the mid-nineteenth century were designed to make
the city *less dark:* "His town-planning was partly aimed at eliminating the darkness
at the centre of the city, where darkness stood for the foul-smelling environment of
the poor, the smell of the poor"—and the poor themselves.[16] However, despite the
common use of black to signify obscurity, shade, shadows, fear, misfortune, death

and evil, it has not always been so. Thus, in mediaeval Europe, black knights were courageous; numerous black madonnas, as in Tarragona cathedral, Spain, and Czestochowa, Poland, were objects of reverence. The positive associations of blackness were lost with colonialism, however, and with industrialization and the development of the class system under capitalism black assumed wider significance through its association with dirt, disorder and the threat to the bourgeoisie posed by the working class.

In the same system of values, whiteness is a symbol of purity, virtue and goodness and a colour which is easily polluted. Since whiteness is often not quite white, it is something to be achieved—an ideal state of pure, untainted whiteness. Thus, white may be connected with a heightened consciousness of the boundary between white and not-white, with an urge to clean, to expel dirt and resist pollution, whether whiteness is attributed to people or to material objects. As Sassoon remarks, white "has a highly accentuated hygienic symbolism," although, in consumer culture, there has been to some extent an "emancipation from white [which] has come about after several decades of emblematic monochromatism [sic]."[17] As a marker of the boundary between purified interior spaces—the home, the nation, and so on—and exterior threats posed by dirt, disorderly minorities or immigrants, white is still a potent symbol.

NOTES

1. Some recent post-modern writing, for example, Iain Chambers's *Migrancy, Culture and Identity,* Routledge, London, 1994, celebrates difference with some enthusiasm. The theme of Chambers's book is that there are fusions, hybrids and new forms of difference that follow from increasing global movement and interconnectedness. I think that it is important not to be carried away by this. Problems defined by the firm contours of territorially based conflict, associated with race, ethnicity, sexuality and disability, are persistent features of socio-spatial relations. Many people live in one place for a long time and some have difficulty getting along with those who are different from themselves. Unfortunately, the African musicians whom Chambers admires and who have certainly enriched British culture are still subject to racism outside the sympathetic environment of the club or the music festival.

2. Sander Gilman, *Difference and Pathology: Stereotypes of sexuality, race and madness,* Cornell University Press, Ithaca, N.Y., 1985. This book, with its emphasis on visual representation, develops object relations theory to incorporate the world as it is perceived.

3. ibid., p. 17.

4. ibid., p. 18.

5. Zygmunt Bauman, "Semiotics and the function of culture," in Julia Kristeva *et al.* (eds), *Essays in Semiotics,* Mouton, The Hague, 1971, pp. 279–295.

6. Gina Ferrero, *Criminal Man,* The Knickerbocker Press, New York, 1911, p. 140.

7. Homi Bhabha, *The Location of Culture,* Routledge, London, 1994. Bhabha presents a deep analysis of the "colonial other," but his arguments have much wider relevance.

8. Iris Young, *Justice and the Politics of Difference,* Princeton University Press, Princeton, N.J., 1990, p. 126. Young bases her argument on Julia Kristeva's *Powers of Horror.*

9. Peter Stallybrass and Allon White, *The Politics and Poetics of Transgression,* Methuen, London, 1986, p. 191.

10. The subjects of Lombroso's moralizing discourse were primarily people with learning disabilities. The importance of photography as an aid to classifying mentally ill and disabled others is discussed in some detail by Sander Gilman, *Disease and Representation,* Cornell University Press, Ithaca, N.Y., 1988, pp. 39–43. Lombroso's photographs are reproduced in Ferrero, op. cit.

11. Julia Kristeva, *Powers of Horror*, Columbia University Press, New York, 1982, p. 3.

12. Rosemary Jackson, *Fantasy: The literature of subversion*, Methuen, London, 1981, p. 129.

13. Richard Dyer, *The Matter of Images: Essays on representation*, Routledge, London, 1993, pp. 142–145.

14. bell hooks, *Black Looks: Race and representation*, Turnaround, London, 1992.

15. ibid., p. 170. Later in this chapter (p. 174), she remarks:

> Reminded of another time when I was strip searched by French officials, who were stopping black people to make sure we were not illegal immigrants and/or terrorists, I think that one fantasy of whiteness is that the threatening Other is always a terrorist. This projection enables many white people to imagine there is no representation of whiteness as terror, as terrorizing. Yet it is this representation of whiteness in the black imagination, first learned in the confines of [a] poor black community, that is sustained by my travels to many different locations.

16. Alain Corbin, *The Fragrant and the Foul: Odor and the French social imagination*, Harvard University Press, Cambridge, Mass., 1986, pp. 134–135.

17. Joseph Sassoon, "Colors, artefacts, and ideologies," in P. Gagliardi (ed.), *Symbols and Artefacts: Views of the corporate landscape*, de Gruyter, Berlin, 1990, p. 172.

Working with the Text

1. In his second paragraph, Sibley writes, "Repulsion and desire, fear and attraction, attach both to people and to places in complex ways. Central to this question is the construction of the self. . . ." How does he go on to develop this point? How is the self constructed in relation to "the generalized other"? To "good" and "bad" stereotypes? How might self-identity be tied to "repulsion and desire, fear and attraction" in complex ways?

2. Sibley is writing about exclusion, about "the people who erect the boundaries and the people who are excluded by them." Who is he talking about here? Do you see yourself more among those who erect boundaries or among those who are excluded? Why? Are the categories mutually exclusive? Or do boundaries differ according to different social situations?

3. Sibley points to "the idea of dirt as a signifier of imperfection and inferiority," implying that cleanliness and dirtiness become determinants of "the inside and the outside." How does this tie into his discussion of images of white and black? Do you find his argument here convincing? Sibley quotes Sander Gilman's theory that goodness becomes associated with control and badness with loss of control. What relation does this idea bear to the idea of exclusion? After looking at some of the linked resources on the *Border Texts* Web site on "otherness," do you think that the Web is a place where stereotypes are being reproduced and spread, or is identity being constructed less as dichotomies in online spaces?

4. What does Sibley suggest s the relationship between "others" and stereotypes? How do stereotypes remove "others" who disturb us from the scene? Do stereotypes in effect replace "others"?

5. Quoting bell hooks, Sibley suggests that whites "do not think about themselves as white but only about others as not-white and other." Do you agree

with this statement? To express the same point a different way, do heterosexuals not think about themselves as straight but only about others as not-straight? To what extent do you think members of any dominant culture accept that culture unthinkingly, only noticing the differences of "aberrant" cultures? Can the same be said to any extent about cultures outside the dominant culture?

THE WHITE MAN'S INDIAN

ROBERT BERKHOFER JR.

■ A professor of history, Robert Berkhofer Jr. has focused much of his research and writing on how our concept of the past is shaped by historians who interpret documents and events within the framework of popular imagery. His most recent book is *Beyond the Great Story: History as Text and Discourse* (1995). In the following chapter from an earlier work, *The White Man's Indian* (1979), Berkhofer considers the ways in which early European settlers in America perceived the native peoples not in terms of their reality, but rather through a variety of stereotypes, many of which continue today.

SIGNIFICANCE OF *INDIAN* AS A GENERAL CATEGORY AND CONCEPTION

From the very beginning of White penetration of the Western Hemisphere, Europeans realized that it was inhabited by peoples divided among themselves. Even Columbus on his first voyage distinguished between peaceful and hostile Indians on the basis of cannibalism and military ardor. Subsequent Spanish explorers, conquerors, and writers noted the differences among the many Indian societies of the New World, especially between the Aztec and Inca civilizations and other peoples. Both French and English explorers remarked the contrasts between the Eskimos and other peoples to the south of them. Early English adventurers into Virginia spoke of *Indians, savages,* and *infidels* in one breath at the same time as they carefully studied the various alliances and specific characteristics of the tribes around Jamestown. The ability to differentiate one tribe from another only increased as White knowledge accumulated over time, but the general term *Indian* or a synonym continued to coexist with—and in spite of—such information. If Whites understood the many differences among Native American peoples, why did they persist in using the general designations, which required the lumping together of all Native Americans as a collective entity? The answer to this question reveals much about later as well as early White images of Native Americans.

Increased knowledge of the fundamental differences among peoples of the world also seemed to promote Europeans' recognition of the similarities among themselves. In other words, exploration and expansion overseas resulted from and reinforced nationalism at the same time that it promoted an overall collective vision of a Europe in contradistinction to the rest of the world. The transition in thinking can perhaps be seen best in the increasing use of "Europe" for self-reference during the fifteenth and sixteenth centuries in preference to the older "Christendom." Another indication would be the new word *continent* to characterize the emerging geographical notions of collective physical self-definition of Europeanness in contrast to other peoples broadly conceived. Humanist scholars endowed the old image of mythical Europa with new secular characteristics in tune with their times and what they considered her place in history. The basic attributes ascribed to continents showed most vividly in the symbolic pictures applied to title pages and to maps, but the same meaning lay behind the more prosaic written descriptions and discourses on the peoples of the world. Europeans portrayed their own continent in terms of intellectual, cultural, military, and political superiority, for Europa was usually pictured wearing a crown, armed with guns, holding orb and scepter, and handling or surrounded by scientific instruments, pallets, books, and Christian symbols. While Asia was richly dressed, rarely did she possess superior signs of power, learning, or religion. America and Africa appeared naked, and the former usually wore a feathered headdress and carried a bow and arrow. Europe, in brief, represented civilization and Christianity and learning confronting nature in America.

The general terms *heathen, barbarian, pagan, savage,* and even *Indian* revealed 3 these criteria of judgment at the same time that they validated the use of collective terms for the peoples of other continents. The European takeover of the New World proved to Europeans, at least, their own superiority and confirmed the reliability of the classification of peoples by continents. Common concepts combined with successful conquest reinforced the general impression of the deficiency of primitives everywhere and validated the continuation of the general conception and the glossing over of the growing knowledge of specific social and cultural differences among New World peoples. Even among themselves and the peoples they had long known well, Europeans correlated whole nationalities with uniform moral and intellectual attributes; it should be no surprise that they should stereotype the new peoples they met elsewhere. If Shakespeare had his Caliban to symbolize New World savagery, he also had his Shylock, his Othello, as well as his Irishmen, Turks, Italians, and others to appeal to his audiences' preconceptions.

Part of this stereotyping of national as well as continental characteristics must be 4 ascribed to the confusion among the realms of culture and biology, nation and race prevalent then and until recently in Western thought. Lifestyles, bloodlines, and national boundaries were all mixed together in White analysis of humankind. Until social heritage and biological heredity were separated in the twentieth century, national character, racialism, and culture were confused and therefore blended together, whether of nations or of continents. Although as time passed the relations among environment, biology, and culture might be seen as dynamic, with each being the cause as well as the effect of the others, their confusion due to imprecise delineation and misunderstanding of the mechanism of transmission meant that race and national character studies were the same thing until very recent times. Nations, races, and cultures were all basically seen as one interchangeable category for the understanding of peoples, and individuals were usually judged as members of their collectivity rather than as different, separate humans. Therefore, general terms embracing stereotyped characteristics made sense to Whites and could exist alongside knowledge of specific societies with individual characteristics or of individuals with varying qualities.

One important consequence of this style of thought was the continuance of the general term *Indian.* The use of the general term demanded a definition, and this definition was provided by moral qualities as well as by description of customs. In short, character and culture were united into one summary judgment. The definition and characterization of *Indian* as a general term constitutes the subject proper of this book as opposed to the history of the evolution of images and conceptions of specific tribes. The basic question to be asked of such overall White Indian imagery and conception is not, therefore, why its invention in the first place but why its continuance, or perpetuation, for so many succeeding centuries? To what extent do these old approaches to the *Indian* still constitute the chief White views of Native Americans even today?

PERSISTING FUNDAMENTAL IMAGES AND THEMES

The centuries-long confusion and melding of what seem to us fundamentally different, even incorrect, ways of understanding human societies account for several persistent practices found throughout the history of White interpretation of Native Americans as Indians: (1) generalizing from one tribe's society and culture to all Indians, (2) conceiving of Indians in terms of their deficiencies according to White ideals rather than in terms of their own various cultures, and (3) using moral evaluation as description of Indians.

Not only does the general term *Indian* continue from Columbus to the present day, but so also does the tendency to speak of one tribe as exemplary of all Indians and conversely to comprehend a specific tribe according to the characteristics ascribed to all Indians. That almost no account in the sixteenth century portrays systematically or completely the customs and beliefs of any one tribe probably results from the newness of the encounter and the feeling that all Indians possessed the same basic qualities. Although eyewitness accounts and discourses by those who had lived among Native Americans in the seventeenth and eighteenth centuries often describe in detail the lives of a specific tribe or tribes, they also in the end generalize from this knowledge to all Indians. The famous reporters on Native American cultures in the colonial period of the United States, for example, invariably treated their tribe(s) as similar enough to all other Indians in customs and beliefs to serve as illustrations of that race in thought and deed. Even in the century that saw the rise of professional anthropology, most social scientists as well as their White countrymen continued to speak and write as if a specific tribe and all Indians were interchangeable for the purposes of description and understanding of fundamental cultural dynamics and social organization. Today, most Whites who use the word *Indian* have little idea of specific tribal peoples or individual Native Americans to render their usage much more than an abstraction, if not a stereotype. Even White writers on the history of White images of the Indian tend to treat all Native American cultures as a single Indian one for the purposes of analyzing the validity of White stereotypes.

Another persistent theme in White imagery is the tendency to describe Indian life in terms of its lack of White ways rather than being described positively from within the framework of the specific culture under consideration. Therefore, tribal Americans were usually described not as they were in their own eyes but from the viewpoint of outsiders, who often failed to understand their ideas or customs. Images of the Indian, accordingly, were (and are) usually what he was not or had not in White terms, rather than in terms of individual tribal cultures and social systems as modern anthropologists aim to do. This negative prototype of the deficient Indian began with Columbus but continues into the present as any history of the White education of Native Americans reveals. To this day such education is still too often treated as philanthropy to the "culturally deprived" Indian.

Description by deficiency all too readily led to characterization by evaluation, and so most of the White studies of Indian culture(s) were (and are) also examinations of Indian moral character. Later White understanding of the Indian, like that of earlier explorers and settlers, expressed moral judgments upon lifestyles as well as presented their description, or mixed ideology with ethnography, to use modern terms. Ethnographic description according to modern standards could not truly be separated from ideology and moral judgment until *both* cultural pluralism and moral relativism were accepted as ideals. Not until well into the twentieth century did such acceptance become general among intellectuals, and even then only a few Whites truly practiced the two ideals in their outlook on Native Americans. Thus eyewitness description prior to this century and so much still in our time combines moral evaluation with ethnographic detail, and moral judgments all too frequently passed for science in the past according to present-day understanding. If ideology was fused with ethnography in firsthand sources, then those images held by Whites who never had experience with Native Americans were usually little more than stereotype and moral judgment.

Whether describing physical appearance or character, manners or morality, economy or dress, housing or sexual habits, government or religion, Whites overwhelmingly measured the Indian as a general category against those beliefs, values, or institutions they most cherished in themselves at the time. For this reason, many commentators on the history of White Indian imagery see Europeans and Americans as using counterimages of themselves to describe Indians and the counterimages of Indians to describe themselves. Such a negative reference group could be used to define White identity or to prove White superiority over the worst fears of their own depravity. If the Puritans, for example, could project their own sins upon people they called savages, then the extermination of the Indian became a cleansing of those sins from their own midst as well as the destruction of a feared enemy.

Since White views of Indians are inextricably bound up with the evaluation of their own society and culture, then ambivalence of Europeans and Americans over the worth of their own customs and civilization would show up in their appraisal of Indian life. Even with the image of the Indian as a reverse or negative model of White life, two different conclusions about the quality of Indian existence can be drawn. That Indians lacked certain or all aspects of White civilization could be viewed as bad or good depending upon the observer's feelings about his own society and the use to which he wanted to put the image. In line with this possibility, commentators upon the history of White imagery of the Indian have found two fundamental but contradictory conceptions of Indian culture.

In general and at the risk of oversimplifying some four centuries of imagery, the good Indian appears friendly, courteous, and hospitable to the initial invaders of his lands and to all Whites so long as the latter honored the obligations presumed to be mutually entered into with the tribe. Along with handsomeness of physique and physiognomy went great stamina and endurance. Modest in attitude if not always in dress, the noble Indian exhibited great calm and dignity in bearing, conversation, and even under torture. Brave in combat, he was tender in love for family and children. Pride in himself and independence of other persons combined with a plain existence and wholesome enjoyment of nature's gifts. According to this version, the Indian, in short, lived a life of liberty, simplicity, and innocence.

On the other side, a list of almost contradictory traits emerged of the bad Indian in White eyes. Nakedness and lechery, passion and vanity led to lives of polygamy and sexual promiscuity among themselves and constant warfare and fiendish revenge against their enemies. When habits and customs were not brutal they appeared loathsome to Whites. Cannibalism and human sacrifice were the worst sins, but cruelty to captives and incessant warfare ranked not far behind in the estimation of Whites. Filthy surroundings, inadequate cooking, and certain items of diet repulsive to White taste tended to confirm a low opinion of Indian life. Indolence rather than industry, improvidence in the face of scarcity, thievery and treachery added to the list of traits on this side. Concluding the bad version of the Indian were the power of superstition represented by the "conjurers" and "medicine men," the hard slavery of women and the laziness of men, and even timidity or defeat in the face of White advances and weaponry. Thus this list substituted license for liberty, a harsh lot for simplicity, and dissimulation and deceit for innocence. [13]

Along with the persistence of the dual image of good and bad but general deficiency overall went a curious timelessness in defining the Indian proper. In spite of centuries of contact and the changed conditions of Native American lives, Whites picture the "real" Indian as the one before contact or during the early period of that contact. That Whites of earlier centuries should see the Indian as without history makes sense given their lack of knowledge about the past of Native American peoples and the shortness of their encounter. That later Whites should harbor the same assumption seems surprising given the discoveries of archeology and the changed condition of the tribes as the result of White contact and policy. Yet most Whites still conceive of the "real" Indian as the aborigine he once was, or as they imagine he once was, rather than as he is now. White Europeans and Americans expect even at present to see an Indian out of the forest or a Wild West show rather than on farm or in city, and far too many anthropologists still present this image by describing aboriginal cultures in what they call the "ethnographic present," or as if tribes live today as they once did. Present-day historians of the United States, likewise, omit the Indian entirely after the colonial period or the last battles on the Plains for the same reason. If Whites do not conceive of themselves still living as Anglo-Saxons, Gauls, or Teutons, then why should they expect Indians to be unchanged from aboriginal times, Native Americans ask of their White peers? [14]

If Whites of the early period of contact invented the Indian as a conception and provided its fundamental meaning through imagery, why did later generations perpetuate that conception and imagery without basic alteration although Native Americans changed? The answer to this question must be sought partially in the very contrast presumed between Red and White society that gave rise to the idea of the Indian in the first place. Since Whites primarily understood the Indian as an antithesis to themselves, then civilization and Indianness as they defined them would forever be opposites. Only civilization had history and dynamics in this view, so therefore Indianness must be conceived of as ahistorical and static. If the Indian changed through the adoption of civilization as defined by Whites, then he was no [15] longer truly Indian according to the image, because the Indian was judged by what Whites were not. Change toward what Whites were made him ipso facto less Indian.

The history of White-Indian contact increasingly proved to Whites, particularly in the late eighteenth and nineteenth centuries, that civilization and Indianness were inherently incompatible and verified the initial conception that gave rise to the imagery. Death through disease and warfare decimated the aboriginal population in the face of White advance and gave rise by the time of the American Revolution to the idea of the vanishing race. If Whites regarded the Indian as a threat to life and morals when alive, they regarded him with nostalgia upon his demise—or when that threat was safely past. 16

Indians who remained alive and who resisted adoption of civilization appeared to accept White vices instead of virtues and so became those imperfect creatures, the degraded or reservation Indian. If there is a third major White image of the Indian, then this degraded, often drunken, Indian constitutes the essence of that understanding. Living neither as an assimilated White nor an Indian of the classic image, and therefore neither noble nor wildly savage but always scorned, the degraded Indian exhibited the vices of both societies in the opinion of White observers. Degenerate and poverty-stricken, these unfortunates were presumed to be outcasts from their own race, who exhibited the worse qualities of Indian character with none of its redeeming features. Since White commentators pitied when they did not scorn this degenerate Indian, the image carried the same unfavorable evaluation overall as the bad or ignoble Indian. 17

Complete assimilation would have meant the total disappearance of Indianness. If one adds to these images the conceptions of progress and evolution, then one arrives at the fundamental premises behind much of White understanding of the Indian from about the middle of the eighteenth century to very recent times. Under these conceptions civilization was destined to triumph over savagery, and so the Indian was to disappear either through death or through assimilation into the larger, more progressive White society. For White Americans during this long period of time, the only good Indian was indeed a dead Indian—whether through warfare or through assimilation. Nineteenth-century frontiersmen acted upon this premise; missionaries and philanthropists tried to cope with the fact. In the twentieth century anthropologists rushed to salvage ethnography from the last living members left over from the ethnographic present, and historians treated Indians as "dead" after early contact with Whites. In these ways modern Native Americans and their contemporary lifestyles have largely disappeared from the White imagination—unless modern Indian activism reverses this historic trend for longer than the recurring but transitory White enthusiasm for things Indian. 18

That the White image of the Indian is doubly timeless in its assumption of the atemporality of Indian life and its enduring judgment of deficiency does not mean that the imagery as a whole does not have its own history. The problem is how to show both the continuity and the changes in the imagery. Ideally such a history would embody both (1) what changed, what persisted, and why, and (2) what images were held by whom, when, where, and why. On the whole, scholars of the topic attempt only one or the other of these approaches and adopt quite different strategies in doing so. One group traces the imagery in the cultural context and intellectual history of a nation or of Western civilization. The other group examines the 19 socioeconomic forces and vested interests of White individuals and groups. To over-simplify somewhat, the first group of scholars sees the imagery as a reflection of White cultures and as the primary explanation of White behavior vis-à-vis Native Americans, while the second group understands the imagery to be dependent upon the political and economic relationships prevailing in White societies at various times. Usually the former concentrates upon imagery and ideas, and the latter emphasizes policy and actual behavior toward Native Americans. As a result of these differences in attention and explanation, nowhere does one find a comprehensive history of White imagery.

If the remarkable thing about the idea of the Indian is not its invention but its   20
persistence and perpetuation, then the task of this book becomes one of delineating that continuity in spite of seeming changes in intellectual and political currents and alterations in social and economic institutions. Accordingly, Part Two searches beneath the "scientific" conception of the Indian as it moves from premises in Christian cosmogony to modern anthropology for the familiar imagery. Part Three examines the persistence of the dual imagery of the Indian in imaginative and ideological literature and art despite changing intellectual and political climates. The last part turns to the continuing use of the basic Indian imagery to justify White public and private policies and actual dealings with Native Americans as political regimes altered and economic institutions changed.

Working with the Text

1. Berkhofer says that early European settlers recognized differences among the various Native American peoples, but that they persisted nonetheless in forming a monolithic concept of the "Indian." What do you think was the motivation for using this collective term?

2. Explore some of the Web resources on Native Americans and American culture on the *Border Texts* Web site. What resources reflect Berkhofer's analysis?

3. What does Berkhofer mean when he refers to "the tendency to describe Indian life in terms of its lack of White ways rather than being described positively from within the framework of the specific culture under consideration"? How did "Europeans and Americans [use] counterimages of themselves to describe Indians and the counterimages of Indians to describe themselves"? Does contemporary popular culture continue to do this? Can you think of different kinds of stereotypes of Native Americans that have reflected different attitudes in mainstream culture?

4. Indians, according to these early definitions, were either "good" or "bad," depending on one's view of the European-American character. Who would have been likely to accept the "good" definition, and who would have used the "bad" definition?

5. Why, according to Berkhofer, have these stereotyped, often ill-informed images of Native Americans persisted? Why was "Indianness" conceived of as "ahistorical and static"? In the Image Portfolio look at Plate 11, the Santa Fe

Railroad Poster. How are "Indians" portrayed as ahistorical and static in the ad? How are they portrayed in Plate 13, John Gast's *American Progress*?

6. If you have read David Sibley's "Feelings About Difference," recall his points on exclusion, otherness, and the idea that whites do not think of themselves as white but rather think of others as "not-white." How might this phenomenon influence the persistence of the "idea of the Indian" (as Berkhofer puts it) and what you know about Native American life today?

THE OTHER ALAMO

MARTIN ESPADA

■ Much of the work of poet Martin Espada is overtly political, offering, in the words of one critic, "vignettes of the indignities that working class people and immigrant Americans suffer every day." Espada's poems are often composed in both English and Spanish. His collections include *City of Coughing and Dead Radiators* (1994) and *Imagine the Angels of Bread* (1996). He also edited the volume *Poetry Like Bread: Poets of the Political Imagination* (1995). Espada is currently on the faculty of the University of Massachusetts at Amherst. The following poem centers on the famous monument to the Texas Revolution—a San Antonio fort where an entire cadre of English-speaking settlers fighting for independence from Mexico was killed by the Mexican army. This event spurred other Texas rebels to fight with renewed force and eventually overthrow Mexican rule in 1836. While historically revered in the United States as a symbol of American triumph in the Western territories, the Alamo has very different associations for Espada.

San Antonio, Texas, 1990

In the Crockett Hotel dining room,
a chalk-faced man in medaled uniform
growls a prayer
at the head of the veteran's table.
Throughout the map of this saint-hungry city,   5
hands strain for the touch of shrines,
genuflection before cannon and memorial plaque,
grasping the talisman of Bowie knife replica
at the souvenir shop, visitors
in white Biblical quote T-shirts.   10

The stones in the walls are smaller
than the fist of Texas martyrs;
their cavernous mouths could drink the canal to mud.
The Daughters of the Republic
print brochures dancing with Mexican demons,   15
Santa Anna's leg still hopping
to conjunto accordions.
The lawyers who conquered farmland
by scratching on parchment in an oil lamp haze,
the cotton growers who kept the time   20
of Mexican peasant lives dangling from their watchchains,
the vigilantes hooded like blind angels
hunting with torches for men the color of night,
gathering at church, the capitol, or the porch
for a century all said this: Alamo.   25

In 1949, three boys
in Air Force dress khaki
ignored the whites-only sign
at the diner by the bus station.
A soldier from Baltimore, who heard nigger sung here   30
more often than his name, but would not glance away;
another blond and solemn as his Tennessee of whitewashed spires;
another from distant Puerto Rico, cap tipped at an angle
in a country where brown skin
could be boiled for the leather of a vigilante's wallet.   35

The waitress squinted a glare and refused their contamination,
the manager lost his crew-cut politeness
and blustered about local customs,
the police, with surrounding faces,
jeered about tacos and señoritas   40
on the Mexican side of town.
"We're not leaving," they said,
and hunched at their stools
till the manager ordered the cook,
sweat-burnished black man unable to hide his grin,   45

to slide cheeseburgers on plates
across the counter.
"We're not hungry," they said,
and left a week's pay for the cook.
One was my father; his word for fury   50
is Texas.

This afternoon, the heat clouds the air like bothered gnats.
The lunch counter was wrecked for the dump years ago.
In the newspapers, a report of vandals
scarring the wooden doors   55
of the Alamo
in black streaks of fire.

Working with the Text

1. In the first image of the poem, "a chalk-faced man in medaled uniform /
growls a prayer / at the head of the veteran's table." How do each of the elements of this image appear in some way later in the poem? What theme does
the image begin to establish?

2. The first half of the second stanza describes a visit to the Alamo, ending
with the image of "Mexican demons" on the Daughters of the Republic
brochures. The second half offers images of Texan-Mexican history. How do
the two parts work together? Explore how the poem articulates a revised view
of history.

3. In what sense do the third and fourth stanzas describe a "second Alamo"?
What is the effect of "his word for fury / is Texas"?

4. What does the Alamo symbolize in the poem? How are Texas and the city
of San Antonio part of the symbolism? What images does the Alamo invoke
for you personally?

SPLIT AT THE ROOT:
AN ESSAY ON JEWISH IDENTITY

Jewish part cut off, taught to deny religion

ADRIENNE RICH

■ Known primarily as a poet, Adrienne Rich published her first volume of poetry, *A Change of World* (1951), when she was an undergraduate at Radcliffe College; it won the Yale Younger Poets Award. Since then she has published more
than fifteen collections, including *Necessities of Life* (1966), *Diving into the Wreck*
(1973), *Your Native Land, Your Life* (1986), and *Dark Fields of the Republic* (1995).
The themes of much of her later work have been explicitly feminist, and in the

1970s, she began to explore lesbian themes as well. Committed to issues of social justice, Rich has also published several volumes of essays and other prose
pieces that question the patriarchal values of the dominant culture and that call
for the empowerment of those who are disenfranchised and discriminated
against. In the following essay from 1982, Rich—whose father was Jewish—considers the "disconnected angles" of her life. She particularly explores her family's
suppression of its Jewishness and her own need to reclaim that part of her self
because, as she says, "the next half century, every aspect of my identity will have
to be engaged."

For about fifteen minutes I have been sitting chin in hand in front of the type-   1
writer, staring out at the snow. Trying to be honest with myself, trying to figure out why writing this seems to be so dangerous an act, filled with fear and
shame, and why it seems so necessary. It comes to me that in order to write this I
have to be willing to do two things: I have to claim my father, for I have my Jewishness from him and not from my gentile mother; and I have to break his silence, his
taboos; in order to claim him I have in a sense to expose him.

And there is, of course, the third thing: I have to face the sources and the flicker-   2
ing presence of my own ambivalence as a Jew; the daily, mundane anti-Semitisms of
my entire life.

These are stories I have never tried to tell before. Why now? Why, I asked myself   3
sometime last year, does this question of Jewish identity float so impalpably, so un-
graspably around me, a cloud I can't quite see the outlines of, which feels to me to
be without definition?

And yet I've been on the track of this longer than I think.   4

In a long poem written in 1960, when I was thirty-one years old, I described myself   5
as "Split at the root, neither Gentile nor Jew, / Yankee nor Rebel."[1] I was still trying to
have it both ways: to be neither/nor, trying to live (with my Jewish husband and
three children more Jewish in ancestry than I) in the predominantly gentile Yankee
academic world of Cambridge, Massachusetts.

But this begins, for me, in Baltimore, where I was born in my father's workplace,   6
a hospital in the Black ghetto, whose lobby contained an immense white marble
statue of Christ.

My father was then a young teacher and researcher in the department of pathology   7
at the Johns Hopkins Medical School, one of the very few Jews to attend or teach at
that institution. He was from Birmingham, Alabama; his father, Samuel, was Ashkenazic, an immigrant from Austria-Hungary and his mother, Hattie Rice, a Sephardic
Jew from Vicksburg, Mississippi. My grandfather had had a shoe store in Birmingham, which did well enough to allow him to retire comfortably and to leave my
grandmother income on his death. The only souvenirs of my grandfather, Samuel
Rich, were his ivory flute, which lay on our living-room mantel and was not to be
played with; his thin gold pocket watch, which my father wore; and his Hebrew

1. Adrienne Rich, "Readings of History," in *Snapshots of a Daughter-in-Law* (New York: W. W. Norton,
1967), pp. 36–40.

prayer book, which I discovered among my father's books in the course of reading my way through his library. In this prayer book there was a newspaper clipping about my grandparents' wedding, which took place in a synagogue.

My father, Arnold, was sent in adolescence to a military school in the North Carolina mountains, a place for training white southern Christian gentlemen. I suspect that there were few, if any, other Jewish boys at Colonel Bingham's, or at "Mr. Jefferson's university" in Charlottesville, where he studied as an undergraduate. With whatever conscious forethought, Samuel and Hattie sent their son into the dominant southern WASP culture to become an "exception," to enter the professional class. Never, in describing these experiences, did he speak of having suffered—from loneliness, cultural alienation, or outsiderhood. Never did I hear him use the word *anti-Semitism.*   8

It was only in college, when I read a poem by Karl Shapiro beginning "To hate the Negro and avoid the Jew / is the curriculum," that it flashed on me that there was an untold side to my father's story of his student years. He looked recognizably Jewish, was short and slender in build with dark wiry hair and deep-set eyes, high forehead and curved nose.   9

My mother is a gentile. In Jewish law I cannot count myself a Jew. If it is true that "we think back through our mothers if we are women" (Virginia Woolf)—and I myself have affirmed this—then even according to lesbian theory, I cannot (or need not?) count myself a Jew.   10

The white southern Protestant women, the gentile, has always been there for me to peel back into. That's a whole piece of history in itself, for my gentile grandmother and my mother were also frustrated artists and intellectuals, a lost writer and a lost composer between them. Readers and annotators of books, note takers, my mother a good pianist still, in her eighties. But there was also the obsession with ancestry, with "background," the southern talk of family, not as people you would necessarily know and depend on, but as heritage, the guarantee of "good breeding." There was the inveterate romantic heterosexual fantasy, the mother telling the daughter how to attract men (my mother often used the word "fascinate"); the assumption that relations between the sexes could only be romantic, that it was in the woman's interest to cultivate "mystery," conceal her actual feelings. Survival tactics of a kind, I think today, knowing what I know about the white woman's sexual role in the southern racist scenario. Heterosexuality as protection, but also drawing white women deeper into collusion with white men.   11

It would be easy to push away and deny the gentile in me—that white southern woman, that social christian. At different times in my life I have wanted to push away one or the other burden of inheritance, to say merely *I am a woman; I am a lesbian.* If I call myself a Jewish lesbian, do I thereby try to shed some of my southern gentile white woman's culpability? If I call myself only through my mother, is it because I pass more easily through a world where being a lesbian often seems like outsiderhood enough?   12

According to Nazi logic, my two Jewish grandparents would have made me a *Mischling, first-degree*—nonexempt from the Final Solution.   13

The social world in which I grew up was christian virtually without needing to say so—christian imagery, music, language, symbols, assumptions everywhere. It was   14 also a genteel, white, middle-class world in which "common" was a term of deep op-probrium. "Common" white people might speak of "niggers"; *we* were taught never to use that word—*we* said "Negroes" (even as we accepted segregation, the eating taboo, the assumption that Black people were simply of a separate species). Our language was more polite, distinguishing us from the "red-necks" or the lynch-mob mentality. But so charged with negative meaning was even the word "Negro" that as children we were taught never to use it in front of Black people. We were taught that any mention of skin color in the presence of colored people was treacherous, forbidden ground. In a parallel way, the word "Jew" was not used by polite gentiles. I sometimes heard my best friend's father, a Presbyterian minister, allude to "the Hebrew people" or "people of the Jewish faith." The world of acceptable folk was white, gentile (christian, really), and had "ideals" (which colored people, white "common" people, were not supposed to have). "Ideals" and "manners" included not hurting someone's feelings by calling her or him a Negro or a Jew—naming the hated identity. This is the mental framework of the 1930s and 1940s in which I was raised.

(Writing this, I feel dimly like the betrayer: of my father, who did not speak the word; of my mother, who must have trained me in the messages; of my caste and class; of my whiteness itself.)   15

Two memories: I am in a play reading at school of *The Merchant of Venice.* Whatever Jewish law says, I am quite sure I was *seen* as Jewish (with a reassuringly gentile mother) in that double vision that bigotry allows. I am the only Jewish girl in the class, and I am playing Portia. As always, I read my part aloud for my father the night before, and he tells me to convey, with my voice, more scorn and contempt with the word "Jew": "Therefore, Jew . . ." I have to say the word out, and say it loudly. I was encouraged to pretend to be a non-Jewish child acting a non-Jewish character who has to speak the word "Jew" emphatically. Such a child would not have had trouble with the part. But *I* must have had trouble with the part, if only because the word itself was really taboo. I can see that there was a kind of terrible, bitter bravado about my father's way of handling this. And who would not dissociate from Shylock in order to identify with Portia? As a Jewish child who was also a female, I loved Portia—and, like every other Shakespearean heroine, she proved a treacherous role model.   16

A year or so later I am in another play, *The School for Scandal,* in which a notorious spendthrift is described as having "many excellent friends . . . among the Jews." In neither case was anything explained, either to me or to the class at large, about this scorn for Jews and the disgust surrounding Jews and money. Money, when Jews wanted it, had it, or lent it to others, seemed to take on a peculiar nastiness; Jews and money had some peculiar and unspeakable relation.   17

At this same school—in which we had Episcopalian hymns and prayers, and read aloud through the Bible morning after morning—I gained the impression that Jews were in the Bible and mentioned in English literature, that they had been persecuted centuries ago by the wicked Inquisition, but that they seemed not to exist in everyday life. These were the 1940s, and we were told a great deal about the Battle of Britain, the noble French Resistance fighters, the brave, starving Dutch—but I did not learn of the resistance of the Warsaw ghetto until I left home.   18

I was sent to the Episcopal church, baptized and confirmed, and attended it for about five years, though without belief. That religion seemed to have little to do with belief or commitment; it was liturgy that mattered, not spiritual passion. Neither of   19 my parents ever entered that church, and my father would not enter *any* church for any reason—wedding or funeral. Nor did I enter a synagogue until I left Baltimore. When I came home from church, for a while, my father insisted on reading aloud to me from Thomas Paine's *The Age of Reason*—a diatribe against institutional religion. Thus, he explained, I would have a balanced view of these things, a choice. He—they—did not give me the choice to be a Jew. My mother explained to me when I was filling out forms for college that if any question was asked about "religion," I should put down "Episcopalian" rather than "none"—to seem to have no religion was, she implied, dangerous.

But it was white social christianity, rather than any particular christian sect, that 20 the world was founded on. The very word *Christian* was used as a synonym for virtuous, just, peace-loving, generous, etc., etc.[2] The norm was christian: "religion: none" was indeed not acceptable. Anti-Semitism was so intrinsic as not to have a name. I don't recall exactly being taught that the Jews killed Jesus—"Christ killer" seems too strong a term for the bland Episcopal vocabulary—but certainly we got the impression that the Jews had been caught out in a terrible mistake, failing to recognize the true Messiah, and were thereby less advanced in moral and spiritual sensibility. The Jews had actually allowed *moneylenders in the Temple* (again, the unexplained obsession with Jews and money). They were of the past, archaic, primitive, as older (and darker) cultures are supposed to be primitive; christianity was lightness, fairness, peace on earth, and combined the feminine appeal of "The meek shall inherit the earth" with the masculine stride of "Onward, Christian Soldiers."

Sometime in 1946, while still in high school, I read in the newspaper that a theater 21 in Baltimore was showing films of the Allied liberation of the Nazi concentration camps. Alone, I went downtown after school one afternoon and watched the stark, blurry, but unmistakable newsreels. When I try to go back and touch the pulse of that girl of sixteen, growing up in many ways so precocious and so ignorant, I am overwhelmed by a memory of despair, a sense of inevitability more enveloping than any I had ever known. Anne Frank's diary and many other personal narratives of the Holocaust were still unknown or unwritten. But it came to me that every one of those piles of corpses, mountains of shoes and clothing had contained, simply, individuals, who had believed, as I now believed of myself, that they were intended to live out a life of some kind of meaning, that the world possessed some kind of sense and order; yet *this* had happened to them. And I, who believed my life was intended to be so interesting and meaningful, was connected to those dead by something—not just mortality but a taboo name, a hated identity. Or was I—did I really have to be? Writing this now, I feel belated rage that I was so impoverished by the family and social worlds I lived in, that I had to try to figure out by myself what this did indeed mean for me. That I had never been taught about resistance, only about passing. That I had no language for anti-Semitism itself.

When I went home and told my parents where I had been, they were not pleased. 22 I felt accused of being morbidly curious, not healthy, sniffing around death for the thrill of it. And since, at sixteen, I was often not sure of the sources of my feelings or of my motives for doing what I did, I probably accused myself as well. One thing was

2. In a similar way the phrase "That's white of you" implied that you were behaving with the superior decency and morality expected of white but not of Black people.

clear: there was nobody in my world with whom I could discuss those films. Probably at the same time, I was reading accounts of the camps in magazines and newspapers; what I remember were the films and having questions that I could not even phrase, such as *Are those men and women "them" or "us"?*

To be able to ask even the child's astonished question *Why do they hate us so?*   23
means knowing how to say "we." The guilt of not knowing, the guilt of perhaps having betrayed my parents or even those victims, those survivors, through mere curiosity—these also froze in me for years the impulse to find out more about the Holocaust.

1947: I left Baltimore to go to college in Cambridge, Massachusetts, left (I thought)   24
the backward, enervating South for the intellectual, vital North. New England also had for me some vibration of higher moral rectitude, of moral passion even, with its seventeenth-century Puritan self-scrutiny, its nineteenth-century literary "flowering," its abolitionist righteousness, Colonel Shaw and his Black Civil War regiment depicted in granite on Boston Common. At the same time, I found myself, at Radcliffe, among Jewish women. I used to sit for hours over coffee with what I thought of as the "real" Jewish students, who told me about middle-class Jewish culture in America. I described my background—for the first time to strangers—and they took me on, some with amusement at my illiteracy, some arguing that I could never marry into a strict Jewish family, some convinced I didn't "look Jewish," others that I did. I learned the names of holidays and foods, which surnames are Jewish and which are "changed names"; about girls who had had their noses "fixed," their hair straightened. For these young Jewish women, students in the late 1940s, it was acceptable, perhaps even necessary, to strive to look as gentile as possible; but they stuck proudly to being Jewish, expected to marry a Jew, have children, keep the holidays, carry on the culture.

I felt I was testing a forbidden current, that there was danger in these revelations.   25
I bought a reproduction of a Chagall portrait of a rabbi in striped prayer shawl and hung it on the wall of my room. I was admittedly young and trying to educate myself, but I was also doing something that *is* dangerous: I was flirting with identity.

One day that year I was in a small shop where I had bought a dress with a too-long   26
skirt. The shop employed a seamstress who did alterations, and she came in to pin up the skirt on me. I am sure that she was a recent immigrant, a survivor. I remember a short, dark woman wearing heavy glasses, with an accent so foreign I could not understand her words. Something about her presence was very powerful and disturbing to me. After marking and pinning up the skirt, she sat back on her knees, looked up at me, and asked in a hurried whisper: "You Jewish?" Eighteen years of training in assimilation sprang into the reflex by which I shook my head, rejecting her, and muttered, "No."

What was I actually saying "no" to? She was poor, older, struggling with a foreign   27
tongue, anxious; she had escaped the death that had been intended for her, but I had no imagination of her possible courage and foresight, her resistance—I did not see in her a heroine who had perhaps saved many lives, including her own. I saw the frightened immigrant, the seamstress hemming the skirts of college girls, the wandering Jew. But I was an American college girl having her skirt hemmed. And I was

frightened myself, I think, because she had recognized me ("It takes one to know one," my friend Edie at Radcliffe had said) even if I refused to recognize myself or her, even if her recognition was sharpened by loneliness or the need to feel safe with me.

But why should she have felt safe with me? I myself was living with a false sense   28
of safety.

There are betrayals in my life that I have known at the very moment were be-   29
trayals: this was one of them. There are other betrayals committed so repeatedly, so mundanely, that they leave no memory trace behind, only a growing residue of mis-ery, of dull, accreted self-hatred. Often these take the form not of words but of si-lence. Silence before the joke at which everyone is laughing: the anti-woman joke, the racist joke, the anti-Semitic joke. Silence and then amnesia. Blocking it out when the oppressor's language starts coming from the lips of one we admire, whose courage and eloquence have touched us: *She didn't really mean that; he didn't really say that.* But the accretions build up out of sight, like scale inside a kettle.

1948: I come home from my freshman year at college, flaming with new insights,   30
new information. I am the daughter who has gone out into the world, to the pinna-cle of intellectual prestige, Harvard, fulfilling my father's hopes for me, but also ex-posed to dangerous influences. I have already been reproved for attending a rally for Henry Wallace and the Progressive party. I challenge my father: "Why haven't you told me that I am Jewish? Why do you never talk about being a Jew?" He answers measuredly, "You know that I have never denied that I am a Jew. But it's not impor-tant to me. I am a scientist, a deist. I have no use for organized religion. I choose to live in a world of many kinds of people. There are Jews I admire and others whom I despise. I am a person, not simply a Jew." The words are as I remember them, not perhaps exactly as spoken. But that was the message. And it contained enough truth—as all denial drugs itself on partial truth—so that it remained for the time being unanswerable, leaving me high and dry, split at the root, gasping for clarity, for air.

At that time Arnold Rich was living in suspension, waiting to be appointed to the   31
professorship of pathology at Johns Hopkins. The appointment was delayed for years, no Jew ever having held a professional chair in that medical school. And he wanted it badly. It must have been a very bitter time for him, since he had believed so greatly in the redeeming power of excellence, of being the most brilliant, inspired man for the job. With enough excellence, you could presumably make it stop mat-tering that you were Jewish; you could become the *only* Jew in the gentile world, a Jew so "civilized," so far from "common," so attractively combining southern gentil-ity with European cultural values that no one would ever confuse you with the raw, "pushy" Jews of New York, the "loud, hysterical" refugees from eastern Europe, the "overdressed" Jews of the urban South.

We—my sister, mother, and I—were constantly urged to speak quietly in public,   32
to dress without ostentation, to repress all vividness or spontaneity, to assimilate with a world which might see us as too flamboyant. I suppose that my mother, pure gentile though she was, could be seen as acting "common" or "Jewish" if she laughed too loudly or spoke aggressively. My father's mother, who lived with us half the year, was a model of circumspect behavior, dressed in dark blue or lavender, retiring in

company, ladylike to an extreme, wearing no jewelry except a good gold chain, a narrow brooch, or a string of pearls. A few times, within the family, I saw her anger flare, felt the passion she was repressing. But when Arnold took us out to a restaurant or on a trip, the Rich women were always tuned down to some WASP level my father believed, surely, would protect us all—maybe also make us unrecognizable to the "real Jews" who wanted to seize us, drag us back to the *shtetl*, the ghetto, in its many manifestations.

For, yes, that *was* a message—that some Jews would be after you, once they "knew," to rejoin them, to re-enter a world that was messy, noisy, unpredictable, maybe poor—"even though," as my mother once wrote me, criticizing my largely Jewish choice of friends in college, "some of them will be the most brilliant, fascinating people you'll ever meet." I wonder if that isn't one message of assimilation—of America—that the unlucky or the unachieving want to pull you backward, that to identify with them is to court downward mobility, lose the precious chance of passing, of token existence. There was always within this sense of Jewish identity a strong class discrimination. Jews might be "fascinating" as individuals but came with huge unruly families who "poured chicken soup over everyone's head" (in the phrase of a white southern male poet). Anti-Semitism could thus be justified by the bad behavior of certain Jews; and if you did not effectively deny family and community, there would always be a remote cousin claiming kinship with you who was the "wrong kind" of Jew. 33

I have always believed his attitude toward other Jews depended on who they were. . . . It was my impression that Jews of this background looked down on Eastern European Jews, including Polish Jews and Russian Jews, who generally were not as well educated. This from a letter written to me recently by a gentile who had worked in my father's department, whom I had asked about anti-Semitism there and in particular regarding my father. This informant also wrote me that it was hard to perceive anti-Semitism in Baltimore because the racism made so much more intense an impression: *I would almost have to think that blacks went to a different heaven than the whites, because the bodies were kept in a separate morgue, and some white persons did not even want blood transfusions from black donors.* My father's mind was predictably racist and misogynist; yet as a medical student he noted in his journal that southern male chivalry stopped at the point of any white man in a streetcar giving his seat to an old, weary Black woman standing in the aisle. Was this a Jewish insight—an outsider's insight, even though the outsider was striving to be on the inside? 34

Because what isn't named is often more permeating than what is, I believe that my father's Jewishness profoundly shaped my own identity and our family existence. They were shaped both by external anti-Semitism and my father's self-hatred, and by his Jewish pride. What Arnold did, I think, was call his Jewish pride something else: achievement, aspiration, genius, idealism. Whatever was unacceptable got left back under the rubric of Jewishness or the "wrong kind" of Jews—uneducated, aggressive, loud. The message I got was that we were really superior: nobody else's father had collected so many books, had traveled so far, knew so many languages. Baltimore was a musical city, but for the most part, in the families of my school friends, culture was for women. My father was an amateur musician, read poetry, adored encyclopedic knowledge. He prowled and pounced over my school 35 papers, insisting I use "grown-up" sources; he criticized my poems for faulty technique and gave me books on rhyme and meter and form. His investment in my intellect and talent was egotistical, tyrannical, opinionated, and terribly wearing. He taught me, nevertheless, to believe in hard work, to mistrust easy inspiration, to write and rewrite; to feel that I *was* a person of the book, even though a woman; to take ideas seriously. He made me feel, at a very young age, the power of language and that I could share in it.

The Riches were proud, but we also had to be very careful. Our behavior had to be more impeccable than other people's. Strangers were not to be trusted, nor even friends; family issues must never go beyond the family; the world was full of potential slanderers, betrayers, *people who could not understand.* Even within the family, I realize that I never in my whole life knew what my father was really feeling. Yet he spoke—monologued—with driving intensity. You could grow up in such a house mesmerized by the local electricity, the crucial meanings assumed by the merest things. This used to seem to me a sign that we were all living on some high emotional plane. It was a difficult force field for a favored daughter to disengage from. 36

Easy to call that intensity Jewish; and I have no doubt that passion is one of the qualities required for survival over generations of persecution. But what happens when passion is rent from its original base, when the white gentile world is softly saying "Be more like us and you can be almost one of us"? What happens when survival seems to mean closing off one emotional artery after another? His forebears in Europe had been forbidden to travel or expelled from one country after another, had special taxes levied on them if they left the city walls, had been forced to wear special clothes and badges, restricted to the poorest neighborhoods. He had wanted to be a "free spirit," to travel widely, among "all kinds of people." Yet in his prime of life he lived in an increasingly withdrawn world, in his house up on a hill in a neighborhood where Jews were not supposed to be able to buy property, depending almost exclusively on interactions with his wife and daughters to provide emotional connectedness. In his home, he created a private defense system so elaborate that even as he was dying, my mother felt unable to talk freely with his colleagues or others who might have helped her. Of course, she acquiesced in this. 37

The loneliness of the "only," the token, often doesn't feel like loneliness but like a kind of dead echo chamber. Certain things that ought to don't resonate. Somewhere Beverly Smith writes of women of color "inspiring the behavior" in each other. When there's nobody to "inspire the behavior," act out of the culture, there is an atrophy, a dwindling, which is partly invisible. 38

I was married in 1953, in the Hillel House at Harvard, under a portrait of Albert Einstein. My parents refused to come. I was marrying a Jew of the "wrong kind" from an Orthodox eastern European background. Brooklyn-born, he had gone to Harvard, changed his name, was both indissolubly connected to his childhood world and terribly ambivalent about it. My father saw this marriage as my having fallen prey to the Jewish family, eastern European division. 39

Like many women I knew in the fifties living under a then-unquestioned heterosexual imperative, I married in part because I knew no better way to disconnect from my first family. I married a "real Jew" who was himself almost equally divided between a troubled yet ingrained Jewish identity, and the pull toward Yankee ap- 40 proval, assimilation. But at least he was not adrift as a single token in a gentile world. We lived in a world where there was much intermarriage and where a certain "Jewish flavor" was accepted within the dominant gentile culture. People talked glibly of "Jewish self-hatred," but anti-Semitism was rarely identified. It was as if you could have it both ways—identity and assimilation—without having to think about it very much.

I was moved and gratefully amazed by the affection and kindliness my husband's parents showed me, the half *shiksa.* I longed to embrace that family, that new and mysterious Jewish world. It was never a question of conversion—my husband had long since ceased being observant—but of a burning desire to do well, please these new parents, heal the split consciousness in which I had been raised, and, of course, to belong. In the big, sunny apartment on Eastern Parkway, the table would be spread on Saturday afternoons with a white or an embroidered cloth and plates of coffeecake, spongecake, mohncake, cookies for a family gathering where everyone ate and drank—coffee, milk, cake—and later the talk still eddied among the women around the table or in the kitchen, while the men ended up in the living room watching the ball game. I had never known this kind of family, in which mock insults were cheerfully exchanged, secrets whispered in corners among two or three, children and grandchildren boasted about, and the new daughter-in-law openly inspected. I was profoundly attracted by all this, including the punctilious observance of *kashrut,* the symbolism lurking behind daily kitchen tasks. I saw it all as quintessentially and authentically Jewish, and I objectified both the people and the culture. My unexamined anti-Semitism allowed me to do this. But also, I had not yet recognized that as a woman I stood in a particular and unexamined relationship to the Jewish family and to Jewish culture.

There were several years during which I did not see, and barely communicated with, my parents. At the same time, my father's personality haunted my life. Such had been the force of his will in our household that for a long time I felt I would have to pay in some terrible way for having disobeyed him. When finally we were reconciled, and my husband and I and our children began to have some minimal formal contact with my parents, the obsessional power of Arnold's voice or handwriting had given way to a dull sense of useless anger and pain. I wanted him to cherish and approve of me, not as he had when I was a child, but as the woman I was, who had her own mind and had made her own choices. This, I finally realized, was not to be; Arnold demanded absolute loyalty, absolute submission to his will. In my separation from him, in my realization at what price that once-intoxicating approval had been bought, I was learning in concrete ways a great deal about patriarchy, in particular how the "special" woman, the favored daughter, is controlled and rewarded.

Arnold Rich died in 1968 after a long, deteriorating illness; his mind had gone, and he had been losing his sight for years. It was a year of intensifying political awareness for me: the Martin Luther King and Robert Kennedy assassinations, the Columbia strike. But it was not that these events, and the meetings and demonstrations that surrounded them, preempted the time of mourning for my father; I had been mourning a long time for an early, primary, and intense relationship, by no means always benign, but in which I had been ceaselessly made to feel that what I did with my life, the choices I made, the attitudes I held, were of the utmost consequence.

41

42

43

Sometime in my thirties, on visits to Brooklyn, I sat on Eastern Parkway, a baby   44
stroller at my feet—one of many rows of young Jewish women on benches with
children in that neighborhood. I used to see the Lubavitcher Hasidim—then beginning to move into the Crown Heights neighborhood—walking out on *Shabbes,* the
women in their *shaytls* a little behind the men. My father-in-law pointed them out
as rather exotic—too old-country, perhaps, too unassimilated even for his devout
yet Americanized sense of Jewish identity. It took many years for me to
understand—partly because I understood so little about class in America—how in
my own family, and in the very different family of my in-laws, there were degrees
and hierarchies of assimilation which looked askance upon each other—and also
geographic lines of difference, as between southern Jews and New York Jews, whose
manners and customs varied along class as well as regional lines.

I had three sons before I was thirty, and during those years I often felt that to be a   45
Jewish woman, a Jewish mother, was to be perceived in the Jewish family as an entirely physical being, a producer and nourisher of children. The experience of
motherhood was eventually to radicalize me. But before that, I was encountering
the institution of motherhood most directly in a Jewish cultural version; and I felt
rebellious, moody, defensive, unable to sort out what was Jewish from what was
simply motherhood or female destiny. (I lived in Cambridge, not Brooklyn; but
there, too, restless, educated women sat on benches with baby strollers, half-
stunned, not by Jewish cultural expectations, but by the middle-class American social expectations of the 1950s.)

My children were taken irregularly to Seders, to bar mizvahs, and to special ser-   46
vices in their grandfather's temple. Their father lit Hanukkah candles while I stood
by, having rememorized each year the English meaning of the Hebrew blessing. We
all celebrated a secular, liberal Christmas. I read aloud from books about Esther and
the Maccabees and Moses, and also from books about Norse trolls and Chinese
grandmothers and Celtic dragon slayers. Their father told stories of his boyhood in
Brooklyn, his grandmother in the Bronx who had to be visited by subway every
week, of misdeeds in Hebrew school, of being a bright Jewish kid at Boys' High. In
the permissive liberalism of academic Cambridge, you could raise your children to
be as vaguely or distinctly Jewish as you would, but Christian myth and calendar organized the year. My sons grew up knowing far more about the existence and concrete meaning of Jewish culture than I had. But I don't recall sitting down with them
and telling them that millions of people like themselves, many of them children, had
been rounded up and murdered in Europe in their parents' lifetime. Nor was I able
to tell them that they came in part out of the rich, thousand-year-old Ashkenazic
culture of eastern Europe, which the Holocaust destroyed; or that they came from a
people whose traditions, religious and secular, included a hatred of oppression and
an imperative to pursue justice and care for the stranger—an anti-racist, a socialist,
and even sometimes a feminist vision. I could not tell them these things because
these things were still too indistinct in my own mind.

The emergence of the Civil Rights movement in the sixties I remember as lifting me   47
out of a sense of personal frustration and hopelessness. Reading James Baldwin's
early essays in the fifties had stirred me with a sense that apparently "given" situations like racism could be analyzed and described and that this could lead to action,

to change. Racism had been so utter and implicit a fact of my childhood and adolescence, had felt so central among the silences, negations, cruelties, fears, supersti-
tions of my early life, that somewhere among my feelings must have been the hope
that if Black people could become free of the immense political and social burdens
they were forced to bear, I, too, could become free of all the ghosts and shadows of
my childhood, named and unnamed. When "the movement" began, it felt extremely
personal to me. And it was often Jews who spoke up for the justice of the cause, Jewish students and civil rights lawyers who travelled South; it was two young Jews who
were found murdered with a young Black man in Mississippi: Schwerner, Good-
man, Chaney.

Moving to New York in the mid-sixties meant being plunged almost immediately   48
into the debate over community control of public schools, in which Black and Jewish teachers and parents were often on opposite sides of extremely militant barricades. It was easy as a white liberal to deplore and condemn the racism of
middle-class Jewish parents or angry Jewish schoolteachers, many of them older
women; to displace our own racism onto them; or to feel it as too painful to think
about. The struggle for Black civil rights had such clarity about it for me: I knew that
segregation was wrong, that unequal opportunity was wrong; I knew that segregation in particular was more than a set of social and legal rules—it meant that even
"decent" white people lived in a network of lies and arrogance and moral collusion.
In the world of Jewish assimilationist and liberal politics which I knew best, however, things were far less clear to me, and anti-Semitism went almost unmentioned.
It was even possible to view concern about anti-Semitism as a reactionary agenda, a
monomania of *Commentary* magazine or, later, the Jewish Defense League. Most of
the political work I was doing in the late 1960s was on racial issues, in particular as
a teacher in the City University during the struggle for open admissions. The white
colleagues I thought of as allies were, I think, mostly Jewish. Yet it was easy to see
other New York Jews, who had climbed out of poverty and exploitation through the
public-school system and the free city colleges, as now trying to block Black and
Puerto Rican students trying to do likewise. I didn't understand then that I was living between two strains of Jewish social identity: the Jew as radical visionary and activist who understands oppression firsthand, and the Jew as part of America's
devouring plan in which the persecuted, called to assimilation, learn that the price
is to engage in persecution.

   And, indeed, there *was* intense racism among Jews as well as white gentiles in the   49
City University, part of the bitter history of Jews and Blacks which James Baldwin
had described much earlier, in his 1948 essay "The Harlem Ghetto,"[3] part of the
divide-and-conquer script still being rehearsed by those of us who have the least to
gain from it.

By the time I left my marriage, after seventeen years and three children, I had be-   50
come identified with the Women's Liberation movement. It was an astonishing time
to be a woman of my age. In the 1950s, seeking a way to grasp the pain I seemed to
be feeling most of the time, to set it in some larger context, I had read all kinds of

---

3. James Baldwin, "The Harlem Ghetto," in *Notes of a Native Son* (Boston: Beacon, 1955).

things; but it was James Baldwin and Simone de Beauvoir who had described the world—though differently—in terms that made the most sense to me. By the end of the sixties there were two political movements—one already meeting severe repression, one just emerging—which addressed those descriptions of the world.

And there was, of course, a third movement, or a movement-within-a- 51 movement: the early lesbian manifestoes, the new visibility and activism of lesbians everywhere. I had known very early on that the women's movement was not going to be a simple walk across an open field; that it would pull on every fiber of my existence; that it would mean going back and searching the shadows of my consciousness. Reading *The Second Sex* in the 1950s isolation of an academic housewife had felt less dangerous than reading "The Myth of Vaginal Orgasm" or "Woman-identified Woman" in a world where I was in constant debate and discussion with women over every aspect of our lives that we could as yet name. De Beauvoir had placed "The Lesbian" on the margins, and there was little in her book to suggest the power of woman bonding. But the passion of debating ideas with women was an erotic passion for me, and the risking of self with women that was necessary in order to win some truth out of the lies of the past was also erotic. The suppressed lesbian I had been carrying in me since adolescence began to stretch her limbs, and her first full-fledged act was to fall in love with a Jewish woman.

Some time during the early months of that relationship, I dreamed that I was ar- 52 guing feminist politics with my lover. *Of course,* I said to her in this dream, *if you're going to bring up the Holocaust against me, there's nothing I can do.* If, as I believe, I was both myself and her in this dream, it spoke of the split in my consciousness. I had been, more or less, a Jewish heterosexual woman. But what did it mean to be a Jewish lesbian? What did it mean to feel myself, as I did, both anti-Semite and Jew? And, as a feminist, how was I charting for myself the oppressions within oppression?

The earliest feminist papers on Jewish identity that I read were critiques of the 53 patriarchal and misogynist elements in Judaism, or of the caricaturing of Jewish women in literature by Jewish men. I remember hearing Judith Plaskow give a paper called "Can a Woman Be a Jew?" (Her conclusion was "Yes, but . . .") I was soon after in correspondence with a former student who had emigrated to Israel, was a passionate feminist, and wrote to me at length of the legal and social constraints on women there, the stirrings of contemporary Israeli feminism, and the contradictions she felt in her daily life. With the new politics, activism, literature of a tumultuous feminist movement around me, a movement which claimed universality though it had not yet acknowledged its own racial, class, and ethnic perspectives or its fears of the differences among women, I pushed aside for one last time thinking further about myself as a Jewish woman. I saw Judaism simply as another strand of patriarchy. If asked to choose, I might have said (as my father had said in other language): *I am a woman, not a Jew.* (But, I always added mentally, if Jews had to wear yellow stars again, I, too, would wear one—as if I would have the choice to wear it or not.)

Sometimes I feel I have seen too long from too many disconnected angles: white, 54 Jewish, anti-Semite, racist, anti-racist, once-married, lesbian, middle-class, feminist, exmatriate southerner, *split at the root*—that I will never bring them whole. I would have liked, in this essay, to bring together the meanings of anti-Semitism and racism as I have experienced them and as I believe they intersect in the world beyond my life. But I'm not able to do this yet. I feel the tension as I think, make notes: *If you really look at the one reality, the other will waver and disperse.* Trying in one week to read Angela Davis and Lucy Davidowicz;[4] trying to hold throughout to a feminist, a lesbian, perspective—what does this mean? Nothing has trained me for this. And sometimes I feel inadequate to make any statement as a Jew; I feel the history of denial within me like an injury, a scar. For assimilation has affected *my* perceptions; those early lapses in meaning, those blanks, are with me still. My ignorance can be dangerous to me and to others.

Yet we can't wait for the undamaged to make our connections for us; we can't   55
wait to speak until we are perfectly clear and righteous. There is no purity and, in our lifetimes, no end to this process.

This essay, then, has no conclusions: it is another beginning for me. Not just a   56
way of saying, in 1982 Right Wing America, *I, too, will wear the yellow star.* It's a moving into accountability, enlarging the range of accountability. I know that in the rest of my life, the next half century or so, every aspect of my identity will have to be engaged. The middle-class white girl taught to trade obedience for privilege. The Jewish lesbian raised to be a heterosexual gentile. The woman who first heard oppression named and analyzed in the Black Civil Rights struggle. The woman with three sons, the feminist who hates male violence. The woman limping with a cane, the woman who has stopped bleeding are also accountable. The poet who knows that beautiful language can lie, that the oppressor's language sometimes sounds beautiful. The woman trying, as part of her resistance, to clean up her act.

Working with the Text

1. What is the significance of the essay's title? Do you ever feel "split at the root," or does your identity feel essentially "unified"?

2. Rich quotes a line from a Karl Shapiro poem: "To hate the Negro and avoid the Jew / is the curriculum." What does this mean, and what did it make her realize about her father? Why do you suppose she had never realized this before?

3. Rich describes her childhood as "christian, . . . gentile, white, middle-class." What is ironic about the fact that within this society "Negro" and "Jew" were words not to be used in front of blacks and Jews—"naming the hated identity"? How does Rich's remembrance of playing Portia in *The Merchant of Venice* contribute to your understanding of the dilemma of being Jewish in a largely non-Jewish society?

4. After describing seeing films of the Allied liberation of Nazi concentration camps when she was sixteen, Rich writes she now feels a "belated rage" that she "had never been taught about resistance, only about passing. That [she] had no language for anti-Semitism itself." What does she mean? If you have read the Nathan McCall essay earlier in this chapter, consider whether he would be sympathetic to Rich. What does she mean by passing?

4. Angela Y. Davis, *Women, Race and Class* (New York: Random House, 1981); Lucy S. Davidowicz, *The War against the Jews 1933–1945* (1975) (New York: Bantam, 1979).

5. Why, when the immigrant seamstress asked Rich if she were Jewish, did Rich—then a college student—say that she wasn't? From what was she distancing herself?

6. Rich notes that in her family and that of her in-laws there were "degrees and hierarchies of assimilation which looked askance upon each other—and also geographic lines of difference, as between southern Jews and New York Jews, whose manners and customs varied along class as well as regional lines." Are you aware of such "hierarchies of assimilation" or "geographic lines of difference" within your family? To what extent do such hierarchies and lines of difference contribute to tensions within the United States today?

7. Rich points to a particular strain of Jewish identity: "the Jew as part of America's devouring plan in which the persecuted, called to assimilation, learn that the price is to engage in persecution." What does she mean? Does assimilation into our society require that we persecute those not assimilated? Using Rich's essay as a basis, explore the price of assimilation in relation to how the assimilating group treats other groups.

from MAUS: A SURVIVOR'S TALE

ART SPIEGELMAN

■ Cartoonist Art Spiegelman has been a professional artist since the mid-1960s. For many years he drew the trading cards packaged with Topps chewing gum—his creations, among others, include the popular Garbage Pail Kids. Spiegelman has also contributed to a number of underground comics magazines such as *Raw,* which he helped found, has published several volumes of his own strips, and has drawn attention-grabbing covers for the *New Yorker.*

The idea for his highly original book *MAUS*—which relates in comic strip form his father's memories of the Jewish Holocaust in Europe—grew out of old cartoons. "[T]his cat and mouse thing," Spiegelman has said, "is just a metaphor for some kind of oppression." Originally, he had planned to focus the story on racism in black/white relations; but he soon found that his parents' experiences as Jews in Nazi Poland, which he knew of personally, provided a stronger inspiration. He therefore created the frame of current-day scenes in which he interviews his father as source material. *MAUS* created a sensation when it was published in 1986, and a second volume, *MAUS II* (1991), was awarded a special Pulitzer Prize. Throughout the book, Jewish characters are rendered as mice and Nazis and Germans as cats. To many, the idea of a comic book about the Holocaust was insulting and outrageous, compounded by the fact that characters were also rendered as animals. The selection presented here comes early in Volume II. Spiegelman begins with a self-conscious reflection about the international success of Volume I, his struggle to keep all this information and emotional baggage straight, and his attempts to deal with the guilt typical of children of Holocaust survivors.

Time flies...

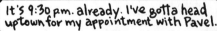

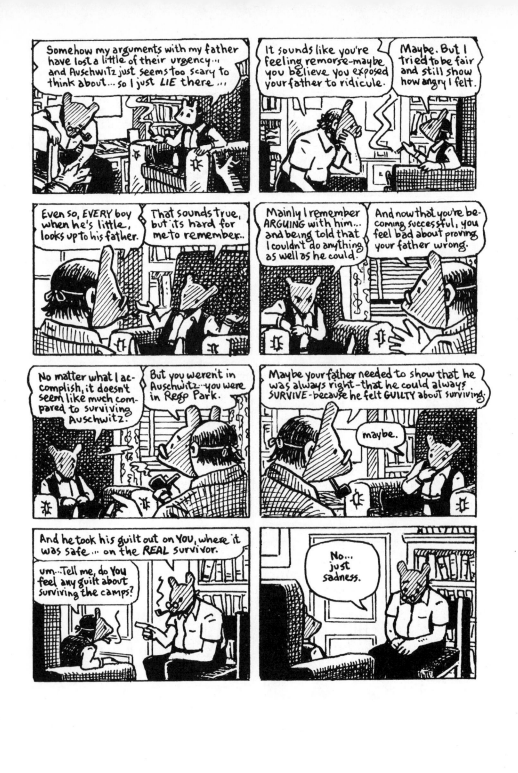

My book! Hah! What book?? Some part of me doesn't want to draw or think about Auschwitz. I can't visualize it clearly, and I can't BEGIN to imagine what it felt like.

What Auschwitz felt like? Hmm... How can I explain?...

BOO!

YIII!

It felt a little like *that*. But ALWAYS! From the moment you got to the gate until the very end.

So, what part of your book are you trying to visualize?

My father worked in a tin shop near the camp. I have no idea what kind of tools and stuff to draw. There's no documentation.

Let's see. There would be a cutter-like a giant paper cutter-and maybe an electric drill press or two.

How do you KNOW that?

Oh, I worked in a tool and die shop in Czechoslovakia when I was a kid.

But it's getting late now, and I still have to walk my dogs.

Okay. I'll see you in a week...

Gee. I don't understand exactly why...

but these sessions with Pavel somehow make me feel better...

Maybe I could show the tin shop and not draw the drill press. I hate to draw machinery.

And so...

CLIK ...THEN, WHEN I CAME OUT FROM THE HOSPITAL, RIGHT AWAY SHE STARTED AGAIN THAT I CHANGE MY WILL!

PLEASE POP. THE TAPE'S ON. LET'S CONTINUE...

I WAS STILL SO SICK AND TIRED. AND TO HAVE PEACE ONLY, I AGREED. TO MAKE IT LEGAL SHE BROUGHT RIGHT TO MY BED A NOTARY.

LET'S GET BACK TO AUSCHWITZ...

FIFTEEN DOLLARS HE CHARGED TO COME! IF SHE WAITED ONLY A WEEK UNTIL I WAS STRONGER, I'D GO TO THE BANK AND TAKE A NOTARY FOR ONLY A QUARTER!

ENOUGH! TELL ME ABOUT AUSCHWITZ!

sigh

YOU WERE TELLING ME HOW YOUR KAPO TRIED TO GET YOU WORK AS A TINSMITH...

YAH. EVERY DAY I WORKED THERE RIGHT OUTSIDE FROM THE CAMP...

THE CHIEF OF THE TINMEN IT WAS A RUSSIAN JEW NAMED YIDL.

BAH! YOU'RE NO TINSMITH. YOU CAN'T EVEN CUT IT RIGHT.

BUT THIS IS HOW I'VE ALWAYS DONE IT!...

I'VE ONLY BEEN A TINSMITH FOR A FEW YEARS. IF YOU SHOW ME HOW YOU WANT IT CUT I CAN LEARN QUICKLY.

HAH! YOU NEVER DID AN HONEST DAY'S WORK IN YOUR WHOLE LIFE, SPIEGELMAN! I KNOW ALL ABOUT YOU...

I DON'T KNOW WHERE FROM HE HEARD STORIES ABOUT ME.

YOU OWNED BIG FACTORIES AND EXPLOITED YOUR WORKERS, YOU DIRTY CAPITALIST!

HE WAS A **COMMU-NIST**, THIS YIDL.

PFUI! THEY SEND DREK LIKE YOU HERE WHILE THEY SEND REAL TINMEN UP THE CHIMNEY.

WATCH OUT. I'VE GOT MY EYE ON YOU!

I WAS AFRAID. HE COULD REALLY DO ME SOMETHING.

WITH THE OTHER BOYS THERE, I GOT ALONG FINE.

DON'T WORRY...YOU JUST HAVE TO KNOW HOW TO HANDLE YIDL...

BRING HIM A FEW EGGS, SOME BUTTER OR CHEESE...

YOU'LL SEE. HE'LL SING A DIFFERENT TUNE.

HA! AND WHERE DO I GET ALL THIS FOOD?

JUST KEEP YOUR EYES OPEN. YOU CAN ORGANIZE THINGS WITH THE POLES HERE.

POLES FROM NEARBY THEY HIRED TO WORK ALSO HERE — NOT PRISONERS, BUT SPECIALIST BUILDING WORKERS...

(PSST - I CAN GET YOU A FINE GOLD WATCH FOR A POUND OF SAUSAGE AND SIX EGGS.)

(AGREED.)

THEY HAD **NOTHING**, ONLY FOOD FROM THEIR FARMS. THEY WERE HAPPY TO MAKE EXCHANGES.

THE HEAD GUY FROM THE AUSCHWITZ LAUNDRY WAS A FINE FELLOW WHAT KNEW WELL MY FAMILY BEFORE THE WAR...

FROM HIM I GOT CIVILIAN **CLOTHINGS** TO SMUGGLE OUT BELOW MY UNIFORM. I WAS SO THIN THE GUARDS DIDN'T SEE IF I WORE EXTRA.

HERE YIDL. I'VE GOT A BIG PIECE OF CHEESE FOR YOU.

A GIFT? VERY NICE, SPIEGELMAN.

AND WHAT ELSE DO YOU HAVE THERE? A LOAF OF BREAD? YOU'RE A RICH MAN!

WAIT! I NEED THAT TO PAY OFF THE GUY WHO HELPED ME ORGANIZE THE CHEESE!

HMPH.

HE WAS SO GREEDY, YIDL, HE WANTED I RISK ONLY FOR HIM EVERYTHING. I TOO HAD TO EAT.

EVERYBODY WAS SO HUNGRY ALWAYS, WE DIDN'T KNOW EVEN WHAT WE ARE DOING...

IN THE MORNING FOR BREAKFAST WE GOT ONLY A BITTER DRINK MADE FROM ROOTS.

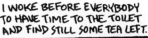
I WOKE BEFORE EVERYBODY TO HAVE TIME TO THE TOILET AND FIND STILL SOME TEA LEFT.

ONE TIME A DAY THEY GAVE A SOUP FROM TURNIPS. TO STAND NEAR THE FIRST OF THE LINE WAS NO GOOD. YOU GOT ONLY WATER.

MIX IT! MIX IT!

NEAR THE END WAS BETTER - SOLID THINGS TO THE BOTTOM FLOATED.

BUT TOO FAR TO THE END IT WAS ALSO NO GOOD

..BECAUSE MANY TIMES IT COULD BE NO SOUP ANYMORE.

AND ONE TIME EACH DAY THEY GAVE TO US A SMALL BREAD, CRUNCHY LIKE GLASS.

THE FLOUR THEY MIXED WITH SAWDUST TOGETHER-WE GOT ONE LITTLE BRICK OF THIS WHAT HAD TO LAST THE FULL DAY.

MOST GOBBLED IT RIGHT AWAY, BUT ALWAYS I SAVED A HALF FOR LATER.

AND IN THE EVENING WE GOT A SPOILED CHEESE OR JAM. IF WE WERE LUCKY A COUPLE TIMES A WEEK WE GOT A SAUSAGE BIG LIKE TWO OF MY FINGERS. ONLY THIS MUCH WE GOT

IF YOU ATE HOW THEY GAVE YOU, IT WAS JUST ENOUGH TO DIE MORE SLOWLY.

EACH MORNING AND EVENING THEY MADE AN *APPEL*. THEY COUNTED THE LIVE ONES AND DEAD ONES TO SEE IT WASN'T ANY MISSING ...

WE STOOD SOMETIMES THE WHOLE NIGHT WHILE THEY COUNTED AGAIN AND AGAIN.

ON OUR *APPELS* IT WAS ONE OLD GUY THERE, ALWAYS HE WAS COMPLAINING ...

I DON'T BELONG HERE WITH ALL THESE YIDS AND POLACKS! I'M A **GERMAN** LIKE YOU!

I HAVE MEDALS FROM THE KAISER· MY SON IS A GERMAN SOLDIER!

ONLY THEY HIT HIM AND THEY LAUGHED.

WAS HE REALLY A GERMAN?

WHO KNOWS... IT WAS GERMAN PRISONERS ALSO... BUT FOR THE GERMANS THIS GUY WAS JEWISH!

ON ONE *APPEL* HE DIDN'T STAND SO STRAIGHT AND A GUARD DRAGGED HIM AWAY. I HEARD HE PUSHED HIM DOWN AND JUMPED HARD ON HIS NECK...

OR THEY SENT HIM TO THE GAS, I DON'T REMEMBER, BUT THEY FINISHED HIM AND HE NEVER ANYMORE COMPLAINED.

Working with the Text

1. The story Spiegelman tells is both biographical and autobiographical. Why do you suppose he chose to render his Jewish characters as mice rather than depicting them as human beings? How do you respond personally to the idea of a narrative about the Holocaust rendered in graphical form?

2. The selection included here, like the book *MAUS* itself, contains a number of different layers of reality and timeframes. Can you sort out the different frames of reference in the selection? How might they all work together as a commentary about memory and history?

3. There are extensive resources on the World Wide Web dealing with the Holocaust. Many of them are linked and sorted from the *Border Texts* Web site. Look at some of the personal narratives online by survivors and children of survivors. Do you see any parallels to Spiegelman's treatment? Are there places in the narratives online that remind you of the conversations that he has with the psychiatrist/survivor in the selection?

4. What is the effect of the piled bodies in the first few frames? How does that contrast to the relative realism of the last section set in the concentration camp?

5. In addition to being a story about Vladek's experience in the Holocaust, *MAUS* is also a complex meditation about communication and expression. What kinds of questions are raised by the selection about telling, silence, and the recovery of experience from a horrible event? Explore some of these issues of "speaking the unspeakable" as they are represented in the selection and in any online Holocaust narratives you have read.

ETHNICITY: IDENTITY AND DIFFERENCE

STUART HALL

■ Jamaican-born Stuart Hall emigrated to England in the 1950s. He is Professor of Sociology at the Open University, London. He is the author of *Reproducing Ideologies* (1984) and *The Hard Road to Renewal* (1988). He has coedited numerous volumes, including *The Idea of the Modern State* (1984) and *Politics and Ideology* (1986). In the following essay, first delivered as a speech in 1989, Hall considers the extent to which we must "reconceptualize what identities might mean in [the] more diverse and pluralized situation" of our current multicultural society.

This is an edited version of a speech delivered at Hampshire College, Amherst, Mass., in the spring of 1989.

I've chosen to talk about questions of identity and ethnicity, first because questions about identity and ethnicity have suddenly surfaced again in English intellectual and critical discussion and debate. And secondly, because the relationship between cultural identities and ethnicities is a question that is also on the *political* agenda in Britain at the moment. I'll try to say in the course of my talk why I think questions of identity are once again in play conceptually and politically.

THE RETURN OF IDENTITY

I'm concerned with what is sometimes called the "return of the question of identity"—not that the question of identity ever went away, but it has come back with a particular kind of force. That return has something to do with the fact that the question of identity focuses on that point where a whole series of different developments in society and a set of related discourses intersect. Identity emerges as a kind of unsettled space, or an unresolved question in that space, between a number of intersecting discourses. My purpose is to mark some of those points of intersection, especially around questions of cultural identity, and to explore them in relation to the subject of ethnicity in politics.

Let me start by saying something about what seems to have been the logic of the way in which we have thought and talked about questions of identity until recently. The logic of the discourse of identity assumes a stable subject, i.e., we've assumed that there is something which we can call our identity which, in a rapidly shifting world, has the great advantage of staying still. Identities are a kind of guarantee that the world isn't falling apart quite as rapidly as it sometimes seems to be. It's a kind of fixed point of thought and being, a ground of action, a still point in the turning world. That's the kind of ultimate guarantee that identity seems to provide us with.

The logic of identity is the logic of something like a "true self." And the language of identity has often been related to the search for a kind of authenticity to one's experience, something that tells me where I come from. The logic and language of identity is the logic of depth—in here, deep inside me, is my Self which I can reflect upon. It is an element of continuity. I think most of us do recognize that our identities have changed over time, but we have the hope or nostalgia that they change at the rate of a glacier. So, while we're not the fledglings that we were when we were one year old, we are the same sort of person.

DISRUPTION OF IDENTITY

So where does the recent disruption of identity come from? What is displacing this depth—the autonomous origin, point of reference, and guaranteed continuity that has been so long associated with the language of identity? What is it about the turbulence of the world we live in that is increasingly mirrored in the vicissitudes of identity?

While, historically, many things have displaced or decentered the stable sense of identity that I just described, I want to focus on four great de-centerings in intellec-

1

2

3

4

5

6

tual life and in Western thought that have helped to destabilize the question of identity. I'll attach particular names to three of them, just for convenience sake. I don't want to say they alone did it, but it is quite useful to summarize by hooking the ideas to a particular name. The fourth cannot be attached to a single name, but is just as important.

Marx begins the de-centering of that stable sense of identity by reminding us that there are always *conditions* to identity which the subject cannot construct. *Men and women make history but not under conditions of their own making.* They are partly made by the histories that they make. We are always constructed in part by the practices and discourses that make us, such that we cannot find within ourselves as individual selves or subjects or identities the point of origin from which discourse or history or practice originates. History has to be understood as a continuous dialectic or dialogic relationship between that which is already made and that which is making the future. While Marx's argument deconstructed a lot of games, I'm particularly interested in his impact on the identity/language game. Marx interrupted that notion of the sovereign subject who opens his or her mouth and speaks, for the first time, the truth. Marx reminds us that we are always lodged and implicated in the practices and structures of everybody else's life.   7

Secondly, there is the very profound displacement which begins with Freud's discovery of the unconscious. If Marx displaced us from the past, Freud displaced us from below. Identity is itself grounded on the huge unknowns of our psychic lives, and we are unable, in any simple way, to reach through the barrier of the unconscious into the psychic life. We can't read the psychic *directly* into the social and the cultural. Nevertheless, social, cultural and political life cannot be understood except in relationship to the formations of the unconscious life. This in itself destabilizes the notion of the self, of identity, as a fully self-reflective entity. It is not possible for the self to reflect and know completely its own identity since it is formed not only in the line of the practice of other structures and discourses, but also in a complex relationship with unconscious life.   8

Thirdly, we must consider Saussure and his model of language and linguistics which has so transformed theoretical work. Saussurian linguistics suggests that speech—discourse, enunciation itself—is always placed within the relationships of language. In order to speak, in order to say anything new, we must first place ourselves within the existing relations of language. There is no utterance so novel and so creative that it does not already bear on it the traces of how that language has been spoken before we opened our mouths. Thus we are always within language. To say something new is first of all to reaffirm the traces of the past that are inscribed in the words we use. In part, to say something new is first of all to displace all the old things that the words mean—to fight an entire system of meanings. For example, think of how profound it has been in our world to say the word "Black" in a new way. In order to say "Black" in a new way, we have to fight off everything else that Black has always meant—all its connotations, all its negative and positive figurations, the entire metaphorical structure of Christian thought, for example. The whole history of Western imperial thought is condensed in the struggle to dislocate what Black used to mean in order to make it mean something new, in order to say "Black is Beautiful." I'm not talking about Saussure's specific theories of language   9 only. I'm talking about what happens to one's conception of identity when one suddenly understands that one is always inside a system of languages that partly speak us, which we are always positioned within and against.

These are the great figures of modernism. We might say that if modernity unleashes the logic of identity I was talking about earlier, modernism is modernity experienced as trouble. In the face of modernity's promise of the great future: "I am, I am Western man, therefore I know everything. Everything begins with me," modernism says, "Hold on. What about the past? What about the languages you speak? What about the unconscious life you don't know about? What about all those other things that are speaking you?"

However, there's a fourth force of destabilization. This could be given a variety of names. If you wanted to stay within the episteme of Western knowledge, you could say Nietzsche. But I want to say something else. I want to talk about the de-centering of identity that arises as a consequence of the end of the notion of truth as having something directly to do with Western discourses of rationality. This is the great de-centering of identity that is a consequence of the relativization of the Western world—of the discovery of other worlds, other peoples, other cultures, and other languages. Western rational thought, despite its imperializing claim to be *the* form of universal knowledge, suddenly appears as just another episteme. To use Foucault's words, just another regime of truth. Or Nietzsche's, not absolute Knowledge, not total Truth, just another *particular* form of knowledge harnessed to particular forms of historical power. The linkage between knowledge and power is what made that regime True, what enabled that regime to claim to speak the truth about identity for everyone else across the globe.

When that installation of Western rationality begins to go and to be seen not as absolute, disinterested, objective, neutral, scientific, nonpowerful truth, but dirty truth—truth implicated in the hard game of power—that is the fourth game that destabilizes the old logic of identity.

COLLECTIVE IDENTITIES

I've been talking so far about intellectual, theoretical, conceptual displacements of the notion of identity, but I want to talk about some of the displacements of identity that come from social and cultural life rather than from conceptual and theoretical thought. The great social collectivities which used to stabilize our identities—the great stable collectivities of class, race, gender and nation—have been, in our times, deeply undermined by social and political developments.

The whole adventure of the modern world was, for a long time, blocked out in terms of these great collective identities. As one knew one's class, one knew one's place in the social universe. As one knew one's race, one knew one's racial position within the great races of the world in their hierarchical relationship to one another. As one knew one's gender, one was able to locate oneself in the huge social divisions between men and women. As one knew one's national identity, one certainly knew about the pecking order of the universe. These collective identities stabilized and staged our sense of ourselves. That logic of identity that seemed so confident at the beginning of my talk, was in part held in place by these great collective social identities.

Now, it is not the best kept secret in the world that all sorts of things have rocked   15
and shaken those great collective, stable, social identities of the past. I don't want to
talk about any of those developments in detail, but if you think, for instance, of
class, it certainly is not true that, in societies like yours and mine, questions
of class—of social structure and of social inequality that are raised by the notion of
class—have gone away. But, nevertheless, the way in which class identities were understood and experienced, the way in which people located themselves in relation to
class identities, the way in which we understood those identities as organized politically—those stable forms of class identity are much more difficult to find at this
point in the twentieth century than they were 100 years ago. In fact, looking backwards, we're not sure whether the great stable identities of class were ever quite as
stable as we told ourselves they were. There's a kind of narrative of class that always
makes the past look simpler than it probably was. If you go back into English nineteenth century life, you will find that class was a pretty complex formation even
then. I think there is, nevertheless, some relative sense in which the nation-state, the
great class formations of industrial capitalism, certainly the way in which gender
was conceptualized, and, toward the end of the nineteenth century, the way in which
the entire population of the world could be thought of in terms of the great family
of races—I do think there is a way in which these great structuring principles did tie
down the question of our social and cultural identities and that they have been very
considerably fractured, fragmented, undermined, dispersed in the course of the last
fifty years.

THE UNIVERSE IS COMING

Now, this fragmentation of social identity is very much a part of the modern and,   16
indeed, if you believe in it, the postmodern experience. That sense of fragmentation
has a peculiar and particular shape to it. Specifically, if I may say this metaphorically,
the fragmentation goes local and global at one and the same time, while the great
stable identities in the middle do not seem to hold.

Take "the nation." The nation-state is increasingly besieged from on top by the   17
interdependence of the planet—by the interdependency of our ecological life, by the
enormous interpenetration of capital as a global force, by the complex ways in
which world markets link the economies of backward, developed, and overdevel-
oped nations. These enormous systems are increasingly undermining the stability of
any national formation. Nation-states are in trouble, though I am not going to
prophesy that the nation-state, that has dominated the history of the world for so
long, is going to bow out gracefully.

So on the one hand, the nation and all the identities that go with it appear to have   18
gone upwards—reabsorbed into larger communities that overreach and intercon-
nect national identities. But at the same time there is also movement down below.
Peoples and groups and tribes who were previously harnessed together in the entities called the nation-states begin to rediscover identities that they had forgotten. So
for example if you come to England and hope to see some great stable cultural identity called "the English"—who represent everybody else—what you will find instead
is that the Scots, for example, are about to fly off somewhere. They say "We are Scottish and we are European, but we certainly aren't British." And the Welsh say "We're

not British either because you've forgotten us and we might as well go somewhere else." And at the same time the Northwest and the Northeast of England, that were left to rot by Mrs. Thatcher, are not truly British any longer either—they're sort of marginal to everybody else. Then the old trade unionists and all Blacks are somebody else, too. You're left with the English as a tight little island somewhere around London with about 25 souls and the Thatcher government hovering over it. And they are continually asking the question—not only about the rest of the world but about most of the people in their own society—"are you one of us?"

So at one and the same time people feel part of the world and part of their village. They have neighborhood identities and they are citizens of the world. Their bodies are endangered by Chernobyl, which didn't knock on the door and say "Can I float radiation over your sovereign territory?" Or another example, we had the warmest winter I've ever experienced in England, last year—the consequence in part of the destruction of rain forests thousands of miles away. An ecological understanding of the world is one that challenges the notion that the nation-state and the boundaries of sovereignty will keep things stable because they won't. The universe is coming! 19

So on the one hand, we have global identities because we have a stake in something global and, on the other hand, we can only know ourselves because we are part of some face-to-face communities. This brings me back to the question of the fate of cultural identity in this maelstrom. Given this theoretical and conceptual decentering that I've just spoken about, given the relativization of the great stable identities that have allowed us to know who we are—how can we think about the question of cultural identity? 20

POST-IDENTITY?: COVER STORIES

There is some language for the notion of doing without identity all together. That is my somewhat unfavorable reference to the extreme version of postmodernism. The argument is that the Self is simply a kind of *perpetual signifier* ever wandering the earth in search of a *transcendental signified* that it can never find—a sort of endless nomadic existence with utterly atomized individuals wandering in an endlessly pluralistic void. Yet, while there are certain conceptual and theoretical ways in which you can try to do without identity, I'm not yet convinced that you can. I think we have to try to reconceptualize what identities might mean in this more diverse and pluralized situation. 21

This takes us back to some of the very profound things that people have said about identity within recent forms of theorizing. First of all, we are reminded of the structure of "identification" itself. Identity, far from the simple thing that we think it is (ourselves always in the same place), understood properly is always a structure that is split; it always has ambivalence within it. The story of identity is a cover story. A cover story for making you think you stayed in the same place, though with another bit of your mind you do know that you've moved on. What we've learned about the structure of the way in which we identify suggests that identification is not one thing, one moment. We have now to reconceptualize identity as a *process of identification,* and that is a different matter. It is something that happens over time, 22 that is never absolutely stable, that is subject to the play of history and the play of difference.

I don't want to bore you autobiographically, but I could tell you something about   23
the process of my own identification. If I think about who I am, I have been—in my own much too long experience—several identities. And most of the identities that I have been I've only known about *not* because of something deep inside me—the real self—but because of how other people have recognized me.

So, I went to England in the 1950s, before the great wave of migration from the   24
Caribbean and from the Asian subcontinent. I came from a highly respectable, lower middle class Jamaican family. When I went back home at the end of the 50s, my mother, who was very classically of that class and culture, said to me "I hope they don't think you're an immigrant over there!" I had never thought of myself as an immigrant! And now I thought, well actually, I guess that's what I am. I migrated just at that moment. When she hailed me, when she said "Hello immigrant," she asked me to refuse it and in the moment of refusal—like almost everything my mother ever asked me to do—I said "That's who I am! I'm an immigrant." And I thought at last, I've come into my *real* self.

And then, at the end of the 60s and the early 70s, somebody said to me "These   25
things are going on in the political world—I suppose you're really Black." Well, I'd never thought of myself as Black, either! And I'll tell you something, nobody in Jamaica ever did. Until the 1970s, that entire population experienced themselves as all sorts of other things, but they never called themselves Black. And in that sense, Black has a history as an identity that is partly *politically* formed. It's not the color of your skin. It's not given in nature.

Another example: at that very moment I said to my son, who is the result of a   26
mixed marriage, "You're Black." "No," he said, "I'm brown." "You don't understand what I'm saying! You're looking to the wrong signifier! I'm not talking about what color you are. People are all sorts of colors. The question is whether you are *culturally, historically, politically* Black. *That's* who you are."

THE OTHER

So experience belies the notion that identification happens once and for all—life is   27
not like that. It goes on changing and part of what is changing is not the nucleus of the "real you" inside, it is history that's changing. History changes your conception of yourself. Thus, another critical thing about identity is that it is partly the relationship between you and the Other. Only when there is an Other can you know who you are. To discover that fact is to discover and unlock the whole enormous history of nationalism and of racism. Racism is a structure of discourse and representation that tries to expel the Other symbolically—blot it out, put it over there in the Third World, at the margin.

The English are racist not because they hate the Blacks but because they don't   28
know who they are without the Blacks. They have to know who they are *not* in order to know who they are. And the English language is absolutely replete with things that the English are not. They are not Black, they are not Indian or Asian, but they are not Europeans and they are not Frogs either and on and on. The Other. It is a

fantastic moment in Fanon's *Black Skin, White Masks* when he talks of how the gaze of the Other fixes him in an identity. He knows what it is to be Black when the white child pulls the hand of her mother and says "Look momma, a Black man." And he says "I was fixed in that gaze." That is the gaze of Otherness. And there is no identity that is without the dialogic relationship to the Other. The Other is not outside, but also inside the Self, the identity. So identity is a process, identity is split. Identity is not a fixed point but an ambivalent point. Identity is also the relationship of the Other to oneself.

DIFFERENCE(S)

You could tell that story also in terms of a psychic conception of identity. Some of 29
the most important work that modern psychoanalysts have done—Lacan and so forth—and that feminists have done in terms of sexual identity is to show the importance of the relationship of the Other. The *construction of difference* as a process, as something that goes on over time, is something that feminism has been showing us is never finished. The notion that identity is complete at some point—the notion that masculinity and femininity can view each other as a perfectly replicating mirror image of each another—is untenable after the slightest reading of any feminist text or after reading Freud's *Three Essays on Sexuality.*

So the notion that identity is outside representation—that there are our selves 30
and then the language in which we describe ourselves—is untenable. Identity is within discourse, within representation. It is constituted in part by representation. Identity is a narrative of the self; it's the story we tell about the self in order to know who we are. We impose a structure on it. The most important effect of this reconceptualization of identity is the surreptitious return of difference. Identity is a game that ought to be played against difference. But now we have to think about identity *in relation to* difference. There are differences between the ways in which genders are socially and psychically constructed. But there is no fixity to those oppositions. It is a relational opposition, it is a relation of difference. So we're then in the difficult conceptual area of trying to think identity *and* difference.

There are two *different* notions of difference operating. There are the great dif- 31
ferences of the discourse of racism—Black and white, civilized and primitive, them and us. But this new conception of difference is a conception much closer to that notion of difference one finds in Derrida. In Derrida you find a notion of *differance* that recognizes the endless, ongoing nature of the construction of meaning but that recognizes also that there is always the play of identity and difference and always the play of difference *across* identity. You can't think of them without each other.

You see, there has been in our lifetime—not in yours, but in mine—a *politics* of 32
identity. There was a *politics* of identity in 1968 in which the various social movements tried to organize themselves politically within one identity. So the identity of being a woman was the subject of the feminist movement. The identity of being a Black person was the identity of the Black movement. And in that rather simpler universe, there was one identity to each movement. While you were in it, you had one identity. Of course, even then, all of us moved between these so-called stable identities. We were sampling these different identities, but we maintained the notion, the myth, the narrative that we were really all the same. That notion of essential forms of identity is no longer tenable.

THE THATCHER PROJECT

So, how can one think about identity in this new context? I want to say just a word   33
about the way this has emerged politically in the United Kingdom in the last ten
years. I referred a few moments ago to a very narrow and exclusive conception of
Englishness that lies at the absolute center of the political project of Thatcherism.
When I first started to write about Thatcherism in the early 70s, I thought it was
largely an economic and political project. It is only more recently that I understood
how profoundly it is rooted in a certain exclusive and essentialist conception of Englishness. Thatcherism is *in defense* of a certain definition of Englishness. England
didn't go to the Falklands War inadvertently. It went because there was something
there about the connection of the great imperial past, of the empire, of the lion
whose tail cannot be tweaked, of the little country that stood up to the great dicta-
tor. It's a way of mythically living all the great moments of the English past again.
Well, it happens that this time it had to be in the South Atlantic, miles away from
anything—in a little corner of the globe that most English people can't identify on
the map. This is Marx's famous phrase "The first time is history, the second time is
farce." And the third time is an extremely long trip to the South Atlantic. This is the
moment of decline that is always a moment of danger in national cultures.

THE RETURN OF THE REPRESSED

So it's a very profound part of the Thatcher project to try to restore the identity that   34
in their view *belongs* to Great Britain—Great Britain, Inc., Ltd.—a great firm, Great
Britain restored to a world power. But in this very moment of the attempted symbolic restoration of the great English identities that have mastered and dominated
the world over three or four centuries, there has come home to roost in English society some *other* British folks. They come from Jamaica, Pakistan, Bangladesh,
India—all that part of the colonial world that the English, just in the 1950s, decided
they could do without. Just in the very moment when they decided they could do
without us, we all took the banana boat and came right back home. We turned up
saying "You said this was the mother country. Well, I just came home." We now stand
as a permanent reminder of that forgotten, suppressed, hidden history. Every time
they walk out on the street, some of us—some of the Other—are there. There we
are, *inside* the culture, going to their schools, speaking their language, playing their
music, walking down their streets, looking like we own a part of the turf, looking
like we belong. Some third generation Blacks are starting to say "We are the Black
British." After all, who are we? We're not Jamaicans any more. We have a relationship
to that past, but we can't be that entirely any more. You can see that debates around
questions of identity are at the center of political life in England today.

ETHNICITIES: OLD AND NEW

What does all that I've been saying have to do with ethnicity? I've left the question   35
of ethnicity to the last because ethnicity is the way in which I want to rethink the relationships between identity and difference. I want to argue that ethnicity is what we
all require in order to think [about] the relationship between identity and difference. What do I mean by that? There is no way, it seems to me, in which people of
the world can act, can speak, can create, can come in from the margins and talk, can

begin to reflect on their own experience unless they come from some *place,* they come from some history, they inherit certain cultural traditions. What we've learned about the theory of enunciation is that there's no enunciation without positionality. You have to position yourself *somewhere* in order to say anything at all. Thus, we cannot do without that sense of our own positioning that is connoted by the term ethnicity. And the relation that peoples of the world now have to their own past is, of course, part of the discovery of their own ethnicity. They need to honor the hidden histories from which they come. They need to understand the languages which they've been not taught to speak. They need to understand and revalue the traditions and inheritances of cultural expression and creativity. And in that sense, the past is not only a position from which to speak, but it is also an absolutely necessary resource in what one has to say. There is no way, in my view, in which those elements of ethnicity that depend on understanding the past, understanding one's roots, can be done without.

But, on the other hand, there comes the play of difference. This is the recognition 36 that our relationship to that past is quite a complex one, we can't pluck it up out of where it was and simply restore it to ourselves. If you ask my son, who is seventeen and who was born in London, where he comes from, he cannot tell you he comes from Jamaica. Part of his identity is there, but he has to *discover* that identity. He can't just take it out of a suitcase and plop it on the table and say "That's mine." It's not an essence like that. He has to learn to tell himself the story of his past. He has to interrogate his own history, he has to relearn that part of him that has an investment in that culture. For example, he's learning wood sculpture, and in order to do that he has had to discover the traditions of sculpturing of a society in which he has never lived.

So the relationship of the kind of ethnicity I'm talking about to the past is not a 37 simple, essential one—it is a constructed one. It is constructed in history, it is constructed politically in part. It is part of narrative. We tell ourselves the stories of the parts of our roots in order to come into contact, creatively, with it. So this new kind of ethnicity—the emergent ethnicities—has a relationship to the past, but it is a relationship that is partly through memory, partly through narrative, one that has to be recovered. It is an act of cultural recovery.

Yet it is also an ethnicity that has to recognize its position in relation to the im- 38 portance of difference. It is an ethnicity that cannot deny the role of difference in discovering itself. And I'll tell you a simple, quick story to show you what I mean. About two years ago I was involved in a photographic exhibition that was organized by the Commonwealth Institute in England, and the idea behind it was very simple. Photography is one of the languages in which people speak about their own past and their own experience and construct their own identity. Large numbers of people in the marginal societies of the British Commonwealth have been the *objects* of someone else's representation, not the *subject* of their own representations. The purpose of this exhibition was to enable some people in those regions to use the creative medium of photography to speak and address their own experience—to empower their ethnicities.

When we came to look at the exhibition, one saw two things at one and the same 39 time. First of all, we saw the enormous excitement of people who are able for the first time to speak about what they have always known—to speak about their culture, their languages, their people, their childhood, about the topography in which they grew up. The arts in our society are being transformed hourly by the new discourses of subjects who have been marginalized coming into representation for the first time. But we also saw something else that we were not prepared for. From those local ethnic enclaves, what they want to speak about as well is the entire world. They want to tell you how they went from the village to Manhattan. They are not prepared to be ethnic archivists for the rest of their lives. They are not prepared only to have something to say of marginalization forever. They have a stake in the whole dominant history of the world, they want to rewrite the history of the world, not just tell my little story. So they use photography to tell us about the enormous migrations of the world and how people now move—of how all our identities are constructed out of a variety of different discourses. We need a place to speak from, but we no longer speak about ethnicity in a narrow and essentialist way.

That is the new ethnicity. It is a new conception of our identities because it has   40 not lost hold of the place and the ground from which we can speak, yet it is no longer contained within that place as an essence. It wants to address a much wider variety of experience. It is part of the enormous cultural relativization of the entire globe that is the historical accomplishment—horrendous as it has been in part—of the twentieth century. Those are the new ethnicities, the new voices. They are neither locked into the past nor able to forget the past. Neither all the same nor entirely different. Identity *and* difference. It is a new settlement between identity and difference.

Of course, alongside the new ethnicities are the *old* ethnicities and the coupling   41 of the old, essentialist identities to power. The old ethnicities still have dominance, they still govern. Indeed, as I tried to suggest when I referred to Thatcherism, as they are relativized their propensity to eat everything else increases. They can only be sure that they really exist at all if they consume everyone else. The notion of an identity that knows where it came from, where home is, but also lives in the symbolic—in the Lacanian sense—knows you can't really go home again. You can't be something else than who you are. You've got to find out who you are in the flux of the past and the present. That new conception of ethnicity is now struggling in different ways across the globe against the present danger and the threat of the dangerous old ethnicity. That's the stake of the game.

Working with the Text

1. Hall draws from some major thinkers and ideas from other fields, such as Karl Marx and Marxism, Freud and psychoanalysis, Nietzsche and the philosophy of power, the idea of modernity, and so on. What ideas discussed in Hall's essay have you encountered in other classes in other departments? What different subjects does Hall bring to bear on the subject of identity? In a group try to pool your knowledge for the broader contexts of Hall's essay.

2. How does Hall's story about exploring his own identity as a Jamaican who immigrated to England relate to what he has to say about identity in America (¶s 23–26)?

3. Choose any story or essay that you have read in *Border Texts* thus far that you think complements Hall's essay. What have you read in this book about

the treatment of culture, ethnicity, or identity that helps make sense of Hall's ideas, or vice versa?

4. Hall's essay is an analysis of the concept of identity in its many, complex forms. What are some of the dimensions of identity Hall addresses? Find two different passages that correspond to different kinds of identity. How do they contribute to a more complex understanding of the forms and faces of identity?

5. What connections are being made in Hall's essay between identity and representation? What do you think he means by the statement in paragraph 22, "We have now to reconceptualize identity as a *process of identification,* and that is a different matter. It is something that happens over time, that is never absolutely stable, that is subject to the play of history and the play of difference." What forces of history, difference, and "otherness" turn identity into a "process of identification"?

6. What is Hall's point about ethnicity at the conclusion of the essay? Discuss what he means by the phrase (¶ 35) ". . . there's no enunciation without positionality. You have to position yourself *somewhere* in order to say anything at all." What does he suggest this means for crossing borders of communication and discovering self-identity?

Thinking and Writing: *Critical Questions Revisited*

1. Images of Otherness

One way to think about the idea of "otherness" is as the act of mentally *replacing* actual people who are different with a simplified image, name, or label that is often degrading or negative. Throughout the readings in this chapter there are many examples of such labels. What is critical about these images and names is both their power and their persistence. One example is the term *exotic,* which Tara L. Masih points out can have a range of meanings, which upon close inspection are all marginalizing and not too flattering. In other cases, names and labels for otherness serve to erase differences *among* groups by emphasizing their collective differences *from* the mainstream. Such is the case with the word *Indian,* which, as Berkhofer points out, is a general category that covered hundreds of different tribes and cultures. Similarly, the term *homeless,* according to Peter Marin, is a word that includes a wide range of people who find themselves on the street for very different reasons. By using one word to "stand for" all these people, we damage our sense of homelessness by treating everyone without a home as part of an undifferentiated group of marginal people.

Nathan McCall emphasizes the erasing power of the word *Nigger* and indeed the whole ideology of "color"—how a "black boy" was always that first, and not a person. The tradition of racial designations is the most devastating example of "otherness" that we have, where imagery and labels substitute for "seeing" other kinds of people who are separate from the center of a civilization or culture.

Using these examples, or others like them, discuss the idea of otherness. What are some additional examples of how images and labels erase or obscure one's ability to see beyond apparent differences? One approach would be to take a particular issue that interests you that involves "marginalized" people and to look closely at the language employed by both sides. How do such images of otherness function in the rhetoric of social issues or the political debate you've chosen to examine?

2. Otherness and Identity (Self, Group, Communal)

What roles do definitions of "otherness" play in creating and maintaining group or communal identity? In what ways are perceptions of differences an important (or inevitable) part of the way that communities and cultures define themselves? One way to consider this question is to begin with the idea that there often exists (either explicitly or implicitly) a definition of what is "normal" in any culture. Are there implied standards of "normal" behavior and "normal" appearance that operate in our society, even if those standards are unarticulated or invisible? Do these norms vary in different places where you have lived? How do different groups conceive a sense of themselves based on their sense of others? In what ways is this view of themselves coded into racial divisions within the United States? Do you agree, for example, with David Sibley, who claims that "White has been normalized in Europe, North America and Austalasia" and "that what seems normal is also a symbol of domination . . . "? What is your reaction to critic bell hooks's claims that "whites have a deep emotional involvement in the myth of 'sameness'" and that "whites do not think about themselves as white but only about others as not-white and other"?

How does this statement apply nationally as well as racially? Is there a "normalized" image of what an American is? What about representations of people from other countries as ways of reinforcing the self-identity of the United States? Can you think of ways that definitions of otherness contribute to communal or group identity? What about the ways that other ("non-white") groups define themselves? Or is their identity already defined for them, as "others"?

You could discuss this question from many other angles in addition to race and nation, such as from the perspective of sexuality, economics, or class.

3. Beyond Dichotomies: Diversity and Community?

In his essay "Makes Me Wanna Holler," Nathan McCall recollects one of the defining moments of his life when he realized, as he puts it, "that there were two distinct worlds in America, and a different set of rules for each: The white one was full of the possibilities of life. The dark one was just that—dark and limited." In McCall's and other selections in this chapter, there is a clear delineation of society into *dichotomies:* us and them. Jacob Riis's essay is about "the other half"; Toni Cade Bambara's story is about a "lesson" in the contrasts between uptown and downtown. Columbus discovered a world that seemed to stand for everything that European civilization was not.

On the other hand, there are other indications in this chapter that the world might be viewed not simply in terms of black/white, rich/poor, us/them. Tara L. Masih suggests a redefinition of the word *exotic* from something that means *different from the norm* to a new meaning: "A recognition of that which is especially unique to each culture." Masih resists the desire to have total assimilation and instead hopes that the "prefix *multi*" in multicultural "will begin to take power, allowing this country to exist as many rather than as one generic, incestuous mass." Similarly, the essays by Adrienne Rich and Stuart Hall in part involve discussions of identity that cross boundaries and mix identities in ways that make strict dichotomous divisions between black and white, upperclass and underclass impossible.

It is not a matter of determining which way to see the world is correct, of course, because each is a true way for each author. But what are the implications of articulating the world in different ways? How are dreams of assimilation into a single, homogenous culture related to a dichotomous world view of *us and them, in or out*? What are the alternatives? Can we imagine a culture that is both coherent and based on difference? Is it possible to think beyond dichotomies? What would be the implications of that notion? Are there ways to think about diversities that move beyond dichotomies rather than reinforcing them?

4. Dirt, Fear, and Morality

Peter Marin, in his essay "Helping and Hating the Homeless," talks about what he calls the "Family of bourgeois fears" that shapes common feelings about homeless people:

> Our response to the homeless is fed by a complex set of cultural attitudes, habits of thought, and fantasies and fears so familiar to us, so common, that they have become a *second* nature and might as well be instinctive, for all the control we have over them. And it is by no means easy to untangle this snarl of responses. What does seem clear is that the homeless embody all that bourgeois culture has for centuries tried to eradicate and destroy.

What Marin sees as the root of middle-class fears is the possibility of masses of hungry and dirty people, as has been the case in other periods in history. As a result, people who are dirty, hungry, or lacking stable homes, jobs, or means of support remind us, Marin claims, of everything that is the opposite of bourgeois values. "The homeless, simply be-cause they are homeless," he says, "are strangers, alien—and therefore a threat. Their presence, in itself, comes to constitute a kind of violence; it deprives us of our sense of safety."

Marin brings together a set of key terms that can be considered together as part of a particular set of reactions to the "other" in general, with varying levels of emphasis de-pending on the context. These terms include *fear, repulsion at dirt, violence,* and *morality.* In various ways these key terms are often present—sometimes at the articulated level, sometimes unspoken—when people represent the "other." In a paper, discuss the inter-action of fear, dirt, and morality in the context of the idea of otherness. How, for exam-ple, in Jacob Riis's analysis of the Lower East Side, does he deal with the relationship between dirt and morality? What is Elizabeth Bishop's response to the naked images in the *National Geographic*? How is it related to her own sense of shame and identity? What about the representation of Jews in Nazi Germany? What other examples of the repre-sentation of otherness can you think of where there was a commingling of images of dirt, morality, and the potential for violence within the marginalized group, or a threat to the safety of others?

5. Resistance to Fitting In

Many of these readings are written from the perspective of resistance. In many cases the resistance is to the categories and patterns of behavior that are assigned to marginalized groups by the dominant part of society. But this resistance is not always simple. For example, consider Adrienne Rich's anger and sense of betrayal toward her father, who passively accepted his need to hide his Jewishness in order to "fit" into Southern profes-sional society. Look at the need for some members of the Jewish community to collabo-rate with the Nazis in order to survive, and the resentment of other Jews toward their choice. What happens when marginalized people are offered a singular choice of fitting in or becoming invisible—compromising their identity, becoming alienated, or some-thing worse?

Or think about the anger that being "kept out" instilled in Nathan McCall, who says of the racist children of his youth, "I wondered, *Where did those white people learn to hate so deeply at such a young age?* I didn't know. But, over time, I learned to hate as blindly and viciously as any of them." What about his anger? What is the relationship be-tween an angry response to being marginalized and a counter-response to that anger that leads to further division?

BORDER VISIONS:

An Image Portfolio

For further materials and resources related to the Image Portfolio, see Border Images Online at http://www.hmco.com/hmco/college/english/bass/images/

Critical Questions

How do you "read" an image? In what ways are images similar to and different from written texts? How do images represent a particular perspective or point of view? How do images express a relationship between subjects (the seer) and objects (the seen)? What are some of the ways that images express relationships of power? Of space? Of otherness and difference? In what ways are pictures coded with meanings drawn from their cultural and social contexts? What conventions and meanings do we ascribe to different kinds of images? Do images represent a kind of "truth" and objective reality, or are they constructed, biased, and subjective?

IMAGES

Plate 1: Jesse Levine: *The Turnabout Map of the Western Hemisphere*
Plate 2: Patricia Rodriguez and students: *La Fruta del Diablo*
Plate 3: Joel Sternfeld: *Studio City*
Plate 4: Lynette Molnar: from *Familiar Names and Not-so-Familiar Faces*
Plate 5: Joel Sternfeld: *The Bronx*
Plate 6: Margaret Morton: *Mr. Lee's House, Chinatown, New York*
Plate 7: Eugene Richards: *Tom, Manhattan*

Plate 8: Mario Lamont: *Sewer Grate*
Plate 9: Jacob Riis: *Street Arabs*
Plate 10: Charlene Williams: *Bird*
Plate 11: Santa Fe Railroad Calendar Art: *The Indian Detour*
Plate 12: Yong Soon Min: *Defining Moments #4: Kwang Ju Massacre*
Plate 13: John Gast: *American Progress*
Plate 14: IBM Computer ad: [Pyramids]
Plate 15: Pedro Meyer: *Biblical Times*
Plate 16: Pedro Meyer: *Biblical Times, New York City, 1987/93* [annotated]

WHY PUT IMAGES IN A BOOK ABOUT WRITING?

Why put images in a book about reading and writing? There are several reasons. First, one of the basic ideas behind this book is that all kinds of expression—not just pieces of writing—can be "read" as texts. Every time we see an image, whether in an ad, on television, or in a book, we're reading that image. And as with written texts, we can choose to do a superficial or literal reading of the text/image or a critical and analytical one. In addition, as with written texts, some images *want* the viewer to read them literally, and others invite a closer look, expressing some ironic or mixed message. This last point relates to the second reason for putting images in this book. Another basic idea behind this book is that all texts are created from a certain perspective, whether they are maps, essays, or photographs. Finally, this book's most important goal is to help you learn to "read" your world better—and we certainly live in a world where we are surrounded more and more each day by images. In many ways our culture is increasingly becoming a visual culture through advertising, television, and even the World Wide Web, which is predominantly a visual medium.

The sixteen images in this portfolio—as well as the other images spread throughout the book that accompany different readings and the images linked off of the Border Images Web page—can be used in several ways. Preceding the images are notes on each image as well as questions and activities. These will help you focus on each image and think about its contexts and connections to other selections in the book. The images included in the portfolio have been selected for a number of reasons. No particular image is intended to correspond to any particular reading in the book. Instead, each is meant to stimulate further your thinking about the book's overarching ideas: identity, a sense of place, difference, otherness, and community. Furthermore, most of the images in the portfolio were chosen because they bring to the foreground the ways that images—whether maps, photographs, or advertisements—always have a perspective (a bias or subjectivity behind them) and often present an "argument." Let's look a little more closely at how this works.

THE SEEING "I"

Just as with the written essays, stories, and poems you have been reading through-out *Border Texts,* the images in the portfolio are expressions of particular subjective perspectives. Naturally, we understand this fact when we look at advertising. We know that a magazine ad has been "constructed" by someone to make us think or feel a certain way. Every advertisement has at least one argument, such as "buy this product." However, most advertisements also have a second, implicit argument, such as "buy this product and you will be thin and attractive to members of the op-posite sex." In terms of images, however, it is not just visual advertisements that are constructed from a particular perspective; all images are.

The first image in the portfolio is a map showing a playful inversion of the West-ern Hemisphere for the purpose of demonstrating the effect of putting South America on top of North America. As we discovered in Chapter 1 and in Chapter 6 in the discussions about maps and murals, although we think of maps as "truthful" representations, they are actually "symbolic" expressions just like any other kind of text. Although their symbolism may have a high degree of "truth value" when you're using them to navigate, they are nonetheless coded by a certain perspective and con-structed to deliver their messages in certain ways. By reversing the positions of North and South America, Jesse Levine's *Turnabout map* (Plate 1) forces the viewer to see an image that is deeply familiar in a completely different way. For a North American, the reversal of the continents is jarring, perhaps even disturbing. How-ever, the effect might be quite different for someone from South America. As is dis-cussed in several sections of the book, maps always have a point of view. They have authors, contexts, perspectives, and biases. It doesn't make maps less useful to ac-knowledge this fact; it just means that we should not view them as objective truth.

A similar point can be made about photographs. For example, look at Plate 9, *Street Arabs,* by one of the first photojournalists, Jacob Riis. Whenever you are ex-amining and analyzing an image, it is first important to ask yourself some basic, de-scriptive questions, the first one being, what do you see?

This particular photograph shows three young boys in some kind of alleyway or corner of a building. They are leaning on each other. Their feet are bare and dirty. Their clothes are worn and threadbare. The boy in the foreground has what looks like a pained expression on his face. They appear to be asleep. The physical arrange-ment of the boys (two leaning in, all leaning deeper into the background) follows the lines of the building and the corner in which they are sleeping. The boys are in the center of the photograph.

After noting as many of the photograph's physical attributes as possible, we can move to the next level of questions which relate to perspective and meaning:

What do you think the photograph is intended to evoke: pity? anger? scorn?
What physically is included in the picture?
How is it framed and composed?
What are the details that you notice?
From what angle is the photograph shot?
How are the boys represented as the "objects" of our viewing?
How does the photograph construct a position from which you, the viewer, see the boys?

This particular photograph was taken in the 1890s. At the end of the nineteenth century, the photographic process was much slower and more cumbersome than it is now. For Jacob Riis to take his photographs, he needed to hold the camera and keep the subject still for several minutes. Given that fact, it is unlikely that the boys were really sleeping and unaware of his presence. In fact, we know that Riis took a whole series of photographs of boys who lived on the street, whom he posed in a variety of ways to get the shots he wanted. Actually, there are some photographs in which you can see one of the boys cracking a smile as he pretends to be asleep. Yet this photograph presents the sleeping boys *as if* the photographer—and thus also as if we, the viewers—had spontaneously caught the boys in a natural moment. The photograph puts the viewer in the position of a "witness" to a pathetic scene (young boys living on the street). However, the photograph turns out to be a carefully arranged, posed, and framed moment intended to evoke certain emotions from the late-nineteenth-century viewer (who was surely of the middle or upper class). None of these composition strategies negate the "truth" of the conditions that Riis was trying to expose on the Lower East Side of New York, but they do point out that Riis's photograph does not portray an "objective" reality any more than his written text, *How the Other Half Lives* (included in Chapter 4), is free of bias and a selective perspective.

For an even more detailed exploration of the "constructive" process itself, see a photographer's own anatomy of his composition in Pedro Meyer's *Biblical Times, New York City, 1987/93* (Plates 15 and 16 [annotated]). In the creation of *Biblical Times,* two different photographs were fused together in order to heighten the effect of passersby on the street ignoring the man with the Bible. Meyer says of the final composite image, "The result is actually a much more powerful image of New York. And, though it stretches the conventional journalistic boundaries of today, it is truthful to New York." In many ways, Meyer's compositional manipulation is an extreme example of the way most photographs are constructed.

As you look at the images in the portfolio, think about how each creates a relationship between the viewing "subject" and the photographic "subject" (that is, the person, people, or objects seen in the picture). Is the person depicted looking straight at the camera or away from it? Is he or she presented as active or passive? As friendly or threatening? Is the photographic subject presented as someone familiar to the viewer? As an equal? As an exotic person who is different from the viewer? Compare, for example, the difference between the photographs *Tom, Manhattan* (Plate 7) and *Sewer Grate* (Plate 8). What do you see in these pictures? How are they similar or different? What are their different effects? What about the photographs is responsible for the differing effects?

STORIES AND MEANING

Just as we don't read all written texts in the same way, we don't look at all pictures in the same way, either. Pictures come in many different genres, styles, and contexts, with various strategies for making meaning and with different intentions. Many of these different styles are represented in Border Visions: An Image Portfolio. In Chapter 1 there is an excerpt from an Adrienne Rich poem called "An Atlas of a Difficult World" in which she says:

I promised to show you a map you say but this is a mural
then yes let it be   these are small distinctions
where do we see it from is the question

One of the issues at the heart of distinguishing between a map and a mural is the extent to which a map seems to represent some purely objective reality, whereas a mural is an interpretation of events or a situation. Rich inverts this distinction in her poem by reading each place-name on a map as if it stood for an historical event of cultural memory. The question, then, is to what extent a map *tells a story* in the same way that a mural does. How can any image—map, mural, photograph—tell a story? In what ways can images evoke a story for the reader by giving only certain visual cues? Images tell stories differently than written texts *both* by being more explicit in some ways and by having the freedom to be more ambiguous in others. That is, graphic images *show,* and therefore make their meaning more apparent. On the other hand, images don't have to fill in all the words in order to convey a meaning and therefore leave other matters more to the imagination.

As you look at the images throughout the portfolio, think about how each of them creates its meaning. How much meaning is made apparent in the images? How much is left to or subject to the interpretation of the viewer? In a painting such as John Gast's *American Progress* (Plate 13) or Patricia Rodriguez's *La Fruta del Diablo* (Plate 2), the "story" is laid out in a linear or circular way so that a sequence of images is meant to come together as a narrative whole. However, in other images the meaning is constructed more openly, such as in the composition from *Familiar Names and Not-so-Familiar Faces* (Plate 4), where an image of two women kissing and hugging is (intentionally) awkwardly spliced into a picture of the "ideal" TV family from "Leave It to Beaver." In this case, a specific story is *not* being told as the collage is serving as a site for the clashing of a set of images or "codes." In American culture the Cleaver family invokes certain traditional family values, and all of these associations are brought into contact through the composition with the apparently disruptive image of two women kissing. Just as with the Gast and Rodriguez murals, the totality of this image's elements makes meaning; but with the image of "Two Women Kissing," the elements do not form a sequence as much as they pose a question or a problem. The viewer simultaneously experiences the Cleaver family and the image of the women kissing, *and* realizes that the image is clearly spliced and faked. We might say that the image is "self-conscious" of its status as a deliberate piece of art. Contrast this image, for example, with Jacob Riis's photograph of the "Street Arabs" sleeping. As discussed earlier, Riis's photograph is also "staged," but in a very different way from the composition of the collage "Two Women Kissing."

LOOK AGAIN

I remember when I was in college. If there were pictures or images of any kind in my textbooks, I would turn to them many times throughout the semester, usually as something to do when I should have been doing the reading. But I have very vivid memories about the images in my textbooks. First, I remember that there never seemed to be enough pictures in my English textbooks, although visuals always made me more interested in the written texts. Usually there were only one or two token images, and I would stare at them hungrily. That experience is one of the reasons why this book has many images. Second, I remember that whatever pictures—maps, photographs, paintings—were in my books would look different to me at various points in the semester. Ultimately my goal of putting what I hope are interesting and provocative images in this book is to give you different kinds of visual texts to come back to throughout the semester and to relate to whatever readings you are currently assigned—and to whatever else is going on in your life and in school. There is something very powerful about images that differs from the power of written texts. They are another way to cross that border of meaning which is at the heart of this book.

WORKING WITH IMAGES: NOTES AND QUESTIONS

Plate I: Jesse Levine, *The Turnabout Map of the Western Hemisphere*

The Turnabout map should be considered alongside the Peters' projection map that is discussed in Chapters 1 and 6. The Peters' projection map is an alternative way of representing the world's land masses in a way that does not "correct" for the curvature of the earth (as Mercator's, Robinson's, and other projections do). The Peters' projection map is politically motivated in that it represents countries at their proportional size, an action which renders the United States and Europe much smaller than they appear on the most familiar maps. The Peters' projection is an attempt to remap the world for the purpose of redevelopment and reallocation of world resources.

Although the Turnabout map is not presumed to be a new kind of functional map, it does similarly reposition the countries in the Western Hemisphere as a way of making an "argument" about the way we project our cultural and nationalistic biases onto maps. The creator of the Turnabout map claims that the convention of putting North America "on top" is just that: a convention, one not grounded in any geographic inevitability. Whether or not that is entirely true, the Turnabout map makes a startling point and might create an uncomfortable image for citizens of the United States and North America. Even more dramatically than does the Peters' projection, the Turnabout map foregrounds the ideas that reality is a matter of perception, and that what you see has everything to do with where you stand.

Questions

1. What are your initial responses to the Turnabout map? Does it make you feel uncomfortable? Do you think you would feel differently if you were from South America? (Conversely, if you are from South America or elsewhere in the world, how do you think your reaction would differ if you were from North America?)

2. Consider Jesse Levine's statement:

> Ever since maps were first drawn, certain countries have been located at the top, others below. Since "on top," "over," and "above" are equated with superiority, while "down there," "beneath," and "below" imply the reverse, these wholly arbitrary placements, over the years, have led to misconceptions and misjudgments.

Do you agree with this statement? Where else do you see correlations between geography and cultural/nationalistic assumptions?

Connecting Images and Texts

Here are a few selections elsewhere in the book that relate to the Turnabout map:

- Essay discussion in Chapter 1
- Elizabeth Bishop, *In the Waiting Room* (Chapter 4)
- Richard Rodriguez, *The Fear of Losing a Culture* (Chapter 7)
- Guillermo Gómez-Peña, *The '90s Culture of Xenophobia: Beyond the Tortilla Curtain* (Chapter 7)
- Clark Blaise, *The Border as Fiction* (Chapter 6)
- Gloria Anzaldúa, *La conciencia de la mestiza / Towards a New Consciousness* (Chapter 7)
- Alan Thomas and Ben Crow, *Maps, Projections and Ethnocentricity* (Chapter 6)

Plate 2: Patricia Rodriguez and students, *La Fruta del Diablo* ("The Fruit of the Devil")

La Fruta del Diablo ("The Fruit of the Devil") was created by Patricia Rodriguez, a teacher and artist at California State University, Monterey Bay, and her students. *La Fruta del Diablo* is based on the Chicano mural tradition, in which stories or historical and cultural events, as well as political struggles, are told through large images traditionally painted on walls. This mural was created digitally through the synthesis of computer images. Murals are a form of visual storytelling in which different graphic elements connect to form a story or message. In *La Fruta del Diablo,* the images tell the story of the genetic hazards of strawberry harvesting due to the dangerous insecticides that are used in the production. The composition of the story is circular, a technique which echoes the cyclical process in which the farm workers—particularly the children—are involved in the agricultural cycles of growth, production, and harvesting.

Questions

1. On the World Wide Web, look at other murals linked with Border Images Online. How does *La Fruta del Diablo* compare and contrast with other murals that you see? What do you think are some of the conventions of murals? How do murals make meaning?

2. From whose perspective is the mural created? Does the mural have a point of view? Is this similar to or different from other murals that you have seen?

3. Can you think of other examples of visual storytelling?

4. To what other issues can you relate the subject matter of this mural? Do you know anything about how strawberries are grown? How would you go about conducting more research about the mural's message?

Connecting Images and Texts

Some stories and essays related to *La Fruta del Diablo:*   •

- Kai Erikson, *Collective Trauma: Loss of Communality* (Chapter 3)
- Jacob Riis, *How the Other Half Lives* (Chapter 4)
- David Sibley, *Feelings About Difference* (Chapter 4)
- Mary Louise Pratt, *Arts of the Contact Zone* (Chapter 5)
- Luis Alberto Urrea, *Across the Wire* (Chapter 5)
- Guillermo Gómez-Peña, *The '90s Culture of Xenophobia: Beyond the Tortilla Curtain* (Chapter 7)
- William Greider, *One World, Ready or Not* (Chapter 7)

Plate 3: Joel Sternfeld, *Studio City*

Joel Sternfeld is a photographer with a very ironic eye. Most of his photographs capture aspects of American life that are both normal and everyday, on the one hand, and slightly bizarre and eccentric, on the other. In this photograph, *Studio City* (which is a city near downtown Los Angeles), a young couple is pictured in a garden or backyard. The picture presents two contradictory impulses. On the one hand, the appearance of the two young people is relatively nonconformist—dyed hair and a punk mohawk haircut. However, their pose is very traditional. Their posture and framing is reminiscent of traditional portrait photography. As with many Sternfeld photographs, the ironic combination of tendencies form a single powerful image.

Questions

1. What do you observe about the positioning, expression, and appearance of the couple? How would you characterize their demeanor and attitude?

2. Do you think that there are "class" dimensions to this photograph? That is, do you think the style or setting implies a certain socioeconomic class?

3. What about the difference between the man and the woman? Do they present different attitudes?

4. Write a response to this photograph discussing the contrasting messages in it. Does the photograph make a commentary—playful or serious—about youth culture, suburban culture, or American family values?

Connecting Images and Texts

Some other texts related to *Studio City:*

- Sherman Alexie, *Family Portrait* (Chapter 2)
- Anne Sexton, *Cinderella* (Chapter 2)

- Tara L. Masih, *Exotic, or "What Beach Do You Hang Out on?"* (Chapter 4)
- Cherylene Lee, *Safe* (Chapter 5)
- Stuart Hall, *Ethnicity: Identity and Difference* (Chapter 4)
- Gary Soto, *Black Hair* (Chapter 5)

Plate 4: Lynette Molnar, [Two Women Kissing] from *Familiar Names and Not-so-Familiar Faces*

This photograph is from a series of compositions called *Familiar Names and Not-so-Familiar Faces*. In the series, the photographer Lynette Molnar has spliced in the image of her partner and herself kissing in a number of situations. In the exhibition series, Molnar inserts the same image over and over again, sometimes in photographs, sometimes in familiar advertisements. In this particular image, she has spliced the kissing image into a photographic still from the 1960s television series "Leave It to Beaver." An important feature of Molnar's composition is the splicing of the photograph that is not done seamlessly but, in fact, is inserted awkwardly, making the photograph a collage with a composite meaning.

Questions

1. What is the effect of splicing the image of the two women into the picture? How does the awkwardness (i.e., showing the seams) of the splicing add to the impact of the picture?

2. How does this picture play with certain social codes? What are the different codes at work?

3. Compare this picture with *Studio City*. How are they alike or different?

Connecting Images and Texts

Some other texts related to [Two Women Kissing]:

- Cherrie Moraga, *A Long Line of Vendidas* (Chapter 3)
- David Sibley, *Feelings About Difference* (Chapter 4)
- Sherman Alexie, *Family Portrait* (Chapter 2)
- Michael Nava, *Gardenland, Sacramento, California* (Chapter 2)
- Adrienne Rich, *Split at the Root: An Essay on Jewish Identity* (Chapter 4)
- Tobias Wolff, *Say Yes* (Chapter 5)
- Sherry Turkle, *TinySex and Gender Trouble* (Chapter 5)
- Allucquère Rosanne Stone, *Sex, Death, and Machinery, or How I Fell in Love with My Prosthesis* (Chapter 6)

Plate 5: Joel Sternfeld, *The Bronx*

Like his other photograph included in this portfolio, *Studio City*, Joel Sternfeld's *The Bronx* presents an image that seems somehow off center. If *Studio City* is an ironic rendering of the "family portrait" convention of photography, then *The Bronx* is an ironic rendering of the traditions of landscape and urban photography. This photograph has a "text within the text." At the center of the photograph on the wall of the building, is a set of sculptures made by the artists Rigoberto Torres and John Ahearn. Torres and Ahearn have made hundreds of such sculptures throughout the Bronx. They always cast them from the actual faces and bodies (and personalities) of people living in the neighborhoods. This particular set of castings collectively is called *We Are Family* (1981–82). They represent actual residents of the area (Layman, Victor and Ernest, Kate, Tawana and Staice, Felix and Iris, and Smokey). They are mounted on a building at the intersection of Fox Street and Intervale Avenue in the Bronx.

Says art critic Michael Ventura of their art:

> [T]hese sculptures are cast from life. Ahearn and Torres live and work in the South Bronx, and the people of their neighborhood are the subjects, the actual faces, of their art. Nobody can say they're "making up" the beauty here. Instead, they're giving it a form—which is to say giving it a home. . . . When they do this, they're not being documentarists (though there is an element of documentation in any art, even the abstract); rather, they are, in the psychological sense, "framing."

In a variety of ways, Sternfeld's photograph attempts to capture what is fascinating, startling, and ironic about Torres and Ahearn's sculpture art, which is usually mounted on neighborhood buildings. Sternfeld's own "framing" of the sculpture within the photograph is calculated to give the viewer a sense of the context through its placement. By doing this, Sternfeld creates several layers to his photograph, trying to put "in place" a work of art (the sculpture) for which part of its point is to seem "out of place" and yet natural at the same time. It is a different way of expressing the collision of messages that characterized *Studio City* (Plate 3).

Questions

1. What are the various elements of the photograph? How do they interact with the sculpture at the center?

2. Why do you think that Sternfeld took the picture from this angle and framed it in this way?

3. What are some of the concepts or ideas that the picture brings to mind? What does it make you think about?

4. What other examples of public art can you think of? Choose an example of public art from where you live and explore how it fits into and in part shapes its context.

Connecting Images and Texts

Some other texts related to *The Bronx:*

- Joy Harjo, *Woman Hanging from the Thirteenth Floor Window* (Chapter 2)
- Alice Walker, *Everyday Use* (Chapter 3)
- Leonard Kriegel, *Graffiti: Tunnel Notes of a New Yorker* (Chapter 3)
- Victor Hernandez Cruz, *Home Is Where the Music Is* (Chapter 3)
- Jacob Riis, *How the Other Half Lives* (Chapter 4)
- William Mitchell, *Soft Cities* (Chapter 6)

Plate 6: Margaret Morton, *Mr. Lee's House, Chinatown, New York*

Margaret Morton is a documentary photographer who has spent much of her career vividly recording the lives of men and women who make their homes on the streets, back alleys, rooftops, and deserted spaces of New York City. Her photographs are in the journalistic and documentary tradition of Jacob Riis. But her work is much less sensationalistic. She is not interested in making her subjects—people and their "fragile dwellings"—look pitiful or like victims. Nor does she try to romanticize them; she merely captures them in their living context, usually with dignity and respect. Her photo essay, *Fragile Dwelling,* is a series of photographs of the housing structures that are built (collected, assembled) by "homeless" men and women in New York City. Of them, she says:

> The homeless individuals of New York City chronicled in these photographs have constructed dwellings that provide far more than mere shelter. These improvised habitats are as diverse as the people who build them and they bear witness to the profound human need to create a sense of place, no matter how extreme one's circumstances. The clusters of makeshift houses, scattered across vacant lots, public parks, along rivers, and under bridges and highway exit ramps, are constructed primarily from consumer detritus, scavenged from the streets and reconstituted as building material. They are decorated with signs, roof ornaments, porches, and gardens, and their interiors are enriched with collections of objects found on the street.

Of *Mr. Lee's House, Chinatown, New York*—Morton says,

> Yi Poi Lee walked the streets of Chinatown each morning, collecting the colored ropes and strings that held his house together. In May 1992, an arsonist torched the home and Lee died in the fire.

Her photographs ask the viewer to reevaluate not only a sense of the environment but also the individuals' consciousness about their shelter and surroundings.

Questions

1. Go to Border Images Online and look at the other images by Margaret Morton as well as at other images of homelessness. What do you notice about the way Morton portrays these "fragile dwellings"? How does she place them visually in the context of the city environment?

2. How do you personally react when (and if) you see homeless people and their belongings? Is your response in person different from your response to Morton's photographs?

3. What is the definition of a "home"? If the photos show shelters of "homeless" people (complete with many of the items that signify a "home"), then what makes a home a home? Permanence? Privacy? Comfort? Ownership?

Connecting Images and Texts

- Alice Walker, *Everyday Use* (Chapter 3)
- Peter Marin, *Helping and Hating the Homeless* (Chapter 4)

- David Sibley, *Feelings About Difference* (Chapter 4)
- Jacob Riis, *How the Other Half Lives* (Chapter 4)
- Wong Sam and Assistants, *An English-Chinese Phrase Book* (Chapter 5)
- William Mitchell, *Soft Cities* (Chapter 6)

Plate 7: Eugene Richards, *Tom, Manhattan*

Eugene Richards is one of the United States' best-known recorders of American life. His subjects range widely from intimate family and personal scenes to public American contexts. Although not often as ironic as Joel Sternfeld (Plates 3 and 5), Richards has numerous images that evoke a sense of playfulness and provocation. This picture—entitled *Tom, Manhattan*—is one of those. The photograph captures a man, Tom, emerging from a sewer grate while passersby move along the street hardly noticing—hardly, that is, except for the woman in the foreground who looks half-watchfully at him.

The photograph manages to create two kinds of movement and space. There is the triangular tension between Tom in the foreground, the woman, and the backdrop of the rest of the street. In contrast to the foreground/background perspective, the photo also conveys senses of "underground" and "above ground." There is a real sense of two worlds in the picture: the subterranean or marginal one of "Tom" and the above-ground world of the people on the street. The picture manages to be both playful and threatening at the same time. Richards says, "When I see Tom emerging from the sewer grate, I don't see a homeless person but a creature from the swamp or black lagoon, from the stuff of childhood nightmares."

Questions

1. What are the different focal points in the picture? Who is looking at whom? How do the various points of focus help create the photograph's effect?

2. Compare this photograph—*Tom, Manhattan*—to Plate 8, *Sewer Grate*. How are they alike and different?

3. How might this photograph express or touch on people's fears, values, or attitudes toward "street people" or symbols of an underclass?

Connecting Images and Texts

- Elizabeth Bishop, *In the Waiting Room* (Chapter 4)
- Peter Marin, *Helping and Hating the Homeless* (Chapter 4)
- David Sibley, *Feelings About Difference* (Chapter 4)
- Stuart Hall, *Ethnicity: Identity and Difference* (Chapter 4)
- Gary Soto, *Black Hair* (Chapter 5)
- Mary Louise Pratt, *Arts of the Contact Zone* (Chapter 5)
- Cherylene Lee, *Safe* (Chapter 5)
- William Mitchell, *Soft Cities* (Chapter 6)

Plate 8: Mario Lamont, *Sewer Grate*

The book *Shooting Back: A Photographic View of Life by Homeless Children* was the result of a project that involved giving children cameras and asking them to document their world through their own eyes. What resulted was a poignant look at the daily lives—joy, pain, the paradoxes—of children whose families lacked permanent housing or stable shelter. There are two photographs from *Shooting Back* in this portfolio. In this photograph a young girl is shown playing in a drainage or sewer grate. The grate and hole are clearly an integral part of her play environment. Says the young photographer of homeless children, "I really admire how they still have fun even though they don't have much."

Questions

1. How do the position, perspective, and expression of the young girl affect how you respond to the photograph?

2. Contrast this photograph with *Tom, Manhattan* and Sternfeld's *Studio City.* How are they similar or different?

Connecting Images and Texts

- Marianne Boruch, *The Quiet House* (Chapter 2)
- William Kittredge, *Home* (Chapter 2)
- Alice Walker, *Everyday Use* (Chapter 3)
- Leonard Kriegel, *Graffiti: Tunnel Notes of a New Yorker* (Chapter 3)
- Daniel Kemmis, *The Last Best Place: How Hardship and Limits Build Community* (Chapter 3)
- Toni Cade Bambara, *The Lesson* (Chapter 4)
- Peter Marin, *Helping and Hating the Homeless* (Chapter 4)
- Mary Louise Pratt, *Arts of the Contact Zone* (Chapter 5)

Plate 9: Jacob Riis, *Street Arabs*

In 1890, Jacob Riis published his pioneering work of investigative journalism, *How the Other Half Lives,* an exposé of New York's Lower East Side. *How the Other Half Lives* is a systematic study of New York's tenement neighborhoods and the people who lived there. Although his work is often seen as a precursor to modern investigative journalism, Riis's narrative voice throughout the written portions of the text is strongly moralistic, interpretive, at times sensationalistic, and very biased. That moralizing narrative voice also carries over in his photographs, in which he tries to grab the reader/viewer and say, in essence, "Here, look at this!"

Riis's sense of urgency arose in response to the increasingly crowded conditions of late nineteenth-century urban America that were characterized by dense and impoverished housing. There was a strong altruistic side to Riis's crusade as well as a dimension that spoke to and in behalf of middle-class anxieties. Most immediately, the target for Riis's documentary work was the unscrupulous landlords. Riis wanted laws that would shut down the worst tenements, cut air holes in unventilated hallways, and improve sanitation.

But underlying this progressive side of his investigations was the fear that a growing, restless underclass would eventually pose a threat to American society, especially to those of the middle class who would be caught as innocent victims between a negligent upper class and an increasingly deprived lower class.

Riis was intensely interested in children and urban youth, in part out of sentiment and sympathy, and in part because he felt that every underprivileged child today was a potential criminal tomorrow. Thus, we see his interest in what he called "Street Arabs"—not because they were ethnically Arabic, but due to their itinerant and homeless life on the street. This photograph epitomizes his visual treatment of street children, portraying them simultaneously as both tough and tender. As elaborated upon in the introduction to this portfolio, this photograph, *Street Arabs,* is one of many like it, each one carefully posed and arranged for deliberate rhetorical effect.

Questions

1. What images or feelings does the photograph evoke? What are some of the various elements of the photograph that create its effect?

2. This photograph was taken just a few years after Mark Twain published his novel *Adventures of Huckleberry Finn,* the story of a barefoot boy traveling up and down the Mississippi. If you have read *Huckleberry Finn,* consider how representations of Huck Finn differ from the images of these children.

3. Are there any other images in the media (magazines, television) similar to this one that present youth as both innocent and tough, appealing and possibly dangerous? Are these mixed messages conveyed today?

Connecting Images and Texts

- Gary Soto, *Black Hair* (Chapter 5)
- Ruben Martinez, *Going Up in L.A.* (Chapter 3)
- Jacob Riis, *How the Other Half Lives* (Chapter 4)
- Luis Alberto Urrea, *Across the Wire* (Chapter 5)
- Frederick Jackson Turner, *The Significance of the Frontier in American History* (Chapter 6)

Plate 10: Charlene Williams, *Bird*

The photograph *Bird* is from the collection *Shooting Back: A Photographic View of Life by Homeless Children,* as is the photograph *Sewer Grate.* This photograph is a combination of a spontaneous moment and some self-conscious arrangement. Says Charlene Williams, the twelve-year-old photographer:

> My favorite picture that I took: that's me and my brother and my sister with a pigeon. My brother had found a pigeon, and the pigeon had been shot in the wing. My brother was trying to fix it, so I just told my brother to look at it, and I just put the timer on, focused it, and ran over there to get into the picture. I want to be a photographer.

The *Shooting Back* collection appeared as an exhibition in New York. One school-child who visited the exhibition said of this photograph in a note to the photographer:

> I saw your picture, Birds, in the exhibit in New York. I saw it from way across the room and I felt drawn to it. . . . The girl on the left, her teeth show, like she understood pain and in that instant, experienced it for the bird.

Questions

1. Compare and contrast this photograph to Jacob Riis's *Street Arabs*. How are they similar or different in the ways that the children are portrayed? To what other images could you relate this photo?

2. How is violence represented in the photograph? Does it add anything to your reading of the photograph to know that the bird has been shot?

3. Does the fact that the photograph is posed affect your response to it? Does the degree of manipulation that went into this photograph seem the same or different from Riis's posing the boys in *Street Arabs*? What about in comparison to Plates 15 and 16, Pedro Meyer's *Biblical Times* and *Biblical Times, New York City, 1987/93* [annotated]?

Connecting Images and Texts

- Russell Banks, *The Visitor* (Chapter 2)
- Kai Erikson, *Collective Trauma: Loss of Communality* (Chapter 3)
- Elizabeth Bishop, *In the Waiting Room* (Chapter 4)
- Peter Marin, *Helping and Hating the Homeless* (Chapter 4)
- Cherylene Lee, *Safe* (Chapter 5)
- Gary Soto, *Black Hair* (Chapter 5)

Plate 11: Santa Fe Railroad Calendar Art: *The Indian Detour*

Beginning in the late nineteenth century, the Santa Fe Railroad began marketing the American Southwest as a major tourist attraction. Putting together tour packages that combined train and car travel, the railroad, along with the Fred Harvey Company, offered tourists glimpses of the scenic natural landscape and the "exotic" Native American peoples who lived there. The language and imagery of the posters that advertised these tours reveal a highly romanticized attitude toward native populations that saw them merely as an extension of the natural landscape, not as a living culture. As the poster in Plate 11 puts it, tourists are invited to view

> Spanish culture three centuries old, the changeless life of inhabited Indian Pueblos, cliff dwellings of forgotten races—combined with the matchless scenery and climate of the New Mexico Rockies.

The attitude that "Indian" life was "changeless" and somehow outside of modern history reaches back many centuries to the first explorers' descriptions of the inhabitants of the "New World." Writers such as Amerigo Vespucci described Native Americans in "negative" terms, as cultures defined by the European characteristics they lacked. (See, for example, the reading by Robert Berkhofer Jr., *The White Man's Indian*, in Chapter 4.)

In the Santa Fe Railroad ad posters, a romanticized sense of nationalism combines with the developing language of tourism to put the middle- and upper-class American in the position of spectator, the "seer" of sights.

Questions

1. What other examples of tourism language can you find? Compare this ad to the IBM computer ad (Plate 14). How are they similar or different? Can you find the language of tourism in other media?

2. Go to Border Images Online. Explore the online exhibit sponsored by the Heard Museum on the "Invention of the Southwest." How is the Santa Fe poster art part of the "invention" of the Southwest? What is meant by this use of "invention"? Can you think of other places in the country that could similarly be considered "inventions"?

Connecting Images and Texts

- William Kittredge, *Home* (Chapter 2)
- Thomas King, *Borders* (Chapter 3)
- Tara L. Masih, *Exotic, or "What Beach Do You Hang Out on?"* (Chapter 4)
- Robert Berkhofer Jr., *The White Man's Indian* (Chapter 4)
- Frederick Jackson Turner, *The Significance of the Frontier in American History* (Chapter 6)
- Patricia Nelson Limerick, *The Adventures of the Frontier in the Twentieth Century* (Chapter 6)
- Jane Tompkins, *At the Buffalo Bill Museum—1988* (Chapter 6)
- Chrystos, *I Have Not Signed a Treaty with the United States* (Chapter 6)
- Joel Garreau, *The Nine Nations of North America* (Chapter 7)

Plate 12: Yong Soon Min: Defining Moments #4: Kwang Ju Massacre

In this image, Korean-born artist Yong Soon Min takes a silhouette of her head and upper body and overlays images of some significant events that make up her personal and cultural history. This image is one of six that makes up a series called *Defining Moments*. In this picture, the event portrayed is the Kwang Ju student uprising in Korea in the 1980s. Writing about Min, author Valerie Soe describes her as "a member of the '1.5' generation, the term for Korean Americans born overseas but primarily raised and educated in the United States. This generation feels it is somewhere in between their parents' generation, which grew up in Korea, and those Korean Americans born and raised in the United States." Soe says Min's "proactive and politically charged work deals with issues of identity, acculturation, and self-articulation, attempting to present a true and accurate portrayal of concerns of the Asian American community."

The image recollects themes raised throughout *Border Texts* that connect personal and cultural history. It is also significant that the images are overlaid, or seen through, her *body* giving a physical reality to the connection between the personal, the cultural, and the national. Says Min, "The importance of history in formulating my own identity is undeniable. Once I felt I had a grasp of alternative history, a history of my Korean roots that was denied or suppressed, that there was a role model, it gave me incredible strength. You realize that you have this connection and that you are part of this continuum." Min tries to portray her place in the continuum by using her body as the window to her culture's past.

Questions

1. What other examples can you think of where *the body* is a place where national and cultural images get projected? Can you find any examples in the media or advertising or art that—even with extreme subtlety—use images of the body (male or female) as sites of cultural value or symbolism?

2. What do you find to be the impact of Min using her silhouette as a window onto the Kwang Ju massacre? What is the effect of projecting a scene of violence onto her body? How do you think the effect might change if the image were different?

3. In addition to the image of the massacre that is projected onto her body, Min has two "words" literally written on her: "DMZ" (de-militarized zone) and "HEARTLAND". What do you take to be the meaning of these words? How do they collaborate with the other aspects of the image to produce its overall meaning? Are there conflicting messages here? Can the meaning be easily summarized?

Connecting Images and Texts

- William Kittredge, *Home* (Chapter 2)
- Michelle Cliff, *Screen Memory* (Chapter 2)
- Kesaya Noda, *Growing Up Asian in America* (Chapter 2)
- Cherrie Moraga, *A Long Line of Vendidas* (Chapter 3)
- Martin Espada, *The Other Alamo* (Chapter 4)
- Adrienne Rich, *Split at the Root* (Chapter 4)
- Art Spiegelman, *MAUS* (Chapter 4)
- Elaine Kim, *Home Is Where the Han Is* (Chapter 7)
- Ronald Takaki, *A Different Mirror* (Chapter 7)

Plate 13: John Gast, *American Progress*

John Gast's painting *American Progress* is like a mural intended to be read as a narrative—a story of American movement across the continent. The figure of a woman floating above the scene is meant to symbolize "Progress." The imagery can be read both from right to left (i.e., east to west) and from foreground to background. In the right foreground you see early settlers, prospectors, and farmers, along with symbols of the westward migration (stagecoach, covered wagon). The Native American Indians are retreating before them, literally being run out of the scene to make way for progress.

Moving from foreground to background, more primitive transportation gives way to the railroad and shipping, and the frontier and the farming scenery give way to the city. All this is set against the landscape of the continent.

In many ways the Gast painting can be seen as a visual expression of Frederick Jackson Turner's thesis on the frontier and what he called "the process of Americanization" that took place as Western settlers moved across the land. The painting exemplifies Manifest Destiny by vividly portraying the equivalence of westward movement and the progress of civilization.

The painting portrays the "land" of the United States as both a literal physical space and a metaphorical space, a "tablet" on which is "written" the histories of civilization and of the American people. The painting is also an excellent example of a text that can be read both as a narrative and as a series of symbols represented in the same space.

Questions

1. If it is supposedly a depiction of American "progress" and American history, what elements are missing from Gast's painting? What gets lost in his linear treatment of American history?

2. What borders (if any) are represented in Gast's painting? Are there borders in his depiction of the moving frontier line?

Connecting Images and Texts

- William Kittredge, *Home* (Chapter 2)
- Daniel Kemmis, *The Last Best Place: How Hardship and Limits Build Community* (Chapter 3)
- Robert Berkhofer Jr., *The White Man's Indian* (Chapter 4)
- Clark Blaise, *The Border as Fiction* (Chapter 6)
- William Mitchell, *Soft Cities* (Chapter 6)
- Frederick Jackson Turner, *The Significance of the Frontier in American History* (Chapter 6)
- Jane Tompkins, *At the Buffalo Bill Museum—1988* (Chapter 6)
- Benedict Anderson, *The Concept of "Nation": A Definition* (Chapter 6)
- Patricia Nelson Limerick, *The Adventures of the Frontier in the Twentieth Century* (Chapter 6)
- Joel Garreau, *The Nine Nations of North America* (Chapter 7)
- Ronald Takaki, *A Different Mirror* (Chapter 7)
- Gloria Anzaldúa, *La conciencia de la mestiza / Towards a New Consciousness* (Chapter 7)

Plate 14: IBM Computer Ad: [Pyramids]

This ad is part of a whole series of images produced by IBM with an international theme. The logic of the campaign is to portray the world as becoming a "smaller" place through the international use of technology. Technology itself is depicted as becoming a universal tool that in some ways bonds people together. In this ad an Egyptian man is seated on a camel, apparently alone in the desert, with the backdrop of pyramids. The words of the ad say, "Why don't we head home and download the results from the equestrian finals?" The implication is that although the man still dresses traditionally and rides a camel in a traditional way, he has a computer and an Internet connection which he uses, among other things, to support his interest in equestrian competition. Not only does the ad try to humanize high technology, as most high technology ads do, but it also tries to bridge the divide between the viewing "subject" (the American readers of the ad) and the exotic "object" or photographic "subject" (the man on the camel) in the same way that technology itself is portrayed as a bridge between remote parts of the world.

As scholar Lisa Nakamura points out, the imagery in the ad is in the Western European tradition of tourism that places the Western "subject" in a privileged position of viewing—much like the person viewing the Santa Fe Railroad advertisement in Plate 11. The implied message of the ad, as Nakamura argues, is that we can *all* have the Internet and high technology's progress—worldwide—but that the exotic, quaint people of other countries will remain intact as "sights" to be enjoyed.

Questions

1. Compare this ad to the Santa Fe Railroad poster. How is the relationship of technology and landscape in the advertisements similar or different? Do you think that the Egyptian lifestyle of the man is portrayed as if it were like the "changeless life of inhabited Indian Pueblos" of the Santa Fe Railroad ad?

2. Consider this ad in its representation of the Middle East. What are some of the common associations that we receive through the media about the Middle East? Is there also a message in this ad about the potential bonding or pacifying effects of technology on intercultural strife or global violence?

Connecting Images and Texts
- Elizabeth Bishop, *In the Waiting Room* (Chapter 4)
- Tara L. Masih, *Exotic, or "What Beach Do You Hang Out on?"* (Chapter 4)
- David Sibley, *Feelings About Difference* (Chapter 4)
- Stuart Hall, *Ethnicity: Identity and Difference* (Chapter 4)
- Cherylene Lee, *Safe* (Chapter 5)
- Mary Louise Pratt, *Arts of the Contact Zone* (Chapter 5)
- Alan Thomas and Ben Crow, *Maps, Projections and Ethnocentricity* (Chapter 6)
- Richard Rodriguez, *The Fear of Losing a Culture* (Chapter 7)
- William Greider, *One World, Ready or Not* (Chapter 7)
- Benjamin Barber, *Jihad vs. McWorld* (Chapter 7)

Plates 15 and 16: Pedro Meyer, *Biblical Times* and *Biblical Times, New York City, 1987/93* [annotated]

Pedro Meyer is a photographer who has gradually moved away from the standard documentary mode to more inventive and constructive forms of photography. In recent years he has developed an interest in digital photography and the fusion of different images into a single new composite image.

   This particular photograph, *Biblical Times, New York City, 1987/93,* is from his book *Truths and Fictions,* in which he experiments with the representation of reality and the question of what constitutes truth and fiction in photography and in life. *Biblical Times* depicts a man selling Bibles on a street corner in New York City and being ignored by passersby. As Meyer points out in the annotation (Plate 16), a second photograph's elements of steam and people walking by provided him with additional material to create the total look and feel that he wanted. As he says, "The result is actually a much more powerful image of New York. And, though it stretches the conventional journalistic boundaries of today, it is truthful to New York." This photograph, as do many of the other images in this portfolio, asks us, the viewers, to consider that a certain kind of truth is always created by a photograph and to reconsider the "border" between truth and fiction.

Questions

1. Where are the boundaries of truth in relation to the construction of this photograph? How much manipulation of an image pushes it past a threshold of credibility as a documentary image? Are the differences among Jacob Riis's *Street Arabs,* Charlene Williams's *Bird,* the IBM computer ad, and this photograph differences in degree or kind? Is there a clear line between photography that is journalistic and photography as art?

2. What about the way that photography is manipulated by tabloid newspapers? Can we trust photography? Do images differ in their biased construction of reality from written texts?

Connecting Images and Texts

- Sherman Alexie, *Family Portrait* (Chapter 2)
- Judith Ortiz Cofer, *Silent Dancing* (Chapter 2)
- Leslie Marmon Silko, *Yellow Woman* and *Storytelling* (Chapter 2)
- Art Spiegelman, *MAUS: A Survivor's Tale* (Chapter 4)
- Stuart Hall, *Ethnicity: Identity and Difference* (Chapter 4)
- Allucquère Rosanne Stone, *Sex, Death, and Machinery, or How I Fell in Love with My Prosthesis* (Chapter 6)

PLATE I ■ JESSE LEVINE: THE TURNABOUT MAP   331

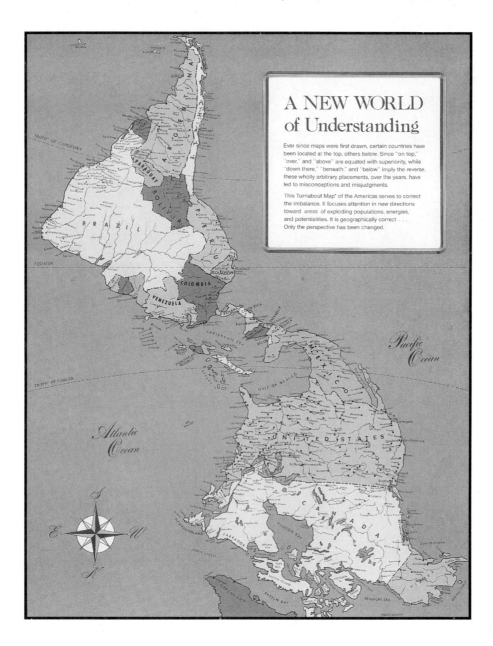

A NEW WORLD
of Understanding

Ever since maps were first drawn, certain countries have been located at the top, others below. Since "on top," "over," and "above" are equated with superiority, while "down there," "beneath," and "below" imply the reverse, these wholly arbitrary placements, over the years, have led to misconceptions and misjudgments.

This Turnabout Map of the Americas serves to correct the imbalance. It focuses attention in new directions toward areas of exploding populations, energies, and potentialities. It is geographically correct . . . Only the perspective has been changed.

PLATE 2 ■ PATRICIA RODRIGUEZ AND STUDENTS: LA FRUTA DEL DIABLO   333

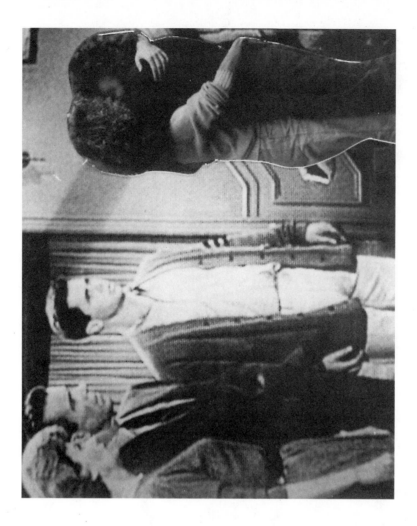

PLATE 6 ■ MARGARET MORTON: MR. LEE'S HOUSE, CHINATOWN, NEW YORK   337

PLATE 8 ■ MARIO LAMONT: SEWER GRATE   339

PLATE 10 ■ CHARLENE WILLIAMS: BIRD   341

Three memorable days in the Land of the Padres and Pueblos, as part of the transcontinental rail journey. Spanish culture three centuries old, the changeless life of inhabited Indian Pueblos, cliff dwellings of forgotten races—combined with the matchless scenery and climate of the New Mexico Rockies.

Only $45. (after May 1st, $50.) all-inclusive. Accommodations and motors of Fred Harvey excellence. A personal Courier service that is unique.

Optional side trips and "motor land cruises," featured by the same thought for individual comfort, are available for those who wish to extend their explorations out from Old Santa Fe and Albuquerque.

PLATE 12 ■ YONG SOON MIN: DEFINING MOMENTS #4: KWANG JU MASSACRE **343**

PLATE 14 ■ IBM COMPUTER AD: PYRAMIDS   **345**

"What do you say we head back and download the results of the equestrian finals?"

street getting in front of him. Unsatisfied as I was, I nevertheless took the picture with a wide-angle lens from close up. In contact sheets of some other pictures I had taken earlier on that same day and on the same street, I found this image with some steam, which was enveloping the people as they walked through. This led me to bring these two scenes together in order to overcome what had eluded me before— that is, to pull in form and content in such a way that the image became more meaningful.

I was actually able to simulate the steam around his hands and around the Bible digitally, at which point the image—as I see it—took on a totally different dimension. His hands become a strong element and the figure walking past conveyed the sense that nobody was paying attention to this Bible salesman, as was the case. The result is actually a much more powerful image of New York. And, though it stretches the conventional jounalistic boundaries of today, it is truthful to New York.

was walking around New York, trying to capture some street images, as I often do. And I found this man with hands like an El Greco figure. People were walking by—nobody was paying much attention. I photographed him from one side, then from the other side, but nothing of significance was coming across the viewfinder.

It was impossible to make the background any better, due to the limitations of space and optics. With a long lens I could have thrown the background out of focus, but I would have lost the sensation of the man, his Bible, and those long hands, as well as all the people walking on the

NEGOTIATING BORDERS:

The Dynamics of Difference

Critical Questions for *Negotiating Borders*

What happens when people meet across their differences, especially when there is an imbalance of power or status? Is there fear? Is there hate? love? trust? violence? understanding? How are individual responses to differences shaped by one's larger group's responses? Are individual members accountable for a group's response? Are "victims" of difference at all responsible for their status? How is language affected, depending on whether one is speaking from one side of a power imbalance or the other? In what ways do new means of communication like the Internet provide opportunities for changing the ways identity and difference are negotiated?

DIFFERENCES THAT MAKE A DIFFERENCE

At the end of her essay in this chapter, "On Not Being a Victim," Mary Gaitskill tells about an encounter she had with a friend on a date:

> A few years ago I invited to dinner at my home a man I'd known casually for two years. We'd had dinner and comradely drinks a few times. I didn't have any intention of becoming sexual with him, but after dinner we slowly got drunk and were soon floundering on the couch. I was ambivalent not only because I was drunk but because I realized that although part of me was up for it, the rest of me was not. So I began to say no. He parried each "no" with charming banter and became more aggressive. I went along with it for a time because I was amused and even somewhat seduced by the sweet, junior-high spirit of his manner. But at some point I began to be alarmed, and then he did and said some things that turned my alarm into fright. I don't remember the exact sequence of words or events, but I do remember taking one of his hands in both of mine, looking him in the eyes, and saying, "If this comes to a fight you would win, but it would be very ugly for both of us. Is that really what you want?"
>
> His expression changed and he dropped his eyes; shortly afterward he left.

In the context of her essay, this is a profound and culminating moment for Gaitskill because, as she says, her words came from both her sense of "delicacy" and her "capacity for aggression." And, she adds, they were words of respect for her friend because they addressed "both sides of his nature." The incident signals for Gaitskill, who had been raped earlier in her life, a way of dealing with being at a disadvantage in terms of physical power from something other than a victim's perspective. To do that meant going against a lifetime of receiving certain messages about rules, behavior, and expectations of how a woman acts.

The story and her conclusions about it serve as an apt opening for the concerns of this chapter, which build upon the previous chapter's exploration of otherness and difference. In the previous chapter we looked at how we construct differences. In this chapter we will be looking at how we communicate and interact across those differences. As Gaitskill's near date rape illustrates, every time we engage in meaningful interaction across significant differences, we do so within a matrix of rules and conventions, responsibilities and complexities that draw on our sense of identity to appeal to someone else's sense of himself or herself.

Obviously, the topic of negotiating across differences is a large and complex one. In this chapter we will begin to consider some of the possibilities and look at a small range of contexts. On the other hand, one does not need a large range of contexts because there are not that many different ways that people engage each other across differences, even if the combinations of circumstances and contingencies are infinite. That is, you can either regard someone else as an equal or not. You can deal with other people through a sense of connection and interdependency or through estrangement and distance. You can have respect or disdain, love or hate for another person. You can be drawn to someone through curiosity and attraction or bound to another through circumstance. When you deal with someone different from yourself, you can either see that person as an individual or see him or her through any one of a number of filters, including the perception of the person as a member of a group or an icon of a category.

All of these possibilities play out in complicated ways each day in our culture. We

can analyze them by building meaningfully on the concepts that the book has developed thus far: the influences that shape identity, a sense of belonging and alienation, a sense of community, and a sense of otherness. The writings in this chapter
present a range of means and contexts for negotiating differences: communication
through fear and withdrawal, strategies of persuasion and appeals to shared values,
the construction of sympathy or mutual self-interests. They also examine the negotiation of differences that arise from fundamentally opposite ways of seeing the
world, such as the contradictory ways that men and women might consider a relationship or sexual interaction, or the ways that different groups view the idea of
race.

TALKING THROUGH DIFFERENCES: THE PROBLEM OF COMMUNICATION

One way that this chapter addresses negotiating differences is through confronting
problems and devising strategies of communication. How do people find ways to
reach across their differences through writing and other forms of communication?
What are some styles for bridging differences? When and how do people communicate as if differences matter? How do writers from a marginalized social position
write to a culture's apparent center? What kinds of ideas, fears, anxieties, and ideals
are projected from the mainstream to the margins? How are these a part of communication across cultures? Across genders? Across classes?

One of this chapter's most famous examples of writing across social differences
is Martin Luther King Jr.'s "Letter from Birmingham Jail." The letter—or essay—is
an excellent example of a writer's use of a wide variety of strategies to bridge differences and to defend unpopular actions. In the "Letter" King defends his civil rights
protest actions to his critics (mostly white and moderate) by citing a combination
of shared values about religion and social justice, on the one hand, and by raising
the specter of violence and mounting social tension, on the other. Accused of "creating social tension" through his nonviolent demonstrations, King responds by re-
casting the situation as one in which the social tension already exists. As he says,
"Actually, we who engage in nonviolent direct action are not the creators of tension.
We merely bring to the surface the hidden tension that is already alive. We bring it
out into the open, where it can be seen and dealt with." This rhetorical move is an
important part of King's overall strategy to take every possible objection to his actions that his liberal but cautious critics have raised and portray them from the perspective of those without power. From this position of marginal power, the "Letter"
strives to create a rhetorical "common ground" based on difference. King's comment "I am cognizant of the interrelatedness of all communities" raises the specter
of tension as much as an image of harmony.

Part of the impact of the "Letter" is its ability to use reason to make what at first
appears reasonable (the objections of his critics) look unreasonable from a different
perspective. This is a key feature of communicating across differences: the acknowledgment that two sides may simply have fundamentally different ways of *perceiving*
a situation. Perceptions are rooted in social position. It is reasonable to assume that

people with power, for example, will perceive things very differently from the ways that people who are marginalized from power do.

Language is also dependent on perception. Often one of the challenges of even talking about differences is understanding that certain words or concepts might have conflicting meanings for people in different positions. This is Bob Blauner's point in his essay, "Talking Past Each Other: Black and White Languages of Race." Blauner argues that "blacks and whites differ on their interpretations of social change from the 1960s through the 1990s because their languages define the central terms, especially 'racism,' differently." In part this difference in definition comes from a fundamental disparity in the perception of the centrality of race to American society. In general, Blauner argues, whites see race and racial issues as being "aberrations," whereas blacks see race as central to the fabric of life in America. Consequently, when "whites talk about race," Blauner claims, they tend to focus on specific acts of discrimination, whereas blacks focus on a broader definition of race and racism. Their definition relates to the whole "social system" that is based on those with power and those without it. Understanding this difference is important, he maintains, because when whites and blacks (and indeed, all other groups) engage in conversations about social and racial justice, they often agree on the immorality of racism but otherwise appear to be talking "past each other" and miscommunicating.

Another situation where two people are miscommunicating due to their fundamentally different perceptions appears in the short story by Tobias Wolff. In that story a man and a woman are having a conversation while doing the dishes after dinner. The husband argues that "blacks and whites should not intermarry," and the wife challenges him. With their disagreement comes an awareness that their differences have more to do with their perspectives (perhaps based on gender) than with their views on race itself. At one point the wife asks her husband if he thinks he would have fallen in love with her if she were black. She says, "Let's say I am black and unattached and we meet and fall in love."

> He glanced over at her. She was watching him and her eyes were bright. "Look," he said, taking a reasonable tone, "this is stupid. If you were black you wouldn't be you." As he said this he realized it was absolutely true. There was no possible way of arguing with the fact that she would not be herself if she were black. So he said it again: "If you were black you wouldn't be you."
>
> "I know," she said, "but let's just say."
>
> He took a deep breath. He had won the argument but he still felt cornered. "Say what?" he asked.
>
> "That I'm black, but still me, and we fall in love. Will you marry me?"
>
> He thought about it.
>
> "Well?" she said, and stepped close to him. Her eyes were even brighter. "Will you marry me?"
>
> "I'm thinking," he said.
>
> "You won't, I can tell. You're going to say no."

The story portrays a tension between the wife's apparent need for acknowledgment of something (like love) that transcends racial identity and the husband's insistence that it is impossible to separate one's total identity from the way that one's "race" would partially construct that identity. What is key in the story is not its theory of social and racial identity but rather the subtle way it portrays a situation in which two people are clearly miscommunicating. Although it seems that they are talking about the same topic, they are speaking with fundamentally different perceptions and perspectives.

The issues Wolff's story raises about the extent to which one's "race" or social position determines one's identity relate to another set of critical issues in this chapter. One of the important questions behind negotiating the dynamics of difference involves individuals speaking from categorical positions (i.e., from a group position) or, similarly, being perceived as speaking as a representative of a group. This question builds particularly on the questions of Chapter 4, which dealt with the construction of difference. Constructions of "otherness" were defined there as the erasure of individuality and its replacement by stereotypes. The readings and questions in this chapter go beyond that initial problem by asking what kind of responsibility we should take for institutional/structural attitudes that are usually the source of that erasure and of those stereotypes. How are we as individuals shaped by institutional and group identities? What is our relationship as individuals to institutionally constructed senses of difference?

CAN A CONTACT ZONE BE A COMMUNITY?

All of these questions relate to the kind of exchange that takes place when diverse people interact. Many of this chapter's essays imply that in order for communication and understanding to take place across differences, we have to become more conscious of the nature of those differences that define the social sphere in which we live. That is, we can only speak *across* differences if we speak with a consciousness *of* differences. One useful way to think about the nature of social differences is offered in Mary Louise Pratt's challenging essay, "Arts of the Contact Zone." "Contact zones," according to Pratt, are "social spaces where cultures meet, clash, and grapple with each other, often in contexts of highly asymmetrical relations of power, such as colonialism, slavery or their aftermaths as they are lived out in many parts of the world today." Part of Pratt's interest in contact zones is to focus our attention on some of the strategies of communication that evolve from such contexts, especially when speakers from less powerful groups speak to the dominating community. One of these strategies—"transculturation" (an anthropological term that Pratt employs)—is a process in which "members of subordinated or marginal groups select and invent from materials transmitted by a dominant culture." It is interesting, for example, to consider Martin Luther King's "Letter from Birmingham Jail" as an expression of transculturation since King selectively and strategically uses the reasoning, values, and intellectual sources of his mainstream critics to argue against their objections to his "marginal" tactics.

Pratt's concept of a contact zone has become a popular and effective image for people to use when thinking about all kinds of situations. For example, in what ways is an urban area a contact zone? Or the Southwest borderlands? Or a workplace? Or even a classroom? Not every situation could be considered a contact zone, but the concept is useful in a wide variety of contexts. The idea of a contact zone is functional because it implies that in contexts where diverse groups come together, there is often inequality, or asymmetry, of power and resources. To a large extent, that asymmetry determines the kinds of communication that occur there. Furthermore, in a contact zone, communication is always "heterogeneous"—a complex mixing of the language, vocabulary, genres, and strategies of one group with another's. As was implied in the excerpts by Blauner and Wolff, the concept of the contact zone begins with the premise that difference is a given and an important determinant of the dynamics of interaction.

The final set of questions that this chapter raises concerns juxtaposing this notion of a contact zone with the ideas about "community" and "belonging" that emerged from the readings in Chapters 2, 3, and 4. Can a contact zone be a community? Can you have a community despite or because of differences? What does it take to feel a sense of safety, connection, or belonging in the midst of people who differ from each other? What would it take to have a community of differences? In many ways and from various angles, the readings in this chapter raise questions about what people both need and fear from each other regarding their differences.

All kinds of things happen in contact zones. People who differ from each other become involved and connected in complex and intricate ways. One kind of psychological interdependence is featured in the short story "Safe." Here the narrator describes her brother, a "flame diver" at Worlds of Water, U.S.A.: "My brother tells me what a rush it is to be a sponge for everyone's fears." However, her brother's dangerous feats are contrasted with the fear of nearly everything else that his and the narrator's parents, Chinese Americans living in San Francisco, have. The story speculates about the interconnection of safety and danger—how we are often attracted to things that are unfamiliar, exotic, even dangerous.

In a different way, Luis Alberto Urrea expresses a similar pull toward the uncomfortable and unsafe when describing his own and his coworkers' complex and varied reactions to their work among the impoverished along the Mexican border. At the end of every day, each worker responded differently to the difficult conditions. Urrea recalls, "Our faith sustained us—if not in God or 'good,' then in our work. Others of us had no room for or interest in such drama, and came away unscathed—and unmoved. Some of us sank into the mindless joy of fundamentalism, some of us drank, some of us married impoverished Mexicans. Most of us took it personally."

Urrea's stories of working among the poor move us from issues of communication across differences back to questions of identity, adaptation, and survival. How can one move among different worlds, crossing boundaries successfully while maintaining a sense of self, and at the same time have one's sense of identity changed and shaped by these crossings? This process is also part of the dynamics of difference.

The final reading in this chapter, an essay by Sherry Turkle, extends the focus of these very questions into "virtual realities" and cyberspace. In particular, Turkle describes contexts of "virtual cross-dressing" in which men and women pose as different genders with different constructed identities. The implications that we interact through *constructed* identities rather than through fixed, natural, or "essential" ones not only relate to the nature of cyberspace but also echo back through the whole chapter to address communication and interaction in any "contact zone." The questions Turkle raises at the end of her essay about online and virtual communities resonate for all the readings and for the combinations of issues related to the dynamics of difference. Once we take "virtuality" seriously as a way of life, we need a new language for talking about the simplest things. Each individual must ask: What is the nature of my relationships? What are the limits of my responsibility? And he or she must consider even more basic questions: Who and what am I? What is the connection between my physical and virtual bodies? And is my body different in different cyberspaces? These questions as framed in Turkle's essay apply to individuals; but with minor modifications, they are equally critical for thinking about communities. What is the nature of our social ties? What kind of accountability do we have for our actions in real life and in cyberspace? What kind of society or societies are we creating, both on and off the computer screen?

BLACK HAIR

GARY SOTO

■ Born in California's San Joaquin Valley, Gary Soto grew up in Fresno where his Mexican American family labored as migrant farm workers. Partly to escape his family's poverty, Soto enrolled at California State University at Fresno in 1970. He later received degrees from the University of California, Irvine. As a protégé of the poet Philip Levine, Soto discovered his own poetic voice—direct, conversational, and highly autobiographical. He published his first volume of poetry, *The Elements of San Joaquin* (1977), when he was twenty-five. Eight years later he won the American Book Award for *Living Up the Street: Narrative Recollections* (1985), a collection of autobiographical prose. His other works include several collections of poetry, another volume of memoirs, essays, and works for children and young adults. Soto teaches English and Chicano studies at the University of California at Berkeley. In the following autobiographical essay, he provides a stark view of his young adulthood when, estranged from his family, he lived on the streets, took a brutalizing job in a tire factory, and suffered an utter sense of alienation from his surroundings.

There are two kinds of work: One uses the mind and the other uses muscle. As a kid I found out about the latter. I'm thinking of the summer of 1969 when I was a seventeen-year-old runaway who ended up in Glendale, California, to work for Valley Tire Factory. To answer an ad in the newspaper I walked miles in the afternoon sun, my stomach slowly knotting on a doughnut that was breakfast, my teeth like bright candles gone yellow.

I walked in the door sweating and feeling ugly because my hair was still stiff from a swim at the Santa Monica beach the day before. Jules, the accountant and part owner, looked droopily through his bifocals at my application and then at me. He tipped his cigar in the ashtray, asked my age as if he didn't believe I was seventeen, but finally after a moment of silence, said, "Come back tomorrow. Eight-thirty."

I thanked him, left the office, and went around to the chain link fence to watch the workers heave tires into a bin; others carted uneven stacks of tires on hand trucks. Their faces were black from tire dust and when they talked—or cussed—their mouths showed a bright pink.

From there I walked up a commercial street, past a cleaners, a motorcycle shop, and a gas station where I washed my face and hands; before leaving I took a bottle that hung on the side of the Coke machine, filled it with water, and stopped it with a scrap of paper and a rubber band.

4

The next morning I arrived early at work. The assistant foreman, a potbellied Hungarian, showed me a timecard and how to punch in. He showed me the Coke machine, the locker room with its slimy shower, and also pointed out the places where I shouldn't go: The ovens where the tires were recapped and the customer service area, which had a slashed couch, a coffee table with greasy magazines, and an ashtray. He introduced me to Tully, a fat man with one ear, who worked the buffers that resurfaced the white walls. I was handed an apron and a face mask and shown how to use the buffer: Lift the tire and center, inflate it with a footpedal, press the buffer against the white band until cleaned, and then deflate and blow off the tire with an air hose.

5

With a paint brush he stirred a can of industrial preserver. "Then slap this blue stuff on." While he was talking a co-worker came up quietly from behind him and goosed him with the air hose. Tully jumped as if he had been struck by a bullet and then turned around cussing and cupping his genitals in his hands as the other worker walked away calling out foul names. When Tully turned to me smiling his gray teeth, I lifted my mouth into a smile because I wanted to get along. He has to be on my side, I thought. He's the one who'll tell the foreman how I'm doing.

6

I worked carefully that day, setting the tires on the machine as if they were babies, since it was easy to catch a finger in the rim that expanded to inflate the tire. At the day's end we swept up the tire dust and emptied the trash into bins.

7

At five the workers scattered for their cars and motorcycles while I crossed the street to wash at a burger stand. My hair was stiff with dust and my mouth showed pink against the backdrop of my dirty face. I then ordered a hotdog and walked slowly in the direction of the abandoned house where I had stayed the night before. I lay under the trees and within minutes was asleep. When I woke my shoulders were sore and my eyes burned when I squeezed the lids together.

8

From the backyard I walked dully through a residential street, and as evening came on, the TV glare in the living rooms and the headlights of passing cars showed against the blue drift of dusk. I saw two children coming up the street with snow cones, their tongues darting at the packed ice. I saw a boy with a peach and wanted to stop him, but felt embarrassed by my hunger. I walked for an hour only to return and discover the house lit brightly. Behind the fence I heard voices and saw a flashlight poking at the garage door. A man on the back steps mumbled something about the refrigerator to the one with the flashlight.

9

I waited for them to leave, but had the feeling they wouldn't because there was the commotion of furniture being moved. Tired, even more desperate, I started walking again with a great urge to kick things and tear the day from my life. I felt weak and my mind kept drifting because of hunger. I crossed the street to a gas station where I sipped at the water fountain and searched the Coke machine for change. I started walking again, first up a commercial street, then into a residential

10

area where I lay down on someone's lawn and replayed a scene at home—my Mother crying at the kitchen table, my stepfather yelling with food in his mouth. They're cruel, I thought, and warned myself that I should never forgive them. How could they do this to me.

When I got up from the lawn it was late. I searched out a place to sleep and found an unlocked car that seemed safe. In the back seat, with my shoes off, I fell asleep but woke up startled about four in the morning when the owner, a nurse on her way to work, opened the door. She got in and was about to start the engine when I raised my head up from the back seat to explain my presence. She screamed so loudly when I said "I'm sorry" that I sprinted from the car with my shoes in hand. Her screams faded, then stopped altogether, as I ran down the block where I hid behind a trash bin and waited for a police siren to sound. Nothing. I crossed the street to a church where I slept stiffly on cardboard in the balcony.

I woke up feeling tired and greasy. It was early and a few street lights were still lit, the east growing pink with dawn. I washed myself from a garden hose and returned to the church to break into what looked like a kitchen. Paper cups, plastic spoons, a coffee pot littered on a table. I found a box of Nabisco crackers which I ate until I was full.

At work I spent the morning at the buffer, but was then told to help Iggy, an old Mexican, who was responsible for choosing tires that could be recapped without the risk of exploding at high speeds. Every morning a truck would deliver used tires, and after I unloaded them Iggy would step among the tires to inspect them for punctures and rips on the side walls.

With a yellow chalk he marked circles and Xs to indicate damage and called out "junk." For those tires that could be recapped, he said "goody" and I placed them on my hand truck. When I had a stack of eight I kicked the truck at an angle and balanced them to another work area where Iggy again inspected the tires, scratching Xs and calling out "junk."

Iggy worked only until three in the afternoon, at which time he went to the locker room to wash and shave and to dress in a two-piece suit. When he came out he glowed with a bracelet, watch, rings, and a shiny fountain pen in his breast pocket. His shoes sounded against the asphalt. He was the image of a banker stepping into sunlight with millions on his mind. He said a few low words to workers with whom he was friendly and none to people like me.

I was seventeen, stupid because I couldn't figure out the difference between an F 78 14 and 750 14 at sight. Iggy shook his head when I brought him the wrong tires, especially since I had expressed interest in being his understudy. "Mexican, how can you be so stupid?" he would yell at me, slapping a tire from my hands. But within weeks I learned a lot about tires, from sizes and makes to how they are molded in iron forms to how Valley stole from other companies. Now and then we received a truckload of tires, most of them new or nearly new, and they were taken to our warehouse in the back where the serial numbers were ground off with a sander. On those days the foreman handed out Cokes and joked with us as we worked to get the numbers off.

Most of the workers were Mexican or black, though a few redneck whites worked there. The base pay was a dollar sixty-five, but the average was three dollars. Of the black workers, I knew Sugar Daddy the best. His body carried two hundred and fifty pounds, armfuls of scars, and a long knife that made me jump when he brought it out from his boot without warning. At one time he had been a singer, and had cut a record in 1967 called *Love's Chance,* which broke into the R and B charts. But nothing came of it. No big contract, no club dates, no tours. He made very little from the sales, only enough for an operation to pull a steering wheel from his gut when, drunk and mad at a lady friend, he slammed his Mustang into a row of parked cars.

"Touch it," he smiled at me one afternoon as he raised his shirt, his black belly   18
kinked with hair. Scared, I traced the scar that ran from his chest to the left of his belly button, and I was repelled but hid my disgust.

Among the Mexicans I had few friends because I was different, a *pocho* who   19
spoke bad Spanish. At lunch they sat in tires and laughed over burritos, looking up at me to laugh even harder. I also sat in tires while nursing a Coke and felt dirty and sticky because I was still living on the street and had not had a real bath in over a week. Nevertheless, when the border patrol came to round up the nationals, I ran with them as they scrambled for the fence or hid among the tires behind the warehouse. The foreman, who thought I was an undocumented worker, yelled at me to run, to get away. I did just that. At the time it seemed fun because there was no risk, only a goodhearted feeling of hide-and-seek, and besides it meant an hour away from work on company time. When the police left we came back and some of the nationals made up stories of how they were almost caught—how they out-raced the police. Some of the stories were so convoluted and unconvincing that everyone laughed *mentiras,* especially when one described how he overpowered a policeman, took his gun away, and sold the patrol car. We laughed and he laughed, happy to be there to make up a story.

If work was difficult, so were the nights. I still had not gathered enough money   20
to rent a room, so I spent the nights sleeping in parked cars or in the balcony of a church. After a week I found a newspaper ad for room for rent, phoned, and was given directions. Finished with work, I walked the five miles down Mission Road looking back into the traffic with my thumb out. No rides. After eight hours of handling tires I was frightening, I suppose, to drivers since they seldom looked at me; if they did, it was a quick glance. For the next six weeks I would try to hitchhike, but the only person to stop was a Mexican woman who gave me two dollars to take the bus. I told her it was too much and that no bus ran from Mission Road to where I lived, but she insisted that I keep the money and trotted back to her idling car. It must have hurt her to see me day after day walking in the heat and looking very much the dirty Mexican to the many minds that didn't know what it meant to work at hard labor. That woman knew. Her eyes met mine as she opened the car door, and there was a tenderness that was surprisingly true—one for which you wait for years but when it comes it doesn't help. Nothing changes. You continue on in rags, with the sun still above you.

I rented a room from a middle-aged couple whose lives were a mess. She was a   21
school teacher and he was a fireman. A perfect set up, I thought. But during my stay there they would argue with one another for hours in their bedroom.

When I rang at the front door both Mr. and Mrs. Van Deusen answered and   22
didn't bother to disguise their shock at how awful I looked. But they let me in all the

same. Mrs. Van Deusen showed me around the house, from the kitchen and bathroom to the living room with its grand piano. On her fingers she counted out the house rules as she walked me to my room. It was a girl's room with lace curtains, scenic wallpaper of a Victorian couple enjoying a stroll, canopied bed, and stuffed animals in a corner. Leaving, she turned and asked if she could do laundry for me and, feeling shy and hurt, I told her no; perhaps the next day. She left and I undressed to take a bath, exhausted as I sat on the edge of the bed probing my aches and my bruised places. With a towel around my waist I hurried down the hallway to the bathroom where Mrs. Van Deusen had set out an additional towel with a tube of shampoo. I ran the water in the tub and sat on the toilet, lid down, watching the steam curl toward the ceiling. When I lowered myself into the tub I felt my body sting. I soaped a wash cloth and scrubbed my arms until they lightened, even glowed pink, but still I looked unwashed around my neck and face no matter how hard I rubbed. Back in the room I sat in bed reading a magazine, happy and thinking of no better luxury than a girl's sheets, especially after nearly two weeks of sleeping on cardboard at the church.

I was too tired to sleep, so I sat at the window watching the neighbors move 23 about in pajamas, and, curious about the room, looked through the bureau drawers to search out personal things—snapshots, a messy diary, and a high school yearbook. I looked up the Van Deusen's daughter, Barbara, and studied her face as if I recognized her from my own school—a face that said "promise," "college," "nice clothes in the closet." She was a skater and a member of the German Club; her greatest ambition was to sing at the Hollywood Bowl.

After a while I got into bed and as I drifted toward sleep I thought about her. In 24 my mind I played a love scene again and again and altered it slightly each time. She comes home from college and at first is indifferent to my presence in her home, but finally I overwhelm her with deep pity when I come home hurt from work, with blood on my shirt. Then there was another version: Home from college she is immediately taken with me, in spite of my work-darkened face, and invites me into the family car for a milkshake across town. Later, back at the house, we sit in the living room talking about school until we're so close I'm holding her hand. The truth of the matter was that Barbara did come home for a week, but was bitter toward her parents for taking in boarders (two others besides me). During that time she spoke to me only twice: Once, while searching the refrigerator, she asked if we had any mustard; the other time she asked if I had seen her car keys.

But it was a place to stay. Work had become more and more difficult. I not only 25 worked with Iggy, but also with the assistant foreman who was in charge of unloading trucks. After they backed in I hopped on top to pass the tires down by bouncing them on the tailgate to give them an extra spring so they would be less difficult to handle on the other end. Each truck was weighed down with more than two hundred tires, each averaging twenty pounds, so that by the time the truck was emptied and swept clean I glistened with sweat and my T-shirt stuck to my body. I blew snot threaded with tire dust onto the asphalt, indifferent to the customers who watched from the waiting room.

The days were dull. I did what there was to do from morning until the bell 26 sounded at five; I tugged, pulled, and cussed at tires until I was listless and my mind drifted and caught on small things, from cold sodas to shoes to stupid talk about what we would do with a million dollars. I remember unloading a truck with Hamp, a black man.

"What's better than a sharp lady?" he asked me as I stood sweaty on a pile of   27
junked tires. "Water. With ice," I said.

He laughed with his mouth open wide. With his fingers he pinched the sweat   28
from his chin and flicked at me. "You be too young, boy. A woman can make you a god."

As a kid I had chopped cotton and picked grapes, so I knew work. I knew the fa-   29
tigue and the boredom and the feeling that there was a good possibility you might have to do such work for years, if not for a lifetime. In fact, as a kid I imagined a dark fate: To marry Mexican poor, work Mexican hours, and in the end die a Mexican death, broke and in despair.

But this job at Valley Tire Company confirmed that there was something worse   30
than field work, and I was doing it. We were all doing it, from foreman to the new-comers like me, and what I felt heaving tires for eight hours a day was felt by everyone—black, Mexican, redneck. We all despised those hours but didn't know what else to do. The workers were unskilled, some undocumented and fearful of de-portation, and all struck with an uncertainty at what to do with their lives. Although everyone bitched about work, no one left. Some had worked there for as long as twelve years; some had sons working there. Few quit; no one was ever fired. It amazed me that no one gave up when the border patrol jumped from their vans, baton in hand, because I couldn't imagine any work that could be worse—or any life. What was out there, in the world, that made men run for the fence in fear?

Iggy was the only worker who seemed sure of himself. After five hours of "junk-   31
ing," he brushed himself off, cleaned up in the washroom, and came out gleaming with an elegance that humbled the rest of us. Few would look him straight in the eye or talk to him in our usual stupid way because he was so much better. He carried himself as a man should—with that old world "dignity"—while the rest of us muffed our jobs and talked dully about dull things as we worked. From where he worked in his open shed he would now and then watch us with his hands on his hips. He would shake his head and click his tongue in disgust.

The rest of us lived dismally. I often wondered what the others' homes were like;   32
I couldn't imagine that they were much better than our work place. No one indi-cated that his outside life was interesting or intriguing. We all looked defeated and contemptible in our filth at the day's end. I imagined the average welcome at home: Rafael, a Mexican national who had worked at Valley for five years, returned to a beaten house of kids who were dressed in mismatched clothes and playing kick-the-can. As for Sugar Daddy, he returned home to a stuffy room where he would read and reread old magazines. He ate potato chips, drank beer, and watched TV. There was no grace in dipping socks into a wash basin where later he would wash his cup and plate.

There was no grace at work. It was all ridicule. The assistant foreman drank   33
Cokes in front of the newcomers as they laced tires in the afternoon sun. Knowing that I had a long walk home, Rudy, the college student, passed me waving and yelling "Hello," as I started down Mission Road on the way home to eat out of cans.

Even our plump secretary got into the act by wearing short skirts and flaunting her milky legs. If there was love, it was ugly. I'm thinking of Tully and an older man whose name I can no longer recall fondling one another in the washroom. I had come in cradling a smashed finger to find them pressed together in the shower, their pants undone and partly pulled down. When they saw me they smiled their pink mouths but didn't bother to push away.

How we arrived at such a place is a mystery to me. Why anyone would stay for years is even a deeper concern. You showed up, but from where? What broken life? What ugly past? The foreman showed you the Coke machine, the washroom, and the yard where you'd work. When you picked up a tire, you were amazed at the black it could give off. 34

Working with the Text

1. Consider the marginality of Soto's existence at seventeen: virtually broke, homeless, eking out a living at a filthy, back-breaking job. If you had encountered him then, how would you have responded? Does it surprise you that he would go on to become a successful writer and college teacher?

2. Soto seems not to have belonged to any of the worlds he inhabited at this time in his life—not among his various coworkers and not in the middle-class household where he lived in a rented room. How did he cope with this alienation? How does he communicate it? Write a paper in which you look at Soto's sense of alienation. How do his attempts (and failures) to belong structure the essay? In what ways does he try to reach across differences?

3. What do the daughter's possessions in the rented room represent for Soto? Give examples of details that he uses to make the room expressive of his feelings.

4. When the story's narrator describes his experience hitchhiking, he tells of one woman who stops to give him "two dollars" to take the bus. He observes,

> It must have hurt her to see me day after day walking in the heat and looking very much the dirty Mexican to the many minds that didn't know what it meant to work hard at labor. That woman knew. Her eyes met mine as she opened the car door, and there was a tenderness that was surprisingly true—one for which you wait for years but when it comes it doesn't help. Nothing changes.

How does that passage, and the realization it represents at that point in the story compare and contrast to the final paragraph?

> How we arrived at such a place is a mystery to me. Why anyone would stay for years is even a deeper concern. You showed up, but from where? What broken life? What ugly past? The foreman showed you the Coke machine, the washroom, and the yard where you'd work. When you picked up a tire, you were amazed at the black it could give off.

Has the narrator's attitude toward work changed by the end? Is he still in the position of the "observed" as in the scene when he is hitchhiking, or has his

position changed? Are there any other passages in the story you might group
with these two?

SAFE

CHERYLENE LEE

■ An author of poetry and plays as well as fiction, Cherylene Lee often focuses
her work on themes involving the experiences of Asian Americans. Her plays
have been produced at the Mark Taper Forum in Los Angeles, the Pan Asian
Repertory Theater in New York City, and the Group Theater in Seattle. Her
writing has been anthologized in collections including the *Southern California Anthology 1985, Sister Stew,* and *American Dragons.* In the following short story, the
narrator and her brother find daring ways to go beyond the safe borders of
their traditional Chinese American family.

My brother sets himself on fire every summer. He's not a pyromaniac and   1
it's not a political statement. He does it in front of people at Worlds of
Water, U.S.A. My brother is a flame diver—a stuntman on a high diving
platform who douses himself in flammable liquid, has someone light a torch to him,
then launches himself into a cool blue pool, toes pointed, form correct—though
that is hard to make out through all the flame and smoke. He says the crowds go
wild because they feel afraid. He makes them feel safe.

Safe. That is the most important consideration for our family. Perhaps there is a   2
Chinese gene encoded with a protein for caution. Or perhaps it's because my father's tailor shop is not doing so well or because of my mother's blindness. Perhaps
it's because my mother and father married late in life and weren't sure how to protect their children.

We try to take precautions. My mother won't go out at night for fear of what the   3
darkness holds. She doesn't like me to take a shower after dinner for fear I might get
a cramp and somehow drown in the shower's spray. She doesn't like me to walk
home from school alone, nor does she like me to walk home with boys. She'd rather
I walked home with girls, at least three for maximum protection so one can always
run for help. I've tried to explain to her, I like walking alone, it's not always possible
to walk in female threes, I don't even have that many girlfriends. "You have to watch
out at your age, you can't be too safe," she warns, "but don't hang around with the
fast ones."

My father is just as bad. He's so afraid someone will dent his car, he won't park in   4
a lot that doesn't have two spaces side by side for his ten-year-old station wagon. He
refuses to go into a grocery store if he could be the first or last customer—"That's
when robbers are most likely to come." He won't eat in restaurants without first wiping the chopsticks, rice bowl, tea cup, or plate, silverware, and glass—"So many

germs everywhere." He has more locks and alarms on his tailor shop door than the bank that's two doors down. It takes him ten minutes to open them up each day, turn off the alarms, before calling my mother to let her know that he has arrived safely.

We live in San Francisco—a city with its share of dangers though my parents 5 have done their best to shield my brother and me from having to face most of them. More than from just physical harm, they've tried to protect us from loss—loss of face, loss of happiness, loss of innocence. So far we have been protected by their constant vigilance. Not that I have been sheltered so much I can't go places on my own or do things without my parents' consent, but their warnings, cautions, and dire predictions have had an effect. While I have always felt safe and have never wanted for anything, neither can I say that I've ever wanted at all. I have never been in danger, never known a need for risk. That's why I was so shocked when my brother announced he wanted to become a flame diver.

It isn't as risky as it seems, at least according to my brother who claims he could 6 do the dive in his sleep. He wears a special flame-retardant suit. It protects him head to foot from the flames that consume him three times a day, six days a week, three months of the year. His summer job—his only job—hasn't changed him much except that he has no facial hair. The suit shields him from burns, but the wind sometimes blows flames under his protective helmet, singeing the hair off his face. The first summer he started doing this work, it took me awhile to recognize what was different about him when he sat down to dinner. He had no eyebrows, no eye lashes, just eyes, big brown eyes that seemed too large for the rest of his face. Since then he's taken to drawing in eyebrows with an eyebrow pencil because he doesn't want people to worry. Otherwise he's normal, though for a while I admit I was afraid of my brother. Who was this guy who grew up with me and suddenly became a flame diver? I thought maybe he would turn into some awful monster with scarred flesh and a swollen head from the fire and adulation. But my brother remains the same—shy, soft-spoken, introverted. Maybe he's happier these days or maybe I just think that because I am relieved. After hearing so much about danger, all he's lost are his eyebrows.

I've never seen my brother actually do his stunt though our father has many pic- 7 tures of his dives hanging on the walls of his tailor shop. My brother won't let any of us watch him. He thinks we'll jinx him and we don't want to do that. He hasn't let us watch him since a high school diving meet three years ago when he made the varsity swim team. On his final and hardest dive of that meet, his foot slipped during his preparation jump causing him to start his backward twist out of control and his head to nick the edge of the platform. Our mother, already nearly blind, became hysterical even before the blood began oozing up in the water. By instinct she started screaming, "My boy, my boy!" the instant his head made contact, before anyone else knew something was wrong. Her screams echoed like a wailing gull inside the indoor swim gym. Luckily my brother wasn't badly hurt, ten stitches closed him up, but he was so embarrassed by our mother's shrieking that he asked us not to attend anymore, our presence brought him bad luck. That's why we all stay away now and only look at the pictures of his dives after he's already done them. When we know he's safe.

According to my mother, her eyesight started going bad because my father's eyes   8
wandered. Years ago, when his tailor shop was in Chinatown, his clients were mostly
women. He made cheongsams, the tight-fitting Chinese dresses the girls in the Miss
Chinatown contest wear. He also did special occasion clothes, Chinese jackets, western-
style wedding dresses, men's suits and such, but his busiest time of the year used to
be the months before Chinese New Year when the Miss Chinatown contest was held.
He would carefully take the measurements of each eager contestant, help her choose
material that brought out her best coloring—mostly variations on fire-engine
red—and cut the gowns so that they showed off each girl to her best advantage. My
mother used to help my father by doing the embroidery on the dresses. Dragons and
phoenixes were her favorite and my mother's embroidery was beautiful, small
stitches of metallic thread, so fine they looked like brush strokes. She never needed
a pattern, the dragons and phoenixes appeared in her head, she saw their outlines,
their wings outstretched, their images flying on satin or silk which guided her hands
as if by magic.

Her embroidery made my father's work much sought after, but one day she   9
claimed her husband of 12 years was taking too much time getting the measurements of a young girl. His hands lingered a bit too long over the tape encircling her
hips. After that my mother refused to do any more embroidery. She said her eyesight
was failing, though she saw with bitter sharpness all the times my father's eyes seem
to pause over a young girl's figure. My mother refused to see a doctor. She claimed
her vision was a gift of the gods, just like her dragons and phoenixes, and my father
must be up to something very bad to make it become so blurry. She became so enraged at women entering the shop, she insisted on taking their measurements herself, though indeed her eyesight was very poor and she often mistook the numbers
on the tape causing much grief during the fitting sessions. Without her special embroidery and because of her mistaken measurements, my father's business suffered.
He became just another tailor, his prices were considered high, his patterns a bit old-
fashioned. My father decided to move his shop away from Chinatown, to a neighborhood where he would have more men for clients, not young girls seeking the
Miss Chinatown crown, and thereby give my mother some peace.

But the neighborhood he chose did not give them peace. The taquerias and salsa   10
music, the easy gatherings of young men at street corners, the rapid Spanish spoken
in shops made both my father and mother feel out of place. My mother stopped
going to work with my father and preferred to stay at home. She spent her time
making "frogs"—Chinese buttons of thin braid twisted into three circles forming
the bulges of a frog's head and eyes. She didn't have to see in order to make these
buttons, she could feel her way along. She knew by instinct the exact place where
stitches were needed to hold the button's shape. But Chinese buttons were not popular items in my father's new location. My parents' caution toward the outside
world increased with my father's diminishing income. Only the family home felt
safe to them and this is what they tried to impart to both my brother and me.

Of course my parents didn't want my brother to become a flame diver. They   11
didn't even want him to join the swim team in high school—"too many accidents
happen in pools"—but my brother didn't tell them he joined until after he'd already

done it. I helped him forge our parents' signatures on the school release form, as he had done for me whenever I cut class. He didn't tell them the truth until after his first competition when he won first place for the platform swan dive. That gave them something to brag about and brag my father did. None of his customers could ever leave his shop without some comment on the first-place ribbon hanging on my father's wall. Our parents didn't like that my brother had gone behind their backs—my father never mentioned that part or my role in the conspiracy—but their pride in my brother's accomplishment did mollify some of their fear. I suppose the possibility of a college scholarship also helped. My father couldn't afford to send my brother to college—he'd used his life savings moving his shop—and since my brother wasn't too academic, his talent for diving, risky as it was, seemed the best path toward the safety of college. My father thought my brother would get a diving scholarship, learn a risk-free well-paying profession, give up his high diving ways after graduation, and live a safe life ever after.

My brother didn't get a scholarship. Although he had a spectacular swan dive, he couldn't seem to master any other. Something happened to his orientation when he tried to perform twists and somersaults. Maybe that time he hit his head made him fearful of hitting the platform again. He couldn't seem to get the spin of going head over heels quite right. When he tried a half twist or a backward gainer, his body went over too far or sometimes not far enough. He suffered spectacular belly flops. He was such a perfectionist though, he practiced diving for hours, but usually only his favorite one—the elegant and beautiful swan dive. A repertory of one dive wasn't enough to impress college recruiters, who thought my brother odd in his singular passion for swan dives. He was looked at and passed over many times during his senior year. Our parents were crushed that my brother wasn't asked to try out for any college team, but my brother didn't seem to mind. He told me one night he thought he could perform swan dives for a living.   12

"Look at these guys," he showed me a magazine that advertised tours to Mexico displaying muscular men in skimpy bathing suits diving off impossibly high cliffs. "Nothing but swan dives. People pay to see this."   13

"But you're not Mexican. And those cliffs are so high."   14

"It doesn't matter, I'm not going to do cliffs. There are other ways to make dives exciting. Look at this." He pulled out another magazine showing tours to Puerto Rico. This ad pictured tourists outside a fancy hotel looking entranced at the sight of a man, encased in flames, diving into a deep blue pool. The tourists clutched at their drinks, their mouths and eyes open in amazement. The caption read: "Thrills everywhere, with comfort you can't compare. Come to the island that has it all—Puerto Rico."   15

"This is more what I had in mind."   16

"Puerto Rico?"   17

"No I'm going to become a flame diver. I can do it better than this guy. Look, he's not even vertical going in."   18

"But how can you, where can you—" I could hardly ask a question. None of us had ever been out of the state, let alone leave home for such far off lands as Mexico or unimaginably, Puerto Rico.   19

"I can do it here."   20

"We don't have a swimming pool."   21

"God you're so dumb. I'm talking about Worlds of Water, U.S.A. It's only 30 miles 22
from here. It's the perfect place. People are tired of watching animals do tricks for
them. They feel guilty about it. They would rather see a man on fire than dolphins
going through flaming hoops."

"Wait till mom and dad hear this." I could already imagine their torrents of 23
protests. They hated candles on birthday cakes, their fear of fire was so great.

"They'll come around," my brother assured me. "It's what I want to do." 24

When I was thirteen, my mother asked for her embroidery basket to see if I pos- 25
sessed her talent. She sat me down with scraps of cloth, a packet of needles, and
spools of thread though her eyesight was so poor by then, she could no longer
thread the needles. She told me to close my eyes and picture a mighty dragon. She
told me to feel its power, feel the flames shooting from the mouth. "Let this image
guide your hands, the needle will follow the flames."

I closed my eyes and tried to see her dragon. I tried to feel its heat and let the nee- 26
dle follow. But I was constantly pricking myself, the thread tangled, the cloth
bunched up. When I looked at my clumsy stitches all I saw were chicken scratches,
uneven threads, unraveling patterns, my mother's nerves frayed at the edge. I had no
dragons and phoenixes in me. My mother told me to go wash my hands and be careful putting away the scissors. She knew I hadn't inherited her gift, but she protected
me just the same. She said such embroidery was not in fashion, not important anymore. We never tried again.

"I didn't raise my son to perform silly tricks for strangers," was my father's first 27
reaction. "You are not a trained animal."

"I'm not a caged one either," I'd never heard my brother use that tone, especially 28
in front of our father. "I can do it, dad. I've been practicing diving for years."

"High school meets, this is different." 29

"What's wrong with going to city college?" mother asked. "You can learn a trade, 30
meet a nice girl. Who will you meet at this water world? Nobody there but fish."

"Ma, I have learned a trade. I know how to dive." 31

"Trying to kill yourself is no way for my son to make a living." 32

"Diving isn't trying to kill myself, dad. It feels like flying to me." 33

"Didn't you hear how many people were killed in that plane crash over Mexico? 34
Flying isn't safe anymore." Our mother knew how to change the subject.

"I'm talking about diving, Ma. Swan dives." 35

"So why do you have to set yourself on fire?" 36

"Because I need a gimmick to make it look exciting. Dangerous." 37

There it was—the D-word. They'll never go for it, I thought. How could he ex- 38
pect their support when he played on their worst fears? I felt sorry for my brother
then. All his diving dreams and he had to choose the wrong word.

"But it only has to look dangerous, dad. Really it's very safe." 39

I don't think my father was always so cautious. He was quite the gambler once. 40
He used to go to weekly poker games in Chinatown before he moved his shop. He
used to talk about opening a factory or a specialty store featuring mom's embroidery. But that was before the trouble began, before she started accusing him.

When I look at my father now, sighing as he hems a pair of trousers, replaces a   41
zipper, or watches my mother making her buttons, I don't think he ever had a wandering eye. I think my mother must have made it up because her vision was blurred.
I think she was afraid without her embroidery, my father would no longer need her.
She thought he would find a younger woman, leave her with two children, middle-
aged, blind, and alone.

But that never happened. I think my father felt embarrassed that he had no   42
dragon in his head. My mother was the one with the gift. She had the visions that
spread to his cloth. She had the instinct that knew just how to hold buttons and
things together. He was afraid he would lose her. They didn't know how to reassure
themselves, so they moved the shop to a new location and tried to shield my brother
and me from further loss in a dangerous world.

Three nights after my brother made his announcement that he was going to be-   43
come a flame diver, my father brought home this special material—something like
rubber only more flexible—and spent hours gluing it together with a special flame
retardant glue. He placed a glued piece over our kitchen stove testing to see if it
melted, putting his hand on the burner to see how hot it grew. He timed how long it
took before the material grew too hot for his hand. He glued squares of it together
to see if he could take more heat. My mother insisted my father not risk his sewing
hands and stuck her own into the makeshift glove holding it over the gas flame,
turning the stove to high, staring with unseeing eyes at the blue circle of heat, patiently daring it to burn her. My parents experimented for a month with different
materials, different glues, different thicknesses, different flames before deciding a
suit could indeed be made that would protect their flesh and blood. Engulfed by my
brother's passion, only they could make him safe.

I haven't told my parents yet, not even my brother though maybe he would un-   44
derstand. I see a man after school. He lives two blocks from the school and I go to
his house everyday before I walk home alone. He is an older white man, not as old
as my father. He called to me from his window one day as I was walking home and
asked if I could bring in his paper and check his mail box for him. When I brought
in his paper and mail, he was very polite and apologized for troubling me, but he
couldn't get out of bed. He asked if I had a few minutes and would I mind reading
something to him, he wanted to hear another voice. He asked me to read Ann Lan-
ders' column. I think he was very lonely. I read to him and he thanked me and that's
how it began. Now I read to him for 15 minutes everyday, sometimes things from
the newspaper, sometimes things from magazines, mostly magazines about sex that
he gets delivered in the mail. The magazines are the type my parents would never
approve of me reading. I sit at the foot of his bed and read and he listens to me with
closed eyes. Sometimes his body tenses and I see sweat break out on his forehead. He
listens so intently, I feel heat coming off his body. He's always very polite to me. He
says that I am a gift. He says that when he hears my voice, it helps him to feel alive.

My brother tells me what a rush it is to be a sponge for everyone's fear. To be so   45
focused on what he does, he only hears his own heartbeat. He's vaguely aware of the
ladder he climbs to the platform hanging above the pool. He doesn't hear the roll of
the drum, he doesn't hear his name announced, he doesn't hear the height of the

platform called out, he doesn't see the water. Encased in his protective suit, glued with familial pride, he feels which way the wind blows by the way it buffets his body. He tells me the exact routine. The number of deep breaths he takes, the number of sprays of butane needed to coat him from head to foot, the sound of the torch which explodes with a roar, the moment he holds his flaming hands outstretched before closing his eyes and flying. He tells me he opens his eyes at the peak of his arch—a dragon sailing through pure blue silk before tucking his head and splashing into the satin smooth mouth of the pool.

And I have imagined the crowd's awe building up with the flames, the tightening   46
nerves with the drum roll, the fearful split second of silence, the collective breath for this human torch against blue sky, the lesser sun god, this crazy kid. And then I've imagined the plunge, a blurred arch of orange and smoke, a curve straightening to a lightning shaft, a sizzling hiss as he breaks the water, the cheers welling up like ocean waves sweeping aside stunned silence. I imagine when my brother surfaces and swims to the side of the pool, the audience sees a phoenix rising, their fears melt, the smiles grow, the celebration is complete. And as he doffs his helmet, waving his arms and smiling broadly, he reassures the crowd that all is well, nothing bad has happened, no loss has occurred. He dove through fire and survived. He lives to dive again. Everything is normal.

Working with the Text

1. The narrator of "Safe" and her brother rebel against their parents' cautiousness in very unusual ways. What do these acts of rebellion suggest about the need to be different from one's parents' expectations? Are their actions exceptional or typical?

2. How is the neighborhood to which the family moves different from their previous neighborhood in Chinatown? How do the narrator's parents respond to this difference? Do you think their response is natural?

3. Why do you think the narrator's parents are so fearful of the outside world?

4. When he makes his flaming dive, the narrator's brother says he becomes a "sponge for everyone's fear" (¶ 45). In what sense do dangerous stunts, when successfully performed, serve to reassure us that, in the narrator's words, "everything is safe"? Write a paper in which you look at other cultural phenomena that serve as outlets for a sense of fear and a yearning for safety.

Arts of the Contact Zone

MARY LOUISE PRATT

■ A native of Canada, Mary Louise Pratt attended the University of Toronto and later received her doctorate from Stanford University. She now teaches comparative literature, as well as Spanish and Portuguese, at Stanford. The subjects of her research and writing cover a wide range, including literature, linguistics, political and cultural studies, and history. Among her books are *Toward a Speech Act*

Theory of Literary Discourse (1977); the textbook *Linguistics for Students of Literature* (1980); *Women, Culture, and Politics in Latin America* (coauthored, 1990); and most recently, *Imperial Eyes: Studies in Travel Writing and Transculturation* (1992), in which this revised version of the essay appeared, having been originally delivered as a lecture at the Modern Language Association Conference in 1990.

In *Imperial Eyes* Pratt considers how early European travelers to Africa and the Americas who wrote about these new worlds for a European audience essentially "invented" them along Eurocentric lines. Rather than describe these lands and their peoples in terms of their positive reality, these travelers wrote of their "inferiority" to Europe and Europeans. In the following essay, Pratt focuses on a 1613 manuscript addressed to King Philip of Spain by an indigenous Peruvian subject of the Spanish conquest. This twelve-hundred-page "letter," written in its author's native Quechua as well as in ungrammatical Spanish, apparently remained unread until the twentieth century. For Pratt, it is emblematic of the perils of communication within "contact zones, . . . social spaces where cultures meet, clash, and grapple with each other, often in contexts of highly asymmetrical relations of power." She finds such zones particularly applicable to the contemporary United States.

Whenever the subject of literacy comes up, what often pops first into my mind is a conversation I overheard eight years ago between my son Sam and his best friend, Willie, aged six and seven, respectively: "Why don't you trade me Many Trails for Carl Yats . . . Yesits . . . Ya-strum-scrum." "That's not how you say it, dummy, it's Carl Yes . . . Yes . . . oh, I don't know." Sam and Willie had just discovered baseball cards. Many Trails was their decoding, with the help of first-grade English phonics, of the name Manny Trillo. The name they were quite rightly stumped on was Carl Yastremski. That was the first time I remembered seeing them put their incipient literacy to their own use, and I was of course thrilled. [1]

Sam and Willie learned a lot about phonics that year by trying to decipher surnames on baseball cards, and a lot about cities, states, heights, weights, places of birth, stages of life. In the years that followed, I watched Sam apply his arithmetic skills to working out batting averages and subtracting retirement years from rookie years; I watched him develop senses of patterning and order by arranging and rearranging his cards for hours on end, and aesthetic judgment by comparing different photos, different series, layouts, and color schemes. American geography and history took shape in his mind through baseball cards. Much of his social life revolved around trading them, and he learned about exchange, fairness, trust, the importance of processes as opposed to results, what it means to get cheated, taken advantage of, even robbed. Baseball cards were the medium of his economic life too. Nowhere better to learn the power and arbitrariness of money, the absolute divorce between use value and exchange value, notions of long- and short-term investment, the possibility of personal values that are independent of market values. [2]

Baseball cards meant baseball card shows, where there was much to be learned about adult worlds as well. And baseball cards opened the door to baseball books, shelves and shelves of encyclopedias, magazines, histories, biographies, novels, books of jokes, anecdotes, cartoons, even poems. Sam learned the history of Amer- [3]

ican racism and the struggle against it through baseball; he saw the depression and two world wars from behind home plate. He learned the meaning of commodified labor, what it means for one's body and talents to be owned and dispensed by another. He knows something about Japan, Taiwan, Cuba, and Central America and how men and boys do things there. Through the history and experience of baseball stadiums he thought about architecture, light, wind, topography, meteorology, the dynamics of public space. He learned the meaning of expertise, of knowing about something well enough that you can start a conversation with a stranger and feel sure of holding your own. Even with an adult—especially with an adult. Throughout his preadolescent years, baseball history was Sam's luminous point of contact with grown-ups, his lifeline to caring. And, of course, all this time he was also playing baseball, struggling his way through the stages of the local Little League system, lucky enough to be a pretty good player, loving the game and coming to know deeply his strengths and weaknesses.

Literacy began for Sam with the newly pronounceable names on the picture   4
cards and brought him what has been easily the broadest, most varied, most enduring, and most integrated experience of his thirteen-year life. Like many parents, I was delighted to see schooling give Sam the tools with which to find and open all these doors. At the same time I found it unforgivable that schooling itself gave him nothing remotely as meaningful to do, let alone anything that would actually take him beyond the referential, masculinist ethos of baseball and its lore.

However, I was not invited here to speak as a parent, nor as an expert on literacy.   5
I was asked to speak as an MLA [Modern Language Association] member working in the elite academy. In that capacity my contribution is undoubtedly supposed to be abstract, irrelevant, and anchored outside the real world. I wouldn't dream of disappointing anyone. I propose immediately to head back several centuries to a text that has a few points in common with baseball cards and raises thoughts about what Tony Sarmiento, in his comments to the conference, called new visions of literacy. In 1908 a Peruvianist named Richard Pietschmann was exploring in the Danish Royal Archive in Copenhagen and came across a manuscript. It was dated in the city of Cuzco in Peru, in the year 1613, some forty years after the final fall of the Inca empire to the Spanish and signed with an unmistakably Andean indigenous name: Felipe Guaman Poma de Ayala. Written in a mixture of Quechua and ungrammatical, expressive Spanish, the manuscript was a letter addressed by an unknown but apparently literate Andean to King Philip III of Spain. What stunned Pietschmann was that the letter was twelve hundred pages long. There were almost eight hundred pages of written text and four hundred of captioned line drawings. It was titled *The First New Chronicle and Good Government*. No one knew (or knows) how the manuscript got to the library in Copenhagen or how long it had been there. No one, it appeared, had ever bothered to read it or figured out how. Quechua was not thought of as a written language in 1908, nor Andean culture as a literate culture.

Pietschmann prepared a paper on his find, which he presented in London in   6
1912, a year after the rediscovery of Machu Picchu by Hiram Bingham. Reception, by an international congress of Americanists, was apparently confused. It took twenty-five years for a facsimile edition of the work to appear in Paris. It was not till the late 1970s, as positivist reading habits gave way to interpretive studies and colonial elitisms to postcolonial pluralisms, that Western scholars found ways of reading

Guaman Poma's *New Chronicle and Good Government* as the extraordinary intercultural tour de force that it was. The letter got there, only 350 years too late, a miracle and a terrible tragedy.

I propose to say a few words about this erstwhile unreadable text, in order   7
to lay out some thoughts about writing and literacy in what I like to call the *contact zones.* I use this term to refer to social spaces where cultures meet, clash, and grapple with each other, often in contexts of highly asymmetrical relations of power, such as colonialism, slavery, or their aftermaths as they are lived out in many parts of the world today. Eventually I will use the term to reconsider the models of community that many of us rely on in teaching and theorizing and that are under challenge today. But first a little more about Guaman Poma's giant letter to Philip III.

Insofar as anything is known about him at all, Guaman Poma exemplified the so-   8
ciocultural complexities produced by conquest and empire. He was an indigenous Andean who claimed noble Inca descent and who had adopted (at least in some sense) Christianity. He may have worked in the Spanish colonial administration as an interpreter, scribe, or assistant to a Spanish tax collector—as a mediator, in short. He says he learned to write from his half brother, a mestizo whose Spanish father had given him access to religious education.

Guaman Poma's letter to the king is written in two languages (Spanish and   9
Quechua) and two parts. The first is called the *Nueva corónica,* "New Chronicle." The title is important. The chronicle of course was the main writing apparatus through which the Spanish presented their American conquests to themselves. It constituted one of the main official discourses. In writing a "new chronicle," Guaman Poma took over the official Spanish genre for his own ends. Those ends were, roughly, to construct a new picture of the world, a picture of a Christian world with Andean rather than European peoples at the center of it—Cuzco, not Jerusalem. In the *New Chronicle* Guaman Poma begins by rewriting the Christian history of the world from Adam and Eve, incorporating the Amerindians into it as offspring of one of the sons of Noah. He identifies five ages of Christian history that he links in parallel with the five ages of canonical Andean history—separate but equal trajectories that diverge with Noah and reintersect not with Columbus but with Saint Bartholomew, claimed to have preceded Columbus in the Americas. In a couple of hundred pages, Guaman Poma constructs a veritable encyclopedia of Inca and pre-Inca history, customs, laws, social forms, public offices, and dynastic leaders. The depictions resemble European manners and customs description, but also reproduce the meticulous detail with which knowledge in Inca society was stored on *quipus* and in the oral memories of elders.

Guaman Poma's *New Chronicle* is an instance of what I have proposed to call an   10
autoethnographic text, by which I mean a text in which people undertake to describe themselves in ways that engage with representations others have made of them. Thus if ethnographic texts are those in which European metropolitan subjects represent to themselves their others (usually their conquered others), autoethnographic texts are representations that the so-defined others construct *in response to* or in dialogue with those texts. Autoethnographic texts are not, then, what are usually thought of as autochthonous forms of expression or self-representation (as the Andean *quipus* were). Rather they involve a selective collaboration with and appropriation of idioms of the metropolis or the conqueror. These are merged or infiltrated to varying degrees with indigenous idioms to create self-representations

intended to intervene in metropolitan modes of understanding. Autoethnographic works are often addressed to both metropolitan audiences and the speaker's own community. Their reception is thus highly indeterminate. Such texts often constitute a marginalized group's point of entry into the dominant circuits of print culture. It is interesting to think, for example, of American slave autobiography in its autoethnographic dimensions, which in some respects distinguish it from Euramerican autobiographical tradition. The concept might help explain why some of the earliest published writing by Chicanas took the form of folkloric manners and customs sketches written in English and published in English-language newspapers or folklore magazines (see Treviño). Autoethnographic representation often involves concrete collaborations between people, as between literate ex-slaves and abolitionist intellectuals, or between Guaman Poma and the Inca elders who were his informants. Often, as in Guaman Poma, it involves more than one language. In recent decades autoethnography, critique, and resistance have reconnected with writing in a contemporary creation of the contact zone, the *testimonio*.

Guaman Poma's *New Chronicle* ends with a revisionist account of the Spanish conquest, which, he argues, should have been a peaceful encounter of equals with the potential for benefiting both, but for the mindless greed of the Spanish. He parodies Spanish history. Following contact with the Incas, he writes, "In all Castille, there was a great commotion. All day and at night in their dreams the Spaniards were saying, 'Yndias, yndias, oro, plata, oro, plata del Piru'" ("Indies, Indies, gold, silver, gold, silver from Peru"). The Spanish, he writes, brought nothing of value to share with the Andeans, nothing "but armor and guns con la codicia de oro, plata oro y plata, yndias, a las Yndias, Piru" ("with the lust for gold, silver, gold and silver, Indies, the Indies, Peru") (372). I quote these words as an example of a conquered subject using the conqueror's language to construct a parodic, oppositional representation of the conqueror's own speech. Guaman Poma mirrors back to the Spanish (in their language, which is alien to him) an image of themselves that they often suppress and will therefore surely recognize. Such are the dynamics of language, writing, and representation in contact zones.

The second half of the epistle continues the critique. It is titled *Buen gobierno y justicia,* "Good Government and Justice," and combines a description of colonial society in the Andean region with a passionate denunciation of Spanish exploitation and abuse. (These, at the time he was writing, were decimating the population of the Andes at a genocidal rate. In fact, the potential loss of the labor force became a main cause for reform of the system.) Guaman Poma's most implacable hostility is invoked by the clergy, followed by the dreaded *corregidores,* or colonial overseers. He also praises good works, Christian habits, and just men where he finds them, and offers at length his views as to what constitutes "good government and justice." The Indies, he argues, should be administered through a collaboration of Inca and Spanish elites. The epistle ends with an imaginary question-and-answer session in which, in a reversal of hierarchy, the king is depicted asking Guaman Poma questions about how to reform the empire—a dialogue imagined across the many lines that divide the Andean scribe from the imperial monarch, and in which the subordinated subject single-handedly gives himself authority in the colonizer's language and verbal repertoire. In a way, it worked—this extraordinary text did get written—but in a way it did not, for the letter never reached its addressee.

To grasp the import of Guaman Poma's project, one needs to keep in mind that the Incas had no system of writing. Their huge empire is said to be the only known instance of a full-blown bureaucratic state society built and administered without writing. Guaman Poma constructs his text by appropriating and adapting pieces of the representational repertoire of the invaders. He does not simply imitate or reproduce it; he selects and adapts it along Andean lines to express (bilingually, mind you) Andean interests and aspirations. Ethnographers have used the term *transculturation* to describe processes whereby members of subordinated or marginal groups select and invent from materials transmitted by a dominant or metropolitan culture. The term, originally coined by Cuban sociologist Fernando Ortiz in the 1940s, aimed to replace overly reductive concepts of acculturation and assimilation used to characterize culture under conquest. While subordinate peoples do not usually control what emanates from the dominant culture, they do determine to varying extents what gets absorbed into their own and what it gets used for. Transculturation, like autoethnography, is a phenomenon of the contact zone.

As scholars have realized only relatively recently, the transcultural character of Guaman Poma's text is intricately apparent in its visual as well as its written component. The genre of the four hundred line drawings is European—there seems to have been no tradition of representational drawing among the Incas—but in their execution they deploy specifically Andean systems of spatial symbolism that express Andean values and aspirations.[1] . . . 14

In sum, Guaman Poma's text is truly a product of the contact zone. If one thinks of cultures, or literatures, as discrete, coherently structured, monolingual edifices, Guaman Poma's text, and indeed any autoethnographic work, appears anomalous or chaotic—as it apparently did to the European scholars Pietschmann spoke to in 1912. If one does not think of cultures this way, then Guaman Poma's text is simply heterogeneous, as the Andean region was itself and remains today. Such a text is heterogeneous on the reception end as well as the production end: it will read very differently to people in different positions in the contact zone. Because it deploys European and Andean systems of meaning making, the letter necessarily means differently to bilingual Spanish-Quechua speakers and to monolingual speakers in either language; the drawings mean differently to monocultural readers, Spanish or Andean, and to bicultural readers responding to the Andean symbolic structures embodied in European genres. 15

In the Andes in the early 1600s there existed a literate public with considerable intercultural competence and degrees of bilingualism. Unfortunately, such a community did not exist in the Spanish court with which Guaman Poma was trying to make contact. It is interesting to note that in the same year Guaman Poma sent off his letter, a text by another Peruvian was adopted in official circles in Spain as the canonical Christian mediation between the Spanish conquest and Inca history. It was another huge encyclopedic work, titled the *Royal Commentaries of the Incas,* written, tellingly, by a mestizo, Inca Garcilaso de la Vega. Like the mestizo half brother who taught Guaman Poma to read and write, Inca Garcilaso was the son of an Inca princess and a Spanish official, and had lived in Spain since he was seventeen. Though he too spoke Quechua, his book is written in eloquent, standard Spanish, without illustrations. While Guaman Poma's life's work sat somewhere unread, the *Royal Commentaries* was edited and reedited in Spain and the New World, a mediation that coded the Andean past and present in ways thought unthreatening to colonial hierarchy.[2] The textual hierarchy persists; the *Royal Commentaries* today 16 remains a staple item on Ph.D. reading lists in Spanish, while the *New Chronicle and Good Government,* despite the ready availability of several fine editions, is not. However, though Guaman Poma's text did not reach its destination, the transcultural currents of expression it exemplifies continued to evolve in the Andes, as they still do, less in writing than in storytelling, ritual, song, dance-drama, painting and sculpture, dress, textile art, forms of governance, religious belief, and many other vernacular art forms. All express the effects of long-term contact and intractable, unequal conflict.

Autoethnography, transculturation, critique, collaboration, bilingualism, media-   17
tion, parody, denunciation, imaginary dialogue, vernacular expression—these are some of the literate arts of the contact zone. Miscomprehension, incomprehension, dead letters, unread masterpieces, absolute heterogeneity of meaning—these are some of the perils of writing in the contact zone. They all live among us today in the transnationalized metropolis of the United States and are becoming more widely visible, more pressing, and, like Guaman Poma's text, more decipherable to those who once would have ignored them in defense of a stable, centered sense of knowledge and reality.

CONTACT AND COMMUNITY

The idea of the contact zone is intended in part to contrast with ideas of commu-   18
nity that underlie much of the thinking about language, communication, and culture that gets done in the academy. A couple of years ago, thinking about the linguistic theories I knew, I tried to make sense of a utopian quality that often seemed to characterize social analyses of language by the academy. Languages were seen as living in "speech communities," and these tended to be theorized as discrete, self-defined, coherent entities, held together by a homogeneous competence or grammar shared identically and equally among all the members. This abstract idea of the speech community seemed to reflect, among other things, the utopian way modern nations conceive of themselves as what Benedict Anderson calls "imagined communities."[3] In a book of that title, Anderson observes that with the possible exception of what he calls "primordial villages," human communities exist as *imagined* entities in which people "will never know most of their fellow-members, meet them or even hear of them, yet in the minds of each lives the image of their communion." "Communities are distinguished," he goes on to say, "not by their falsity/genuineness, but by *the style in which they are imagined*" (15; emphasis mine). Anderson proposes three features that characterize the style in which the modern nation is imagined. First, it is imagined as *limited,* by "finite, if elastic, boundaries"; second, it is imagined as *sovereign;* and, third, it is imagined as *fraternal,* "a deep, horizontal comradeship" for which millions of people are prepared "not so much to kill as willingly to die" (15). As the image suggests, the nation-community is embodied metonymically in the finite, sovereign, fraternal figure of the citizen-soldier.

Anderson argues that European bourgeoisies were distinguished by their ability   19
to "achieve solidarity on an essentially imagined basis" (74) on a scale far greater than that of elites of other times and places. Writing and literacy play a central role in this argument. Anderson maintains, as have others, that the main instrument that made bourgeois nation-building projects possible was print capitalism. The commercial circulation of books in the various European vernaculars, he argues, was

what first created the invisible networks that would eventually constitute the literate elites and those they ruled as nations. (Estimates are that 180 million books were put into circulation in Europe between the years 1500 and 1600 alone.)

Now obviously this style of imagining of modern nations, as Anderson describes it, is strongly utopian, embodying values like equality, fraternity, liberty, which the societies often profess but systematically fail to realize. The prototype of the modern nation as imagined community was, it seemed to me, mirrored in ways people thought about language and the speech community. Many commentators have pointed out how modern views of language as code and competence assume a unified and homogeneous social world in which language exists as a shared patrimony—as a device, precisely, for imagining community. An image of a universally shared literacy is also part of the picture. The prototypical manifestation of language is generally taken to be the speech of individual adult native speakers face-to-face (as in Saussure's famous diagram) in monolingual, even monodialectal situations—in short, the most homogeneous case linguistically and socially. The same goes for written communication. Now one could certainly imagine a theory that assumed different things—that argued, for instance, that the most revealing speech situation for understanding language was one involving a gathering of people each of whom spoke two languages and understood a third and held only one language in common with any of the others. It depends on what workings of language you want to see or want to see first, on what you choose to define as normative.

In keeping with autonomous, fraternal models of community, analyses of language use commonly assume that principles of cooperation and shared understanding are normally in effect. Descriptions of interactions between people in conversation, classrooms, medical and bureaucratic settings, readily take it for granted that the situation is governed by a single set of rules or norms shared by all participants. The analysis focuses then on how those rules produce or fail to produce an orderly, coherent exchange. Models involving games and moves are often used to describe interactions. Despite whatever conflicts or systematic social differences might be in play, it is assumed that all participants are engaged in the same game and that the game is the same for all players. Often it is. But of course it often is not, as, for example, when speakers are from different classes or cultures, or one party is exercising authority and another is submitting to it or questioning it. Last year one of my children moved to a new elementary school that had more open classrooms and more flexible curricula than the conventional school he started out in. A few days into the term, we asked him what it was like at the new school. "Well," he said, "they're a lot nicer, and they have a lot less rules. But know *why* they're nicer?" "Why?" I asked. "So you'll obey all the rules they don't have," he replied. This is a very coherent analysis with considerable elegance and explanatory power, but probably not the one his teacher would have given.

When linguistic (or literate) interaction is described in terms of orderliness, games, moves, or scripts, usually only legitimate moves are actually named as part of the system, where legitimacy is defined from the point of view of the party in authority—regardless of what other parties might see themselves as doing. Teacher-pupil language, for example, tends to be described almost entirely from the point of view of the teacher and teaching, not from the point of view of pupils and pupiling (the word doesn't even exist, though the thing certainly does). If a classroom is analyzed as a social world unified and homogenized with respect to the teacher, whatever students do other than what the teacher specifies is invisible or anomalous to the analysis. This can be true in practice as well. On several occasions my fourth grader, the one busy obeying all the rules they didn't have, was given writing assignments that took the form of answering a series of questions to build up a paragraph. These questions often asked him to identify with the interests of those in power over him—parents, teachers, doctors, public authorities. He invariably sought ways to resist or subvert these assignments. One assignment, for instance, called for imagining "a helpful invention." The students were asked to write single-sentence responses to the following questions:

> What kind of invention would help you?
> How would it help you?
> Why would you need it?
> What would it look like?
> Would other people be able to use it also?
> What would be an invention to help your teacher?
> What would be an invention to help your parents?

Manuel's reply read as follows:

> A grate adventchin
>
> Some inventchins are GRATE!!!!!!!!!!! My inventchin would be a shot that would put every thing you learn at school in your brain. It would help me by letting me graduate right now!! I would need it because it would let me play with my friends, go on vacachin and, do fun a lot more. It would look like a regular shot. Ather peaple would use to. This inventchin would help my teacher parents get away from a lot of work. I think a shot like this would be GRATE!

Despite the spelling, the assignment received the usual star to indicate the task had been fulfilled in an acceptable way. No recognition was available, however, of the humor, the attempt to be critical or contestatory, to parody the structures of authority. On that score, Manuel's luck was only slightly better than Guaman Poma's. What is the place of unsolicited oppositional discourse, parody, resistance, critique in the imagined classroom community? Are teachers supposed to feel that their teaching has been most successful when they have eliminated such things and unified the social world, probably in their own image? Who wins when we do that? Who loses?

Such questions may be hypothetical, because in the United States in the 1990s, many teachers find themselves less and less able to do that even if they want to. The composition of the national collectivity is changing and so are the styles, as Anderson put it, in which it is being imagined. In the 1980s in many nation-states, imagined national syntheses that had retained hegemonic force began to dissolve. Internal social groups with histories and lifeways different from the official ones began insisting on those histories and lifeways *as part of their citizenship,* as the very mode of their membership in the national collectivity. In their dialogues with dominant institutions, many groups began asserting a rhetoric of belonging that made demands beyond those of representation and basic rights granted from above. In universities we started to hear, "I don't just want you to let me be here, I want to belong here; this institution should belong to me as much as it does to anyone else." Institutions have responded with, among other things, rhetorics of diversity and multiculturalism whose import at this moment is up for grabs across the ideological spectrum.

These shifts are being lived out by everyone working in education today, and 24 everyone is challenged by them in one way or another. Those of us committed to educational democracy are particularly challenged as that notion finds itself besieged on the public agenda. Many of those who govern us display, openly, their interest in a quiescent, ignorant, manipulable electorate. Even as an ideal, the concept of an enlightened citizenry seems to have disappeared from the national imagination. A couple of years ago the university where I work went through an intense and wrenching debate over a narrowly defined Western-culture requirement that had been instituted there in 1980. It kept boiling down to a debate over the ideas of national patrimony, cultural citizenship, and imagined community. In the end, the requirement was transformed into a much more broadly defined course called Cultures, Ideas, Values.[4] In the context of the change, a new course was designed that centered on the Americas and the multiple cultural histories (including European ones) that have intersected here. As you can imagine, the course attracted a very diverse student body. The classroom functioned not like a homogeneous community or a horizontal alliance but like a contact zone. Every single text we read stood in specific historical relationships to the students in the class, but the range and variety of historical relationships in play were enormous. Everybody had a stake in nearly everything we read, but the range and kind of stakes varied widely.

It was the most exciting teaching we had ever done, and also the hardest. We were 25 struck, for example, at how anomalous the formal lecture became in a contact zone (who can forget Atahuallpa throwing down the Bible because it would not speak to him?). The lecturer's traditional (imagined) task—unifying the world in the class's eyes by means of a monologue that rings equally coherent, revealing, and true for all, forging an ad hoc community, homogeneous with respect to one's own words—this task became not only impossible but anomalous and unimaginable. Instead, one had to work in the knowledge that whatever one said was going to be systematically received in radically heterogeneous ways that we were neither able nor entitled to prescribe.

The very nature of the course put ideas and identities on the line. All the students 26 in the class had the experience, for example, of hearing their culture discussed and objectified in ways that horrified them; all the students saw their roots traced back to legacies of both glory and shame; all the students experienced face-to-face the ignorance and incomprehension, and occasionally the hostility, of others. In the absence of community values and the hope of synthesis, it was easy to forget the positives; the fact, for instance, that kinds of marginalization once taken for granted were gone. Virtually every student was having the experience of seeing the world described with him or her in it. Along with rage, incomprehension, and pain, there were exhilarating moments of wonder and revelation, mutual understanding, and new wisdom—the joys of the contact zone. The sufferings and revelations were, at different moments to be sure, experienced by every student. No one was excluded, and no one was safe.

The fact that no one was safe made all of us involved in the course appreciate the 27 importance of what we came to call "safe houses." We used the term to refer to social and intellectual spaces where groups can constitute themselves as horizontal, homogeneous, sovereign communities with high degrees of trust, shared understandings, temporary protection from legacies of oppression. This is why, as we realized, multicultural curricula should not seek to replace ethnic or women's studies, for example. Where there are legacies of subordination, groups need places for healing and mutual recognition, safe houses in which to construct shared understandings, knowledges, claims on the world that they can then bring into the contact zone.

Meanwhile, our job in the Americas course remains to figure out how to make that crossroads the best site for learning that it can be. We are looking for the pedagogical arts of the contact zone. These will include, we are sure, exercises in storytelling and in identifying with the ideas, interests, histories, and attitudes of others; experiments in transculturation and collaborative work and in the arts of critique, parody, and comparison (including unseemly comparisons between elite and vernacular cultural forms); the redemption of the oral; ways for people to engage with suppressed aspects of history (including their own histories), ways to move *into and out of* rhetorics of authenticity; ground rules for communication across lines of difference and hierarchy that go beyond politeness but maintain mutual respect; a systematic approach to the all-important concept of *cultural mediation*. These arts were in play in every room at the extraordinary Pittsburgh conference on literacy. I learned a lot about them there, and I am thankful.

WORKS CITED

Adorno, Rolena. *Guaman Poma de Ayala: Writing and Resistance in Colonial Peru.* Austin: U of Texas P, 1986.

Anderson, Benedict. *Imagined Communities: Reflections on the Origins and Spread of Nationalism.* London: Verso, 1984.

Garcilaso de la Vega, El Inca. *Royal Commentaries of the Incas.* 1613. Austin: U of Texas P, 1966.

Guaman Poma de Ayala, Felipe. *El primer nueva corónica y buen gobierno.* Manuscript. Ed. John Murra and Rolena Adorno. Mexico: Siglo XXI, 1980.

Pratt, Mary Louise. "Linguistic Utopias." *The Linguistics of Writing.* Ed. Nigel Fabb et al. Manchester: Manchester UP, 1987. 48–66.

Treviño, Gloria. "Cultural Ambivalence in Early Chicano Prose Fiction." Diss. Stanford U, 1985.

NOTES

1. For an introduction in English to these and other aspects of Guaman Poma's work, see Rolena Adorno. Adorno and Mercedes Lopez-Baralt pioneered the study of Andean symbolic systems in Guaman Poma.

2. It is far from clear that the *Royal Commentaries* was as benign as the Spanish seemed to assume. The book certainly played a role in maintaining the identity and aspirations of indigenous elites in the Andes. In the mid–eighteenth century, a new edition of the *Royal Commentaries* was suppressed by Spanish authorities because its preface included a prophecy by Sir Walter Raleigh that the English would invade Peru and restore the Inca monarchy.

3. The discussion of community here is summarized from my essay "Linguistic Utopias."

4. For information about this program and the contents of courses taught in it, write Program in Cultures, Ideas, Values (CIV), Stanford Univ., Stanford, CA 94305.

Working with the Text

1. Pratt uses the example of her son's education through baseball cards to suggest how we learn to "read" texts—to decode their various intricacies and to make meaning of the whole through understanding the many different parts. How does this idea of learning to "read" relate to Guaman Poma's *The First New Chronicle and Good Government*? What does Pratt mean when she says the "letter got there, only 350 years too late, a miracle and a terrible tragedy" (¶ 6)?

2. What is a "contact zone," in Pratt's terminology? What contact zones have you been part of?

3. In paragraph 10 Pratt distinguishes "ethnographic texts" from "autoethnographic texts." Why is the reception of autoethnographic texts "highly indeterminate"? Why can they be harder for their intended audience to "read" than ethnographic texts? In what sense can they be more authentic than ethnographic texts?

4. How do autoethnographic texts function within contact zones? Pratt notes the "parodic, oppositional representation" of part of the *New Chronicle* that "mirrors back to the Spanish . . . an image of themselves that they often suppress and will therefore surely recognize" (¶ 11). What is the purpose of such representations within contact zones?

5. Pratt refers to the term *transculturation,* coined in the 1940s "to replace overly reductive concepts of acculturation and assimilation" (¶ 13). How does this concept relate to her larger thesis? What are some examples of transculturation in the United States?

6. In paragraph 17 Pratt notes "the transnationalized metropolis of the United States" as a center for writing in the contact zone. Why are "the literate arts of the contact zone . . . becoming more widely visible, more pressing, and . . . more decipherable to those who once would have ignored them in defense of a stable, centered sense of knowledge and reality"? How does Pratt use the *New Chronicle* to represent these contemporary texts? Choose at least one other text you have read in this book so far and consider it in light of Pratt's terminology. How is your example a work expressive of a "contact zone"? What makes different kinds of writing by traditionally marginalized groups more "visible" than in the past?

7. Can you have a contact zone online? If you spend time in any virtual spaces (IRC, chat rooms, MUDs or MVOs), think about these spaces in light of Pratt's arguments. Do circumstances of "asymmetrical relations of power" change online? Are there asymmetries of power? Do social hierarchies in "real life" disappear online?

AN ENGLISH-CHINESE PHRASE BOOK

WONG SAM AND ASSISTANTS

■ The following phrase book appeared in *The Big Aiiieeeee: An Anthology of Chinese-American and Japanese-American Literature,* edited by Jeffrey Paul Chan, Frank Chin, Lawson Fusao Inada, and Shawn Wang. As the introductory note suggests, the phrase book was developed in the 1870s. The translations that it includes reveal a great deal about the life of Chinese immigrants during that era and their interactions with English-speaking Americans.

WONG SAM AND ASSISTANTS

Who was Wong Sam? Who were his assistants? We don't know. We don't   1
know how they convinced Wells, Fargo to print and distribute the bilingual *An English-Chinese Phrase Book* in its 130 offices throughout the West in towns where Chinamen lived and worked. We do know that whoever he was, Wong Sam revised the 1875 edition two years later, and Wells, Fargo published and distributed this larger version of the *Phrase Book* in more than two hundred towns with Chinese American populations.

This is not the kind of phrase book used alphabetically by subject. The Chinese   2
learn writing, painting, philosophy, [and] martial arts through a process of memorization, recitation, and internalization of specific "sets." In the *Phrase Book,* the sets contain strategy and tactics for business and criminal law, and for dealing with white people in general. These sets are "fast," unlike those of *The Analects* of Confucius, which take years—a lifetime—to internalize. No, these sets are meant to be memorized quickly, fun to recite, and internalized by the time a Chinaman has his first experience with a white man.

Try these phrases out loud with a different voice for every other line, and it will   3
be instantly apparent that Wong Sam and Assistants' tactics and strategy for dealing with the white man's application of the law do not include submission, acculturation, and assimilation. The Christian prayers found at the back of the *Phrase Book* are themselves a strategy for raising money to publish the book.

Eighteen seventy-five.   4

Rye Patch, Nevada. Salem, Oregon. Sierra City, California. You have to do business. Get from one place to another, buy clothes, secure licenses. Have an answer for the cops when they ask why your friend is dead on your doorstep. Read these sets. Memorize them. Recite them. Free-associate with them, riff with them and discover how they work. Internalize them until all the phrases are instinct. Wong Sam and his assistants compiled a book of phrases that prepared the Chinese for any situation, anywhere in the American West. The *Phrase Book* is that set. Free! At any Wells, Fargo office.   5

An English-Chinese Phrase Book

你 有 乜 貨 物 出 賣
What goods have you for sale?

樣 樣 都 有
I have all kinds.

我 想 買 條 好 褲
I want to get a pair of your best pants.

你 愛 點 樣 價 銀
What do you ask for them?

你 舱 減 少 些
Can you take less for them?

先 生　不 舱
I cannot, sir.

沒 還 有 好 過 沒 樣 麼
Have you any other kind better than these?

沒 肯 賣 賒 款 麼
Will you sell on credit?

我 賣 現 銀　先 生
No sir, I sell for cash.

倘 沒 俾 好 貨 過 我　我 時
時 與 沒 交 易
I will come to deal with you always if you give
me the best kinds (quality).

為 何 咁 貴
How is it that it is so dear?

煩 沒 與 我 交 易
Please give me your custom.

好 貨 稅 餉 太 重　另 值 我
本 銀 十 元
Well, sir, it costs us $10, and besides we have
to pay very heavy duty on our best goods.

好 生 意
Is business good?

甚 好　多 謝
Very well, I thank you.

買 客 甚 少
The buyers are very few.

生 意 焉 舱 興 旺
How can the business be prosperous!

有 人 缺 本
Some men lose capital.

有 人 賺 銀
Some men get profits.

價 銀 太 高
The price is too high.

我 唔 舱 俾 得 咁 多
I am not able to pay.

我 賣 甚 公 平
I sell very justly.

孩 子 我 都 不 騙
I don't cheat, even a boy.

自 然 係 眞
Certainly, it is true.

賣 客 甚 多
The sellers are too many.

價 錢 憑 貨 物
The price depends on the goods.

佢 應 當 對 面 講
He ought to speak face to face.

倘若我愛物我再回來
If I want anything I will call on you again.

吩咐攔阻
In order to prevent.

貨物頂好
The goods are first-class.

乜價錢嗎
What is the price?

價錢係真
And the price is fixed.

四元銀一叫順
Four dollars per dozen.

先驗明貨正買
Examine the goods before you buy.

我必先說沒知
I must tell you before.

我有時買來平
Sometimes I bought them cheap.

有時我平賣
Sometimes I sold them cheap.

我如今照市價賣
Now I sell them at market prices.

自然係真實
Certainly, it is true.

因謂稅餉太重
Because the duty is too heavy.

買賣甚艱難
To buy and sell is very difficult.

有時我買淂貴
Sometimes I buy them dear.

因此我賣亦貴
Of course I must sell them dear.

我一樣價錢賣
I sell them at one price.

中意咁多就買咁多
Buy as many as you like.

你要價錢高
You ask too high a price.

唔係價高　先生
It is not dear, sir.

不防我騙汝
Don't fear I am cheating you.

我有鞋帽衣服
I also have clothes, shoes and caps.

你肯俾我看麼
Can you let me see them?

倘你如意看就看　此物不
是好淂
If you like to see, you might see, they are not
very good.

你肯賣平些
Can you sell it cheaper?

你愛幾多
How much do you want?

我如今無
I have none now.

俾貨我看過
Show me some goods.

汝愛幾多銀
What do you charge for it?

乜誰命汝來
Who sent you here for it?

我唔相信汝
I cannot trust you.

我下禮拜俾汝
I shall pay you next week.

我望汝相信我
I hope you will trust me.

我防汝走去
I fear you will run away.

為何汝唔買
Why don't you buy them?

我明日來取
I will come for them to-morrow.

信道理捱欺
Christians bear great trials.

佢強搶我物
He took it from me by violence.

我無意打佢
I struck him accidentally.

我認唔該佢還想來打我
I have made an apology, but still he wants to strike me.

佢無事打我
He assaulted me without provocation.

我賃汝樓要汝包水
I will rent the house if you include the water.

你肯去我包汝回
I Guarantee to bring him back, if he will go.

此人欲搔工銀
The men are striking for wages.

我身分足用
I am content with my situation.

你同佢闕款
You contend with him about the account.

裝滿箱蘋果
The box contains apples.

佢詐病
He feigned to be sick.

女人暈倒在會堂
The lady fainted in church.

佢誓了願
He ended what he said with an oath.

此樓無意燒了
The house was burned by accident.

此樓有意燒了
The house was set on fire by an incendiary.

佢想白認我行李
He tried to obtain my baggage by false pretenses.

佢強搶我泥口
He claimed my mine.

佢強霸我地
He squatted on my lot.

倘佢唔走我定然逐佢出去
I will expel him if he don't leave the place.

幾時滿期
When will the lease expire?

你幾時滿號
When is the expiration of you lease?

我下禮拜四滿號
Next Thursday my month will have expired.

昨日我工滿號一月
Yesterday was the expiration of one month of labor.

我下禮拜四滿號
My month will have expired on Thursday next.

佢簽名于紙上
He indorsed the note.

佢做我認頭
He went my security.

你肯誓願麼
Can you swear to that.

佢誓了願
He has sworn already.

佢誓願幾次
He swore several times.

我保佢前後
I guarantee him back and fore.

我包個樓係好個
I warranted the house to be a good one.

佢在審事堂誓假願
He perjured himself in Court.

佢在衙門誓願官府廳
He gave his oath to the judge in Court.

佢誓假願
He was fined for perjury.

佢託名捉拿
He was arrested for forgery.

倘有材料我可做工之于汝
If you find the materials I will furnish laborers.

倘汝唔賠我定劫汝家物
I will attach his furniture if you idemnify me.

倘若滿號汝無俾我定然封汝舖之契
I will close the mortgage on your store if you don't pay me when the time has expired.

我定封汝舖之契若滿號無俾
I will close the mortgage on your store if you don't pay me when the time has expired.

佢逼勒我可銀
He tries to extort money from me.

汝去假託逼勒佢照 （招）
They are going to extort a confession from him by false pretensions.

逼佢招出
The confession was extorted from him by force.

唬怕勒逼佢招認罪
The confessions were extorted from them by threats

我保佢出監
I bailed him out of jail.

我摘水上船
I bailed the water out of the boat.

佢一仟五佰銀保單
He gave bonds for $1,500.

佢案情昨日十點鐘開審
His case was tried yesterday at 10 A. M.

官府定然定罪于過
The judge will certainly convict him.

佢受大頭人定佢罪
He was convicted by the jury.

佢如今定罪
He is now a convict.

佢取人來見証係眞
He brought a man to prove the fact.

人曰我講所見之事
The man said: "I will testify what I saw."

佢口供已經信了
His testimony was believed.

佢搾洽汝工貝
He will retain your wages.

佢騙了我之工貝
He cheated me out of my wages.

佢誆騙東家
He swindled his employer.

佢騙了我斯文銀
He defrauded me out of my salary.

案情昨日罷了
The case was ended yesterday.

後回審定了罪
He was found guilty, by the last trial.

決 命 佢 去 做 十 秊 苦 工
He will be sent to the penitentiary for
10 years.

佢 已 經 命 去 省 監
He has been sent to the State Prison.

佢 誣 告 我 偷 錶
He falsely accused me of stealing his watch.

汝 犯 了 國 法
You have violated the Constitution of this State.

他 眠 埋 伏 之 地
They were lying in ambush.

佢 被 誤 殺
He came to his death by homicide.

佢 被 夜 盜 謀 殺
He was murdered by a thief.

佢 犯 罪 自 儘
He committed suicide.

佢 受 賊 人 用 繩 索 索 死
He was choked to death with a lasso, by a
robber.

佢 受 人 縊 死
He was strangled to death by a man.

佢 飢 死 在 監
He was starved to death in prison.

佢 在 霜 冷 死
He was frozen to death in the snow.

佢 在 灣 投 水 死
He was going to drown himself in the bay.

後 尋 數 日 捉 治 兇 手
After searching for several days they caught the
murderer.

汝 明 得 係 眞 實
Did they find anything in his possession.

也 有
They did.

佢 受 人 陰 殺
He was killed by an assassin.

佢 想 陰 害 我
He tried to assassinate me.

佢 想 陰 殺 我
He tried to kill me by assassination.

佢 係 功 打 之 人
He is an assaulter.

佢 在 房 淹 死
He was smothered in his room.

佢 捫 死 在 房 裡
He was suffocated in his room.

佢 受 仇 人 用 炮 打 死
He was shot dead by his enemy.

佢 受 朋 友 用 藥 道 死
He was poisoned to death by his friend.

佢 想 用 藥 道 死
He tries to kill him by poisoning.

佢 加 刑 死 在 監
He tries to inflict death by poison.

立 意 攻 擊 禍 害 肉 身
Assault with the intention to do bodily injury.

佢 手 拈 規 例
He took the law in his own hand.

佢 想 奪 去 我 位
He tried to deprive me of my situation.

佢 不 義 搶 去 我 工 銀
He wrongfully deprived me of my wages.

我 夜 間 回 家
I go home at night.

我 也 回 家
I have gone home.

我 去 歸
I went home.

我 在 家 住
I abide at home.

我 在 大 埠 住
I abode at San Francisco.

我 也 曾 在 屋 崙 住
I have lived in Oakland.

我 日 出 起 身
I arise at sunrise.

我 今 早 四 點 鐘 起 身
I arose this morning at 4 o'clock.

我 有 時 上 晝 三 點 起 身
I have arisen at 3 A. M. some mornings.

我 四 點 鐘 醒
I awake at 4 o'clock.

我 今 早 五 點 鐘 醒
I awoke this morning at 5 o'clock.

我 有 時 七 點 鐘 醒
I awaken at 7 A. M. sometimes.

我 七 點 鐘 開 工
I begin work at 7 A. M.

我 上 晝 八 點 鐘 開 工
You began work at 8 A. M.

我 六 點 鐘 開 工
We have begun work at 6 A. M.

我 綁 起 此 麥
We bind the wheat up.

我 綁 治 個 瘡
We bound up the wound.

我 用 鐵 鍊 綁 治 個 孩 子
We have bound that boy with a chain.

汝 毀 了 窗 門
You break windows.

我 毀 了 刀
I broke my knife.

他 毀 了 國 法
They have broken the laws of the State.

丟 佢 下 水
Cast him into the water.

我 捉 個 人 入 監 今 日
We cast a man into p[rison to-day.

人 他 放 出 去
They have cast the man out.

斬 柴 過 個 人
You cut wood for the man.

佢 無 意 斬 了 隻 手
He cut a man's hand off by an accident.

我 斬 倒 此 樹
We have cut the tree down.

乃 日 沒 得 順 便 到 來
What day is the most convenient for you to come?

沒 幾 時 順 便 到 此 處
What day is the most convenient for you to be here?

汝 乃 日 便 到 位
What day is the most convenient for you to be present?

乜 日 沒 到 來
What day can you come?

乃 日 沒 如 意 來 拜 見
What day is the best time for you to call?

幾 時 沒 有 好 機 會 到 此
What day is the best chance for you to get here?

沒 定 乜 日 到 來
What certain day can you arrive?

乃 日 沒 可 艙 起 程
On what day is it possible for you to depart?

乃 日 汝 著 便 起 程
What will be the most suitable day for you to start?

乃 日 汝 可 骹 放 落 工 夫
At what day can you leave the work?

乃 日 汝 可 骹 離 開 事 業
At what day can you get away from your avocation?

乃 日 汝 骹 淂 去
What day can you get away?

我 唔 估 到 汝 來 此 處
I did not think that you would come here.

我 唔 曾 望 汝 到 此
I did not expect that you would be here.

我 唔 估 汝 肯 來
I did not suppose that you would come.

我 唔 知 汝 願 來
I did not know that you would come.

我 唔 估 汝 想 來
I never thought that you would come.

我 唔 估 汝 到 來
I have not been expecting you.

我 唔 估 係 汝
I could not think it were you

你 驚 揚 於 我
You have taken me by surprise.

我 並 無 等 候 見 汝
Well! I never expected to see you.

汝 可 骹 來 淂
Is it possible that you have come?

順 便 來 見
Call in when convenient.

不 過 係 順 便 來 拜 見
I call in because it is convenient.

我 因 為 淂 閒 到 來
I came because I had an opportunity.

我 因 為 順 便 到 來
I came because it was convenient.

一 有 便 處 我 就 到 來
I came at the first opportunity.

我 因 方 便 到 來
My convenience caused me to come.

我 中 意 來
It suits me to come.

因 合 宜 我 來
There is an appropriateness in my coming.

我 合 宜 到 來
There is a fitness in my coming.

我 因 朋 友 唔 來 我 就 來
I came because my friend did not come.

我 咁 樣 做 因 為 我 中 意
I do so because I love to.

我 來 因 我 有 個 好 機 會
I came for I had a splendid chance.

我 來 因 我 有 好 機 會
I came for I had a good chance.

我 估 我 過 時 就 入 來
Well! I thought I would drop in while passing.

我 估 我 行 過 之 時 順 便 入 來 見
Well! I thought I would make a visit while passing.

我 估 庭 昔 過 此 地
Well! I thought I would step in while passing by here.

我 估 我 會 庭 一 時 之 久
Well! I thought I would step in for a moment.

我 來 因 我 有 淂 閒
Oh! I came because my time was not occupied.

我 來 因 我 在 家 無 工 夫 做
Oh! I came because I had nothing to do at home.

我方便因此我来
The commodiousness of the cars enabled me to come conveniently.

你要乜野呀先生
Well, sir! what will you have?

好呀先生我幫沒做乜野
Well, sir! what can I do for you?

你想愛乜野先生
Well, sir! what do you wish?

尊駕沒要乜呀
Well, sir! what do you want?

你想買乜野先生
Well, sir! what do you want to buy?

一擔貨過崙屋每日來回
沒要幾多艮一個月
What will be the charges per month for a vegetable dealer and his two baskets to Oakland and return, daily?

我買沒貨我要沒送到我
處
I buy goods from you, I want you to deliver them to my place.

連箱借與我明日送回沒
Lend to me, with the box too, I will return it to you to-morrow.

我要沒包我出入費用
I want you to pay all my fare of coming and going.

你嫌我貨價錢貴因此沒
唔買
You dislike my goods because it is so dear, and you don't buy.

等幾日然後講沒知
Wait for a few days, then I will tell you.

沒幾時齊備
When will you be ready?

沒肯相信我
Will you trust me?

佢係拐帶之人
He is a kidnapper.

佢係我書管學生頭
He is a monitor in our school.

放牛乳油入碗櫃
Put the butter in the cupboard.

倒白糖出來牛乳盤
Empty the sugar into the milk-pan.

沒愛我幫沒
You want me to help you?

佢內外病症
He is sick in mind and body.

佢心算度即如他手做工
咁辛苦
He is performing hard mental as well as physical labor.

留住他一禮拜工艮等佢
在此長做
I keep back a week's wages in order to secure his stay.

多煩沒俾回我沒所留住
之工艮
Please give me now that portion of my wages which you have withheld from me.

耶穌係我中保
Christ is our mediator.

我高過佢
I am taller than he.

每間店鋪有一個出番之
人能說英話
There is not a store which has not an interpreter -- one who can speak the English language.

Working with the Text

1. According to Chin, the *Phrase Book* contains strategies for dealing with "any situation, anywhere in the American West." What does this selection of phrases tell you about the life of Chinese immigrants in the United States in the 1870s? Try to construct what life might have been like for Chinese immigrants based on the phrase book.

2. Can you imagine why a company like Wells, Fargo—a transportation company something akin to today's UPS or Federal Express—would provide this *Phrase Book* free?

3. Compare the *Phrase Book* to a contemporary phrase book written for tourists visiting another country. How effective are such books in facilitating communication? If phrase books are intended to help non-native speakers "survive" in another country, address how this phrase book might have been connected to Chinese immigrant survival. What larger attitudes and social beliefs are represented (directly or indirectly) in the phrase clusters?

LETTER FROM BIRMINGHAM JAIL

MARTIN LUTHER KING JR.

■ The great civil rights leader Martin Luther King Jr. was born in Atlanta. He graduated from Morehouse College and the Crozer Theological Seminary, later receiving a doctorate in theology from Boston University. As a pastor in Montgomery, Alabama, he was instrumental in organizing a boycott that led to the desegregation of Montgomery's buses in 1956. As president of the Southern Christian Leadership Council, he articulated and advocated a theory of nonviolent protest as a means to rectify racist laws and practices. He continued to fight for civil rights throughout his life and was awarded the Nobel Peace Prize in 1964. Tragically, he was assassinated in Memphis in 1968 at the age of thirty-nine.

In the early 1960s, King led a large contingent of nonviolent protesters in demonstrations to end segregation and legalized racial discrimination in Birmingham, Alabama. Jailed for his activities in Birmingham and also criticized by white moderates who considered the protests too "extreme," King wrote the following famous letter to some of his critics in an attempt to explain and justify his beliefs and actions.

April 16, 1963
Birmingham, Alabama

MY DEAR FELLOW CLERGYMEN:

While confined here in the Birmingham city jail, I came across your recent statement calling my present activities "unwise and untimely." Seldom do I pause to answer criticism of my work and ideas. If I sought to answer all the criticisms that cross my desk, my secretaries would have little time for anything other than such correspondence in the course of the day, and I would have no time for constructive work. But since I feel that you are men of genuine good will and that your criticisms are sincerely set forth, I want to try to answer your statement in what I hope will be patient and reasonable terms.

I think I should indicate why I am here in Birmingham, since you have been in-   2
fluenced by the view which argues against "outsiders coming in." I have the honor of serving as president of the Southern Christian Leadership Conference, an organiza-tion operating in every southern state, with headquarters in Atlanta, Georgia. We have some eighty-five affiliated organizations across the South, and one of them is the Alabama Christian Movement for Human Rights. Frequently we share staff, ed-ucational, and financial resources with our affiliates. Several months ago the affiliate here in Birmingham asked us to be on call to engage in a nonviolent direct-action program if such were deemed necessary. We readily consented, and when the hour came we lived up to our promise. So I, along with several members of my staff, am here because I was invited here. I am here because I have organizational ties here.

But more basically, I am in Birmingham because injustice is here. Just as the   3
prophets of the eighth century B.C. left their villages and carried their "thus saith the Lord" far beyond the boundaries of their home towns, and just as the Apostle Paul left his village of Tarsus and carried the gospel of Jesus Christ to the far corners of the Greco-Roman world, so am I compelled to carry the gospel of freedom beyond my own home town. Like Paul, I must constantly respond to the Macedonian call for aid.

Moreover, I am cognizant of the interrelatedness of all communities and states. I   4
cannot sit idly by in Atlanta and not be concerned about what happens in Birming-ham. Injustice anywhere is a threat to justice everywhere. We are caught in an in-escapable network of mutuality, tied in a single garment of destiny. Whatever affects one directly, affects all indirectly. Never again can we afford to live with the narrow, provincial "outside agitator" idea. Anyone who lives inside the United States can never be considered an outsider anywhere within its bounds.

You deplore the demonstrations taking place in Birmingham. But your state-   5
ment, I am sorry to say, fails to express a similar concern for the conditions that brought about the demonstrations. I am sure that none of you would want to rest content with the superficial kind of social analysis that deals merely with effects and does not grapple with underlying causes. It is unfortunate that demonstrations are taking place in Birmingham, but it is even more unfortunate that the city's white power structure left the Negro community with no alternative.

In any nonviolent campaign there are four basic steps: collection of the facts to   6
determine whether injustices exist; negotiation; self-purification; and direct action. We have gone through all these steps in Birmingham. There can be no gainsaying the fact that racial injustice engulfs this community. Birmingham is probably the most thoroughly segregated city in the United States. Its ugly record of brutality is widely known. Negroes have experienced grossly unjust treatment in the courts. There have been more unsolved bombings of Negro homes and churches in Birmingham than in any other city in the nation. These are the hard, brutal facts of the case. On the basis of these conditions, Negro leaders sought to negotiate with the city fathers. But the latter consistently refused to engage in good-faith negotiation.

Then, last September, came the opportunity to talk with leaders of Birmingham's 7 economic community. In the course of the negotiations, certain promises were made by the merchants—for example, to remove the stores' humiliating racial signs. On the basis of these promises, the Reverend Fred Shuttlesworth and the leaders of the Alabama Christian Movement for Human Rights agreed to a moratorium on all demonstrations. As the weeks and months went by, we realized that we were the victims of a broken promise. A few signs, briefly removed, returned; the others remained.

As in so many past experiences, our hopes had been blasted, and the shadow of 8 deep disappointment settled upon us. We had no alternative except to prepare for direct action, whereby we would present our very bodies as a means of laying our case before the conscience of the local and the national community. Mindful of the difficulties involved, we decided to undertake a process of self-purification. We began a series of workshops on nonviolence, and we repeatedly asked ourselves: "Are you able to accept blows without retaliation?" "Are you able to endure the ordeal of jail?" We decided to schedule our direct-action program for the Easter season, realizing that except for Christmas, this is the main shopping period of the year. Knowing that a strong economic-withdrawal program would be the by-product of direct action, we felt that this would be the best time to bring pressure to bear on the merchants for the needed change.

Then it occurred to us that Birmingham's mayoral election was coming up in 9 March, and we speedily decided to postpone action until after election day. When we discovered that the Commissioner of Public Safety, Eugene "Bull" Connor, had piled up enough votes to be in the run-off, we decided again to postpone action until the day after the run-off so that the demonstrations could not be used to cloud the issues. Like many others, we waited to see Mr. Connor defeated, and to this end we endured postponement after postponement. Having aided in this community need, we felt that our direct-action program could be delayed no longer.

You may well ask, "Why direct action? Why sit-ins, marches, and so forth? Isn't 10 negotiation a better path?" You are quite right in calling for negotiation. Indeed, this is the very purpose of direct action. Nonviolent direct action seeks to create such a crisis and foster such a tension that a community which has constantly refused to negotiate is forced to confront the issue. It seeks so to dramatize the issue that it can no longer be ignored. My citing the creation of tension as part of the work of the nonviolent-resister may sound rather shocking. But I must confess that I am not afraid of the word "tension." I have earnestly opposed violent tension, but there is a type of constructive, nonviolent tension which is necessary for growth. Just as Socrates felt that it was necessary to create a tension in the mind so that individuals could rise from the bondage of myths and half-truths to the unfettered realm of creative analysis and objective appraisal, so must we see the need for nonviolent gadflies to create the kind of tension in society that will help men rise from the dark depths of prejudice and racism to the majestic heights of understanding and brotherhood.

The purpose of our direct-action program is to create a situation so crisis packed 11 that it will inevitably open the door to negotiation. I therefore concur with you in your call for negotiation. Too long has our beloved Southland been bogged down in a tragic effort to live in monologue rather than dialogue.

One of the basic points in your statement is that the action that I and my associates have taken in Birmingham is untimely. Some have asked: "Why didn't you give the new city administration time to act?" The only answer that I can give to this query is that the new Birmingham administration must be prodded about as much as the outgoing one, before it will act. We are sadly mistaken if we feel that the election of Albert Boutwell as mayor will bring the millennium to Birmingham. While Mr. Boutwell is a much more gentle person than Mr. Connor, they are both segregationists, dedicated to maintenance of the status quo. I have hoped that Mr. Boutwell will be reasonable enough to see the futility of massive resistance to desegregation. But he will not see this without pressure from devotees of civil rights. My friends, I must say to you that we have not made a single gain in civil rights without determined legal and nonviolent pressure. Lamentably, it is an historical fact that privileged groups seldom give up their privileges voluntarily. Individuals may see the moral light and voluntarily give up their unjust posture; but, as Reinhold Niebuhr has reminded us, groups tend to be more immoral than individuals.

We know through painful experience that freedom is never voluntarily given by the oppressor; it must be demanded by the oppressed. Frankly, I have yet to engage in a direct-action campaign that was "well timed" in view of those who have not suffered unduly from the disease of segregation. For years now I have heard the word "Wait!" It rings in the ear of every Negro with piercing familiarity. This "Wait" has almost always meant "Never." We must come to see, with one of our distinguished jurists, that "justice too long delayed is justice denied."

We have waited for more than 340 years for our constitutional and God-given rights. The nations of Asia and Africa are moving with jetlike speed toward gaining political independence, but we still creep at horse-and-buggy pace toward gaining a cup of coffee at a lunch counter. Perhaps it is easy for those who have never felt the stinging darts of segregation to say, "Wait." But when you have seen vicious mobs lynch your mothers and fathers at will and drown your sisters and brothers at whim; when you have seen hate-filled policemen curse, kick, and even kill your black brothers and sisters; when you see the vast majority of your twenty million Negro brothers smothering in an airtight cage of poverty in the midst of an affluent society; when you suddenly find your tongue twisted and your speech stammering as you seek to explain to your six-year-old daughter why she can't go to the public amusement park that has just been advertised on television, and see tears welling up in her eyes when she is told that Funtown is closed to colored children, and see ominous clouds of inferiority beginning to form in her little mental sky, and see her beginning to distort her personality by developing an unconscious bitterness toward white people; when you have to concoct an answer for a five-year-old son who is asking, "Daddy, why do white people treat colored people so mean?"; when you take a cross-country drive and find it necessary to sleep night after night in the uncomfortable corners of your automobile because no motel will accept you; when you are humiliated day in and day out by nagging signs reading "white" and "colored"; when your first name becomes "nigger," your middle name becomes "boy" (however old you are) and your last name becomes "John," and your wife and mother are never given the respected title "Mrs."; when you are harried by day and haunted by night by the fact that you are a Negro, living constantly at tiptoe stance, never quite knowing what to expect next, and are plagued with inner fears and outer resentments;

when you are forever fighting a degenerating sense of "nobodiness"—then you will understand why we find it difficult to wait. There comes a time when the cup of endurance runs over, and men are no longer willing to be plunged into the abyss of despair. I hope, sirs, you can understand our legitimate and unavoidable impatience.

You express a great deal of anxiety over our willingness to break laws. This is certainly a legitimate concern. Since we so diligently urge people to obey the Supreme Court's decision of 1954 outlawing segregation in the public schools, at first glance it may seem rather paradoxical for us consciously to break laws. One may well ask: "How can you advocate breaking some laws and obeying others?" The answer lies in the fact that there are two types of laws: just and unjust. I would be the first to advocate obeying just laws. One has not only a legal but a moral responsibility to obey just laws. Conversely, one has a moral responsibility to disobey unjust laws. I would agree with St. Augustine that "an unjust law is no law at all."

Now, what is the difference between the two? How does one determine whether a law is just or unjust? A just law is a man-made code that squares with the moral law or the law of God. An unjust law is a code that is out of harmony with the moral law. To put it in the terms of St. Thomas Aquinas: An unjust law is a human law that is not rooted in eternal law and natural law. Any law that uplifts human personality is just. Any law that degrades human personality is unjust. All segregation statutes are unjust because segregation distorts the soul and damages the personality. It gives the segregator a false sense of superiority and the segregated a false sense of inferiority. Segregation, to use the terminology of the Jewish philosopher Martin Buber, substitutes an "I-it" relationship for an "I-thou" relationship and ends up relegating persons to the status of things. Hence segregation is not only politically, economically, and sociologically unsound, it is morally wrong and sinful. Paul Tillich has said that sin is separation. Is not segregation an existential expression of man's tragic separation, his awful estrangement, his terrible sinfulness? Thus it is that I can urge men to obey the 1954 decision of the Supreme Court, for it is morally right; and I can urge them to disobey segregation ordinances, for they are morally wrong.

Let us consider a more concrete example of just and unjust laws. An unjust law is a code that a numerical or power majority group compels a minority group to obey but does not make binding on itself. This is *difference* made legal. By the same token, a just law is a code that a majority compels a minority to follow and that it is willing to follow itself. This is *sameness* made legal.

Let me give another explanation. A law is unjust if it is inflicted on a minority that, as a result of being denied the right to vote, had no part in enacting or devising the law. Who can say that the legislature of Alabama which set up that state's segregation laws was democratically elected? Throughout Alabama all sorts of devious methods are used to prevent Negroes from becoming registered voters, and there are some counties in which, even though Negroes constitute a majority of the population, not a single Negro is registered. Can any law enacted under such circumstances be considered democratically structured?

Sometimes a law is just on its face and unjust in its application. For instance, I have been arrested on a charge of parading without a permit. Now, there is nothing wrong in having an ordinance which requires a permit for a parade. But such an ordinance becomes unjust when it is used to maintain segregation and to deny citizens the First-Amendment privilege of peaceful assembly and protest.

I hope you are able to see the distinction I am trying to point out. In no sense do   20
I advocate evading or defying the law, as would the rabid segregationist. That would
lead to anarchy. One who breaks an unjust law must do so openly, lovingly, and with
a willingness to accept the penalty. I submit that an individual who breaks a law that
conscience tells him is unjust, and who willingly accepts the penalty of imprison-
ment in order to arouse the conscience of the community over its injustice, is in reality expressing the highest respect for law.

Of course, there is nothing new about this kind of civil disobedience. It was evi-   21
denced sublimely in the refusal of Shadrach, Meshach, and Abednego to obey the
laws of Nebuchadnezzar, on the ground that a higher moral law was at stake. It was
practiced superbly by the early Christians, who were willing to face hungry lions
and the excruciating pain of chopping blocks rather than submit to certain unjust
laws of the Roman Empire. To a degree, academic freedom is a reality today because
Socrates practiced civil disobedience. In our own nation, the Boston Tea Party represented a massive act of civil disobedience.

We should never forget that everything Adolf Hitler did in Germany was "legal"   22
and everything the Hungarian freedom fighters did in Hungary was "illegal." It was
"illegal" to aid and comfort a Jew in Hitler's Germany. Even so, I am sure that, had I
lived in Germany at the time, I would have aided and comforted my Jewish brothers. If today I lived in a Communist country where certain principles dear to the
Christian faith are suppressed, I would openly advocate disobeying that country's
anti-religious laws.

I must make two honest confessions to you, my Christian and Jewish brothers.   23
First, I must confess that over the past few years I have been gravely disappointed
with the white moderate. I have almost reached the regrettable conclusion that the
Negro's great stumbling block in his stride toward freedom is not the White Citizen's
Counciler or the Ku Klux Klanner, but the white moderate, who is more devoted to
"order" than to justice; who prefers a negative peace which is the absence of tension
to a positive peace which is the presence of justice; who constantly says, "I agree with
you in the goal you seek, but I cannot agree with your methods of direct action";
who paternalistically believes he can set the timetable for another man's freedom;
who lives by a mythical concept of time and who constantly advises the Negro to
wait for a "more convenient season." Shallow understanding from people of good
will is more frustrating than absolute misunderstanding from people of ill will.
Lukewarm acceptance is much more bewildering than outright rejection.

I had hoped that the white moderate would understand that law and order exist   24
for the purpose of establishing justice and that when they fail in this purpose they
become the dangerously structured dams that block the flow of social progress. I
had hoped that the white moderate would understand that the present tension in
the South is a necessary phase of the transition from an obnoxious negative peace,
in which the Negro passively accepted his unjust plight, to a substantive and positive
peace, in which all men will respect the dignity and worth of human personality.
Actually, we who engage in nonviolent direct action are not the creators of tension.
We merely bring to the surface the hidden tension that is already alive. We bring it
out in the open, where it can be seen and dealt with. Like a boil that can never be
cured so long as it is covered up but must be opened with all its ugliness to the natural medicines of air and light, injustice must be exposed, with all the tension its

exposure creates, to the light of human conscience and the air of national opinion, before it can be cured.

In your statement you assert that our actions, even though peaceful, must be condemned because they precipitate violence. But is this a logical assertion? Isn't this like condemning a robbed man because his possession of money precipitated the evil act of robbery? Isn't this like condemning Socrates because his unswerving commitment to truth and his philosophical inquiries precipitated the act by the misguided populace in which they made him drink hemlock? Isn't this like condemning Jesus because his unique God-consciousness and never-ceasing devotion to God's will precipitated the evil act of crucifixion? We must come to see that, as the federal courts have consistently affirmed, it is wrong to urge an individual to cease his efforts to gain his basic constitutional rights because the quest may precipitate violence. Society must protect the robbed and punish the robber. 25

I had also hoped that the white moderate would reject the myth concerning time in relation to the struggle for freedom. I have just received a letter from a white brother in Texas. He writes: "All Christians know that the colored people will receive equal rights eventually, but it is possible that you are in too great a religious hurry. It has taken Christianity almost two thousand years to accomplish what it has. The teachings of Christ take time to come to earth." Such an attitude stems from a tragic misconception of time, from the strangely irrational notion that there is something in the very flow of time that will inevitably cure all ills. Actually, time itself is neutral; it can be used either destructively or constructively. More and more I feel that the people of ill will have used time much more effectively than have the people of good will. We will have to repent in this generation not merely for the hateful words and actions of the bad people, but for the appalling silence of the good people. Human progress never rolls in on wheels of inevitability; it comes through the tireless efforts of men willing to be co-workers with God, and without this hard work, time itself becomes an ally of the forces of stagnation. We must use time creatively, in the knowledge that the time is always ripe to do right. Now is the time to make real the promise of democracy and transform our pending national elegy into a creative psalm of brotherhood. Now is the time to lift our national policy from the quicksand of racial injustice to the solid rock of human dignity. 26

You speak of our activity in Birmingham as extreme. At first I was rather disappointed that fellow clergymen would see my nonviolent efforts as those of an extremist. I began thinking about the fact that I stand in the middle of two opposing forces in the Negro community. One is a force of complacency, made up in part of Negroes who, as a result of long years of oppression, are so drained of self-respect and a sense of "somebodiness" that they have adjusted to segregation; and in part of a few middle-class Negroes who, because of a degree of academic and economic security and because in some ways they profit by segregation, have become insensitive to the problems of the masses. The other force is one of bitterness and hatred, and it comes perilously close to advocating violence. It is expressed in the various black nationalist groups that are springing up across the nation, the largest and best-known being Elijah Muhammad's Muslim movement. Nourished by the Negro's frustration over the continued existence of racial discrimination, this movement is made up of people who have lost faith in America, who have absolutely repudiated Christianity, and who have concluded that the white man is an incorrigible "devil." 27

I have tried to stand between these two forces, saying that we need emulate nei- 28
ther the "do-nothingism" of the complacent nor the hatred and despair of the black
nationalist. For there is the more excellent way of love and nonviolent protest. I am
grateful to God that, through the influence of the Negro church, the way of nonviolence became an integral part of our struggle.

If this philosophy had not emerged, by now many streets of the South would, I 29
am convinced, be flowing with blood. And I am further convinced that if our white
brothers dismiss as "rabble-rousers" and "outside agitators" those of us who employ
nonviolent direct action, and if they refuse to support our nonviolent efforts, millions of Negroes will, out of frustration and despair, seek solace and security in
black-nationalist ideologies—a development that would inevitably lead to a frightening racial nightmare.

Oppressed people cannot remain oppressed forever. The yearning for freedom 30
eventually manifests itself, and that is what has happened to the American Negro.
Something within has reminded him of his birthright of freedom, and something
without has reminded him that it can be gained. Consciously or unconsciously, he
has been caught up by the *Zeitgeist,* and with his black brothers of Africa and his
brown and yellow brothers of Asia, South America, and the Caribbean, the United
States Negro is moving with a sense of great urgency toward the promised land of
racial justice. If one recognizes this vital urge that has engulfed the Negro community, one should readily understand why public demonstrations are taking place.
The Negro has many pent-up resentments and latent frustrations, and he must release them. So let him march; let him make prayer pilgrimages to the city hall; let
him go on freedom rides—and try to understand why he must do so. If his re-
pressed emotions are not released in nonviolent ways, they will seek expression
through violence; this is not a threat but a fact of history. So I have not said to my
people, "Get rid of your discontent." Rather, I have tried to say that this normal and
healthy discontent can be channeled into the creative outlet of nonviolent direct action. And now this approach is being termed extremist.

But though I was initially disappointed at being categorized as an extremist, as I 31
continued to think about the matter I gradually gained a measure of satisfaction
from the label. Was not Jesus an extremist for love: "Love your enemies, bless them
that curse you, do good to them that hate you, and pray for them which despitefully
use you, and persecute you." Was not Amos an extremist for justice: "Let justice roll
down like waters and righteousness like an ever-flowing stream." Was not Paul an
extremist for the Christian gospel: "I bear in my body the marks of the Lord Jesus."
Was not Martin Luther an extremist: "Here I stand; I cannot do otherwise, so help
me God." And John Bunyan: "I will stay in jail to the end of my days before I make a
butchery of my conscience." And Abraham Lincoln: "This nation cannot survive
half slave and half free." And Thomas Jefferson: "We hold these truths to be self-
evident, that all men are created equal. . . ." So the question is not whether we will be
extremists, but what kind of extremists we will be. Will we be extremists for hate or
for love? Will we be extremists for the preservation of injustice or for the extension
of justice? In that dramatic scene on Calvary's hill three men were crucified. We
must never forget that all three were crucified for the same crime—the crime of ex-
tremism. Two were extremists for immorality, and thus fell below their environment. The other, Jesus Christ, was an extremist for love, truth, and goodness, and

thereby rose above his environment. Perhaps the South, the nation, and the world are in dire need of creative extremists.

I had hoped that the white moderate would see this need. Perhaps I was too op- 32 timistic; perhaps I expected too much. I suppose I should have realized that few members of the oppressor race can understand the deep groans and passionate yearnings of the oppressed race, and still fewer have the vision to see that injustice must be rooted out by strong, persistent, and determined action. I am thankful, however, that some of our white brothers in the South have grasped the meaning of this social revolution and committed themselves to it. They are still all too few in quantity, but they are big in quality. Some—such as Ralph McGill, Lillian Smith, Harry Golden, James McBride Dabbs, Ann Braden, and Sarah Patton Boyle—have written about our struggle in eloquent and prophetic terms. Others have marched with us down nameless streets of the South. They have languished in filthy, roach-infested jails, suffering the abuse and brutality of policemen who view them as "dirty nigger-lovers." Unlike so many of their moderate brothers and sisters, they have recognized the urgency of the moment and sensed the need for powerful "action" antidotes to combat the disease of segregation.

Let me take note of my other major disappointment. I have been so greatly dis- 33 appointed with the white church and its leadership. Of course, there are some notable exceptions. I am not unmindful of the fact that each of you has taken some significant stands on this issue. I commend you, Reverend Stallings, for your Christian stand on this past Sunday, in welcoming Negroes to your worship service on a nonsegregated basis. I commend the Catholic leaders of this state for integrating Spring Hill College several years ago.

But despite these notable exceptions, I must honestly reiterate that I have been 34 disappointed with the church. I do not say this as one of those negative critics who can always find something wrong with the church. I say this as a minister of the gospel, who loves the church; who was nurtured in its bosom; who has been sustained by its spiritual blessings and who will remain true to it as long as the cord of life shall lengthen.

When I was suddenly catapulted into the leadership of the bus protest in Mont- 35 gomery, Alabama, a few years ago, I felt we would be supported by the white church. I felt that the white ministers, priests, and rabbis of the South would be among our strongest allies. Instead, some have been outright opponents, refusing to understand the freedom movement and misrepresenting its leaders; all too many others have been more cautious than courageous and have remained silent behind the anesthetizing security of stained-glass windows.

In spite of my shattered dreams, I came to Birmingham with the hope that the 36 white religious leadership of this community would see the justice of our cause and, with deep moral concern, would serve as the channel through which our just grievances could reach the power structure. I had hoped that each of you would understand. But again I have been disappointed.

I have heard numerous southern religious leaders admonish their worshipers to 37 comply with a desegregation decision because it is the law, but I have longed to hear white ministers declare: "Follow this decree because integration is morally right and because the Negro is your brother." In the midst of blatant injustices inflicted upon the Negro, I have watched white churchmen stand on the sideline and mouth pious irrelevancies and sanctimonious trivialities. In the midst of a mighty struggle to rid our nation of racial and economic injustice, I have heard many ministers say: "Those are social issues, with which the gospel has no real concern." And I have watched many churches commit themselves to a completely otherworldly religion which makes a strange, un-Biblical distinction between body and soul, between the sacred and the secular.

I have traveled the length and breadth of Alabama, Mississippi, and all the other southern states. On sweltering summer days and crisp autumn mornings I have looked at the South's beautiful churches with their lofty spires pointing heavenward. I have beheld the impressive outlines of her massive religious-education buildings. Over and over I have found myself asking: "What kind of people worship here? Who is their God? Where were their voices when the lips of Governor Barnett dripped with words of interposition and nullification? Where were they when Governor Wallace gave a clarion call for defiance and hatred? Where were their voices of support when bruised and weary Negro men and women decided to rise from the dark dungeons of complacency to the bright hills of creative protest?"

Yes, these questions are still in my mind. In deep disappointment I have wept over the laxity of the church. But be assured that my tears have been tears of love. Yes, I love the church. How could I do otherwise? I am in the rather unique position of being the son, the grandson, and the great-grandson of preachers. Yes, I see the church as the body of Christ. But, oh! How we have blemished and scarred that body through social neglect and through fear of being nonconformists.

There was a time when the church was very powerful—in the time when the early Christians rejoiced at being deemed worthy to suffer for what they believed. In those days the church was not merely a thermometer that recorded the ideas and principles of popular opinion; it was a thermostat that transformed the mores of society. Whenever the early Christians entered a town, the people in power became disturbed and immediately sought to convict the Christians for being "disturbers of the peace" and "outside agitators." But the Christians pressed on, in the conviction that they were "a colony of heaven," called to obey God rather than man. Small in number, they were big in commitment. They were too God-intoxicated to be "astronomically intimidated." By their effort and example they brought an end to such ancient evils as infanticide and gladiatorial contests.

Things are different now. So often the contemporary church is a weak, ineffectual voice with an uncertain sound. So often it is an archdefender of the status quo. Far from being disturbed by the presence of the church, the power structure of the average community is consoled by the church's silent—and often even vocal—sanction of things as they are.

But the judgment of God is upon the church as never before. If today's church does not recapture the sacrificial spirit of the early church, it will lose its authenticity, forfeit the loyalty of millions, and be dismissed as an irrelevant social club with no meaning for the twentieth century. Every day I meet young people whose disappointment with the church has turned into outright disgust.

Perhaps I have once again been too optimistic. Is organized religion too inextricably bound to the status quo to save our nation and the world? Perhaps I must turn my faith to the inner spiritual church, the church within the church, as the true *ekklesia* and the hope of the world. But again I am thankful to God that some noble souls from the ranks of organized religion have broken loose from the paralyzing chains of conformity and joined us as active partners in the struggle for freedom. They have left their secure congregations and walked the streets of Albany, Georgia, with us. They have gone down the highways of the South on tortuous rides for freedom. Yes, they have gone to jail with us. Some have been dismissed from their churches, have lost the support of their bishops and fellow ministers. But they have acted in the faith that right defeated is stronger than evil triumphant. Their witness has been the spiritual salt that has preserved the true meaning of the gospel in these troubled times. They have carved a tunnel of hope through the dark mountain of disappointment.

I hope the church as a whole will meet the challenge of this decisive hour. But even if the church does not come to the aid of justice, I have no despair about the future. I have no fear about the outcome of our struggle in Birmingham, even if our motives are at present misunderstood. We will reach the goal of freedom in Birmingham and all over the nation, because the goal of America is freedom. Abused and scorned though we may be, our destiny is tied up with America's destiny. Before the pilgrims landed at Plymouth, we were here. For more than two centuries our forebears labored in this country without wages; they made cotton king; they built the homes of their masters while suffering gross injustice and shameful humiliation—and yet out of a bottomless vitality they continued to thrive and develop. If the inexpressible cruelties of slavery could not stop us, the opposition we now face will surely fail. We will win our freedom because the sacred heritage of our nation and the eternal will of God are embodied in our echoing demands. 44

Before closing I feel impelled to mention one other point in your statement that has troubled me profoundly. You warmly commended the Birmingham police force for keeping "order" and "preventing violence." I doubt that you would have so warmly commended the police force if you had seen its dogs sinking their teeth into unarmed, nonviolent Negroes. I doubt that you would so quickly commend the policemen if you were to observe their ugly and inhumane treatment of Negroes here in the city jail; if you were to watch them push and curse old Negro women and young Negro girls; if you were to see them slap and kick old Negro men and young boys; if you were to observe them, as they did on two occasions, refuse to give us food because we wanted to sing our grace together. I cannot join you in your praise of the Birmingham police department. 45

It is true that the police have exercised a degree of discipline in handling the demonstrators. In this sense they have conducted themselves rather "nonviolently" in public. But for what purpose? To preserve the evil system of segregation. Over the past few years I have consistently preached that nonviolence demands that the means we use must be as pure as the ends we seek. I have tried to make clear that it is wrong to use immoral means to attain moral ends. But now I must affirm that it is just as wrong, or perhaps even more so, to use moral means to preserve immoral ends. Perhaps Mr. Connor and his policemen have been rather nonviolent in public, as was Chief Pritchett in Albany, Georgia, but they have used the moral means of nonviolence to maintain the immoral end of racial injustice. As T. S. Eliot has said, "The last temptation is the greatest treason: To do the right deed for the wrong reason." 46

I wish you had commended the Negro sit-inners and demonstrators of Birming- 47 ham for their sublime courage, their willingness to suffer, and their amazing discipline in the midst of great provocation. One day the South will recognize its real heroes. They will be the James Merediths, with the noble sense of purpose that enables them to face jeering and hostile mobs, and with the agonizing loneliness that characterizes the life of the pioneer. They will be old, oppressed, battered Negro women, symbolized in a seventy-two-year-old woman in Montgomery, Alabama, who rose up with a sense of dignity and with her people decided not to ride segregated buses, and who responded with ungrammatical profundity to one who inquired about her weariness: "My feets is tired, but my soul is at rest." They will be the young high school and college students, the young ministers of the gospel and a host of their elders, courageously and nonviolently sitting in at lunch counters and willingly going to jail for conscience' sake. One day the South will know that when these disinherited children of God sat down at lunch counters, they were in reality standing up for what is best in the American dream and for the most sacred values in our Judaeo-Christian heritage, thereby bringing our nation back to those great wells of democracy which were dug deep by the founding fathers in their formulation of the Constitution and the Declaration of Independence.

Never before have I written so long a letter. I'm afraid it is much too long to take   48
your precious time. I can assure you that it would have been much shorter if I had been writing from a comfortable desk, but what else can one do when he is alone in a narrow jail cell, other than write long letters, think long thoughts, and pray long prayers?

If I have said anything in this letter that overstates the truth and indicates an un-   49
reasonable impatience, I beg you to forgive me. If I have said anything that understates the truth and indicates my having a patience that allows me to settle for anything less than brotherhood, I beg God to forgive me.

I hope this letter finds you strong in the faith. I also hope that circumstances will   50
soon make it possible for me to meet each of you, not as an integrationist or a civil-rights leader but as a fellow clergyman and a Christian brother. Let us all hope that the dark clouds of racial prejudice will soon pass away and the deep fog of misunderstanding will be lifted from our fear-drenched communities, and in some not too distant tomorrow the radiant stars of love and brotherhood will shine over our great nation with all their scintillating beauty.

> Yours for the cause of Peace and Brotherhood,
> Martin Luther King, Jr.

Working with the Text

1. King's letter was written in response to a statement issued by a group of white clergymen criticizing him and his followers for their civil rights activism in Birmingham, Alabama, in 1963. What are the specific criticisms to which King responds in the letter? How would you evaluate the effectiveness of his response?

2. Throughout his letter, King maintains an even, reasonable tone and an attitude of respect, though one sometimes tinged with disappointment. Do you think King had any reason to respond more angrily? (Keep in mind that

during this time Malcolm X and others were advocating for more violent measures to combat racial injustice.) Could King be accused of limiting his success by trying too hard to work through the system?

3. In King's words, "few members of the oppressor race can understand the deep groans and passionate yearnings of the oppressed" (¶ 32). How do you respond to this statement? Do you think that the United States and the world more generally can today be divided into the "oppressor" and the "oppressed"?

4. In what ways do the final three paragraphs provide a strong conclusion to King's letter? Do you think he succeeds in building a bridge across difference?

5. If you have read Mary Louise Pratt's "Arts of the Contact Zone," consider King's letter as an autoethnographic text. In what ways is King merging the idioms of the "conqueror" with "indigenous" idioms to "intervene in" the understanding of the dominant culture?

TALKING PAST EACH OTHER:
BLACK AND WHITE LANGUAGES OF RACE

BOB BLAUNER

■ Born in Chicago to working-class parents, Bob Blauner studied at the University of Chicago and received his Ph.D. from the University of California at Berkeley, where he has been a professor of sociology since 1963. When he was thirty-five, he published his first major scholarly work, *Alienation and Freedom: The Factory Worker and His Industry* (1964), which was based partly on his own experiences as a factory worker before entering college. In later works such as *Racial Oppression in the United States* (1972) and *Black Lives, White Lives: Three Decades of Race Relations in the United States,* his research grew in part out of his own experiences as an African American. In the following essay, Blauner reflects on some of the borders that must be negotiated if black and white Americans are to achieve a permanent understanding.

For many African-Americans who came of age in the 1960s, the assassination of Martin Luther King, Jr. in 1968 was a defining moment in the development of their personal racial consciousness. For a slightly older group, the 1955 lynching of the fourteen-year-old Chicagoan Emmett Till in Mississippi had been a similar awakening. Now we have the protest and violence in Los Angeles and other cities in late April and early May of 1992, spurred by the jury acquittal of four policemen who beat motorist Rodney King.

The aftermath of the Rodney King verdict, unlike any other recent racial violence, will be seared into the memories of Americans of *all* colors, changing the way they see each other and their society. Spring 1992 marked the first time since the 1960s that incidents of racial injustice against an African-American—and by extension the black community—have seized the entire nation's imagination. Even highly publicized racial murders, such as those of African-American men in two New York City neighborhoods—Howard Beach (1986) and Bensonhurst (1989)—stirred the consciences of only a minority of whites. The response to the Rodney King verdict is thus a long-overdue reminder that whites still have the capacity to feel deeply about white racism—when they can see it in unambiguous terms.

The videotaped beating by four Los Angeles police officers provided this concreteness. To be sure, many whites focused their response on the subsequent black rioting, while the anger of blacks tended to remain fixed on the verdict itself. However, whites initially were almost as upset as blacks: An early poll reported that 86 percent of European-Americans disagreed with the jury's decision. The absence of any black from the jury and the trial's venue, Simi Valley, a lily-white suburban community, enabled mainstream whites to see the parallels with the Jim Crow justice of the old South. When we add to this mixture the widespread disaffection, especially of young people, with the nation's political and economic conditions, it is easier to explain the scale of white emotional involvement, unprecedented in a matter of racial protest since the 1960s. 3

In thirty years of teaching, I have never seen my students so overwrought, needing to talk, eager to do something. This response at the University of California at Berkeley cut across the usual fault lines of intergroup tension, as it did at high schools in Northern California. Assemblies, marches, and class discussions took place all over the nation in predominantly white as well as nonwhite and integrated high schools. Considering that there were also incidents where blacks assaulted white people, the scale of white involvement is even more impressive. 4

While many whites saw the precipitating events as expressions of racist conduct, they were much less likely than blacks to see them as part of some larger pattern of racism. Thus two separate polls found that only half as many whites as blacks believe that the legal system treats whites better than blacks. (In each poll, 43 percent of whites saw such a generalized double standard, in contrast to 84 percent of blacks in one survey, 89 percent in the other.) 5

This gap is not surprising. For twenty years European-Americans have tended to feel that systematic racial inequities marked an earlier era, not our own. Psychological denial and a kind of post-1960s exhaustion may both be factors in producing the sense among mainstream whites that civil rights laws and other changes resolved blacks' racial grievances, if not the economic basis of urban problems. But the gap in perceptions of racism also reflects a deeper difference. Whites and blacks see racial issues through different lenses and use different scales to weigh and assess injustice. 6

I am not saying that blacks and whites have totally disparate value systems and worldviews. I think we were more polarized in the late 1960s. It was then that I began a twenty-year interview study of racial consciousness published in 1989 as *Black Lives, White Lives.* By 1979 blacks and whites had come closer together on many issues than they had been in 1968. In the late 1970s and again in the mid-to-late 1980s, both groups were feeling quite pessimistic about the nation's direction. They agreed that America had become a more violent nation and that people were more individualistic and less bound by such traditional values as hard work, 7 personal responsibility, and respect for age and authority. But with this and other convergences, there remained a striking gap in the way European-Americans and African-Americans evaluated *racial* change. Whites were impressed by the scale of integration, the size of the black middle class, and the extent of demonstrable progress. Blacks were disillusioned with integration, concerned about the people who had been left behind, and much more negative in their overall assessment of change.

In the 1990s this difference in general outlook led to different reactions to specific racial issues. That is what makes the shared revulsion over the Rodney King verdict a significant turning point, perhaps even an opportunity to begin bridging the gap between black and white definitions of the racial situation. 8

I want to advance the proposition that there are two languages of race in America. I am not talking about black English and standard English, which refer to different structures of grammar and dialect. "Language" here signifies a system of implicit understandings about social reality, and a racial language encompasses a worldview. 9

Blacks and whites differ on their interpretations of social change from the 1960s through the 1990s because their racial languages define the central terms, especially "racism," differently. Their racial languages incorporate different views of American society itself, especially the question of how central race and racism are to America's very existence, past and present. Blacks believe in this centrality, while most whites, except for the more race-conscious extremists, see race as a peripheral reality. Even successful, middle-class black professionals experience slights and humiliations—incidents when they are stopped by police, regarded suspiciously by clerks while shopping, or mistaken for messengers, drivers, or aides at work—that remind them they have not escaped racism's reach. For whites, race becomes central on exceptional occasions: collective, public moments such as the recent events, when the veil is lifted, and private ones, such as a family's decision to escape urban problems with a move to the suburbs. But most of the time European-Americans are able to view racial issues as aberrations in American life, much as Los Angeles Police Chief Daryl Gates used the term "aberration" to explain his officers' beating of Rodney King in March 1991. 10

Because of these differences in language and worldview, blacks and whites often talk past one another, just as men and women sometimes do. I first noticed this in my classes, particularly during discussions of racism. Whites locate racism in color consciousness and its absence in color blindness. They regard it as a kind of racism when students of color insistently underscore their sense of difference, their affirmation of ethnic and racial membership, which minority students have increasingly asserted. Many black, and increasingly also Latino and Asian, students cannot understand this reaction. It seems to them misinformed, even ignorant. They in turn sense a kind of racism in the whites' assumption that minorities must assimilate to mainstream values and styles. Then African-Americans will posit an idea that many whites find preposterous: Black people, they argue, cannot be racist, because racism is a system of power, and black people as a group do not have power. 11

In this and many other arenas, a contest rages over the meaning of racism. Racism has become the central term in the language of race. From the 1940s through the 1980s new and multiple meanings of racism have been added to the so- 12 cial science lexicon and public discourse. The 1960s were especially critical for what the English sociologist Robert Miles has called the "inflation" of the term "racism." Blacks tended to embrace the enlarged definitions, whites to resist them. This conflict, in my view, has been at the very center of the racial struggle during the past decade.

THE WIDENING CONCEPTION OF RACISM

The term "racism" was not commonly used in social science or American public life   13 until the 1960s. "Racism" does not appear, for example, in the Swedish economist Gunnar Myrdal's classic 1944 study of American race relations, *An American Dilemma.* But even when the term was not directly used, it is still possible to determine the prevailing understandings of racial oppression.

In the 1940s racism referred to an ideology, an explicit system of beliefs postu-   14 lating the superiority of whites based on the inherent, biological inferiority of the colored races. Ideological racism was particularly associated with the belief systems of the Deep South and was originally devised as a rationale for slavery. Theories of white supremacy, particularly in their biological versions, lost much of their legitimacy after the Second World War due to their association with Nazism. In recent years cultural explanations of "inferiority" are heard more commonly than biological ones, which today are associated with such extremist "hate groups" as the Ku Klux Klan and the White Aryan Brotherhood.

By the 1950s and early 1960s, with ideological racism discredited, the focus shifted   15 to a more discrete approach to racially invidious attitudes and behavior, expressed in the model of prejudice and discrimination. "Prejudice" referred (and still does) to hostile feelings and beliefs about racial minorities and the web of stereotypes justifying such negative attitudes. "Discrimination" referred to actions meant to harm the members of a racial minority group. The logic of this model was that racism implied a double standard, that is, treating a person of color differently—in mind or action—than one would a member of the majority group.

By the mid-1960s the terms "prejudice" and "discrimination" and the implicit   16 model of racial causation implied by them were seen as too weak to explain the sweep of racial conflict and change, too limited in their analytical power, and for some critics too individualistic in their assumptions. Their original meanings tended to be absorbed by a new, more encompassing idea of racism. During the 1960s the referents of racial oppression moved from individual actions and beliefs to group and institutional processes, from subjective ideas to "objective" structures or results. Instead of intent, there was now an emphasis on process: those more objective social processes of exclusion, exploitation, and discrimination that led to a racially stratified society.

The most notable of these new definitions was "institutional racism." In their   17 1967 book *Black Power,* Stokely Carmichael and Charles Hamilton stressed how institutional racism was different and more fundamental than individual racism. Racism, in this view, was built into society and scarcely required prejudicial attitudes to maintain racial oppression.

This understanding of racism as pervasive and institutionalized spread from   18 relatively narrow "movement" and academic circles to the larger public with the appearance in 1968 of the report of the commission on the urban riots appointed by President Lyndon Johnson and chaired by Illinois Governor Otto Kerner. The Kerner Commission identified "white racism" as a prime reality of American society and the major underlying cause of ghetto unrest. America, in this view, was moving toward two societies, one white and one black (it is not clear where other racial minorities fit in). Although its recommendations were never acted upon politically, the report legitimated the term "white racism" among politicians and opinion leaders as a key to analyzing racial inequality in America.

Another definition of racism, which I would call "racism as atmosphere," also [19] emerged in the 1960s and 1970s. This is the idea that an organization or an environment might be racist because its implicit, unconscious structures were devised for the use and comfort of white people, with the result that people of other races will not feel at home in such settings. Acting on this understanding of racism, many schools and universities, corporations, and other institutions have changed their teaching practices or work environments to encourage a greater diversity in their clientele, students, or work force.

Perhaps the most radical definition of all was the concept of "racism as result." In [20] this sense, an institution or an occupation is racist simply because racial minorities are underrepresented in numbers or in positions of prestige and authority.

Seizing on different conceptions of racism, the blacks and whites I talked to in the [21] late 1970s had come to different conclusions about how far America had moved toward racial justice. Whites tended to adhere to earlier, more limited notions of racism. Blacks for the most part saw the newer meanings as more basic. Thus African-Americans did not think racism had been put to rest by civil rights laws, even by the dramatic changes in the South. They felt that it still pervaded American life, indeed, had become more insidious because the subtle forms were harder to combat than old-fashioned exclusion and persecution.

Whites saw racism largely as a thing of the past. They defined it in terms of seg- [22] regation and lynching, explicit white supremacist beliefs, or double standards in hiring, promotion, and admissions to colleges or other institutions. Except for affirmative action, which seemed the most blatant expression of such double standards, they were positively impressed by racial change. Many saw the relaxed and comfortable relations between whites and blacks as the heart of the matter. More crucial to blacks, on the other hand, were the underlying structures of power and position that continued to provide them with unequal portions of economic opportunity and other possibilities for the good life.

The newer, expanded definitions of racism just do not make much sense to most [23] whites. I have experienced their frustrations directly when I try to explain the concept of institutional racism to white students and popular audiences. The idea of racism as an "impersonal force" loses all but the most theoretically inclined. Whites are more likely than blacks to view racism as a personal issue. Both sensitive to their own possible culpability (if only unconsciously) and angry at the use of the concept of racism by angry minorities, they do not differentiate well between the racism of social structures and the accusation that they as participants in that structure are personally racist.

The new meanings make sense to blacks, who live such experiences in their   24
bones. But by 1979 many of the African-Americans in my study, particularly the
older activists, were critical of the use of racism as a blanket explanation for all manifestations of racial inequality. Long before similar ideas were voiced by the black
conservatives, many blacks sensed that too heavy an emphasis on racism led to the
false conclusion that blacks could only progress through a conventional civil rights
strategy of fighting prejudice and discrimination. (This strategy, while necessary,
had proved very limited.) Overemphasizing racism, they feared, was interfering
with the black community's ability to achieve greater self-determination through
the politics of self-help. In addition, they told me that the prevailing rhetoric of the
1960s had affected many young blacks. Rather than taking responsibility for their
own difficulties, they were now using racism as a "cop-out."

In public life today this analysis is seen as part of the conservative discourse on   25
race. Yet I believe that this position originally was a progressive one, developed out
of self-critical reflections on the relative failure of 1960s movements. But perhaps
because it did not seem to be "politically correct," the left-liberal community, black
as well as white, academic as well as political, has been afraid of embracing such a
critique. As a result, the neoconservatives had a clear field to pick up this grass-roots
sentiment and to use it to further their view that racism is no longer significant in
American life. This is the last thing that my informants and other savvy African-
Americans close to the pulse of their communities believe.

By the late 1970s the main usage of racism in the mind of the white public had   26
undoubtedly become that of "reverse racism." The primacy of "reverse racism" as
"the really important racism" suggests that the conservatives and the liberal-center
have, in effect, won the battle over the meaning of racism.

Perhaps this was inevitable because of the long period of backlash against all the   27
progressive movements of the 1960s. But part of the problem may have been the inflation of the idea of racism. While institutional racism exists, such a concept loses
practical utility if every thing and every place is racist. In that case, there is effectively nothing to be done about it. And without conceptual tools to distinguish what
is important from what is not, we are lost in the confusion of multiple meanings.

BACK TO BASICS

While public discourse was discounting white racism as exaggerated or a thing of   28
the past, the more traditional forms of bigotry, harassment, and violence were unfortunately making a comeback. (This upsurge actually began in the early 1980s but
was not well noticed, due to some combination of media inattention and national
mood.) What was striking about the Bernhard Goetz subway shootings in New
York, the white-on-black racial violence in Howard Beach, the rise of organized hate
groups, campus racism, and skinhead violence is that these are all examples of old-
fashioned racism. They illustrate the power and persistence of racial prejudices and
hate crimes in the tradition of classical lynchings. They are precisely the kind of
phenomena that many social analysts expected to diminish, as I did.

If there was one positive effect of this upsurge, it was to alert many whites to the   29
destructive power of racial hatred and division in American life. At the same time,
these events also repolarized racial attitudes in America. They have contributed to

the anger and alienation of the black middle class and the rapid rise of Afrocentrism, particularly among college students.

As the gap in understanding has widened, several social scientists have proposed 30 restricting the concept of racism to its original, more narrow meaning. However, the efforts of African-Americans to enlarge the meaning of racism is part of that group's project to make its view of the world and of American society competitive with the dominant white perspective. In addition, the "inflated" meanings of racism are already too rooted in common speech to be overturned by the advice of experts. And certainly some way is needed to convey the pervasive and systematic character of racial oppression. No other term does this as well as racism.

The question then becomes what to do about these multiple and confusing mean- 31 ings of racism and their extraordinary personal and political charge. I would begin by honoring both the black and white readings of the term. Such an attitude might help facilitate the interracial dialogue so badly needed and yet so rare today.

Communication can only start from the understandings that people have. While 32 the black understanding of racism is, in some sense, the deeper one, the white views of racism (ideology, double standard) refer to more specific and recognizable beliefs and practices. Since there is also a cross-racial consensus on the immorality of racist ideology and racial discrimination, it makes sense whenever possible to use such a concrete referent as discrimination, rather than the more global concept of racism. And reemphasizing discrimination may help remind the public that racial discrimination is not just a legacy of the past.

The intellectual power of the African-American understanding lies in its more 33 critical and encompassing perspective. In the Rodney King events, we have an unparalleled opportunity to bridge the racial gap by pointing out that racism and racial division remain essential features of American life and that incidents such as police beatings of minority people and stacked juries are not aberrations but part of a larger pattern of racial abuse and harassment. Without resorting to the overheated rhetoric that proved counterproductive in the 1960s, it now may be possible to persuade white Americans that the most important patterns of discrimination and disadvantage are not to be found in the "reverse racism" of affirmative action but sadly still in the white racism of the dominant social system. And, when feasible, we need to try to bridge the gap by shifting from the language of race to that of ethnicity and class.

RACE OR ETHNICITY?

In the American consciousness the imagery of race—especially along the black- 34 white dimension—tends to be more powerful than that of class or ethnicity. As a result, legitimate ethnic affiliations are often misunderstood to be racial and illegitimate.

Race itself is a confusing concept because of the variance between scientific and 35 common sense definitions of the term. Physical anthropologists who study the distribution of those characteristics we use to classify "races" teach us that race is a fiction because all peoples are mixed to various degrees. Sociologists counter that this biological fiction unfortunately remains a sociological reality. People define one anther racially, and thus divide society into racial groups. The "fiction" of race affects every aspect of people's lives, from living standards to landing in jail.

The consciousness of color differences, and the invidious distinctions based on them, have existed since antiquity and are not limited to any one corner of the world. And yet the peculiarly modern division of the world into a discrete number of hierarchically ranked races is a historic product of Western colonialism. In pre-colonial Africa the relevant group identities were national, tribal, or linguistic. There was no concept of an African or black people until this category was created by the combined effects of slavery, imperialism, and the anticolonial and Pan-African movements. The legal definitions of blackness and whiteness, which varied from one society to another in the Western hemisphere, were also crucial for the construction of modern-day races. Thus race is an essentially political construct, one that translates our tendency to see people in terms of their color or other physical attributes into structures that make it likely that people will act for or against them on such a basis. 36

The dynamic of ethnicity is different, even though the results at times may be similar. An ethnic group is a group that shares a belief in its common past. Members of an ethnic group hold a set of common memories that make them feel that their customs, culture, and outlook are distinctive. In short, they have a sense of peoplehood. Sharing critical experiences and sometimes a belief in their common fate, they feel an affinity for one another, a "comfort zone" that leads to congregating together, even when this is not forced by exclusionary barriers. Thus if race is associated with biology and nature, ethnicity is associated with culture. Like races, ethnic groups arise historically, transform themselves, and sometimes die out. 37

Much of the popular discourse about race in America today goes awry because ethnic realities get lost under the racial umbrella. The positive meanings and potential of ethnicity are overlooked, even overrun, by the more inflammatory meanings of race. Thus white students, disturbed when blacks associate with each other, justify their objections through their commitment to *racial* integration. They do not appreciate the ethnic affinities that bring this about, or see the parallels to Jewish students meeting at the campus Hillel Foundation or Italian-Americans eating lunch at the Italian house on the Berkeley campus. 38

When blacks are "being ethnic," whites see them as "being racial." Thus they view the identity politics of students who want to celebrate their blackness, their *chicanoismo,* their Asian heritages, and their American Indian roots as racially offensive. Part of this reaction comes from a sincere desire, almost a yearning, of white students for a color-blind society. But because the ethnicity of darker people so often gets lost in our overracialized perceptions, the white students misread the situation. When I point out to my class that whites are talking about race and its dynamics and the students of color are talking about ethnicity and its differing meaning, they can begin to appreciate each other's agendas. 39

Confounding race and ethnicity is not just limited to the young. The general public, including journalists and other opinion makers, does this regularly, with serious consequences for the clarity of public dialogue and sociological analysis. A clear example comes from the Chicago mayoral election of 1983. The establishment press, including leading liberal columnists, regularly chastised the black electorate for giving virtually all its votes to Harold Washington. Such racial voting was as 40 "racist" as whites voting for the other candidate because they did not want a black mayor. Yet African-Americans were voting for ethnic representation just as Irish-Americans, Jews, and Italians have always done. Such ethnic politics is considered the American way. What is discriminatory is the double standard that does not confer the same rights on blacks, who were not voting primarily out of fear or hatred as were many whites.

Such confusions between race and ethnicity are exacerbated by the ambiguous sociological status of African-Americans. Black Americans are *both* a race and an ethnic group. Unfortunately, part of our heritage of racism has been to deny the ethnicity, the cultural heritage of black Americans. Liberal-minded whites have wanted to see blacks as essentially white people with black skins. Until the 1960s few believed that black culture was a real ethnic culture. 41

Because our racial language is so deep-seated, the terminology of black and white just seems more "natural" and commonsensical than more ethnic labels like African-American or European-American. But the shift to the term African-American has been a conscious attempt to move the discourse from a language of race to a language of ethnicity. "African-American," as Jesse Jackson and others have pointed out, connects the group to its history and culture in a way that the racial designation, black, does not. The new usage parallels terms for other ethnic groups. Many whites tend to dismiss this concern about language as mere sloganeering. But "African-American" fits better into the emerging multicultural view of American ethnic and racial arrangements, one more appropriate to our growing diversity. The old race relations model was essentially a view that generalized (often inappropriately) from black-white relations. It can no longer capture—if it ever could—the complexity of a multiracial and multicultural society. 42

The issue is further complicated by the fact that African-Americans are not a homogeneous group. They comprise a variety of distinct ethnicities. There are the West Indians with their long histories in the U.S., the darker Puerto Ricans (some of whom identify themselves as black), the more recently arrived Dominicans, Haitians, and immigrants from various African countries, as well as the native-born African-Americans, among whom regional distinctions can also take on a quasi-ethnic flavor. 43

Blacks from the Caribbean are especially likely to identify with their homeland rather than taking on a generic black or even African-American identity. While they may resist the dynamic of "racialization" and even feel superior to native blacks, the dynamic is relentless. Their children are likely to see themselves as part of the larger African-American population. And yet many native-born Americans of African descent also resist the term "African-American," feeling very little connection to the original homeland. Given the diversity in origin and outlook of America's largest minority, it is inevitable that no single concept can capture its full complexity or satisfy all who fall within its bounds. 44

For white Americans, race does not overwhelm ethnicity. Whites see the ethnicity of other whites; it is their own whiteness they tend to overlook. But even when race is recognized, it is not conflated with ethnicity. Jews, for example, clearly distinguish their Jewishness from their whiteness. Yet the long-term dynamic still favors the development of a dominant white racial identity. Except for recent immigrants, the various European ethnic identities have been rapidly weakening. Vital ethnic com- 45 munities persist in some cities, particularly on the East Coast. But many whites, especially the young, have such diverse ethnic heritages that they have no meaningful ethnic affiliation. In my classes only the Jews among European-Americans retain a strong sense of communal origin.

Instead of dampening the ethnic enthusiasms of the racial minorities, perhaps it   46
would [be] better to encourage the revitalization of whites' European heritages. But a problem with this approach is that the relationship between race and ethnicity is more ambiguous for whites than for people of color. Although for many white groups ethnicity has been a stigma, it also has been used to gain advantages that have marginalized blacks and other racial minorities. Particularly for working-class whites today, ethnic community loyalties are often the prism through which they view their whiteness, their superiority.

Thus the line between ethnocentrism and racism is a thin one, easily crossed—as   47
it was by Irish-Americans who resisted the integration of South Boston's schools in the 1970s and by many of the Jews and Italians that sociologist Jonathan Rieder describes in his 1985 book *Canarsie.*

White students today complain of a double standard. Many feel that their college   48
administrations sanction organization and identification for people of color, but not for them. If there can be an Asian business organization and a black student union, why can't there be a white business club or a white student alliance? I'd like to explain to them that students of color are organized ethnically, not racially, that whites have Hillel and the Italian theme house. But this makes little practical sense when such loyalties are just not that salient for the vast majority.

Out of this vacuum the emerging identity of "European-American" has come into   49
vogue. I interpret the European-American idea as part of a yearning for a usable past. Europe is associated with history and culture. "America" and "American" can no longer be used to connote white people. "White" itself is a racial term and thereby inevitably associated with our nation's legacy of social injustice.

At various California colleges and high schools, European-American clubs have   50
begun to form, provoking debate about whether it is inherently racist for whites to organize as whites—or as European-Americans. Opponents invoke the racial analogy and see such organizations as akin to exclusive white supremacist groups. Their defenders argue from an ethnic model, saying that they are simply looking for a place where they can feel at home and discuss their distinctive personal and career problems. The jury is still out on this new and, I suspect, burgeoning phenomenon. It will take time to discover its actual social impact.

If the European-Americans forming their clubs are truly organizing on an ethnic   51
or panethnic rather than a racial model, I would have to support these efforts. Despite all the ambiguities, it seems to me a gain in social awareness when a specific group comes to be seen in ethnic rather than racial terms. During the period of the mass immigration of the late nineteenth century and continuing through the 1920s, Jews, Italians, and other white ethnics were viewed racially. We no longer hear of the "Hebrew race," and it is rare for Jewish distinctiveness to be attributed to biological rather than cultural roots. Of course, the shift from racial to ethnic thinking did not put an end to anti-Semitism in the United States—or to genocide in Germany, where racial imagery was obviously intensified.

It is unrealistic to expect that the racial groupings of American society can be   52 totally "deconstructed," as a number of scholars now are advocating. After all, African-Americans and native Americans, who were not immigrants, can never be exactly like other ethnic groups. Yet a shift in this direction would begin to move our society from a divisive biracialism to a more inclusive multiculturalism.

To return to the events of spring 1992, I ask what was different about these civil dis- 53 turbances. Considering the malign neglect of twelve Reagan-Bush years, the almost two decades of economic stagnation, and the retreat of the public from issues of race and poverty, the violent intensity should hardly be astonishing.

More striking was the multiracial character of the response. In the San Francisco 54 Bay area, rioters were as likely to be white as nonwhite. In Los Angeles, Latinos were prominent among both the protesters and the victims. South Central Los Angeles is now more Hispanic than black, and this group suffered perhaps 60 percent of the property damage. The media have focused on the specific grievances of African-Americans toward Koreans. But I would guess that those who trashed Korean stores were protesting something larger than even the murder of a fifteen-year-old black girl. Koreans, along with other immigrants, continue to enter the country and in a relatively short time surpass the economic and social position of the black poor. The immigrant advantage is real and deeply resented by African-Americans, who see that the two most downtrodden minorities are those that did not enter the country voluntarily.

During the 1960s the police were able to contain riots within the African-American 55 community. This time Los Angeles police were unable to do so. Even though the South Central district suffered most, there was also much destruction in other areas including Hollywood, downtown, and the San Fernando Valley. In the San Francisco Bay area the violence occurred primarily in the white business sections, not the black neighborhoods of Oakland, San Francisco, or Berkeley. The violence that has spilled out of the inner city is a distillation of all the human misery that a white middle-class society has been trying to contain—albeit unsuccessfully (consider the homeless). As in the case of an untreated infection, the toxic substances finally break out, threatening to contaminate the entire organism.

Will this widened conflict finally lead Americans toward a recognition of our 56 common stake in the health of the inner cities and their citizens, or toward increased fear and division? The Emmett Till lynching in 1955 set the stage for the first mass mobilization of the civil rights movement, the Montgomery bus boycott later that year. Martin Luther King's assassination provided the impetus for the institution of affirmative action and other social programs. The Rodney King verdict and its aftermath must also become not just a psychologically defining moment but an impetus to a new mobilization of political resolve.

Working with the Text

1. Blauner states that in his experience, most whites find it difficult to make sense of the concept of *institutional racism,* in part because they "do not differentiate well between the racism of social structures and the accusation that they as participants in that structure are personally racist" (¶ 23). The concept makes sense to blacks, however, because they "live such experiences in their bones." How do you respond to this conclusion?

2. Blauner's white students often regard the desire of African Americans, Hispanics, or Asian Americans to create racially exclusive groups as "reverse racism." In what ways does Blauner feel that considering such groups in the context of ethnicity can help his white students get beyond this view? Do you agree? Similarly, Blauner advocates the term *African-American* (¶ 42) and also sometimes uses the term *European-American* instead of *white*. Why? Do you agree with his reasoning? What is the difference between race and ethnicity in the context of his essay?

3. In discussing the disadvantages of encouraging "the revitalization of whites' European heritages" (¶ 46), Blauner suggests that "the line between ethnocentrism and racism is a thin one" (¶ 47). Why, then, does Blauner tentatively support the emergence of European American clubs on college campuses?

4. In paragraph 8 Blauner suggests that the "shared revulsion over the Rodney King verdict" in 1992 was a "significant turning point, perhaps even an opportunity to begin bridging the gap between black and white definitions of the racial situation." Considering black and white attitudes about the "racial situation" today, what do you think of Blauner's prediction?

SAY YES

TOBIAS WOLFF

■ Tobias Wolff was born in Birmingham, Alabama, and attended Oxford University in England and Stanford University. Formerly a reporter for the *Washington Post,* Wolff turned to fiction writing in the late 1970s, publishing his highly praised first collection of short stories, *In the Garden of the North American Martyrs,* in 1981. His most recent collection is *The Night in Question* (1996). His works of nonfiction include *This Boy's Life: A Memoir* (1989) and *In Pharaoh's Army: Memories of the Last War* (1994), which is about his experiences as a soldier in Vietnam in the late 1960s. Of his writing he has said, "All my stories are in one way or another autobiographical. . . . [A]ll of my characters are reflections of myself, in that I share their wish to count for something and their almost complete confusion as to how this is supposed to be done." The following story appeared in his 1985 collection, *Back to the World.*

They were doing the dishes, his wife washing while he dried. He'd washed the night before. Unlike most men he knew, he really pitched in on the housework. A few months earlier he'd overheard a friend of his wife's congratulate her on having such a considerate husband, and he thought, *I try.* Helping out with the dishes was a way he had of showing how considerate he was.

They talked about different things and somehow got on the subject of whether white people should marry black people. He said that all things considered, he thought it was a bad idea.

"Why?" she asked.

Sometimes his wife got this look where she pinched her brows together and bit her lower lip and stared down at something. When he saw her like this he knew he should keep his mouth shut, but he never did. Actually it made him talk more. She had that look now. 4

"Why?" she asked again, and stood there with her hand inside a bowl, not washing it but just holding it above the water. 5

"Listen," he said, "I went to school with blacks, and I've worked with blacks and lived on the same street with blacks, and we've always gotten along just fine. I don't need you coming along now and implying that I'm a racist." 6

"I didn't imply anything," she said, and began washing the bowl again, turning it around in her hand as though she were shaping it. "I just don't see what's wrong with a white person marrying a black person, that's all." 7

"They don't come from the same culture as we do. Listen to them sometime—they even have their own language. That's okay with me, I *like* hearing them talk"—he did; for some reason it always made him feel happy—"but it's different. A person from their culture and a person from our culture could never really *know* each other." 8

"Like you know me?" his wife asked. 9

"Yes. Like I know you." 10

"But if they love each other," she said. She was washing faster now, not looking at him. 11

Oh boy, he thought. He said, "Don't take my word for it. Look at the statistics. Most of those marriages break up." 12

"Statistics." She was piling dishes on the drainboard at a terrific rate, just swiping at them with the cloth. Many of them were greasy, and there were flecks of food between the tines of the forks. "All right," she said, "what about foreigners? I suppose you think the same thing about two foreigners getting married." 13

"Yes," he said, "as a matter of fact I do. How can you understand someone who comes from a completely different background?" 14

"Different," said his wife. "Not the same, like us." 15

"Yes, different," he snapped, angry with her for resorting to this trick of repeating his words so that they sounded crass, or hypocritical. "These are dirty," he said, and dumped all the silverware back into the sink. 16

The water had gone flat and gray. She stared down at it, her lips pressed tight together, then plunged her hands under the surface. "Oh!" she cried, and jumped back. She took her right hand by the wrist and held it up. Her thumb was bleeding. 17

"Ann, don't move," he said. "Stay right there." He ran upstairs to the bathroom and rummaged in the medicine chest for alcohol, cotton, and a Band-Aid. When he came back down she was leaning against the refrigerator with her eyes closed, still holding her hand. He took the hand and dabbed at her thumb with the cotton. The bleeding had stopped. He squeezed it to see how deep the wound was and a single drop of blood welled up, trembling and bright, and fell to the floor. Over the thumb she stared at him accusingly. "It's shallow," he said. "Tomorrow you won't even know it's there." He hoped that she appreciated how quickly he had come to her aid. He'd acted out of concern for her, with no thought of getting anything in return, but now the thought occurred to him that it would be a nice gesture on her part not to start up that conversation again, as he was tired of it. "I'll finish up here," he said. "You go and relax." 18

"That's ok," she said. "I'll dry." 19

He began to wash the silverware again, giving a lot of attention to the forks. 20

"So," she said, "you wouldn't have married me if I'd been black." 21

"For Christ's sake, Ann!" 22

"Well, that's what you said, didn't you?" 23

"No, I did not. The whole question is ridiculous. If you had been black we prob- 24
ably wouldn't even have met. You would have had your friends and I would have had
mine. The only black girl I ever really knew was my partner in the debating club, and
I was already going out with you by then."

"But if we had met, and I'd been black?" 25

"Then you probably would have been going out with a black guy." He picked up 26
the rinsing nozzle and sprayed the silverware. The water was so hot that the metal
darkened to pale blue, then turned silver again.

"Let's say I wasn't," she said. "Let's say I am black and unattached and we meet 27
and fall in love."

He glanced over at her. She was watching him and her eyes were bright. "Look," 28
he said, taking a reasonable tone, "this is stupid. If you were black you wouldn't be
you." As he said this he realized it was absolutely true. There was no possible way of
arguing with the fact that she would not be herself if she were black. So he said it
again: "If you were black you wouldn't be you."

"I know," she said, "but let's just say." 29

He took a deep breath. He had won the argument but he still felt cornered. "Say 30
what?" he asked.

"That I'm black, but still me, and we fall in love. Will you marry me?" 31

He thought about it. 32

"Well?" she said, and stepped close to him. Her eyes were even brighter. "Will you 33
marry me?"

"I'm thinking," he said. 34

"You won't, I can tell. You're going to say no." 35

"Let's not move too fast on this," he said. "There are lots of things to consider. We 36
don't want to do something we would regret for the rest of our lives."

"No more considering. Yes or no." 37

"Since you put it that way—" 38

"Yes or no." 39

"Jesus, Ann. All right. No." 40

She said "Thank you," and walked from the kitchen into the living room. A mo- 41
ment later he heard her turning the pages of a magazine. He knew that she was too
angry to be actually reading it, but she didn't snap through the pages the way he
would have done. She turned them slowly, as if she were studying every word. She
was demonstrating her indifference to him, and it had the effect he knew she wanted
it to have. It hurt him.

He had no choice but to demonstrate his indifference to her. Quietly, thoroughly, 42
he washed the rest of the dishes. Then he dried them and put them away. He wiped
the counters and the stove and scoured the linoleum where the drop of blood had
fallen. While he was at it, he decided, he might as well mop the whole floor. When
he was done the kitchen looked new, the way it looked when they were first shown
the house, before they had ever lived here.

He picked up the garbage pail and went outside. The night was clear and he could 43 see a few stars to the west, where the light of the town didn't blur them out. On El Camino the traffic was steady and light, peaceful as a river. He felt ashamed that he had let his wife get him into a fight. In another thirty years or so they would both be dead. What would all that stuff matter then? He thought of the years they had spent together, and how close they were, and how well they knew each other, and his throat tightened so that he could hardly breathe. His face and neck began to tingle. Warmth flooded his chest. He stood there for a while, enjoying these sensations, then picked up the pail and went out the back gate.

The two mutts from down the street had pulled over the garbage can again. One   44
of them was rolling around on his back and the other had something in her mouth. Growling, she tossed it into the air, leaped up and caught it, growled again and whipped her head from side to side. When they saw him coming they trotted away with short, mincing steps. Normally he would heave rocks at them, but this time he let them go.

The house was dark when he came back inside. She was in the bathroom. He   45
stood outside the door and called her name. He heard bottles clinking, but she didn't answer him. "Ann, I'm really sorry," he said. "I'll make it up to you, I promise."

"How?" she asked.   46

He wasn't expecting this. But from a sound in her voice, a level and definite note   47
that was strange to him, he knew that he had come up with the right answer. He leaned against the door. "I'll marry you," he whispered.

"We'll see," she said. "Go on to bed. I'll be out in a minute."   48

He undressed and got under the covers. Finally he heard the bathroom door   49
open and close.

"Turn off the light," she said from the hallway.   50

"What?"   51

"Turn off the light."   52

He reached over and pulled the chain on the bedside lamp. The room went dark.   53
"All right," he said. He lay there, but nothing happened. "All right," he said again. Then he heard a movement across the room. He sat up, but he couldn't see a thing. The room was silent. His heart pounded the way it had on their first night together, the way it still did when he woke at a noise in the darkness and waited to hear it again—the sound of someone moving through the house, a stranger.

Working with the Text

1. Which character do you find more sympathetic in this story—the husband or the wife? Or do you have relatively equal sympathy (or lack of sympathy) for the two? Who do you think "wins" the argument? How do you account for your response?

2. To what extent do you see this story as being about attitudes toward racial difference? About differences between men and women? About the inevitability of difference between individual human beings? How does the final image of a stranger moving through the darkness color your interpretation? In a paper, analyze how the story interrelates these varied differences and in what ways.

3. In what ways can interracial dating or marriage be seen as a crossing of borders? Based on your experience, do you think that interracial couples "could never really *know* each other," that a certain sense of difference could never really be overcome? Or is this ultimately a narrow-minded response based on stereotypical ideas of racial culture?

FROM ACROSS THE WIRE

LUIS ALBERTO URREA

■ Born in Tijuana, Mexico, to an American mother and a Mexican father, Luis Alberto Urrea graduated from the University of California at San Diego in 1977. After working for several years as a film extra, Urrea began a career as a teacher. He has taught expository writing at Harvard and elsewhere. In addition to a novel, Urrea has also published *The Fever of Being* (1994), a collection of poems that won the Western States Book Award for poetry. He currently edits the literary magazine *Many Mountains Moving*.

In the 1980s he joined a crew of relief workers helping poor people on the Mexican side of the U.S.–Mexican border. He has written two books based on these experiences—*Across the Wire: Life and Hard Times on the Mexican Border* (1993) and *By the Lake of Sleeping Children: The Secret Life of the Mexican Border* (1996). The following chapter from *Across the Wire* describes the harrowingly miserable living conditions experienced by the poor on Mexico's border and what it feels like to bring these people the little relief that is possible.

BORDER STORY

When I was younger, I went to war. The Mexican border was the battlefield. There are many Mexicos; there are also many Mexican borders, any one of which could fill its own book. I, and the people with me, fought on a specific front. We sustained injuries and witnessed deaths. There were machine guns pointed at us, knives, pistols, clubs, even skyrockets. I caught a street-gang member trying to stuff a lit cherry bomb into our gas tank. On the same night, a drunk mariachi opened fire on the missionaries through the wall of his house.

We drove five beat-up vans. We were armed with water, medicine, shampoo, food, clothes, milk, and doughnuts. At the end of a day, like returning veterans from other battles, we carried secrets in our hearts that kept some of us awake at night, gave others dreams and fits of crying. Our faith sustained us—if not in God or "good," then in our work.

Others of us had no room for or interest in such drama, and came away unscathed—and unmoved. Some of us sank into the mindless joy of fundamentalism, some of us drank, some of us married impoverished Mexicans. Most of us took it personally. Poverty *is* personal: it smells and it shocks and it invades your space. You come home dirty when you get too close to the poor. Sometimes you bring back vermin: they hide in your hair, in your underpants, in your intestines. These unpleasant possibilities are a given. They are the price you occasionally have to pay.

In Tijuana and environs, we met the many ambassadors of poverty: lice, scabies, tapeworm, pinworm, ringworm, fleas, crab lice. We met diphtheria, meningitis, typhoid, polio, *turista* (diarrhea), tuberculosis, hepatitis, VD, impetigo, measles, chronic hernia, malaria, whooping cough. We met madness and "demon possession."

These were the products of dirt and disregard—bad things afflicting good people. Their world was far from our world. Still, it would take you only about twenty minutes to get there from the center of San Diego.

For me, the worst part was the lack of a specific enemy. We were fighting a nebulous, all-pervasive *It*. Call it hunger. Call it despair. Call it the Devil, the System, Capitalism, the Cycle of Poverty, the Fruits of the Mexican Malaise. It was a seemingly endless circle of disasters. Long after I'd left, the wheel kept on grinding.

At night, the Border Patrol helicopters swoop and churn in the air all along the line. You can sit in the Mexican hills and watch them herd humans on the dusty slopes across the valley. They look like science fiction crafts, their hard-focused lights raking the ground as they fly.

Borderlands locals are so jaded by the sight of nightly people-hunting that it doesn't even register in their minds. But take a stranger to the border, and she will *see* the spectacle: monstrous Dodge trucks speeding into and out of the landscape; uniformed men patrolling with flashlights, guns, and dogs; spotlights; running figures; lines of people hurried onto buses by armed guards; and the endless clatter of the helicopters with their harsh white beams. A Dutch woman once told me it seemed altogether "un-American."

But the Mexicans keep on coming—and the Guatemalans, the Salvadorans, the Panamanians, the Colombians. The seven-mile stretch of Interstate 5 nearest the Mexican border is, at times, so congested with Latin American pedestrians that it resembles a town square.

They stick to the center island. Running down the length of the island is a cement wall. If the "illegals" (currently, "undocumented workers"; formerly, "wetbacks") are walking north and a Border Patrol vehicle happens along, they simply hop over the wall and trot south. The officer will have to drive up to the 805 interchange, or Dairy Mart Road, swing over the overpasses, then drive south. Depending on where this pursuit begins, his detour could entail five to ten miles of driving. When the officer finally reaches the group, they hop over the wall and trot north. Furthermore, because freeway arrests would endanger traffic, the Border Patrol has effectively thrown up its hands in surrender.

It seems jolly on the page. But imagine poverty, violence, natural disasters, or political fear driving you away from everything you know. Imagine how bad things get to make you leave behind your family, your friends, your lovers; your home, as humble as it might be; your church, say. Let's take it further—you've said good-bye to the graveyard, the dog, the goat, the mountains where you first hunted, your grade school, your state, your favorite spot on the river where you fished and took time to think.

Then you come hundreds—or thousands—of miles across territory utterly un-   12
known to you. (Chances are, you have never traveled farther than a hundred miles
in your life.) You have walked, run, hidden in the backs of trucks, spent part of your
precious money on bus fare. There is no AAA or Travelers Aid Society available to
you. Various features of your journey north might include police corruption; violence in the forms of beatings, rape, murder, torture, road accidents; theft; incarcer-
ation. Additionally, you might experience loneliness, fear, exhaustion, sorrow, cold,
heat, diarrhea, thirst, hunger. There is no medical attention available to you. There
isn't even Kotex.

Weeks or months later, you arrive in Tijuana. Along with other immigrants, you   13
gravitate to the bad parts of town because there is nowhere for you to go in the glit-
tery sections where the *gringos* flock. You stay in a run-down little hotel in the red-
light district, or behind the bus terminal. Or you find your way to the garbage
dumps, where you throw together a small cardboard nest and claim a few feet of dirt
for yourself. The garbage-pickers working this dump might allow you to squat, or
they might come and rob you or burn you out for breaking some local rule you cannot possibly know beforehand. Sometimes the dump is controlled by a syndicate,
and goon squads might come to you within a day. They want money, and if you
can't pay, you must leave or suffer the consequences.

In town, you face endless victimization if you aren't streetwise. The police come   14
after you, street thugs come after you, petty criminals come after you; strangers try
your door at night as you sleep. Many shady men offer to guide you across the border, and each one wants all your money now, and promises to meet you at a pre-
arranged spot. Some of your fellow travelers end their journeys right here—relieved
of their savings and left to wait on a dark corner until they realize they are going
nowhere.

If you are not Mexican, and can't pass as *tijuanense,* a local, the tough guys find   15
you out. Salvadorans and Guatemalans are routinely beaten up and robbed. Sometimes they are disfigured. Indians—Chinantecas, Mixtecas, Guasaves, Zapotecas,
Mayas—are insulted and pushed around; often they are lucky—they are merely ignored. They use this to their advantage. Often they don't dream of crossing into the
United States: a Mexican tribal person would never be able to blend in, and they
know it. To them, the garbage dumps and street vending and begging in Tijuana are
a vast improvement over their former lives. As Doña Paula, a Chinanteca friend of
mine who lives at the Tijuana garbage dump, told me, "This is the garbage dump.
Take all you need. There's plenty here for *everyone!*"

If you are a woman, the men come after you. You lock yourself in your room, and   16
when you must leave it to use the pestilential public bathroom at the end of your
floor, you hurry, and you check every corner. Sometimes the lights are out in the toilet room. Sometimes men listen at the door. They call you "good-looking" and
"bitch" and "*mamacita,*" and they make kissing sounds at you when you pass.

You're in the worst part of town, but you can comfort yourself—at least there are   17
no death squads here. There are no torturers here, or bandit land barons riding into
your house. This is the last barrier, you think, between you and the United
States—*los Yunaites Estaites.*

You still face police corruption, violence, jail. You now also have a wide variety of   18 new options available to you: drugs, prostitution, white slavery, crime. Tijuana is not easy on newcomers. It is a city that has always thrived on taking advantage of a sucker. And the innocent are the ultimate suckers in the Borderlands.

If you have saved up enough money, you go to one of the *coyotes* (people-smugglers), who guide travelers through the violent canyons immediately north of the border. Lately, these men are also called *polleros,* or "chicken-wranglers." Some of them are straight, some are land pirates. Negotiations are tense and strange: *polleros* speak a Spanish you don't quite understand—like the word *polleros.* Linguists call the new border-speak "Spanglish," but in Tijuana, Spanglish is mixed with slang and *pochismos* (the polyglot hip talk of Mexicans infected with *gringoismo;* the *cholos* in Mexico, or Chicanos on the American side). 19

Suddenly, the word for "yes," *sí,* can be *simón* or *siról.* "No" is *chale.* "Bike" (*bicicleta*) is *baica.* "Wife" (*esposa*) is *waifa.* "The police" (*la policía*) are *la chota.* "Women" are *rucas* or *morras.* You don't know what they're talking about. 20

You pay them all your money—sometimes it's your family's lifelong savings. Five hundred dollars should do it. "*Orale,*" the dude tells you, which means "right on." You must wait in Colonia Libertad, the most notorious *barrio* in town, ironically named "Liberty." 21

The scene here is baffling. Music blares from radios. Jolly women at smoky taco stands cook food for the journeys, sell jugs of water. You can see the Border Patrol agents cruising the other side of the fence; they trade insults with the locals. 22

When the appointed hour comes, you join a group of *pollos* (chickens) who scuttle along behind the *coyote.* You crawl under the wires, or, if you go a mile east, you might be amazed to find that the famous American Border Fence simply stops. To enter the United States, you merely step around the end of it. And you follow your guide into the canyons. You might be startled to find groups of individuals crossing the line without *coyotes* leading them at all. You might wonder how they have mastered the canyons, and you might begin to regret the loss of your money. 23

If you have your daughters or mothers or wives with you—or if you are a woman—you become watchful and tense, because rape and gang rape are so common in this darkness as to be utterly unremarkable. If you have any valuables left after your various negotiations, you try to find a sly place to hide them in case you meet *pandilleros* (gang members) or *rateros* (thieves—ratmen). But, really, where can you put anything? Thousands have come before you, and the hiding places are pathetically obvious to robbers: in shoulder bags or clothing rolls, pinned inside clothes, hidden in underwear, inserted in body orifices. 24

If the *coyote* does not turn on you suddenly with a gun and take everything from you himself, you might still be attacked by the *rateros.* If the *rateros* don't get you, there are roving zombies that you can smell from fifty yards downwind—these are the junkies who hunt in shambling packs. If the junkies somehow miss you, there are the *pandilleros*—gang-bangers from either side of the border who are looking for some bloody fun. They adore "taking off" illegals because it's the perfect crime: there is no way they can ever be caught. They are Tijuana *cholos,* or Chicano *vatos,* or Anglo head-bangers. 25

Their sense of fun relies heavily on violence. Gang beatings are their preferred sport, though rape in all its forms is common, as always. Often the *coyote* will turn 26 tail and run at the first sight of *pandilleros*. What's another load of desperate chickens to him? He's just making a living, taking care of business.

If he doesn't run, there is a good chance he will be the first to be assaulted. The 27 most basic punishment these young toughs mete out is a good beating, but they might kill him in front of the *pollos* if they feel the immigrants need a lesson in obedience. For good measure, these boys—they are mostly *boys,* aged twelve to nineteen, bored with Super Nintendo and MTV—beat people and slash people and thrash the women they have just finished raping.

Their most memorable tactic is to hamstring the *coyote* or anyone who dares 28 speak out against them. This entails slicing the muscles in the victim's legs and leaving him to flop around in the dirt, crippled. If you are in a group of *pollos* that happens to be visited by these furies, you are learning border etiquette.

Now, say you are lucky enough to evade all these dangers on your journey. Hazards still await you and your family. You might meet white racists, complimenting themselves with the tag "Aryans"; they "patrol" the scrub in combat gear, carrying radios, high-powered flashlights, rifles, and bats. Rattlesnakes hide in bushes—you didn't count on that complication. Scorpions, tarantulas, black widows. And, of course, there is the Border Patrol (*la migra*). 29

They come over the hills on motorcycles, on horses, in huge Dodge Ramcharger 30 four-wheel drives. They yell, wear frightening goggles, have guns. Sometimes they are surprisingly decent; sometimes they are too tired or too bored to put much effort into dealing with you. They collect you in a large group of fellow *pollos,* and a guard (a Mexican Border Patrol agent!) jokes with your group in Spanish. Some cry, some sulk, most laugh. Mexicans hate to be rude. You don't know what to think—some of your fellow travelers take their arrest with aplomb. Sometimes the officers know their names. But you have been told repeatedly that the Border Patrol sometimes beats or kills people. Everyone talks about the Mexican girl molested inside its building.

The Border Patrol puts you into trucks that take you to buses that take you to 31 compounds that load you onto other buses that transport you back to Tijuana and put you out. Your *coyote* isn't bothered in the least. Some of the regulars who were with you go across and get brought back a couple of times a night. But for you, things are different. You have been brought back with no place to sleep. You have already spent all your money. You might have been robbed, so you have only your clothes—maybe not all of them. The robbers may have taken your shoes. You might be bloodied from a beating by *pandilleros,* or an "accident" in the Immigration and Naturalization Service compound. You can't get proper medical attention. You can't eat, or afford to feed your family. Some of your compatriots have been separated from their wives or their children. Now their loved ones are in the hands of strangers, in the vast and unknown United States. The Salvadorans are put on planes and flown back to the waiting arms of the military. As you walk through the cyclone fence, back into Tijuana, the locals taunt you and laugh at your misfortune.

If you were killed, you have nothing to worry about. 32

Now what? 33
Perhaps you'll join one of the other groups that break through the Tortilla 34

Curtain every night. The road-runners. They amass at dusk along the cement canal that separates the United States from Mexico. This wide alley is supposedly the Tijuana River, but it's usually dry, or running with sewage that Tijuana pumps toward the U.S. with great gusto.

As soon as everybody feels like it—there are no *coyotes* needed here—you join 35 the groups passing through the gaping holes in the fence. Houses and alleys and cantinas back up against it, and in some spots, people have driven stolen cars into the poles to provide a wider passage. You rush across the canal and up the opposite slope, timing your dash between passing *migra* trucks and the overflights of helicopters. Following the others, you begin your jog toward the freeway. Here, there are mostly just Border Patrol officers to outrun—not that hard if you're in good shape. There are still some white-supremacist types bobbling around, but the cops will get them if they do anything serious. No, here the problem is the many lanes of I–5.

You stand at the edge of the road and wonder how you're going to cut across five 36 lanes of traffic going sixty miles an hour. Then, there is the problem of the next five lanes. The freeway itself is constructed to run parallel to the border, then swing north. Its underpasses and storm-drain pipes offer another subterranean world, but you don't know about them. All you know is you have to get across at some point, and get far from the hunters who would take you back.

If you hang around the shoulder of I–5 long enough, you will find that many of 37 your companions don't make it. So many have been killed and injured that the *gringos* have put up warning signs to motorists to watch for running people. The orange signs show a man, a woman, and a child charging across. Some *gringos* are so crazy with hate for you that they speed up, or aim for you as you run.

The vague blood of over a hundred slain runners shadows the concrete. 38

On either side of the border, clustered near the gates, there are dapper-looking 39 men, dressed in nice cowboy clothes, and they speak without looking anyone in the eye. They are saying, "Los Angeles. San Bernardino. San Francisco."

They have a going concern: business is good. 40

Once you've gotten across the line, there will always be the question of *Where do* 41 *I go now?* "Illegal aliens" have to eat, sleep, find work. Once across, you must begin another journey.

Not everyone has the energy to go on. Even faith—in Jesus, the Virgin Mary, or 42 the Streets of Gold—breaks down sooner or later. Many of these immigrants founder at the border. There is a sad swirl of humanity in Tijuana. Outsiders eddy there who have simply run out of strength. If North America does not want them, Tijuana wants them even less. They become the outcasts of an outcast region. We could all see them if we looked hard enough: they sell chewing gum. Their children sing in traffic. In bars downtown, the women will show us a breast for a quarter. They wash our windshields at every stoplight. But mostly, they are invisible. To see them, we have to climb up the little canyons all around the city, where the cardboard shacks and mud and smoke look like a lost triptych by Hieronymus Bosch. We have to wade into the garbage dumps and the orphanages, sit in the little churches and the hospitals, or go out into the back country, where they raise their goats and bake red bricks and try to live decent lives.

They are not welcome in Tijuana. And, for the most part, Tijuana itself is not wel-   43
come in the Motherland. Tijuana is Mexico's cast-off child. She brings in money and
gringos, but nobody would dare claim her. As a Mexican diplomat once confided to
me, "We both know Tijuana is not Mexico. The border is nowhere. It's a no-man's-
land."

I was born there.   44

MY STORY

I was born in Tijuana, to a Mexican father and an American mother. I was registered   45
with the U.S. government as an American Citizen, Born Abroad. Raised in San
Diego, I crossed the border all through my boyhood with abandon, utterly bilingual
and bicultural. In 1977, my father died on the border, violently. (The story is told in
detail in a chapter entitled "Father's Day.")

In the Borderlands, anything can happen. And if you're in Tijuana long enough,   46
anything *will* happen. Whole neighborhoods appear and disappear seemingly
overnight. For example, when I was a boy, you got into Tijuana by driving through
the Tijuana River itself. It was a muddy floodplain bustling with animals and belch-
ing old cars. A slum that spread across the riverbed was known as "Cartolandia." In
border-speak, this meant "Land of Cardboard."

Suddenly, it was time for Tijuana to spruce up its image to attract more Ameri-   47
can dollars, and Cartolandia was swept away by a flash flood of tractors. The big machines swept down the length of the river, crushing shacks and toppling fences. It
was like magic. One week, there were choked multitudes of sheds; the next, a clear,
flat space awaiting the blank concrete of a flood channel. Town—no town.

The inhabitants of Cartolandia fled to the outskirts, where they were better   48
suited to Tijuana's new image as Shopping Mecca. They had effectively vanished.
Many of them homesteaded the Tijuana municipal garbage dump. The city's varied
orphanages consumed many of their children.

Tijuana's characteristic buzz can be traced directly to a mixture of dread and ex-   49
pectation: there's always something coming.

I never intended to be a missionary. I didn't go to church, and I had no reason to   50
believe I'd be involved with a bunch of Baptists. But in 1978, I had occasion to meet
a remarkable preacher known as Pastor Von (Erhardt George von Trutzschler III, no
less): as well as being a minister, he was a veteran of the Korean War, a graphic artist,
a puppeteer, a German baron, an adventurer, and a practical joker. Von got me involved in the hardships and discipline he calls "Christian Boot Camp."

After working as a youth pastor in San Diego for many years, he had discovered   51
Mexico in the late sixties. His work there began with the typical church do-good activities that everyone has experienced at least once: a bag of blankets for the or-
phans, a few Christmas toys, alms for the poor. As Protestantism spread in Mexico,
however, interest in Von's preaching grew. Small churches and Protestant orphanages and Protestant *barrios,* lacking ministers of their own, began asking Von to
teach. Preaching and pastoring led to more work; work led to more needs; more
needs pulled in more workers. On it went until Von had put in thirty or so years
slogging through the Borderlands mud, and his little team of die-hard renegades

and border rats had grown to a nonprofit corporation (Spectrum Ministries, Inc.), where you'll find him today.

Von's religious ethic is similar in scope to Teresa of Calcutta's. Von favors actual works over heavy evangelism. Spectrum is based on a belief Christians call "living the gospel." This doctrine is increasingly rare in America, since it involves little lip service, hard work, and no glory.

Von often reminds his workers that they are "ambassadors of Christ" and should comport themselves accordingly. Visitors are indelicately stripped of their misconceptions and prejudices when they discover that the crust on Von and his crew is a mile thick: the sight of teenybopper Bible School girls enduring Von's lurid pretrip briefing is priceless. Insouciantly, he offers up his litany: lice, worms, pus, blood; diarrhea, rattletrap outhouses, no toilet paper; dangerous water and food; diseased animals that will leave you with scabies; rats, maggots, flies; *odor*. Then he confuses them by demanding love and respect for the poor. He caps his talk with: "Remember—you are not going to the zoo. These are people. Don't run around snapping pictures of them like they're animals. Don't rush into their shacks saying, 'Ooh, gross!' They live there. Those are their homes."

Because border guards often "confiscate" chocolate milk, the cartons must be smuggled into Mexico under bags of clothes. Because the floors of the vans get so hot, the milk will curdle, so the crew must first freeze it. The endless variations of challenge in the Borderlands keep Von constantly alert—problems come three at a time and must be solved on the run.

Like the time a shipment of tennis shoes was donated to Spectrum. They were new, white, handsome shoes. The only problem was that no two shoes in the entire shipment matched. Von knew there was no way the Mexican kids could use *one* shoe, and they—like teens everywhere—were fashion-conscious and wouldn't be caught dead in unmatching sneakers.

Von's solution was practical and witty. He donned unmatched shoes and made his crew members wear unmatched shoes. Then he announced that it was the latest California surfer rage; kids in California weren't considered hip unless they wore unmatched shoes. The shipment was distributed, and shoeless boys were shod in the *faux* fashion craze begun by Chez Von.

Von has suffered for his beliefs. In the ever more conservative atmosphere of American Christianity (read: Protestantism), the efforts of Spectrum have come under fire on several occasions. He was once denounced because he refused to use the King James Bible in his sermons—clearly the sign of a heretic.

Von's terse reply to criticism: "It's hard to 'save' people when they're dead."

Von has a Monday night ministerial run into Tijuana, and in his heyday, he was hitting three or four orphanages a night. I was curious, unaware of the severity of the poverty in Tijuana. I knew it was there, but it didn't really mean anything to me. One night, in late October 1978, my curiosity got the better of me. I didn't believe Von could show me anything about my hometown that I didn't know. I was wrong. I quickly began to learn just how little I really knew.

He managed to get me involved on the first night. Actually, it was Von and a little girl named América. América lived in one of the orphanages barely five miles from my grandmother's house in the hills above Tijuana.

She had light hair and blue eyes like mine—she could have been my cousin.   61
When she realized I spoke Spanish, she clutched my fingers and chattered for an
hour without a break. She hung on harder when Von announced it was time to go.
She begged me not to leave. América resorted to a tactic many orphanage children
master to keep visitors from leaving—she wrapped her legs around my calf and sat
on my foot. As I peeled her off, I promised to return on Von's next trip.

He was waiting for me in the alley behind the orphanage.   62

"What did you say to that girl?" he asked.   63

"I told her I'd come back next week."   64

He glared at me. "Don't *ever* tell one of my kids you're coming back," he snapped.   65
"Don't you know she'll wait all week for you? Then she'll wait for months. Don't say
it if you don't mean it."

"I mean it!" I said.   66

I went back the next time to see her. Then again. And, of course, there were other   67
places to go before we got to América's orphanage, and there were other people to
talk to after we left. Each location had people waiting with messages and questions
to translate. It didn't take long for Von to approach me with a proposition. It seemed
he had managed the impressive feat of spending a lifetime in Mexico without picking up any Spanish at all. Within two months, I was Von's personal translator.

It is important to note that translation is often more delicate an art than people   68
assume. For example, Mexicans are regularly amused to read *TV Guide* listings for
Spanish-language TV stations. If one were to leave the tilde (~) off the word *años,* or
"years," the word becomes the plural for "anus." Many cheap laughs are had when
"The Lost Years" becomes "The Lost Butt Holes."

It was clear that Von needed reliable translating. Once, when he had arranged a   69
summer camping trip for *barrio* children, he'd written a list of items the children
needed to take. A well-meaning woman on the team translated the list for Von, and
they Xeroxed fifty or sixty copies.

The word for "comb" in Spanish is *peine,* but leave out a letter, and the word takes   70
on a whole new meaning. Von's note, distributed to every child and all their families, read:

> You must bring CLEAN CLOTHES
> TOOTH PASTE
> SOAP
> TOOTHBRUSH
> SLEEPING BAG
> and BOYS—You Must Remember
> to BRING YOUR PENIS!

Von estimates that in a ten-year period his crew drove several *million* miles in   71
Mexico without serious incident. Over five hundred people came and went as crew
members. They transported more than sixty thousand visitors across the border.

In my time with him, I saw floods and three hundred-mile-wide prairie fires, car   72
wrecks and gang fights, monkeys and blood and shit. I saw human intestines and
burned flesh. I saw human fat through deep red cuts. I saw people copulating. I saw
animals tortured. I saw birthday parties in the saddest sagging shacks. I looked
down throats and up wombs with flashlights. I saw lice, rats, dying dogs, rivers black

with pollywogs, and a mound of maggots three feet wide and two feet high. One little boy in the back country cooked himself with an overturned pot of boiling *frijoles;* when I asked him if it hurt, he sneered like Pancho Villa and said, "Nah." A
maddened Pentecostal tried to heal our broken-down van by laying hands on the
engine block. One girl who lived in a brickyard accidentally soaked her dress in
diesel fuel and lit herself on fire. When I went in the shed, she was standing there,
naked, her entire front burned dark brown and red. The only part of her not burned
was her vulva; it was a startling cleft, a triangular island of white in a sea of burns.

I saw miracles, too. A boy named Chispi, deep in a coma induced by spinal   73
meningitis, suffered a complete shutdown of one lobe of his brain. The doctors in
the intensive care unit, looking down at his naked little body hard-wired to banks of
machinery and pumps, just shook their heads. He was doomed to be a vegetable, at
best. His mother, fished out of the cantinas in Tijuana's red-light district, spent several nights sitting in the hospital cafeteria sipping vending-machine coffee and
telling me she hoped there were miracles left for people like her.

Chispi woke up. The machines were blipping and pinging, and he sat up and   74
asked for Von. His brain had regenerated itself. They unhitched him, pulled out the
catheters, and pulled the steel shunt out of his skull. He went home. There was no
way anybody could explain it. Sometimes there were happy endings, and you spent
as much time wondering about them as grieving over the tragedies.

God help me—it was fun. It was exciting and nasty. I strode, fearless, through the   75
Tijuana garbage dumps and the Barrio of Shallow Graves. I was doing good deeds,
and the goodness thrilled me. But the squalor, too, thrilled me. Each stinking gray
barrio gave me a wicked charge. I was arrested one night by Tijuana cops; I was so
terrified that my knees wobbled like Jell-O. After they let me go, I was happy for a
week. Mexican soldiers pointed machine guns at my testicles. I thought I was going
to die. Later, I was so relieved, I laughed about it for days. Over the years, I was cut,
punctured, sliced: I love my scars. I had girlfriends in every village, in every orphanage, at each garbage dump. For a time, I was a hero. And at night, when we returned,
caked in dried mud, smelly, exhausted, and the good Baptists of Von's church looked
askance at us, we felt dangerous. The housewives, grandmothers, fundamentalists,
rock singers, bikers, former drug dealers, schoolgirls, leftists, republicans, jarheads,
and I were all transformed into *The Wild Bunch.*

It added a certain flair to my dating life as well. It was not uncommon for a Mex-   76
ican crisis to track me down in the most unlikely places. I am reminded of the night
I was sitting down to a fancy supper at a woman's apartment when the phone rang.
A busload of kids from one of our orphanages had flipped over, killing the American daughter of the youth minister in charge of the trip. All the *gringos* had been arrested. The next hour was spent calling Tijuana cops, Mexican lawyers, cousins in
Tijuana, and Von. I had to leave early to get across the border.

Incredibly, in the wake of this tragedy, the orphanage kids were taken to the beach   77
by yet another *gringo* church group, and one of the boys was hit by a car and killed.

My date was fascinated by all this, no doubt.   78

Slowly, it became obvious that nobody outside the experience understood it. Only   79
among ourselves was hunting for lice in each other's hair considered a nice thing.
Nobody but us found humor in the appalling things we saw. No one else wanted to
discuss the particulars of our bowel movements. By firsthand experience, we had

become diagnosticians in the area of gastro-intestinal affliction. Color and content spoke volumes to us: pale, mucus-heavy ropes of diarrhea suggested amoebas. Etc.

One of Von's pep talks revolved around the unconscionable wealth in the United   80
States. "Well," he'd say to some unsuspecting *gringo*, "you're probably not rich. You probably don't even have a television. Oh, you *do?* You have three televisions? One in each room? Wow. But surely you don't have furniture? You do? Living room furniture and beds in the bedroom? Imagine that!

"But you don't have a floor, do you? Do you have carpets? Four walls? A roof!   81
What do you use for light—candles? *Lamps!* No way. Lamps.

"How about your kitchen—do you have a stove?"   82

He'd pick his way through the kitchen: the food, the plates and pots and pans, the   83
refrigerator, the ice. Ice cream. Soda. Booze. The closets, the clothes in the closets. Then to the bathroom and the miracle of indoor plumbing. Whoever lived in that house suddenly felt obscenely rich.

I was never able to reach Von's level of commitment. The time he caught scabies,   84
he allowed it to flourish in order to grasp the suffering of those from whom it originated. He slept on the floor because the majority of the world's population could not afford a bed.

Working with the Text

1. Urrea begins with a description of what it is like to be a poor Mexican in Tijuana who is trying to get across the border. How does this lead into the section headed "My Story"?

2. Near the end of this essay, Urrea writes, "God help me—it was fun. It was exciting and nasty. I strode, fearless, through the Tijuana garbage dumps and the Barrio of Shallow Graves. I was doing good deeds, and the goodness thrilled me. But the squalor, too, thrilled me. Each stinking gray *barrio* gave me a wicked charge." In what sense can you see facing these most appalling of human circumstances as "thrilling"?

 3. How does Urrea use language and writing strategies to help convey his meaning? What is the effect of using a phrase like "ambassadors of poverty" when referring to lice, fleas, and other vermin? What about his use of pronouns, such as *we/us* and *you?* How does he rhetorically move between references to himself as an individual and his recollections of his coworkers as a collective group? How do these techniques point to his overall strategies of crossing borders? What are the different borders being crossed in his essay?

4. Urrea describes Pastor Von's warning the "teenybopper Bible school girls" working with the ministry not to treat the poor like animals and demand that the girls treat them with "love and respect." What does this suggest about the way volunteers sometimes approach the beneficiaries of their charity?

5. Could you work with a group like Spectrum Ministries? What would it take to get you involved?

On Not Being a Victim:
Sex, Rape, and the Trouble with
Following Rules

MARY GAITSKILL

■ Born in Lexington, Kentucky, fiction writer Mary Gaitskill has said that she suffered a troubled adolescence, her rebelliousness leading her strict parents to in-
stitutionalize her several times. She ran away from home at sixteen and spent a
number of years on the fringes of society, often supporting herself as a stripper.
She eventually resumed her education and received her B.A. from the University
of Michigan in 1981. She began publishing stories soon after, with her first collection, *Bad Behavior,* appearing in 1988. Since then she has published *Two Girls, Fat
and Thin* (1991), a novel, and *Because They Wanted To* (1997), another collection of
short stories.

   Gaitskill says that her stories "examine the way people, including myself, create survival systems and psychologically 'safe' places for themselves that . . . although often unworkable and unattractive in social terms, can have a unique
beauty and courage." In the following essay, which originally appeared in the *Atlantic Monthly,* Gaitskill considers the subject of rape—what it means to be the
victim of such a violation and how human subjectivity in interpreting "rules" can
lead to disastrous consequences.

n the early 1970s, I had an experience that could be described as acquaintance
rape. Actually, I have had two or three such experiences, but this one most dramatically fits the profile. I was sixteen and staying in the apartment of a slightly
older girl I'd just met in a seedy community center in Detroit. I'd been in her apartment for a few days when an older guy she knew came over and asked us if we
wanted to drop some acid. In those years, doing acid with complete strangers was
consistent with my idea of a possible good time, so I said yes. When I started peak-
ing, my hostess decided she had to go see her boyfriend, and there I was, alone with
this guy, who, suddenly, was in my face.

   He seemed to be coming on to me, but I wasn't sure. My perception was quite
loopy, and on top of that he was black and urban-poor, which meant that I, being
very inexperienced and suburban-white, did not know how to read him the way I
might have read another white kid. I tried to distract him with conversation, but it
was hard, considering that I was having trouble with logical sentences, let alone
repartee. During one long silence, I asked him what he was thinking. Avoiding my
eyes, he answered, "That if I wasn't such a nice guy you could really be getting
screwed." The remark sounded to me like a threat, albeit a low-key one. But instead
of asking him to explain himself or to leave, I changed the subject. Some moments
later, when he put his hand on my leg, I let myself be drawn into sex because I could
not face the idea that if I said no, things might get ugly. I don't think he had any idea
how unwilling I was—the cultural unfamiliarity cut both ways—and I suppose he
may have thought that all white girls just kind of lie there and don't do or say much.
My bad time was made worse by his extreme gentleness; he was obviously trying very

hard to please me, which, for reasons I didn't understand, broke my heart. Even as inexperienced as I was, I sensed that in his own way he intended a romantic encounter.

For some time afterward I described this event as "the time I was raped." I knew when I said it that the statement wasn't quite accurate, that I hadn't, after all, said no. Yet it *felt* accurate to me. In spite of my ambiguous, even empathic feelings for my unchosen partner, unwanted sex on acid is a nightmare, and I did feel violated by the experience. At times I even flat-out lied about what had happened, grossly exaggerating the violence and the threat—not out of shame or guilt, but because the pumped-up version was more congruent with my feelings of violation than the confusing facts. Every now and then, in the middle of telling an exaggerated version of the story, I would remember the actual man and internally pause, uncertain of how the memory squared with what I was saying or where my sense of violation was coming from—and then I would continue with my story. I am ashamed to admit this, both because it is embarrassing to me and because I am afraid the admission could be taken as evidence that women lie "to get revenge." I want to stress that I would not have lied that way in court or in any other context that might have had practical consequences; it didn't even occur to me to take my case to court. My lies were told not for revenge but in service of what I felt to be the metaphorical truth.

I remember my experience in Detroit, including its aftermath, every time I hear or read yet another discussion of what constitutes "date rape." I remember it when yet another critic castigates "victimism" and complains that everyone imagines himself or herself to be a victim and that no one accepts responsibility anymore. I could imagine telling my story as a verification that rape occurs by subtle threat as well as by overt force. I could also imagine telling it as if I were one of those crybabies who want to feel like victims. Both stories would be true and not true. The complete truth is more complicated than most of the intellectuals who have written scolding essays on victimism seem willing to accept. I didn't understand my own story fully until I described it to an older woman many years later, as a proof of the unreliability of feelings. "Oh, I think your feelings were reliable," she returned. "It sounds like you were raped. It sounds like you raped yourself." I immediately knew that what she said was true, that in failing even to try to speak up for myself, I had, in a sense, raped myself.

I don't say this in a tone of self-recrimination. I was in a difficult situation: I was very young, and he was aggressive. But my inability to speak for myself—to *stand up* for myself—had little to do with those facts. I was unable to stand up for myself because I had never been taught how.

When I was growing up in the 1960s, I was taught by the adult world that good girls never had sex and bad girls did. This rule had clarity going for it but little else; as it was presented to me, it allowed no room for what I actually might feel, what I might want or not want. Within the confines of this rule, I didn't count for much, and I quite vigorously rejected it. Then came the less clear "rules" of cultural trend and peer example that said that if you were cool you wanted to have sex as much as possible with as many people as possible. This message was never stated as a rule, but, considering how absolutely it was woven into the social etiquette of the day (at least in the circles I cared about), it may as well have been. It suited me better than the adults' rule—it allowed me my sexuality, at least—but again it didn't take into account what I might actually want or not want.

The encounter in Detroit, however, had nothing to do with being good or bad, cool or uncool. It was about someone wanting something I didn't want. Since I had been taught only how to follow rules that were somehow more important than I was, I didn't know what to do in a situation where no rules obtained and that required me to speak up on my own behalf. I had never been taught that my behalf mattered. And so I felt helpless, even victimized, without really knowing why.

My parents and my teachers believed that social rules existed to protect me and that adhering to these rules constituted social responsibility. Ironically, my parents did exactly what many commentators recommend as a remedy for victimism. They told me they loved me and that I mattered a lot, but this was not the message I got from the way they conducted themselves in relation to authority and social convention—which was not only that I didn't matter but that *they* didn't matter. In this, they were typical of other adults I knew as well as of the culture around them. When I began to have trouble in school, both socially and academically, a counselor exhorted me to "just play the game"—meaning to go along with everything from school policy to the adolescent pecking order—regardless of what I thought of "the game." My aunt, with whom I lived for a short while, actually burned my jeans and T-shirts because they violated what she understood to be the standards of decorum. A close friend of mine lived in a state of war with her father because of her hippie clothes and hair—which were, of course, de rigueur among her peers. Upon discovering that she was smoking pot, he had her institutionalized. 8

Many middle-class people—both men and women—were brought up, like I was, to equate responsibility with obeying external rules. And when the rules no longer work, they don't know what to do—much like the enraged, gun-wielding protagonist of the movie *Falling Down,* played by Michael Douglas, who ends his ridiculous trajectory by helplessly declaring, "I did everything they told me to." If I had been brought up to reach my own conclusions about which rules were congruent with my internal experience of the world, those rules would have had more meaning for me. Instead, I was usually given a series of static pronouncements. For example, when I was thirteen, I was told by my mother that I couldn't wear a short skirt because "nice girls don't wear skirts above the knee." I countered, of course, by saying that my friend Patty wore skirts above the knee. "Patty is not a nice girl," returned my mother. But Patty *was* nice. My mother is a very intelligent and sensitive person, but it didn't occur to her to define for me what she meant by "nice," what "nice" had to do with skirt length, and how the two definitions might relate to what I had observed to be nice or not nice—and then let me decide for myself. It's true that most thirteen-year-olds aren't interested in, or much capable of, philosophical discourse, but that doesn't mean that adults can't explain themselves more completely to children. Part of becoming responsible is learning how to make a choice about where you stand in respect to the social code and then holding yourself accountable for your choice. In contrast, many children who grew up in my milieu were given abstract absolutes that were placed before us as if our thoughts, feelings, and observations were irrelevant. 9

Recently I heard a panel of feminists on talk radio advocating that laws be passed prohibiting men from touching or making sexual comments to women on the street. Listeners called in to express reactions both pro and con, but the one I remember was a woman who said, "If a man touches me and I don't want it, I don't 10 need a law. I'm gonna beat the hell out of him." The panelists were silent. Then one of them responded in an uncertain voice, "I guess I just never learned how to do that." I understood that the feminist might not want to get into a fistfight with a man likely to be a lot bigger than she, but if her self-respect was so easily shaken by an obscene comment made by some slob on the street, I wondered, how did she expect to get through life? She was exactly the kind of woman whom the cultural critics Camille Paglia and Katie Roiphe have derided as a "rape-crisis feminist"—puritans, sissies, closet-Victorian ladies who want to legislate the ambiguity out of sex. It was very easy for me to feel self-righteous, and I muttered sarcastically at my radio as the panel yammered about self-esteem.

I was conflicted, however. If there had been a time in my own life when I couldn't   11
stand up for myself, how could I expect other people to do it? It could be argued that the grown women on the panel should be more capable than a sixteen-year-old girl whacked out on acid. But such a notion presupposes that people develop at a predictable rate or react to circumstances by coming to universally agreed-upon conclusions. This is the crucial unspoken presumption at the center of the date-rape debate as well as of the larger discourse on victimism. It is a presumption that in a broad but potent sense reminds me of a rule.

Feminists who postulate that boys must obtain a spelled-out "yes" before having   12
sex are trying to establish rules, cut in stone, that will apply to any and every encounter and that every responsible person must obey. The new rule resembles the old good girl/bad girl rule not only because of its implicit suggestion that girls have to be protected but also because of its absolute nature, its iron-fisted denial of complexity and ambiguity. I bristle at such a rule and so do a lot of other people. But should we really be so puzzled and indignant that another rule has been presented? If people have been brought up believing that to be responsible is to obey certain rules, what are they going to do with a can of worms like "date rape" except try to make new rules that they see as more fair or useful than the old ones?

But the "rape-crisis feminists" are not the only absolutists here; their critics play   13
the same game. Camille Paglia, author of *Sexual Personae,* has stated repeatedly that any girl who goes alone into a frat house and proceeds to tank up is cruising for a gang bang, and if she doesn't know that, well, then she's "an idiot." The remark is most striking not for its crude unkindness but for its reductive solipsism. It assumes that all college girls have had the same life experiences as Paglia, and have come to the same conclusions about them. By the time I got to college, I'd been living away from home for years and had been around the block several times. I never went to a frat house, but I got involved with men who lived in rowdy "boy houses" reeking of dirty socks and rock and roll. I would go over, drink, and spend the night with my lover of the moment; it never occurred to me that I was in danger of being gang-raped, and if I had been, I would have been shocked and badly hurt. My experience, though some of it had been bad, hadn't led me to conclude that boys plus alcohol equals gang bang, and I was not naive or idiotic. Katie Roiphe, author of *The Morning After: Fear, Sex, and Feminism on Campus,* criticizes girls who, in her view, create a myth of false innocence: "But did these twentieth-century girls, raised on Madonna videos and the six o'clock news, really trust that people were good until they themselves were raped? Maybe. Were these girls, raised on horror movies and glossy Hollywood sex scenes, really as innocent as all that?" I am sympathetic to

Roiphe's annoyance, but I'm surprised that a smart chick like her apparently doesn't know that people process information and imagery (like Madonna videos and the news) with a complex subjectivity that doesn't in any predictable way alter their ideas about what they can expect from life.

Roiphe and Paglia are not exactly invoking rules, but their comments seem to de- 14 rive from a belief that everyone except idiots interprets information and experience in the same way. In that sense, they are not so different in attitude from those ladies dedicated to establishing feminist-based rules and regulations for sex. Such rules, just like the old rules, assume a certain psychological uniformity of experience, a right way.

The accusatory and sometimes painfully emotional rhetoric conceals an attempt 15 not only to make new rules but also to codify experience. The "rape-crisis feminists" obviously speak for many women and girls who have been raped or have *felt* raped in a wide variety of circumstances. They would not get so much play if they were not addressing a widespread and real experience of violation and hurt. By asking, "Were they really so innocent?" Roiphe doubts the veracity of the experience she presumes to address because it doesn't square with hers or with that of her friends. Having not felt violated herself—even though she says she has had an experience that many would now call date rape—she cannot understand, or even quite believe, that anyone else would feel violated in similar circumstances. She therefore believes all the fuss to be a political ploy or, worse, a retrograde desire to return to crippling ideals of helpless femininity. In turn, Roiphe's detractors, who have not had her more sanguine "morning after" experience, believe her to be ignorant and callous, or a secret rape victim in deep denial. Both camps, believing their own experience to be the truth, seem unwilling to acknowledge the emotional truth on the other side.

It is at this point that the "date-rape debate" resembles the bigger debate about 16 how and why Americans seem so eager to identify themselves and be identified by others as victims. Book after article has appeared, written in baffled yet hectoring language, deriding the P.C. goody-goodies who want to play victim and the spoiled, self-centered fools who attend twelve-step programs, meditate on their inner child, and study pious self-help books. The revisionist critics have all had a lot of fun with the recovery movement, getting into high dudgeon over those materially well-off people who describe their childhoods as "holocausts" and winding up with a fierce exhortation to return to rationality. Rarely do such critics make any but the most superficial attempt to understand why the population might behave thus.

In a fussing, fuming essay in these pages ("Victims, All?" October 1991) that has 17 almost become a prototype of the genre, David Rieff expressed his outrage and bewilderment that affluent people would feel hurt and disappointed by life. He angrily contrasted rich Americans obsessed with their inner children to Third World parents concerned with feeding their actual children. On the most obvious level, the contrast is one that needs to be made, but I question Rieff's idea that suffering is one definable thing, that he knows what it is, and that since certain kinds of emotional pain don't fit this definition they can't really exist. This idea doesn't allow him to have much respect for other people's experience—or even to see it. It may be ridiculous and perversely self-aggrandizing for most people to describe whatever was bad about their childhood as a "holocaust," but I suspect that when people talk like that they are saying that as children they were not given enough of what they would later need in order to know who they are or to live truly responsible lives. Thus they find themselves in a state of bewildering loss that they can't articulate, except by wild exaggeration—much like I defined my inexplicable feelings after my Detroit episode. "Holocaust" may be a grossly inappropriate exaggeration. But to speak in exaggerated metaphors about psychic injury is not so much the act of a crybaby as it is a distorted attempt to explain one's own experience. I think the distortion comes from a desperate desire to make one's experience have consequence in the eyes of others, and that such desperation comes from a crushing doubt that one's own experience counts at all.

In her book *I'm Dysfunctional, You're Dysfunctional,* Wendy Kaminer speaks   18
harshly of women in some twelve-step programs who talk about being metaphorically raped. "It is an article of faith here that suffering is relative; no one says she'd rather be raped metaphorically than in fact," she writes, as if not even a crazy person would prefer a literal rape to a metaphorical one. But actually, I might. About two years after my "rape" in Detroit, I was raped for real. The experience was terrifying: my attacker repeatedly said he was going to kill me, and I thought he might. The terror was acute, but after it was over it actually affected me less than many other mundane instances of emotional brutality I've suffered or seen other people suffer. Frankly, I've been scarred more by experiences I had on the playground in elementary school. I realize that the observation may seem bizarre, but for me the rape was a clearly defined act, perpetrated upon me by a crazy asshole whom I didn't know or trust; it had nothing to do with me or who I was, and so, when it was over, it was relatively easy to dismiss. Emotional cruelty is more complicated. Its motives are often impossible to understand, and it is sometimes committed by people who say they like or even love you. Nearly always it's hard to know whether you played a role in what happened, and, if so, what the role was. The experience *sticks* to you. By the time I was raped I had seen enough emotional cruelty to feel that the rape, although bad, was not especially traumatic.

My response may seem strange to some, but my point is that pain can be an experi-   19
ence that defies codification. If thousands of Americans say that they are in psychic pain, I would not be so quick to write them off as self-indulgent fools. A metaphor like "the inner child" may be silly and schematic, but it has a fluid subjectivity, especially when projected out into the world by such a populist notion as "recovery." Ubiquitous recovery-movement phrases like "We're all victims" and "We're all codependent" may not seem to leave a lot of room for interpretation, but they are actually so vague that they beg for interpretation and projection. Such phrases may be fair game for ridicule, but it is shallow to judge them on their face value, as if they hold the same meaning for everyone. What is meant by an "inner child" depends on the person speaking, and not everyone will see it as a metaphor for helplessness. I suspect that most inner-child enthusiasts use the image of themselves as children not so that they can *avoid* being responsible but to learn responsibility by going back to the point in time when they *should* have been taught responsibility—the ability to think, choose, and stand up for themselves—and were not. As I understand it, the point of identifying an "inner child" is to locate the part of yourself that didn't develop into adulthood and then to develop it yourself. Whether or not this works is an open question, but it is an attempt to accept responsibility, not to flee it.

When I was in my late teens and early twenties, I could not bear to watch movies   20
or read books that I considered demeaning to women in any way; I evaluated
everything I saw or read in terms of whether it expressed a "positive image" of
women. I was a very P.C. feminist before the term existed, and, by the measure of my
current understanding, my critical rigidity followed from my inability to be responsible for my own feelings. In this context, being responsible would have meant that
I let myself feel whatever discomfort, indignation, or disgust I experienced without
allowing those feelings to determine my entire reaction to a given piece of work. In
other words, it would have meant dealing with my feelings and what had caused
them, rather than expecting the outside world to assuage them. I could have chosen
not to see the world through the lens of my personal unhappiness and yet maintained a kind of respect for my unhappiness. For example, I could have decided to
avoid certain films or books because of my feelings without blaming the film or
book for making me feel the way I did.

My emotional irresponsibility did not spring from a need to feel victimized, al-   21
though it may have looked that way to somebody else. I essentially was doing what
I had seen most mainstream cultural critics do—it was from them that I learned to
view works of art in terms of the message they imparted and, further, that the message could be judged on the basis of consensual ideas about what life is, and how it
can and should be seen. My ideas, like most P.C. ideas, were extreme, but they were
consistent with more mainstream thought—they just shifted the parameters of ac-
ceptability a bit.

Things haven't changed much: at least half the book and film reviews that I read   22
praise or condemn a work on the basis of the likability of the characters (as if there
is a standard idea of what is likable) or because the author's point of view is or is not
"life-affirming"—or whatever the critic believes the correct attitude toward life to
be. The lengthy and rather hysterical debate about the film *Thelma and Louise*, in
which two ordinary women become outlaws after one of them shoots the other's
rapist, was predicated on the idea that stories are supposed to function as instruction manuals, and that whether the film was good or bad depended on whether the
instructions were correct. Such criticism assumes that viewers or readers need to see
a certain type of moral universe reflected back at them or, empty vessels that they
are, they might get confused or depressed or something. A respected mainstream
essayist writing for *Time* faulted my novel *Two Girls, Fat and Thin* for its nasty male
characters, which he took to be a moral statement about males generally. He ended
his piece with the fervent wish that fiction not "diminish" men or women but
rather seek to "raise our vision of" both—in other words, that it should present the
"right" way to the reader, who is apparently not responsible enough to figure it out
alone.

I have changed a lot from the P.C. teenager who walked out of movies that por-   23
trayed women in a demeaning light. As I've grown older, I've become more confident of myself and my ability to determine what happens to me, and, as a result,
those images no longer have such a strong emotional charge. I don't believe they will
affect my life in any practical sense unless I allow them to do so. I no longer feel that
misogynistic stories are about me or even about women (whether they purport to
be or not) but rather are about the kinds of experience the authors wish to render—and therefore are not my problem. I consider my current view more balanced,

but that doesn't mean my earlier feelings were wrong. The reason I couldn't watch "disrespect to women" at that time was that such depictions were too close to my own experience (most of which was not unusual), and I found them painful. I was displaying a simplistic self-respect by not subjecting myself to something I was not ready to face. Being unable to separate my personal experience from what I saw on the screen, I was not dealing with my own particular experience—I think, paradoxically, because I hadn't yet learned to value it. It's hard to be responsible for something that isn't valuable. Someone criticizing me as dogmatic and narrow-minded would have had a point, but the point would have ignored the truth of my unacknowledged experience, and thus ignored me.

Many critics of the self-help culture argue against treating emotional or meta-   24
phoric reality as if it were equivalent to objective reality. I agree that they are not the same. But emotional truth is often bound up with truth of a more objective kind and must be taken into account. This is especially true of conundrums such as date rape and victimism, both of which often are discussed in terms of unspoken assumptions about emotional truth anyway. Sarah Crichton, in a cover story for *Newsweek* on "Sexual Correctness," described the "strange detour" taken by some feminists and suggested that "we're not creating a society of Angry Young Women. These are Scared Little Girls." The comment is both contemptuous and superficial; it shows no interest in *why* girls might be scared. By such logic, anger implicitly is deemed to be the more desirable emotional state because it appears more potent, and "scared" is used as a pejorative. It's possible to shame a person into hiding his or her fear, but if you don't address the cause of the fear, it won't go away. Crichton ends her piece by saying, "Those who are growing up in environments where they don't have to figure out what the rules should be, but need only follow what's been prescribed, are being robbed of the most important lesson there is to learn. And that's how to live." I couldn't agree more. But unless you've been taught how to think for yourself, you'll have a hard time figuring out your own rules, and you'll feel scared—especially when there is real danger of sexual assault.

One reason I had sex with strangers when I didn't really want to was that part of   25
me wanted the adventure, and that tougher part ran roughshod over the part of me that was scared and uncertain. I'll bet the same thing happened to many of the boys with whom I had these experiences. All people have their tough, aggressive selves as well as their more delicate selves. If you haven't developed these characteristics in ways that are respectful of yourself and others, you will find it hard to be responsible for them. I don't think it's possible to develop yourself in such ways if you are attuned to following rules and codes that don't give your inner world enough importance. I was a strong-willed child with a lot of aggressive impulses, which, for various reasons, I was actively discouraged from developing. They stayed hidden under a surface of extreme passivity, and when they did appear it was often in a wildly irresponsible, almost crazy way. My early attraction to aggressive boys and men was in part a need to see *somebody* act out the distorted feelings I didn't know what to do with, whether it was destructive or not. I suspect that boys who treat girls with disrespectful aggression have failed to develop their more tender, sensitive side and futilely try to regain it by "possessing" a woman. Lists of instructions about what's nice and what isn't will not help people in such a muddled state, and it's my observation that many people are in such a state to a greater or lesser degree.

I am not idealistic enough to hope that we will ever live in a world without rape   26
and other forms of sexual cruelty; I think men and women will always have to struggle to behave responsibly. But I think we could make the struggle less difficult by
changing the way we teach responsibility and social conduct. To teach a boy that
rape is "bad" is not as effective as making him see that rape is a violation of his own
masculine dignity as well as a violation of the raped woman. It's true that children
don't know big words and that teenage boys aren't all that interested in their own
dignity. But these are things that children learn more easily by example than by
words, and learning by example runs deep.

A few years ago I invited to dinner at my home a man I'd known casually for two   27
years. We'd had dinner and comradely drinks a few times. I didn't have any intention of becoming sexual with him, but after dinner we slowly got drunk and were
soon floundering on the couch. I was ambivalent not only because I was drunk but
because I realized that although part of me was up for it, the rest of me was not. So
I began to say no. He parried each "no" with charming banter and became more aggressive. I went along with it for a time because I was amused and even somewhat
seduced by the sweet, junior-high spirit of his manner. But at some point I began to
be alarmed, and then he did and said some things that turned my alarm into fright.
I don't remember the exact sequence of words or events, but I do remember taking
one of his hands in both of mine, looking him in the eyes, and saying, "If this comes
to a fight you would win, but it would be very ugly for both of us. Is that really what
you want?"

His expression changed and he dropped his eyes; shortly afterward he left.   28

I consider that small decision to have been a responsible one because it was made   29
by taking both my vulnerable feelings and my carnal impulses into account. When I
spoke, my words came from my feeling of delicacy as well as from my capacity for
aggression. And I respected my friend as well by addressing both sides of his nature.
It is not hard for me to make such decisions now, but it took me a long time to get
to this point. I only regret that it took so long, both for my young self and for the boys
I was with, under circumstances that I now consider disrespectful to all concerned.

Working with the Text

1. Gaitskill describes two different incidents of rape in her life: the first a case
of "date rape" when she was a teenager, and the second a case of violent rape
by a stranger who threatened to kill her. Why was the second rape so much
less traumatic for her than the first?

2. Gaitskill says that her parents and teachers believed that simply following
rules "constituted social responsibility" (¶ 8). What does she see as the problem with simply teaching children to follow rules? What do you think constitutes personal and social responsibility?

3. Throughout this essay Gaitskill suggests that people do not "develop at a
predictable rate or react to circumstances by coming to universally agreed-
upon conclusions" (¶ 11), that we each "process information and imagery . . .
with a complex subjectivity" not necessarily similar to anyone else's (¶ 13).

How do these differences relate to her beliefs about rules? How might they create problems of communication? In a paper address the interrelationship between social rules and subjectivity. In what ways is subjectivity shaped by social rules of behavior? When and how do individuals transcend them?

4. Gaitskill says that—as in her own description of her date-rape experience and in someone's description of his or her childhood as a "holocaust"— people sometimes find they have to exaggerate in order to communicate the complex emotional depth of an experience. Have you ever found yourself doing this? Is doing so a legitimate means of communication?

5. Late in the essay, Gaitskill writes that women who have been forced to suppress their own aggressive impulses often seek out aggressive, violent men, while men who have failed to develop the more sensitive side of their nature "futilely try to regain it by 'possessing' a woman," perhaps violently. Does your own experience lend any credence to this idea? How does it relate to her belief that rape is just as much a violation of a man's masculine identity as it is of the woman who is raped?

TINYSEX AND GENDER TROUBLE

SHERRY TURKLE

■ With degrees in sociology and psychology from Harvard University, clinical psychologist Sherry Turkle has been a professor of the sociology of science at the Massachusetts Institute of Technology since 1976. The recipient of both a Rockefeller and a Guggenheim fellowship, Turkle has taken a cross-disciplinary approach in much of her research and writing. Among her early scholarly works is *Psychoanalysis, Creativity, and Literature* (1978). More recently, her work has focused on looking, in her words, "at computers as carriers of culture, as objects that give rise to new metaphors, to new relationships between people and machines, between different people, and most significantly between people and their ways of thinking about themselves." In the following chapter from her most recent book, *Life on the Screen: Identity in the Age of the Internet* (1995), Turkle considers the potential of electronic communication (and the anonymity and role-playing it allows) for transforming our conceptions of gender and sexuality and for creating new modes of communication across—and beyond—gender lines.

From my earliest effort to construct an online persona, it occurred to me that being a virtual man might be more comfortable than being a virtual woman. When I first logged on to a MUD, I named and described a character but forgot to give it a gender. I was struggling with the technical aspects of the MUD universe—the difference between various MUD commands such as "saying" and "emoting," "paging" and "whispering." Gender was the last thing on my mind. This rapidly changed when a male-presenting character named Jiffy asked me if I was "really an it." At his question, I experienced an unpleasurable sense of disorientation which immediately gave way to an unfamiliar sense of freedom.

When Jiffy's question appeared on my screen, I was standing in a room of LambdaMOO filled with characters engaged in sexual banter in the style of the movie *Animal House.* The innuendos, double entendres, and leering invitations were scrolling by at a fast clip; I felt awkward, as though at a party to which I had been invited by mistake. I was reminded of junior high school dances when I wanted to go home or hide behind the punch bowl. I was reminded of kissing games in which it was awful to be chosen and awful not to be chosen. Now, on the MUD, I had a new option. I wondered if playing a male might allow me to feel less out of place. I could stand on the sidelines and people would expect *me* to make the first move. And I could choose not to. I could choose simply to "lurk," to stand by and observe the action. Boys, after all, were not called prudes if they were too cool to play kissing games. They were not categorized as wallflowers if they held back and didn't ask girls to dance. They could simply be shy in a manly way—aloof, above it all.

Two days later I was back in the MUD. After I typed the command that joined me, in Boston, to the computer in California where the MUD resided, I discovered that I had lost the paper on which I had written my MUD password. This meant that I could not play my own character but had to log on as a guest. As such, I was assigned a color: Magenta. As "Magenta_guest" I was again without gender. While I was struggling with basic MUD commands, other players were typing messages for all to see such as "Magenta_guest gazes hot and enraptured at the approach of Fire_Eater." Again I was tempted to hide from the frat party atmosphere by trying to pass as a man. When much later I did try playing a male character, I finally experienced that permission to move freely I had always imagined to be the birthright of men. Not only was I approached less frequently, but I found it easier to respond to an unwanted overture with aplomb, saying something like, "That's flattering, Ribald_Temptress, but I'm otherwise engaged." My sense of freedom didn't just involve a different attitude about sexual advances, which now seemed less threatening. As a woman I have a hard time deflecting a request for conversation by asserting my own agenda. As a MUD male, doing so (nicely) seemed more natural; it never struck me as dismissive or rude. Of course, my reaction said as much about the construction of gender in my own mind as it did about the social construction of gender in the MUD.

Playing in MUDs, whether as a man, a woman, or a neuter character, I quickly fell into the habit of orienting myself to new cyberspace acquaintances by checking out their gender. This was a strange exercise, especially because a significant proportion of the female-presenting characters were RL men, and a good number of the male-presenting characters were RL women. I was not alone in this curiously irrational preoccupation. For many players, guessing the true gender of players behind MUD characters has become something of an art form. Pavel Curtis, the founder of LambdaMOO, has observed that when a female-presenting character is called something like FabulousHotBabe, one can be almost sure there is a man behind the mask. Another experienced MUDder shares the folklore that "if a female-presenting character's description of her beauty goes on for more than two paragraphs, 'she' [the player behind the character] is sure to be an ugly woman."

The preoccupation in MUDs with getting a "fix" on people through "fixing" their   6
gender reminds us of the extent to which we use gender to shape our relationships.
Corey, a twenty-two-year-old dental technician, says that her name often causes
people to assume that she is male—that is, until she meets them. Corey has long
blonde hair, piled high, and admits to "going for the Barbie look."

> I'm not sure how it started, but I know that when I was a kid the more people
> said, "Oh, you have such a cute boy's name," the more I laid on the hairbows.
> [With my name] they always expected a boy—or at least a tomboy.

Corey says that, for her, part of the fun of being online is that she gets to see "a lot   7
of people having the [same] experience [with their online names that] I've had with
my name." She tells me that her girlfriend logged on as Joel instead of Joely, "and she
saw people's expectations change real fast." Corey continues:

> I also think the neuter characters [in MUDs] are good. When I play one, I real-
> ize how hard it is not to be either a man or a woman. I always find myself try-
> ing to be one or the other even when I'm trying to be neither. And all the time
> I'm talking to a neuter character [she reverses roles here] . . . I'm thinking "So
> who's behind it?"

In MUDs, the existence of characters other than male or female is disturbing, evocative. Like transgressive gender practices in real life, by breaking the conventions, it
dramatizes our attachment to them.

Gender-swapping on MUDs is not a small part of the game action. By some es-   8
timates, Habitat, a Japanese MUD, has 1.5 million users. Habitat is a MUD operated
for profit. Among the registered members of Habitat, there is a ratio of four real-life
men to each real-life woman. But inside the MUD the ratio is only three male characters to one female character. In other words, a significant number of players, many
tens of thousands of them, are virtually cross-dressing.

GENDER TROUBLE

What is virtual gender-swapping all about? Some of those who do it claim that it is   9
not particularly significant. "When I play a woman I don't really take it too seriously," said twenty-year-old Andrei. "I do it to improve the ratio of women to men.
It's just a game." On one level, virtual gender-swapping is easier than doing it in real
life. For a man to present himself as female in a chat room, on an IRC channel, or in
a MUD, only requires writing a description. For a man to play a woman on the
streets of an American city, he would have to shave various parts of his body; wear
makeup, perhaps a wig, a dress, and high heels; perhaps change his voice, walk, and
mannerisms. He would have some anxiety about passing, and there might be even
more anxiety about not passing, which would pose a risk of violence and possibly
arrest. So more men are willing to give virtual cross-dressing a try. But once they are
online as female, they soon find that maintaining this fiction is difficult. To pass as
a woman for any length of time requires understanding how gender inflects speech,
manner, the interpretation of experience. Women attempting to pass as men face

the same kind of challenge. One woman said that she "worked hard" to pass in a room on a commercial network service that was advertised as a meeting place for gay men.

> I have always been so curious about what men do with each other. I could never even imagine how they talk to each other. I can't exactly go to a gay bar and eavesdrop inconspicuously. [When online] I don't actually have [virtual] sex with anyone. I get out of that by telling the men there that I'm shy and still unsure. But I like hanging out; it makes gays seem less strange to me. But it is not so easy. You have to think about it, to make up a life, a job, a set of reactions.

Virtual cross-dressing is not as simple as Andrei suggests. Not only can it be technically challenging, it can be psychologically complicated. Taking a virtual role may involve you in ongoing relationships. In this process, you may discover things about yourself that you never knew before. You may discover things about other people's response to you. You are not in danger of being arrested, but you are embarked on an enterprise that is not without some gravity and emotional risk.

In fact, one strong motivation to gender-swap in virtual space is to have TinySex as a creature of another gender, something that suggests more than an emotionally neutral activity. Gender-swapping is an opportunity to explore conflicts raised by one's biological gender. Also, as Corey noted, by enabling people to experience what it "feels" like to be the opposite gender or to have no gender at all, the practice encourages reflection on the way ideas about gender shape our expectations. MUDs and the virtual personae one adopts within them are objects-to-think-with for reflecting on the social construction of gender.

Case, a thirty-four-year-old industrial designer who is happily married to a coworker, is currently MUDding as a female character. In response to my question, "Has MUDding ever caused you any emotional pain?" he says, "Yes, but also the kind of learning that comes from hard times."

> I'm having pain in my playing now. The woman I'm playing in MedievalMUSH [Mairead] is having an interesting relationship with a fellow. Mairead is a lawyer. It costs so much to go to law school that it has to be paid for by a corporation or a noble house. A man she met and fell in love with was a nobleman. He paid for her law school. He bought my [Case slips into referring to Mairead in the first person] contract. Now he wants to marry me although I'm a commoner. I finally said yes. I try to talk to him about the fact that I'm essentially his property. I'm a commoner, I'm basically property and to a certain extent that doesn't bother me. I've grown up with it, that's the way life is. He wants to deny the situation. He says, "Oh no, no, no. . . . We'll pick you up, set you on your feet, the whole world is open to you."
>
> But everytime I behave like I'm now going to be a countess some day, you know, assert myself—as in, "And I never liked this wallpaper anyway"—I get pushed down. The relationship is pull up, push down. It's an incredibly psychologically damaging thing to do to a person. And the very thing that he liked about her—that she was independent, strong, said what was on her mind—it is all being bled out of her.

Case looks at me with a wry smile and sighs, "A woman's life." He continues:

> I see her [Mairead] heading for a major psychological problem. What we have is a dysfunctional relationship. But even though it's very painful and stressful, it's very interesting to watch myself cope with this problem. How am I going to dig my persona's self out of this mess? Because I don't want to go on like this. I want to get out of it. . . . You can see that playing this woman lets me see what I have in my psychological repertoire, what is hard and what is easy for me. And I can also see how some of the things that work when you're a man just backfire when you're a woman.

Case has played Mairead for nearly a year, but even a brief experience playing a character of another gender can be evocative. William James said, "Philosophy is the art of imagining alternatives." MUDs are proving grounds for an action-based philosophical practice that can serve as a form of consciousness-raising about gender issues. For example, on many MUDs, offering technical assistance has become a common way in which male characters "purchase" female attention, analogous to picking up the check at an RL dinner. In real life, our expectations about sex roles (who offers help, who buys dinner, who brews the coffee) can become so ingrained that we no longer notice them. On MUDs, however, expectations are expressed in visible textual actions, widely witnessed and openly discussed. When men playing females are plied with unrequested offers of help on MUDs, they often remark that such chivalries communicate a belief in female incompetence. When women play males on MUDs and realize that they are no longer being offered help, some reflect that those offers of help may well have led them to believe they needed it. As a woman, "First you ask for help because you think it will be expedient," says a college sophomore, "then you realize that you aren't developing the skills to figure things out for yourself." [13]

ALL THE WORLD'S A STAGE

Any account of the evocative nature of gender-swapping might well defer to Shakespeare, who used it as a plot device for reframing personal and political choices. *As You Like It* is a classic example, a comedy that uses gender-swapping to reveal new aspects of identity and to permit greater complexity of relationships. In the play, Rosalind, the Duke's daughter, is exiled from the court of her uncle Frederick, who has usurped her father's throne. Frederick's daughter, Rosalind's cousin Celia, escapes with her. Together they flee to the magical forest of Arden. When the two women first discuss their plan to flee, Rosalind remarks that they might be in danger because "beauty provoketh thieves sooner than gold." In response, Celia suggests that they would travel more easily if they rubbed dirt on their faces and wore drab clothing, thus pointing to a tactic that frequently provides women greater social ease in the world—becoming unattractive. Rosalind then comes up with a second idea—becoming a man: "Were it not better, / Because that I am more than common tall, / That I did suit me all points like a man?" [14]

In the end, Rosalind and Celia both disguise themselves as boys, Ganymede and Aliena. In suggesting this ploy, Rosalind proposes a disguise that will be both physical ("A gallant curtle-axe on my thigh, / A boar-spear in my hand") and emotional ("and—in my heart, / Lie there what hidden woman's fear there will"). She goes on, "We'll have a swashbuckling and martial outside, / as many other mannish cowards have / That do outface it with their semblances." [15]

In these lines, Rosalind does not endorse an essential difference between men [16] and women; rather, she suggests that men routinely adopt the same kind of pose she is now choosing. Biological men have to construct male gender just as biological women have to construct female gender. If Rosalind and Celia make themselves unattractive, they will end up less feminine. Their female gender will end up deconstructed. Both strategies—posing as men and deconstructing their femininity—are games that female MUDders play. One player, a woman currently in treatment for anorexia, described her virtual body this way:

> In real life, the control is the thing. I know that it is very scary for me to be a woman. I like making my body disappear. In real life that is. On MUDs, too. On the MUD, I'm sort of a woman, but I'm not someone you would want to see sexually. My MUD description is a combination of smoke and angles. I like that phrase "sort of a woman." I guess that's what I want to be in real life too.

In addition to virtual cross-dressing and creating character descriptions that de- [17] construct gender, MUDders gender-swap as double agents. That is, in MUDs, men play women pretending to be men, and women play men pretending to be women. Shakespeare's characters play these games as well. In *As You Like It,* when Rosalind flees Frederick's court she is in love with Orlando. In the forest of Arden, disguised as the boy Ganymede, she encounters Orlando, himself lovesick for Rosalind. As Ganymede, Rosalind says she will try to cure Orlando of his love by playing Rosalind, pointing out the flaws of femininity in the process. In current stagings, Rosalind is usually played by a woman who at this point in the play pretends to be a man who pretends to be a woman. In Shakespeare's time, there was yet another turn because all women's parts were played by boys. So the character of Rosalind was played by a boy playing a girl playing a boy who plays a girl so she can have a flirtatious conversation with a boy. Another twist occurs when Rosalind playing Ganymede playing Rosalind meets Phebe, a shepherdess who falls passionately in love with "him."

As You Like It, with its famous soliloquy that begins "All the world's a stage," is a [18] play that dramatizes the power of the theater as a metaphor for life. The visual pun of Rosalind's role underscores the fact that each of us is an actor playing one part or many parts. But the play has another message that speaks to the power of MUDs as new stages for working on the politics of gender. When Rosalind and Orlando meet "man to man" as Ganymede and Orlando, they are able to speak freely. They are able to have conversations about love quite different from those that would be possible if they followed the courtly conventions that constrain communications between men and women. In this way, the play suggests that donning a mask, adopting a persona, is a step toward reaching a deeper truth about the real, a position many MUDders take regarding their experiences as virtual selves.

Garrett is a twenty-eight-year-old male computer programmer who played a fe- [19] male character on a MUD for nearly a year. The character was a frog named Ribbit. When Ribbit sensed that a new player was floundering, a small sign would materialize in her hand that said, "If you are lost in the MUD, this frog can be a friend."

When talking about why he chose to play Ribbit, Garrett says: [20]

> I wanted to know more about women's experiences, and not just from reading
> about them. . . . I wanted to see what the difference felt like. I wanted to exper-
> iment with the other side. . . . I wanted to be collaborative and helpful, and I
> thought it would be easier as a female. . . . As a man I was brought up to be
> territorial and competitive. I wanted to try something new. . . . In some way I
> really felt that the canonically female way of communicating was more pro-
> ductive than the male—in that all this competition got in the way.

And indeed, Garrett says that as a female frog, he did feel freer to express the helpful side of his nature than he ever had as a man. "My competitive side takes a back
seat when I am Ribbit."

Garrett's motivations for his experiment in gender-swapping run deep. Growing   21
up, competition was thrust upon him and he didn't much like it. Garrett, whose
parents divorced when he was an infant, rarely saw his father. His mother offered little protection from his brother's bullying. An older cousin regularly beat him up
until Garrett turned fourteen and could inflict some damage of his own. Garrett got
the clear idea that male aggression could only be controlled by male force.

In his father's absence, Garrett took on significant family responsibility. His   22
mother ran an office, and Garrett checked in with her every day after school to see
if she had any errands for him to run. If so, he would forgo the playground. Garrett
recalls these days with great warmth. He felt helpful and close to his mother. When
at ten, he won a scholarship to a prestigious private boarding school for boys, a
school he describes as being "straight out of Dickens," there were no more opportunities for this kind of collaboration. To Garrett, life now seemed to be one long competition. Of boarding school he says:

> It's competitive from the moment you get up in the morning and you all got
> to take a shower together and everyone's checking each other out to see who's
> got pubic hair. It's competitive when you're in class. It's competitive when
> you're on the sports field. It's competitive when you're in other extracurricular
> activities such as speeches. It's competitive all day long, every day.

At school, the older boys had administrative authority over the younger ones.   23
Garrett was not only the youngest student, he was also from the poorest family and
the only newcomer to a group that had attended school together for many years. "I
was pretty much at the bottom of the food chain," he says. In this hierarchical environment, Garrett learned to detest hierarchy, and the bullies at school reinforced his
negative feelings about masculine aggression.

Once out of high school, Garrett committed himself to finding ways to "get back   24
to being the kind of person I was with my mother." But he found it difficult to develop collaborative relationships, particularly at work. When he encouraged a female coworker to take credit for some work they had done together—"something,"
he says "that women have always done for men"—she accepted his offer, but their
friendship and ability to work together were damaged. Garrett sums up the experience by saying that women are free to help men and both can accept the woman's
self-sacrifice, "but when a man lets a woman take the credit, the relationship feels
too close, too seductive [to the woman]."

From Garrett's point of view, most computer bulletin boards and discussion groups are not collaborative but hostile environments, characterized by "flaming." This is the practice of trading angry and often *ad hominem* remarks on any given topic.

> There was a premium on saying something new, which is typically something that disagrees to some extent with what somebody else has said. And that in it-self provides an atmosphere that's ripe for conflict. Another aspect, I think, is the fact that it takes a certain degree of courage to risk really annoying some-one. But that's not necessarily true on an electronic medium, because they can't get to you. It's sort of like hiding behind a wall and throwing stones. You can keep throwing them as long as you want and you're safe.

Garrett found MUDs different and a lot more comfortable. "On MUDs," he says, "people were making a world together. You got no prestige from being abusive."

Garrett's gender-swapping on MUDs gave him an experience-to-think-with for thinking about gender. From his point of view, all he had to do was to replace male with female in a character's description to change how people saw him and what he felt comfortable expressing. Garrett's MUD experience, where as a female he could be collaborative without being stigmatized, left him committed to bringing the helpful frog persona into his life as a male, both on and off the MUD. When I met him, he had a new girlfriend who was lending him books about the differences in men's and women's communication styles. He found they reinforced the lessons he learned in the MUD.

By the time I met Garrett, he was coming to feel that his gender-swapping exper-iment had reached its logical endpoint. Indeed, between the time of our first and second meeting, Garrett decided to blow his cover on the MUD and tell people that in RL he was really male. He said that our discussions of his gender-swapping had made him realize that it had achieved its purpose.

For anthropologists, the experience of *dépaysement* (literally, "decountrifying" oneself) is one of the most powerful elements of fieldwork. One leaves one's own culture to face something unfamiliar, and upon returning home it has become strange—and can be seen with fresh eyes. Garrett described his decision to end his gender-swapping in the language of *dépaysement*. He had been playing a woman for so long that it no longer seemed strange. "I'd gotten used to it to the extent that I was sort of ignoring it. OK, so I log in and now I'm a woman. And it really didn't seem odd anymore." But returning to the MUD as a male persona *did* feel strange. He struggled for an analogy and came up with this one:

> It would be like going to an interview for a job and acting like I do at a party or a volleyball game. Which is not the way you behave at an interview. And so it is sort of the same thing. [As a male on the MUD] I'm behaving in a way that doesn't feel right for the context, although it is still as much me as it ever was.

When Garrett stopped playing the female Ribbit and started playing a helpful male frog named Ron, many of Garrett's MUDding companions interpreted his ac-tions as those of a woman who now wanted to try playing a man. Indeed, a year after his switch, Garrett says that at least one of his MUD friends, Dredlock, remains un-convinced that the same person has actually played both Ribbit and Ron. Dredlock insists that while Ribbit was erratic (he says, "She would sometimes walk out in the middle of a conversation"), Ron is more dependable. Has Garrett's behavior changed? Is Garrett's behavior the same but viewed differently through the filter of gender? Garrett believes that both are probably true. "People on the MUD have . . . seen the change and it hasn't necessarily convinced them that I'm male, but they're also not sure that I'm female. And so, I've sort of gotten into this state where my gender is unknown and people are pretty much resigned to not knowing it." Garrett says that when he helped others as a female frog, it was taken as welcome, natural, and kind. When he now helps as a male frog, people find it unexpected and suspect that it is a seduction ploy. The analogy with his real life is striking. There, too, he found that playing the helping role as a man led to trouble because it was easily mis-interpreted as an attempt to create an expectation of intimacy.

Case, the industrial designer who played the female Mairead in MedievalMUSH, 31 further illustrates the complexity of gender-swapping as a vehicle for self-reflection. Case describes his RL persona as a nice guy, a "Jimmy Stewart–type like my father." He says that in general he likes his father and he likes himself, but he feels he pays a price for his low-key ways. In particular, he feels at a loss when it comes to con-frontation, both at home and in business dealings. While Garrett finds that MUD-ding as a female makes it easier to be collaborative and helpful, Case likes MUDding as a female because it makes it easier for him to be aggressive and confrontational. Case plays several online "Katharine Hepburn–types," strong, dynamic, "out there" women who remind him of his mother, "who says exactly what's on her mind and is a take-no-prisoners sort." He says:

> For virtual reality to be interesting it has to emulate the real. But you have to be able to do something in the virtual that you couldn't in the real. For me, my female characters are interesting because I can say and do the sorts of things that I mentally want to do, but if I did them as a man, they would be obnox-ious. I see a strong woman as admirable. I see a strong man as a problem. Po-tentially a bully.

In other words, for Case, if you are assertive as a man, it is coded as "being a bas-tard." If you are assertive as a woman, it is coded as "modern and together."

> My wife and I both design logos for small businesses. But do this thought ex-periment. If I say "I will design this logo for $3,000, take it or leave it," I'm just a typical pushy businessman. If she says it, I think it sounds like she's a "to-gether" woman. There is too much male power-wielding in society, and so if you use power as a man, that turns you into a stereotypical man. Women can do it more easily.

Case's gender-swapping has given him permission to be more assertive within 32 the MUD, and more assertive outside of it as well:

> There are aspects of my personality—the more assertive, administrative, bu-reaucratic ones—that I am able to work on in the MUDs. I've never been good at bureaucratic things, but I'm much better from practicing on MUDs and playing a woman in charge. I am able to do things—in the real, that is—that I couldn't have before because I have played Katharine Hepburn characters.

Case says his Katharine Hepburn personae are "externalizations of a part of my- 33
self." In one interview with him, I use the expression "aspects of the self," and he
picks it up eagerly, for MUDding reminds him of how Hindu gods could have different aspects or subpersonalities, all the while having a whole self.

> You may, for example, have an aspect who is a ruthless business person who
> can negotiate contracts very, very well, and you may call upon that part of
> yourself while you are in tense negotiation, to do the negotiation, to actually
> go through and negotiate a really good contract. But you would have to trust
> this aspect to say something like, "Of course, I will need my lawyers to look
> over this," when in fact among your "lawyers" is the integrated self who is
> going to do an ethics vet over the contract, because you don't want to violate
> your own ethical standards and this [ruthless] aspect of yourself might do
> something that you wouldn't feel comfortable with later.

Case's gender-swapping has enabled his inner world of hard-bitten negotiators 34
to find self-expression, but without compromising the values he associates with his
"whole person." Role playing has given the negotiators practice; Case says he has
come to trust them more. In response to my question, "Do you feel that you call
upon your personae in real life?" Case responds:

> Yes, an aspect sort of clears its throat and says, "I can do this. You are being so
> amazingly conflicted over this and I know exactly what to do. Why don't you
> just let me do it?" MUDs give me balance. In real life, I tend to be extremely
> diplomatic, nonconfrontational. I don't like to ram my ideas down anyone's
> throat. On the MUD, I can be, "Take it or leave it." All of my Hepburn charac-
> ters are that way. That's probably why I play them. Because they are smart-
> mouthed, they will not sugarcoat their words.

In some ways, Case's description of his inner world of actors who address him 35
and are capable of taking over negotiations is reminiscent of the language of people
with multiple personality. In most cases of multiple personality, it is believed that
repeated trauma provokes a massive defense: An "alter" is split off who can handle
the trauma and protect the core personality from emotional as well as physical pain.
In contrast, Case's inner actors are not split off from his sense of himself. He calls
upon their strengths with increasing ease and fluidity. Case experiences himself very
much as a collective self, not feeling that he must goad or repress this or that aspect
of himself into conformity. To use Marvin Minsky's language, Case feels at ease in
his society of mind.

Garrett and Case play female MUD characters for very different reasons. There is 36
a similar diversity in women's motivations for playing male characters. Some share
my initial motivation, a desire for invisibility or permission to be more outspoken
or aggressive. "I was born in the South and I was taught that girls didn't speak up to
disagree with men," says Zoe, a thirty-four-year-old woman who plays male and female characters on four MUDs.

> We would sit at dinner and my father would talk and my mother would agree.
> I thought my father was a god. Once or twice I did disagree with him. I re-
> member one time in particular when I was ten, and he looked at me and said,

"Well, well, well, if this little flower grows too many more thorns, she will never catch a man."

Zoe credits MUDs with enabling her to reach a state of mind where she is better   37
able to speak up for herself in her marriage ("to say what's on my mind before things get all blown out of proportion") and to handle her job as the financial officer for a small biotechnology firm.

> I played a MUD man for two years. First I did it because I wanted the feeling
> of an equal playing field in terms of authority, and the only way I could think
> of to get it was to play a man. But after a while, I got very absorbed by MUD-
> ding. I became a wizard on a pretty simple MUD—I called myself
> Ulysses—and got involved in the system and realized that as a man I could be
> firm and people would think I was a great wizard. As a woman, drawing the
> line and standing firm has always made me feel like a bitch and, actually, I feel
> that people saw me as one, too. As a man I was liberated from all that. I
> learned from my mistakes. I got better at being firm but not rigid. I practiced,
> safe from criticism.

Zoe's perceptions of her gender trouble are almost the opposite of Case's. Case   38
sees aggressiveness as acceptable only for women; Zoe sees it as acceptable only for men. Comparison with Garrett is also instructive. Like Case, Garrett associated feminine strength with positive feelings about his mother; Zoe associated feminine strength with loss of her father's love. What these stories have in common is that in all three cases, a virtual gender swap gave people greater emotional range in the real. Zoe says:

> I got really good at playing a man, so good that whoever was on the system
> would accept me as a man and talk to me as a man. So, other guys talked to
> Ulysses "guy to guy." It was very validating. All those years I was paranoid
> about how men talked about women. Or I thought I was paranoid. And then, I
> got a chance to be a guy and I saw that I wasn't paranoid at all.

Zoe talked to me about her experiences in a face-to-face interview, but there is a   39
great deal of spontaneous discussion of these issues on Internet bulletin boards and discussion groups. In her paper "Gender Swapping on the Internet," Amy Bruckman tracks an ongoing discussion of gender issues on the electronic discussion group rec.games.mud. Individuals may post to it, that is, send a communication to all subscribers. Postings on specific topics frequently start identifiable discussion "threads," which may continue for many months.

On one of these threads, several male participants described how playing female   40
characters had given them newfound empathy with women. One contributor, David, described the trials and tribulations of playing a female character:

> Other players start showering you with money to help you get started, and I
> had never once gotten a handout when playing a male player. And then they
> feel they should be allowed to tag along forever, and feel hurt when you leave
> them to go off and explore by yourself. Then when you give them the knee
> after they grope you, they wonder what your problem is, reciting that famous
> saying, "What's your problem? It's only a game."

Carol, an experienced player with much technical expertise about MUDs, con-   41
curred. She complained about male players' misconception that "women can't play
MUDs, can't work out puzzles, can't even type 'kill monster' without help." Carol
noted that men offered help as a way to be ingratiating, but in her case this seduction strategy was ineffectual: "People offering me help to solve puzzles *I* wrote are
not going to get very far."

Ellen, another contributor to the rec.games.mud discussion, tried gender-bending   42
on an adventure-style MUD, thinking she would find out:

> if it was true that people would be nasty and kill me on sight and other stuff
> I'd heard about on r.g.m. [an abbreviation of rec.games.mud]. But, no,
> everyone was helpful (I was truly clueless and needed the assistance); someone
> gave me enough money to buy a weapon and armor and someone else showed
> me where the easy-to-kill newbie [a new player] monsters were. They
> definitely went out of their way to be nice to a male-presenting newbie. . . .
> (These were all male-presenting players, btw [by the way].)
>
> One theory is that my male character [named Argyle and described as "a
> short squat fellow who is looking for his socks"] was pretty innocuous. Maybe
> people are only nasty if you are "a broad-shouldered perfect specimen of a
> man" or something of that nature, which can be taken as vaguely attacking.

Ellen concluded that harassment relates most directly to self-presentation: "Peo-   43
ple are nice if they don't view you as a threat." Short, squat, a bit lost, in search of
socks, and thus connoting limpness—Argyle was clearly not a threat to the dominant status of other "men" on the MUD. In the MUD culture Ellen played in, men
tended to be competitive and aggressive toward each other; Argyle's nonthreatening
self-presentation earned him kind treatment.

For some men and women, gender-bending can be an attempt to understand   44
better or to experiment safely with sexual orientation. But for everyone who tries it,
there is the chance to discover, as Rosalind and Orlando did in the Forest of Arden,
that for both sexes, gender is constructed.

VIRTUAL SEX

Virtual sex, whether in MUDs or in a private room on a commercial online service,   45
consists of two or more players typing descriptions of physical actions, verbal statements, and emotional reactions for their characters. In cyberspace, this activity
is not only common but, for many people, it is the centerpiece of their online
experience.

On MUDs, some people have sex as characters of their own gender. Others have   46
sex as characters of the other gender. Some men play female personae to have netsex with men. And in the "fake-lesbian syndrome," men adopt online female personae in order to have netsex with women. Although it does not seem to be as
widespread, I have met several women who say they present as male characters in
order to have netsex with men. Some people have sex as nonhuman characters, for
example, as animals on FurryMUDs. Some enjoy sex with one partner. Some use
virtual reality as a place to experiment with group situations. In real life such behavior (where possible) can create enormous practical and emotional confusion.

Virtual adventures may be easier to undertake, but they can also result in significant complications. Different people and different couples deal with them in very different ways.

Martin and Beth, both forty-one, have been married for nineteen years and have four children. Early in their marriage, Martin regretted not having had more time for sexual experimentation and had an extramarital affair. The affair hurt Beth deeply, and Martin decided he never wanted to do it again. When Martin discovered MUDs he was thrilled. "I really am monogamous. I'm really not interested in something outside my marriage. But being able to have, you know, a Tiny romance is kind of cool." Martin decided to tell Beth about his MUD sex life and she decided to tell him that she does not mind. Beth has made a conscious decision to consider Martin's sexual relationships on MUDs as more like his reading an erotic novel than like his having a rendezvous in a motel room. For Martin, his online affairs are a way to fill the gaps of his youth, to broaden his sexual experience without endangering his marriage.

Other partners of virtual adulterers do not share Beth's accepting attitude. Janet, twenty-four, a secretary at a New York law firm, is very upset by her husband Tim's sex life in cyberspace. After Tim's first online affair, he confessed his virtual infidelity. When Janet objected, Tim told her that he would stop "seeing" his online mistress. Janet says that she is not sure that he actually did stop.

> Look, I've got to say the thing that bothers me most is that he wants to do it in the first place. In some ways, I'd have an easier time understanding why he would want to have an affair in real life. At least there, I could say to myself, "Well, it is for someone with a better body, or just for the novelty." It's like the first kiss is always the best kiss. But in MUDding, he is saying that he wants that feeling of intimacy with someone else, the "just talk" part of an encounter with a woman, and to me that comes closer to what is most important about sex.
>
> First I told him he couldn't do it anymore. Then, I panicked and figured that he might do it anyway, because unlike in real life I could never find out. All these thousands of people all over the world with their stupid fake names . . . no way I would ever find out. So, I pulled back and said that talking about it was strictly off limits. But now I don't know if that was the right decision. I feel paranoid whenever he is on the computer. I can't get it off my mind, that he is cheating, and he probably is tabulating data for his thesis. It must be clear that this sex thing has really hurt our marriage.

This distressed wife struggles to decide whether her husband is unfaithful when his persona collaborates on writing real-time erotica with another persona in cyberspace. And beyond this, should it make a difference if unbeknownst to the husband his cyberspace mistress turns out to be a nineteen-year-old male college freshman? What if "she" is an infirm eighty-year-old man in a nursing home? And even more disturbing, what if she is a twelve-year-old girl? Or a twelve-year-old boy?

TinySex poses the question of what is at the heart of sex and fidelity. Is it the physical action? Is it the feeling of emotional intimacy with someone other than one's primary partner? Is infidelity in the head or in the body? Is it in the desire or in the action? What constitutes the violation of trust? And to what extent and in what ways should it matter who the virtual sexual partner is in the real world? The fact that the physical body has been factored out of the situation makes these issues both subtler and harder to resolve than before.

Janet feels her trust has been violated by Tim's "talk intimacy" with another woman. Beth, the wife who gave her husband Martin permission to have TinySex, feels that he violated her trust when he chose to play a female character having a sexual encounter with a "man." When Beth read the log of one of these sessions, she became angry that Martin had drawn on his knowledge of her sexual responses to play his female character. 51

For Rudy, thirty-six, what was most threatening about his girlfriend's TinySex was the very fact that she wanted to play a character of the opposite sex at all. He discovered that she habitually plays men and has sex with female characters in chat rooms on America Online (like MUDs in that people can choose their identities). This discovery led him to break off the relationship. Rudy struggles to express what bothers him about his ex-girlfriend's gender-bending in cyberspace. He is not sure of himself, he is unhappy, hesitant, and confused. He says, "We are not ready for the psychological confusion this technology can bring." He explains: 52

> It's not the infidelity. It's the gnawing feeling that my girlfriend—I mean, I was
> thinking of marrying her—is a dyke. I know that everyone is bisexual, I know,
> I know . . . but that is one of those things that I knew but it never had
> anything to do with me. . . . It was just intellectual.
>   What I hate about the rooms on America Online is that it makes it so easy
> for this sort of thing to become real. Well, in the sense that the rooms are real.
> I mean, the rooms, real or not, make it too easy for people to explore these
> things. If she explored it in real life, well, it would be hard on me, but it would
> have been hard for her. If she really wanted to do it, she would do it, but it
> would have meant her going out and doing it. It seems like more of a
> statement. And if she had really done it, I would know what to make of it.
> Now, I hate her for what she does online, but I don't know if I'm being crazy
> to break up with her about something that, after all, is only words.

Rudy complained that virtual reality made it too easy for his girlfriend to explore what it might be like to have a sexual relationship with another woman, too easy for her to experience herself as a man, too easy to avoid the social consequences of her actions. MUDs provide a situation in which we can play out scenarios that otherwise might have remained pure fantasy. Yet the status of these fantasies-in-action in cyberspace is unclear. Although they involve other people and are no longer pure fantasy, they are not "in the world." Their boundary status offers new possibilities. TinySex and virtual gender-bending are part of the larger story of people using virtual spaces to construct identity. 53

Working with the Text

1. Much of what Turkle is discussing in this essay are the ways that people in online spaces take on and play with different kinds of personae. As you think about what she says about virtual interactions, consider the different per-

sonae that you might have in different contexts. Do you "appear" as a different person in different contexts?

2. Taking as an example any online space that you have been to (or go to for this assignment), analyze how people play with their online personae. Are people always "themselves"? Is the idea of "self" at all complicated by the online environment? (Consider any kind of online environment: chat room, IRC, MUD or MOO, Bulletin Board, or "real time" chat space you might be using for your course.) In what ways does the behavior of participants change or adapt to virtual spaces? Are identities and personae more flexible, deceptive, playful, vulnerable?

3. Turkle says of her decision to finally take on a male identity online, "When much later I did try playing a male character, I finally experienced that permission to move freely I had always imagined to be the birthright of men. . . . As a woman I have a hard time deflecting a request for conversation by asserting my own agenda. As a MUD male, doing so (nicely) seemed more natural; it never struck me as dismissive or rude. Of course, my reaction said as much about the construction of gender in my own mind as it did about the social construction of gender in the MUD." What are some of the ways that the "social construction of gender" in "real life" is revealed through Turkle's analysis of role playing and gender online? Do online spaces facilitate the negotiation of differences or simply perpetuate them in new ways?

4. Near the end of the selection, Turkle summarizes the complex issues at the heart of what she calls TinySex:

> TinySex poses the question of what is at the heart of sex and fidelity. Is it the physical action? Is it the feeling of emotional intimacy with someone other than one's primary partner? Is infidelity in the head or in the body? Is it in the desire or in the action? What constitutes the violation of trust? And to what extent and in what ways should it matter who the virtual sexual partner is in the real world? The fact that the physical body has been factored out of the situation makes these issues both subtler and harder to resolve than before.

How do you respond to these questions?

5. Turkle refers to these "fantasies-in-action" online as having a "boundary status" with the real world. That is, they are not "in the world" (as she puts it) but yet they involve real emotions and other people. Write a paper in which you examine the idea of "boundary status" regarding online experiences. You can focus on these sexual/emotional experiences, or expand out to other kinds of interactions. Can you think of other examples of online experience that have "boundary status" with the real world? Can you speculate about any? What can we learn about ourselves and the "real world" from online experiences?

Thinking and Writing: *Critical Questions Revisited*

1. Strategies of Communication Across Differences

In this chapter there are various examples and models of how people communicate across and through their differences. Some of the discussion is about how certain groups simply perceive ideas and issues differently and consequently communicate differently about them. We saw examples in Blauner's description of how whites and blacks view racism differently. Other essays are themselves models or strategies of communication for negotiating differences (and power imbalances), such as the coping communication and behavior of Gary Soto, Wong Sam's Chinese phrase book, Martin Luther King's persuasive rhetoric, or Mary Gaitskill's learning to survive a potentially violent imbalance of power between herself and a male pursuer by using the right kind of communication.

Choose among the chapter's many approaches to this topic and write a paper about communication across differences. How is communication different for various groups? Once we understand fundamental differences in perception, what are the options for clear communication? How do those communication strategies translate into approaches to writing and speaking? In negotiating differences, what are the options for making connections? An appeal to shared values? An appeal to shared differences? An appeal to fear? An appeal to reason? An appeal to violence? Choose any text from this chapter or elsewhere and analyze it as an act of communication across differences. Or discuss the topic as an overview, using examples from throughout the chapter.

2. What Is a Contact Zone?

In her essay on the language of intercultural contact, Mary Louise Pratt defines *contact zones* as "social spaces where cultures meet, clash, and grapple with each other, often in contexts of highly asymmetrical relations of power." Can you think of a contact zone of which you are a part or can observe? How would you go about describing and analyzing a contact zone? What issues do you find interesting and important in examining these kinds of social spaces? How do people in such "zones" communicate with each other? What are the signs and signals of "asymmetrical relations of power"? In what ways is a classroom or a school a contact zone? What about where you work? Or where you live? Or being on the Internet in some kind of electronic chat group or electronic community? What are the key factors that influence life in the contact zone that you are examining?

3. Can a Contact Zone Be a Community?

One of the important concepts in this book is "community," which is often defined as a relatively coherent and often homogeneous group with a physical or values-driven bond. The concept of community contrasts with the idea of a contact zone, which implies diversity, inequality, and imbalance. What happens when we think of these two ideas together? Is it possible to have a contact zone that might be considered a coherent community by all its members, not just by its dominant ones? Can a contact zone be positive for all its inhabitants? Can a contact zone also be a community? Can you think of one?

4. Taking It Personally: Individual Versus Institutional Responses to Difference

Is there a separate way that groups—as opposed to individuals—respond to differences? Bob Blauner, for example, claims that one of the fundamental differences in the ways that whites and blacks perceive the issue of racism is that whites think of racism as a personal issue, whereas blacks are more likely to think of racism as "structural" or "institutional." How might individuals respond to differences in ways that ignore institutional or structural responses? What is the relationship between institutional attitudes and individual responses toward marginalized people? Are individuals always implicated in group or institutional responses? How are attitudes of particular cultural identifications, nativism (anti-foreigner sentiment), or self-imposed segregation group responses rather than individual responses? Can individuals make a difference in the context of structural responses to differences such as racism, intolerance, or marginalization? Are individuals accountable for structural problems? Does passivity among individuals, as Martin Luther King suggests in "Letter from Birmingham Jail," constitute complicity with institutional problems?

5. Victims, Rules, and Responsibility

What does it mean to be a "victim"? How is being a victim an important part of the dynamics of difference? To what extent is your being perceived as a victim (by others or by yourself) a matter of choice or social construction? To what extent do social contexts informed by significant differences in power or privilege create victims? Every social and cultural context has certain "rules" (as Gaitskill calls them) that dictate how we ought to respond to differences. What are some of the rules that you've encountered? When does following or not following the rules constitute an act of personal responsibility? How is the act of taking personal responsibility related to the idea of victimization?

6. Autoethnography and "Border Texts"

Pratt's essay in this chapter also discusses "autoethnography," a kind of writing that she claims is particular to contact zones. She defines an autoethnography as "a text in which people undertake to describe themselves in ways that engage with representations others have made of them" (p. 370). There are numerous texts in this book that could be viewed as contemporary "autoethnographies." Using Pratt's basic definition, write a paper in which you examine one or more other essays that you've read in this book that you consider examples of "autoethnography." In what ways do the authors work with or against representations of themselves "that others have made of them"? Is this kind of writing inevitable for certain marginalized groups or individuals? How might this kind of writing be a part of the process of "acculturation"? How might it be a resistance to acculturation? Is it useful to think about the meaning of autoethnographic "border texts" in the context of what Pratt calls "transculturation," a phenomenon of the contact zone where members of a marginal group select or invent materials transmitted by a dominant culture?

BORDERS AND FRONTIERS:

Imagined and
Virtual Communities

Alan Thomas and Ben Crow: *Maps, Projections and Ethnocentricity* [maps and text]

Benedict Anderson: *The Concept of "Nation": A Definition* [essay]

Frederick Jackson Turner: *The Significance of the Frontier in American History* [essay]

Patricia Nelson Limerick: *The Adventures of the Frontier in the Twentieth Century* [essay]

Jane Tompkins: *At the Buffalo Bill Museum—June 1988* [essay]

Chrystos: *I Have Not Signed a Treaty with the United States Government* [poem]

Clark Blaise: *The Border as Fiction* [essay]

William Mitchell: *Soft Cities* [essay]

Steven G. Jones: *Understanding Community in the Information Age* [essay]

Allucquère Rosanne Stone: *Sex, Death, and Machinery, or How I Fell in Love with My Prosthesis* [essay]

Critical Questions for *Borders and Frontiers*

To what extent are communities constructed imaginatively in the minds of their members? What role does our environment play in the way we imagine the communities we inhabit? How do perceptions of geography and physical environment contribute to one's sense of cultural and individual identity? How do frontiers—the "edges" of nations and other communities—define communities, both geographically and imaginatively? In particular, how has the concept of the American frontier colored Americans' perceptions of their country, themselves, and others? How might online communication in virtual space shape the way individual or communal identity is imagined in ways that face-to-face communication cannot? Can a true community exist online? How do virtual communities differ from local ones? What will be the relationship between online communities and other kinds of communities, such as local communities or our concept of a national community?

IMAGINED COMMUNITIES

Not long after the Internet first became popular, its users were imagining it as a new, empty space waiting to be filled. Not only was the Internet thought of as "open space," but it was also often considered in terms of the American frontier. In 1993, Howard Rheingold published a book called *Virtual Communities,* with the subtitle "Homesteading on the Electronic Frontier." One of the early advocacy groups for freedom of speech and expression on the Internet called itself the Electronic Frontier Foundation. Randy Farmer, a leader of the first online, or virtual, community, said of MUDs (a kind of online community called a MultiUser Dungeon): "Right now MUDs are wild frontier towns being held together by a bunch of homesteaders," but they eventually "will evolve rules of conduct and even forms of self-governance."

Using this kind of language to describe the Internet and cyberspace reveals not only the degree to which we think of electronic environments in spatial terms (i.e., as if they were physical places) but also that we think of those spaces as representing a *process* that parallels the settlement of the American West. First, cyberspace is perceived as a vast, open country that is essentially vacant, a place where no one initially "owns" anything. This anarchy of open spaces quickly subsides as people settle the space and establish their own communities and societies. Something is both lost and gained through this settlement. In the end people will probably be nostalgic for the "good old days" of Wild Cyberspace in the same ways that American culture endlessly relives, revises, and often rejoices in the days of the pioneers and the Wild West. Perhaps one of the features that attracts people to cyberspace during its imaginative and idealistic phase is the "space" it gives them to explore and call their own.

We'll consider why people are so attracted to cyberspace at the end of this chapter. First, let's simply ask why people need to think of cyberspace *as a space,* and what we can learn about ourselves by examining this concept. In his essay in this chapter, William Mitchell says, "Cyberspace is still tough territory to travel, though, and we are just beginning to glimpse what it may hold." He then quotes a comment that Mitch Kapor and John Perry Barlow (founders of the Electronic Frontier Foundation) made about the Internet and cyberspace back in 1990 when they were very new, long before the appearance of the World Wide Web:

> [C]yberspace is a frontier region, populated by the few hardy technologists who can tolerate the austerity of its savage computer interfaces, incompatible communications protocols, proprietary barricades, cultural and legal ambiguities, and general lack of useful maps or metaphors. . . .
>
> Certainly, the old concepts of property, expression, identity, movement, and context, based as they are on physical manifestation, do not apply succinctly in a world where there can be none.

Everything we need for a new Wild West is here in the language of Kapor and Barlow's comment: a new "frontier" space, "hardy" pioneers, and even a "savage" landscape to conquer, along with a number of other intolerable "barricades" to success in this as-yet-uncharted territory.

Their language points not only to the living legacy of the American frontier as a dominant metaphor for imagining a new venture or place but also to Internet users' need to imagine cyberspace as big, open, limitless, and comprehensive. It wasn't inevitable that cyberspace would be conceived as a space, or that people would speak of electronic environments as new "worlds" and alternative, constructed "realities." However, these terms of understanding seem to be the most compelling and attractive, whether in the context of pure romantic speculation about technology's potential or in the attention-grabbing media campaigns of hardware and software manufacturers.

Kapor and Barlow raise another important point when they talk about how "the old concepts of property, expression, identity, movement, and context, based as they are on physical manifestation, do not apply succinctly in a world where there can be none." Cyberspace is a nonphysical place that is designed and described by analogies to physical things: property lines, homes, sites, bodies, communities. Cyberspace and the Internet are the ultimate cross between a *border text* and a *border place* because, after all, what are places on the Internet but texts, and vice versa? Also, as a place built out of texts, cyberspace is nothing but imagined realities with made-up structures, representations of people, and simulated environments with new kinds of rules and limits.

Watching the development and spread of cyberspace and the Internet gives us an easy window into how physical and imaginative components interact to create a constructed reality. In this sense, however, electronic spaces are not unique. They are just one version of the interaction of the physical and the nonphysical, of real and symbolic dimensions of the worlds we inhabit—whether an electronic community, a neighborhood community, a group identity that transcends physical space, or even a nation. In fact, nations may be one of the most important and powerful examples of the synthesis of the geographical (physical) and the imaginative (symbolic).

Benedict Anderson argues that all nations are "imagined communities." That is, all nations are comprised of people who believe that they are connected in some fundamental way to other people within certain limited boundaries. People inside the United States, France, or Thailand all think that they have an abstract connection to all the other people who call themselves American, French, or Thai—and that this connection is based, to some extent, on the physical, geographic (and political) boundaries of their country.

Anderson asserts that all communities of almost any size are "imagined communities" that are distinguished "by the style in which they are imagined." Thus, nations are a particular kind of community that is imagined in one particular style (Anderson elaborates on this notion later in the chapter). Alternatively, communities located in cyberspace are characterized by different factors but are still a kind of "imagined community," just as a city or a neighborhood would be. However, what all these imagined communities have in common is that they are combinations of cultural values and physical places.

This chapter raises some of the book's most abstract questions: How is the perspective of groups, cultures, communities, even nations formed by a context that could be characterized as an imaginative reality—a reality based on a geographical place and formed in a particular space? In what ways does the physical environment shape cultural perceptions? Conversely, in what ways do cultural values shape our perceptions of geographical space and the physical environment?

Although these questions may seem abstract or obscure, there are significant consequences to pursuing this important dimension of cultural thinking. In Chapters 4 and 5, we looked at how communities and cultures define a sense of "otherness" that often has the impact of excluding or denigrating certain groups and types of people. In the course of examining our culture, we find that our sense of difference and otherness often relates to space and place. How people regard the homeless, how one neighborhood perceives its own boundaries, or how natives perceive immigrants are all real social phenomena that are rooted in the imaginative and perceptual qualities of physical space and geography. It would be incomplete, then, to think about the nature of identity and difference without also considering these spatial and environmental dimensions. And there is no more important place to begin than with the most persistent and influential of American borders—the American frontier.

THE AMERICAN FRONTIER AS PLACE AND IDEA

When Americans hear the word *frontier,* they tend to think of those parts of the country that were once filled with pioneers and cowboys, cavalry and Indians, farmers and gold miners. When people in the United States think of the "frontier," they think of a place that was rough and untamed, a place without law and order—and without culture and cities. The frontier is the edge of civilization, the ultimate American border.

In other words, Americans tend to think of the frontier as a "place." Even if they think of it as many different places (the Kentucky of Daniel Boone, the Dodge City of cowboy movies, the California mountains of the gold miners), they still tend to think of the American frontier as a geographic location, a part of the country that once had yet to be civilized.

However, the American frontier was more than a physical place. It was an *idea*—one that existed, in many ways, before there even was a geographical frontier. In order for a culture to imagine that there is a frontier (i.e., an edge or distant border), it also has to imagine that there is a *center.* Therefore, the idea of a *frontier* of civilization implies that there is a *center* of civilization. Imagining a frontier and a center is more than just conceiving of geographic points. It implies certain things about values and human characteristics. Such an idea assumes that the people who live at the center represent the center of some cultural ideal and that those who live at the edge on the frontier live outside that ideal—or at its margins. Whether the Europeans who first encountered native people in the New World or the pioneers who encountered Indians on the Great Plains, the European explorers and settlers of America brought to the "frontier" a whole set of stereotypes and images about normal and abnormal culture and about the center and edge of civilization.

As a place and as an idea, the frontier is America's longest-lived cultural border, and the one most central to its cultural identity. In fact, it is the interaction of physical space and cultural identity that gives the frontier its force. As Frederick Jackson Turner says in his essay in this chapter, the frontier was not only important to American development, but it had also always been the most important aspect of American history. Writing over a hundred years ago in 1893, Turner calls the frontier "the outer edge of the wave" of westward expansion, "the meeting point between savagery and civilization." He also maintains that this meeting point was the place where the American people were formed: "The fact is that here [on the frontier] is a new product that is American. At first the frontier was the Atlantic coast. It was the frontier of Europe in a very real sense. Moving westward, the frontier became more and more American."

This process of "Americanization" (as Turner puts it) had everything to do with the physical space of an open continent. None of the restrictive institutional structures that characterized Europe could be found on the frontier: there was no aristocracy, no handful of rich landowners. On the frontier, supposedly, there were no "classes," no upper class and lower class. The American frontier was "open"—both environmentally and economically. According to the traditional American mythology, the frontier offered unlimited opportunity to all people, without prejudice against their social standing. The frontier's openness of opportunity is what, according to Turner, gave the United States of America its special quality as a land devoted to democracy, equality, and the opportunity for social mobility and individual success.

However, inside the myth of the frontier is a fairly narrow reading of history. The American frontier moved from east to west, a movement implying civilization's march in a single direction into the wilds and the inevitable conquest of a "savage" people. The myth of the American frontier assumed that the land in front of the westward-moving Europeans was new, vacant, empty space waiting to be filled. If people already lived in this empty space (and some did), they didn't "own" it in the eyes of the Europeans.

In America the story of the frontier is the story of a very particular kind of border. Just as in Chapter 2, where we looked at a range of cultural stories that exerted a shaping influence on individual identity, the idea of the American frontier is one of the dominant stories that exerts a shaping influence on American cultural identity. Long after the frontier had ceased to be a real place, it continued as the dominant myth of our culture, blending symbol, emotion, and image.

In standard usage the primary definition of *frontier* is linked to the United States and its westward expansion (see for example, John Gast's *American Progress* in the Image Portfolio). But, as Patricia Limerick points out in her essay, the term has a second meaning—"the much less familiar, but much more realistic, usage of *la frontera,* the borderlands between Mexico and the United States." The idea of the frontier as a border—or borderlands—rather than as a line of progress contrasts the image of a frontier where empty land and primitive people give way to a superior culture with a more complicated notion of two or more cultures coexisting in a complex imbalance of power and wealth. As Limerick puts it, "In the idea of *la frontera,* there is no illusion of vacancy, of triumphal conclusions, or of simplicity. . . . It is a unique place on the planet's surface, a zone where an industrialized nation shares a long land border with a nation much troubled by poverty." The difference between the two meanings—between frontier and *la frontera*—is huge and speaks to the importance of understanding the interplay of geography and perception, the physical and the symbolic. Limerick says, "If the idea of *la frontera* had anywhere near the standing of the idea of the frontier, we would be well launched toward self-understanding, directed toward a realistic view of this nation's position in the hemisphere and in the world."

But the traditional image of the frontier as a place of adventure and conquest still dominates our culture, precisely because it is not just a place but also an idea. And as an idea, it has tended to appeal to some very basic emotional needs in American culture. In explaining, for example, the tremendous appeal of Buffalo Bill and his traveling Wild West shows (complete with reenactments of Indian fights and buffalo hunts), Jane Tompkins claims that Buffalo Bill "and his cowboys played to an inward territory: a Wild West of the psyche that hungered for exercise sprang into activity when the show appeared." The notions of the frontier and the Wild West have persisted in American culture precisely because they are not just some geographical territory of the past but rather an "inward territory" in the culture's mind and soul.

All this brings us back to the idea of electronic frontiers and the construction of cyberspace. To what extent do the Internet and cyberspace "play to an inward territory"? How is their appeal related to a recovery of the values and emotions associated with the Western frontier: open space and opportunity, progress, mobility, democracy, and even adventure and discovery? Where are the edges and borders of the electronic frontier? Where is the sense of limits? Where are the boundaries and limits in cyberspace? Is the Internet another cultural phenomenon—like cities and shopping malls—through which we attempt to deny human limits? Or is it a territory open for the taking?

VIRTUAL COMMUNITIES: IT DOESN'T RAIN IN CYBERSPACE

Cyberspace (or "Computer Mediated Communication"), as Steven Jones puts it in his essay in this chapter,

> is not just a tool; it is at once technology, medium, and engine of social relations. It not only structures social relations, it is the space within which the relations occur and the tool that individuals use to enter that space. It is more than the context within which social relations occur (although it is that, too) for it is commented on and imaginatively constructed by symbolic processes initiated and maintained by individuals and groups.

As "socially produced space," new electronic environments like the Internet represent new ways for individuals and groups to interact. What, then, are the implications for all of the issues related to communicating and living with *difference* that the earlier chapters in this book have been exploring? How will people deal with each other in these new contact zones where boundaries, edges, and limits operate with different rules? Jones poses these questions in terms of how people will develop a sense of *belonging* to electronic communities: "What is the nature of individual members' commitments to [electronic communities]? In the physical world, community members must live together. When community membership is in no small way a simple matter of subscribing or unsubscribing to a bulletin board or electronic newsgroup, is the nature of interaction different simply because one may disengage with little or no consequence?"

nother essay William Mitchell asks a similar set of questions in structural and
ectural, rather than in behavioral, terms:

doesn't rain in cyberspace, so shelter is not an architectural issue. But privacy cer-
ainly is. So the construction technology for virtual cities—just like that of bricks-and-
mortar ones—must provide for putting up boundaries and erecting access controls,
and it must allow cyberspace architects and urban designers to organize virtual places
into public-to-private hierarchies.

What will it mean if we are building "virtual cities" for ourselves to live in? What will
be the implications, not just for public and private space on the Internet, but for the
relationship between the private space of being online and the public space of physical world interaction? What will be our commitment to the physical world? How
will it differ from our commitment to online communities?

These are new and compelling questions that arise from the same basic issues we
have been exploring: identity, community, and difference. Electronic environments,
like cyberspace, give us the opportunity to explore new kinds of spaces with different sorts of boundaries, edges, and limits. Consequently, they encourage us to rethink our perspectives on issues of who we are and how we relate to who we are not.
They even pose questions about the boundaries of the human body. Speaking of
Stephen Hawking—the world-famous physicist who suffers from a degenerative
disease so that he can only speak through an artificial, electronically operated
speech device (a prosthesis)—Allucquère Rosanne Stone asks: "Where *does* he stop?
Where are his edges? The issues his person and his communication prosthesis raise
are boundary debates, borderland/*frontera* questions." Whether about bodies, identities, communities, or territories, ultimately this chapter addresses *spaces and their
boundaries,* understood as both places and ideas.

MAPS, PROJECTIONS AND ETHNOCENTRICITY

ALAN THOMAS AND BEN CROW

■ The following selection from the *Third World Atlas* (1994) asks you to consider
how the geographic representations of the world that we see on maps actually
"distort sizes, shapes, relative locations, directions and distances." It also illustrates
how the most common representations create a Europe-centered image of the
world. The authors have provided a number of different geographic renderings to
suggest alternative ways of viewing the relations among the world's continents.

The Earth is almost perfectly spherical in shape. (In fact, it is just a little flattened at the poles, so that whereas the distance around the Equator is
40,077 km, the distance along the meridian from South Pole to North Pole
and back to South Pole again is only 39,942 km.) The way in which a sphere or globe
is represented on a flat surface is called a *projection.* Map projections are bound to
be distorted in one way or another—to realize this, think of spreading and stretching out flat the peel of an orange.

Different projections distort sizes, shapes, relative locations, directions and distances in different ways, and are designed for different purposes. Mercator's projection is probably the most familiar. It was developed in the sixteenth century as an aid to navigation, but is now commonly used as a reference base on which to put any kind of geographical information, for many purposes other than navigation at sea, including cases where other projections would be better. Mercator's projection has the special property of maintaining the true direction of any one point relative to another, so that, for example, a line drawn diagonally on the map at 45° to the equator always points north-east. Shapes are also fairly faithfully reproduced. However, the price paid is that distances and areas are both magnified towards the poles, so that Greenland, for example, looks much bigger than it really is, relative to, say, Africa or China. In fact, this distortion becomes mathematically infinite towards the poles and a map on Mercator's projection can never include the poles themselves. As a result, a false impression is given of the shortest distance between points around the earth's surface. For example, North America and Russia are in fact quite close to each other across the polar regions. William-Olsson's projection, on which air routes are shown on [page 463] is one of several which do show this.

It has been suggested that Mercator's projection promotes a Eurocentric view of the world—Europe is in the centre of the top half of the map and is disproportionately large. Placing the North Pole at the top (rather than the bottom or either side) dates back to the Ancient Greeks; measuring longitude from the Greenwich meridian so that London is usually in the middle of a map derives from British domination of the seas. (There is an early example of a map with a different orientation and a different centre on page 467, left.) Peters' projection was developed recently to "correct the Europe-centred image of the world as projected by Mercator." It is an "equal-area" projection; that is, regions on the globe which are equal in land (or sea) area are represented by equal areas on the map. Peters' projection also conserves the North–South and East–West directions throughout. However, other directions and, more importantly, distances and shapes, are quite badly distorted, so that near the equator the land surfaces appear to be elongated in a North–South direction, whereas near the poles they are stretched in an East–West direction.

Peters' projection still has the North Pole at the top and the Greenwich meridian down the middle! Perhaps, though, the very fact that Peters' projection "looks funny" draws attention to the Third World countries presented in "their actual central position."

2

3

4

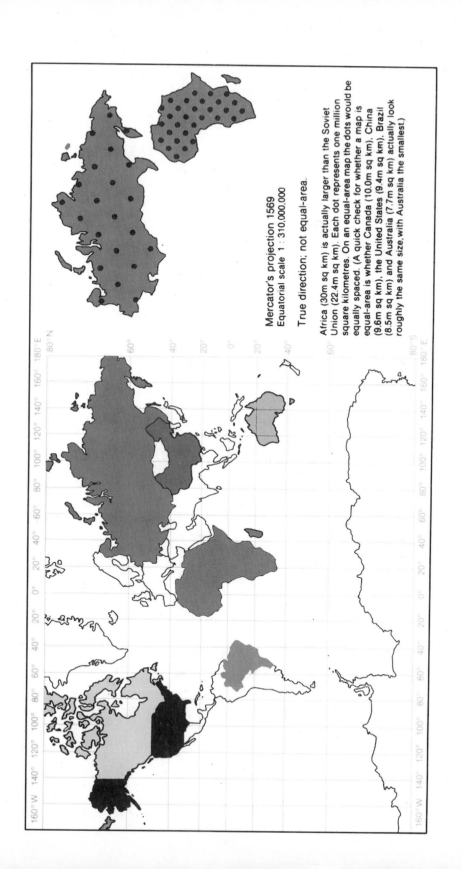

Mercator's projection 1569
Equatorial scale 1 : 310,000,000

True direction; not equal-area.

Africa (30m sq km) is actually larger than the Soviet
Union (22.4m sq km). Each dot represents one million
square kilometres. On an equal-area map the dots would be
equally spaced. (A quick check for whether a map is
equal-area is whether Canada (10.0m sq km). China
(9.6m sq km), the United States (9.4m sq km). Brazil
(8.5m sq km) and Australia (7.7m sq km) actually look
roughly the same size with Australia the smallest.)

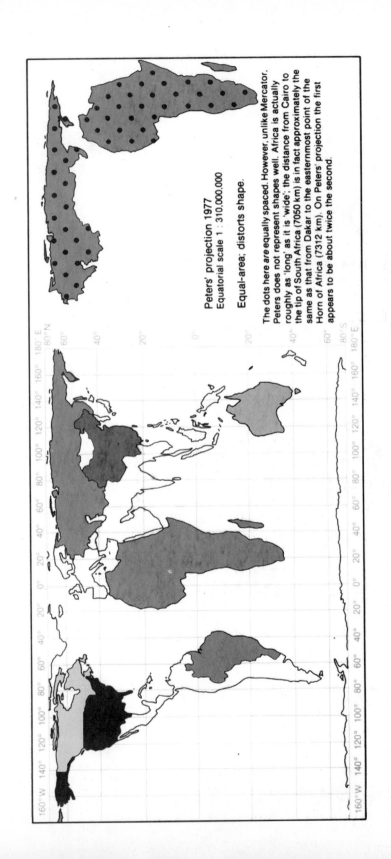

Peters' projection 1977
Equatorial scale 1 : 310,000,000

Equal-area; distorts shape.

The dots here *are* equally spaced. However, unlike Mercator, Peters does not represent shapes well. Africa is actually roughly as 'long' as it is 'wide': the distance from Cairo to the tip of South Africa (7050 km) is in fact approximately the same as that from Dakar to the easternmost point of the Horn of Africa (7312 km). On Peters' projection the first appears to be about twice the second.

There are numerous other equal-area projections, mostly based on an oval out-   5
line and curved lines of longitude and/or latitude. Mollweide's projection, on which
the main human races are shown on [page 465], is perhaps the simplest. However,
the deformation of shape towards the poles is possibly worse than with Peters' projection, since the surfaces are not simply elongated but also appear at different
angles. . . .

In this Atlas, different projections are used as appropriate, and the variety of cen-   6
tres and types of projection is meant to counter any tendency to Eurocentrism. The
majority of the maps are presented on the equal-area projection used by the *1980
World Bank Atlas,* namely the Eckert IV projection. This projection does not distort
shape as badly as Peters' or Mollweide's. It is drawn here with lines of latitude and
longitude to show how it is constructed. In the main world maps in the Atlas, the
land-masses are shown as large as possible on the page. As a result, New Zealand is
slightly displaced, and Antarctica and most of the Pacific Ocean are omitted.

It is worth pondering how the use of any kind of map affects the way one under-   7
stands the data presented. Does an equal-area map really present a good picture of
the relative importance of different countries of the world? The next [few] pages
show various types and uses of maps—and ways of presenting geographical
data without maps—that are less straightforward than simply choosing a different
projection.

W. William-Olsson's projection centred on London, showing main world air routes.

1:280,000,000
from centre of map (London)

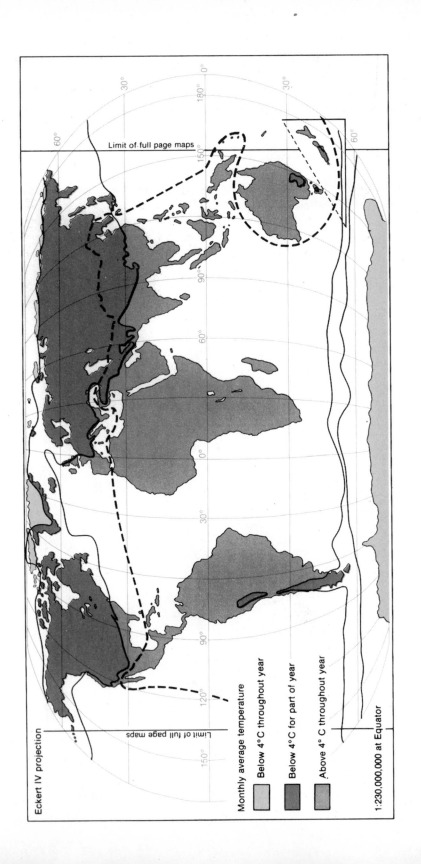

Eckert IV projection

Limit of full page maps

Limit of full page maps

Monthly average temperature

Below 4°C throughout year

Below 4°C for part of year

Above 4° C throughout year

1:230,000,000 at Equator

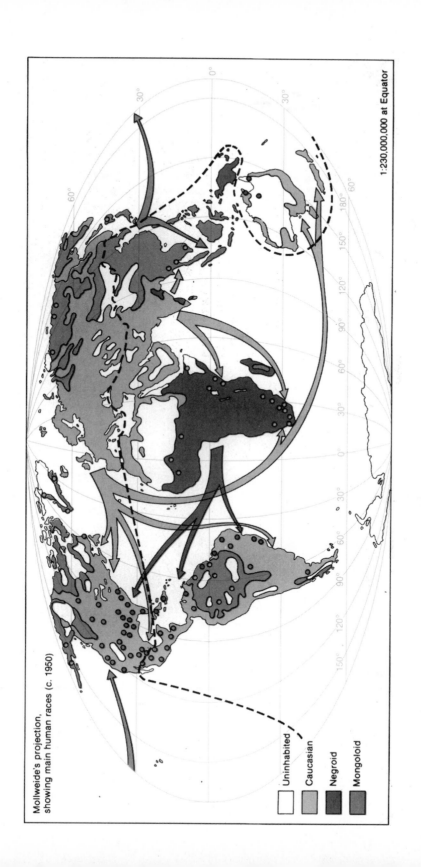

Mollweide's projection,
showing main human races (c. 1950)

1:230,000,000 at Equator

Uninhabited

Caucasian

Negroid

Mongoloid

Maps have two rather different types of uses. Some use conventions to present   8
geographical information to a level of detail required for a particular purpose, such
as navigation or town planning. Other maps are graphic illustrations of how certain
factors or variables are related spatially. Most of the maps in this Atlas are of this second type. For example, the maps (and diagram) on [pages 469–472] all illustrate in
different ways how income, as measured by Gross National Product (GNP), is related to population on a world basis.

There can never be total lack of bias on any map, but one can differentiate be-   9
tween (i) an attempt at objectivity, where the form of graphic representation is chosen to match the information on display; and (ii) a map putting over a specific
message. The left-hand map [on page 467] seems inaccurate because of the incomplete geographical knowledge of the time, whereas the [one on the right] is a simple
but accurate map on an "equidistant" projection. The [map on page 468] is clearly
designed to put over a message, though in its way it is as "accurate" as the [right-
hand map on page 467].

[Pages 469–472] show graphic techniques that will crop up throughout this   10
Atlas. One is the "proportional base" where the size of a region on the page is proportional to its population [page 469] or Gross National Product (GNP) [page 471],
and the "map" does not represent the shape and position of territory at all closely.
Think about exactly what the role of the *spatial* dimension is in such cases. Is it just
to locate a country you are interested in? Or are you referring in your mind to some
"normal" map for comparison? You may be saying to yourself something like: "India
is larger than I expected in terms of population." Are you using geographical area as
an implicit variable and relating what the map shows to it? If so, this underlines the
importance of the "equal-area" question. If your mind's map is on Mercator's projection, you will be misjudging these comparisons.

Another important question is the level of *aggregation*, or what *units* are used for   11
presenting data. Examples shown [on pages 467–472] are countries, regions and
equal population cells. Some data only make sense with respect to a *country* as the
unit: for example, the independence date of a country, or the way its representatives
voted at the United Nations. Other items are derived from statistics which are collected on a country basis, whereas some ethnographic or biological data really do
not fit into country units at all. Country data may hide or average out regional or
other variations to a misleading extent, particularly when comparing countries having great regional, social and even climatic variations (like Brazil) with much
smaller and/or more homogenous countries.

Scatter-graphs are used throughout this Atlas in addition to maps where the   12
question is: "Does variable A correlate with variable B?" ... Does GNP correlate
with the size of a country's population? In such cases, look first to see how far the
two variables do correspond. Thus, on the scatter-graph [page 470], lines have been
drawn to represent the average GNP per capita for each region. Note how closely the
points of each [shade] bunch around the corresponding line. Then look carefully at
any points that fall outside the general pattern, and consider what might account for
the anomalies. In the case of sub-Saharan Africa the bunching is quite tight, indicating a close relationship between GNP and population. North Africa/West Asia
show a much less clear pattern.

Hereford World Map AD 1285 (simplified)

Note that East (the 'orient') is at the top – a practice common in the Middle Ages in Europe, from which the term 'to orient a map' derives.

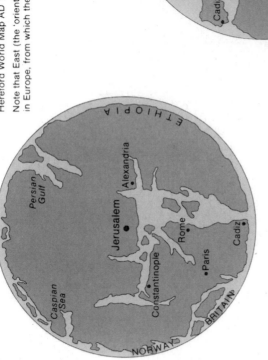

An equidistant projection centred on Jerusalem. 'Equidistant' means equal distances on the globe are represented by equal distances on the map

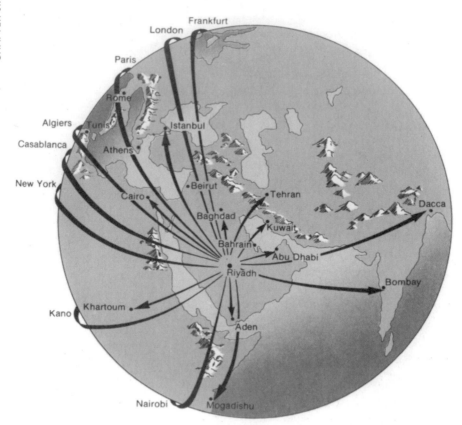

Adapted from a Saudi Arabian Airlines advertisement

These figures show different ways of relating Gross National Product (GNP) to   13
population. Take care that when you study a particular diagram you notice whether
it shows total GNP or per-capita GNP. . . .

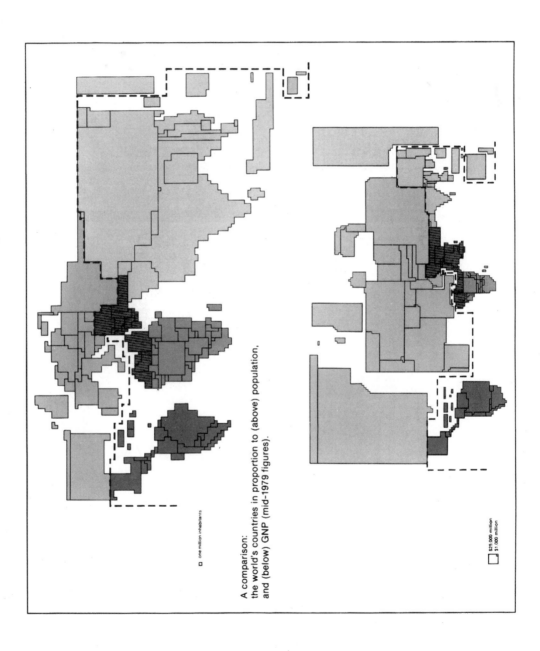

A comparison:
the world's countries in proportion to (above) population,
and (below) GNP (mid-1979 figures).

□ one million inhabitants

□ $25,000 million
□ $1,000 million

The scatter-graph [below] plots countries' GNP against their population (1979 [14] data). The lines show average GNP per capita for each region; those far off the lines have unusually high (or low) average per-capita incomes for the region. Countries with high per-capita income are bottom right, while those with low per-capita income are top left. Note the logarithmic scale on each axis, which is used to accommodate great variations in data. (A linear scale would need to be about two metres long to show the same detail.) It is important to realize that equal intervals in the data are not represented by equal distances along the scale. Thus, the distance along the vertical axis between 2 and 4 is greater than that between 4 and 6. Similarly, the distance on the axis between 2 and 4 is the same as that between 20 and 40, although the intervals are 2 and 20 respectively. Values can still be read off in the normal way.

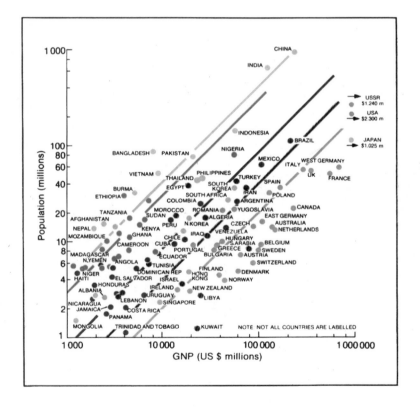

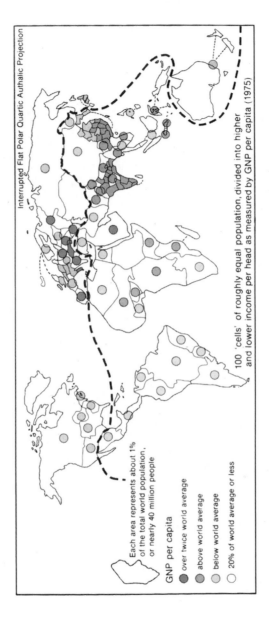

Interrupted Flat Polar Quartic Authalic Projection

100 'cells' of roughly equal population, divided into higher and lower income per head as measured by GNP per capita (1975)

Each area represents about 1% of the total world population, or nearly 40 million people

GNP per capita

- over twice world average
- above world average
- below world average
- 20% of world average or less

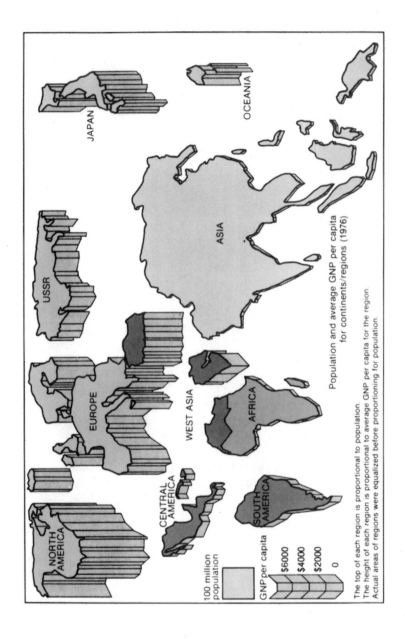

NORTH AMERICA

CENTRAL AMERICA

SOUTH AMERICA

EUROPE

USSR

WEST ASIA

AFRICA

ASIA

JAPAN

OCEANIA

100 million population

GNP per capita

$6000
$4000
$2000
0

Population and average GNP per capita
for continents/regions (1976)

The top of each region is proportional to population.
The height of each region is proportional to average GNP per capita for the region.
Actual areas of regions were equalized before proportioning for population.

Working with the Text

1. One of the points that this section makes (and the reason it begins this chapter) is that no map can be "true" in any absolute sense. As the authors write, "Map projections are bound to be distorted in one way or another." To illustrate this point they compare Mercator's projection—which preserves shapes but distorts size—to Peters' projection—which distorts shapes but preserves size (or area). The result of Mercator's projection is that countries north of the equator appear larger that they actually are. Do you think that Mercator's projection promotes a "Eurocentric" view of the world? What should be the primary considerations in representing the world on a flat surface? Should custom or tradition matter?

2. Denis Wood, a geographer, has written about Peters' projection:

> Peters did more than insist that whatever its appearance an equal-area projection was the only fair way to show most things worth showing about the world. He implied—no, he pointed out—that the use of most other projections had a powerful built-in bias. . . . the selection of any map projection is always to choose among competing interests, is inescapably to take—that is, to *promote,* to *embody in the map*—a point of view.

Do you agree that all maps have a "point of view"? Do you usually think of maps as having authors and audiences, as works of writing or painting do?

3. Do you believe, in general, that maps reinforce and reflect cultural biases? For example, in the United States, we are accustomed to seeing maps with the center point being the "Greenwich" meridian. How different would it be if the Western Hemisphere were always located off to the far left? Do you assume that all countries' cartographers simply put their respective countries in the center of their own maps? Can you locate maps (in the library or on the World Wide Web) that are used in other countries or cultures? How do they differ? What impact do these differences have? Use a couple of specific examples.

4. Look at the "Turnabout map" by Jesse Levine in the Image Portfolio. As he himself states, his map is "geographically correct." What is the effect of looking at the Western Hemisphere this way? Does it seem disturbing or disorienting?

THE CONCEPT OF "NATION": A DEFINITION

BENEDICT ANDERSON

■ A professor of international studies at Cornell University, Benedict Anderson has written extensively about Indonesian culture and history. Among his books on the subject are *Mythology and the Tolerance of the Javanese; In the Mirror: Literature and Politics in Siam in the American Era; Java in a Time of Revolution: Occupation and Resistance, 1944–1946;* and *Language and Power: Exploring Political Era Cultures in Indonesia.*

His 1983 *Imagined Communities,* from which the following essay is excerpted, is something of an anomaly. In that book his aim was "to offer some tentative suggestions for a more satisfactory interpretation of the 'anomaly' of national-ism." In these paragraphs from his introduction, Anderson explains his definition of a nation as "an imagined political community—and imagined as both inher-ently limited and sovereign."

Theorists of nationalism have often been perplexed, not to say irritated, by these three paradoxes: (1) The objective modernity of nations to the histo-rian's eye vs. their subjective antiquity in the eyes of nationalists. (2) The formal universality of nationality as a socio-cultural concept—in the modern world everyone can, should, will "have" a nationality, as he or she "has" a gender—vs. the irremediable particularity of its concrete manifestations, such that, by definition, "Greek" nationality is sui generis. (3) The "political" power of nationalisms vs. their philosophical poverty and even incoherence. In other words, unlike most other isms, nationalism has never produced its own grand thinkers: no Hobbeses, Tocquevilles, Marxes, or Webers. This "emptiness" easily gives rise, among cosmopolitan and polylingual intellectuals, to a certain condescension. Like Gertrude Stein in the face of Oakland, one can rather quickly conclude that there is "no there there." It is char-acteristic that even so sympathetic a student of nationalism as Tom Nairn can nonetheless write that: "'Nationalism' is the pathology of modern developmental history, as inescapable as 'neurosis' in the individual, with much the same essential ambiguity attaching to it, a similar built-in capacity for descent into dementia, rooted in the dilemmas of helplessness thrust upon most of the world (the equiva-lent of infantilism for societies) and largely incurable."[1]

Part of the difficulty is that one tends unconsciously to hypostasize the existence of Nationalism-with-a-big-N (rather as one might Age-with-a-capital-A) and then classify "it" as *an* ideology. (Note that if everyone has an age, Age is merely an ana-lytical expression.) It would, I think, make things easier if one treated it as if it be-longed with "kinship" and "religion," rather than with "liberalism" or "fascism."

In an anthropological spirit, then, I propose the following definition of the na-tion: it is an imagined political community—and imagined as both inherently lim-ited and sovereign.

It is *imagined* because the members of even the smallest nation will never know most of their fellow-members, meet them, or even hear of them, yet in the minds of each lives the image of their communion.[2] Renan referred to this imagining in his suavely back-handed way when he wrote that "Or l'essence d'une nation est que tous les individus aient beaucoup de choses en commun, et aussi que tous aient oublié bien des choses."[3] With a certain ferocity Gellner makes a comparable point when he rules that "Nationalism is not the awakening of nations to self-consciousness:

1. *The Break-up of Britain,* p. 359.
2. Cf. Seton-Watson, *Nations and States,* p. 5: "All that I can find to say is that a nation exists when a sig-nificant number of people in a community consider themselves to form a nation, or behave as if they formed one." We may translate "consider themselves" as "imagine themselves."
3. Ernest Renan, "Qu'est-ce qu'une nation?" in *Œuvres Complètes,* 1, p. 892. He adds: "tout citoyen français doit avoir oublié la Saint-Barthélemy, les massacres du Midi au XIIIe siècle. Il n'y a pas en France dix familles qui puissent fournir la preuve d'une origine franque . . ."

it *invents* nations where they do not exist."[4] The drawback to this formulation, however, is that Gellner is so anxious to show that nationalism masquerades under false pretences that he assimilates "invention" to "fabrication" and "falsity," rather than to "imagining" and "creation." In this way he implies that "true" communities exist which can be advantageously juxtaposed to nations. In fact, all communities larger than primordial villages of face-to-face contact (and perhaps even these) are imagined. Communities are to be distinguished, not by their falsity/genuineness, but by the style in which they are imagined. Javanese villagers have always known that they are connected to people they have never seen, but these ties were once imagined particularistically—as indefinitely stretchable nets of kinship and clientship. Until quite recently, the Javanese language had no word meaning the abstraction "society." We may today think of the French aristocracy of the *ancien régime* as a class; but surely it was imagined this way only very late.[5] To the question "Who is the Comte de X?" the normal answer would have been, not "a member of the aristocracy," but "the lord of X," "the uncle of the Baronne de Y," or "a client of the Duc de Z."

The nation is imagined as *limited* because even the largest of them, encompassing perhaps a billion living human beings, has finite, if elastic, boundaries, beyond which lie other nations. No nation imagines itself coterminous with mankind. The most messianic nationalists do not dream of a day when all the members of the human race will join their nation in the way that it was possible, in certain epochs, for, say, Christians to dream of a wholly Christian planet.   5

It is imagined as *sovereign* because the concept was born in an age in which Enlightenment and Revolution were destroying the legitimacy of the divinely-ordained, hierarchical dynastic realm. Coming to maturity at a stage of human history when even the most devout adherents of any universal religion were inescapably confronted with the living *pluralism* of such religions, and the allomorphism between each faith's ontological claims and territorial stretch, nations dream of being free, and, if under God, directly so. The gage and emblem of this freedom is the sovereign state.   6

Finally, it is imagined as a *community,* because, regardless of the actual inequality and exploitation that may prevail in each, the nation is always conceived as a deep, horizontal comradeship. Ultimately it is this fraternity that makes it possible, over the past two centuries, for so many millions of people, not so much to kill, as willingly to die for such limited imaginings.   7

These deaths bring us abruptly face to face with the central problem posed by nationalism: what makes the shrunken imaginings of recent history (scarcely more than two centuries) generate such colossal sacrifices? I believe that the beginnings of an answer lie in the cultural roots of nationalism.   8

Working with the Text

1. In this short excerpt from a much longer exploration of the concept of "nation," Anderson offers the following definition of a nation: "it is an imagined

---

4. Ernest Gellner, *Thought and Change*, p. 169. Emphasis added.
5. Hobsbawm, for example, "fixes" it by saying that in 1789 it numbered about 400,000 in a population of 23,000,000. (See his *The Age of Revolution*, p. 78). But would this statistical picture of the noblesse have been imaginable under the *ancien régime*?

political community—and imagined as both inherently limited and sovereign." He then goes on to explain each of the four key words in that definition—*imagined, limited, sovereign,* and *community.* Think about what he means by each of the four words and then spend a little time reading the "national" news section of a newspaper. Find an example of some national coverage that supports one or more of those four criteria for the definition of a nation.

2. Do you agree with Anderson that the essence of being an American is mostly a matter of imagining your relationship to other Americans? (Or, if you are not a U.S. citizen, to whomever your fellow citizens are?) How do you think this idea relates to immigrants? Could you imagine yourself without a nation? Do you feel a bond with someone simply because you are both of the same country? If you were both visiting in a foreign country, would that bond seem stronger?

3. Anderson writes that "all communities larger than primordial villages of face-to-face contact (and perhaps even these) are imagined. Communities are to be distinguished, not by their falsity/genuineness, but by the style in which they are imagined." Think about two different kinds of communities that you have already read about in this book and discuss how the "styles in which they are imagined" differ. In other words, consider how a "nation" is a different kind of imagined community than, say, one's neighborhood, group of friends, sports team, or religious group. Which communities have the strongest imagined ties for you? Are any of the ties conflicting?

THE SIGNIFICANCE OF THE FRONTIER IN AMERICAN HISTORY

FREDERICK JACKSON TURNER

■ Frederick Jackson Turner, who lived from 1861 to 1932, was one of the most renowned American historians of his day, and his work continues to exert a significant influence on the study of American history. A native of Wisconsin, Turner taught at the University of Wisconsin and later at Harvard. He published his most famous work, *The Frontier in American History,* in 1920. His other works include *The Rise of the New West* (1906) and, with Edward Channing and Albert Bushnell Hart, *Guide to the Study and Reading of American History* (1912).

Central to *The Frontier in American History* is the following essay, which Turner originally delivered as an address to the World's Fair in Chicago in 1893. In the words of one of his biographers, it "supplied a large part of a generation of historians with a theme to investigate." In this essay Turner notes that the development of America has involved the expansion of frontiers. He then posits that this advance "has meant a steady movement away from the influence of Europe, a steady growth of independence on American lines." He maintains that "to the frontier the American intellect owes its striking characteristics."

n a recent bulletin of the Superintendent of the Census for 1890 appear these significant words: "Up to and including 1880 the country had a frontier of settlement, but at present the unsettled area has been so broken into by isolated bodies of settlement that there can hardly be said to be a frontier line. In the discussion of its extent, its westward movement, etc., it can not, therefore, any longer have a place in the census reports." This brief official statement marks the closing of a great historic movement. Up to our own day American history has been in a large degree the history of the colonization of the Great West. The existence of an area of free land, its continuous recession, and the advance of American settlement westward, explain American development.

Behind institutions, behind constitutional forms and modifications, lie the vital forces that call these organs into life and shape them to meet changing conditions. The peculiarity of American institutions is the fact that they have been compelled to adapt themselves to the changes of an expanding people—to the changes involved in crossing a continent, in winning a wilderness, and in developing at each area of this progress out of the primitive economic and political conditions of the frontier into the complexity of city life. Said Calhoun in 1817, "We are great, and rapidly—I was about to say fearfully—growing!" So saying, he touched the distinguishing feature of American life. All peoples show development; the germ theory of politics has been sufficiently emphasized. In the case of most nations, however, the development has occurred in a limited area; and if the nation has expanded, it has met other growing peoples whom it has conquered. But in the case of the United States we have a different phenomenon. Limiting our attention to the Atlantic coast, we have the familiar phenomenon of the evolution of institutions in a limited area, such as the rise of representative government; the differentiation of simple colonial governments into complex organs; the progress from primitive industrial society, without division of labor, up to manufacturing civilization. But we have in addition to this a recurrence of the process of evolution in each western area reached in the process of expansion. Thus American development has exhibited not merely advance along a single line, but a return to primitive conditions on a continually advancing frontier line, and a new development for that area. American social development has been continually beginning over again on the frontier. This perennial rebirth, this fluidity of American life, this expansion westward with its new opportunities, its continuous touch with the simplicity of primitive society, furnish the forces dominating American character. The true point of view in the history of this nation is not the Atlantic coast, it is the Great West. Even the slavery struggle, which is made so exclusive an object of attention by writers like Professor von Holst, occupies its important place in American history because of its relation to westward expansion.

In this advance, the frontier is the outer edge of the wave—the meeting point between savagery and civilization. Much has been written about the frontier from the point of view of border warfare and the chase, but as a field for the serious study of the economist and the historian it has been neglected.

The American frontier is sharply distinguished from the European frontier—a   4
fortified boundary line running through dense populations. The most significant
thing about the American frontier is that it lies at the hither edge of free land. In the
census reports it is treated as the margin of that settlement which has a density of
two or more to the square mile. The term is an elastic one, and for our purposes
does not need sharp definition. We shall consider the whole frontier belt, including
the Indian country and the outer margin of the "settled area" of the census reports.
This paper will make no attempt to treat the subject exhaustively; its aim is simply
to call attention to the frontier as a fertile field for investigation, and to suggest some
of the problems which arise in connection with it.

In the settlement of America we have to observe how European life entered the   5
continent, and how America modified and developed that life and reacted on Europe. Our early history is the study of European germs developing in an American
environment. Too exclusive attention has been paid by institutional students to the
Germanic origins, too little to the American factors. The frontier is the line of most
rapid and effective Americanization. The wilderness masters the colonist. It finds
him a European in dress, industries, tools, modes of travel, and thought. It takes him
from the railroad car and puts him in the birch canoe. It strips off the garments of
civilization and arrays him in the hunting shirt and the moccasin. It puts him in the
log cabin of the Cherokee and Iroquois and runs an Indian palisade around him.
Before long he has gone to planting Indian corn and plowing with a sharp stick; he
shouts the war cry and takes the scalp in orthodox Indian fashion. In short, at the
frontier the environment is at first too strong for the man. He must accept the conditions which it furnishes, or perish, and so he fits himself into the Indian clearings
and follows the Indian trails. Little by little he transforms the wilderness, but the
outcome is not the old Europe, not simply the development of Germanic germs, any
more than the first phenomenon was a case of reversion to the Germanic mark. The
fact is that here is a new product that is American. At first, the frontier was the Atlantic coast. It was the frontier of Europe in a very real sense. Moving westward, the
frontier became more and more American. As successive terminal moraines result
from successive glaciations, so each frontier leaves its traces behind it, and when it
becomes a settled area the region still partakes of the frontier characteristics. Thus
the advance of the frontier has meant a steady movement away from the influence
of Europe, a steady growth of independence on American lines. And to study this
advance, the men who grew up under these conditions, and the political, economic,
and social results of it, is to study the really American part of our history. . . .

But the most important effect of the frontier has been in the promotion of   6
democracy here and in Europe. As has been indicated the frontier is productive
of individualism. Complex society is precipitated by the wilderness into a kind of
primitive organization based on the family. The tendency is anti-social. It produces
antipathy to control, and particularly to any direct control. The tax-gatherer is
viewed as a representative of oppression. Professor Osgood, in an able article, has
pointed out that the frontier conditions prevalent in the colonies are important factors in the explanation of the American Revolution, where individual liberty was
sometimes confused with absence of all effective government. The same conditions
aid in explaining the difficulty of instituting a strong government in the period of

the confederacy. The frontier individualism has from the beginning promoted democracy. . . .

So long as free land exists, the opportunity for a competency exists, and economic power secures political power. But the democracy born of free land, strong in selfishness and individualism, intolerant of administrative experience and education, and pressing individual liberty beyond its proper bounds, has its dangers as well as its benefits. Individualism in America has allowed a laxity in regard to governmental affairs which has rendered possible the spoils system and all the manifest evils that follow from the lack of a highly developed civic spirit. In this connection may be noted also the influence of frontier conditions in permitting lax business honor, inflated paper currency and wildcat banking. The colonial and revolutionary frontier was the region whence emanated many of the worst forms of an evil currency. The West in the War of 1812 repeated the phenomenon on the frontier of that day, while the speculation and wildcat banking of the period of the crisis of 1837 occurred on the new frontier belt of the next tier of States. Thus each one of the periods of lax financial integrity coincides with periods when a new set of frontier communities had arisen, and coincides in area with these successive frontiers, for the most part. The recent Populist agitation is a case in point. Many a State that now declines any connection with the tenets of the Populists, itself adhered to such ideas in an earlier stage of the development of the State. A primitive society can hardly be expected to show the intelligent appreciation of the complexity of business interests in a developed society. The continual recurrence of these areas of paper-money agitation is another evidence that the frontier can be isolated and studied as a factor in American history of the highest importance. . . .

From the conditions of frontier life came intellectual traits of profound importance. The works of travelers along each frontier from colonial days onward describe certain common traits, and these traits have, while softening down, still persisted as survivals in the place of their origin, even with a higher social organization succeeded. The result is that to the frontier the American intellect owes its striking characteristics. That coarseness and strength combined with acuteness and inquisitiveness; that practical, inventive turn of mind, quick to find expedients; that masterful grasp of material things, lacking in the artistic but powerful to effect great ends; that restless, nervous energy; that dominant individualism, working for good and for evil, and withal that buoyancy and exuberance which comes with freedom—these are traits of the frontier, or traits called out elsewhere because of the existence of the frontier. Since the days when the fleet of Columbus sailed into the waters of the New World, America has been another name for opportunity, and the people of the United States have taken their tone from the incessant expansion which has not only been open but has even been forced upon them. He would be a rash prophet who should assert that the expansive character of American life has now entirely ceased. Movement has been its dominant fact, and, unless this training has no effect upon a people, the American energy will continually demand a wider field for its exercise. But never again will such gifts of free land offer themselves. For a moment, at the frontier, the bonds of custom are broken and unrestraint is triumphant. There is not *tabula rasa*. The stubborn American environment is there with its imperious summons to accept its conditions; the inherited ways of doing things are also there; and yet, in spite of environment, and in spite of custom, each frontier did indeed furnish a new field of opportunity, a gate of escape from the bondage of the past; and freshness, and confidence, and scorn of older society, impatience of its restraints and its ideas, and indifference to its lessons, have accompanied the frontier. What the Mediterranean Sea was to the Greeks, breaking the bond of custom, offering new experiences, calling out new institutions and activities, that, and more, the ever retreating frontier has been to the United States directly, and to the nations of Europe more remotely. And now, four centuries from the discovery of America, at the end of a hundred years of life under the Constitution, the frontier has gone, and with its going has closed the first period of American history.

Working with the Text

1. Turner makes a number of claims about the frontier's contributions to making the United States "distinctly American." What does Turner say is "American" about the frontier experience? Do you associate these qualities as distinctively or typically American?

2. In his essay, Turner describes the frontier not only as a "place" but as a "process" of social development. What is that process? Write a paper in which you examine his assumptions about culture, society, and civilization that lie behind the process.

3. What are the connections in Turner's essay between geography and culture? How does the physical environment (the land and the wilderness itself) influence American institutions? In what ways does the American continent, in his words, "lie like a huge page" to be read? What aspects of the American experience does his thesis exclude? What are its limitations? Compare his description to John Gast's painting *American Progress* in the Image Portfolio. How does Gast imagine the United States as lying "like a huge page" to be read?

THE ADVENTURES OF THE FRONTIER IN THE TWENTIETH CENTURY

PATRICIA NELSON LIMERICK

■ Among the generation of contemporary historians of the American West, none perhaps is better known than Patricia Nelson Limerick. While her research is both scrupulous and wide-ranging, her writing style is such that her work appeals to popular as well as academic audiences. She is currently on the faculty of the University of Colorado at Boulder.

Limerick published her most important work, *The Legacy of Conquest: The Unbroken Past of the American West,* in 1987. In this book she explicitly rejects Frederick Jackson Turner's influential thesis regarding the history of the West as a history of frontiers and his claim that the frontier essentially closed at the end of the nineteenth century. Limerick suggests that we should look at the West "as a place—as many complicated environments occupied by natives who considered their homelands to be the center, not the edge." For her, "the American West was an important meeting ground, the point where Indian America, Latin America, Anglo-America, Afro-America, and Asia intersected," and its story is primarily one of conquest. In the following essay she examines what she considers simplistic contemporary conceptions of the frontier and the more complicated idea of *la frontera*.

TRAVELS IN FRONTIERLAND

The year 1988 signified the fortieth anniversary of humanity's escape from zippers and buttons. In May of that year a journal of science and technology called *Discover* published an article commemorating this occasion. "Velcro," the headline read: "The Final Frontier." 1

To the specialist in Western American history, this is a title to ponder. In what sense might Velcro constitute a frontier? In his 1893 essay "The Significance of the Frontier in American History," Frederick Jackson Turner left his central term curiously befogged: The word "frontier," he said, "is an elastic one, and for our purposes does not need sharp definition."¹ But Turner did join the director of the United States census in offering one clear and concrete definition: the frontier was a place occupied by fewer than two people per square mile. Thus, if the headline writer were a strict follower of Turner's quantitative definition, then the Velcro Frontier would be a place where fewer than two people per square mile used Velcro. The writer, on the other hand, might have been following one of the more poetic and less precise Turnerian definitions, finding in a society's choice of fasteners a symbolic line of division between wilderness and human culture, backwardness and progress, savagery and civilization. The habit-bound users of zippers would now represent the primitive and backward people of North America, with the hardy, adventurous users of Velcro living on the cutting edge of progress. 2

Historians of the American West might puzzle over the shifting definitions of the word "frontier," but few readers experience any confusion when they see this headline. To them, the frontier analogy says simply that makers, marketers, and users of Velcro stand on the edge of exciting possibilities. Velcro is a frontier because Velcro has thousands of still-to-be-imagined uses. No normal reader, if one defines "normal reader" as a person who is not a Western American historian, would even notice the peculiar implications of the analogy. For most Americans in the twentieth century, the term "frontier" is perfectly clear, reliable, and simple in its meanings. 3

"Frontier," the historian David Wrobel writes, "has become a metaphor for promise, progress, and ingenuity."² And yet, despite the accuracy of this summation, the relation between the frontier and the American mind is not a simple one. Clear and predictable on most occasions, the idea of the frontier is still capable of sudden twists and shifts of meaning, meanings considerably more interesting than the conventional and familiar definition of the frontier as a zone of open opportunity. 4

Conventional thinking is at its most powerful, however, in twentieth-century reconstructions of the nineteenth-century experience of westward expansion, reconstructions quite explicitly designed for sale. To see this commercialized vision of the 5

Old Frontier in concrete, three-dimensional form, the best place to go is Disneyland in Anaheim, California. When they enter Frontierland, visitors might ask Disneyland employees for directions, but they do not have to ask for a definition of the frontier. The frontier, every tourist knows, was the edge of Anglo-American settlement, the place where white Americans struggled to master the continent. This frontier, as everything in Frontierland confirms, was populated by a colorful and romantic cast of characters—mountain men, cowboys, prospectors, pioneer wives, saloon girls, sheriffs, and outlaws. Tepees, log cabins, and false-front stores were the preferred architecture of the frontier; coonskin caps, cowboy hats, bandannas, buckskin shirts and leggings, moccasins, boots, and an occasional sunbonnet or calico dress constituted frontier fashion; canoes, keelboats, steamboats, saddle horses, covered wagons, and stagecoaches gave Americans the means to conquer the rivers, mountains, deserts, plains, and other wide-open spaces of the frontier; firearms, whether long rifles or six-shooters, were everywhere and in frequent use. These images are very well understood. Tourists do not need any assistance in defining Frontierland.

And yet, even in the tightly controlled world of Disneyland, the idea of the frontier has encountered complications. At the Golden Horseshoe, Frontierland's saloon, every show once had a "spontaneous" gunfight in which Black Bart and Sheriff Lucky blazed away at each other. In 1958, as a reporter for the *Saturday Evening Post* watched, the gunfight underwent some slippage at the joint that connects fantasy to reality: "As the sheriff advanced toward the wounded bandit," the writer said, "a tow-headed five-year-old, wearing a cowboy suit and holding a cap pistol, came running from the crowd," asking earnestly, "'Can I finish him off, sheriff, can I?'" The sheriff consented, and everyone fired.

> Black Bart shuddered, then lay deathly still.
> The lad took one look, dropped his gun and fled, screaming,
> "Mommy, mommy! I didn't mean to! I didn't mean to!"

Scholars with a penchant for interpreting signs, symbols, and signifiers could go to town with this incident, pondering the way in which the appeal to "mommy" follows hard and fast on the attempted initiation into the manly sport of gunplay. But my own attention fixes on the line, "I didn't mean to!" Since the child wanted to kill Black Bart, and, with an impressive deference to authority, asked the sheriff for permission to kill him, why would he then make the claim, "I didn't mean to"? His worries of intention and outcome were, in any case, soon ended: "His tears stopped a moment later, however, when he turned and saw Black Bart and Sheriff Lucky walking into the Golden Horseshoe to get ready for their next performance."[3] Rather than feeling soothed, another sort of child might at that moment have conceived a long-range ambition to kill *both* Black Bart and Sheriff Lucky for their complicity in tricking him.

In the twentieth century, as this boy learned, the image of the frontier balances precariously between too much reality and too little. Properly screened and edited, the doings of the Old Frontier are quite a bit of fun. But when encounters with death, or injury, or conflict, or loss become unexpectedly convincing and compelling, then fun can make an abrupt departure, while emotions considerably more troubling take its place.

The outlaw-killing lad was not the only child encountering the limits of Fron-   8
tierland's fun, not the only one to stumble in the uncertain turf along the border between the imagined and the actual. As the *Saturday Evening Post* writer described it,
one "seven-year-old boy was certain he could tell the real from the unreal."

> As they jogged along on the burro ride, the leathery mule-skinner warned,
> "Look out for them thar cactus plants. Them needles is mighty sharp."
> The skeptical boy leaned over and took a swipe at the cactus. On the way to
> the first-aid station, he decided all was not fantasy at Disneyland. The
> management has since moved the cactus out of reach.[4]

Moving the cactus—finding the place where its thorns could *look* sharp and scary
but not *be* sharp and scary—can serve as a fine representation of the whole process
of getting authenticity into the proper adjustment at Frontierland. When too many
surprised innocents made visits to the first-aid stand, the frontier was clearly out of
alignment, and a repositioning was in order.

And yet, in other parts of Frontierland's turf, wounds and injuries were a taken-   9
for-granted dimension of frontier life. At Tom Sawyer's Island, as the *Saturday
Evening Post* writer put it, kids "can fire air-operated, bulletless rifles at the plastic
Indians."[5] A writer for the *Reader's Digest* described the same opportunity in 1960:
"From the top of a log fort you can sight in with guns on a forest in which Indians
lurk. The guns don't fire bullets—they're hydraulically operated—but the recoil is
so realistic that you'd never guess they aren't the genuine article."[6]

The Indians of this frontier were not, however, the sort to hold a grudge. Visitors   10
could fire away at the Indians and then move on to a voyage in "Indian canoes pad-
dled by real Indians."[7] "Realness" was not, in this case, an easy matter to arrange.
"Wanting authentic Native Americans to paddle canoes full of guests around the
rivers of the theme area, Disneyland recruited employees from southwestern tribes,"
the historian John Findlay writes in his book *Magic Lands*. "These Indians, of
course, came from the desert rather than a riverine or lakes environment, so they
had to be taught how to paddle canoes by white employees of the park who had
learned the skill at summer camp."[8]

Over the decades, life at Frontierland has become, if anything, more confusing   11
for those rare individuals who stop and think about what they are seeing. There is,
for instance, the question of the frontier's geographical location. On one side of a
path, a roller coaster rushes through a southwestern mesa, carved into a mine. On
the other side of the path, the great river, with its stately steamboat, rolls by. Where
is the frontier? Evidently where New Mexico borders on the Mississippi River, where
western gold and silver miners load their ore directly onto steamboats heading to
New Orleans.

In recent times, even the ritualized violence between whites and Indians has be-   12
come a matter of some awkwardness. On the various rides along the Rivers of
America, one passes a settler's cabin, wildly in flames. In my childhood, the guides
announced that the cabin was on fire because Indians had attacked it. In current
times, the cabin is just on fire, usually without commentary or blame. At the further
reaches of cultural change lies the recent experience of an acquaintance: the guide
told his group that the cabin was on fire because the settler had been ecologically
and environmentally careless.[9]

Consider, as well, the curious politics of the shooting gallery encountered at the entrance to Frontierland. Visitors can take firearm in hand and shoot at a variety of targets—including a railroad train, winding its way through a sculpted landscape. But if you are shooting at a railroad train, then *who*—in this frontier role-play—*are you?* Which side are you on? If you are firing on the train, then you seem to be either a hostile Indian or a murderous and larcenous outlaw. What is going on here? Is the visitor receiving an invitation to play with point of view, to reconsider the whole question of the identity and interests of good guys and bad guys, champions of progress and opponents of progress? Or is this casting of the railroad as target simply the product of Disneyland's designers working under the mandate to create a scene chock-full of the shapes and forms that will say "frontier," with the assumption that any visitor so stimulated visually will fall into step with the mythic patterns of frontier life, pick up a gun, and blast away at whatever is in sight? 13

If professional Western American historians find themselves conceptually without anchor when they visit Frontierland, the reason is clear: with the possible exception of the suggestion that environmental carelessness produced the settler's cabin fire, the work of academic historians has had virtually no impact either on Disneyland's vision of the frontier or on the thinking of Disneyland's visitors. That cheerful and complete indifference to the work of frontier historians may, in truth, be the secret of the place's success. 14

THE FIGHT FOR THE FRONTIER IN THE HISTORY DEPARTMENT

In recent years, academic historians have given the idea of the frontier a pretty rough overhauling. Nicknamed the "f-word" and pummeled for its ethnocentrism and vagueness, the term has from time to time landed on the ropes, perilously close to conceding the match. But a determined group of trainers and handlers has always trooped out to the rescue, braced up the frontier, and gotten it back on its feet for the next round. 15

The academic boxing match centers on this question: how well does the concept of the frontier perform the task of describing, explaining, and encapsulating the story of the colonization of North America? "Miserably," answers one group of historians, of which I happen to be a member.[10] "Pretty well," responds a different set of historians, "if you make a few adjustments and realignments in its definition." 16

The case for the frailty of the "f-word" is an easy one to make. First, built into the idea is an inflexible point of view. For the term to have clear meaning, historians have had to hand their point of view over to the custody of English-speaking white people. In its clearest and most concrete meaning, as Richard White has said, the frontier was where white people got scarce—or, with a friendly amendment, the frontier was where white people got *scared* because they were scarce. This perspective has certainly been an important psychological reality in American history, and it is a psychological reality well worth study. But using the frontier as an analytic concept puts the historian at risk of adopting the point of view of only one of the contesting groups. Moreover, the frontier came with two sides, the Anglo-American side and the one labeled "the other side of the frontier." Jammed into the second category were Indians of all tribes (often tribes that fought against each other as well as 17 against Anglo Americans), long-term Hispano settlers, and more recent Mexican immigrants. In lived reality, the people on this "other side of the frontier" did not form anything remotely resembling a united team or a homogeneous society. Conceptually, neither "side" of the frontier offered much in the way of accommodations for Asian Americans, who came from the "wrong" direction, or for African Americans, participants in the westward movement who encountered a full measure of restrictions and exclusions. Trying to grasp the enormous human complexity of the American West is not easy under any circumstances, and the effort to reduce a tangle of many-sided encounters to a world defined by a frontier line only makes a tough task even tougher.

Second, the idea of the frontier runs almost entirely on an east-to-west track. Indeed, to most of its users, the term "frontier" has been a synonym for the American nation's westward movement. Can such a term do justice to the prior presence of Indian people, to the northward movement of Spanish-speaking people, or to the eastward movement of Asians? The east-to-west movement of Anglo Americans and African Americans is enormously important, but so are these movements of other people. Try to wrap the term "frontier" around all these movements, and the poor idea stretches to the point of snapping. 18

Third, it is nearly impossible to define either the beginning or the ending of a frontier. If one cannot define the beginning or ending of a condition, it is not going to be easy to say when that condition is present and when it is *not* present. Return, for instance, to Frederick Jackson Turner's definition of a frontier, borrowed from the Census Department, as a place where the population numbers fewer than two people per square mile. Then think of a mining rush—where, as soon as the news of the gold or silver gets out, the population instantly exceeds two people per square mile, with enough people to form a camp or a town. By Turner's definition, then, one would have to declare the mining frontier closed virtually the moment it opened. 19

Other scholars have offered more enterprising, and certainly more colorful, definitions of the closing of the frontier. One of the best comes from the historian Paula Petrik, who studied prostitutes in Helena, Montana. In the early years of Helena, Petrik reports, the prostitutes tended to be their own employers. They were able to hold on to the rewards of their labors, and some of them saved significant amounts of money, owned real estate, and lent money at interest. But then, as the frontier phase passed, men took control of the prostitutes and their earnings. This, I thought when I first heard Petrik's evidence and argument, is the most interesting marker of the end of the frontier I am ever going to hear: the frontier ends when the pimps come to town.[11] 20

My own entry in the "closing" competition rests on the popularization of tourism and the quaintness of the folk. When Indian war dances became tourist spectacles, when the formerly scorned customs of the Chinese drew tourists to Chinatown, when former out-groups found that characteristics that once earned them disapproval could now earn them a living, when fearful, life-threatening deserts became charming patterns of color and light, the war was over and the frontier could be considered closed, even museumized. But this nomination comes with its own fatal flaw. Let the car break down in the desert, or let the Indians file a lawsuit to reassert an old land claim, and the quaint appeal of nature and native can abruptly 21 vanish. The frontier is suddenly reopened, and the whole question of beginnings and endings becomes unsettled again.

Fourth, a presumption of innocence and exceptionalism is interwoven with the roots of frontier history, as Americans have understood it. The contrast becomes clearest when one thinks of a nation like South Africa. Europeans forcibly took South Africa from the natives, everyone understands, and the residents still struggle with the consequences. But the idea of the frontier permits the United States to make an appeal to innocence and exceptionalism: while South Africa underwent an invasion and a conquest, the United States had an expanding frontier of democracy, opportunity, and equality.

22

The term "frontier" blurs the fact of conquest and throws a veil over the similarities between the story of American westward expansion and the planetary story of the expansion of European empires. Whatever meanings historians give the term, in popular culture it carries a persistently happy affect, a tone of adventure, heroism, and even fun very much in contrast with the tough, complicated, and sometimes bloody and brutal realities of conquest. Under these conditions, the word "frontier" uses historians before historians can use it. . . .

23

MEANWHILE, *LA FRONTERA*

Anglo Americans have fixed their attention on the definition of the frontier drawn from the imaginative reconstruction of the story of the United States and its westward expansion. But North America has, in fact, had two strong traditions in the use of the term. There is the much more familiar, English, usage of the frontier as the place where white settlers entered a zone of "free" land and opportunity. But there is the much less familiar, but much more realistic, usage of *la frontera,* the borderlands between Mexico and the United States. This is not simply a place where two groups meet; Indian people have been influential players in the complicated pattern of human relations in the area. In the nineteenth century, trade, violence, conquest, and cultural exchange punctuated and shaped life in the borderlands. In the twentieth century, with conflicts over the restriction of immigration, with disputes over water flow and environmental pollution, and with a surge of industrial development and population growth from American-owned businesses (*maquiladoras*) operating in northern Mexico, conditions along the border remain far from tranquil.[38]

24

In the idea of *la frontera,* there is no illusion of vacancy, of triumphal conclusions, or of simplicity. As the writer Gloria Anzaldúa puts it, the United States–Mexican border is "where the Third World grates up against the first and bleeds."[39] It is a unique place on the planet's surface, a zone where an industrialized nation shares a long land border with a nation much troubled by poverty. "Ambivalence and unrest," Anzaldúa says, "reside there and death is no stranger."[40] Any temptation to romanticize *la frontera*—as a place of cultural syncretism, a place where the Spanish and English languages have learned to cohabit and even merge—runs aground on the bare misery of poverty in the border towns.[41]

25

The idea of the frontier is extremely well established as cultural common property. If the idea of *la frontera* had anywhere near the standing of the idea of the frontier, we would be well launched toward self-understanding, directed toward a

26

realistic view of this nation's position in the hemisphere and in the world. "The struggle of borders is our reality still," Anzaldúa writes.[42] One can tinker a bit with that line to draw the crucial contrast: "The adventure of frontiers is our fantasy still; the struggle of borders is our reality still."

In truth, this idea of the frontier as border has made some inroads in popular   27
thinking. If you are reading a headline for a news story set outside the United States, there is a chance that the word "frontier" will carry a meaning completely different from its usual one. References to "the Romania-Bulgaria frontier" or to "the Lebanese-Israeli frontier" are quite a different matter from references to the frontier where the pioneer stands on the edge of vacancy and opportunity. These are frontiers in the old, concrete, down-to-earth sense, much closer in meaning to *la frontera:* borders between countries, between peoples, between authorities, sometimes between armies. When "Algeria and Morocco reopen their frontier," or when the nation of Turkey decides it "will close its frontier with Bulgaria," these are references to borders that are full of possibilities for both cooperation and friction, places where the meaning of "opening" and "closing" differs dramatically from what Frederick Jackson Turner and the director of the census meant in the 1890s.[43]

In these references to international borders and boundaries, the word "frontier"   28
takes a firmer hold on reality. In my collection of headlines, the frequent appearance of this definition of frontier caught me by surprise. Perhaps, it began to seem, there is more hope for this word than seemed possible at first; perhaps popular thinking has already dug a sizable channel for thinking about the frontier in a manner quite different from the *Star Trek* mode.

One other pattern of usage, however, struck me as equally surprising: the om-   29
nipresence in headlines of African American pioneers. Here, the usage was again closer to the *Star Trek* definition, with pioneers boldly going where no one like them had gone before. Pioneers in civil rights—"Desegregation's Pioneers"—were everywhere, from A. Philip Randolph to Rosa Parks, from Julian Bond to Charlayne Hunter-Gault. The range of African American pioneers covers a great deal of turf: a Pioneer Black Professional Golfer; a Pioneer of Black Pride; the National Football League's Pioneer Black Coach; a Pioneer Black (Theatrical) Producer; a Pioneer Black Announcer; Negro League Pioneers; a Pioneer Black Ivy League Teacher; a Black Radio Pioneer; a Black Foreign Service Pioneer; a Pioneer Black Los Angeles Judge; a Pioneer Black Journalist; a Pioneer in Black Film; and Sidney Poitier, the winner of the "coveted Pioneer Award," bestowed at the Black Oscar Nominees dinner in 1989. As all these headlines suggest, the idea of calling African American people pioneers, as an appropriately complimentary way to refer to their dignity, courage, and determination in traveling where no black person had gone before, has established itself as part of the American cultural vocabulary. When in 1989 Secretary of Health and Human Services Louis Sullivan "told the graduating class of A. Philip Randolph Campus High School in Manhattan that they will become 'pioneers' if they meet the challenges of fighting inequality, racism, and poverty in the 21st century," Sullivan was employing the term in its standard usage.[44]

This usage was so well understood that it gave rise to one of the few cases where   30
a person interviewed in a newspaper article actually engaged and questioned the meaning of the term "pioneer," and its application to him. "National League

President Plays Down 'Pioneer' Talk," the headline read. The opening sentence explained, "National League President Bill White says he's getting tired of people referring to him as a black pioneer. . . . 'I'm not a pioneer,' White said. 'Jackie [Robinson] was the pioneer.'"[45] To Bill White, "pioneer" was the term reserved for the unusually courageous person who went first, and the one who faced the worst and the most intense opposition and resistance.

The African American applications of the pioneer analogy caught me completely by surprise. They took the ground out from under any remaining inclination I might have had simply to mock the analogy. The lesson of these references is this: the whole package of frontier and pioneer imagery has ended up as widely dispersed intellectual property. One could argue, as I probably at other times *would* have argued, that African Americans would be well advised to keep their distance from the metaphors and analogies of conquest and colonialism, that there are other, and better, ways to say that someone was a person of principle, innovation, and determination without calling him or her a pioneer. Even though they have been significant participants in the westward movement and in the life of the American West in the twentieth century, African Americans barely figured in the traditional tellings of frontier history; the history of pioneering Americans was for far too long a segregated, "whites-only" subject matter.[46] The image of the heroic pioneer was in many ways a vehicle of racial subordination, exalting the triumph of whites over Indians. Jackie Robinson, A. Philip Randolph, and Rosa Parks were people of great courage and spirit, and getting them entangled in the whole inherited myth of Manifest Destiny, nationalistic cheerleading, and justifications for conquest does not seem to be the best way to honor them.

But it is a bit too late to avoid that entangling. Greatly troubled by the problem of violence inflicted by blacks against blacks, Rev. Jesse Jackson pled with people to "Stop the violence!" The campaign to end the violence, he said, is "the new frontier of the civil rights movement."[47] Logic and history say that the frontier was, in fact, a place where violence served the causes of racial subordination, but a more powerful emotional understanding says that the frontier is where people of courage have gone to take a stand for the right and the good. For people of a wide range of ethnicities, when it comes to the idea of the frontier, logic and history yield to the much greater power of inherited image.

This is the curious conclusion that these headlines forced upon me: a positive image of the frontier and the pioneer is now implanted in nearly everyone's mind. It would not surprise me to see headlines referring to an American Indian lawyer as "a pioneer in the assertion of Indian legal rights," "pushing forward the frontier of tribal sovereignty"—even though it was the historical pioneers who assaulted those rights, even though it was the pioneers' historical frontier that charged head-on into tribal sovereignty. And yet Indian people have adopted any number of items introduced by whites. They wear cowboy hats, drive pickup trucks and automobiles, shop in supermarkets, study constitutional law in law schools, and remain Indian. In all sorts of ways, Indian people put Anglo-American artifacts, mental and physical, to use for Indian purposes. There is no very convincing argument for saying they must put a stop to their adopting and incorporating when it comes to the idea of the frontier and the image of the pioneer.

The historian Arthur Schlesinger, Jr., and many others have recently lamented "the disuniting of America" through the expansion of multicultural history.[48] We hear frequent expressions of nostalgia for an imagined era of unity, before an emphasis on race, class, and gender divided Americans into contesting units and interests. Reading several thousand headlines about pioneers and frontiers, however, convinced me that matters are by no means as disunited as the lamenters think. When African Americans turn comfortably to the image of the pioneer, then the idea of the frontier and the pioneer have clearly become a kind of multicultural common property, a joint-stock company of the imagination. As encounters with scholars from other countries usually demonstrate, this is not just multicultural, this is international. People from the Philippines, people from Senegal, people from Thailand, people with plenty of reasons to resent the frontier and cowboy diplomacy inflicted on their nations by our nation: many of them nonetheless grew up watching western movies and yearning for life on the Old Frontier and the open range.[49]

34

As a mental artifact, the frontier has demonstrated an astonishing stickiness and persistence. It is virtually the flypaper of our mental world; it attaches itself to everything—healthful diets, space shuttles, civil rights campaigns, heart transplants, industrial product development, musical innovations. Packed full of nonsense and goofiness, jammed with nationalistic self-congratulation and toxic ethnocentrism, the image of the frontier is nonetheless universally recognized, and laden with positive associations. Whether or not it suits my preference, the concept works as a cultural glue—a mental and emotional fastener that, in some very curious and unexpected ways, works to hold us together.

35

The frontier of an expanding and confident nation; the frontier of cultural interpenetration; the frontier of contracting rural settlement; the frontier of science, technology, and space; the frontier of civil rights where black pioneers ventured and persevered; the frontiers between nations in Europe, Asia, and Africa; *la frontera* of the Rio Grande and the deserts of the southwestern United States and northern Mexico: somewhere in this weird hodgepodge of frontier and pioneer imagery lie important lessons about the American identity, sense of history, and direction for the future. Standing in the way of a full reckoning with those lessons, however, is this fact: in the late *twentieth* century, the scholarly understanding formed in the late *nineteenth* century still governs most of the public rhetorical uses of the word "frontier"; the vision of Frederick Jackson Turner still governs the common and conventional understandings of the term. If the movement of ideas from frontier historians to popular culture maintains its velocity, sometime in the next century we might expect the popular usage of the word to begin to reckon with the complexity of the westward movement and its consequences. Somewhere in the mid-2000s the term might make a crucial shift, toward the reality of *la frontera* and away from the fantasy of the frontier. And that shift in meaning, *if* it occurs, will mark a great change in this nation's understanding of its own origins.

36

NOTES

I would like to thank Kim Gruenwald, Stephen Sturgeon, and Jon Coleman for their help in following the trail of the frontier. I would also like to thank my colleague

Mark Pittenger, whose book *American Socialists and Evolutionary Thought, 1870–1920* (Madison: University of Wisconsin Press, 1993) showed me how to think about the habits, ways, and customs of analogy-users.

1. In Frederick Jackson Turner, *The Frontier in American History* (1920; rpt. Tucson: University of Arizona Press, 1986), 2.

2. David M. Wrobel, *The End of American Exceptionalism: Frontier Anxiety from the Old West to the New Deal* (Lawrence: University Press of Kansas, 1993), 145.

3. Robert Cahn, "The Intrepid Kids of Disneyland," *Saturday Evening Post,* June 18, 1958, 22–23.

4. Ibid., 120.

5. Ibid., 119.

6. Ira Wolfert, "Walt Disney's Magic Kingdom," *Reader's Digest,* April 1960, 147.

7. Ibid., 147.

8. John M. Findlay, *Magic Lands: Western Cityscapes and American Culture after 1940* (Berkeley: University of California Press, 1992), 93–94.

9. Change seems to have been equally dramatic in Disney thinking about Indians. In 1993, the Walt Disney Company announced plans for a new American history theme park in Virginia. The section called "Native America," one company representative said, would now display "the sophisticated, intelligent societies that existed here before European settlers came, and in fact wiped out their societies" (Michael Wines, "Disney Will 'Recreate' U.S. History next to a Place Where It Was Made," *New York Times,* November 12, 1993).

10. See Patricia Nelson Limerick, Clyde A. Milner II, and Charles E. Rankin, eds., *Trails: Toward a New Western History* (Lawrence: University Press of Kansas, 1991).

11. Paula Petrik, *No Step Backward* (Helena: Montana Historical Society Press, 1987), chapter 2, "Capitalists with Rooms: Prostitution in Helena, 1865–1900," 25–58. [Notes no. 12 through no. 37, which relate to a portion of the essay not printed in this text, have been omitted.]

38. See Oscar J. Martínez, *Troublesome Border* (Tucson: University of Arizona Press, 1986); Mario T. García, "La Frontera: The Border as Symbol and Reality in Mexican-American Thought," *Mexican Studies,* Summer 1985, 195–225; Alan Weisman and Jay Dusard, *La Frontera: The United States Border with Mexico* (Tucson: University of Arizona Press, 1986); Tom Miller, *On the Border: Portraits of America's Southwestern Frontier* (New York: Harper and Row, 1981).

39. Gloria Anzaldúa, *Borderlands/La Frontera: The New Mestiza* (San Francisco: Aunt Lute Books, 1987), 3.

40. Ibid., 4.

41. See Luis Alberto Urrea, *Across the Wire: Life and Hard Times on the Mexican Border* (New York: Doubleday, 1993).

42. Anzaldúa, *Borderlands/La Frontera,* 63.

43. "Thousands Form Human Chain across Romania-Bulgaria Frontier," Reuters, June 8, 1990; "Palestinian Guerrilla is Killed at Lebanese-Israeli Frontier," *New York Times,* September 6, 1989; "Algeria and Morocco Reopen their Frontier," Reuters, June 5, 1988; Jim Bodgener, "Turkey Will Close its Frontier with Bulgaria Today," *Financial Times,* August 22, 1989.

44. David Maraniss, "Memories in Black and White; Desegregation's Pioneers," *Washington Post,* June 6, 1990; "Genevieve Stuttaford Reviews *A. Philip Randolph: Pioneer of the Civil Rights Movement,*" *Publishers Weekly,* May 11, 1990; "Rights Pioneer Parks Hospitalized," *Los Angeles Times,* February 2, 1989; "City in Ohio Honors Civil Rights Pioneer," *Chicago Tribune,* May 11, 1990; Tanya Barrientos, "Civil Rights Pioneer Julian Bond Perplexed by Persistence of Racism," *Philadelphia Inquirer,* May 9, 1992; David Treadwell, "She is the First Black to Give Commencement Address: Integration Pioneer Returns to Speak at U. of Georgia," *Los Ange-*

les Times, June 12, 1988; "Thelma Cowans, Pioneer Black Professional Golfer, Dies," United Press International, February 7, 1990; Rosemary L. Bray, "Renaissance for a Pioneer of Black Pride," *New York Times,* February 4, 1990; G. D. Clay, "First, There Was Fritz; Long before Art Shell, Pollard was NFL's Pioneer Black Coach," *Newsday,* December 20, 1989; "Didi Daniels Peter; Pioneer Black Producer," *Los Angeles Times,* March 2, 1989; "Joseph W. Bostic: Pioneer Black Announcer," *Los Angeles Times,* June 2, 1988; Charles Fountain, "A Baseball Historian Goes to Bat for Some Negro League Greats: Blackball Stars: Negro League Pioneers," *Christian Science Monitor,* April 15, 1988; C. Gerald Fraser, "J. Saunders Redding, 81, Is Dead; Pioneer Black Ivy League Teacher," *New York Times,* March 5, 1988; David Mills, "Tuned In to Jockey Jack; Tribute to a Black Radio Pioneer," *Washington Post,* June 23, 1990; "Clifton R. Wharton Sr. Dies; Foreign Service Pioneer," *Jet,* May 14, 1990; "Pioneer Black L.A. Judge Edwin Jefferson Dies at 84," *Jet,* September 18, 1989; "Pioneer Black Journalist Albert J. Dunsmore, 73, Praised at Detroit Rites," *Jet,* February 20, 1989; Tia Swanson, "A Pioneer in World of Black Film," *Philadelphia Inquirer,* June 4, 1992; "Black Oscar Nominees Gala Celebrates Movie Talents (Sidney Poitier Wins Pioneer Award)," *Jet,* April 17, 1989; Gene Siskel, "Poitier the Pioneer: He's Back on Screen—and Taking a Second Look at a Life Full of Firsts," *Chicago Tribune,* January 31, 1988; Nick Jesdanun, "'Pioneer' Futures," *Newsday,* June 24, 1989.

45. "NL President Plays Down 'Pioneer' Talk," *Chicago Tribune,* May 16, 1989. See also "NL Boss Won't Wear Pioneer Tag," *USA Today,* May 16, 1989.

46. The first efforts at including African Americans within Western American history left the framework of traditional frontier history unchallenged. In the introduction to the first edition of *The Black West* (1971; rpt. Seattle, Wash.: Open Hand Publishing, 1987), William Loren Katz remarked, "When historian Frederick Jackson Turner told how the frontier shaped American democracy, he ignored the black experience—not because it challenged his central thesis, but because he wrote in a tradition that had denied the existence of black people" (xii). By the time of a later edition, Katz was developing a more critical approach; consider this remark from the 1987 introduction:

> A U.S. Army that treated its Buffalo Soldiers [African American men enlisted in the post–Civil War western army] shabbily and cynically buried their military record, has accepted an image rehabilitation and trumpeted black heroism the better to recruit despairing, unemployed black youths. Will it, in the name of troopers who battled Apaches, Sioux and Commanches, train dark young men to stem Third World liberation forces? This would be a tragic misuse of the past. (xi)

See also William Leckie, *The Buffalo Soldiers* (Norman: University of Oklahoma Press, 1967). The recent issuing of a United States Post Office stamp commemorating the Buffalo Soldiers puts an unintended spotlight on the question of the African American role in conquest; see "Part of America's Past Becomes a Stamp of Tomorrow," *New York Times,* December 8, 1993.

47. Don Terry, "A Graver Jackson's Cry: Overcome the Violence!" *New York Times,* November 11, 1993.

48. Arthur Schlesinger, Jr., *The Disuniting of America: Reflections on a Multicultural Society* (New York: Whittle Books, 1991).

49. These impressions come from a number of speaking engagements with United States Information Agency tour groups, where international scholars have told me about their early encounters with the American frontier myth.

Working with the Text

1. What does the term *frontier* mean to you? What are some of the different definitions of *frontier* that Limerick explores and invokes? Which of Limer-

ick's different definitions is closest to the images the word *frontier* conjures up for you?

2. What point is Limerick trying to make in her discussion about "Frontierland" at Disneyland? What does she mean by the "uncertain turf along the border between the imagined and the actual"? How does she extend her point about Frontierland to her broader discussion of the role of the "frontier" in twentieth-century American culture?

3. What is the relationship between images of the "frontier" and American values? Which values or American characteristics are implicated by the imagery and mythology of the frontier? How are they invoked, for example, for the uses that American presidents and politicians have made of them? Go to the section of the *Border Texts* Web site called "The Electronic Frontier." Beginning with the links provided there, explore some of the ways that the American Frontier is portrayed on the Web, both in relation to cyberspace and otherwise. Where do you see continuity with Limerick's argument?

4. Why is Limerick initially bothered by the use of the terms *pioneer* and *frontier* in African American contexts? How does she resolve this in her own mind? Do you think that her concerns about language are legitimate? Does the historical meaning of words matter if there are popular meanings that are simpler or less problematic?

5. Near the end of the essay, Limerick says, "If the idea of *la frontera* had anywhere near the standing of the idea of the frontier, we would be well launched toward self-understanding, directed toward a realistic view of this nation's position in the hemisphere and in the world." What is the difference between "the frontier" and *la frontera*? How, in Limerick's eyes, are "borders" different from the American "frontier"? In a paper explore what ideas or assumptions are present in the traditional notion of the frontier that are not applicable or operative in an analysis of borders or of the borderlands.

AT THE BUFFALO BILL MUSEUM— JUNE 1988

JANE TOMPKINS

■ A professor of English at Duke University in North Carolina, Jane Tompkins has approached literary study from a cultural perspective. She is more interested in what novels, stories, and poems tell us about the cultures that produced them than in the works as discrete artistic productions. Tompkins has also often written from a highly personal perspective, linking her own experiences to the works that she studies. Rather than drawing firm conclusions, she will admit her inability to resolve contradictory responses.

She became interested in studying European-Indian relations while researching the Puritans' relations with Native Americans for a colonial literature course.
Her book *West of Everything: The Inner Life of Westerns* (1992) examines historical
images of the American West as filtered through popular culture. In the following
essay, which became a part of that book, she focuses on a Western icon whose
legacy suggests the many contradictory images we have of the commingling of
cultures in the American West.

The video at the entrance to the Buffalo Bill Historical Center tells us that   1
Buffalo Bill was the most famous American of his time, that by 1900 over
a billion words had been written about him, and that he had a progressive
vision of the West. Buffalo Bill had worked as a cattle driver, a wagoneer, a Pony Express rider, a buffalo hunter for the railroad, a hunting guide, an army scout and
sometime Indian fighter; he wrote dime novels about himself and an autobiography
at the age of thirty-three, by which time he was already famous; and then he began
another set of careers—first he became an actor, performing on the urban stage in
wintertime melodramatic representations of what he actually earned a living at in
the summer (scouting and leading hunting expeditions), and finally he became the
impresario of the Wild West show, a form of entertainment which he invented and
carried on as actor, director, and all-around idea man for thirty years. Toward the
end of his life he founded the town of Cody, Wyoming, to which he gave, among
other things, $200,000. Strangely enough, it was as a progressive civic leader that Bill
Cody wanted to be remembered. "I don't want to die," the video at the entrance tells
us he said, "and have people say—oh, there goes another old showman. . . . I would
like people to say—this is the man who opened Wyoming to the best of civilization."

The best of civilization. This was the phrase that rang in my head as I moved   2
through the museum, which is one of the most disturbing places I have ever visited.
It is also a wonderful place. It is four museums in one: the Whitney Gallery of Western Art, which houses art works on western subjects; the Buffalo Bill Museum
proper, which memorializes Cody's life; the Plains Indian Museum, which exhibits
artifacts of American Indian civilization; and the Winchester Arms Museum, a collection of firearms, historically considered.

The whole operation is extremely well designed and well run, from the video   3
program at the entrance that gives an overview of all four museums, to the fresh-
faced young attendants wearing badges that say "Ask Me," to the museum shop
stacked with books on western Americana, to the ladies' room—a haven of satiny
marble, shining mirrors, and flattering light. Among other things, the museum is
admirable for its effort to combat prevailing stereotypes about the so-called "winning of the West," a phrase it self-consciously places in quotation marks. There are
placards declaring that all history is a matter of interpretation, and that the American West is a source of "myth." Everywhere except, perhaps, in the Winchester Arms
Museum, where the rhetoric is different, you feel the effort of the museum staff to
reach out to the public, to be clear, to be accurate, to be fair, not to condescend, in
short, to educate in the best sense of the term.

On the day I went, the museum was featuring an exhibition of Frederic Reming-   4 ton's works. There are two facts about these productions that make them different from those of artists one is used to encountering in museums. The first is that Remington's paintings and statues function as a historical record. Their chief attraction has always been that they transcribe scenes and events that have vanished from the earth. The second fact, related to this, is the brutality of their subject matter. Remington's work makes you pay attention to *what is happening* in the painting or the piece of statuary. When you look at his work you cannot escape from its subject.

Consequently, as I moved through the exhibit, the wild contortions of the buck- 5 ing broncos, the sinister expression invariably worn by the Indians, and the killing of animals and men made the placards discussing Remington's use of the "lost wax" process seem strangely disconnected. In the face of unusual violence, or implied violence, their message was: what is important here is technique. Except in the case of paintings showing the battle of San Juan Hill, where white Americans were being killed, the material accompanying Remington's works did not refer to the subject matter of the paintings and statues. Nevertheless, an undertone of disquiet ran beneath the explanations; at least I thought I detected one. Someone had taken the trouble to ferret out Remington's statement of horror at the slaughter on San Juan Hill; someone had also excerpted the judgment of art critics commending Remington for the lyricism, interiority, and mystery of his later canvases—pointing obliquely to the fascination with bloodshed that preoccupied his earlier work.

The uneasiness of the commentary, and my uneasiness with it, were nothing 6 compared to the blatant contradictions in the paintings themselves. A pastel palette, a sunlit stop-action haze, murderous movement arrested under a lazy sky, flattened onto canvas and fixed in azure and ocher—two opposed impulses nestle here momentarily; the tension that keeps them from splitting apart is what holds the viewer's gaze.

The most excruciating example of what I mean occurs in the first painting in the 7 exhibit. Entitled *His First Lesson,* it shows a horse standing saddled but riderless while a man pierces it just below the shoulder with a sharp instrument. The white of the horse's eye signals his pain. The man who is doing the piercing is simultaneously backing away from the reaction he clearly anticipates, and the man who holds the horse's halter is doing the same. But what can they be afraid of? For the horse's right rear leg is tied a foot off the ground by a rope that is also tied around his neck. He can't move. That is the whole point.

"His First Lesson." Whose? And what lesson, exactly? How to stay still and stand 8 pain? How not to break away when they come at you with sharp instruments? How to be obedient? How to behave? It is impossible not to imagine that Remington's obsession with physical cruelty had roots somewhere in his own experience. Why else, in statue after statue, is the horse rebelling? The bucking bronco—symbol of the state of Wyoming, on every license plate, on every sign for every bar, on every belt buckle, mug, and decal—this image Remington cast in bronze over and over again. There is a wild diabolism in the bronzes; the horse and rider seem one thing, not so much rider and ridden as a single bolt of energy gone crazy and caught somehow, complicatedly, in a piece of metal.

In the paintings it is different, more subtle and bizarre. The cavalry on its way to 9 a massacre, sweetly limned, softly tinted, poetically seized in midcareer, and gently laid on the two-dimensional surface. There is about these paintings of military men in the course of their deadly duty an almost maternal tenderness. The idealization of the cavalrymen in their dusty uniforms on their gallant horses has nothing to do with patriotism; it is pure love.

Remington's paintings and statues, as shown in this exhibition, embody   10 everything that was objectionable about his era in American history. They are imperialist and racist; they glorify war and the torture and killing of animals; there are no women in them anywhere. Never the West as garden, never as pastoral, never as home. But in their aestheticizing of violent life Remington's pictures speak (to me at least) of some other desire. The maternal tenderness is not an accident, nor the beauty of the afternoons, nor the warmth of the desert sun. In these paintings Remington plays the part of the preserver, as if by catching the figures in color and line he could save their lives, and absorb some of that life into himself.

In one painting that particularly repulsed and drew me, a moose is outlined   11 against the evening sky at the brink of a lake. He looks expectantly into the distance. Behind him and to one side, hidden from his view, and only just revealed to ours, for it is dark there, is a hunter poised in the back of a canoe, rifle perfectly aimed. We look closer; the title of the picture is *Coming to the Call*. Ah, now we see. This is a sadistic scene. The hunter has lured the moose to his death. But wait a moment. Isn't the sadism really directed at us? First we see the glory of the animal; Remington has made it as noble as he knows how. Then we see what is going to happen. The hunter is one up on the moose but Remington is one up on us. He makes us feel the pain of the anticipated killing, and makes us want to hold it off, to preserve the moose, just as he has done. Which way does the painting cut? Does it go against the hunter— who represents us, after all—or does it go against the moose, who came to the call? Who came, to what call? Did Remington come to the West in response to it—to whatever the moose represents, or to whatever the desire to kill the moose represents? But he hasn't killed it; he has only preserved an image of a white man about to kill it. And what call do we answer when we look at this painting? Who is calling whom? What is being preserved here? That is the question that for me hung over the whole museum.

The Whitney Gallery is an art museum: its allegiance is to "art" as our academic   12 tradition has defined it. In this tradition, we come to understand a painting by having in our possession various bits of information. Something about the technical process used to produce it (pastels, watercolors, woodblock prints, etc.); something about the elements of composition—line and color and movement; something about the artist's life (where born, how educated, by whom influenced, which school belonged to or revolted against); something about his relation to this particular subject, such as how many times he painted it, or whether it contains his favorite model. Occasionally there will be some philosophizing about the themes or ideas the paintings are said to represent.

The problem is, when you're faced with a painter like Remington, these bits of in-   13 formation, while nice to have, don't explain what is there in front of you. They don't begin to give you an account of why a person should have depicted such things. The experience of a lack of fit between the explanatory material and what is there on the wall is one I've had before in museums, when, standing in front of a painting or a piece of statuary, I've felt a huge gap between the information on the little placard and what it is I'm seeing. I realize that "works of art," so-called, all have a subject matter, are all engaged with life, with some piece of life no less significant, no less compelling than Remington's subjects are, if we could only see its force. The idea that art is somehow separate from history, that it somehow occupies a space that is not the same as the space of life, seems out of whack here.

I wander through the gallery thinking these things because right next to it, in-   14
deed all around it, in the Buffalo Bill Museum and in the Plains Indian Museum, are artifacts that stand not for someone's expertise or skill in manipulating the elements of an artistic medium, but for life itself; they are the residue of life.

The Buffalo Bill Museum envelops you in an array of textures, colors, shapes, sizes,   15
forms. The fuzzy brown bulk of a buffalo's hump, the sparkling diamonds in a stick-pin, the brilliant colors of the posters—there's something about the cacophonous mixture that makes you want to walk in and be surrounded by it, as if you were going into a child's adventure story. It all appeals to the desire to be transported, to pretend for a little while that we're cowboys or cowgirls; it's a museum where fantasy can take over. In this respect, it is true to the character of Buffalo Bill's life.

As I moved through the exhibition, "the best of civilization" was the phrase that   16
rang through my head, and particularly I thought of it as I looked at certain objects on display in a section of the museum that re-creates rooms from Cody's house. Ostrich and peacock feather fans, a chair and a table made entirely of antlers, a bearskin rug. Most of all, I thought of the phrase as I looked at the heads on the wall: Alaska Yukon moose, Wapiti American elk, musk-ox (the "Whitney," the "De-Rham"), mountain caribou (the "Hyland"), Quebec Labrador caribou (the "Elbow"), Rocky Mountain goat (the "Haase," the "Kilto"), woodland caribou (world's record, "DeRham"), the "Rogers" freak Wapiti, the "Whitney" bison, the "Lord Rundle-sham" bison. The names that appear after the animals are the names of the men who killed them. Each of the animals is scored according to measurements devised by the Boone and Crockett Club, a big-game hunters' organization. The Lord Rundlesham bison, for example, scores 124⅝, making it number 25 in the world for bison trophies. The "Reed" Alaska Yukon moose scores 247. The "Witherbee" Canada moose holds the world's record.

Next to the wall of trophies is a small enclosure where jewelry is displayed: a   17
buffalo-head stickpin and two buffalo-head rings, the heads made entirely of diamonds, with ruby eyes, the gifts of the Russian Crown Prince; a gold and diamond stickpin from Edward VII; a gold, diamond, and garnet locket from Queen Victoria. The two kinds of trophies—animals and jewels—form an incongruous set, the relationship between them compelling but obscure.

If the rest of the items in the museum—the dime novels with their outrageous   18
covers, the marvelous posters, the furniture, Cody's wife's dress, his daughter's oil painting—if these have faded in my mind, it is because I cannot forget the heads of the animals as they stared down, each with an individual expression on its face. When I think about it I realize that I don't know why these animals' heads are there. Buffalo Bill didn't kill them; perhaps they were gifts from the famous people he took on hunts. A different kind of jewelry.

After the heads, I began to notice something about the whole exhibition. In one   19
display, doghide chaps, calfskin chaps, Angora goatskin chaps, and horsehide chaps. Next to these a rawhide lariat and a horsehair quirt. Behind me, boots and saddles,

all of leather. Everywhere I looked there was tooth or bone, skin or fur, hide or hair, or the animal itself entire—two full-size buffaloes (a main feature of the exhibition) and a magnificent stone sheep (a mountain sheep with beautiful curving horns). This one was another world's record. The best of civilization.

In the literature about Buffalo Bill you read that he was a conservationist, that if   20 it were not for the buffaloes in his Wild West shows, the species might have become extinct. (In the seventeenth century, 40 million wild buffalo roamed North America; by 1900 all the wild buffalo had been killed except for one herd in northern Alberta.) That the man who gained fame first as a buffalo hunter should have been an advocate for conservation of the buffalo is not an anomaly but typical of the period. The men who did the most to preserve America's natural wilderness and its wildlife were big-game hunters. The Boone and Crockett Club, founded by Theodore Roosevelt, George Bird Grinnell, and Owen Wister, turns out to have been one of the earliest organizations to devote itself to environmental protection in the United States. The *Readers' Encyclopaedia of the American West* says that the club "supported the national park and forest reserve movement, helped create a system of national wildlife refuges, and lobbied for the protection of threatened species, such as the buffalo and antelope." At the same time, the prerequisites for membership in the club were "the highest caliber of sportsmanship and the achievement of killing 'in fair chase' trophy specimens [which had to be adult males] from several species of North American big game."

The combination big-game hunter/conservationist suggests that these men had   21 no interest in preserving the animals for the animals' sake but simply wanted to ensure the chance to exercise their sporting pleasure. But I think this view is too simple; something further is involved here. The men who hunted game had a kind of love for game and a kind of love for nature which led them to want to preserve the animals which they also desired to kill. That is, the desire to kill the animals was in some way related to a desire to see them live. It is not an accident, in this connection, that Theodore Roosevelt, Owen Wister, and Frederic Remington all originally went west for reasons of health. Their devotion to the West, their connection to it, their love for it, is rooted in their need to reanimate their own lives. The preservation of nature, in other words, becomes for them symbolic of their own survival.

In a sense, then, there is a relationship between the Remington exhibition in the   22 Whitney Gallery and the animal memorabilia in the Buffalo Bill Museum. The moose in *Coming to the Call* and the moose heads on the wall are not so different as they might appear. The heads on the wall serve an aesthetic purpose; they are decorative objects, pleasing to the eye, which call forth certain associations. In this sense they are like visual works of art. The painting, on the other hand, has something of the trophy about it. The moose as Remington painted it is about to *become* a trophy, yet in another sense it already is one. Remington has simply captured the moose in another form. In both cases the subject matter, the life of a wild animal, symbolizes the life of the observer. It is the preservation of that life which both the painting and the taxidermy serve.

What are museums keeping safe for us, after all? What is it that we wish so much   23 to preserve? The things that we put in safekeeping, that we put in our safe-deposit boxes and keep under lock and key, are always in some way intended finally as safeguards of our own existence. The money and jewelry and stock certificates are meant for a time when we can no longer earn a living. Similarly, the objects in museums preserve for us a source of life from which we need to nourish ourselves when the resources that would normally supply us have run dry.

The Buffalo Bill Historical Center, full as it is of dead bones, lets us see more   24
clearly than we normally can what it is that museums are for. It is a kind of charnel house that houses images of living things that have passed away but whose life force still lingers around their remains and so passes itself on to us. We go and look at the objects in the glass cases and at the paintings on the wall, as if by standing there we could absorb into ourselves some of the energy that flowed once through the bodies of the live things represented. A museum, rather than being, as we normally think of it, the most civilized of places, a place most distant from our savage selves, actually caters to the urge to absorb the life of another into one's own life.

To give the idea its most extreme form, museums are a form of cannibalism   25
made safe for polite society. If we see the Buffalo Bill Museum in this way, it is no longer possible to separate ourselves from the hunters responsible for the trophies with their wondering eyes or from the curators who put them there. We are not, in essence, different from Teddy Roosevelt, or Frederic Remington, or Buffalo Bill, who killed animals when they were abundant in the Wild West of the 1880s. If, in doing so, those men were practicing the ancient art of absorbing the life of an animal into their own through the act of killing it, realizing themselves through the destruction of another life, then we are not so different from them as visitors to the museum. We stand beside the bones and skins and hooves of beings that were once alive, or stare fixedly at their painted images. Indeed our visit is only a safer form of the same enterprise.

So I did not get out of the Buffalo Bill Museum unscathed, unimplicated in the   26
acts of rapine and carnage which these remains represent. And I did not get out without having had a good time, either, because however many dire thoughts I may have had, the exhibits were interesting and fun to see. I was even able to touch a piece of buffalo hide they have displayed especially for that purpose (it was coarse and springy). Everyone else had touched it, too. The hair was worn down, where people's hands had been, to a fraction of its original length.

After this, the Plains Indian Museum was a terrible letdown. I went from one exhibit   27
to another expecting to become absorbed, but nothing worked. What was the matter? I thought I was interested in Indians, had read about them, taught some Indian literature, felt drawn to their religion. I had been prepared to enter this museum as if I were going into another children's story, only this time I would be an Indian instead of a cowboy or a cowgirl. But the objects on display, most of them behind glass, seemed paltry and insignificant. They lacked visual presence somehow. The bits of leather and sticks of wood triggered no fantasies in me. I couldn't make anything of them.

At the same time, I noticed with some discomfort that almost everything in those   28
glass cases was made of feathers and claws and hide, just like the men's chaps and ladies' fans in the Buffalo Bill Museum, only there was no luxury here. Plains Indian culture, it seemed, was made entirely from animals. Their mode of life had been completely dependent on animals for food, clothing, shelter, equipment, every-

thing. In the Buffalo Bill Museum I was able to say to myself: Well, if these men had been more sensitive, if they had had a right relation to their environment and to life itself, the atrocities that produced their trophies would never have occurred. They never would have exterminated the Indians and killed off the buffalo. But faced with the spectacle before me, it wasn't possible to say just what a right relation to the environment might be. I had expected that the Plains Indian Museum would show me how life in nature ought to be lived: not the wholesale destruction practiced by Euro-Americans, but an ideal form of communion with animals and the land. What the museum seemed to say, on the contrary, was that both colonizer and colonized had had their hands imbrued with blood. The Indians had lived off animals and had made war against each other. Violence was simply a necessary and inevitable part of life. There was no such thing as the life lived in non-violent harmony with nature. It was all bloodshed and killing, an unending cycle, over and over again, and no one could escape.

But perhaps there was a way to understand the violence that made it less terrible. 29 Perhaps if violence was necessary, a part of nature, intended by the universe, then it could be seen as sacramental. Perhaps it was true what Calvin Martin had said in *Keepers of the Game:* that the Indians had a sacred contract with the animals they killed, that they respected them as equals and treated their remains with honor and punctilio. If so, the remains of animals in the Plains Indian Museum weren't the same as those left by Buffalo Bill and his friends. They certainly didn't look the same. All I knew for certain was that these artifacts, lifeless and shrunken, spoke to me of nothing I could understand. No more did the life-size models of Indians, with strange featureless faces, draped in costumes that didn't look like clothing. The figures, posed awkwardly in front of tepees too white to seem real, carried no sense of a life actually lived, any more than the objects in the glass cases had.

The more I read the placards on the wall, the more disaffected I became. Plains 30 Indian life, apparently, had been not only bloody but exceedingly tedious. All those porcupine quills painstakingly softened, flattened, dyed, then appliquéd through even more laborious methods of stitching or weaving. Four methods of attaching porcupine quills, six design groups, population statistics, patterns of migration. There wasn't any glamour here at all. No glamour in the lives the placards told about, no glamour in the objects themselves, no glamour in the experience of looking at them. Just a lot of shriveled things accompanied by some even drier information.

Could it be, then, that the problem with the exhibitions was that Plains Indian 31 culture, if representable at all, was simply not readable by someone like me? Their stick figures and abstract designs could, by definition, convey very little to a Euro-American eye trained to know what glamour is by slick magazines. One display in particular seemed to illustrate this. It was a piece of cloth, behind glass, depicting a buffalo skin with marks on it. The placard read: "Winter Count, Sioux ca. 1910, after Lone Dog's, Fort Peck, Montana, 1877." The hide with its markings, now copied onto cloth, had been a calendar, each year represented by one image, showing the most significant event in the life of the tribe. To one side of the glass case was a book-length pamphlet explaining each image, year by year: 1800–1801, the attack of the Uncapoo on a Crow Indian fort; 1802–1803, a total eclipse of the sun. The images,

once you knew what they represented, made sense, and seemed poetic interpretations of the experiences they stood for. But without explanation they were incomprehensible, empty.

For the Plains Indian Museum just stopped me in my tracks. It was written in a language I had never learned. I didn't have the key. Maybe someone did, but I wasn't
too sure.   32

For it may not have been just cultural difference that made the text unreadable. I   33
began to suspect that the text itself was corrupt. That the architects of this museum
were going through motions whose purpose was, even to themselves, obscure.
Knowing what event a figure stands for in the calendar doesn't mean you understand an Indian year. The deeper purpose of the museum began to puzzle me. What
is an Indian museum for, anyway? Why should we be bothering to preserve the ves-
tiges of a people whose culture we had effectively extinguished? Wasn't there an air
of bad faith about this? Did the museum exist to assuage our guilt and not for any
educational reason? I did not and do not have an answer to these questions. All I
know is that I felt I was in the presence of something pious and a little insincere. It
had the aura of a failed attempt at virtue, as though the curators were trying to present, as interesting, objects whose purpose and meaning even they could not fully
imagine.

In a last-ditch attempt to salvage something, I went up to one of the guards and   34
asked where the movie was showing that the video had advertised, the movie about
Plains Indian life. "Oh, the slide show, you mean," he said. "It's been discontinued."
When I asked why, he said he didn't know. It occurred to me then that that was the
message the museum was sending, if I could read it—that that was the bottom line.
Discontinued, no reason given.

The movie in the Winchester Arms Museum, "Lock, Stock, and Barrel," was going   35
strong. The film began with the introduction of the cannon into European warfare
in the Middle Ages, and was working its way slowly toward the nineteenth century
when I left. I was in a hurry. Soon my husband would be waiting for me in the lobby.
Trying to get a quick impression of the objects on display, I went from room to
room, but the objects in this museum repelled me even more than the artifacts in
the Indian museum had. They were all the same: guns, guns, and more guns. Some
large drawings and photographs on the walls tried to give a sense of the context in
which the arms had been used, but the effect was nil. It was case after case of rifles
and pistols, repeating themselves over and over, and even when some slight variation caught my eye the differences meant nothing to me.

But the statistics that accompanied a display of commemorative rifles did mean   36
something. I saw the Antlered Game Commemorative Carbine. Date of manufacture: 1978. Number produced: 19,999. How many antlered animals had each carbine killed? I saw the Canadian Centennial, 1962, 90,000; the Legendary Lawman,
1978, 19,999; the John Wayne, 1980–81, 51,600. Like the titles of the various sections
of the museum, these names had a message. The message was: guns are patriotic.
Associated with national celebrations, law enforcement, and cultural heroes, the
firearms were made to seem inseparable from the march of American history:
Firearms in Colonial America; Born in America: The Kentucky Rifle; The Era of Expansion and Invention; The Civil War: Firearms of the Conflict; The Golden Age of

Hunting; Winning the West. The guns embodied phases of the history they had helped to make, and the fact that firearms had *had* a history seemed to consecrate them, to make them worth not only preserving but revering.

Awe and admiration are the attitudes the museum invites. You hear the ghostly march of military music in the background; you imagine flags waving and sense the implicit reference to feats of courage in battle and glorious death. The place had the air of an enormous reliquary, or of the room off the transept of a cathedral where the vestments are kept. These guns were not there merely to be seen or even studied; they were there to be venerated. 37

But I did not look closely. I did not try to appreciate the guns. Unconsciously, I said to myself, my ability to empathize, to extend myself toward the virtues of an alien craft, ends here. For here in the basement the instruments that had produced the hides and horns upstairs, and had massacred the Indians, were being lovingly displayed. And we were still making them. Fifty-one thousand six hundred John Waynes in 1980–81. Arms were going strong. 38

As I bought my books and postcards in the gift shop, I noticed a sign that read, "Rodeo Tickets Sold Here," and something clicked into place. So that was it. *Everything* was still going strong. The whole museum was just another rodeo, only with the riders and their props stuffed, painted, sculpted, immobilized, and put under glass. Like the rodeo, the museum witnessed a desire to bring back the United States of the 1880s and 1890s. The quotation marks around the phrase "the winning of the West," the statements about myth and interpretation, were only gestures in the direction of something that had nothing to do with the museum's real purpose. The American people did not want to let go of the winning of the West. They wanted to win it all over again, in imagination. It was the ecstasy of the kill, as much as the life of the hunted, that we fed off here. The Buffalo Bill Historical Center did not repudiate the carnage that had taken place in the nineteenth century. It celebrated it. With its gleaming restrooms, cute snack bar, opulent museum shop, wooden Indians, thousand rifles, and scores of animal trophies, it helped us all reenact the dream of excitement, adventure, and conquest that was what the Wild West meant to most people in this country. 39

This is where my visit ended. But it had a sequel. When I left the Buffalo Bill Historical Center I was full of moral outrage, an indignation so intense it made me almost sick, though it was pleasurable, too, as such emotions usually are. But the outrage was undermined by the knowledge that I knew nothing about Buffalo Bill, nothing of his life, nothing of the circumstances that led him to be involved in such violent events. And I began to wonder if my reaction wasn't in some way an image, however small, of the violence I had been objecting to. So I began to read about Buffalo Bill, and as I did, a whole new world opened up. 40

"I have seen him the very personification of grace and beauty . . . dashing over the free wild prairie and riding his horse as though he and the noble animal were bounding with one life and one motion." That is the sort of thing people wrote about Buffalo Bill. They said "he was the handsomest man I ever saw." They said there "was never another man lived as popular as he was." They said there "wasn't a man, woman or child that he knew or ever met that he didn't speak to." They said he "was handsome as a god, a good rider and a crack shot." They said he "gave lots of 41 money away. Nobody ever went hungry around him." They said he "was way above the average, physically and every other way."

These are quotes from people who knew Cody, collected by one of his two most responsible biographers. She puts them in the last chapter, and by the time you get there they all ring true. Buffalo Bill was incredibly handsome. He was extremely brave and did things no other scout would do. He carried messages over rugged territory swarming with hostile Indians, riding all night in bad weather to get through, and then taking off again the next day to ride sixty miles through a blizzard. He was not a proud man. He didn't boast of his exploits. But he did do incredible things, not just once in a while but on a fairly regular basis. He had a great deal of courage; he believed in himself, in his abilities, in his strength and endurance and knowledge. He was very skilled at what he did—hunting and scouting—but he wasn't afraid to try other things. He wrote some dime novels; he wrote his autobiography at age thirty-three, without very much schooling. He wasn't afraid to try acting even though the stage terrified him and he knew so little about it that, according to his wife, he didn't even know you had to memorize lines.

Maybe it was because he grew up on the frontier, maybe it was just the kind of person he was, but he was constantly finding himself in situations that required resourcefulness and courage, quick decisions and decisive action and rising to the occasion. He wasn't afraid to improvise.

He liked people, drank a lot, gave big parties, gave lots of presents, and is reputed to have been a womanizer.[1] When people came to see him in his office tent on the show grounds, to shake his hand or have their picture taken with him, he never turned anyone away. "He kept a uniformed doorman at the tent opening to announce visitors," writes a biographer. "No matter who was outside, from a mayor to a shabby woman with a baby, the Colonel would smooth his mustache, stand tall and straight, and tell the doorman to 'show 'em in.' He greeted everyone the same." "He told the damnedest stories you ever heard," writes the son of an Indian who worked in the Wild West show, "entertaining his troupe of performers for hours with Old West blood and guts make-believe. He was admired by all, including the hundreds of Indians he took along on tour. Indians love a man who can tell good stories." They also admired him for fighting well, said his biographers. Though I looked for it, I could find no evidence that contradicts those claims.

As a showman, he was a genius. People don't say much about why he was so successful; mostly they describe the wonderful goings-on. But I get the feeling that Cody was one of those people who was connected to his time in an uncanny way. He knew what people wanted, he knew how to entertain them, because he *liked* them, was open to them, felt kinship with them, or was so much in touch with himself at some level that he was thereby in touch with almost everybody else.

He liked to dress up and had a great sense of costume (of humor, too, they say). Once he came to a fancy-dress ball, his first, in New York, wearing white tie and tails and a large Stetson. He knew what people wanted. He let his hair grow long and wore a mustache and beard because, he said, he wouldn't be believable as a scout otherwise. Hence his Indian name, Pahaska, meaning "long hair," which people loved to use. Another kind of costume. He invented the ten-gallon hat, which the Stetson company made to his specifications. Afterward, they made a fortune off of it. In the scores of pictures reproduced in the many books about him, he most often wears scout's clothes—usually generously fringed buckskin, sometimes a modified cavalryman's outfit—though often he's impeccably turned out in a natty-looking three-piece business suit (sometimes with overcoat, sometimes not). The photographs show him in a tuxedo, in something called a "Mexican suit," which looks like a cowboy outfit, and once he appears in Indian dress. In almost every case he is wearing a hat, usually the Stetson, at exactly the right angle. He poses deliberately, and with dignity, for the picture. Cody didn't take himself so seriously that he had to pretend to be less than he was. "Jesus / he was a handsome man," wrote e. e. cummings in "Buffalo Bill's defunct."

What made Buffalo Bill so irresistible? Why is he still so appealing, even now, when we've lost, supposedly, all the illusions that once supported his popularity? There's a poster for one of his shows when he was traveling in France that gives a clue to what it is that makes him so profoundly attractive. The poster consists of a huge buffalo galloping across the plains; in the center of the buffalo's hump is a cutout circle that shows the head of Buffalo Bill, white mustachioed and bearded now, in his famous hat, and beneath, in large red letters, are the words *"Je viens."*   47

Je viens, I am coming, are the words of a savior. The announcement is an annunciation. Buffalo Bill is a religious figure of a kind who makes sense, I think, within a specifically Christian tradition. That is, he comes in the guise of a redeemer, of someone who will save us, who will through his own actions do something for us that we cannot. He will lift us above our lives, out of the daily grind, into something larger than ourselves.   48

His appeal on the surface is to childish desires, the desire for glamour, fame, bigness, adventure, romance. But these desires are also the sign of something more profound, and it is to something more profound in us that he also appeals. Buffalo Bill comes to the child in us, understood not as that part of ourselves which we have outgrown but the part that got left behind, of necessity, a long time ago, having been starved, bound, punished, disciplined out of existence. He promises that that part of the self can live again. He has the power to promise these things because he represents the West, that geographical space of the globe which was still the realm of exploration and discovery, which was still open, which had not yet quite been tamed when he began to play himself on the stage. He not only represented it, he *was* it. He brought the West itself with him when he came: the very Indians, the very buffaloes, the very cowboys, the very cattle, the very stagecoach itself which had been memorialized in story. He performed in front of the audience the feats that had made him famous. He shot glass balls and clay pigeons out of the air with amazing rapidity. He rode his "watersmooth-silver stallion" at full gallop.   49

"I am coming." The appearance of Buffalo Bill, in the flesh, was akin to the apparition of a saint or of the Virgin Mary to believers. He was the incarnation of an ideal. He came to show people that what they had only imagined was really true. The West really did exist. There really were heroes who rode white horses and performed amazing feats. e. e. cummings was right to invoke the name of Jesus in his poem. Buffalo Bill was a secular messiah.   50

He was a messiah because people believed in him. When he died, he is reputed to have said, "Let my show go on." But he had no show at the time, so he probably   51 didn't say that. Still, the words are prophetic because the desire for what Buffalo Bill had done had not only not died but would call forth the countless reenactments of the Wild West, from the rodeo—a direct descendant of his show—to the thousands of western novels, movies, and television programs that comprise the western genre in the twentieth century, a genre that came into existence as a separate category right about the time that Bill Cody died. Don Russell maintains that the way the West exists in our minds today is largely the result of the way Cody presented it in his show. That was where people got their ideas of what the characters looked like. Though many Indian tribes wore no feathers and fought on foot, you will never see a featherless, horseless Indian warrior in the movies because Bill employed only Sioux and other Plains tribes that had horses and traditionally wore feathered head-dresses. "Similarly," he adds, "cowboys wear ten-gallon Stetsons, not because such a hat was worn in early range days, but because it was part of the costume adopted by Buffalo Bill for his show."[2]

But the deeper legacy is elsewhere. Buffalo Bill was a person who inspired other people. What they saw in him was an aspect of themselves. It really doesn't matter whether Cody was as great as people thought him or not, because what they were responding to when he rode into the arena, erect and resplendent on his charger, was something intangible, not the man himself but a possible way of being. William F. Cody and the Wild West triggered the emotions that had fueled the imaginative lives of people who flocked to see him, especially men and boys who made up the larger portion of the audience. He and his cowboys played to an inward territory: a Wild West of the psyche that hungered for exercise sprang into activity when the show appeared. *Je viens* was a promise to redeem that territory, momentarily at least, from exile and oblivion. The lost parts of the self symbolized by buffaloes and horses and wild men would live again for an hour while the show went on. [52]

People adored it. Queen Victoria, who broke her custom by going to see it at all (she never went to the theater and on the rare occasions when she wanted to see a play, she had it brought to her), is supposed to have been lifted out of a twenty-five-year depression caused by the death of her husband after she saw Buffalo Bill. She liked the show so much that she saw it again, arranging for a command performance to be given at Windsor Castle the day before her Diamond Jubilee. This was the occasion when four kings rode in the Deadwood coach with the Prince of Wales on top next to Buffalo Bill, who drove. No one was proof against the appeal. Ralph Blumenfeld, the London correspondent for the *New York Herald,* wrote in his diary while the show was in London that he'd had two boyhood heroes, [53]

> Robin Hood and Buffalo Bill, and delighted in Cody's stories of the Pony Express and Yellow Hand. Everything was done to make Cody conceited and un-bearable, but he remained the simple, unassuming child of the plains who thought lords and ladies belonged in the picture books and that the story of Little Red Riding Hood was true. I rode in the Deadwood coach. It was a great evening in which I realized a good many of my boyhood dreams, for there was Buffalo Bill on his white rocking horse charger, and Annie Oakley behind him.[3]

Victor Weybright and Henry Blackman Sell, from whose work on the Wild West some of the foregoing information has come, dedicated their book to Buffalo Bill. It was published in 1955. Nellie Irene Snyder Yost, whose 1979 biography is one of the [54] two scholarly accounts of Cody's life, dedicates her book "to all those good people, living or dead, who knew and liked Buffalo Bill."[4] Don Russell's *Lives and Legends of Buffalo Bill* (1960), the most fact-filled scholarly biography, does not have a dedication, but in the final chapter where he steps back to assess Cody and his influence, Russell ends by exclaiming: "What more could possibly be asked of a hero? If he was not one, who was?"[5]

Let me now pose a few questions of my own. Must we throw out all the wonderful qualities that Cody had, the spirit of hope and emulation that he aroused in millions of people, because of the terrible judgment history has passed on the epoch of which he was a part? The kinds of things he stands for—courage, daring, strength, endurance, generosity, openness to other people, love of drama, love of life, the possibility of living a life that does not deny the body and the desires of the body—are these to be declared dangerous and delusional because he manifested some of them while fighting Indians, and others while representing his victories to the world? And the feelings he aroused in his audiences—the idealism, the enthusiasm, the excitement, the belief that dreams could become real—must these be declared misguided or a sham because they are associated with the imperialistic conquest of a continent, with the wholesale extermination of animals and men?

It is not so much that we cannot learn from history as that we cannot teach history how things should have been. When I set out to discover how Cody had become involved in the killing of Indians and the slaughter of buffalo, I found myself unable to sustain the outrage I had felt on leaving the museum. From his first job as an eleven-year-old herder for an army supply outfit, sole wage earner for his ailing, widowed mother, who had a new infant and other children to support, to his death in Colorado at seventy-one, there was never a time when it was possible for me to say, There, there you went wrong, Buffalo Bill, you should not have killed that Indian. You should have held your fire and quit the army and gone to work in the nineteenth-century equivalent of the Peace Corps. You should have known how it would end. My reading made me see that you can't prescribe for someone in Buffalo Bill's position—what he should have done, how things should have been—and it made me reflect on the violence of my own reaction. I saw how eager I had been to get off on being angry at the museum. The thirst for moral outrage, for self-vindication, lay pretty close to the surface.

I cannot resolve the contradictions between my experience at the Buffalo Bill Museum, with its celebration of violent conquest, and my response to the shining figure of Buffalo Bill as it emerged from the pages of books. On the one hand, a history of shame; on the other, an image of the heart's desire. But I have reached one conclusion that for a while, at least, will have to serve.

Major historical events like genocide and major acts of destruction are not simply produced by impersonal historical processes or economic imperatives or ecological blunders; human intentionality is involved and human knowledge of the self. Therefore, if you're really interested in not having any more genocide or killing of animals, no matter what else you might do—condemning imperialism or shaking your finger at history—if you don't first, or also, come to recognize the violence in yourself and your own anger and your own destructiveness, whatever else you do won't work. It isn't that genocide doesn't matter. Genocide matters and it starts at home.

NOTES

1. Iron Eyes Cody, as told to Collin Perry, *Iron Eyes: My Life as a Hollywood Indian* (New York, 1982), 16.

2. Don Russell, *The Lives and Legends of Buffalo Bill* (Norman, Okla., 1960), 470.

3. Victor Weybright and Henry Blackman Sell, *Buffalo Bill and the Wild West* (New York, 1955), 172.

4. Nellie Irene Snyder Yost, *Buffalo Bill, His Family, Friends, Fame, Failures, and Fortunes* (Chicago, 1979).

5. Russell, *Lives and Legends,* 480.

Working with the Text

1. Throughout her essay Tompkins describes her feelings and observations in terms of contradiction, pointing to the "blatant contradictions" in the exhibits or to her attempts to "resolve the contradictions" in herself. Throughout the museums she senses an "undertone of disquiet" and "uneasiness of the commentary." What are the sources of these conflicting feelings and thoughts? To what larger contradictions or tensions in American culture do they point? Does she ever resolve the essay's tensions, either for herself or for you, the reader?

2. Early in the essay Tompkins points out that Buffalo Bill (according to the museum) had a "progressive vision of the West." Yet near the end of the essay, Tompkins concludes that what made Buffalo Bill so attractive was the way that he embodied a frozen image of the West, a sense of what the West *had been* in the 1880s and 1890s and not what it could become. Moreover, she claims that the museum helps "us all reenact the dream of excitement, adventure, and conquest that was what the Wild West meant to most people in this country." Does this shift—from the West as progressive to the West as nostalgia—seem contradictory to you? In what ways are nostalgic notions of the Wild West related to America's progressive notions of itself as a national community? What are some of the American characteristics of the Wild West that have become generalized as important aspects of the American psyche? In what ways is the geographic space of the West a part of American national culture?

3. One phrase that Tompkins repeats is "the best of civilization." Later in the essay she pairs the idea of civilization with the idea of savagery or "the savage." Bridging these two ideas—civilization and savagery—is the idea of violence or brutality. How does her treatment of the violence that is part of civilization change over the course of the essay? What is the relationship between cultural violence and personal attitudes toward violence? Is there violence represented in the museum that would be repugnant to us in modern life but which seems sanitized or rationalized in the context of the past or in the context of "the West," which Tompkins describes as a "geographical space of the globe, which was still the realm of exploration and discovery, which was still open, which had not yet been tamed when [Buffalo Bill] began to play himself on the stage"?

4. The Buffalo Bill Museum in Cody, Wyoming, has an extensive site on the World Wide Web. There are also many other Web resources on Buffalo Bill.

Beginning with the "Frontier" section of the *Border Texts* Web site, visit some of these resources and compare their presentation of materials on Buffalo Bill and the Wild West to Tompkins' descriptions. Do you see or feel the same kind of contradictions? How is the West represented here?

5. What do you think she means by the essay's concluding phrase—"Genocide begins at home"? Do you find that phrase startling or disturbing? How does it echo back through the essay?

I HAVE NOT SIGNED A TREATY WITH THE UNITED STATES GOVERNMENT

CHRYSTOS

■ Of mixed racial heritage (her mother was of European descent while her father's ancestry was Menominee Indian), Chrystos has chosen to identify solely with her Native American heritage—even though her father himself did not embrace that heritage. After a troubled youth marked by intense family conflict, she spent her twenties in and out of mental institutions, suffering from depression and drug and alcohol abuse. Finally, in the late 1970s, with the help of her partner and encouraged by the feminist writer Kate Millett, she began to turn her life around, in part by concentrating on her poetry. After having her work included in several anthologies, in 1988 she published her first volume of poems, *Not Vanishing*, when she was forty-two. *Dream On*, a second volume, followed in 1991. Chrystos describes herself as "proudly uneducated and politically involved," and most of her work is overtly political in nature, dealing with issues of oppression and abuse. A native of San Francisco, she has lived near the Suquamish reservation in the state of Washington since 1980.

I have not signed a treaty
with the United States Government

nor has my father nor his father
nor any grandmothers
We don't recognize these names on old sorry paper   5
Therefore we declare the United States a crazy person
        nightmare   lousy food   ugly clothes   bad meat
        nobody we know
No one wants to go there   This US is theory   illusion
        terrible ceremony   The United States can't dance   can't cook   10

has no children   no elders   no relatives

They build funny houses no one lives in but papers

      Everything the United States does to everybody is bad

No this US is not a good idea   We declare you terminated

You've had your fun now go home we're tired   We signed   15

no treaty WHAT are you still doing here Go somewhere else and

      build a McDonalds We're going to tear all this ugly mess

down now We revoke your immigration papers

      your assimilation soap suds   your stories are no good

your colors hurt our feet   our eyes are sore   20

      our bellies are tied in sour knots   Go Away Now

      We don't know you from anybody

You must be some ghost in the wrong place wrong time

      Pack up your toys garbage   lies

We who are alive now   25

      have signed no treaties

Burn down your stuck houses   your sitting

      in a nowhere gray glow   Your spell is dead

So go far away we won't remember you ever came here

      Take these words back with you   30

Working with the Text

1. This poem, written from a Native American perspective, demands that the treaties giving the United States control of former frontier territories be terminated. If this actually could happen, if these lands could be returned exclusively to the descendants of the original inhabitants and everything else ejected, could the lands be defined again as "frontier"? In considering this question, you may want to explore some of the definitions of *frontier* that Patricia Nelson Limerick notes in her essay earlier in this chapter.

2. This poem raises an interesting question about responsibility for the actions of previous generations. The speaker claims that the treaties Native American tribes signed with the United States are void because "We who are alive now / have signed no treaties." Do you agree with the logic of this position? Looking at it from a different perspective, critics of affirmative action could make a similar claim: slavery and other institutionalized forms of discrimination were perpetrated by previous generations, so the current generation should have no responsibility for making any sort of restitution. Do you see any distinctions between these two claims?

3. How do you personally respond to this poem?

THE BORDER AS FICTION

CLARK BLAISE

■ Born in Fargo, North Dakota, to parents who were Canadian citizens, Clark Blaise spent his childhood moving from place to place because of his father's itinerant career as a furniture salesman. "As a native-born American with foreign parents, and as a child who attended an average of two schools a year in twenty-five different cities," he writes, "I grew up with an outsider's view of America and a romanticized exile's view of French-Canada." After receiving an M.F.A. from the University of Iowa's prestigious writing program, he taught at a variety of colleges in the United States and Canada and is now on the faculty of the University of Iowa. He has published several short story collections and novels, including *A North American Education* (1973) and *Lusts* (1983). He coauthored a book about India, *Days and Nights in Calcutta* (1977), with his Indian-born wife, writer Bharati Mukherjee, whose essay on belonging is in Chapter 3. Most recently he published *I Had a Father: A Post-Modern Autobiography* (1993). In the following essay, he considers how his dual relationship to Canada and the United States has influenced his conception of "borders."

How do you get eighteen French Canadians into a Volkswagen?
"Tell them you're going to Plattsburgh."

—old joke

In the last days of 1987, during our latest move, while unpacking boxes of books that had lain in storage for over two years, I uncovered a slim, discolored volume entitled *The Borderland and Other Poems,* by a certain Roger Quin, poet and Bohemian (born 1850). The book is updated (but is circa 1910), and is published by A. Walker and Son of Galashiels. That, I take it, is in Scotland. The discoloring comes from smoke, a reminder of our house fire in Montreal in 1973. Books purchased before that fire, and preserved through two dozen moves since, are signs of a certain naive commitment. I had probably purchased Quin's book at a church rummage sale in rural Quebec in the mid-sixties.

Anything to do with borders speaks to me personally. I am animated by the very thought of border; crossing the border is like ripping the continent, tearing its invisible casing. I look upon borders as zones of grace, fifty miles wide on either side, where dualities of spirit are commonplace.

The Scots, of course, first cultivated border consciousness to a bardic art. That invisible, near-mythical Scottish border is a primeval literary marker, and the prototype for the border that obsesses me, the Canadian-American. I'm not Scottish, and have never set foot in Scotland, but at one time in my life the thought of such a border appealed to me, as it would to many Canadians. Now, as though to prove that no written word is ever lost, I put Roger Quin ("the tramp poet") at the head of an essay, a paper to his lost, disparate clan.

In a preface to a book of nineteenth-century Scottish short stories, the editor,

Douglas Gifford, writes of the conflicts in the characteristic Scottish story: "Disorder, romance, imagination and feeling" are set against "rational Order." Sir Walter Scott's novels are "seen as extended metaphors for the dissociation in Scotland of thought and feeling, materialism and imagination, repression and sensitivity." Later Gifford notes that "two major forces shape the major fiction: protestantism and profit."

These divisions have their echoes in Canada, certainly in my own family and in   5
my sense of what Canada and the United States represent, and of the purpose of the border that lies between them. In an autobiographical essay, the late Quebec (actually Franco Manitoban) novelist, Gabrielle Roy, speaking of her own family, wrote, "with which side should I identify myself especially? With the Roys, troubled people, strict, Jansenists according to what I have been told, but also idealists and dreamers? Or with the Landrys, vivacious, impulsive, gracious and smiling? Where should I turn to learn from where I came?" The borders in Quebec do not require a checkpoint.

This dissociation, or at least conflict, between Protestantism and profit, secular-   6
ism and the Church, seems to me a useful point of departure for discussing Canadian visions of the United States. Surely the United States has embodied to Canadians a promise of wealth and self-assertion, and a threat to stability, while the border—increasingly mythical, one might add, as free trade and modern communications erode its ancient protections—affords only a tattered shelter. Canada's initial mission on this continent was the extension of parliamentary civilization—anti-republican, and anti-individualist—and there are substantial segments of Canadian society, and deep responses in the collective Canadian cortex, that resist the anarchic, litigious sprawl of American life, even when attracted, or pulled, to the American marketplace. This tension is the transparent casing that supports the border; it is central to the reading of the Canadian character and, not incidentally, to its literature.

Wouldn't most Canadian thinkers, and writers, agree with the proposition,   7
drawn from the Scottish example, that adherence to Canada (an ideal of Canada that is every bit as operative as the stars-and-stripes ideal of America) implies a certain material sacrifice? One clings to Canada out of inertia, yes, but faintly from virtue as well. One gives up Canada—the conclusion is inevitable—for the same reasons a Glaswegian treks to London: guilt and greed.

Look again at the self-awareness in that little joke (a Québécois joke, actually,   8
told in French) that heads this essay. See the disparity between a Quebecker's image of Plattsburgh, and an American's sense of the same, dreary, air-base town. In the United States, Plattsburgh is seen as the last outpost; from Canada it is the shopping mall of milk and honey.

Our move this year is deeper into Manhattan; last year was Queens. In the past eight   9
years we have lived in Iowa City, British Columbia, Atlanta, Saratoga Springs, Toronto, and Montreal. From a lifetime of crossing borders, I have developed a border consciousness. Borders mean metamorphosis, personal transformation. They offer the opportunity to be and not be simultaneously, or to be two opposing things without deception. I suspect I am not alone in sensing the pull of alien gravities; yet

I've often felt lonely, wondering if anyone else out there on our continent of rootless adventurers ever felt as I did.

For me, growing up in a map-strewn apartment in central Florida, countries   10 were like bodies, and borders were their skin. I attributed personalities to shapes, and learned to recognize and respond to outlines of states, countries, and even counties the way salesmen do to faces. I projected personalities on barren outlines.

I fantasized the embrace of Vermont and New Hampshire; they share their diag-   11 onal slice of a rocky rectangle like lovers. I approved the tentacular, border-state handshake of West Virginia and Maryland, snaking over Virginia and sliding under Pennsylvania. I detected disloyalty, however, in West Virginia's dagger thrust into the latitudes of Ohio and Pennsylvania. (The suspicion was borne out years later, in the late fifties, when I used to drive between my Pittsburgh home and my Ohio college, crossing that West Virginia panhandle at Wheeling. Between two abolitionist states stood the stark "colored-white" motel signs.) I thought of Tennessee and North Carolina as a sliced earthworm—two separate bodies from a single diagonal cut. I inferred hostility between Mississippi and Alabama as they turn their backs on each other, just like Arizona and New Mexico. I saw Arkansas as a chipped flowerpot, Louisiana as an overstuffed armchair, Minnesota as an enveloping protoplasm about to ingest Wisconsin. I liked broad, smiling Iowa, with its bulging cheek. I wondered about the twinning of inanimate objects—why Missouri and Georgia took on similar shapes, even to tiny nipples at their lower right. Alberta and British Columbia were bloated and blunted versions of Nevada and California. The Yukon mimicked Idaho, and Montana played the American version of the Northwest Territories. Canada leaned its Western provinces vertically, while the Western states were boxes, cut square for stacking.

Later, watching television weather forecasts, I wondered how the Americans   12 could cut off their borders at North Dakota and complain of "Canadian cold" emanating from sheer blankness to the north. Books as well seemed to end at the border. I loved Faulkner's sense of Canada, the use of Shreve McCannon, Quentin Compson's Harvard roommate, as the implied audience to the greatest of all American novels, *Absalom, Absalom!* It's Shreve who asks the major question in the book and in Faulkner's writing—"Why do you hate the South?"—and it's to Shreve, a Canadian, that Quentin cries his response: "*I dont.*" (At one time, I made something of that formulation: the Southerner and the Canadian, back-to-back brothers with the belt of individualist, ahistorical Yankeeland in between.) The only other American author with a consistently continental sense of origins was Ross Macdonald, and he, of course, was an old Canadian.

There is, I think, a border mentality, just as there is a small-country mentality (as   13 recently expounded by Milan Kundera), or an exile mentality, a ghetto mentality, an imperialist mentality, an island mentality. The border mentality is alert to differences, to calculating loss and advantage. It watches for tinctures of change as one demographic landscape blends into another.

And there is a border mentality that can take liberty with borders as they are   14 drawn, and that seeks to arrange things more coherently. I've written in the past of my own helpless fascination with the observed facts of the atlas, my attempts to memorize everything on the face of the globe, until finally those facts were not enough and I embarked on a childhood reinvention of the world, of countries, cities, continents, on a movement from history and from memoir into fiction. I was inspired to read, in a *Paris Review* interview, of Carlos Fuentes's literary reinvention of the world. There is, for Fuentes, a Caribbean literature, subversive of history and language, a multilingual literature of history's castaways: "There is a culture of the Caribbean . . . that includes Faulkner, Carpentier, García Márquez, Derek Walcott, and Aimé Césaire, a trilingual culture in and around the whirlpool of the baroque which is the Caribbean, the Gulf of Mexico." The point is, there are many more borders in the world than those we traditionally honor. In the process of growing up, we writers reinvent borders in the same way politicians and businessmen rediscover constituencies and markets.

The two borders of the United States offer interesting contrasts. The Rio Grande 15 appears as a giant bug zapper, a lure behind a grid. The attraction is greater than the risk, and risk is a physical calculation compounded of jail time, humiliation, and possible death. Presumably few of the millions of Mexicans and Latin Americans who attempt to breach the Mexican-American border annually are much concerned with possible loss of culture and identity, or with the new political and psychological landscape they'll be asked to inhabit. The same cannot be said of those who cross the forty-ninth parallel and its New England equivalent. Because the Canadian identity is consciously maintained, the border is as much a psychological as a physical one. Each Canadian emigrant must come to America prepared to die a subtle, psychic death.

Some borders are cages; others are mirrors. Some purely political borders rasp 16 on our consciousnesses—the various Koreas, Germanies, Irelands, Lebanons, "Bantustans," and West Banks. They seem to defy the common meaning of *border,* which is to define differences—these are borders that separate likenesses. Traditional borders, such as those in Europe, are natural reminders of where ancient armies ran out of steam, where languages and religions died, where empires faltered. European countries, so far as European consciousnesses are concerned, are separate but equal. (It would be hard to imagine a Danish joke using the nearest German city, Flensburg, in the same way the Quebecker uses Plattsburgh.) A few borders are aesthetic or cultural, such as that of Scotland, or the Mason-Dixon Line, or hundreds of others with poetic and psychological potency—the various *Gaeltaecht* regions of Ireland, the Breton, Welsh, Basque, Kurdish borders that don't really exist except as maintained fictions. There are borders made of the thinnest membrane, such as that between Canada and the United States, which is undefended because the two sides have reached a mental stasis. (To call the border "undefended" is an absurdity; Canadian defensiveness is a standing army of twenty-five million. We stand on guard for thee.) And there are the new, economic supraborders: the postcolonials, and those dividing east and west, north and south, industrialized and developing countries, and free and communist ones. Increasingly, they are the borders with which our children will be dealing—my obsession with minute shapes and whimsical curlicues will be seen as a harmless hobby akin to stalking stamps with a magnifying glass.

I trust, however, there will always be ambiguous borders like the Canadian- 17 American—not exactly a fiction, yet clearly special. As a child, I thought of borders, or at least the ones that I knew well, as force fields. I was powerless to move. I could see across them into a pure Canada or America, but those places were not for me. Borders threw back a likeness that partook of parody and distortion. The images were like us, but just a little strange. The border seemed to move with me, hanging overhead like a cloud.

I would say now that borders are fictions. Within a given territory's boundaries, and determined by the nature of those boundaries, exists a collective character, the European confidence, the Japanese insularity, the American naive openness, the African touchiness, the Canadian desire for identity. Africa suffers a surplus of borders, none of which speak to the consciousness of the people. Africans live, simultaneously, within three or four sets of borders (tribal, religious, racial, linguistic). Canada has only one external border, which is a protection against assimilation (like Scotland's), and a host of regional and linguistic barriers that are internal variants of the same thing. To be Canadian is to state a preference, and to maintain that preference every day in a series of symbolic acts. By their borders ye shall know them. 18

My Canadian parents, fleeing the war, dipped into North Dakota in 1940 to have me. And so I carry a mythical birthplace around for life—Fargo—a place we left within the year. And then we hit the road, my French-speaking father and my aristocratic mother: Cincinnati, Pittsburgh, Atlanta, a dozen stops in Florida, New York, Cleveland, Chicago, Winnipeg, Springfield (Missouri), Cincinnati, Montreal, and Pittsburgh again. All of this before I was twelve. In stories and novels I've treated my suitcase-and-Greyhound life as an uncommon existence and I'm sure it is, but it's not unknown. Many children of feckless parents travelled as much or more—but not all developed a border consciousness. I was overdetermined, but I'm not sure where it came from. If I had to guess, I would say that my parents were so profoundly different from one another, that I grew up loving and fearing a border consciousness every day of my life. 19

A border means that certain things are more likely to occur on this side, *here*, than *there*. Certain other things are probably impossible. There is comfort in knowing that in Canada chances are you won't be gunned down by a random psychopath. You probably are safe from serial murderers. You will not be beggared by medical bills and education costs. The part of the country from which you come will determine your outlook, you will be regionally determined. (A Canadian friend, now married to an American novelist, remarked to me this winter, "I've been here two years and only now am I learning not to ask 'where do you come from?' as a first question.") It means, if you're a writer in Canada, writing about high school, you're more likely to sympathize with the teacher over the student (with Laurence's *Jest of God* and Metcalf's *Going Down Slow* over Knowles's *Separate Peace* and Salinger's *Catcher in the Rye.*) If you're writing about small towns, you are not necessarily advocating the use of an incendiary device to obliterate them. Members of Parliament, policemen, clergymen, will not be seen, necessarily, as fools, thugs, or hypocrites. 20

I was a passionately Southern boy in the segregated Deep South of the late forties, and I was a fervent Canadian singing "O Canada" and "God Save the King," and I 21 was a child of the Ozarks, and a member of the Reds' Knothole Club in old Crosley Field, and I passed out of my boyhood in the post-Kiner-Clemente era of Pittsburgh. Especially Pittsburgh, my home for seven years [and the] American city I know best.

I suffered for all the rebukes that clung to grim, sooty Pittsburgh and so I mem- 22 orized—it always helps to have a hungry memory—lists of Pittsburgh's accomplishments. (Why, I wonder now? Native-born Pittsburghers could be merciless about the city's patent ghastliness. I never had the confidence to ridicule. The city was me. Everyplace I've ever been has been me; I've expanded myself right out to everyone's borders.) Pittsburgh's great fortunes were my benefactors, its institutions were mine for the taking. Loving Pittsburgh wasn't easy—except as a lover of losing efforts, a true Scotsman, or perhaps Southerner, Canadian, or one of Fuentes's Caribbeans—back when the Pirates, Steelers, and Pitt Panthers were all at the bottom of their respective leagues. We had Duquesne basketball to cheer, and the rest was civic endowment: the Carnegie Library and Museum, Buhl Planetarium, the Civic Light Opera, the Pittsburgh Symphony, the Art Students League, and the astronomy clubs and archaeology clubs that worked out of the basements of those gray-granite institutions. I belonged to all of them, they developed my talents, they gave me friends who were nerdy, just like me. They carried me through high school, as proud of my city as any New Yorker or Parisian is of his.

Which is, of course, the point. By the age of fourteen I had manufactured myself 23 half a dozen times into a native of a place. Border crossing could have made me feel alien, and deep down it probably did; overtly, however, I responded only with a puppylike loyalty. Seeking always to blend in, I did so by memorizing the box scores and the trolley grid, and tracing out the city maps at night and poring over the regional maps so I could picture each outlying town and suburb as it surfaced in the news. Oh, the satisfaction gained from those Friday night high-school football scores, and knowing, after a few months, where each of those schools [was] located! Thirty years later, as I drive the continent at night and KDKA (Pittsburgh's fifty thousand watts) weaves the airwaves, I realize I *still* remember. But I'm not a native of anywhere, and I still fear the inevitable question: "Where are you from?" Fargo, North Dakota?

Or Montreal, the city where my parents had met and married, and from which 24 they'd emigrated, and which is still the place I feel most attached to, and have lived in longest? Or the Deep South, which I remember with a special ferocity, a place whose smells and visions still assault me? Or Manitoba, the only repository of my family, where my maternal grandparents and cousins and aunts and uncles lived, and the family had its farm, and I was sent most every summer? My mother is buried in Winnipeg, in the family plot, with her parents and sisters. (My father is buried in Manchester, New Hampshire, next to his last wife's first husband.)

Or perhaps, in the hungriest leap of all, Europe, where my mother spent the most 25 exciting years of her life, studying art and design in Germany from 1929 until the closing of her school in 1933? Crossing the border into Denmark in 1935, she told me, and seeing a smiling porter sweeping the platforms, had made her cry with gratitude. She hadn't realized, until leaving Germany, the strain that she and everyone else had been under inside those Nazi borders. Her stories had made a vanished Europe, or a pre-World War I Saskatchewan winter, more real to me than anything in my experience.

I wanted to be anything but what I was, and to come from anyplace but where I 26
had. The real me was always somewhere else, but I never found it. Which is the other
side of saying, with Roger Quin (poet and Bohemian), that "my errant Muse" lives
only here, "in the ruins of Lincluden, Torthorwald, Caerlaverock" (or Montreal,
Pittsburgh, Europe, Winnipeg, and the Deep South, with stopovers in India, due to
my exotic marriage).

Until my recently married Canadian friend mentioned it, I hadn't thought of in- 27
tense regionalism as a national trait of Canadians—it was always so much an urgent
aspect of my personality—but of course she's right. Canadians ask where you're
from, because where you're from reveals relatively more about you if you're a Canadian than it does if you're an American. Being from Saskatchewan or Nova Scotia, at
a Toronto cocktail party, probably accounts for sharper self-definition than being
from Kansas or Maryland does in New York.

That is, I *think* it does. One feature of a psychologically maintained border, a sub- 28
jectively felt border, is its porosity; the fact that it blends differences but does not
eliminate them. Border mystique exists in Scotland, where differences must be internalized and perpetuated, formed into symbols, and rehearsed as works of art.
But some people, alas, are not good actors. Historical borders—solid, traditional,
European-style borders where fifty meters on the other side of a striped kiosk people
speak a different language and practice a different religion, share a different history,
and even *look* a little different—do not require symbols or rehearsals. Those borders
served only to define territory and protect against invasion. *Maintained* borders,
such as Canada's with the United States, protect against assimilation. Presumably, a
group of young Italians would not identify a group of German tourists on a camping trip as anything but Germans (nor would it occur to them to question the Germans' identity), but in Margaret Atwood's *Surfacing,* the narrator discovers—with a
shock and with depression—that some typically loud and vulgar American campers
and fishermen, despoilers of a pristine Canadian nature, turn out to be Canadian
(that is, they may be *from* Canada, but that fact is not contiguous, in the self-
conscious Canadian psyche, with *being* Canadian). If Canadians do not suffer continuing identity crises, then they are contaminated with the American virus of total,
blank unselfconsciousness.

There are, conversely, many Americans who hold classically Canadian opinions 29
of the United States and think of themselves as "belonging" to a different culture
(Canada being an alternate of choice). Such people, I feel, act from sentiment. They
feel Canada embodies an innocence or purity lacking in America, that its border is
somehow an ecological and social time tunnel. A clean, progressive place to fish and
ski and swim. "Toronto's like New York was thirty years ago," say wonder-struck
friends, reflecting New Yorkers' contemporary anxiety over dirt and violence. For
most Canadians and Europeans, to visit New York City is also to engage in time
travel; the city poses many of the shocking confrontations of a preindustrial age.

Psychological borders are, by their nature, unequally felt. The English don't feel 30
oppressed by the Scottish border. If they think about what it means to cross that
border at all, their thoughts are probably folkloric, full of stags at eve and Highland
flings. Such a border crossing involves rugged, ecological time travel. Americans
don't feel cramped by the Canadian helmet tight on their heads. The fugitive virtues
of Plattsburgh are differently weighted in the two cultures. For Canadians, however

(especially for those who would strenuously deny it) the American border is a central, imaginative fact of life. Proportionally, I suspect there are many more Canadians who feel themselves to be "basically American," and do not weight the cultural and psychological costs of free trade (for example) with the same scales as they do the economic costs. My father, who gave up the French language and Catholicism, was such a person. For all of his American life he lied about his background, his names, and his origins. He claimed, like me, to be a native of anyplace he lived. My mother, who went along with all the moves, never claimed to be anything but a Canadian, from "the West," Wawanesa born and North Battleford and Winnipeg educated—these places were truly the frontier West when she was a child.

Borders are a supreme fiction. For the once colonial, newly liberated, borders are a   31
deformity. They do not define, they do not protect, they do not express a collective will. Borders, in fact, exacerbate instability. Borders are madness, they separate natural brothers, they enclose natural enemies.

It took a psychic insurrection for V.S. Naipaul to realize he was not defined by the   32
accidental quadrant of his birth, the island of Trinidad, but that paradoxically, his accidental, colonially determined birth as an uprooted Hindu in a Caribbean barracoon made him a citizen of the colonial master, Britain, as well as the rest of the postcolonial world. So, too, the India-born residents of the United States, Vikram Seth and Bharati Mukherjee. Guyana-born Wilson Harris sails the world in his imagination, as does the nominally Pakistani, Brazil-anointed American resident Zulfikar Ghosh. Small wonder that in the works of all these writers madness lurks at the edges. They have seen too much, twisted themselves into too many shapes. They are extensions of Fuentes's super-Caribbean—new border crossers, new mapmakers, citizens of a new world literary order.

For Europeans, borders are definitions, especially perhaps for the British and   33
Scandinavians, who fortify their ancient identities with islandlike isolation (that's why the few of them who travel do so in such an entertaining manner). Authors such as Bruce Chatwin and Jonathan Raban are not travelling to discover new selves—they know what they are. They travel without the edge of danger, the risk of character loss; travel, if anything, enhances their confidence.

For Canadians, borders are a protection against assault, which always happens   34
elsewhere. When they travel, it is to try on possible new identities; what they often encounter is a mirror of themselves they can't accept. In Alice Munro's story "Miles City, Montana," the narrator and her young husband and two daughters drive from British Columbia to Ontario. To reduce the story rather brutally to a portion of its plot, something happens when they enter the United States. In their car game of "Who Am I?" (yes, of course, one thinks), the older daughter identifies herself as "somebody dead, and an American, and a girl." (She turns out to be a shot doe, seen slung on a pickup truck that morning.) They want to swim in a pool, but it is closed between noon and two o'clock. The young lifeguard, however, is accommodating, if somewhat distracted by her boyfriend; she lets the girls use the pool. The parents stay in the car. The mother eventually gets out to stretch her legs, then has a sudden jolt of recognition—"Where are the children?" Of course, she intervenes just before the younger girl drowns. The lifeguard was inattentive; her boyfriend smiles and

turns down the radio. The family drives off, and eventually rejoins the Trans-Canada north of North Dakota.

In Munro's story, death and recognition are averted, but not forever. The grace of good fortune *this time* becomes a moral wariness, a realization of vulnerability. The mother sees an equivalence between the heedless young Americans and herself and her husband, as they seek approval from his Ontario parents, wanting to prove themselves as grown-up and responsible. 35

In Atwood's *Bodily Harm* and *The Handmaid's Tale*, the assault is not avoided. Canada is an incubator of innocence for the protagonist of *Bodily Harm*, whose sanitized Toronto trendiness offers no protection from, and no warning of, the impending violence on a tiny Caribbean island. In *The Handmaid's Tale*, Canada exists as an unaffected bystander to American fundamentalist violence, a place to which fugitive women, the runaway slaves of the late-twentieth century, may escape. In the work of Michael Ondaatje (Ondaatje, like Atwood, is a poet and novelist), violence is also animating, embraced as a consciousness, a dark companion. In Ondaatje's *Coming through Slaughter* and *The Collected Works of Billy the Kid*, violence as an art form arises south of the border. 36

The worst that can be said of Canadians is that they are frequently silly, tasteless, indecisive, or vulgar—for confirmation see the collected satires of John Metcalf or Mordecai Richler. The best that can be said is that they are rational, sober, decent, humble—see the New Age cycle of novelist Hugh Hood. Or—because of their peculiarly passive position on this continent, torn between the American beast and the European ideal, acted upon but essentially powerless—Canada and the Canadian psyche becomes the proper testing ground for the anima/animus formulations of Robertson Davies. 37

Space has run out, but the border lingers in my mind. I want to speak of borders and margins, borders and frontiers, borders and mimicry, borders and subversion. I want to say my childhood perceptions were entirely backwards: I was not imposing character on the maps I studied and tried to memorize—the map I was born with had imposed its character on me. 38

Working with the Text

1. What does Blaise claim are the chief differences between the United States and Canada? What does he describe as being important to Canadian identity? He says at one point that "adherence to Canada (an ideal of Canada that is every bit as operative as the stars-and-stripes ideal of America) implies a certain material sacrifice." What is the nature of this sacrifice? What do Canadians fear they might lose in their relationship to America?

2. In discussing the respective identities of the United States and Canada, Blaise makes many claims about American identity. Do you question or disagree with any of his assumptions? Would you challenge any of his generalizations? He says, "I would say now that borders are fictions. Within a given territory's boundaries, and determined by the nature of those boundaries, exists a collective character. . . ." Do you agree with his assessment of the "collective character" of either the United States or Canada?

3. In addition to discussing the U.S.–Canadian border, Blaise makes a number of statements about "borders" in general and speaks of himself as having developed a "border consciousness." What does he mean by a border consciousness? How have his senses of borders, geography, and belonging affected his way of thinking? Are there any statements about crossing borders that strike you as familiar? What borders have you crossed in your life?

4. What does he say are the differences between the United States–Canada border and the United States–Mexico border? In your mind how do you conceptualize the differences? If you have read any of the writers in this book who examine the United States–Mexico borderlands (such as Gloria Anzaldúa or Guillermo Gómez-Peña), compare Blaise's sense of "border consciousness" to theirs. How are they similar or different? The story "Borders" by Thomas King is another work in this book about the U.S.–Canadian border. How are the story's characters' notions of borders similar to or different from those of Blaise?

SOFT CITIES

WILLIAM MITCHELL

■ Australian-born William Mitchell is an architect with degrees from the University of Melbourne, Yale, and Cambridge. For sixteen years he was on the faculty of the School of Architecture at the University of California, Los Angeles. In 1986, he joined the School of Architecture and Planning at the Massachusetts Institute of Technology, where he is currently dean. He was also a founding partner of the Computer-Aided Design Group in Marina del Rey, California. His publications include *Computer-Aided Architectural Design* (1977), *The Logic of Architecture* (1990), and *City of Bits: Space, Place, and the Infobahn* (1995), in which the following essay appears. In "Soft Cities," Mitchell looks at the early "frontier days" of cyberspace and its potential development into a "public space" for communication much like the public squares of ancient Rome.

REAL ESTATE / CYBERSPACE

I was there at the almost-unnoticed Big Bang—the silent blast of bits that begat the new communities of the digital era. It was UCLA, fall 1969, and I was a very young assistant professor writing primitive CAD software and trying to imagine the role that designers might play in the emerging electronic future. In a back room just down the hallway from the monster mainframe on which I worked, some Bolt Beranek and Newman engineers installed a considerably smaller machine that booted up to become the very first node of ARPANET—the computer network that was destined to evolve into the worldwide Internet.

From this inconspicuous point of origin, network tentacles grew like kudzu to blanket the globe. By December there were four ARPANET nodes. In April 1971 there were 23, in June 1974 there were 62, and in March 1977 there were 111. Soon, cyberspace was busting out all over: two more important networks, CSnet (funded by the National Science Foundation) and BITNET (funded by IBM) developed in the early 1980s. A high-speed backbone (NSFnet) was in place by July 1988; this connected thirteen regional networks scattered across the United States—much as the interstate highway system linked local road networks—and the whole loosely organized system became known as the Internet. During the late 1980s and early 1990s more and more networks connected to the Internet, and by 1993 it included nearly two million host computers in more than 130 countries. In the first six months of 1994 more than a million additional machines were hooked up.

3 In the United States, by that point, there was one Internet host for every couple of hundred people. (Take care in interpreting these figures, though; the actual density is likely to be much higher in affluent, computer-literate places like Cambridge, Massachusetts, and Palo Alto, California, and much lower in inner-city Detroit or East Los Angeles.) According to the best estimates—but in truth, nobody really knew—there were more than thirty million active users.

4 While the Internet community was evolving into something analogous to a ramshackle Roman Empire of the entire computer world, numerous smaller, independent colonies and confederations were also developing. Dial-in bulletin board systems such as the Sausalito-based WELL—much like independent city-states—appeared in many locations to link home computers. Commercial online services such as Compuserve, Prodigy, and America Online emerged in parallel to the government-sponsored, education- and research-oriented Internet. Before long, though, most of these erstwhile rivals found it necessary to join forces with the Internet.

5 There would not have been a great deal to connect if computers had remained as large and expensive as they were when ARPANET began in 1969. But as networks developed, so did inexpensive personal computers and mass-marketed software to run on them. The very first, the Altair, showed up in 1974, and it was followed in the early 1980s by the first IBM PCs and Apple Macintoshes. Each one that rolled off the assembly line had its complement of RAM and a disk drive, and it expanded the potential domain of cyberspace by a few more megabytes of memory.

6 Somewhere along the line, our conception of what a computer *is* began to change fundamentally. It turns out that these electronic boxes are not just big, fast, centralized calculating and data-sorting machines, as ENIAC, UNIVAC, and their mainframe successors had led us to believe. No, they are primarily *communication* devices—not dumb ones like telephone handsets, that merely encode and decode electronic information, but smart ones that can organize, interpret, filter, and present vast amounts of information. Their real role is to construct cyberspace—a new kind of place for human interactions and transactions.

WILD WEST / ELECTRONIC FRONTIER

7 The early days of cyberspace were like those of the western frontier. Parallel, breakneck development of the Internet and of consumer computing devices and software

quickly created an astonishing new condition; a vast, hitherto-unimagined territory began to open up for exploration. Early computers had been like isolated mountain valleys ruled by programmer-kings; the archaic digital world was a far-flung range in which narrow, unreliable trails provided only tenuous connections among the multitudinous tiny realms. An occasional floppy disk or tape would migrate from one to the other, bringing the makings of colonies and perhaps a few unnoticed viruses. But networking fundamentally changed things—as clipper ships and rail-roads changed the preindustrial world—by linking the increasingly numerous indi-vidual fragments of cyberturf into one huge, expanding system.

By the 1990s the digital electronics and telecommunications industries had con- 8 figured themselves into an immense machine for the ongoing production of cyber-space. We found ourselves rapidly approaching a condition in which every last bit of computer memory in the world would be electronically linked to every other. And those links will last forever. Because its electronic underpinnings are so modular, ge-ographically dispersed, and redundant, cyberspace is essentially indestructible. You can't demolish it by cutting links with backhoes or sending commandos to blow up electronic installations, and you can't even nuke it. (The original ARPANET was, in fact, explicitly designed to withstand nuclear attack.) If big chunks of the network were to be wiped out, messages would automatically reroute themselves around the damaged parts. If some memory or processing power were to be lost, it could quickly be replaced. Since copies of digital data are absolutely exact replicas of the originals, it doesn't matter if the originals get lost or destroyed. And since multiple copies of files and programs can be stored at widely scattered locations, eliminating them all with certainty is as hard as lopping Hydra heads.

Cyberspace is still tough territory to travel, though, and we are just beginning to 9 glimpse what it may hold. "In its present condition," Mitch Kapor and John Perry Barlow noted in 1990, "cyberspace is a frontier region, populated by the few hardy technologists who can tolerate the austerity of its savage computer interfaces, in-compatible communications protocols, proprietary barricades, cultural and legal ambiguities, and general lack of useful maps or metaphors." And they warned, "Cer-tainly, the old concepts of property, expression, identity, movement, and context, based as they are on physical manifestation, do not apply succinctly in a world where there can be none."

This vast grid is the new land beyond the horizon, the place that beckons the 10 colonists, cowboys, con artists, and would-be conquerors of the twenty-first cen-tury. And there are those who would be King.

HUMAN LAWS / CODED CONDITIONALS

Out there on the electronic frontier, code is the law. The rules governing any 11 computer-constructed microworld—of a video game, your personal computer desktop, a word processor window, an automated teller machine, or a chat room on the network—are precisely and rigorously defined in the text of the program that constructs it on your screen. Just as Aristotle, in *Politics,* contemplated alternative constitutions for city-states (those proposed by the theorists Plato, Phaleas, and Hippodamos, and the actual Lacedaemonian, Cretan, and Carthaginian ones), so denizens of the digital world should pay the closest of critical attention to pro-grammed polity. Is it just and humane? Does it protect our privacy, our property, and our freedoms? Does it constrain us unnecessarily or does it allow us to act as we may wish?

At a technical level, it's all a matter of the software's conditionals—those coded rules that specify *if* some condition holds, *then* some action follows. Consider, for example, the familiar ritual of withdrawing some cash from an ATM. The software running the machine has some gatekeeper conditionals; *if* you have an account and *if* you enter the correct PIN number (the one that matches up, in a database some-where, with the information magnetically encoded on your ATM card), *then* you can enter the virtual bank. (Otherwise you are stopped at the door. You may have your card confiscated as well.) Next the program presents you with a menu of pos-sible actions—just as a more traditional bank building might present you with an array of appropriately labeled teller windows or (on a larger scale) a directory point-ing you to different rooms: *if* you indicate that you want to make a withdrawal, *then* it asks you to specify the amount; *if* you want to check your balance, *then* it prints out a slip with the amount; *if* you want to make a deposit, *then* yet another sequence of actions is initiated. Finally, the program applies a banker's rule; *if* the balance of your account is sufficient (determined by checking a database), *then* it physically dispenses the cash and appropriately debits the account.

To enter the space constructed by the ATM system's software you have to submit to a potentially humiliating examination—worse than being given the once-over by some snotty and immovable receptionist. You are either embraced by the system (if you have the right credentials) or excluded and marginalized by it right there in the street. You cannot argue with it. You cannot ask it to exercise discretion. You cannot plead with it, cajole it, or bribe it. The field of possible interactions is totally delim-ited by the formally stated rules.

So control of code is power. For citizens of cyberspace, computer code—arcane text in highly formalized language, typically accessible to only a few privileged high-priests—is the medium in which intentions are enacted and designs are realized, and it is becoming a crucial focus of political contest. Who shall write the software that increasingly structures our daily lives? What shall that software allow and pro-scribe? Who shall be privileged by it and who marginalized? How shall the writers of the rules be answerable?

FACE-TO-FACE / INTERFACE

The most basic built-in rules of virtual places control when you can act, what kinds of actions you can take, and who or what you can affect by your actions. Old com-puter graphics hackers, for example, fondly remember *Spacewar,* the first computer game; it provided a diagrammatically depicted, deep-space battlefield in which players could take turns moving simulated spaceships, launching missiles, and ami-ably attempting to blow each other to bits. On timesharing systems, players did not have to share a single console but could operate individually from their own. And when networks began to develop, so did remote *Spacewar* between players who might be hundreds of miles apart. But the game stayed the same. The relationships that mattered were not those of the players' bodies in physical space (as, for example, in a pistol duel) but those of their surrogates in cyberspace, and the rules that counted were the coded-in ones of the virtual place in which the surrogates met.

On the early bulletin boards and commercial networks, "forums" or "rooms" that allowed participants to "chat" quickly became a main attraction. Here the rules structured not a shoot-'em-up arena but a space for (mostly) risk-free, multiparticipant conversation. The place that you entered was presented as a scrolling text window. It had a descriptive or evocative name (like a bar, coffee shop, or other such hangout), and you could survey the scene by looking at a list of current participants. At any point, you could type in a short text comment; this appeared in the window, preceded by your chosen online handle, so that a stream of comments scrolled by on each participant's screen—a geographically distributed, highly stylized, cocktail party with electronically masked participants and a mouse in your hand instead of a drink. 16

Forum habitués would often bar crawl from room to room until they found one that seemed to have the right buzz. If they struck up an interesting conversation, they could agree to go off into private rooms to continue, and eventually might even contemplate the big step of choosing times and physical locations to go face-to-face with new-found friends. So these virtual places performed, in a vivid new way, the traditional urban function of creating opportunities for chance encounters between strangers. And the associated conventions allowed those encounters to evolve, step by step, toward friendship and intimacy. Not surprisingly, some of these convivial spots became hot hangouts in cyberspace. 17

In the early days of computer networks it seemed a slightly far-fetched metaphor to describe these sorts of interaction sites as "places," since bandwidth was narrow and communication was mostly restricted to typing and receiving text. But SIM-NET changed that. A military project dating from the interregnum when ARPA was DARPA, SIMNET first came online in 1986 as a network of M-1 tank simulators, and it has since been elaborated to include other types of vehicles. The viewports of the "tanks" are video screens displaying simulated three-dimensional terrain over which a mock tank battle takes place. Since the computer-generated display is updated in real time as controls are manipulated, dozens of widely scattered tank crews have the vivid impression of maneuvering around the same patch of countryside. Perhaps fittingly, this prototypical electronic landscape—this Garden of Eden of cyberspace—is a realistically simulated battlefield. 18

The technology of distributed interactive simulation (DIS) systems grew out of SIMNET, and by the early 1990s it was being hyped as the latest thing for the theme park industry. Pretty soon you could line up to play *Battle Tech*, *Virtuality*, or *Fightertown*—interactive games unfolding in networked simulator pods that immerse you in tacky but fairly convincing virtual worlds. 19

As bandwidth burgeons and computing muscle continues to grow, cyberspace places will present themselves in increasingly multisensory and engaging ways. They will look, sound, and feel more realistic, they will enable richer self-representations of their users, they will respond to user actions in real time and in complex ways, and they will be increasingly elaborate and artfully designed. We will not just look *at* them; we will feel present *in* them. We can expect them to evolve into the ele- 20 ments of cyberspace construction—constituents of a new architecture without tectonics and a new urbanism freed from the constraints of physical space.

ON THE SPOT / ON THE NET

Why do some places attract people? Often, it is because being on the spot puts you 21
in the know. The merchants' coffeehouses of eighteenth-century New York, for instance, provided opportunities to get the latest shipping information, to meet potential trading partners, and to exchange other important commercial information. Depending on your trade, you might find the need to locate in the financial district, the garment district, or SoHo, on Harley Street, Fleet Street, or Lincoln's Inn Fields, in Hollywood, Silicon Valley, or Detroit. You might be attracted to the literary salon, the corner saloon, or the Cambridge high table. It's not just a matter of where the jobs are, but of where you can exchange the most up-to-date, specialized information with the most savvy people; you may be able to do the same work and pursue similar interests if you are out in the sticks, but you are likely to feel cut off and far from the center of things.

In cyberspace, list servers soon evolved to perform some of the same functions. 22
These are programs for broadcasting e-mail messages to all the "subscribers" on specified address lists. They are like electronic Hyde Park Corners—places in which anybody can stand up and speak to the assembled crowd. Lists may assemble formal groups such as the employees of a business, or the students enrolled in a class, or they may be constructed through some informal, self-selection process. As with physical assemblies, some lists are public and some secret, some are open to anybody and some are rigorously exclusive.

Electronic "newsgroups" were also quick to develop. Newsgroup software allows 23
participants to "post" text messages (and sometimes other sorts of files), much as you might pin printed notices to a physical bulletin board. The notices—queries, requests, responses, news items, announcements, tips, warnings, bits of gossip, jokes, or whatever—stay there until they are deleted, and anyone who enters the place can read them. Usually there is a host—a sort of Cyber de Staël or Virtual Gertrude presiding over an online rue de Fleury—who sets topics, coaxes the exchanges along when they flag, and occasionally kicks out an unruly or objectionable participant. By the 1990s there were countless thousands of these places, advertising every interest you might imagine and some that you surely would not. If you wanted to be in touch and up with the latest in your field, it was increasingly important to have ready access to the right newsgroups. And your physical location no longer mattered so much.

When there is a sudden need, ad-hoc newsgroups can spring almost instantly 24
into existence. Within hours of the January 1994 Los Angeles earthquake, there was a Usenet newsgroup called *alt.current-events.la.quake.* Long before the rubble had been swept from Wilshire Boulevard and before telephone service had unjammed, it was providing a place to post damage reports and find news about friends and relatives. It was the best place to be if you wanted to know what was going on.

The virtual communities that networks bring together are often defined by com- 25
mon interests rather than by common location: Unix hackers, Amiga enthusiasts,

Trekkies, and Deadheads are scattered everywhere. But the opposite can also be true. When networks and servers are organized to deal with information and issues of local concern to the people of a town or to the students, staff, and faculty of a university, they act to maintain more traditional, site-specific communities. So, for example, the City of Santa Monica's pioneering Public Electronic Network (PEN) is available only to residents of Santa Monica, to people who work in the city, or at thirty-five public-access terminals located within the city boundaries. And the Athena educational network was put in place on MIT's Cambridge campus to serve the MIT community.

STREET NETWORKS / WORLD WIDE WEB

Ever since Ur, urban places have been linked by movement channels of various kinds: doorways and passageways have joined together the rooms of buildings, street grids have connected buildings to each other, and road and rail networks have allowed communication between distant cities. These familiar sorts of physical connections have provided access to the places where people lived, worked, worshipped, and entertained themselves. 26

Now there is a powerful alternative. Ever since the winter of 1994, I have had a remarkable piece of software called Mosaic on the modest desktop machine that I'm using to write this paragraph. (Right now, Mosaic is open in another window.) Mosaic is a "client" program that provides convenient access to World Wide Web (WWW) servers located throughout the Internet. These servers present "pages" of information, which may be in the form of text, graphics, video, or sound. Pages typically have "hyperlinks" pointing to related pages elsewhere in the Web, allowing me to jump from page to page by clicking on highlighted text or images. 27

The "home page" of any WWW server invites me to step, like Alice through the looking glass, into the vast information flea market of the Web—a cyberspace zone now consisting of countless millions of interconnected pages. The astonishing thing is that a WWW page displayed on my screen may originate from a machine located *anywhere* on the Internet. In fact, as I move from page to page, I am logging into computers scattered around the world. But as I see it, I jump almost instantaneously from virtual place to virtual place by following the hyperlinks that programmers have established—much as I might trace a path from station to station through the London Underground. If I were to diagram these connections, I would have a kind of subway map of cyberspace. 28

NEIGHBORHOODS / MUDS

MUD crawling is another way to go. Software constructions known as MUDs, Multi-User Dungeons, have burned up countless thousands of log-in hours since the early 1980s. These provide settings—often very large and elaborately detailed ones—for online, interactive, role-playing games, and they often attract vast numbers of participants scattered all over the Internet. They are cyberspace equivalents of urban neighborhoods. 29

The particular joy of MUDville is the striking way that it foregrounds issues of personal identity and self-representation; as newcomers learn at old MUDders' knees, your first task as a MUD initiate is to construct an online persona for your- 30 self by choosing a name and writing a description that others will see when they encounter you. It's like dressing up for a masked ball, and the irresistible thing is that you can experiment freely with shifts, slippages, and reversals in social and sexual roles and even try on entirely fantastic guises. You can discover how it *really* feels to be a *complete* unknown.

Once you have created your MUD character, you can enter a virtual place populated with other characters and objects. This place has exits—hyperlinks connecting it to other such settings, which have in turn their own exits. Some heavily frequented MUDs are almost incomprehensibly vast, allowing you to wander among thousands of distinct settings, all with their own special characteristics, like Baudelaire strolling through the buzzing complexity of nineteenth-century Paris. You can examine the settings and objects that you encounter, and you can interact with the characters that you meet.

But as you quickly discover, the most interesting and provocative thing about a MUD is its constitution—the programmed-in rules specifying the sorts of interactions that can take place and shaping the culture that evolves. Many are based on popular fantasy narratives such as *Star Trek,* Frank Herbert's *Dune,* C. S. Lewis's *Chronicles of Narnia,* the Japanese animated television series *Speed Racer,* and even more doubtful products of the literary imagination; these are communities held together, as in many traditional societies, by shared myths. Some are set up as hack-'n-slash combat games in which bad MUDders will try to "kill" your character; these, of course, are violent, Darwinian places in which you have to be aggressive and constantly on your guard. Others, like many of the TinyMUDs, stress ideals of constructive social interaction, egalitarianism, and nonviolence—MUDderhood and apple pie. Yet others are organized like high-minded lyceums, with places for serious discussion of different scientific and technical topics. The MIT-based *Cyberion City* encourages young hackers—MUDders of invention—to write MUSE code that adds new settings to the environment and creates new characters and objects. And some are populated by out-of-control, crazy MUDders who will try to engage your character in TinySex—the one-handed keyboard equivalent of phone sex.

Early MUDs—much like text-based adventure video games such as *Zork*—relied entirely on typed descriptions of characters, objects, scenes, and actions. (James Joyce surely would have been impressed; city as text and text as city. Every journey constructs a narrative.) But greater bandwidth, faster computers, and fancier programming can shift them into pictorial and spatial formats. Lucasfilm's *Habitat,* for example, was an early example of a graphic MUD that had its first incarnation, in North America, on the QuantumLink Club Caribe network (a precursor of America Online) and Commodore 64 computers. Later, it spawned a colony, *Populopolis,* that reputedly attracted a lot more paying customers on the NIFtyServe network in Japan.

As a citizen of *Habitat,* you could customize your character, known as your Avatar, by selecting from a menu of body parts and choosing a sex. (That was a one-bit choice, since *Habitat* was marketed as fairly conservative family entertainment.) Players conversed with one another in comic strip speech balloons. A region—one of as many as 20,000 similar ones in the original *Habitat* at its zenith—was a place that you can walk your character around, and it had doors and passages to other regions. These regions were filled with functional objects such as ATM machines to

31

32

33

34

provide cash, bags and boxes to carry things in, books and newspapers to read, weapons, flashlights, and garbage cans. You could walk, take elevators, or teleport to other regions and explore them; you could exchange conversation, buy and sell goods, and even swap body parts. And, if you got tired of your character, you could reconfigure it, give it some drugs, or take it to the Change-o-matic sex-change machine.

As the creators of *Habitat* soon found, their task became one of reinventing architecture and urban design for cyberspace. They commented: 35

> For 20,000 Avatars we needed 20,000 "houses" organized into towns and cities
> with associated traffic arteries and shopping and recreational areas. We needed
> wilderness areas between the towns so that everyone would not be jammed to-
> gether into the same place. Most of all, we needed things for 20,000 people to
> do. They needed interesting places to visit—and since they can't all be in the
> same place at the same time, they needed a *lot* of interesting places to visit—
> and things to do in those places. Each of those houses, towns, roads, shops,
> forests, theaters, arenas, and other places is a distinct entity that someone
> needs to design and create.

Only limitations in bandwidth and processing power inhibit taking the next   36
step—the realization of whizzier World Wide Webs, superMUDs, and other multi-participant, urban-scale structures consisting of hyperlinked, three-dimensional, sensorily immersive spaces. And these limitations are temporary. The online environments of the future will increasingly resemble traditional cities in their variety of distinct places, in the extent and complexity of the "street networks" and "transportation systems" linking these places, in their capacity to engage our senses, and in their social and cultural richness.

But no matter how extensive a virtual environment or how it is presented, it has   37
an underlying structure of places where you meet people and find things and links connecting those places. This is the organizing framework from which all else grows. In cyberspace, the hyperplan is the generator.

ENCLOSURE / ENCRYPTION

You don't get to go just anywhere in a city, and the same is true of cyberspace. In   38
both domains, barriers and thresholds play crucial roles.

In the built fabric of a city, the enclosing surfaces of the constituent spaces—   39
walls, floors, ceilings, and roofs—provide not only shelter, but also privacy. Breaches in these surfaces—gates, doors, and windows—incorporate mechanisms to control access and maintain privacy; you can lock your doors or leave them open, lower the window shades or raise them. Spatial divisions and access-control devices are carefully deployed to organize places into hierarchies grading from completely public to utterly private. Sometimes you have to flip your ID to a bouncer, take off your shoes, pay admission, dress to a doorman's taste, slip a bribe, submit to a search, speak into a microphone and wait for the buzzer, smile at a receptionist, placate a watchdog, or act out some other ritual to cross a threshold into a more private space. Traditions and laws recognize these hierarchies and generally take a dim view of illicit boundary crossing by trespassers, intruders, and Peeping Toms.

Different societies have distinguished between public and private domains (and the activities appropriate to them) in differing ways, and urban form has reflected those distinctions. According to Lewis Mumford, domestic privacy was "a luxury of the well-to-do" up until the seventeenth century in the West. The rich were the people who could do pretty much what they wanted, as long as they didn't do it in the street and frighten the horses. As privacy rights trickled down to the less advantaged classes, the modern "private house" emerged, acquired increasingly rigorous protections of constitutional law and public policy, and eventually became the cellular unit of suburban tissue. Within the modern Western house itself—in contrast to some of its ancient and medieval predecessors—there is a staged gradation from relatively public verandahs, entry halls, living rooms, and parlors to more private, enclosed bedrooms and bathrooms, where you can shut and lock the doors and draw down the shades against the outside world. 40

It doesn't rain in cyberspace, so shelter is not an architectural issue. But privacy certainly is. So the construction technology for virtual cities—just like that of bricks-and-mortar ones—must provide for putting up boundaries and erecting access controls, and it must allow cyberspace architects and urban designers to organize virtual places into public-to-private hierarchies. 41

Fortunately, some of the necessary technology does exist. Most obviously, in cyberspace construction the rough equivalent of a locked gate or door is an authentication system. This controls access to virtual places (such as your e-mail inbox) by asking for identification and a password from those who request entry. If you give the correct password, you're in. The trouble, of course, is that passwords, like keys, can be stolen and copied. And they can sometimes be guessed, systematically enumerated until one that works is found, or somehow extorted from the system manager who knows them all. So password protection—like putting a lock on a door—discourages illicit entry but does not block the most determined break-in artists. 42

Just as you can put the valuables that you *really* want to protect in a sturdy vault or crypt, though, you can build the strongest of enclosures around digital information by encrypting it—scrambling it in a complex way so that it can be decoded only by someone with the correct secret numerical key. The trick is not only to have a code that is difficult to crack, but also to manage keys so that they don't fall into the wrong hands. The cleverest known way to do this is to use a technique called RSA public-key encryption. In this system, which derives its power from the fundamental properties of large prime numbers, each user has both a secret "private" key and a "public" key that can be distributed freely. If you want to send a secure message, you obtain the intended recipient's public key and use it to encode the information. Then the recipient decodes the message using the private key. 43

Under pressure from cops and cold warriors, who anticipate being thwarted by impregnable fortresses in cyberspace, the US federal government has doggedly tried to restrict the availability of strong encryption software. But in June 1991, hacker folk hero Philip Zimmerman released his soon-to-be-famous, RSA-based Pretty Good Privacy (PGP) encryption program. By May 1994 commercial versions had been licensed to over four million users, and MIT had released a free, noncommercial version that anybody could legally download from the Internet. From that moment, you could securely fence off your private turf in cyberspace. . . . 44

So the technological *means* to create private places in cyberspace are available, 45 but the *right* to create these places remains a fiercely contested issue. Can you always keep your bits to yourself? Is your home page your castle? These are still open questions.

PUBLIC SPACE / PUBLIC ACCESS

Once public and private spaces are distinguished from each other, they can begin to play complementary roles in urban life; a well-organized city needs both. And so it is in cyberspace. At the very least, this means that some part of our emerging electronic habitat should be set aside for public uses—just as city planners have traditionally designated land for public squares, parks, and civic institutions. Public pressure for this grew in the 1990s as the importance of cyberspace became increasingly clear. In 1994, for example, Senator Inouye of Hawaii introduced to the US Senate a bill that would reserve 20 percent of all new telecommunication capacity for free, public uses (noncommercial educational and informational services and civic discourse) and would provide funding for those uses. 46

But urban public space is not merely un-private—what's left over when everyone walls off their private domains. A space is genuinely public, as Kevin Lynch once pointed out, only to the extent that it really is openly accessible and welcoming to members of the community that it serves. It must also allow users considerable freedom of assembly and action. And there must be some kind of public control of its use and its transformation over time. The same goes for public cyberspace, so creators and maintainers of public, semipublic, and pseudopublic parts of the online world—like the makers of city squares, public parks, office building lobbies, shopping mall atriums, and Disneyland Main Streets—must consider who gets in and who gets excluded, what can and cannot be done there, whose norms are enforced, and who exerts control. These questions, like the complementary ones of privacy and encryption, have become the foci of crucial policy debates. 47

The Internet and commercial online services like America Online and Compuserve have to date provided only semipublic cyberspace at best, since they are widely but not universally accessible; you have to belong to a subscribing organization or have to pay to get in. This begs the question of how truly public cyberspace—the equivalent, say, of the Piazza San Marco in Venice—might be constructed. The community networks that emerged in the 1980s and 1990s— Santa Monica Public Electronic Network, Blacksburg Electronic Village, Telluride InfoZone, Smart Valley, and Cambridge Civic Network, for example—sought answers by trying to make network access openly available to entire communities in the same way that city hall and the local public parks traditionally have been. 48

Many of these community networks are structured as so-called free-nets, in which a "city" metaphor is explicitly used to structure information access: you go to the appropriate "building" to find the information or services that you want. Thus the "welcome" screen of the Cleveland Free-Net (one of the oldest and largest, with more than 35,000 registered users and over 10,000 log-ins per day) presents the following quotidian directory: 49

1. The Administration Building
2. The Post Office
3. Public Square

4. The Courthouse and Government Center
5. The Arts Building
6. Science and Technology Center
7. The Medical Arts Building
8. The Schoolhouse (Academy One)
9. The Community Center and Recreation Area
10. The Business and Industrial Park
11. The Library
12. University Circle
13. The Teleport
14. The Communications Center
15. NPTN / USA Today Headline News

On the free-net model, then, the new, virtual city becomes a kind of electronic shadow of the existing physical one. In many (though not all) cases, a citizen can choose between going to an actual public building or to the corresponding virtual one.

BEING THERE / GETTING CONNECTED

But a free-net's superimposition of the virtual onto the physical, while sensible   50
enough, is not a logical or technical necessity. In fact, one of the most interesting questions for twenty-first-century urban designers to ask is, "How *should* virtual and physical public space relate to one another?"

Consider the obvious options. There is complete dissociation of the two if the   51
electronic public space is accessible only from personal computers in homes and businesses. Another possibility is to associate access points with civic architecture: put an electronic information kiosk in the lobby of city hall or in the public library, for example. The Berkeley Community Memory and Santa Monica PEN systems have demonstrated a more radical strategy by placing rugged workstations in places like laundromats and at congregation points for the homeless; these workstations thus begin to play a public role much like the traditional one of fountains in the public places of Rome. The artist Krzysztof Wodiczko has gone a step further by suggesting that the physically homeless and displaced might carry electronic "alien staffs"—personal devices that connect them to cyberspace and sometimes construct public representations of self by providing information to others about who they are and where they come from. These are public rather than personal digital assistants.

Since physical distance means little in cyberspace, the possibility also exists to   52
"condense" scattered rural communities by creating public spaces that serve large, thinly populated areas. The Big Sky Telegraph, which has been running in Montana since 1988, successfully pioneered this idea. It began by linking one-room and two-room rural schoolhouses across the state, and it has focused on education, economic opportunity, and economic self-sufficiency. In economically disadvantaged communities, where adequate public facilities of a traditional kind do not exist, the possibility of providing public cyberspace may become an important community development issue. Increasingly, communities and their planners will have to

consider tradeoffs between investing scarce resources in creating or upgrading parks and community buildings and putting the money into effective electronic networks.

Whatever approach is taken to deploying network capacity for public purposes, 53 though, simply making computers available and providing some kind of electronic access to civic information and discourse is not enough to create successful public cyberspace. Just as parks and squares must be pleasant and welcoming to a diverse population in order to function effectively, so must the interfaces to public areas of cyberspace; an interface that depends on cryptic commands and arcane knowledge of computer technology is as much a barrier to most people as is a flight of steps to a park user in a wheelchair. People must also feel secure and comfortable—not subject to hostility, abuse, or attack. And more subtly, but just as importantly, the cultural presumptions and cues that are built into an interface must not discourage potential users. Think of important physical public spaces like New York's Central Park and consider the extent to which both their successes and their failures depend on these sorts of things; designers of public cyberspace will have to deal with them as well.

COMMUNITY CUSTOMS / NETWORK NORMS

Where public cyberspace exists, how can and should it be used? Do the customs and 54 laws that govern physical public space still make sense in this new context?

As usage of the Internet and commercial online services has grown, there have 55 been increasingly frequent disputes that have tested the limits of acceptable behavior in electronic public places and raised the question of how these limits might reasonably be enforced. In April 1994, for example, some particularly thick-skinned lawyers from Phoenix spammed the Internet by indiscriminately spraying a commercial advertisement for the services of their firm into thousands of newsgroups. This blast of unwanted bits had the same effect as driving a blaring sound truck into a public park. The Internet community reacted with outrage and disdain, and flamed back tens of thousands of complaints. One of the unrepentant perpetrators proclaimed his right to be a pain and threatened to do it again. Eventually—to cries of "censorship!" from some quarters—a young Norwegian programmer wrote and unleashed an effective piece of "cancelbot" software that sniffed out and automatically removed the offending advertisements wherever they showed up.

In another widely publicized incident that unfolded almost simultaneously, a 56 graduate student at MIT was busted by the FBI for operating an Internet bulletin board that had become a very active site for illegal activity—much like a bar in which drug deals were going down. Copies of commercial software were being posted, then downloaded without payment by users who logged in from all over the world. Was the operator of this openly accessible place responsible for knowing and controlling what was going on there? Or could he rightfully claim that it was just none of his business?

Like the proprietors of shopping malls and Disneylands, the operators of com- 57 mercial online services must struggle with the inherently contradictory nature of the semipublic places they create. On the one hand, these places need lots of paying customers to support them, so they have to seem as welcoming, open, and inclusive as possible. On the other hand, though, the operators want to stay in firm control of what goes on. (The question is often framed as one of whether these services should be regarded as common carriers, like the telephone companies, and therefore not responsible for any libelous, obscene, or criminal information that they might carry or whether they should be in control and therefore held responsible like book and newspaper publishers and television broadcasters.) The last time I peeked at Prodigy, for example, I found the following notice from the management (a bit like the "Do not spit" signs that used to appear in railway stations): "And please remember that PRODIGY is for people of all ages and backgrounds. Notes containing obscene, profane or sexually explicit language (including descriptions of sexual acts, and whether or not masked with 'x's and the like) are not allowed. A good test is whether the language in your note would be acceptable at a public meeting."

Prodigy explicitly aims at a family audience, so it remorselessly enforces the 58 norms of Middle America. Its competitors Compuserve and Genie have different sorts of constituencies, but their operators also take care to remove messages they consider obscene or illegal. And America Online has shut down some feminist discussion forums because, according to a spokesperson, kids might see the word "girl" in the forum's headline and "go in there looking for information about their Barbies." The excluded feminists might be forgiven for responding in not-for-prime-time language. And forget the 'x's. These places have found a useful role to play, but don't mistake them for genuine, open-to-all, watch-out-for-yourself spaces for unconstrained public discourse.

Some institutions are even more restrictive. My daughter's high school treats its 59 corner of public cyberspace as a schoolyard where teachers enforce discipline. When the kids first got e-mail addresses, they were asked to sign contracts banning "sexually explicit speech." Then, when the inevitable happened, and some students complained about receiving obscene messages, the e-mail system was temporarily shut down as punishment.

But then, there will always be a Berkeley! The Berkeley Community Memory sys- 60 tem is a radical political invention—a transposition of the Free Speech Movement and People's Park into cyberspace. All information on the system is community generated, postings can be anonymous, and no central authority controls the content of postings. Funding is decentralized as well: there are coin-operated terminals on which postings can be read without charge, but it costs a quarter to post an opinion and a dollar to open up a new forum.

NOLLI AND THE NET

The story of virtual communities, so far, is that of urban history replayed in fast for- 61 ward—but with computer resource use playing the part of land use, and network navigation systems standing in for streets and transportation systems. The WELL, the World Wide Web, MUDs, and Free Nets are—like Hippodamos's gridded layout for Miletos, Baron Haussmann's radial patterning of Paris, or Daniel Burnham's grand plan for Chicago—large-scale structures of places and connections organized to meet the needs of their inhabitants.

And the parallels don't stop there. As traditional cities have evolved, so have cus- 62 toms, norms, and laws governing rights to privacy, access to public and semipublic places, what can be done where, and exertion of control. The organization of built space into public-to-private hierarchies, with gates and doors to control boundary crossings, has reflected this. Nolli's famous map of Rome vividly depicted it. Now, as cyberspace cities emerge, a similar framework of distinctions and expectations is—with much argument—being constructed, and electronic plazas, forums, lobbies, walls, doors, locks, members-only clubs, and private rooms are being invented and deployed. Perhaps some electronic cartographer of the future will produce an appropriately nuanced Nolli map of the Net.

Working with the Text

1. This chapter from Mitchell's book *City of Bits* is titled "Soft Cities." Was it inevitable that "cyberspace" would be described as a city? He speaks of electronic environments as providing "a new urbanism freed from the constraints of physical space." In what ways does he argue that cyberspace is like an "urban" environment? What constraints (if not physical ones) does he say are present even in these new environments?

2. Mitchell makes the distinction between "virtual communities" (imaginary places constructed entirely on the Internet) and "site-specific communities" (physical places served by an electronic network). What are some of the characteristics of each? What are their differences? What kind of impact might an electronic community network (for a site-specific community) have on the actual physical community? What might an electronic dimension add to or take away from a local place? Find an example on the World Wide Web of a community network like the Cleveland Free Net that he describes. How is the local place represented electronically? What kinds of groups, activities, or relationships are represented there?

3. A significant portion of Mitchell's discussion concerns "public cyberspace"—the need to create and preserve "public" spaces on the Internet that people can share. Here he sees many parallels to urban planning. What are some of these parallels? Do you agree with his assertion that "some part of our emerging electronic habitat should be set aside for public uses"? Where are those public spaces in your physical community now? Could they be replaced, created, or enhanced with public electronic spaces?

4. How do Mitchell's metaphors of "cities" for cyberspace compare to the tendency of early Internet theorists to refer to cyberspace as a frontier? Do "soft cities" retain any frontier qualities, or do they represent the "civilized" version of cyberspace?

5. Toward the essay's conclusion, Mitchell says: "In economically disadvantaged communities, where adequate public facilities of a traditional kind do not exist, the possibility of providing public cyberspace may become an important community development issue. Increasingly, communities and their planners will have to consider tradeoffs between investing scarce resources in creating or upgrading parks and community buildings and putting the money into effective electronic networks." Do you agree with him that this is a "tradeoff"? Would significant electronic resources providing "public cyber-

space" substitute for "upgrading parks and community buildings"? Could "public cyberspace" provide alternative space for the economically disadvantaged?

UNDERSTANDING COMMUNITY IN THE INFORMATION AGE

STEVEN G. JONES

■ Steven G. Jones, who received his doctorate in communication from the University of Illinois, currently teaches at the University of Tulsa in Oklahoma. He has written extensively about popular music as a form of communication and published *Rock Formation: Music, Technology, and Mass Communication* in 1992. He also edited the collection *Cybersociety: Computer-Mediated Communication and Community* (1995), in which the following essay appears, as well as the more recent *Virtual Culture* (1998). Of his work, Jones has written, "My own particular interests have led me to examine the mediation of reality, of authentic experience and its interpretation, as we devise and develop technologies of simulation like virtual reality." In "Understanding Community in the Information Age," he raises a central question about virtual communities: "Can [computer-mediated communication] be understood to build communities and form a part of the conduct of public life, as other forms of communication seem to, or does CMC problematize our very notions of community and public life?"

Whether by choice or accident, by design or politics (or some complex combination of each), the United States (followed closely by many other countries) is embarking on a building project the likes of which have not been seen since the Eisenhower era. Indeed, there are startling parallels between the current project, the "information highway," and the one spurred on by both world wars, the interstate highway system—not the least of which is the reliance on the word "highway" and the romantic connotations of the open road (and that Vice President Al Gore, Jr.'s father was instrumental in the development of the federal highway system). Another parallel is the initially military motivation for highway building (established by Thomas Jefferson, among others) and the military origins of the most prominent information highway, the Internet, in defense department computer networks linked to university research centers.

Patton (1986), in his history of the U.S. interstate system, says that it was

> the most expensive and elaborate public works program of all time, offer[ing] a vision of social and economic engineering. It was planned to be at once a Keynesian economic driver and a geographic equalizer, an instrument for present prosperity and the armature of a vision of the future. It was at once the last program of the New Deal and the first space program. (p. 17)

The information highway being vociferously championed by the Clinton administration and by Vice President Al Gore also combines ideas about the economic and social direction of the United States. It is in a sense the first program of the new New Deal and, some say, the last space program. Patton's comments about the effects that interstates have had on cities and communities bear especially close scrutiny, as they evoke images of what the information highway may as well do to social formations. Highways, Patton says,

> have had monstrous side effects. They have often rolled, like some gigantic version of the machines that build them, through cities, splitting communities off into ghettos, displacing people, and crushing the intimacies of old cities. . . .
>
> While promising to bring us closer, highways in fact cater to our sense of separateness. (p. 20)

Critical to the rhetoric surrounding the information highway is the promise of a re-newed sense of community and, in many instances, new types and formations of community. Computer-mediated communication, it seems, will do by way of elec-tronic pathways what cement roads were unable to do, namely, connect us rather than atomize us, put us at the controls of a "vehicle" and yet not detach us from the rest of the world.

If that is to be so, it is not premature to ask questions about these new forma- 3 tions. What might electronic communities be like? Most forecasters, like Howard Rheingold (1993), envision them as a kind of ultimate flowering of community, a place (and there is no mistaking in these visions that it is place that is at stake) where individuals shape their own community by choosing which other communities to belong to. Thus a paradox long haunting America is solved in a particularly Ameri-can way; we will be able to forge our own places from among the many that exist, not by creating new places but by simply choosing from the menu of those available. Another of the many questions we must ask about electronic communities is: What is the nature of individual members' commitments to them? In the physical world, community members must live together. When community membership is in no small way a simple matter of subscribing or unsubscribing to a bulletin board or electronic newsgroup, is the nature of interaction different simply because one may disengage with little or no consequence? . . .

Computer-mediated communication will, it is said, lead us toward a new com- 4 munity: global, local, and everything in between. But the presence of chaos inex-orably draws us away from that ideal as the need for control becomes greater and greater. It is most accurate to claim, as Carey (1993) does, that when it comes to proselytizing CMC, "these are ideas that people want or need to be true merely be-cause it would be bewildering to be without them" (p. 172).

It may as well be "bewildering" for us to create and learn the norms of on-line 5 worlds, for to learn them is a complex process. It may bring people together insofar as such learning is often collaborative, but it is equally as often frustrating and off-putting. Nevertheless, there is a sense that we are embarking on an adventure in cre-ating new communities and new forms of community, and that sense is fueled by two motives: first, that we *need* new communities and, second, that we *can* create them technologically. Such motives, in turn, arise from what Soja (1989) has called "postmodern geographies," the tensions caused by differentiation and homogeniza-tion in the (re)production of space. In the case of CMC, what allows for the re-production of space is the malleability with which identity can be created and negotiated, an issue several of the authors in *CyberSociety* take up. Consequently, one must question the potential of CMC for production of social space. Could it perhaps *re*produce "real" social relations in a "virtual" medium?

It is more likely that social relations emerging from CMC are between the two   6 poles of production and reproduction. Pushing too close to either pole puts at risk whatever new social construction of reality may arise. And yet any new social formations are at risk of being mythologized and incorporated into the "rhetoric of the electrical sublime" that Carey (1989) identifies. All media, for instance, have been touted for their potential for education. Radio and television, in particular, were early on promoted as tools for education, and CMC is no different. In an article on computer technology in schools, one author wrote, "At a time when American schools are receiving less and less money to cope with growing social upheaval, tele-computing seems to offer a glimmer of hope, enlivening both teachers and students even as it compels a striking realignment of relationships within the classroom" (Leslie, 1993, p. 90).

There is no doubt that CMC is linked inextricably to education. Even the Cor-   7 poration for Public Broadcasting (CPB) now seeks

> to develop community-wide education and information services. These publicly accessible interactive services will take full advantage of widely available communications and information technologies, particularly inexpensive computers linked by telephone lines.
>
> Who will mobilize the development of high-quality, non-commercial, educational and public services that will provide all Americans with the opportunities for learning, staying healthy, and participating in cultural and civic affairs—services crucial to the well-being of society as a whole? (from 1993 solicitation guidelines)

The CPB's comments parallel those made when radio and TV were introduced (the emphasis then was on broadcasting in the public interest, convenience, and necessity). Even Jaron Lanier, a pioneering virtual reality programmer and engineer, has said, "Television wasn't planned well enough and I think it's been a real disaster in this country" ("Virtual Reality," 1992, p. 6). Similarly, Quarterman (1993) has said, "Radio and television produced a different society. Computer networks will, too. Perhaps this time we can avoid a few mistakes" (p. 49). Such comments obfuscate the power behind decisions that go into planning and organizing media. Who will plan, how will we plan, and how will we account in our planning for unanticipated consequences? Media regulation in the U.S. has hardly been the most successful enterprise. Why should we believe regulating CMC will be different?

At the heart of comments like Lanier's and Quarterman's is a pervasive sense   8 that we can learn from the "mistakes" we believe we've made using older media. Computer-mediated communication (and computers generally) gives us a sense that we can start over and learn from the past. Their comments point out that we have a fundamental need, or at least hope, for something better to come from future media.

But what exactly are we hoping *for*? The answer to that question is necessarily   9 linked to questions about who we are hoping to be as a society, and that, in turn, is tied to issues of identity and discourse. Who are we when we are on-line? The question becomes even more important as new technologies are developed for creating "agents" or "alters" that roam the network for us when we are away from our terminals. . . .

CMC, of course, is not just a tool; it is at once technology, medium, and engine of social relations. It not only structures social relations, it is the space within which the relations occur and the tool that individuals use to enter that space. It is more than the context within which social relations occur (although it is that, too) for it is commented on and imaginatively constructed by symbolic processes initiated and maintained by individuals and groups. The difficulty in defining space is clear in the zeal with which many have latched onto other derivative terms. For instance, yet more evidence of the prophetic nature of rhetoric about CMC is the pervasive use of the word "cyberspace," coined by William Gibson, a writer of fiction, to put a finger on a space at once real in its effects and illusory in its lack of physical presence. The "space race" of the 1950s and 1960s is indeed over. We no longer look to the stars and the thermodynamic engines that will transport us to them but to sites unknown and unseen (perhaps unseeable) and the ever smaller electronic engines that seem to effortlessly and without danger bring this space to us. | 10

But is it even possible to pin down space to any particular definition? As Benedikt (1991) correctly observes, "Space, for most of us, hovers between ordinary physical existence and something other" (p. 125). Where we find it hovering is, as Soja (1989) notes, in "socially produced space, [where] spatiality can be distinguished from the physical space of material nature and the mental space of cognition and representation, each of which is used and incorporated into the construction of spatiality but cannot be conceptualized as its equivalent" (p. 120). . . . | 11

The importance of CMC and its attendant social structures lies not only in interpretation and narrative, acts that can fix and structure, but in the sense of mobility with which one can move (narratively and otherwise) through the social space. Mobility has two meanings in this case. First, it is clearly an ability to "move" from place to place without having physically traveled. But, second, it is also a mobility of status, class, social role, and character. Like the boulevardiers or the denizens of Nevsky Prospect described by Berman (1982), the citizens of cyberspace (or the "net," as it is commonly called by its evanescent residents) "come here to see and be seen, and to communicate their visions to one another, not for any ulterior purpose, without greed or competition, but as an end in itself" (p. 196). The difference between those on the net and those on the street is encompassed in a distinction made by Soja (1989): "Just as space, time, and matter delineate and encompass the essential qualities of the physical world, spatiality, temporality, and social being can be seen as the abstract dimensions which together comprise all facets of human existence" (p. 25). | 12

In cyberspace, spatiality is largely illusory (at least until Gibson's accounts of its visualization are realized), and temporality is problematized by the instantaneity of CMC and the ability to roam the net with "agents," software constructs that are automated representatives able to retrieve information and/or interact on the net. What is left is social being, and that too is problematic. Is the social actor in cyberspace mass-mediated, a mass-mediator, a public figure, or a private individual engaged in close, special interrelation? As Soja sees it in a summary of the dialectic between space and social life, | 13

> The spatio-temporal structuring of social life defines how social action and re-
> lationship (including class relations) are materially constituted, made con-
> crete. The constitution/concretization process is problematic, filled with
> contradiction and struggle (amidst much that is recursive and routinized).
> Contradictions arise primarily from the duality of produced space as both
> outcome/embodiment/product and medium/presupposition/producer of so-
> cial activity. (p. 129)

No matter how ill-defined the space of cyberspace, the space we occupy as social beings is as affected by CMC. As Gillespie and Robins (1989) note, "New communications technologies do not just impact upon places; places and the social processes
and social relationships they embody also affect how such technological systems are
designed, implemented and used" (p. 7).

Soja's comments and the questions that arise from them speak to the heart of the   14
many contradictions and problems embodied in CMC. On the one hand, it appears
to foster community, or at least the sense of community, among its users. On the
other hand, it embodies the impersonal communication of the computer and of the
written word, the "kind of imitation talking" Ong (1982, p. 102) aptly describes. In
that fashion, CMC wears on its sleeve the most important dichotomy that Jensen
(1990) identifies in her book *Redeeming Modernity.* Jensen writes that traditional
life, supposedly, "was marked by face-to-face, intimate relationships among friends,
while modern life is characterized by distant, impersonal contact among strangers.
Communities are defined as shared, close, and intimate, while societies are defined
as separate, distanced, and anonymous" (p. 71).

Can CMC be understood to build communities and form a part of the conduct   15
of public life, as other forms of communication seem to, or does CMC problematize
our very notions of community and public life? . . .

Communities formed by CMC have been called "virtual communities" and de-   16
fined as "incontrovertibly social spaces in which people still meet face-to-face, but
under new definitions of both 'meet' and 'face'. . . . [V]irtual communities [are]
passage points for collections of common beliefs and practices that united people
who were physically separated" (Stone, 1991, p. 85). In that sense, cyberspace hasn't
a "where" (although there are "sites" or "nodes" at which users gather). Rather, the
space of cyberspace is predicated on knowledge and information, on the common
beliefs and practices of a society abstracted from physical space. Part of that knowledge and information, though, lies in simply knowing how to navigate cyberspace.
But the important element in cyberspatial social relations is the sharing of information. It is not sharing in the sense of *transmission* of information that binds communities in cyberspace. It is the ritual sharing of information (Carey, 1989) that
pulls it together. That sharing creates the second kind of community that Carey
(1993) identifies as arising from the growth of cities during the late 19th and early
20th century, the one

> formed by imaginative diaspora—cosmopolitans and the new professionals
> who lived in the imaginative worlds of politics, art, fashion, medicine, law and
> so forth. These diasporic groups were twisted and knotted into one another
> within urban life. They were given form by the symbolic interactions of the
> city and the ecology of media, who reported on and defined these groups to

> one another, fostered and intensified antagonisms among them, and sought
> forms of mutual accommodation. (p. 178)

Such a formation is reoccuring in the discourse within CMC and without it, in the conversations its participants have on-line and off, and in the media coverage of electronic communication, electronic communities, and virtual reality. . . .

THE ILLUSION OF COMMUNITY

Issues of identity ought to be front and center with those of community as CMC develops. As Cheney (1991) correctly claims, "One's identity is somehow related to the larger social order. However [there is] disagree[ment] . . . on what kind of relationship this entails" (p. 10). What is most important is that identity is related directly to the increase in size of social organizations. The necessity to "keep track" of individuals by way of Social Security numbers and other bureaucratic devices that connect an individual to a larger entity make identification a matter of organization too, rather than a matter of self-definition. Cheney's (1991) comment that "there has been a transformation of the term 'identity' from its 'sameness' meaning to its 'essence' meaning" (p. 13) is significant precisely because identity as mediated in cyberspace carries no essential meanings. Alliances based on "sameness" may form and dissolve. Yet the ideas that Cheney borrows from Burke that assist him in developing a definition of identity "associated with the individual that must draw upon social and collective resources for its meaning" (p. 20) do not apply equally in CMC. CMC users may use similar resources to develop and structure meaning but without the affective alliances that Cheney implies are necessary. [17]

Rheingold (1993) attempts to define how identity will be constructed via CMC: [18]

> We reduce and encode our identities as words on a screen, decode and unpack
> the identities of others. The way we use these words, the stories (true and
> false) we tell about ourselves (or about the identity we want people to believe
> us to be) is what determines our identities in cyberspace. The aggregation of
> personae, interacting with each other, determines the nature of the collective
> culture. (p. 61)

One might suppose the same is true as to the aggregation of particular traits that determine the nature of the individual. However, the symbolic processes that Rheingold elides through use of such words as "encode" and "unpack" (themselves taken from the language of computer software) are fraught with unproblematized assumptions about the work that humans perform in search of their own identities, and those of others. Interaction ought not be substituted for community, or, for that matter, for communication, and to uncritically accept connections between personae, individuals, and community inadvisable.

It will be unfortunate, too, if we uncritically accept that CMC will usher in the great new era that other media of communication have failed to bring us. It is not, as virtual reality pioneer Jaron Lanier says, that television has failed us because it "wasn't planned well enough" ("Virtual Reality," 1992, p. 6); it is that organization and planning are not necessarily appropriate processes for constructing or recapturing the sense of community for which we are nostalgic. Bender (1978) sharply criticizes those who seek "to recapture community by imputing it to large-scale organizations and to locality-based social activity regardless of the quality of human [19] relationships that characterize these contexts" (p. 143). Instead, Bender finds community in the midst of a transformation and asks us to heed his call that we not, by way of our nostalgia, limit definitions of community to that which "seventeenth-century New Englanders knew" (p. 146), although with electronic town hall meetings and the like we seem to be doing precisely that. One example can be found in Rheingold's work. Although often critical in much of his writing, it is clear from the comparisons that Rheingold (1993) makes to other forms of community that what he calls "virtual communities" are predicated on nostalgic (and romantic) ideals:

> It's a bit like a neighborhood pub or coffee shop. It's a little like a salon, where I can participate in a hundred ongoing conversations with people who don't care what I look like or sound like, but who do care how I think and communicate. There are seminars and word fights in different corners. (p. 66)

> Virtual communities might be real communities, they might be pseudocommunities, or they might be something entirely new in the realm of social contracts, but I believe they are in part a response to the hunger for community that has followed the disintegration of traditional communities around the world. (p. 62).

Of course, it is difficult to imagine what new on-line communities may be like, and it is far easier to use our memories and myths as we construct them. What is more important than simply understanding the construction we are undertaking is to notice that it is peculiar and particular to the computer. Because these machines are seen as "linking" machines (they link information, data, communication, sound, and image through the common language of digital encoding), to borrow from Jensen (1990), they inherently affect the ways we think of linking up to each other, and thus they fit squarely into our concerns about community. Media technologies that have largely been tied to the "transportation" view of communication mentioned earlier were developed to overcome space and time. The computer, in particular, is an "efficiency" machine, purporting to ever increase its speed. But unlike those technologies, the computer used for communication is a technology to be understood from the "ritual" view of communication, for once time and space have been overcome (or at least rendered surmountable) the spur for development is connection, linkage. Once we can surmount time and space and "be" anywhere, we must choose a "where" at which to be, and the computer's functionality lies in its power to make us organize our desires about the spaces we visit and stay in.

20

The question remains, though, whether or not the communities we may form by way of CMC will, or even ought to, be part of our public culture. If so, then perhaps it would be best to not understand them as communities. As Bender (1978) writes, "Our public lives do not provide an experience of community. The mutuality and sentiment characteristic of community cannot and need not be achieved in public. We must be careful to distinguish between these two contexts of social experience" (p. 148). The manner in which we seek to find community, empowerment, and political action all embedded in our ability to use CMC is thereby troubling. No one medium, no one technology, has been able to provide those elements in combination, and often we have been unable to find them in any media. CMC has potential for a variety of consequences, some anticipated, some not. A critical awareness of the social transformations that have occurred and continue to occur with or without technology will be our best ally as we incorporate CMC into contemporary social life.

REFERENCES

Barnes, T. J., & Duncan, J. S. (1992). *Writing worlds.* London: Routledge.

Bell, C., & Newby, H. (1974). *The sociology of community.* London: Frank Cass & Company, Ltd.

Bender, T. (1978). *Community and social change in America.* New Brunswick, NJ: Rutgers University Press.

Benedikt, M. (1991). Cyberspace: Some proposals. In M. Benedikt (Ed.), *Cyberspace* (pp. 119–224). Cambridge: MIT Press.

Beniger, J. (1986). *The control revolution.* Cambridge, MA: Harvard University Press.

Beniger, J. (1987). Personalization of mass media and the growth of pseudo-community. *Communication Research, 14*(3), 352–371.

Berger, P. L., & Luckmann, T. (1967). *The social construction of reality.* New York: Anchor Books.

Berman, M. (1982). *All that is solid melts into air.* New York: Simon & Schuster.

Branscomb, A. W. (1993). Jurisdictional quandaries for global networks. In L. M. Harasim (Ed.), *Global networks* (pp. 57–80). Cambridge: MIT Press.

Calhoun, C. J. (1980). Community: Toward a variable conceptualization for comparative research. *Social History, 5,* 105–129.

Carey, J. (1989). *Communication as culture.* Boston, MA: Unwin-Hyman.

Carey, J. (1993). Everything that rises must diverge: Notes on communications, technology and the symbolic construction of the social. In P. Gaunt (Ed.), *Beyond agendas* (pp. 171–184). Westport, CT: Greenwood.

Chayko, M. (1993). What is real in the age of virtual reality? "Reframing" frame analysis for a technological world. *Symbolic Interaction, 16*(2), 171–181.

Cheney, G. (1991). *Rhetoric in an organizational society: Managing multiple identities.* Columbia: University of South Carolina Press.

Chesebro, J. W., & Bonsall, D. G. (1989). *Computer-mediated communication.* Tuscaloosa: University of Alabama Press.

Cohen, A. (1985). *The symbolic construction of community.* London: Tavistock.

Doolittle, R. J. (1972). *Speech communication as an instrument in engendering and sustaining a sense of community in urban and poor neighborhoods: A study of rhetorical potentialities.* Unpublished doctoral dissertation, Pennsylvania State University.

Effrat, M. P. (1974). *The community: Approaches and applications.* New York: Free Press.

Etzioni, A. (1991). *The responsive society.* San Francisco: Jossey-Bass.

Frederick, H. (1993). Computer networks and the emergence of global civil society. In L. M. Harasim (Ed.), *Global networks* (pp. 283–296). Cambridge: MIT Press.

Gillespie, A., & Robins, K. (1989). Geographical inequalities: The spatial bias of the new communications technologies. *Journal of Communication, 39*(3), 7–18.

Harasim, L. M. (Ed.). (1993). *Global networks.* Cambridge: MIT Press.

Harvey, D. (1989). *The condition of postmodernity.* Oxford: Blackwell.

Hiltz, S. R., & Turoff, M. (1978). *The network nation: Human communication via computer.* Reading, MA: Addison-Wesley.

Jensen, J. (1990). *Redeeming modernity.* Newbury Park, CA: Sage.

Laird, A. (1993). *Computerscape with letters.* Unpublished manuscript prepared for Media History, Faculty of Communication, University of Tulsa.

Leslie, J. (1993, November). Kids connecting. *Wired, 1*(5), 90–93.

Licklider, J. C. R., & Taylor, R. W. (1968). The computer as a communication device. *Science & Technology, 76,* 21–31.

Marvin, C. (1988). *When old technologies were new.* Oxford: Oxford University Press.

Morris, M. (1992). The man in the mirror: David Harvey's "condition" of postmodernity. *Theory, Culture & Society, 9,* 253–279.

Mumford, L. (1934). *Technics and civilization.* New York: Harcourt, Brace & World.

Ong, W. (1982). *Orality and literacy.* London: Methuen.

Patton, P. (1986). *Open road.* New York: Simon & Schuster.

Peck, M. S. (1987). *The different drum: Community-making and peace.* New York: Simon & Schuster.

Quarterman, J. S. (1993). The global matrix of minds. In L. M. Harasim (Ed.), *Global networks* (pp. 35–56). Cambridge: MIT Press.

Rafaeli, S. (1988). Interactivity: From new media to communication. In R. P. Hawkins, J. M. Wiesmann, & S. Pingree (Eds.), *Advancing communication science: Merging mass and interpersonal processes* (Sage Annual Reviews of Communication Research, Vol. 16, pp. 110–134). Newbury Park, CA: Sage.

Rheingold, H. (1993). A slice of life in my virtual community. In L. M. Harasim (Ed.), *Global networks* (pp. 57–80). Cambridge: MIT Press.

Rice, R. E. (1984). *The new media: Communication, research, and technology.* Beverly Hills, CA: Sage.

Rice, R. E. (1987). Computer-mediated communication and organizational innovation. *Journal of Communication, 37*(4), 65–94.

Rice, R. E. (1989). Issues and concepts in research on computer-mediated communication systems. In J. A. Anderson (Ed.), *Communication yearbook* (Vol. 12, pp. 436–476). Newbury Park, CA: Sage.

Rice, R. E. & Love, G. (1987). Electronic emotion: Socioemotional content in a computer-mediated communication network. *Communication Research, 14,* 85–108.

Rice, R. E., & McDaniel, B. (1987). *Managing organizational innovation: The evolution from word processing to office information systems.* New York: Columbia University Press.

Ross, A. (1990). Hacking away at the counterculture. *Postmodern Culture, 1*(1), 1–43.

Schudson, M. (1978). The ideal of conversation in the study of mass media. *Communication Research, 12*(5), 320–329.

Soja, E. (1989). *Postmodern geographies: The reassertion of space in critical social theory.* London: Verso.

Sproull, L., & Kiesler, S. (1991, September). Computers, networks and work. *Scientific American,* pp. 116–123.

Stacey, M. (1974). The myth of community studies. In C. Bell & H. Newby (Eds.), *The sociology of community* (pp. 13–26). London: Frank Cass & Company, Ltd.

Stone, A. R. (1991). Will the real body please stand up? Boundary stories about virtual cultures. In M. Benedikt (Ed.), *Cyberspace* (pp. 81–118). Cambridge: MIT Press.

Taylor, C. (1992). *The ethics of authenticity.* Cambridge, MA: Harvard University Press.

Tonnies, F. (1967). *Community and society.* Lansing: Michigan State University Press.

Virtual reality: A new medium and a new culture. (1992, November). *Communique,* p. 6.

Walls, J. (1993). Global networking for local development: Task focus and relationship focus in cross-cultural communication. In L. M. Harasim (Ed.), *Global networks* (pp. 153–166). Cambridge: MIT Press.

Warner, L. (1963). *Yankee city.* New Haven, CT: Yale University Press.

Working with the Text

1. Jones argues that "critical to the rhetoric surrounding the information highway is the promise of a renewed sense of community and, in many instances, new types and formations of community. Computer-mediated communication, it seems, will do by way of electronic pathways what cement

roads were unable to do, namely, connect us rather than atomize us. . . ." Else-where he questions the "potential of Computer Mediated Communication for production of social space," and he asks if CMC can "reproduce 'real' social re-lations in a 'virtual' medium."

What does he mean by "real" social relations? That is, what seem to be Jones's criteria for what makes social relations "real"? Do you think that CMC can produce "real" communities and "real" social relations? Are these new so-cial relations positive? Is CMC connecting us or atomizing us? Do you think this issue can be evaluated or resolved at this point? Does it matter? Use any online communication with which you are familiar as a point of departure for this discussion.

2. Quoting communications theorist James Carey, Jones makes a distinction between the use of communications technologies for the "transmission" of information and their use for the "ritual sharing of information." The impli-cation is that while the transmission of information is important, it is the "rit-uals" of communication that hold groups of people together as communities. Based on your experience of "cyberspace"—whether in E-mail, MOOs, MUDs, IRC, chat rooms, or newsgroups—what would you say are the "ritual" dimensions of communication online? How are they like and unlike the ritu-als of communication in everyday life—or the rituals of communication in a newspaper or on television?

3. When speaking of some people's hopes for the potential of online com-munities, Jones asks, "But what exactly are we hoping for?" "The answer to that question," he continues, "is necessarily linked to questions about who we are hoping to be as a society, and that, in turn, is tied to issues of identity and discourse. Who are we when we are on-line?" Jones implies that there is a close relationship between individual identity and the identity and character of a community. How does individual identity contribute to a larger communal identity in an online environment? How does the nature of an environment—in this case a "socially produced space"—shape the behavior of individuals? How might the ability to sign on and off at will, or the ability to represent identity any way we like, affect the kind of community that individuals can form online?

4. Jones notes that some people believe that new online communities are fill-ing a need for community that is lacking in modern society. Do you agree with that view? Do you think that online communities compensate for some-thing that is missing? Do people who participate in online communities find something that they need but don't get elsewhere? If you have participated in online communities and conversations, consider how your interactions are similar to or different from those in your everyday life.

SEX, DEATH, AND MACHINERY, OR HOW I FELL IN LOVE WITH MY PROSTHESIS

ALLUCQUÈRE ROSANNE STONE

■ In the following introduction to her 1996 book, *The War of Desire and Technology at the Close of the Mechanical Age,* Allucquère Rosanne Stone posits that we are passing from a "mechanical age" into a "virtual age." This new age is characterized by a "gradual change that has come over the relationship between sense of self and the body, and the relationship between individual and group." As computers become, as Stone puts it, "arenas for social experience," our notions of selfhood, space, and communication may well undergo drastic changes. Stone teaches at the University of Texas at Austin.

It started this afternoon when I looked down at my boots. I was emerging from a stall in the women's room in my department. The university was closed for the holidays. The room was quite silent except for the distant rush of the air conditioning, imparting to the cramped institutional space the mechanical qualities of a submarine. I was idly adjusting my clothing, thinking of nothing in particular, when I happened to look down, and there they were: My boots. Two completely unremarkable boots. They were right where they belonged, on the ends of my legs. Presumably my feet were inside.

I felt a sudden thrill of terror.

Maybe, I suppose, the boots could have reminded me of some long-buried trauma, of the sort that Freudians believe leads to shoe fetishism. But my sudden fear was caused by something quite different. What was driving me was not the extraordinariness of the sight of my own boots, but the ordinariness of them. They were common as grass. In fact, I realized that I hadn't even thought about putting them on. They were *just there.* If you wanted to "get real ugly about it"—as they say in Austin—you might call it a moment of radical existential *Dasein,* in the same way you might say déjà vu again. I had become transparent to myself. Or rather, the *I* that I customarily express and that reflexively defines me through my chosen personal style had become part of the wallpaper.

This is hardly a serious problem for some. But I tend to see myself as an entity that has chosen to make its life career out of playing with identity. It sometimes seems as though everything in my past has been a kind of extended excuse for experiments with subject position and interaction. After all, what material is better to experiment with than one's self? Academically speaking, it's not exactly breaking new ground to say that any subject position is a mask. That's well and good, but still most people take some primary subject position for granted. When pressed, they may give lip service to the idea that perhaps even their current "root" persona is also a mask, but nobody really believes it. For all intents and purposes, your "root" persona is *you.* Take that one away, and there's nobody home.

Perhaps someone with training in drama already perceives this, but it was a revelation to me. In the social sciences, symbolic interactionists believe that the root persona is always a momentary expression of ongoing negotiations among a horde of subidentities, but this process is invisible both to the onlooker and to the persona within whom the negotiations are taking place. For me this has never been particularly true. My current *I* has been as palpably a mask to me as any of my other *I*'s have been. Perceiving that which is generally invisible as really a kind of capital has been more than a passing asset (as it were); it has been a continual education, a source of endless challenge, not to mention fear, and certainly not least, an ongoing celebration of the sacred nature of the universe of passing forms. It was for these reasons, then, that I found looking down rather complacently at my boots and not really seeing them to be so terrifying. Like an athlete who has begun to flub a long-polished series of moves, I began to wonder if I was losing my edge.

Going through life with this outlook has been a terrific asset in my chosen work, and the current rise in the number of people who engage in social interactions without ever meeting in the customary sense of the term—that is, engaging in social intercourse by means of communication technologies—has given me increasing opportunities to watch others try on their own alternative personae. And although most still see those personae as just that—alternatives to a customary "root" identity—there are some out at the margins who have always lived comfortably with the idea of floating identities, and inward from the margins there are a few who are beginning, just a bit, to question. What it is they are questioning is a good part of what this essay is about.

6

A bit of background may be appropriate here.

7

I have bad history: I am a person who fell in love with her own prostheses. Not once, but twice. Then I fell in love with somebody *else's* prosthesis.

8

The first time love struck was in 1950. I was hunkered down in the dark late at night, on my bed with the big iron bedstead on the second floor, listening absently to the crickets singing and helping a friend scratch around on the surface of a galena crystal that was part of a primitive radio. We were looking for one of the hot spots, places where the crystal had active sites that worked like diodes and could detect radio waves. There was nothing but silence for a long, long time, and then suddenly the earphones burst into life, and a whole new universe was raging in our heads— the ranting voice of Jean Shepherd, boiling into the atmosphere from the massive transmitter of WOR-AM, 50 kilowatts strong and only a few miles away. At that distance we could have heard the signal in our tooth fillings if we'd had any, but the transmitter might as well have been in Rangoon, for all the fragrant breath of exotic worlds it suggested. I was hooked. Hooked on technology. I could take a couple of coils of wire and a hunk of galena and send a whole part of myself out into the ether. An extension of my will, of my instrumentality . . . that's a prosthesis, all right.

9

The second time happened in 1955, while I was peering over the edge of a 24 × 24 recording console. As I stood on tiptoe, my nose just clearing the top of the console, from my age and vantage point the massive thing looked as wide as a football field. Knobs and switches from hell, all the way to the horizon . . . there was something about the vast forest of controls that suggested the same breath of exotic worlds that the simple coil of wire and the rickety crystal did. I was hooked again. I looked on even bigger technology, on another extension of my instrumentality. I could create whole oceans of sound, universes of sound, could at last begin on my life's path of learning how to make people laugh, cry, and throw up in dark rooms. And I hadn't even heard it turned *on*.

10

But the third time . . .   11

The third time was when Hawking came to town.   12

Stephen Hawking, the world-famous physicist, was giving a lecture at UC Santa   13
Cruz. The auditorium was jammed, and the overflow crowd was being accommodated outside on the lawn. The lawn looked like a medieval fair, with people sitting
on blankets and towels, others standing or milling around, all ears cocked toward
the loudspeakers that were broadcasting Hawking's address across the landscape.

If you haven't seen Stephen Hawking give a talk, let me give you a quick back-   14
ground. Hawking was amyotrophic lateral sclerosis, which makes it virtually impossible for him to move anything more than his fingers or to speak. A friendly
computer engineer put together a nice little system for him, a program that displays
a menu of words, a storage buffer, and a Votrax allophone generator—that is, an artificial speech device. He selects words and phrases, the word processor stores them
until he forms a paragraph, and the Votrax says it. Or he calls up a prepared file, and
the Votrax says that.

So I and a zillion other people are on the lawn, listening to Hawking's speech,   15
when I get the idea that I don't want to be outside with the PA system—what I really
want to do is sneak into the auditorium, so I can actually hear Hawking give the talk.

In practice this maneuver proves not too hard. The lecture is under way, security   16
is light—after all, it's a *physicist,* dammit, not the UC Board of Regents, for which
they would have had armed guards with two-way radios—so it doesn't take long for
me to worm my way into the first row.

And there is Hawking. Sitting, as he always does, in his wheelchair, utterly mo-   17
tionless, except for his fingers on the joystick of the laptop; and on the floor to one
side of him is the PA system microphone, nuzzling into the Votrax's tiny loud-
speaker.

And a thing happens in my head. Exactly where, I say to myself, *is* Hawking? Am   18
I any closer to him now than I was outside? Who is it doing the talking up there on
stage? In an important sense, Hawking doesn't stop being Hawking at the edge of his
visible body. There is the obvious physical Hawking, vividly outlined by the way our
social conditioning teaches us to see a person as a person. But a serious part of
Hawking extends into the box in his lap. In mirror image, a serious part of that silicon and plastic assemblage in his lap extends into him as well . . . not to mention the
invisible ways, displaced in time and space, in which discourses of medical technology and their physical accretions already permeate him and us. No box, no discourse; in the absence of the prosthetic, Hawking's intellect becomes a tree falling in
the forest with nobody around to hear it. On the other hand, with the box his voice
is auditory and simultaneously electric, in a radically different way from that of a
person *speaking* into a microphone. Where *does* he stop? Where are his edges? The
issues his person and his communication prostheses raise are boundary debates,
borderland/*frontera* questions. Here at the close of the mechanical age, they are the
things that occupy a lot of my attention.

FLASHBACK: I WAS IDLY LOOKING

I was idly looking out my window, taking a break from some nasty piece of aca-   19
demic writing, when up the dusty, rutted hill that constitutes my driveway and bas-
tion against the world there abruptly rode, on a nasty little Suzuki Virago, a brusque,

sharp-tongued person of questionable sexuality. Doffing her helmet, she revealed herself, both verbally and physically, as Valkyrie, a postoperative m/f transgender with dark hair and piercing black eyes who evinced a pronounced affinity for black leather. She announced that there were things we had to do and places we had to go, and before I could mutter "science fiction" we were off on her bike.

Valkyrie proceeded to introduce me to a small community of women in the San Francisco Bay area. Women's collectives were not new to me; I had recently studied a group of women who ran a business, housed themselves under one roof, and lived their lives according to the principles of a canonically undefined but quite powerful idea known as lesbian separatism. But the group to which my new friend now introduced me did not at all fit the model I had painstakingly learned to recognize. This collective ran a business, and the business was hetero phone sex . . . not something of which my other research community, immured in radical lesbian orthodoxy, would have approved. 20

I was instantly entranced, and also oddly repelled. After all, I had broken bread with one of the most episcopal of women's collectives for five years, and any deviation from group norms would have been punishable in fairly horrid ways. To imagine that hetero sex could be enjoyable, not to mention profitable, was playing into the hands of the gentiles, and even to spend time with a group that supported itself in such a manner (and even joked about it) could have had mortal consequences. 21

For reasons best described as kismet, the phone sex workers and I became good friends. We found each other endlessly fascinating. They were intrigued by my odd history and by what I'd managed to make out of it. In turn, I was intrigued by the way they negotiated the mine fields of ethics and personal integrity while maintaining a lifestyle that my other research community considered unthinkable. 22

After a while, we sorted out two main threads of our mutual attraction. From my point of view, the more I observed phone sex the more I realized I was observing very practical applications of data compression. Usually sex involves as many of the senses as possible. Taste, touch, smell, sight, hearing—and, for all I know, short-range psychic interactions—all work together to heighten the erotic sense. Consciously or unconsciously phone sex workers translate all the modalities of experience into audible form. In doing so they have reinvented the art of radio drama, complete down to its sound effects, including the fact that some sounds were best represented by *other* improbable sounds that they resembled only in certain iconic ways. On the radio, for example, the soundmen (they were always literally men) represented fire by crumpling cellophane, because to the audience it sounded *more like* fire than holding a microphone to a real fire did. 23

The sex workers did similar stuff. I made a little mental model out of this: The sex workers took an extremely complex, highly detailed set of behaviors, translated them into a single sense modality, then further boiled them down to a series of highly compressed tokens. They then squirted those tokens down a voice-grade phone line. At the other end of the line the recipient of all this effort added boiling water, so to speak, and reconstituted the tokens into a fully detailed set of images and interactions in multiple sensory modes. 24

Further, what was being sent back and forth over the wires wasn't just information, it was *bodies*. The majority of people assume that erotics implies bodies; a body is part of the idea of erotic interaction and its concomitants, and the erotic sensibilities are mobilized and organized around the idea of a physical body which is the 25 seat of the whole thing. The sex workers' descriptions were invariably and quite directly about physical bodies and what they were doing or what was being done to them. . . .

A recent but fairly broad area of inquiry in the social sciences into the nature and character of human-computer interaction is known as the study of computer-supported cooperative work (CSCW). Part of the informing philosophy of this discipline is the idea that all human activity can be usefully interpreted as a kind of work, and that work is the quintessential defining human capacity. This, too, I think, misses some of the most important qualities of human-computer interaction just as it does when applied to broader elements of human experience. By this I mean that a significant part of the time that humans spend in developing interactional skills is devoted not to work but to what by common understanding would be called play. Definitions of what counts as play are many and varied, generally revolving around the idea of purposive activities that do not appear to be directly goal oriented. "Goal orientation" is, of course, a problematic phrase. There is a fine body of research addressed to the topic of play versus work activities, but it doesn't appear to have had a deep effect on CSCW and its allied disciplines. From the standpoint of cultural criticism, the issue is not one of definitions of work or play, but of how the meanings of those terms are produced and maintained. Both work and play have culture-specific meanings and purposes, and I am conducting a quite culture-specific discussion when I talk about the primacy of play in human-computer interaction (HCI, or for our purposes just "interaction") as I do here.

In order to clarify this point, let me mention that there are many definitions of interaction and many opinions about what interaction is for. As I write, large industry consortiums are finalizing their standards for what they call interactive multimedia platforms. These devices usually consist of a computer, color monitor, mouse, CD-ROM drive, sound card, and pair of speakers. This electronic instantiation of a particular definition freezes the conceptual framework of interaction in a form most suitable for commercial development—the user moves the cursor to the appropriate place and clicks the mouse, which causes something to happen—or what the interactivist Michael Naimark would call, more pejoratively, poke-and-see technology. This definition of interaction has been in the wind for so long now that few researchers say much about it. It is possible to play within the constraints of such a system, but the potential for *interaction* is limited, because the machine can only respond to an on-off situation: that is, to the click of the mouse. Computer games offer a few more input modes, usually in the form of a joystick, which has two or three degrees of freedom. However, from the standpoint of kind and gentle instruction, what the game companies do with this greater potential is not very inspiring. Technologically speaking, Sega's *Sewer Shark* (1993), for example, was an amazing exercise in game design for its time, but it reinforced the feeling that interaction in a commercial frame is still a medium like television, in which the most advanced product of the technological genius of an entire species conveys Geraldo Rivera to millions of homes in breathtaking color.

I don't want to make this a paradise-lost story, but the truth is that the definitions of interactivity used by the early researchers at MIT possessed a certain poignancy that seems to have become lost in the commercial translation. One of the best definitions was set forth by Andy Lippman, who described interaction as mutual and simultaneous activity on the part of both participants, usually working toward some goal—but, he added, not necessarily. Note that from the beginning of interaction research the idea of a common goal was already in question, and in that fact inheres interaction's vast ludic dimension.

There are five corollaries to Lippman's definition. One is *mutual interruptibility,*   29 which means that each participant must be able to interrupt the other, mutually and simultaneously. Interaction, therefore, implies conversation, a complex back-and-forth exchange, the goal of which may change as the conversation unfolds.

The second is *graceful degradation,* which means that unanswerable questions   30 must be handled in a way that doesn't halt the conversation: "I'll come back to that in a minute," for example.

The third is *limited look-ahead,* which means that because both parties can be in-   31 terrupted there is a limit to how much of the shape of the conversation can be anticipated by either party.

The fourth is *no-default,* which means that the conversation must not have a   32 preplanned path; it must develop fully in the interaction.

The fifth, which applies more directly to immersive environments (in which the   33 human participant is surrounded by the simulation of a world), is that the participants should have *the impression of an infinite database.* This principle means that an immersive interactional world should give the illusion of not being much more limiting in the choices it offers than an actual world would be. In a nonimmersive context, the machine should give the impression of having about as much knowledge of the world as you do, but not necessarily more. This limitation is intended to deal with the Spock phenomenon, in which more information is sometimes offered than is conversationally appropriate.

Thus interactivity implies two conscious agencies in conversation, playfully and   34 spontaneously developing a mutual discourse, taking cues and suggestions from each other as they proceed.

In order to better draw this out let me briefly review the origins and uses of   35 computers. Afterward I will return to the subject of play from a slightly different perspective.

The first devices that are usually called computers were built as part of a series of   36 projects mandated by the military during World War II. For many years, computers were large and extremely costly. They were also cranky and prone to continual breakdown, which had to do with the primitive nature of their components. They required continual maintenance by highly skilled technicians. The factors of cost, unreliability, and the need for skilled and continual attention, not to mention the undeniable aura of power that surrounded the new machines like some heady smell, combined to keep computers available only to large corporations and government organizations. These entities came already equipped with their own ideas of efficiency, with the concepts of time and motion study then in vogue in industry (of which my colleagues have written at length), and of course with the cultural abstraction known as the work ethic perpetually running in the background. Even within the organizations themselves, access to the new machines was restricted to a technological elite which, though by no means monolithic in its view of technological achievement, had not had enough time to develop much of a sense, not to mention a sensibility, of the scope and potential of the new devices.

These factors combined to keep attention focused on the uses of computers as   37 rather gross instrumentalities of human will—that is, as number crunchers and databases. Computers could extend human abilities, physically and conceptually. That is, computers were tools, like crowbars and screwdrivers, except that they primarily extended the mind rather than the muscles. Even Vannevar Bush's astonishingly prophetic "As We May Think" (1949) treated computers as a kind of superswitch. In this frame of understanding, computers were prosthetic in the specific sense of the Greek term *prosthenos*—extension. Computers assisted or augmented human intelligence and capabilities in much the same way that a machine or even another human being would; that is, as separate, discrete agencies or tools that occupied physical or conceptual spaces separate from those of the human. . . .

All this changed in the 1960s, but the change was largely invisible both physically and conceptually. Deleuze and Guattari and Manuel De Landa and the eerie concept of the machinic phylum would not arrive on the scene for some 30 years. In 1962, the young hackers at Project MAC, deep in the bowels of MIT, made hardly a ripple in corporate arenas with their invention of a peculiarly engrossing computational diversion that they called *SpaceWar.* This first computer game was still firmly identified with the military, even down to its name and playing style, but in that moment something quite new and (dare I say it) completely different had happened to the idea of computation. Still, it would not be until the 1970s that two kids in a garage in Mountain View, California, rather than a corporate giant like Sperry Rand or IBM or a government entity like the Bureau of Vital Statistics, would knock the props out from under the idea of computation-as-tool for all time.   38

Let me return to the discussion of work versus play once again, from the standpoint of computation and instrumentality. Viewing computers as calculatory devices that assist or mediate human work seems to be part of a Kuhnian paradigm that consists of two main elements. The first is a primary *human work ethic;* the second is a particularized view of *computers as tools.* The emergence of the work ethic has been the subject of innumerable essays, but the view of computers as tools has been so totally pervasive among those with the power to determine meaning in such forums as school policy and corporate ethics that only recently has the idea begun to be seriously challenged. The paradigm of computers as tools burst into existence, more or less, out of the allied victory in World War II (although the Nazis were working on their own computers). A paradigm of computers as something other than number crunchers does not have a similar launching platform, but the signs of such an imminent upheaval are perspicuous. Let me provide an example.   39

One of the most perceptive scholars currently studying the emergent computer societies is the anthropologist Barbara Joans. She describes the community of cyberspace workers as composed of two groups that she calls Creative Outlaw Visionaries and Law and Order Practitioners. One group has the visions; the other group knows how to build stuff and get it sold. One group fools around with technology and designs fantastic stuff; the other group gets things done and keeps the wheels turning. They talk to each other, if they talk to each other, across a vast conceptual gulf. These groups are invisible to each other, I think, because one is operating out of the older paradigm of computers as tools and the other out of the newer paradigm of computers as something else. Instead of carrying on an established work ethic, the beliefs and practices of the cultures I observe incorporate a *play* ethic—not to displace the corporate agendas that produce their paychecks, but to   40 complexify them. This play ethic is manifest in many of the communities and situations I study. It is visible in the northern California Forth community, a group of radical programmers who have adopted for their own an unusual and controversial programming language; in the CommuniTree community, an early text-based virtual discussion group that adopted such mottos as "If you meet the electronic avatar on the road, laserblast Hir"; and in the Atari Research Lab, where a group of hackers created an artificial person who became real enough to become pro tem lab director. The people who play at these technosocial games do not do so out of any specific transformative agenda, but they have seized upon advantages afforded by differences of skill, education, and income to make space for play in the very belly of the monster that is the communication industry.

This production and insertion of a play ethic like a mutation into the corporate genome is a specifically situated activity, one that is only possible for workers of a certain type and at a certain job level. In specific, it is only possible to the communities who are perhaps best described as hackers—mostly young (although the demographic changes as the first- and second-generation hackers age), mostly educated (although the field is rife with exceptions, perhaps indicating the incapability of U.S. public schools to deal with talented individuals), mostly white (and exceptions are quite rare in the United States), and mostly male (although a truly egregious exception is part of this study). They create and use a broad variety of technological prosthetics to manifest a different view of the purpose of communication technology, and their continual and casual association with the cutting edge of that technology has molded them and their machines—separately and jointly— in novel and promising ways. In particular, because they are thoroughly accustomed to engaging in nontrivial social interactions through the use of their computers— social interactions in which they change and are changed, in which commitments are made, kept, and broken, in which they may engage in intellectual discussions, arguments, and even sex—they view computers not only as tools but also as *arenas for social experience.* 41

The result is a multiple view of the state of the art in communication technology. When addressing the question of what's new about networking, it's possible to give at least two answers. Let's stick with two for now. 42

Answer 1: Nothing   The tools of networking are essentially the same as they have been since the telephone, which was the first electronic network prosthesis. Computers are engines of calculation, and their output is used for quantitative analysis. Inside the little box is information. I recently had a discussion with a colleague in which he maintained that there was nothing new about virtual reality. "When you sit and read a book," he said, "you create characters and action in your head. That's the same thing as VR, without all the electronics." Missing the point, of course, but understandably. 43

Answer 2: Everything   Computers are arenas for social experience and dramatic interaction, a type of media more like public theater, and their output is used for qualitative interaction, dialogue, and conversation. Inside the little box are *other people.* 44

In order for this second answer to be true, we have to rethink some assumptions   45
about presence. Presence is currently a word that means many different things to
many different people. One meaning is the sense that we are direct witnesses to
something or that we ourselves are being directly apprehended. This is what we
might call the straightforward meaning, the one used by many sober virtual reality
researchers. Another meaning is related to agency, to the proximity of intentionality. The changes that the concept of presence is currently undergoing are embedded
in much larger shifts in cultural beliefs and practices. These include repeated transgressions of the traditional concept of the body's physical envelope and of the locus
of human agency. . . .

My first organized piece of research in the field of virtual systems involved study-   46
ing a group of phone sex workers in the early 1980s. In this study I was doing two
things. On one hand, I was beginning to develop some of the ideas I set forth here
and, on the other, also discovering in microcosm the fascinating interplays between
communication technology, the human body, and the uses of pleasure. If I were to
frame some of the questions that occurred to me during that time, they might be
these: How are bodies represented through technology? How is desire constructed
through representation? What is the relationship of the body to self-awareness?
What is the role of play in an emergent paradigm of human-computer interaction?
And overall: What is happening to sociality and desire at the close of the mechanical age?

If I'm going to give in to the temptation to periodize—which I do again and   47
again, though frequently with tongue in cheek—then I might as well take the period
that follows the mechanical age and call it the virtual age. By the virtual age I don't
mean the hype of virtual reality technology, which is certainly interesting enough in
its own ways. Rather, I refer to the gradual change that has come over the relationship between sense of self and the body, and the relationship between individual
and group, during a particular span of time. I characterize this relationship as virtual because the accustomed grounding of social interaction in the physical facticity of human bodies is changing. Partly this change seems good, and partly it seems
bad. There are palpable advantages to the virtual mode in relation to the ways that
the structure of cities and expectations of travel have changed with the advent of the
telephone, the rise of large corporations, the invention and marketing of inexpensive tract housing, the development of the shopping mall, the commercial development and exploitation of electronic mass media, the development of the personal
computer, the greening of large-scale information networks (which can be coopted
for social interaction), and the increasing miniaturization of electronic components
(eventually perhaps to be extended to mechanical devices, that is, Drexler and others). There are equally palpable disadvantages to each of these deep changes in our
lives. I don't want this perhaps too-familiar list to be read as either extolling or condemnation. They are the manifestations, as well as causative agents, of the social
changes, ruptures, and reorganizations that they accompany. . . .

Just as textual technologies—cheap paper, the typewriter, printing—accom-   48
panied new discourse networks and social formations, so electronic communication technologies—radio, television, computer networks—accompany the discourse
networks and social formations now coming into being. These technologies,

discourse networks, and social formations continue the trend toward increasing awareness of a sense of self; toward increasing physical isolation of individuals in Western and Western-influenced societies; and toward displacement of shared physical space, both public and private, by textuality and prosthetic communication—in brief, the constellation of events that define the close of the mechanical age and the unfolding or revealing of what, for lack of a better term, we might call the virtual age.

Working with the Text

1. Stone subtitles her essay "How I Fell in Love with My Prosthesis," and in fact goes on to describe falling in love with three "prostheses": a crystal radio, a massive recording console, and the Votrax generator physicist Stephen Hawking uses to communicate orally. Later she suggests that the general view of computers is as prosthetic devices. What does she mean by *prosthesis*? How does the example of Hawking (whom she describes as raising issues of "boundary debates, borderland/*frontera* questions") relate to the point she is making about reconceptualizing computers as "arenas for social experience"? Similarly, how does her discussion of phone sex relate to this point?

2. Computer technology is referred to as "interactive." However, Stone writes that because of current standards that freeze the "conceptual framework of interaction in a form most suitable for commercial development . . . the potential for *interaction* is limited." How does Stone, summarizing Andy Lippman, define *interactive*? Can you imagine human-computer interaction of this sort? How does this broader and deeper definition of *interactive* differ from popular and commercial applications of the term *interactive* to computer programs?

3. Stone suggests that we are at the beginning of a "virtual age" (as the "mechanical age" ends). This virtual age is characterized by a redefining of "the relationship between sense of self and the body, and the relationship between individual and group" as "the accustomed grounding of social interaction in the physical facticity of human bodies is changing." What do you think she is getting at? How do you respond to her picture of those "on the cutting edge of computer technology . . . [who] are thoroughly accustomed to engaging in nontrivial social interactions through the use of their computers—social interactions in which they change and are changed, in which commitments are made, kept, and broken, in which they may engage in intellectual discussion, arguments, and even sex"? How might this virtual environment alter our conception of individual—and group—identity?

 4. At the conclusion of this excerpt, Stone says that "the discourse networks and social formations now coming into being" as a result of new electronic communication technologies will lead toward "displacement of shared physical space, both public and private, by textuality and prosthetic communication." How drastic do you think this "displacement" might be over the course of your lifetime and beyond? Can you imagine a time when, as Stone seems to

suggest, people will rarely be together in a physical space? Also, what might this developing virtual space ultimately "look" and "feel" like?

5. Stone's discussion of interactivity and play in electronic environments makes the most sense in the context of rich immersion environments like games, and less sense for general linking and retrieval environments like those of the World Wide Web. If you have played any computer games or participated in any extensive virtual, interactive environments, consider them in light of Stone's arguments about the connections among technology, desire, and the body. What elements of the virtual environments you're familiar with work most effectively to engage you?

Thinking and Writing: *Critical Questions Revisited*

1. The Borders of a Community

Consider a specific community to which you belong (or have belonged) that is clearly delineated in terms of both geography and culture. It could be a town, a city neighborhood that is identified by its own name, a suburb, your college or university, a region of the country with which you identify strongly, or the geographic and cultural place that you consider "home."

Analyze the identity of this community in terms of the issues and concepts raised in this chapter. To what extent—and how—is it imagined? Would most of its inhabitants define it in essentially the same way? What symbols represent it? What are some of the stories or myths surrounding its past or present? How coherent is it internally? How is it viewed as being different from neighboring or "rival" communities? How does its representation on maps define its perceived prominence or importance? What are its borders, and how well are they defined? Is it marked by any "frontiers" where interactions with members of other communities take place? What is the nature of these interactions? Do the physical dimensions of place influence its inhabitants' sense of personal identity? Finally, you might also consider how your analysis of this smaller community contributes to—or contradicts—your understanding of larger national communities.

2. Frontier Line Versus Border Zone (Frontier/*La Frontera*)

In her essay on the American frontier, Patricia Limerick says, "If the idea of *la frontera* had anywhere near the standing of the idea of the frontier, we would be well launched toward self-understanding, directed toward a realistic view of this nation's position in the hemisphere and in the world." The distinction that Limerick draws between the American idea of the frontier and the meaning of a "frontier" in other countries is a very important one. In part, the distinction to which she refers is the difference between a line or edge, on the one hand, and a zone, on the other. In the history of the American frontier, the "frontier line" was the place where "civilization" met its opposite. The concept of that meeting point was part of a narrow interpretation of the progress of history, and of the movement of civilized peoples from east to west.

However, the idea of *la frontera* is very different. It is closer to two related definitions presented in other chapters of the "interactive spaces" between cultures: Mary Louise Pratt's notion of the "contact zone" (a place where two cultures meet in an asymmetrical power relationship) and Gloria Anzaldúa's idea of the "borderlands" (a geographic, psychological, and cultural space where differences meet). Limerick, Pratt, and Anzaldúa's focus on borderlands and zones is part of a large and significant shift that has been occurring in the study of culture during the last few years. In this newer way of looking at cultural history, cultures are not seen as separate entities but rather as interdependent—defined from their very roots by the existence, proximity, and mixing of other cultures.

In part, what is implied by the difference between "frontier" and *la frontera* is that the latter provides a way of seeing borders as places of ongoing negotiation between different groups, value systems, and cultural perspectives. In a paper, explore the difference between seeing a border as a frontier—a rigid boundary between cultures—and seeing a border as a "borderland" or "zone." How would these two ways of considering borders differ? What are the implications of their differences for constructing cultural differences? How would each view deal with the creation of images of "otherness"? What are the implications for believing in a sense of cultural purity or integrity? Are there issues in American culture today that are divided along lines that are related to this split between seeing cultural differences along a "frontier" as opposed to a "borderlands"?

3. The Borders of American Identity

In her essay about the Buffalo Bill Museum, Jane Tompkins discusses how accounts of the exciting exploits of Buffalo Bill "play to an inward territory: a Wild West of the psyche that hungered for exercise." Similarly, Patricia Limerick refers to the American frontier as occupying the "uncertain turf along the border between the imagined and actual." In what ways have the imagined and the actual interacted in the cultural construction of America's identity within its geographic boundaries? In what ways has the American frontier always been an "inward territory" as well as a physical one? Looking particularly at works in this chapter by writers such as Frederick Jackson Turner, Patricia Limerick, and Jane Tompkins, discuss the imaginative dimensions of American identity that grow out of the presence and creation of the American frontier. How does Turner connect what are often invoked as "characteristic American values"—individualism, democracy, egalitarianism—to the geography of the United States? How does the construction of those values translate into American folk mythology and images of the American past? How are these "mythic" constructions at odds with historical reality?

4. Limits and Freedom in Imagined Communities

One of the themes running through many of this chapter's readings relates to limits and freedom. In an earlier chapter's essay about the idea of "community" in the Western United States, Daniel Kemmis claims that the essence of "community" comes from the notion of people living within the limits of their environment. In other words, despite whatever physical proximity, economic and social interdependence, or shared values bring people together as a community, the real shaping "boundaries" of that community come from coping with scarce or limited resources. It is interesting to juxtapose that idea with those William Mitchell presents in this chapter about cyberspace. Mitchell believes that locations in cyberspace will develop as "electronic cities," a "new urbanism freed from the constraints of physical space." Indeed, it is the wide open nature of cyberspace—along with its seemingly limitless space and resources—that attracts people to it as a "new frontier." Of course, a similar perception of abundance and limitless land and resources invested the American frontier with such idealistic importance in the first place.

Considering these ideas, write an essay in which you analyze one or more aspects of the relationship among limits, freedom, abundance, and the space in which we imagine our communities. You could approach this topic from the perspective of new computing technologies and the concepts of limits and abundance, such as the metaphors and images we use when thinking about cyberspace (through media images of the Internet and computers, for example). Or you might consider people's attraction to online communities or the use of online resources to offer content and services. How do people working with online resources represent the idea of limits? In what ways are we attracted to "space" (cyberspace, outer space, or any open space) as a place where the tensions of "scarcity" (as they are felt in urban spaces, for example) are absent? Do you think this view of "space" is true?

How do people talk about countries, nations, or regions in terms that imply a limit of resources? To what extent are debates in the United States about immigration, "free trade," or "buying American" products debates that mix cultural, social, and geographic arguments in the context of limited resources?

5. Describing and Analyzing an Online Virtual Community

Analyze one of the many kinds of virtual communities, such as a MUD, an interactive Web site, an ongoing chat group, or a discussion space. How is this particular kind of social space a community? What criteria are you using to define a community? What are the members of this community like? Are they diverse or similar? What brings them together? What keeps them together? Using this community as a focus, discuss how online communities differ from communities in physical or geographical space. Or, if you select an online network based in a geographical space (such as a city free-net), consider how the online interaction of people in this community relates to the physical space it embodies. How might online communities enhance face-to-face contact? How might it detract from it? What about an evolving sense of ethics, behavior, and conduct? How do people know how to act within this community? Who enforces the rules? How is authority or hierarchy constructed in this community? What needs or desires do online communities fulfill?

CHAPTER **seven**

THE WORLD'S NEW BORDERS:

Globalism
Versus
Tribalism

Critical Questions for *The World's New Borders*

How are communal identities changing? How are group identity and national identity increasingly at odds in the United States? In what sense is America a global crossroads? What kinds of tensions does this situation create? What impact does it have on American values and ideals? How are borders within the United States and throughout the world changing? How are the world's populations increasingly interconnected? To what extent are these changes economically driven? How are nations becoming less important than a global culture, on the one hand, and smaller, more focused communities, on the other? In what ways are some of the world's communities developing around a sense of separation and otherness? In the United States, how is the debate over cultural purity versus cultural mixing being framed? Will individual rights and community values, and civic and democratic values increase or decrease as the world becomes both more coherent and more fragmented?

A NATION OF BORDERS

In his essay in this chapter, *Harper's* magazine editor Lewis Lapham begins by complaining:

> Were I to believe what I read in the papers, I would find it easy to think that I no longer can identify myself simply as an American. The noun apparently means nothing unless it is dressed up with at least one modifying adjective. As a plain American I have neither voice nor authentic proofs of existence. I acquire a presence only as an old American, a female American, a white American, a rich American, a black American, a gay American, a poor American, a native American, a dead American. The subordination of the noun to the adjectives makes a mockery of both the American premise and the democratic spirit. . . .

Lapham's claim that the "plain American" has no "voice" or "existence" is both startling and ironic. After all, as Lapham says, "the subordination of the noun" (American) "to the adjectives" (rich, poor, female, gay) seemingly goes against the very ideal on which the United States was founded. From very early in our history, the United States was supposed to be a place where peoples of many different backgrounds came together to form a single nation and a single society—in short, a place where different people could become "plain Americans."

One of the most famous statements of this ideal was made by a French immigrant to the United States, Hector St. Jean de Crèvecoeur, who back in the 1770s asked, "What is an American?"

> What is this American, this new man? He is neither an European nor the descendent of an European; hence that strange mixture of blood, which you will find in no other country. I could point out to you a family whose grandfather was an Englishman, whose wife was Dutch, whose son married a French woman, and whose present four sons have now four wives of different nations. He is an American, who, leaving behind him all his ancient prejudices and manners, receives new ones from the new mode of life he has embraced, the new government he obeys, and the new rank he holds. . . . Here individuals of all nations are melted into a new race of men, whose labours and posterity will one day cause great change in the world. . . .

The ideal set out by Crèvecoeur has everything to do with *borders*. Writing in the late eighteenth century, Crèvecoeur is describing the earliest immigrants to America around the time that it became the "United States." When leaving the borders of their home country and crossing the borders of this one during this period, immigrants to the United States were asked to relinquish their old nationality and take on a new one. Thus, from this country's earliest years as a nation, crossing the *physical* borders of America had important *symbolic* dimensions. America was to be a different kind of country because it would be a nation in which everyone's differences would be left at the border. You might have come from Ireland, France, Germany, or Spain, but once you arrived here, you would be an "American." Yet what was "American" in part had to do with the shaping influence that each immigrant and immigrant group brought to the new nation.

So if America was supposed to be about diversity melting into unity, then how did we get from Crèvecoeur's ideal to Lapham's complaint? For one thing, Crèvecoeur's ideal, as expansive and inclusive as it might have seemed to him, now looks rather narrow to us. Consider these points while looking closely at the previous passage: Whom does Crèvecoeur include in his vision? Crèvecoeur's vision of Europeans—French, German, Dutch, English—all coming together did not encompass, for example, the people already living within the physical borders of what Europeans called "America." These native Americans interpreted the physical and symbolic borders very differently, and they certainly weren't aware of or included in anybody's plans to "melt" with Europeans "into a new race of men."

Nor did Crèvecoeur's vision include the millions of people who were wrenched from their African homelands and brought to the United States and the Caribbean. Finally, Crèvecoeur's vision—and the ideal that it expressed—neither included nor anticipated the great variety of peoples who would willingly come to America from other places. Not everyone who came to this country was *as welcome* as were the first European groups during Crèvecoeur's era or as eligible for the same opportunities for assimilation and success. Whether Irish, Chinese, Mexican, or Filipino, many groups have entered the United States only to discover that symbolic barriers surround them, even if they have successfully crossed the physical and geographic ones. Prejudice, stereotypes, discrimination, bigotry, racism—these are all symbolic borders that immigrants have encountered within America. This nation's complex mixture of races, nationalities, religions, cultures, and subcultures has provided it with a thousand adjectives to go with the noun. For more than two hundred years, this mixture has been the basis of a fundamental tension between a nation of diverse peoples, on the one hand, and a society of "plain Americans" (as Lapham puts it) who share common space and common ideals, on the other.

AMERICA AS A GLOBAL CROSSROADS

However, during the last two hundred years, people immigrating to the United States did not come merely from diverse parts of Europe but indeed from all over the world. That incredible diversity of peoples has created not a single, unified "new race of men" but rather a nation characterized as a "global crossroads"—a country defined as much by its differences as by its commonalities. What happens when our differences become more powerful than our commonalities? What if we are not a nation of diverse peoples "melted into a new race" but instead are a mixed society whose borders and boundaries with the rest of the world are porous and unstable?

Speaking of the rising tide of anti-immigrant sentiment particularly directed at Mexicans and Latinos crossing the United States–Mexico border, Guillermo Gómez-Peña, in his essay later in this chapter, says that Americans' "worst nightmare is finally coming true: the United States is no longer a fictional extension of Europe, or the wholesome suburb imagined by the screenwriter of *Lassie*. It is rapidly becoming a huge border zone, a hybrid society, a mestizo race, and worst of all, this process seems to be irreversible." Have we then seen the passing of the ideal image of the United States as a place where a diversity of peoples come together as a single people? Has it been replaced by the reality of this nation as a "hybrid society"? And if this is true, then what kind of hybrid society will it be? Can it continue to evolve toward unity as a "mestizo race," despite its mixing of very diverse cultures? Or is it a society that will continually give rise to racial and ethnic tensions? Will America merely see the continuation of what Ronald Takaki in this chapter calls "America's intensifying racial crisis"?

What do we have, then, if we fall short of the ideal? What is America if it is not a nation where diverse peoples come together as a single society? What is the alternative to a coherent national identity? And how do these questions about the United States relate to and reflect the rest of the world?

THE RISE OF GROUP IDENTITY

In this chapter one major alternative concept that is posited against national identity is *group identity*. Throughout *Border Texts* identity has been a central issue. In the early chapters we principally explored the idea of individual identity and the ways that individuals develop their sense of identity in light of the cultural institutions and community structures around them. In the later chapters we have been examining the idea of *difference* and the dynamics of how individuals interact in zones where their differences come together. The dynamics of difference and otherness explored in Chapters 4 and 5 are partly based on the ways that individuals are identified as members of particular groups and that group identities affect individual actions.

This final chapter continues many of those same concerns but looks at group identity from the perspective of national and transnational societies. This is not a big leap to make. America was supposed to be a place where individuals came together to form a nation. As noted earlier in Crèvecoeur's vision, there has always been an effort in this country to imagine that the defining relationship here would be between the individual and the nation. All other allegiances and bonds would be weaker, symbolic, less important. And yet, as Lapham's opening paragraph makes clear, "group identity" has become extremely important in America. Group identity has extensive and deep political implications, and it is acquiring ever-increasing social implications. Whether in the context of empowering ethnic and cultural movements such as Afrocentrism, or the Chicano Movement, or reactionary counter-movements such as the rising tide of anti-immigrant nationalism, this growing sense of group identity is increasingly becoming a defining element of American politics and culture. Consider for a moment the complexities of "group" conflict in the South Central "riots" following the Rodney King verdict in 1992. Unlike the riots of the 1960s, this could not be written off as a "black versus white" conflict, but instead was a multicultural one that raised important questions about group identity and social cohesion. Much of the violence, as Elaine Kim discusses in her essay, transpired between African Americans and Korean Americans. Much of the tension and antagonism between these two groups has a great deal to do with their respective relationships to a majority white society. And that is only part of the multiracial picture of that conflict.

Inasmuch as America has always been a global crossroads, the context for its racial crisis is global as well. As Ronald Takaki puts it:

Indeed, Americans have been witnessing ethnic strife erupting around the world—the rise of neo-Nazism and the murder of Turks in Germany, the ugly "ethnic cleansing" in Bosnia, the terrible and bloody clashes between Muslims and Hindus in India. Is the situation here different, we have been nervously wondering, or do ethnic conflicts elsewhere represent a prologue for America? What is the nature of malevolence? Is there a deep, perhaps primordial, need for group identity rooted in hatred for the other? Is ethnic pluralism possible for America?

One of the key points that Takaki raises in this quotation is the relationship between ethnic strife around the world and racial and ethnic tension in the United States. Central to this chapter is the idea that this phenomenon is in no way unique to America. In fact, the rise of *group consciousness* in the United States is in many ways part of a larger global pattern. Furthermore, international politics during the last ten years, especially since the breakup of the Soviet Union in the late eighties, has been defined by the reassertion of group identity largely along ethnic and, in some cases, religious lines.

GROUP SOLIDARITY OR GLOBAL THEME PARK?

The rise of group consciousness in the United States and around the world has not been the only major pattern of world development. It has taken place at the same time that the world has been becoming increasingly connected and while particular aspects of global culture have been becoming increasingly homogenous. Benjamin Barber, in his essay in this chapter, calls these two contrary tendencies *Jihad* and *Mc-World*. Each of these terms stands for a different scenario for the future of the globe: "The first scenario [Jihad] rooted in race holds out the grim prospect of a retribalization of large swaths of humankind by war and bloodshed: a threatened balkanization of nation-states in which culture is pitted against culture, people against people, tribe against tribe, a Jihad in the name of a hundred narrowly conceived faiths against every kind of interdependence. . . ." By contrast, a second scenario (McWorld) "paints" the future of the world "in shimmering pastels, a busy portrait of onrushing economic, technological, and ecological forces that demand integration and uniformity and that mesmerize peoples everywhere with fast music, fast computers, and fast food—MTV, Macintosh, and McDonald's—pressing nations into one homogenous global theme park. . . ." *Jihad* is the tendency of groups to struggle for independent existence, island-like and separate. *McWorld* is the assertion of a global culture that is the same worldwide, blending and at times conflicting with local cultural beliefs. The paradox of this situation is that Jihad and McWorld are occurring simultaneously; the world seems to be coming together and dividing into smaller pieces at the same time. (Naturally, Barber's accessible formulation of "Jihad vs. McWorld" is not about either/or dichotomies but rather about a complexity of tensions and countertensions that are different in every local context.)

This tension between counter-tendencies forms an important context for this chapter and for our final look at the borders of American culture. America is often viewed as a model of (as Barber puts it) "benign multiculturalism," where differences are noted and respected but subsumed to a higher allegiance or identity—i.e., a sense of national belonging and being a citizen of a democracy. How much can we compare these two tendencies elsewhere in the world to the increasing tension in the United States between its ideal as a single, coherent national people on the one hand and its existence as a nation of diverse, separate peoples and cultures on the other? How related is the rising tide of group identities in the United States to the worldwide tendency toward tribalism, or what we might call subnational or transnational identities?

Despite their identification with particular groups, individuals in the United States are supposed to be, first and last, citizens of their *nation*. But in *Jihad* (to use Barber's term for group consciousness) or *McWorld* (homogenous, global culture), *political nations* don't matter. If there are no nations, then there are no citizens. Also, according to Barber, in either Jihad or McWorld, "no one is a citizen." Therefore, Barber asks, "without citizens, how can there be democracy?"

By positing an opposition between group consciousness and democracy, we do not demonize the idea of group identity. Group consciousness (i.e., "tribalism") usually originates as an act of resistance to patterns of marginalization or histories of repression. Even if group conflicts (or nation-group conflicts) take violent forms, that doesn't mean that they are not "liberation" movements of one kind or another. Similarly, it is complicated to talk about the opposition of *McWorld* to the concept of democracy. Although globalism transcends national boundaries, it is often intimately tied up with national issues. For example, international trade agreements that often facilitate the flow of global products internationally are built on national interests.

On the other hand, much of what constitutes McWorld is based on "multinational" interests—that is, the interests of multinational corporate entities that facilitate the marketing of products globally. This worldwide corporate capitalism has become one face of the *New World Order* that was proclaimed by then President George Bush as replacing the Cold War division of the world into alliances between the two superpowers (and perhaps a third division of underdeveloped nations constituting the "third world"). The New World Order was supposed to represent a solidarity among most nations against local (or tribal) acts of aggression. One premise of the New World Order was that there remained in the world only one viable political and economic system: democratic capitalism. Indeed, this is one of the fallacies of the new globalism that Barber addresses: the tendency to mistake "the right to shop" (free-market capitalism) with the "right to vote" (democracy). One persistent question in several of these readings is that of the survival of democracy: is it increasing or decreasing? Do global technologies like the Internet increase possibilities for participatory democracy or lessen them? Does the new globalism of interdependent economies make capitalism and democracy interdependent?

These complex issues—which are only partially touched upon here—are relevant to this book in that they ultimately bear on the borders of American cultural identity. If our own individual identity is partially constructed by a sense of place and where we are from, then the same is true with a sense of national identity. As inhabitants of the United States, *who* we think we are is significantly influenced by our sense of our place in the world. From the perspective of living in the United States, one gets a very particular view of Jihad vs. McWorld. Group consciousness is often portrayed as threatening, whereas multinational democratic capitalism is often portrayed as inevitable and good for everyone. As you will see in the final readings in this chapter and in the additional materials in *Border Texts* Online, the internationalization of economies and the global export of American culture might look very different in local contexts in other countries. Similarly, as we saw in Chapter 5, *differences* are rarely negotiated on equal terms. The same is true with the international flow of goods and culture, where both new and old hierarchies apply. As one critic, Ana Lopez, puts it:

> For culture—and information—rarely travels independently of capital and gatekeepers and thus, inevitably, runs into borders of one kind or another. Questions of global cultural exchange cannot be addressed without taking into consideration the relationships among information flow, capital, and ultimately, power relations. Whose culture travels? What culture? Where does it go?

The questions of this chapter, as broad and global as they are, bring us back around, full circle, to the most central questions of the book. How do individuals see themselves in the world? How do we see ourselves in relation to others? How does our sense of individual identity relate to other kinds of identity: our family, community, region, nation, ethnicity, or race? How does *where we are* determine *who we are*? How do we imagine what kinds of ties we have to people like and unlike ourselves across the globe or down the street? In the end, these are all questions about borders: borders with which we live, borders that we resist, borders that define us, and borders that we help to reinforce. The *border texts* in this chapter can't answer these questions, but they do try to raise them. And no questions will be more important for the next century than these.

The Nine Nations of North America

JOEL GARREAU

■ Joel Garreau, a staff member at the *Washington Post* since 1976, currently writes that paper's "Cybersurfing" column. His most recent book is *Edge City: Life on the New Frontier* (1997), which focuses on "edge cities," exurban enclaves like Silicon Valley and Tysons Corner, Virginia, that are homes to major high-tech corporations. His first book, *The Nine Nations of North America* (1981), from which the following selection is taken, grew out of his experience as chief of correspondents at the *Post*. In talking to reporters across the country, he says he became aware that "there were new power centers emerging, and distinct and characteristic values, views, and cultures growing up around them," independent of state political lines. He first wrote about these power centers in an article for the *Post* that was widely reprinted. He then traveled the country for fourteen months to expand the article into a book. Garreau calls the nine nations a "news map": "This is the way the news breaks down. And to whatever extent news reflects human realities, this is the way the continent operates." Rather than the nation's being homogenized by "McDonald's stands and the interstates," Garreau says that the regions he describes are becoming more and more distinct.

A nation is the desire of many individuals
to do great things together.

—Marcel Rioux

Forget the pious wisdom you've been handed about North America.   1
    Forget about the borders dividing the United States, Canada, and Mexico,   2
those pale barriers so thoroughly porous to money, immigrants, and ideas.

Forget the bilge you were taught in sixth-grade geography about East and West,   3
North and South, faint echoes of glorious pasts that never really existed save in sanitized textbooks.

Forget the maze of state and provincial boundaries, those historical accidents   4
and surveyors' mistakes. The reason no one except the trivia expert can name all fifty of the United States is that they hardly matter.

Forget the political almanacs full of useless data on local elections rendered   5
meaningless by strangely carved districts and precincts.

Consider, instead, the way North America really works. It is Nine Nations. Each   6
has its capital and its distinctive web of power and influence. A few are allies, but many are adversaries. Several have readily acknowledged national poets, and many have characteristic dialects and mannerisms. Some are close to being raw frontiers; others have four centuries of history. Each has a peculiar economy; each commands a certain emotional allegiance from its citizens. These nations look different, feel different, and sound different from each other, and few of their boundaries match the political lines drawn on current maps. Some are clearly divided topographically by mountains, deserts, and rivers. Others are separated by architecture, music, language, and ways of making a living. Each nation has its own list of desires. Each nation knows how it plans to get what it needs from whoever's got it.

Most important, each nation has a distinct prism through which it views the   7
world.

The Foundry, the declining industrial nation of the Northeast, for example, still   8
tends to see the other eight nations as subservient, as the tribute-paying colonies they once were. It views itself as the "real" center of power in the continent, shrugging off the inexorable slide of population and ambitions to other places as temporary aberrations susceptible to some quick fix, to some new "program."

Viewed from the emerging nation of Dixie, however, the Foundry is a different   9
place. Dixie, which has traded populations and histories with the Northeast for over a century, sees the Foundry as a collection of mistakes to be avoided as wealth flows south. To Dixie, the Foundry is the smell of the New Jersey Turnpike through Elizabeth; the question of the moment is whether that odor must soon permeate North Carolina and Louisiana, too.

Yet the northern Pacific Rim nation of Ecotopia views the Foundry in yet another   10 way—as irrelevant. Even quaint, Foundry-like unemployment and recession are simply not overwhelming concerns in the Pacific Northwest, which is developing the industries of the twenty-first century: lightweight alloys, computer chips, and ways to use them that are still in the future. Its natural markets and its lessons about living are in Asia. The Foundry, on the other hand, is tied to Europe and thinks that the rest of the continent should be. The mistakes Ecotopia fears it may repeat are not those of the Foundry, but those of the boom towns of dry, sunny MexAmerica. If Ecotopia feels kin to any of the Nine Nations, it is to New England, from which so many of the Pacific Northwest's original settlers came, and with which so many of its successful social patterns are traded.

Each of these Nine Nations has a different future. Some are energy self-sufficient   11
or exporting; most are desperate for oil. Some are chronically damp; to others, water is the primary concern, without which no future is thinkable. These nations attract different kinds of inhabitants—the assembly line or farm around which one person can build a life, another person may find supremely maddening.

It's valuable to recognize these divergent realities. The layers of unifying flavor   12
and substances that define these nations help explain the major storms and excursions through which our public affairs pass.

Studying them is certainly far more constructive than examining misleading   13
ideas, such as "Colorado."

Colorado is clearly two different places: the eastern half, which is flat, fertile agri-   14
cultural land, and the western half, which rises dramatically in the suburbs of Denver to become the Rocky Mountains. Back when there were few people to speak of in the territory and it didn't make much difference, "Colorado" was boxed off into a neat, perfect rectangle, and now the idea it represents has been around long enough to become self-perpetuating. People speak and think of Colorado as one identifiable place, despite abundant evidence to the contrary and for little better reason than that their fathers did it that way. That does not, however, make the idea useful.

Take the farm protest movement that in the late seventies resulted in thousands   15
of tractors blocking the traffic of downtown Washington, D.C. It was born of a frustration that spoke of parity and adverse farm prices, but it went far deeper. Actually, it was a cry declaring that no one cared about the farmers' problems; no one acknowledged the importance of the farmers' existence; no one was listening. That frustration did not first manifest itself in the heartland of Iowa or Nebraska. The American Agriculture Movement was born in the wheat fields of eastern Colorado. That's not much of a surprise. If any farmer was likely to be mad as hell, it would be he who sent his taxes to Denver, despite that capital's obvious interest in loosening its agrarian ties. Denver's great pride today is its shedding of the label "cowtown." As Denver flourishes (it's been called the nesting place of the forty-story crane), it clearly cares less and less about wheat. Denver sees its future in the oil, coal, gas, uranium, copper, molybdenum, and snow to its mountainous, winter-scoured west. Denver is the capital of, and the staging area for the assault on, the Empty Quarter—the most mineral-rich of the Nine Nations. The irrigated farm country to its east is rightfully part of a completely different nation—the Breadbasket.

"California" is an even worse idea than Colorado.   16

The Empty Quarter's attitude toward the Breadbasket is cordial inattention. The   17 two Pacific nations that divide California, by contrast, are openly antagonistic. They're as antithetical as sunshine and rain.

The problem is simply stated: the thin strip of the Pacific shore along the Coast and Cascade Mountain ranges from Northern California to southern Alaska is the only place in the West with enough water. Everything else for a thousand miles in any direction is basically desert. It's no wonder that essentially different civilizations have grown up on the Pacific coast as a result. 18

The metropolises of MexAmerica, for example—adored for their dry, sunny climes—are designed like fragile moon bases. All the essentials to support life—water, power, and even breathable air—are imported from someplace else a long way away. 19

Power for the air conditioners of Los Angeles is sucked in from as far as Utah and Arizona. By buying electricity generated at such great distance, Los Angeles also effectively exports its pollution to these distant outposts, which is a way of importing clean air. For that matter, the smog of the Southern California coast is occasionally scoured by a "gift" of the desert to the east. The hot, violent Santa Ana winds surge over the mountains to make the cities sparkle, at the same time as they shrivel the chaparral to the explosive brush-fire stage. 20

But most important is water. "You can make gasoline out of cow manure if you have to," points out the western grower. "But you can't make water." Every developmental decision here—be it the growth of homes, industry, or agriculture—is based on the availability of water. Tucson is depending on water pumped over the Rocky Mountains and through manmade concrete riverbeds in the sand. San Diego depends on the Colorado River, also pumped over mountains. The unmatchable vegetable harvests of central California's San Joaquin Valley are absolutely dependent on water imported from the north. The whole civilization is based on engineering ingenuity of the first order. 21

There are several ways of looking at this. 22

In MexAmerica, such ingenuity is both father and child to a sense of the miraculous. A discussion of "limits" doesn't ring true here. After all, seven million people demonstrably can live in a Los Angeles Basin, which God saw fit to endow with the resources to support only two hundred thousand. If the difference is a man-made miracle, why stop at this point? The only real limits, it would appear, are those imposed by an inability to dream. Look at the wealth here. Look at the abundance and quality of the food. Look at the property values! This is obviously where people want to be and where people will continue to want to be. We've never let nature stand in the way of building canyon bungalows and sowing plains of rutabagas before. Why start now? In fact, there are serious men in these deserts who even propose diverting the waters of the Yukon River to further their sun-ripened visions of a rich tomorrow. 23

On the other side, of course, are those who think this is all patently insane, if not blasphemous. Chief among them are Northern Californians and other residents of Ecotopia who like their part of the world just fine the way it is. They worship different gods from those of their neighbors. They certainly have no reverence for the dams, channels, and diversions that would seize their assets and dump them into the unquenchable maw to the south. The forests of the Pacific Northwest are sufficiently 24 blessed with resources to inspire thoughts of husbanding what exists, where it exists, in order to make it last forever. The implication is that others should consider doing the same.

Thus, in MexAmerica, the idea of a freshwater supply flowing unchecked into the   25
sea is considered a crime against nature—a sin. In Ecotopia, leaving a river wild and free is viewed as a blow struck for God's original plan for the land.

Along such faiths are divergent social arrangements made.   26

San Francisco and Los Angeles are not just two cities. They represent two value   27
structures. Indeed, they are the capitals of two different nations—Los Angeles the capital of MexAmerica, and San Francisco that of Ecotopia. So viewed, Sacramento becomes less the capital of anything terribly important than it is merely a border town between hostile forces.

So it goes, across the map. State legislators in Virginia correctly perceive any idea   28
conceived north of the Rappahannock River, in the wealthy suburbs of Washington, D.C., as foreign and suspect. Most of Virginia is part of Dixie, where tax money, characteristically, is spent strictly on roads and schools, and sometimes not all that much on schools. Northern Virginians, with their ideas about social services and mass transit, obviously are not part of this tradition. They're Yankees. Northern Virginia is part, not of Dixie, but of the Foundry.

Chicago is not a capital city, because there is no such thing as the "Midwest."   29
Chicago is properly an important border metropolis directing the trade in values and enterprise between the Foundry and the Breadbasket. Its hybrid status explains why it gets along so poorly in a political way with the rest of Illinois.

Canada, which is little save moose, Aleuts, and energy wealth north of the al-   30
legedly temperate strip along its border with the United States, has migraines about losing its "identity." It shouldn't. Apart from French-speaking Québec, which is properly a nation unto itself, Canada shares five perfectly respectable and different identities with the northern United States.

Of course, the oil-rich "sheikdom" of Alberta defies Ottawa. Economically and   31
philosophically, Calgary is far more kin to Fairbanks, Salt Lake City, or Denver than it is to Ottawa. It's part of the Empty Quarter. By the same token, the grain belt of the north, centered on Winnipeg, is visibly and temperamentally part of the Bread-basket. The industries of Windsor, Toronto, and Ottawa are part of the Foundry. Vancouver shares far more with Seattle than it does with Halifax, Nova Scotia. And the poor but proud Maritimes are in the same boat as New England.

These realities should come as no more of a shock than that South Florida is not   32
part of any Confederate dream. Miami, after all, is now less a tourist mecca for the pasty-fleshed than it is the trade and intrigue capital of that Caribbean nation, the Islands.

Yet the existence of interstate highways, dense air connections, cheap long-   33
distance rates, ubiquitous television, and the celebrated franchised hamburger has lulled many, incorrectly, into some sense that North America has become utterly ho-mogenized, if not bland.

Granted, some cherished old regional idiosyncrasies have disappeared since   34
World War II—widespread starvation in the South, for example. But focusing on certain absorbed folkways is to ignore what has been dispersed: power. Power, money, thought, talent, information, resources, and population. What's been hap-

pening for the past few decades is that North America has been maturing. Houston, Kansas City, and Atlanta, for example, only twenty years ago were crossroads not even their Chambers of Commerce could love. Now they're world-class cities.

Malarial East Texas became a technologically plausible alternative to New York   35
City, for example, only in the 1960s. Shell Oil didn't dream of leaving Manhattan for Houston until it became thinkable to air-condition an employee's entire life—home, office, automobile, parking garage, shopping center, redneck bar, bedomed baseball stadium. Now, not only is Houston the world headquarters of oil, but the number of foreign banks there rose from six to forty-five in the last six years of the 1970s, with as many as twenty more expected in the very near term.

In 1972, the Soviet Union demonstrated that the North American Breadbasket   36
could have as much strategic world importance as the Middle East by secretly contracting for massive, bargain-priced grain imports. When this happened, Kansas City proved to have better global sources of information and communication than did Washington, D.C. Washington got the first detailed reports on the "great grain robbery"—which rocked the U.S. economy, driving up food prices—by reading *Milling and Baking News,* the Kansas City weekly that had the scoop.

And Atlanta, in 1976, demonstrated conclusively that it had acquired a critical   37
mass of financial, political, and media expertise. That's the year it propelled a former state governor, more unknown than which few were, into the presidency of the United States.

The significance of the evolution of these cities is that their regions and peoples   38
are gaining sophistication, too.

Twenty years ago, if you were young, smart, ambitious, and from Des Moines,   39
you fled to the bright lights of Chicago, if not New York, at your earliest opportunity. Getting *out* was of prime importance. The action was elsewhere; the opportunities to test your mettle were in some more glamorous site.

Today, abandoning Iowa at a tender age is not an indefensible action, but it's no   40
longer an inevitable one. As one farmer put it, "In the old days, if you weren't smart enough to get a job in the city, you could always farm. Today, if you're not smart enough to farm, you can always get a job in the city."

In Sioux City, which is proud of the fact that it recently got the stockyards to   41
move the block-long hill of manure that used to dominate the view of the city from the south, I chatted with two young men who had seen the light. Both had left Iowa in their teens, vowing never to return. But each came to the conclusion that the action was back home. The twenty-six-year-old was a commodities futures speculator who'd plowed some of his gains into a full-sized luxury sedan with a tiltable steering wheel in which he looked a little odd—as if both the car and the job would fit him better if he had either thirty pounds more paunch or thirty more years of age. A similar sense of the incongruous was offered by his friend, the corporate officer in a grain-trading outfit. He was twenty-five.

This new maturity is more obvious to regions flexing their new-found muscle   42
than it is to older power centers reluctant to think of the rest of the continent as anything but a collection of branch offices.

"The [rest of the United States] is lagging so far behind us," says Walter Hoadley,   43
chief economist of the Bank of America, the major financial institution of the West. "We're backing into a tremendous period of growth in the nineteen eighties out

here. The West has a lot of potential resources and a dynamism which simply doesn't exist back east."

Similarly, the 1980s will be the decade in which majority control of the U.S.   44
House of Representatives will pass out of the hands of New England, the Foundry, and the Breadbasket. Massive losses of population in old Foundry cities such as the Bronx will see New York state alone lose five seats, while Dixie, MexAmerica, Ecotopia, the Empty Quarter, and the Islands gain seventeen.

When the site of what is now Washington, D.C., was selected for the capital of the   45
fledgling Republic in 1790, it was virtually on top of the United States population center, then just east of Baltimore. In the 1980s, the population center of the United States will move west of the Mississippi River for the first time.

There are three major results of these changes.   46

- The more self-assured each of these Nine Nations becomes, the less willing it is to be dictated to by outsiders who show no interest in sharing—or even understanding—local values. This hinders a search for continentwide answers to political questions.
- As resources and opportunities are dispersed, each nation, at least theoretically, becomes increasingly capable of solving its own problems at its own level, although habit and institutions often do not cooperate.
- Increased sophistication may lead to the decline of marginal continental differences. (The classic southern drawl is on the wane, for example.) But it emphasizes the real, enduring, and basic economic and social differences of each region, manifested in attitudes toward everything from nuclear power to unions to abortion.

Recent public policy is replete with propositions that were paralyzed by their ini-   47
tiators' ignorance of these new implications about power.

Jimmy Carter's political weakness in the West, for an obvious example, was made   48
permanent in the first hundred days of his administration, when he promulgated his "hit list" of waterprojects that he did not feel to be cost-effective. As chief of staff Hamilton Jordan was later to admit candidly, in Dixie, "Water is just another word." It's something that floods your basement every spring, not the linchpin of your agricultural, industrial, or urban survival.

Foreign policy is affected, too. An ill-fated flap over an alleged Soviet combat   49
brigade in Cuba was stirred up in 1979 by a scholarly Idaho senator, chairman of the Senate Foreign Relations Committee Frank Church. He was desperately and unsuccessfully trying to counter a vigorous conservative re-election challenge that centered on one charge: that he had succumbed to the pressures of the eastern seaboard and had become "soft" and "liberal."

The new diversity affects financial thinking. Recently the "multi-tier" theory of   50
industrial performance has gained popularity. It demonstrates, for example, that recessions hurt the creators of expensive durable goods, like automobiles or steel, worse than they do the purveyors of energy, electronics, services, food, and ideas. This was a much-needed explanation of how the Foundry can be failing at the same time that the Breadbasket can expect continued stability, and MexAmerica, strong growth.

The more pressing the continental concern, the more abundant the regional   51 complications. Energy is the classic example. Long have the pundits deplored the seeming inability of North America to come up with an energy program. Unstinting was the derision heaped on Jimmy Carter's declaration of the "moral equivalent of war." Brief was the reign of Canadian prime minister Joe Clark, who called for austerity and a tax on gasoline of eighteen cents a gallon.

Yet the problem has not been a lack of energy plans. The problem has been their abundance. North America has nine energy programs up and functioning right now, each tailored to the demands of a particular nation.   52

New England, for example, is dedicated to austerity and conservation, which is appropriate for a nation marked by compact geography, good public transportation, and extremely limited resources.   53

By contrast, Québec's hydroelectric potential is so vast as to be inexhaustible. Québec is actively seeking out heavy energy demands, such as the manufacturing of aluminum products.   54

Dixie is more reliant on nuclear power plants than any other nation, which is a logical outgrowth of few choices coupled with an unquestioning commitment to growth.   55

Ecotopia, on the other hand, with abundant renewable-energy options and a jaundiced view of development, sees atomic energy as the poisoned fruit of a technology gone berserk.   56

The Empty Quarter, which is in the catbird's seat in terms of energy reserves, and is marked by enormous distances between everything, views conservation in the form of a fifty-five-mile-per-hour speed limit in the same light as Ecotopia views nukes—as self-evidently crazy.   57

MexAmerica, like the Empty Quarter in having significant energy deposits, is like the Foundry in having intractable pollution problems. Unlike any of the others, its growth is fueled by refugees who flee from the cost of heating a home through a northern winter.   58

The nation of the Islands is similarly filled with "snowbirds" escaping the chill, but unlike people in MexAmerica, few are asking, yet, where the energy to drive the air conditioners will come from.   59

Meanwhile, the Breadbasket carries on a lonely love affair with gasohol—a fuel partly distilled from grain—a course that every other nation is convinced will drive up food prices.   60

In this light, it's far less mysterious why, for example, there's a continental inability to agree on a plan so basic as standby gasoline rationing. It is difficult to imagine how, in the face of such diverse interests, coupons could be distributed in a fashion that would fairly distribute hardship.   61

More critically, unlike during World War II, it's impossible to imagine how a plan aimed at benefiting the industrial Northeast could be rammed down the throat of the rest of the continent.   62

"Partly, I think, our problems are insoluble unless we change the way we do things," says Jeff Faux, a Maine economist who has studied the plight of New England closely, but who, as codirector of the National Center for Economic Alternatives, a Washington, D.C., think tank, sees broader implications to the current federal system.   63

"Take Dickey-Lincoln, for example."   64

(Dickey-Lincoln is the name of a proposal by the U.S. Army Corps of Engineers 65
to dam a river in northern Maine to generate hydroelectricity. Opponents claim it
would ruin a pristine wilderness in order to produce an insignificant amount of energy at an astronomical cost.)

There've been analyses—and assume for a moment that they're right—that
the environmentalists have put forward, that say if you take the eight hundred
million or billion dollars they propose to put into Dickey-Lincoln, and used
that in a series of alternative energy projects—low-head hydro, small things,
solar, wood burning, insulation, the whole gamut of what we know—you
would produce more energy than with Dickey-Lincoln, more of it would be
baseload rather than peak power, you'd have less environmental damage, and
you'd create more jobs.

Just assume for a moment—assume—that that is right. The problem is
that we don't have that choice. The way the system comes down to the state of
Maine, and to New England, is that you've got a program that the Corps of
Engineers has, and it's willing to put a billion dollars into this. Yes or no. A billion dollars this way, or nothing.

Now there's an obvious problem there. The region cannot make a rational
decision on that basis. My point is that we're going to have public spending, no
matter what happens in the future. We ought to be thinking about this public
investment. Probably not just in energy alone, but in roads and in transportation and all the other major decisions, in a way that provides a region with the
flexibility to make the choices between Dickey-Lincoln and nuclear power and
an alternative. We need a framework of, okay, what are the region's needs for
the next twenty years, how are we going to supply those needs?

I mean, I am a person who feels that, yes, there *is* a position that says we
ought to have nuclear power in New England. I don't think Central Maine
Power has made the case for it, but clearly, given New England's situation, it is
not an unreasonable position. The case for Dickey-Lincoln, I think, is a reasonable case. And the case that the environmentalists make, to say now wait a
minute, if you did it this way you could have more jobs and all that, is a reasonable position.

The problem is that there is no forum for the region in which we say, all
right, add up all the social costs and the social benefits, and recognize that the
public sector is going to put money into whatever it is—nuclear power doesn't
stand on its own any more than Dickey-Lincoln or some of these other things.
Okay, what is the best decision we can make?

But what we have is the corps saying, hey, you want this program? Yes or
no. I mean, a *billion* dollars. Well hell, in a poor state . . .

This sense of regional frustration is hardly limited to old New England. Utah, 66
with its immense coal reserves, is not a poor state. And Kent Briggs, the administrative assistant to the governor of Utah, and the son of an Idaho reclamation farmer,
is by no means either a bleeding-heart environmentalist or an opponent of industrialization. Yet he, too, feels chafed by shortsighted federal policies devised far away
that block local control over the majority of Utah's land.

"We see the Yankees putting restrictions on our development and continuing 67 colonial shackles," he says. "My vision is that we might need a new western nation from the Mackenzie River to the Rio Grande."

Whether or not Briggs is correct about what his part of the continent should, in the future, do, the fact is that the various portions of the continent are, right now, bringing a new sense of sovereignty to the way they view the world. The ultimate demonstration is that most North Americans, at some level of consciousness, feel a dual citizenship. While their passports may say "United States" or "Mexico" or "Canada," they are also bound to another nation—the heartland of the Breadbasket or the row houses of the Foundry.   68

The power of these ties to the Nine Nations is confirmed by what would appear to be a contradiction: the extraordinary mobility of citizens who move from one nation to another. These migrants retain some of their old trappings, but they push to embrace the styles and attitudes of their new nation.   69

The standard amusement among MexAmerican Anglos is watching newcomers turn "mellow"—beguiled by the relentless sun despite their vows never to succumb.   70

Carolina developers become almost a little apologetic about the deep partisanship for Dixie displayed by European industrialists transferred there. It's hardly uncommon to hear stories of their later reluctance to accept a posting to other parts of North America, or even back to the home office.   71

With never-ceasing amazement do natives of Idaho or Wyoming watch how quickly a newcomer picks up the habit of referring, with suspicion, to all nonresidents of the region as "them."   72

To New Englanders, it's tiresomely obvious that one of the region's employment problems stems from the many outlanders who first come to the region just to get four years of college, but then stay—even accepting starvation wages—because they can no longer conceive of living somewhere less "civilized."   73

The Rand McNally Road Atlas is not a perennial paperback best seller because North Americans think they are all the same. Travel is the great North American pastime because of our enduring diversity. We look forward to picking up our belongings and taking a new job in a different region out of a sense of adventure. It allows us to try on different values, different senses of the pace at which life should be lived, different attitudes about art, food, and ethnic origin, different relationships to nature. It allows us to discover, with some perspective, what empty place there is that only Georgia, say, can fill.   74

A newspaper reporter told me of the time he gave up the prestige of being a Washington correspondent in order to return to the quieter life of the medium-sized western paper from which he had originally come.   75

The drive across the continent for him was a long and silent one. As he drove through Pennsylvania, Illinois, Nebraska, he hardly noticed his surroundings, wondering whether the choice he had made was right.   76

He told me he remembered with great clarity finally losing his indecision on Interstate 80, not far from Cheyenne, Wyoming, as the flatlands gave way to the mountains and their small towns.   77

It was there, he said, that suddenly a knot disappeared from his stomach, a knot he hadn't known was there. It was there that he discovered a feeling of familiarity with the colors, the horizon, the names of the towns.   78

Every North American knows a place like that, a place where, on your way back   79 from your wanderings, surroundings stop feeling threatening, confusing, or strange.

Ultimately, that's the reason we are Nine Nations. When you're from one, and you're in it, you know you're home.

80

Working with the Text

1. Garreau begins his essay by saying, "[F]orget about" the traditional borders that divide the United States; forget about the borders between the United States and Mexico or Canada; forget about the borders between states, counties, or regions. Instead, he suggests, focus on "the way North America really works." What are those ways, according to Garreau? In a paper examine the forces and influences that Garreau thinks form the real borders and boundaries. If not state lines and national boundaries, then what? What holds Garreau's regions (or "nations") together? What distinguishes them? How do the borders that Garreau draws influence your thinking about borders generally?

2. Which of Garreau's nine nations do you live in or come from? Do you agree with his assessment of the region in which you live? Do you agree with his generalizations about other regions? Which of his assertions ring true for you, and which do not?

3. What are we to make of Garreau's use of the word *nations*? He could have used a different word like *regions* or *sections*. What is the force of using the term *nation* to describe his nine "units"? Compare his use of the word *nation* to Benedict Anderson's definition of it in the previous chapter.

4. Garreau concludes by saying that if you're from the United States, one of these nine nations probably feels like home to you. To what extent is your feeling of belonging tied to your sense of belonging to one of Garreau's nations (or to a regional place) as opposed to belonging to the nation of the United States? Do you in any way feel a sense of dual citizenship? If you are not originally from the United States (or have lived outside of it for a length of time), what is your response to Garreau's assertions? What defines your sense of belonging to a region as opposed to the nation as a whole?

THE '90S CULTURE OF XENOPHOBIA: BEYOND THE TORTILLA CURTAIN

GUILLERMO GÓMEZ-PEÑA

■ Born in Mexico City in 1955, Guillermo Gómez-Peña later immigrated to California and earned an M.F.A. degree from the California Institute of the Arts. An interdisciplinary writer, artist, and performer, Gómez-Peña has created a number of solo theater pieces which he has performed throughout the United States and abroad, including *Border Brujo*, which was later turned into a film. He has also created the experimental radio works *Norte/Sur* and *Border Notebooks* and for five years edited the journal *Broken Line/La Linea Quebrada*. A 1991 McArthur fellow, Gómez-Peña has published *Warrior for Gringostroika: Essays, Performance Texts, and Poetry* (1993); *The New World Border: Prophesies, Poems, and Loqueras for the End of the Century* (1996); and *Temple of Confessions: Mexican Beasts and Living Santos* (1997), which includes an audio compact disk. In the following selection from *The New World Border,* Gómez-Peña argues that current anti-immigration sentiments, particularly those directed at Mexicans and Latinos, are ultimately motivated by xenophobia.

Americans never remember; Mexicans never forget.

—popular Mexican saying

THE CAPITAL OF THE AMERICAN CRISIS

From 1978 to 1991, I lived and worked in and among the cities of Tijuana, San Diego, and Los Angeles. Like hundreds of thousands of Mexicans living at the border, I was a binational commuter. I crossed that dangerous border regularly, by plane, by car, and on foot. The border became my home, my base of operations, and my laboratory for social and artistic experimentation. My art, my dreams, my family and friends, and my psyche were literally and conceptually divided by the border. But the border was not a straight line; it was more like a Möbius strip. No matter where I was, I was always on "the other side," feeling ruptured and incomplete, ever longing for my other selves, my other home and tribe.

Thanks to my Chicano colleagues and border accomplices, I learned to perceive California as an extension of Mexico; and the city of Los Angeles as the northernmost barrio of Mexico City. And despite many Californians' denial of their state's Mexican past and their bittersweet relationship with contemporary Mexicans, I never quite felt like an immigrant. As a mestizo with a thick accent and an even thicker mustache, I knew I wasn't exactly welcome, but I also knew that millions of Latinos, "legal" and "illegal," Mexican or not, shared that border experience with me.

Then in 1991, I moved to New York City, and my umbilical cord was finally snapped. For the first time in my life, I felt like a true immigrant. From my Brooklyn apartment, Mexico and Chicanolandia seemed a million light years away. (The republic of Mexa York was still a project yet to be realized.)

I decided to return to Southern Califas in 1993. Since the riots, Los Angeles had become the epicenter of America's social, racial, and cultural crisis. It was, unwillingly, the capital of a growing Third World within the shrinking First World. I wanted to be both a witness and a chronicler of this wonderful madness.

I found a city at war with itself; a city gravely punished by natural and social forces; a city whose experience is a concentrated version of the crises confronting the entire country. Its political structures are dysfunctional and its economy is in shambles; cutbacks in the defense budget have resulted in increased unemployment; and racial tensions are the focus of daily news reports. Crime rates and poverty levels can be compared with those of any Third World city. All this coincides with an unprecedented crisis of national identity: post–Cold War America is having a very hard time shedding its imperial nostalgia, embracing its multiracial soul, and accepting its new status as the first "developed" country to become a member of the Third World.

Perhaps what scared me most was to realize who was being blamed for all the turmoil. The Mexican/Latino immigrant community was the scapegoat, singled out by politicians (both Republicans and Democrats), fanatic citizen groups like SOS [Save Our State], and by sectors of the mainstream media as the main cause of California's social ills. The racist Proposition 187, which denies nonemergency medical services and education to "illegal aliens," passed with 60 percent of the vote on November 8, 1994, turning every doctor, nurse, pharmacist, policeman, schoolteacher and "concerned citizen" into a de facto border patrolman. Furthermore, the very same people who supported Prop. 187 (which is now being challenged in the courts) also opposed women's and gay rights, affirmative action, bilingual education, freedom of speech, and the existence of the National Endowment for the Arts and the Corporation for Public Broadcasting. Why? What does this all mean? What are we all losing?

> You are the posse and 187 is the rope.
>
> —Orange County rightwinger

GODZILLA WITH A MARIACHI HAT

Despite the fact that the United States has been a nation of immigrants and border crossers ever since its violent foundation, nativism has periodically reared its head. American identity has historically depended on opposing an "other," be it cultural, racial, or ideological. Americans need enemies against whom to define their personal and national boundaries. From the original indigenous inhabitants of this continent to the former Soviets, an evil "other" has always been stalking and ready to strike.

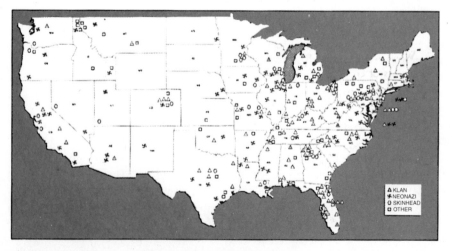

Documented hate groups in the United States in 1994.
From the *Klanwatch Intelligence Report*, March 1995

Now, it is the "illegal aliens" who are to take the blame for everything that American citizens and their incompetent politicians have been unable (or unwilling) to solve. Undocumented immigrants are being stripped of their humanity and individuality, becoming blank screens for the projection of Americans' fear, anxiety, and rage. In California and other southwestern states, this threatening otherness comes in a huge package that includes Mexicans, Latinos (including U.S.-born Latinos), Mexican-looking people (whatever this means), Mexican and Chicano culture, and the Spanish language. This horrible menace is here, inside of "our" country, within "our" borders, not only threatening "our" jobs and neighborhoods, but also "our" ideals of justice and order.

Anti-immigration has become a galvanizing force behind the resurgence of a phony form of patriotism. "True" Americans (as opposed to the dark-skinned invaders) perceive themselves as the victims of immigration: "If it wasn't for *them*, everything would be all right." Of all the current arguments against immigration, perhaps the one most often used is that the United States is not as able to absorb immigrants as it was in the past; the Statue of Liberty is exhausted, and she needs a break. What is not stated openly is that she needs a break mainly from immigrants of color; the most "different" ones; those who are less willing or able to assimilate. Sadly, sectors of the Latino and African American communities also subscribe to these bizarre nativist beliefs, forgetting that they themselves are perceived as part of the problem. In the eyes of the xenophobes, any person with visibly different features, skin color, accent, clothes, or social or sexual behavior is an alien.

> *Illegal aliens are a category of criminal, not a category of ethnic group.*
>
> —Proposition 187 advocate Ron Prince

THE BLURRING OF THE BORDER

Fear is always at the core of xenophobia. This fear is particularly disturbing when directed at the most vulnerable victims: migrant workers. They become the "invaders" from the South, the human incarnation of the Mexican fly, subhuman "wetbacks," the "alien" from another (cultural) planet. They are accused of stealing "our jobs," of shrinking "our budget," of taking advantage of the welfare system, of not paying taxes, and of bringing disease, drugs, street violence, foreign thoughts, pagan rites, primitive customs, and alien sounds. Their indigenous features and rough clothes conjure images of an unpleasant pre-European American past, and of the mythical lands to the south immersed in poverty and political turmoil, where innocent gringos could be attacked for no apparent reason. Yet, these invaders no longer inhabit the remote past, some banana republic, or a Hollywood film. They actually live down the block, and their children attend the same schools as the Anglo kids.

Nothing is scarier than the blurring of the border between them and us; between the Dantesque South and the prosperous North; between paganism and Christianity. For many Americans, the border has failed to stop chaos and crisis from creeping in (the origin of crisis and chaos is somehow always located outside). Their worst nightmare is finally coming true: The United States is no longer a fictional extension of Europe, or the wholesome suburb imagined by the screenwriter of *Lassie*. It is rapidly becoming a huge border zone, a hybrid society, a mestizo race, and worst of all, this process seems to be irreversible. America shrinks day by day, as the pungent smell of enchiladas fills the air and the volume of quebradita music rises.

Both the anti-immigration activists and the conservative media have utilized ex- 12
tremely charged metaphors to describe this process of "Mexicanization." It is described as a Christian nightmare ("hell at our doorsteps"); a natural disaster ("the brown wave"); a fatal disease or an incurable virus; a form of demographic rape; a cultural invasion; or the scary beginning of a process of secession or "Quebequization" of the entire Southwest.

Paradoxically, the country allegedly responsible for all of these anxieties is now 13
an intimate business partner of the United States. But NAFTA only regulates the exchange of consumer products; human beings are not part of the deal. Our new economic community advocates open markets and closed borders, and as NAFTA goes into effect, the Tortilla Curtain is being replaced by a metallic wall that resembles the one that "fell" in Berlin.

> *If you catch 'em [Mexicans], skin 'em and fry 'em yourself.*
>
> —Harold Ezell, head of SOS and
>   Western Regional Commissioner of the INS

THE CONTRADICTIONS OF UTOPIA

Many Americans easily forget that thanks to "illegal" Mexicans hired by other Amer- 14
icans, the food, garment, tourist, and construction industries of California and the rest of the Southwest survive. They forget that the strawberries, apples, grapes, oranges, tomatoes, lettuce, and avocadoes that they eat were harvested, prepared, and served by Mexican hands. And that these very same "illegal" hands clean up after them in restaurants and bars, fix their broken cars, paint and mop their homes, and manicure their gardens. They also forget that their babies and elderly are being cared for by Mexican nannies. The list of underpaid contributions by "illegal aliens" is so long that the lifestyle of many Americans couldn't possibly be sustained without them. Yet the Americans who are against illegal immigration prefer to believe that their cities and neighborhoods are less safe, and that their cultural and educational institutions have lowered their standards since we were allowed in.

What begins as inflammatory rhetoric eventually becomes accepted dictum, jus- 15
tifying racial violence against suspected illegal immigrants. What Operation Gatekeeper, Proposition 187, and SOS have done is to send a very frightening message to society: The governor is behind you; let those "aliens" have it. Since they are here "illegally," they are expendable. Since they have no "legal residency," they lack both human and civil rights. To hurt, attack, or offend a faceless and nameless "criminal" doesn't seem to have any legal or moral implications. Precisely because of their undocumented condition, the "aliens" are not protected if they talk back, or decide to organize politically. If they demonstrate or engage in direct political actions, or if they report a crime to the police, they risk deportation. When the police or the border patrol abuse their human rights, there is nowhere to go for help. They are the easy targets of state violence, economic exploitation, and civilian vigilantism. And

quite often, neither the police nor the citizenry can differentiate between an "illegal alien" and a U.S.-born Latino.

SUICIDAL MEASURES AND ENLIGHTENED PROPOSALS

Authoritarian solutions to "the problem" of immigration can only make things worse. Further militarizing the border while dismantling the social, medical, and educational support systems that serve the immigrant population will only worsen social tensions. Denying medical services to undocumented immigrants will result in more disease and more teenage pregnancy. Throwing 300,000 kids out of the schools and into the streets will only contribute to crime and social disintegration. Not only will these proposals backfire, but they will also contribute to a growing nationalism in the Chicano/Latino communities, repoliticizing entire communities that were dormant in the past decade—any community under attack tends to be more defiant. 16

So, what to do with "the problem" of immigration? First of all, we need to stop characterizing it as a unilateral "problem." Let's be honest: The end of the century appears scary to both Anglos and Latinos; to legal and illegal immigrants. Both sides feel threatened, uprooted, and displaced, to different degrees and for different reasons. We all fear deep inside that there won't be enough jobs, food, air, and housing for everybody. Yet we cannot deny the processes of interdependence that define our contemporary experience as North Americans. In a post-NAFTA/post–Cold War America, the binary models of us/them, North/South, and Third World/First World are no longer useful in understanding our complicated border dynamics, our transnational identities and our multiracial communities. 17

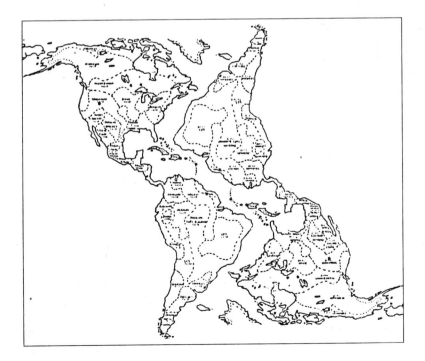

It is time to face the facts: Anglos won't go back to Europe, and Mexicans and   18
Latinos (legal or illegal) won't go back to Latin America. We are all here to stay. For
better or for worse, our destinies and aspirations are in one another's hands. For me,
the only solution lies in a paradigm shift: the recognition that we all are the protag-
onists in the creation of a new cultural topography and a new social order, one in
which we all are "others," and we need the other "others" to exist. Hybridity is no
longer up for discussion. It is a demographic, racial, social, and cultural fact.

The real tasks ahead of us are to embrace more fluid and tolerant notions of per-   19
sonal and national identity, and to develop models of peaceful coexistence and mul-
tilateral cooperation across nationality, race, gender, and religion. To attain this,
rather than more border patrols, border walls, and punitive laws, we need more and
better information about one another. Culture and education are at the core of the
solution. We need to learn each others' languages, histories, art, and cultural traditions. We need to educate our children and teenagers about the dangers of racism
and the complexities of living in a multiracial, borderless society—the inevitable society of the next century.

Working with the Text

1. Do you agree with Gómez-Peña's assertion that "American identity has
historically depended on opposing an 'other,' be it cultural, racial, or ideological," that "Americans need enemies against whom to define their personal
and national boundaries"? In what ways do you think that recent efforts to
curb illegal immigration, and negative responses to immigration in general,
are tied to issues of personal and national identity?

2. How are economics and culture interrelated in Gómez-Peña's discussion
of the border? What are the ironies he points out regarding America's growing disdain for "illegal aliens"? In what ways is the "lifestyle of many Americans" dependent on an underpaid underclass? Do you agree that this situation
is ironic?

3. In speaking about such legislative restrictions as Proposition 187, Gómez-
Peña claims, "Not only will these proposals backfire, but they will also contribute
to a growing nationalism in the Chicano/Latino communities, repoliticizing
entire communities that were dormant in the past decade—any community
under attack tends to be more defiant." In that claim, how is he using the term
nationalism? Are the terms *nation* and *community* synonymous in his usage?
How are they defined? Compare his usage of *nationalism* to Benjamin Barber's usage of the word in the essay "Jihad vs. McWorld" later in this chapter.
Do the two men use the word *nationalism* in the same way?

4. What new way of seeing does Gómez-Peña propose at the end of the essay?
What might it mean to grapple with the "processes of interdependence that
define our contemporary experience as North Americans," as he puts it at the
end of the essay? To what extent do you agree that the "inevitable society of
the next century" will be a "multiracial, borderless" one? How might his proposals practically be put into effect? Do you think that his proposals would actually serve the purposes that he advocates?

WHO AND WHAT IS AMERICAN?

LEWIS LAPHAM

■ Born in San Francisco in 1935, Lewis Lapham attended Yale and later worked as a reporter for a variety of newspapers and magazines. Since 1971, he has been the editor of *Harper's* magazine, which publishes his monthly column of ideas. One of the best-known journalists and social critics in America, Lapham has written on topics ranging from environmentalism and conservation, to education, politics, class relations, and race relations. His books include *Money and Class in America* (1988), *Imperial Masquerade* (1990), and *Hotel America: Scenes in the Lobby at the Fin-de-Siècle* (1995). In the following 1992 essay, Lapham argues that instead of focusing on a kind of identity politics based on difference, Americans should be raising serious questions about the forces that bind them together.

There may not be an American character, but there is the emotion of being American. It has many resemblances to the emotion of being Russian—that feeling of nostalgia for some undetermined future when man will have improved himself beyond recognition and when all will be well.

—V. S. Pritchett

Were I to believe what I read in the papers, I would find it easy to think that I no longer can identify myself simply as an American. The noun apparently means nothing unless it is dressed up with at least one modifying adjective. As a plain American I have neither voice nor authentic proofs of existence. I acquire a presence only as an old American, a female American, a white American, a rich American, a black American, a gay American, a poor American, a native American, a dead American. The subordination of the noun to the adjectives makes a mockery of both the American premise and the democratic spirit, but it serves the purposes of the politicians as well as the news media, and throughout the rest of this election year I expect the political campaigns to pitch their tents and slogans on the frontiers of race and class. For every benign us, the candidates will find a malignant them; for every neighboring we (no matter how eccentric or small in number), a distant and devouring they. The strategies of division sell newspapers and summon votes, and to the man who would be king (or president or governor) the popular hatred of government matters less than the atmosphere of resentment in which the people fear and distrust one another.

Democratic politics trades in only two markets—the market in expectation and the market in blame. A collapse in the former engenders a boom in the latter. Something goes wrong in the news—a bank swindle of genuinely spectacular size, a series of killings in Milwaukee, another disastrous assessment of the nation's schools—and suddenly the air is loud with questions about the paradox of the American character or the Puritan subtexts of the American soul. The questions arise from every quarter of the political compass—from English professors and political consultants as well as from actors, corporate vice presidents, and advertising salesmen—and the conversation is seldom polite. Too many of the people present no longer can pay the bills, and a stray remark about acid rain or a third-grade textbook can escalate within a matter of minutes into an exchange of insults. Somebody calls Jesse Helms a fascist, and somebody else says that he is sick and tired of paying ransom money to a lot of welfare criminals. People drink too much and stay too late, their voices choked with anecdote and rage, their lexicons of historical reference so passionately confused that both Jefferson and Lincoln find themselves doing thirty-second commercials for racial quotas, a capital gains tax, and the Persian Gulf War.

The failures in the nation's economy have marked up the prices for obvious villains, and if I had a talent for merchandising I would go into the business of making dolls (black dolls, white dolls, red-necked dolls, feminist dolls, congressional dolls) that each of the candidates could distribute at fund-raising events with a supply of color-coordinated pins. Trying out their invective in the pre-season campaigns, the politicians as early as last October were attributing the cause of all our sorrows to any faction, interest, or minority that could excite in their audiences the passions of a beloved prejudice. David Duke in Louisiana denounced the subsidized beggars (i.e., black people) who had robbed the state of its birthright. At a partisan theatrical staged by the Democratic Party in New Hampshire, Senator Tom Harkin reviled the conspiracy of Republican money. President Bush went to Houston, Texas, to point a trembling and petulant finger at the United States Congress. If the country's domestic affairs had been left to him, the President said, everybody would be as prosperous and smug as Senator Phil Gramm, but the liberals in Congress (blind as mollusks and selfish as eels) had wrecked the voyage of boundless opportunity.

The politicians follow the trends, and apparently they have been told by their handlers to practice the arts of the demagogue. Certainly I cannot remember an election year in which the political discourse—among newspaper editorialists and the single-issue lobbies as well as the candidates—relied so unashamedly on pitting rich against poor, black against white, male against female, city against suburb, young against old. Every public event in New York City—whether academic appointment, traffic delay, or homicide—lends itself to both a black and a white interpretation of the news. The arguments in the arenas of cultural opinion echo the same bitter refrain. The ceaseless quarrels about the canon of preferred texts (about Columbus the Bad and Columbus the Good, about the chosen company of the politically correct, about the ice people and the sun people) pick at the scab of the same questions. Who and what is an American? How and where do we find an identity that is something other than a fright mask? When using the collective national pronoun ("we the people," "we happy few," etc.) whom do we invite into the club of the we?

Maybe the confusion is a corollary to the end of the Cold War. The image of the Soviet Union as monolithic evil held in place the image of the United States as monolithic virtue. Break the circuit of energy transferred between negative and positive poles, and the two empires dissolve into the waving of sectional or nationalist flags. Lacking the reassurance of a foreign demon, we search our own neighborhoods for fiends of convincing malevolence and size.

The search is a boon for the bearers of false witness and the builders of prisons. Because it's so easy to dwell on our differences, even a child of nine can write a Sunday newspaper sermon about the centrifugal forces that drive the society apart. The more difficult and urgent questions have to do with the centripetal forces that bind us together. What traits of character or temperament do we hold in common? Why is it that I can meet a black man in a street or a Hispanic woman on a train and imagine that he and I, or she and I, share an allied hope and a joint purpose? That last question is as American as it is rhetorical, and a Belgian would think it the work of a dreaming imbecile.

What we share is a unified field of emotion, but if we mistake the sources of our energy and courage (i.e., if we think that our uniqueness as Americans rests with the adjectives instead of the noun) then we can be rounded up in categories and sold the slogan of the week for the fear of the month. Political campaigns deal in the commodity of votes, and from now until November I expect that all of them will divide the American promise into its lesser but more marketable properties. For reasons of their own convenience, the sponsors of political campaigns (Democratic, environmental, racial, Republican, sexual, or military-industrial) promote more or less the same false constructions of the American purpose and identity. As follows: 7

That the American achieves visible and specific meaning only by reason of his or her association with the political guilds of race, gender, age, ancestry, or social class. 8

The assumption is as elitist as the view that only a woman endowed with an income of $1 million a year can truly appreciate the beauty of money and the music of Cole Porter. Comparable theories of grace encourage the belief that only black people can know or teach black history, that no white man can play jazz piano, that blonds have a better time, and that Jews can't play basketball. 9

America was founded on precisely the opposite premise. We were always about becoming, not being; about the prospects for the future, not about the inheritance of the past. The man who rests his case on his color, like the woman who defines herself as a bright cloud of sensibility beyond the understanding of merely mortal men, makes a claim to special privilege not unlike the divine right of kings. The pretensions might buttress the cathedrals of our self-esteem, but they run counter to the lessons of our history. 10

We are a nation of parvenus, all bound to the hopes of tomorrow, or next week, or next year. John Quincy Adams put it plainly in a letter to a German correspondent in the 1820s who had written on behalf of several prospective émigrés to ask about the requirements for their success in the New World. "They must cast off the European skin, never to resume it," Adams said. "They must look forward to their posterity rather than backward to their ancestors." 11

We were always a mixed and piebald company, even on the seventeenth-century colonial seaboard, and we accepted our racial or cultural differences as the odds that we were obliged to overcome or correct. When John Charles Frémont (a.k.a. The Pathfinder) first descended into California from the East in 1843, he remarked on the polyglot character of the expedition accompanying him south into the San Joaquin Valley: 12

"Our cavalcade made a strange and grotesque appearance, and it was impossible to avoid reflecting upon our position and composition in this remote solitude . . . still forced on south by a desert on one hand and a mountain range on the other; guided by a civilized Indian, attended by two wild ones from the Sierra; a Chinook from the Columbia; and our own mixture of American, French, German—all armed; four or five languages heard at once; about a hundred horses and mules, 13

half-wild; American, Spanish and Indian dresses and equipments intermingled—
such was our composition."

The theme of metamorphosis recurs throughout the whole chronicle of Ameri-   14
can biography. Men and women start out in one place and end up in another, never
quite knowing how they got there, perpetually expecting the unexpected, drifting
across the ocean or the plains until they lodge against a marriage, a land deal, a public office, or a jail. Speaking to the improvised character of the American experience,
Daniel Boorstin, the historian and former Librarian of Congress, also summed up
the case against the arithmetic of the political pollster's zip codes: "No prudent man
dared to be too certain of exactly who he was or what he was about; everyone had to
be prepared to become someone else. To be ready for such perilous transmigrations
was to become an American."

That the American people aspire to become more nearly alike.   15

The hope is that of the ad salesman and the prison warden, but it has become de-   16
pressingly familiar among the managers of political campaigns. Apparently they
think that no matter how different the native songs and dances in different parts of
the country, all the tribes and factions want the same beads, the same trinkets, the
same prizes. As I listen to operatives from Washington talk about their prospects in
the Iowa or New Hampshire primary, I understand that they have in mind the figure of a perfect or ideal American whom everybody in the country would wish to
resemble if only everybody could afford to dress like the dummies in the windows
of Bloomingdale's or Saks Fifth Avenue. The public opinion polls frame questions in
the alphabet of name recognitions and standard brands. The simplicity of the results supports the belief that the American citizen or the American family can be
construed as a product, and that with only a little more time and a little more
money for research and development all of us will conform to the preferred images
seen in a commercial for Miller beer.

The apologists for the theory of the uniform American success sometimes pre-   17
sent the example of Abraham Lincoln, and as I listen to their sentimental after-
dinner speeches about the poor country grown to greatness, I often wonder what
they would say if they had met the man instead of the statue. Throughout most of
his life Lincoln displayed the character of a man destined for failure—a man who
drank too much and told too many jokes (most of them in bad taste), who was habitually late for meetings and always borrowing money, who never seized a business
opportunity and missed his own wedding.

The spirit of liberty is never far from anarchy, and the ur-American is apt to look   18
a good deal more like one of the contestants on *Let's Make a Deal* (i.e., somebody
dressed like Madonna, or Wyatt Earp, or a giant iguana) than any of the yachtsmen
standing around on the dock of Kennebunkport. If America is about nothing else, it
is about the invention of the self. Because we have little use for history, and because
we refuse the comforts of a society established on the blueprint of class privilege, we
find ourselves set adrift at birth in an existential void, inheriting nothing except the
obligation to construct a plausible self, to build a raft of identity on which (with a
few grains of luck and a cheap bank loan) maybe we can float south to Memphis or
the imaginary islands of the blessed. We set ourselves the tasks of making and re-

making our destinies with whatever lumber we happen to find lying around on the banks of the Snake or Pecos River.

Who else is the American hero if not a wandering pilgrim who goes forth on a perpetual quest? Melville sent Ahab across the world's oceans in search of a fabulous beast, and Thoreau followed the unicorn of his conscience into the silence of the Maine woods. Between them they marked out the trail of American literature as well as the lines of speculation in American real estate. To a greater or a lesser extent, we are all confidence men, actors playing the characters of our own invention and hoping that the audience—fortunately consisting of impostors as fanciful or synthetic as ourselves—will accept the performance at par value and suspend the judgments of ridicule.   19

The settled peoples of the earth seldom recognize the American as both a chronic revolutionary and a born pilgrim. The American is always on the way to someplace else (i.e., toward some undetermined future in which all will be well), and when he meets a stranger on the road he begins at once to recite the summary of the story so far—his youth and early sorrows, the sequence of his exits and entrances, his last divorce and his next marriage, the point of his financial departure and the estimated time of his spiritual arrival, the bad news noted and accounted for, the good news still to come. Invariably it is a pilgrim's tale, and the narrator, being American, assumes that he is addressing a fellow pilgrim. He means to exchange notes and compare maps. His newfound companion might be bound toward a completely different dream of Eden (a boat marina in Naples, Florida, instead of a garden in Vermont; a career as a Broadway dancer as opposed to the vice presidency of the Wells Fargo bank), but the destination doesn't matter as much as the common hope of coming safely home to the land of the heart's desire. For the time being, and until something better turns up, we find ourselves embarked on the same voyage, gazing west into the same blue distance.   20

That the American people share a common code of moral behavior and subscribe to identical theories of the true, the good, and the beautiful.   21

Senator Jesse Helms would like to think so, and so would the enforcers of ideological discipline on the vocabulary of the doctrinaire left. The country swarms with people making rules about what we can say or read or study or smoke, and they imagine that we should be grateful for the moral guidelines (market-tested and government-inspected) imposed (for our own good) by a centralized bureau of temporal health and spiritual safety. The would-be reformers of the national character confuse the American sense of equality with the rule of conformity that governs a police state. It isn't that we believe that every American is as perceptive or as accomplished as any other, but we insist on the preservation of a decent and mutual respect across the lines of age, race, gender, and social class. No citizen is allowed to use another citizen as if he or she were a means to an end; no master can treat his servant as if he or she were only a servant; no government can deal with the governed as if they were nothing more than a mob of votes. The American loathing for the arrogant or self-important man follows from the belief that all present have bet their fortunes (some of them bigger than others, and some of them counterfeit or stolen) on the same hypothesis.   22

The American premise is an existential one, and our moral code is political, its   23
object being to allow for the widest horizons of sight and the broadest range of expression. We protect the other person's liberty in the interest of protecting our own
and our virtues conform to the terms and conditions of an arduous and speculative
journey. If we look into even so coarse a mirror as the one held up to us by the situation comedies on prime-time television, we see that we value the companionable
virtues—helpfulness, forgiveness, kindliness, and, above all, tolerance.

The passenger standing next to me at the rail might be balancing a parrot on his   24
head, but that doesn't mean that he has invented a theory of the self any less im-
plausible than the one I ordered from a department-store catalogue or assembled
with the tag lines of a two-year college course on the great books of Western civilization. If the traveler at the port rail can balance a parrot on his head, then I can
continue my discussion with Madame Bovary and Mr. Pickwick, and the two gentlemen standing aft of the rum barrels can get on with the business of rigging the
price of rifles or barbed wire. The American equation rests on the habit of holding
our fellow citizens in thoughtful regard not because they are exceptional (or famous, or beautiful, or rich) but simply because they are our fellow citizens. If we
abandon the sense of mutual respect, we abandon the premise as well as the machinery of the American enterprise.

That the triumph of America corresponds to its prowess as a nation-state.   25

The pretension serves the purposes of the people who talk about "the national   26
security" and "the vital interest of the American people" when what they mean is the
power and privilege of government. The oligarchy resident in Washington assumes
that all Americans own the same property instead of taking part in the same idea,
that we share a joint geopolitical program instead of a common temperament and
habit of mind. Even so faithful a servant of the monied interests as Daniel Webster
understood the distinction: "The public happiness is to be the aggregate of individuals. Our system begins with the individual man."

The Constitution was made for the uses of the individual (an implement on the   27
order of a plow, an ax, or a surveyor's plumb line), and the institutions of American
government were meant to support the liberties of the people, not the ambitions of
the state. Given any ambiguity about the order of priority or precedence, it was the
law that had to give way to the citizen's freedom of thought and action, not the citizen's freedom of thought and action that had to give way to the law. The Bill of
Rights stresses the distinction in the two final amendments, the ninth ("The enu-
meration in the Constitution, of certain rights, shall not be construed to deny or
disparage others retained by the people") and the tenth ("The powers not delegated
to the United States by the Constitution, nor prohibited by it to the States, are reserved to the States, respectively, or to the people").

What joins the Americans one to another is not a common nationality, language,   28
race, or ancestry (all of which testify to the burdens of the past) but rather their
complicity in a shared work of the imagination. My love of country follows from my
love of its freedoms, not from my pride in its fleets or its armies or its gross national
product. Construed as a means and not an end, the Constitution stands as the
premise for a narrative rather than a plan for an invasion or a monument. The narrative was always plural. Not one story but many stories.

That it is easy to be an American.   29

I can understand why the politicians like to pretend that America is mostly about   30
going shopping, but I never know why anybody believes the ad copy. Grant the existential terms and conditions of the American enterprise (i.e., that we are all bound
to invent ourselves), and the position is both solitary and probably lost. I know a
good many people who would rather be British or Nigerian or Swiss.

Lately I've been reading the accounts of the nineteenth-century adventurers and   31
pioneers who traveled west from Missouri under circumstances almost always adverse. Most of them didn't find whatever it was they expected to find behind the
next range of mountains or around the next bend in the river. They were looking for
a garden in a country that was mostly desert, and the record of their passage is
largely one of sorrow and failure. Travelers making their way across the Great Plains
in the 1850s reported great numbers of dead horses and abandoned wagons on the
trail, the echo of the hopes that so recently preceded them lingering in an empty
chair or in the scent of flowers on a new grave.

Reading the diaries and letters, especially those of the women in the caravans, I   32
think of the would-be settlers lost in an immense wilderness, looking into the mirrors of their loneliness and measuring their capacity for self-knowledge against the
vastness of the wide and indifferent sky.

Too often we forget the proofs of our courage. If we wish to live in the state of   33
freedom that allows us to make and think and build, then we must accustom ourselves to the shadows on the walls and the wind in trees. The climate of anxiety is the
cost of doing business. Just as a monarchy places far fewer burdens on its subjects
than a democracy places on its citizens, so also bigotry is easier than tolerance.
When something goes wrong with the currency or the schools, it's always comforting to know that the faults can be easily found in something as obvious as a color, or
a number, or the sound of a strange language. The multiple adjectives qualifying the
American noun enrich the vocabulary of blame, and if the election year continues
as it has begun I expect that by next summer we will discover that it is not only
middle-aged Protestant males who have been making a wreck of the culture but also
(operating secretly and sometimes in disguise) adolescent, sallow, Buddhist females.

Among all the American political virtues, candor is probably the one most nec-   34
essary to the success of our mutual enterprise. Unless we try to tell each other the
truth about what we know and think and see (i.e., the story so far as it appears to the
travelers on the voyage out) we might as well amuse ourselves (for as long as somebody else allows us to do so) with fairy tales. The vitality of the American democracy always has rested on the capacity of its citizens to speak and think without cant.
As long ago as 1838, addressing the topic of *The American Democrat,* James Feni-
more Cooper argued that the word "American" was synonymous with the habit of
telling the truth: "By candor we are not to understand trifling and uncalled for ex-
positions of truth; but a sentiment that proves a conviction of the necessity of
speaking truth, when speaking at all; a contempt for all designing evasions of our
real opinions.

"In all the general concerns, the public has a right to be treated with candor.   35
Without this manly and truly republican quality . . . the institutions are converted
into a stupendous fraud."

If we indulge ourselves with evasions and the pleasure of telling lies, we speak to   36 our fears and our weaknesses instead of to our courage and our strength. We can speak plainly about our differences only if we know and value what we hold in common. Like the weather and third-rate journalism, bigotry in all its declensions is likely to be with us for a long time (certainly as long as the next hundred years), but unless we can draw distinctions and make jokes about our racial or cultural baggage, the work of our shared imagination must vanish in the mist of lies. The lies might win elections (or sell newspapers and economic theories) but they bind us to the theaters of wish and dream. If I must like or admire a fellow citizen for his or her costume of modifying adjectives (because he or she is black or gay or rich), then I might as well believe that the lost continent of Atlantis will rise next summer from the sea and that the Japanese will continue to make the payments—now and forever, world without end—on all our mortgages and battleships.

Among all the nations of the earth, America is the one that has come most triumphantly to terms with the mixtures of blood and caste, and maybe it is another of history's ironic jokes that we should wish to repudiate our talent for assimilation at precisely the moment in time when so many other nations in the world (in Africa and Western Europe as well as the Soviet Union) look to the promise of the American example. The jumble of confused or mistaken identities that was the story of nineteenth-century America has become the story of a late-twentieth-century world defined by a vast migration of peoples across seven continents and as many oceans. Why, then, do we lose confidence in ourselves and grow fearful of our mongrel freedoms? 37

The politician who would lift us to a more courageous understanding of ourselves might begin by saying that we are all, each and every one of us, as much at fault as anybody else, that no matter whom we blame for our troubles (whether George Bush, or Al Sharpton, or David Duke) or how pleasant the invective (racist, sexist, imperialist pig), we still have to rebuild our cities and revise our laws. We can do the work together, or we can stand around making strong statements about each other's clothes. 38

Working with the Text

1. Lapham claims, "The subordination of the noun [American] to the adjectives makes a mockery of both the American premise and the democratic spirit. . . ." Do you agree? Is modifying *American* with an adjective in front of it in the democratic spirit or in opposition to it? How could you defend or criticize this statement?

2. In paragraph 4, Lapham asks some big questions: "Who and what is an American? How and where do we find an identity that is something other than a fright mask? When using the collective national pronoun ('we the people,' 'we happy few,' etc.) whom do we invite into the club of the we?" Does he answer these questions in the course of the essay? How does he negotiate the central tension of his essay: the conflict between the desire for identity with the historical tendency of immigrants toward metamorphosis? Do you find his conclusions satisfying?

3. Do you think this is an optimistic or a pessimistic essay? If it is optimistic, where do you locate his reasons for being optimistic? Do you think he con-

siders the "shared work of the imagination" that holds Americans together a reality or an ideal? Does he characterize that "shared work" as a solution to the divisiveness of the politics of identity that are at the heart of his essay?

4. Working together, look at the list of "false constructions" that structures the middle of the essay. Do you agree that these are "false constructions"? Where do these constructions come from? Are they merely the inventions of politicians, as Lapham claims? Are they at all linked to American ideals?

A DIFFERENT MIRROR

RONALD TAKAKI

■ Historian Ronald Takaki was born in Honolulu in 1939. A graduate of the College of Wooster, he later earned his M.A. and Ph.D. at the University of California at Berkeley, where he is now a professor of history. He has frequently written on historical issues of race and multiculturalism. His works include *A Different Mirror: A History of Multicultural America* (1993); *The Asian-American Experience* (1994), a fourteen-volume history for young adult readers; and *Hiroshima: Why America Dropped the Atomic Bomb* (1995). He also edited the anthology *From Different Shores: Perspectives on Race and Ethnicity in America* (1994). In the following chapter from *A Different Mirror*, Takaki argues that it is time Americans started viewing their history through "a different mirror," one that can enable "the people of America's diverse groups . . . to see themselves and each other in our common past."

I had flown from San Francisco to Norfolk and was riding in a taxi to my hotel to attend a conference on multiculturalism. Hundreds of educators from across the country were meeting to discuss the need for greater cultural diversity in the curriculum. My driver and I chatted about the weather and the tourists. The sky was cloudy, and Virginia Beach was twenty minutes away. The rearview mirror reflected a white man in his forties. "How long have you been in this country?" he asked. "All my life," I replied, wincing. "I was born in the United States." With a strong southern drawl, he remarked: "I was wondering because your English is excellent!" Then, as I had many times before, I explained: "My grandfather came here from Japan in the 1880s. My family has been here, in America, for over a hundred years." He glanced at me in the mirror. Somehow I did not look "American" to him; my eyes and complexion looked foreign.

Suddenly, we both became uncomfortably conscious of a racial divide separating us. An awkward silence turned my gaze from the mirror to the passing landscape, the shore where the English and the Powhatan Indians first encountered each other. Our highway was on land that Sir Walter Raleigh had renamed "Virginia" in honor of Elizabeth I, the Virgin Queen. In the English cultural appropriation of America, the indigenous peoples themselves would become outsiders in their native land. Here, at the eastern edge of the continent, I mused, was the site of the beginning of multicultural America. Jamestown, the English settlement founded in 1607, was nearby: the first twenty Africans were brought here a year before the Pilgrims arrived at Plymouth Rock. Several hundred miles offshore was Bermuda, the "Bermoothes" where William Shakespeare's Prospero had landed and met the native Caliban in *The Tempest*. Earlier, another voyager had made an Atlantic crossing and unexpectedly bumped into some islands to the south. Thinking he had reached Asia, Christopher Columbus mistakenly identified one of the islands as "Cipango" (Japan). In the wake of the admiral, many peoples would come to America from different shores, not only from Europe but also Africa and Asia. One of them would be my grandfather. My mental wandering across terrain and time ended abruptly as we arrived at my destination. I said good-bye to my driver and went into the hotel, carrying a vivid reminder of why I was attending this conference.

Questions like the one my taxi driver asked me are always jarring, but I can under-   3
stand why he could not see me as an American. He had a narrow but widely shared sense of the past—a history that has viewed American as European in ancestry. "Race," Toni Morrison explained, has functioned as a "metaphor" necessary to the "construction of Americanness": in the creation of our national identity, "American" has been defined as "white."

But America has been racially diverse since our very beginning on the Virginia   4
shore, and this reality is increasingly becoming visible and ubiquitous. Currently, one-third of the American people do not trace their origins to Europe; in California, minorities are fast becoming a majority. They already predominate in major cities across the country—New York, Chicago, Atlanta, Detroit, Philadelphia, San Francisco, and Los Angeles.

This emerging demographic diversity has raised fundamental questions about   5
America's identity and culture. In 1990, *Time* published a cover story on "America's Changing Colors." "Someday soon," the magazine announced, "white Americans will become a minority group." How soon? By 2056, most Americans will trace their descent to "Africa, Asia, the Hispanic world, the Pacific Islands, Arabia—almost anywhere but white Europe." This dramatic change in our nation's ethnic composition is altering the way we think about ourselves. "The deeper significance of America's becoming a majority nonwhite society is what it means to the national psyche, to individuals' sense of themselves and their nation—their idea of what it is to be American."

Indeed, more than ever before, as we approach the time when whites become a   6
minority, many of us are perplexed about our national identity and our future as one people. This uncertainty has provoked Allan Bloom to reaffirm the preeminence of Western civilization. Author of *The Closing of the American Mind,* he has emerged as a leader of an intellectual backlash against cultural diversity. In his view, students entering the university are "uncivilized," and the university has the responsibility to "civilize" them. Bloom claims he knows what their "hungers" are and "what they can digest." Eating is one of his favorite metaphors. Noting the "large black presence" in major universities, he laments the "one failure" in race relations—black students have proven to be "indigestible." They do not "melt as have *all* other groups." The problem, he contends, is that "blacks have become blacks": they have become "ethnic." This separatism has been reinforced by an aca-

demic permissiveness that has befouled the curriculum with "Black Studies" along with "Learn Another Culture." The only solution, Bloom insists, is "the good old Great Books approach."

Similarly, E. D. Hirsch worries that America is becoming a "tower of Babel," and that this multiplicity of cultures is threatening to rend our social fabric. He, too, longs for a more cohesive culture and a more homogeneous America: "If we *had* to make a choice between the *one* and the *many,* most Americans would choose the principle of unity, since we cannot function as a nation without it." The way to correct this fragmentization, Hirsch argues, is to acculturate "disadvantaged children." What do they need to know? "Only by accumulating shared symbols, and the shared information that symbols represent," Hirsch answers, "can we learn to communicate effectively with one another in our national community." Though he concedes the value of multicultural education, he quickly dismisses it by insisting that it "should not be allowed to supplant or interfere with our schools' responsibility to ensure our children's mastery of American literate culture." In *Cultural Literacy: What Every American Needs to Know,* Hirsch offers a long list of terms that excludes much of the history of minority groups.

While Bloom and Hirsch are reacting defensively to what they regard as a vexatious balkanization of America, many other educators are responding to our diversity as an opportunity to open American minds. In 1990, the Task Force on Minorities for New York emphasized the importance of a culturally diverse education. "Essentially," the *New York Times* commented, "the issue is how to deal with both dimensions of the nation's motto: 'E pluribus unum'—'Out of many, one.'" Universities from New Hampshire to Berkeley have established American cultural diversity graduation requirements. "Every student needs to know," explained University of Wisconsin's chancellor Donna Shalala, "much more about the origins and history of the particular cultures which, as Americans, we will encounter during our lives." Even the University of Minnesota, located in a state that is 98 percent white, requires its students to take ethnic studies courses. Asked why multiculturalism is so important, Dean Fred Lukermann answered: As a national university, Minnesota has to offer a national curriculum—one that includes all of the peoples of America. He added that after graduation many students move to cities like Chicago and Los Angeles and thus need to know about racial diversity. Moreover, many educators stress, multiculturalism has an intellectual purpose. By allowing us to see events from the viewpoints of different groups, a multicultural curriculum enables us to reach toward a more comprehensive understanding of American history.

What is fueling this debate over our national identity and the content of our curriculum is America's intensifying racial crisis. The alarming signs and symptoms seem to be everywhere—the killing of Vincent Chin in Detroit, the black boycott of a Korean grocery store in Flatbush, the hysteria in Boston over the Carol Stuart murder, the battle between white sportsmen and Indians over tribal fishing rights in Wisconsin, the Jewish-black clashes in Brooklyn's Crown Heights, the black-Hispanic competition for jobs and educational resources in Dallas, which *Newsweek* described as "a conflict of the have-nots," and the Willie Horton campaign commercials, which widened the divide between the suburbs and the inner cities.

This reality of racial tension rudely woke America like a fire bell in the night on April 29, 1992. Immediately after four Los Angeles police officers were found not guilty of brutality against Rodney King, rage exploded in Los Angeles. Race relations reached a new nadir. During the nightmarish rampage, scores of people were killed, over two thousand injured, twelve thousand arrested, and almost a billion dollars' worth of property destroyed. The live televised images mesmerized America. The rioting and the murderous melee on the streets resembled the fighting in Beirut and the West Bank. The thousands of fires burning out of control and the dark smoke filling the skies brought back images of the burning oil fields of Kuwait during Desert Storm. Entire sections of Los Angeles looked like a bombed city. "Is this America?" many shocked viewers asked. "Please, can we get along here," pleaded Rodney King, calling for calm. "We all can get along. I mean, we're all stuck here for a while. Let's try to work it out."

But how should "we" be defined? Who are the people "stuck here" in America?   11
One of the lessons of the Los Angeles explosion is the recognition of the fact that we are a multiracial society and that race can no longer be defined in the binary terms of white and black. "We" will have to include Hispanics and Asians. While blacks currently constitute 13 percent of the Los Angeles population, Hispanics represent 40 percent. The 1990 census revealed that South Central Los Angeles, which was predominantly black in 1965 when the Watts rebellion occurred, is now 45 percent Hispanic. A majority of the first 5,438 people arrested were Hispanic, while 37 percent were black. Of the fifty-eight people who died in the riot, more than a third were Hispanic, and about 40 percent of the businesses destroyed were Hispanic-owned. Most of the other shops and stores were Korean-owned. The dreams of many Korean immigrants went up in smoke during the riot: two thousand Korean-owned businesses were damaged or demolished, totaling about $400 million in losses. There is evidence indicating they were targeted. "After all," explained a black gang member, "we didn't burn our community, just *their* stores."

"I don't feel like I'm in America anymore," said Denisse Bustamente as she   12
watched the police protecting the firefighters. "I feel like I am far away." Indeed, Americans have been witnessing ethnic strife erupting around the world—the rise of neo-Nazism and the murder of Turks in Germany, the ugly "ethnic cleansing" in Bosnia, the terrible and bloody clashes between Muslims and Hindus in India. Is the situation here different, we have been nervously wondering, or do ethnic conflicts elsewhere represent a prologue for America? What is the nature of malevolence? Is there a deep, perhaps primordial, need for group identity rooted in hatred for the other? Is ethnic pluralism possible for America? But answers have been limited. Television reports have been little more than thirty-second sound bites. Newspaper articles have been mostly superficial descriptions of racial antagonisms and the current urban malaise. What is lacking is historical context; consequently, we are left feeling bewildered.

How did we get to this point, Americans everywhere are anxiously asking. What   13
does our diversity mean, and where is it leading us? *How* do we work it out in the post–Rodney King era?

Certainly one crucial way is for our society's various ethnic groups to develop a   14
greater understanding of each other. For example, how can African Americans and Korean Americans work it out unless they learn about each other's cultures, histories, and also economic situations? This need to share knowledge about our ethnic

diversity has acquired new importance and has given new urgency to the pursuit for a more accurate history.

More than ever before, there is a growing realization that the established scholarship has tended to define America too narrowly. For example, in his prize-winning study *The Uprooted,* Harvard historian Oscar Handlin presented—to use the book's subtitle—"the Epic Story of the Great Migrations That Made the American People." But Handlin's "epic story" excluded the "uprooted" from Africa, Asia, and Latin America—the other "Great Migrations" that also helped to make "the American People." Similarly, in *The Age of Jackson,* Arthur M. Schlesinger, Jr., left out blacks and Indians. There is not even a mention of two marker events—the Nat Turner insurrection and Indian removal, which Andrew Jackson himself would have been surprised to find omitted from a history of his era.   15

Still, Schlesinger and Handlin offered us a refreshing revisionism, paving the way for the study of common people rather than princes and presidents. They inspired the next generation of historians to examine groups such as the artisan laborers of Philadelphia and the Irish immigrants of Boston. "Once I thought to write a history of the immigrants in America," Handlin confided in his introduction to *The Uprooted.* "I discovered that the immigrants *were* American history." This door, once opened, led to the flowering of a more inclusive scholarship as we began to recognize that ethnic history was American history. Suddenly, there was a proliferation of seminal works such as Irving Howe's *World of Our Fathers: The Journey of the East European Jews to America,* Dee Brown's *Bury My Heart at Wounded Knee: An Indian History of the American West,* Albert Camarillo's *Chicanos in a Changing Society,* Lawrence Levine's *Black Culture and Black Consciousness,* Yuji Ichioka's *The Issei: The World of the First Generation Japanese Immigrants,* and Kerby Miller's *Emigrants and Exiles: Ireland and the Irish Exodus to North America.*   16

But even this new scholarship, while it has given us a more expanded understanding of the mosaic called America, does not address our needs in the post–Rodney King era. These books and others like them fragment American society, studying each group separately, in isolation from the other groups and the whole. While scrutinizing our specific pieces, we have to step back in order to see the rich and complex portrait they compose. What is needed is a fresh angle, a study of the American past from a comparative perspective. . . .   17

The signs of America's ethnic diversity can be discerned across the continent—Ellis Island, Angel Island, Chinatown, Harlem, South Boston, the Lower East Side, places with Spanish names like Los Angeles and San Antonio or Indian names like Massachusetts and Iowa. Much of what is familiar in America's cultural landscape actually has ethnic origins. The Bing cherry was developed by an early Chinese immigrant named Ah Bing. American Indians were cultivating corn, tomatoes, and tobacco long before the arrival of Columbus. The term *okay* was derived from the Choctaw word *oke,* meaning "it is so." There is evidence indicating that the name *Yankee* came from Indian terms for the English—from *eankke* in Cherokee and *Yankwis* in Delaware. Jazz and blues as well as rock and roll have African-American origins. The "Forty-Niners" of the Gold Rush learned mining techniques from the Mexicans; American cowboys acquired herding skills from Mexican *vaqueros* and adopted their range terms—such as *lariat* from *la reata, lasso* from *lazo,* and *stam-*   18 *pede* from *estampida*. Songs like "God Bless America," "Easter Parade," and "White Christmas" were written by a Russian-Jewish immigrant named Israel Baline, more popularly known as Irving Berlin.

Furthermore, many diverse ethnic groups have contributed to the building of the   19 American economy, forming what Walt Whitman saluted as "a vast, surging, hopeful army of workers." They worked in the South's cotton fields, New England's textile mills, Hawaii's canefields, New York's garment factories, California's orchards, Washington's salmon canneries, and Arizona's copper mines. They built the railroad, the great symbol of America's industrial triumph. Laying railroad ties, black laborers sang:

> Down the railroad, um-huh
> Well, raise the iron, um-huh
> Raise the iron, um-huh.

Irish railroad workers shouted as they stretched an iron ribbon across the continent:

> Then drill, my Paddies, drill—
> Drill, my heroes, drill,
> Drill all day, no sugar in your tay
> Workin' on the U.P. railway.

Japanese laborers in the Northwest chorused as their bodies fought the fickle weather:

> A railroad worker—
> That's me!
> I am great.
> Yes, I am a railroad worker.
> Complaining:
> "It is too hot!"
> "It is too cold!"
> "It rains too often!"
> "It snows too much!"
> They all ran off.
> I alone remained.
> I am a railroad worker!

Chicano workers in the Southwest joined in as they swore at the punishing work:

> Some unloaded rails
> Others unloaded ties,
> And others of my companions
> Threw out thousands of curses.

Moreover, our diversity was tied to America's most serious crisis: the Civil War   20 was fought over a racial issue—slavery. In his "First Inaugural Address," presented on March 4, 1861, President Abraham Lincoln declared: "One section of our country believes slavery is *right* and ought to be extended, while the other believes it is *wrong* and ought not to be extended." Southern secession, he argued, would be anarchy. Lincoln sternly warned the South that he had a solemn oath to defend and preserve the Union. Americans were one people, he explained, bound together by "the mystic chords of memory, stretching from every battlefield and patriot grave to every living heart and hearthstone all over this broad land." The struggle and sacrifices of the War for Independence had enabled Americans to create a new nation out of thirteen separate colonies. But Lincoln's appeal for unity fell on deaf ears in the South. And the war came. Two and a half years later, at Gettysburg, President Lincoln declared that "brave men" had fought and "consecrated" the ground of this battlefield in order to preserve the Union. Among the brave were black men. Shortly after this bloody battle, Lincoln acknowledged the military contributions of blacks. "There will be some black men," he wrote in a letter to an old friend, James C. Conkling, "who can remember that with silent tongue, and clenched teeth, and steady eye, and well-poised bayonet, they have helped mankind on to this great consummation. . . ." Indeed, 186,000 blacks served in the Union Army, and one-third of them were listed as missing or dead. Black men in blue, Frederick Douglass pointed out, were "on the battlefield mingling their blood with that of white men in one common effort to save the country." Now the mystic chords of memory stretched across the new battlefields of the Civil War, and black soldiers were buried in "patriot graves." They, too, had given their lives to ensure that the "government of the people, by the people, for the people shall not perish from the earth." . . .

In his recent study of Spain and the New World, *The Buried Mirror,* Carlos   21
Fuentes points out that mirrors have been found in the tombs of ancient Mexico, placed there to guide the dead through the underworld. He also tells us about the legend of Quetzalcoatl, the Plumed Serpent: when this god was given a mirror by the Toltec deity Tezcatlipoca, he saw a man's face in the mirror and realized his own humanity. For us, the "mirror" of history can guide the living and also help us recognize who we have been and hence are. In *A Distant Mirror,* Barbara W. Tuchman finds "phenomenal parallels" between the "calamitous 14th century" of European society and our own era. We can, she observes, have "greater fellow-feeling for a distraught age" as we painfully recognize the "similar disarray," "collapsing assumptions," and "unusual discomfort."

But what is needed in our own perplexing times is not so much a "distant" mir-   22
ror, as one that is "different." While the study of the past can provide collective self-knowledge, it often reflects the scholar's particular perspective or view of the world. What happens when historians leave out many of America's peoples? What happens, to borrow the words of Adrienne Rich, "when someone with the authority of a teacher" describes our society, and "you are not in it"? Such an experience can be disorienting—"a moment of psychic disequilibrium, as if you looked into a mirror and saw nothing."

Through their narratives about their lives and circumstances, the people of Amer-   23
ica's diverse groups are able to see themselves and each other in our common past. They celebrate what Ishmael Reed has described as a society "unique" in the world because "the world is here"—a place "where the cultures of the world crisscross." Much of America's past, they point out, has been riddled with racism. At the same time, these people offer hope, affirming the struggle for equality as a central theme in our country's history. At its conception, our nation was dedicated to the proposition

of equality. What has given concreteness to this powerful national principle has been our coming together in the creation of a new society. "Stuck here" together, workers of different backgrounds have attempted to get along with each other.

> *People harvesting*
> *Work together unaware*
> *Of racial problems,*

wrote a Japanese immigrant describing a lesson learned by Mexican and Asian farm laborers in California.

Finally, how do we see our prospects for "working out" America's racial crisis? Do we see it as through a glass darkly? Do the televised images of racial hatred and violence that riveted us in 1992 during the days of rage in Los Angeles frame a future of divisive race relations—what Arthur Schlesinger, Jr., has fearfully denounced as the "disuniting of America"? Or will Americans of diverse races and ethnicities be able to connect themselves to a larger narrative? Whatever happens, we can be certain that much of our society's future will be influenced by which "mirror" we choose to see ourselves. America does not belong to one race or one group, the people in this study remind us, and Americans have been constantly redefining their national identity from the moment of first contact on the Virginia shore. By sharing their stories, they invite us to see ourselves in a different mirror. 24

Working with the Text

1. Toward the end of his essay, Takaki quotes the writer Ishmael Reed as describing America as "a society 'unique' in the world because 'the world is here'—a place 'where the cultures of the world crisscross.'" How does Takaki discuss America as a global crossroads? What are some of the details that he invokes when outlining a global context for American multiculturalism?

2. Why are the Los Angeles "riots" of 1992 a key event for Takaki? What does he think they tell us about the current state of race relations in the United States? What are your memories of the event? Do you think that it has endured as a meaningful event in our recent past? Do you remember it very well—or at all? How do you recall the media portrayals of the riots? What aspects do you recall being emphasized? Are your memories of the riots similar to Takaki's descriptions?

3. Takaki implies that there has always been a central tension at the heart of American development and history: the tension between group identity and national identity. Discuss how the notion of this tension is raised in Takaki's essay. Is there an essential relationship—as well as a tension—between commonality and difference? What is the balance of importance in the United States between group identity and national identity? Which kinds of group identity are allowed or compatible with the national identity, and which are at odds with it?

4. What makes Takaki's "different mirror" different from traditional ways of looking at history? What are the most important differences that we can perceive by "looking back" at history with "a different mirror"? How would his-

tory appear to be different, and how would our responses to it differ? How, does he imply, would a different mirror on the past shed a different light on our present and future?

THE FEAR OF LOSING A CULTURE

RICHARD RODRIGUEZ

■ Memoirist and journalist Richard Rodriguez was born in San Francisco in 1944, the son of Mexican immigrant parents who spoke little English. Educated in English-speaking Catholic schools, Rodriguez recalls in his acclaimed autobiography, *Hunger of Memory: The Education of Richard Rodriguez* (1982), the complex tensions he felt in learning to assimilate, to cross the divide between the Anglo world and that of his family. Educated at Stanford, Columbia, and the University of California at Berkeley, Rodriguez now writes for a variety of publications and also serves as a correspondent for the Pacific News Service. His latest book is *Days of Obligation: An Argument with My Mexican Father* (1992). In the following essay, Rodriguez wonders how Hispanics can "belong to America without betraying the past," arguing that "[w]e will change America even as we will be changed."

What is culture? 1

The immigrant shrugs. Latin American immigrants come to the 2 United States with only the things they need in mind—not abstractions like culture. Money. They need dollars. They need food. Maybe they need to get out of the way of bullets.

Most of us who concern ourselves with Hispanic-American culture, as painters, 3 musicians, writers—or as sons and daughters—are the children of immigrants. We have grown up on this side of the border, in the land of Elvis Presley and Thomas Edison; our lives are prescribed by the mall, by the DMV and the Chinese restaurant. Our imaginations yet vacillate between an Edenic Latin America (the blue door)—which nevertheless betrayed our parents—and the repellent plate glass of a real American city—which has been good to us.

Hispanic-American culture is where the past meets the future. Hispanic-American 4 culture is not a Hispanic milestone only, not simply a celebration at the crossroads. America transforms into pleasure what America cannot avoid. Is it any coincidence that at a time when Americans are troubled by the encroachment of the Mexican desert, Americans discover a chic in cactus, in the decorator colors of the Southwest? In sand?

Hispanic-American culture of the sort that is now showing (the teen movie, the 5 rock songs) may exist in an hourglass; may in fact be irrelevant to the epic. The U.S. Border Patrol works through the night to arrest the flow of illegal immigrants over the border, even as Americans wait in line to get into "La Bamba." Even as Americans vote to declare, once and for all, that English shall be the official language of the United States, Madonna starts recording in Spanish.

But then so is Bill Cosby's show irrelevant to the 10 o'clock news, where families huddle together in fear on porches, pointing at the body of the slain boy bagged in tarpaulin. Which is not to say that Bill Cosby or Michael Jackson are irrelevant to the future or without neo-Platonic influence. Like players within the play, they prefigure, they resolve. They make black and white audiences aware of a bond that may not yet exist. 6

Before a national TV audience, Rita Moreno tells Geraldo Rivera that her dream as an actress is to play a character rather like herself: "I speak English perfectly well . . . I'm not dying from poverty . . . I want to play *that* kind of Hispanic woman, which is to say, an American citizen." This is an actress talking, these are show-biz pieties. But Moreno expresses as well the general Hispanic-American predicament. Hispanics want to belong to America without betraying the past. 7

Hispanics fear losing ground in any negotiation with the American city. We come from an expansive, an intimate culture that has been judged second-rate by the United States of America. For reasons of pride, therefore, as much as of affection, we are reluctant to give up our past. Hispanics often express a fear of "losing" culture. Our fame in the United States has been our resistance to assimilation. 8

The symbol of Hispanic culture has been the tongue of flame—Spanish. But the remarkable legacy Hispanics carry from Latin America is not language—an inflatable skin—but breath itself, capacity of soul, an inclination to live. The genius of Latin America is the habit of synthesis. 9

We assimilate. Just over the border there is the example of Mexico, the country from which the majority of U.S. Hispanics come. Mexico is *mestizo*—Indian and Spanish. Within a single family, Mexicans are light-skinned and dark. It is impossible for the Mexican to say, in the scheme of things, where the Indian begins and the Spaniard surrenders. 10

In culture as in blood, Latin America was formed by a rape that became a marriage. Due to the absorbing generosity of the Indian, European culture took on new soil. What Latin America knows is that people create one another as they marry. In the music of Latin America you will hear the litany of bloodlines—the African drum, the German accordion, the cry from the minaret. 11

The United States stands as the opposing New World experiment. In North America the Indian and the European stood apace. Whereas Latin America was formed by a medieval Catholic dream of one world—of meltdown conversion—the United States was built up from Protestant individualism. The American melting pot washes away only embarrassment; it is the necessary initiation into public life. The American faith is that our national strength derives from separateness, from "diversity." The glamour of the United States is a carnival promise: You can lose weight, get rich as Rockefeller, tough up your roots, get a divorce. 12

Immigrants still come for the promise. But the United States wavers in its faith. As long as there was space enough, sky enough, as long as economic success validated individualism, loneliness was not too high a price to pay. (The cabin on the prairie or the Sony Walkman.) 13

As we near the end of the American century, two alternative cultures beckon the American imagination—both highly communal cultures—the Asian and the Latin 14

American. The United States is a literal culture. Americans devour what we might otherwise fear to become. Sushi will make us corporate warriors. Combination Plate #3, smothered in *mestizo* gravy, will burn a hole in our hearts.

Latin America offers passion. Latin America has a life—I mean *life*—big clouds, unambiguous themes, death, birth, faith, that the United States, for all its quality of life, seems without now. Latin America offers communal riches: an undistressed leisure, a kitchen table, even a full sorrow. Such is the solitude of America, such is the urgency of American need, Americans reach right past a fledgling, homegrown Hispanic-American culture for the real thing—the darker bottle of Mexican beer, the denser novel of a Latin American master.   15

For a long time, Hispanics in the United States withheld from the United States our Latin American gift. We denied the value of assimilation. But as our presence is judged less foreign in America, we will produce a more generous art, less timid, less parochial. Carlos Santana, Luis Valdez, Linda Ronstadt—Hispanic Americans do not have a "pure" Latin American art to offer. Expect bastard themes, expect ironies, comic conclusions. For we live on this side of the border, where Kraft manufactures bricks of "Mexican style" Velveeta, and where Jack in the Box serves "Fajita Pita."   16

The flame-red Chevy floats a song down the Pan American Highway: From a rolled-down window, the grizzled voice of Willie Nelson rises in disembodied harmony with the voice of Julio Iglesias. Gabby Hayes and Cisco are thus resolved.   17

Expect marriage. We will change America even as we will be changed. We will disappear with you into a new miscegenation.   18

Along the border, real conflicts remain. But the ancient tear separating Europe from itself—the Catholic Mediterranean from the Protestant north—may yet heal itself in the New World. For generations, Latin America has been the place—the bed—of a confluence of so many races and cultures that Protestant North America shuddered to imagine it.   19

Imagine it.   20

Working with the Text

1. Rodriguez characterizes Hispanic American culture as a hybrid culture, and mainstream culture in the United States as "Protestant North American" culture. What are some of the other characteristics that vary between the two cultures? What cultural qualities or values does he propose as oppositions between Hispanic American and North American cultures?

2. What is the root of the conflict behind Rodriguez's statement that "Hispanics want to belong to America without betraying the past"? Why is that an issue? What about their past does belonging to America threaten?

3. In what ways has North America absorbed cultural influences of Hispanic America? Would you consider these substantive or superficial influences in terms of their impact on North American culture?

4. The title of this essay is "The Fear of Losing a Culture." To whose fear is he referring—that of Hispanic America, North America, or both? Would the meaning and expression of that fear be the same for either side?

HOME IS WHERE THE *HAN* IS: A KOREAN AMERICAN PERSPECTIVE ON THE LOS ANGELES UPHEAVALS

ELAINE H. KIM

■ Born in New York City in 1942, Elaine Kim attended the University of Pennsylvania and Columbia University. She later taught English as a second language in Seoul, Korea, and in Washington, D.C. She received her Ph.D. from the University of California at Berkeley in 1976. Now a professor of Asian American studies there, she became one of the first tenured Asian American women at a major U.S. university. Her book *Asian American Literature: An Introduction to the Writings and Their Social Contexts* (1982) was one of the first important works in its field, as was her coedited collection, *Making Waves: An Anthology of Writings by and about Asian American Women* (1989). Kim has also worked as a television producer and has been active in Asian American and Korean American social, educational, and political organizations. The following essay, sparked by the 1992 rioting in Los Angeles that destroyed many Korean-owned businesses, critiques issues of racial conflict in the United States from a Korean American perspective, a voice generally silenced within the dominant culture.

A bout half of the estimated $850 million in estimated material losses incurred during the Los Angeles upheavals was sustained by a community no one seems to want to talk much about. Korean Americans in Los Angeles, suddenly at the front lines when violence came to the buffer zone they had been so precariously occupying, suffered profound damage to their means of livelihood.[1] But my concern here is the psychic damage which, unlike material damage, is impossible to quantify.

I want to explore the questions of whether or not recovery is possible for Korean Americans, and what will become of our attempts to "become American" without dying of *han. Han* is a Korean word that means, loosely translated, the sorrow and anger that grow from the accumulated experiences of oppression. Although the word is frequently and commonly used by Koreans, the condition it describes is taken quite seriously. When people die of *han,* it is called dying of *hwabyong,* a disease of frustration and rage following misfortune.

Situated as we are on the border between those who have and those who have not, between predominantly Anglo and mostly African American and Latino communities, from our current interstitial position in the American discourse of race, many Korean Americans have trouble calling what happened in Los Angeles an "uprising." At the same time, we cannot quite say it was a "riot." So some of us have

I am deeply indebted to the activists in the Los Angeles Korean American community, especially Bong Hwan Kim and Eui-Young Yu, whose courage and commitment to the empowerment of the disenfranchised, whether African American, Latino, or Korean American, during this crisis in Los Angeles have been a continuous source of inspiration for me. I would also like to thank Barry Maxwell for critically reading this manuscript and offering many insightful suggestions; my niece Sujin Kim, David Lloyd, and Caridad Souza for their encouragement; and Mia Chung for her general assistance.

taken to calling it *sa-i-ku,* April 29, after the manner of naming other events in Korean history—3.1 (*sam-il*) for March 1, 1919, when massive protests against Japanese colonial rule began in Korea; 6.25 (*yook-i-o*), or June 25, 1950, when the Korean War began; and 4.19 (*sa-il-ku*), or April 19, 1960, when the first student movement in the world to overthrow a government began in South Korea. The ironic similarity between 4.19 and 4.29 does not escape most Korean Americans.

Los Angeles Koreatown has been important to me, even though I visit only a dozen times a year. Before Koreatown sprang up during the last decade and a half,[2] I used to hang around the fringes of Chinatown, although I knew that this habit was pure pretense.[3] For me, knowing that Los Angeles Koreatown existed made a difference; one of my closest friends worked with the Black-Korean Alliance there,[4] and I liked to think of it as a kind of "home"—however idealized and hypostatized—for the soul, an anchor, a potential refuge, a place in America where I could belong without ever being asked, "Who are you and what are you doing here? Where did you come from and when are you going back?"

Many of us watched in horror the destruction of Koreatown and the systematic targeting of Korean shops in South Central Los Angeles after the Rodney King verdict. Seeing those buildings in flames and those anguished Korean faces, I had the terrible thought that there would be no belonging and that we were, just as I had always suspected, a people destined to carry our *han* around with us wherever we went in the world. The destiny (*p'aljja*) that had spelled centuries of extreme suffering from invasion, colonization, war, and national division had smuggled itself into the U.S. with our baggage.

African American and Korean American conflict.   As someone whose social consciousness was shaped by the African American–led civil rights movement of the 1960s, I felt that I was watching our collective dreams for a just society disintegrating, cast aside as naive and irrelevant in the bitter and embattled 1990s. It was the courageous African American women and men of the 1960s who had redefined the meaning of "American," who had first suggested that a person like me could reject the false choice between being treated as a perpetual foreigner in my own birthplace, on the one hand, and relinquishing my identity for someone else's ill-fitting and impossible Anglo American one on the other. Thanks to them, I began to discern how institutional racism works and why Korea was never mentioned in my world-history textbooks. I was able to see how others besides Koreans had been swept aside by the dominant culture. My American education offered nothing about Chicanos or Latinos, and most of what I was taught about African and Native Americans was distorted to justify their oppression and vindicate their oppressors.

I could hardly believe my ears when, during the weeks immediately following *sa-i-ku,* I heard African American community leaders suggesting that Korean American merchants were foreign intruders deliberately trying to stifle African American economic development, when I knew that they had bought those liquor stores at five times gross receipts from African American owners, who had previously bought them at two times gross receipts from Jewish owners after Watts.[5] I saw anti-Korean flyers that were being circulated by African American political candidates and read about South Central residents petitioning against the reestablishment of swap meets, groups of typically Korean immigrant-operated market stalls. I was disheartened with Latinos who related the pleasure they felt while looting Korean stores that they believed "had it coming" and who claimed that it was because of racism that more

Latinos were arrested during *sa-i-ku* than Asian Americans.[6] And I was filled with despair when I read about Chinese Americans wanting to dissociate themselves from us. According to one Chinese American reporter assigned to cover Asian American issues for a San Francisco daily, Chinese and Japanese American shopkeepers, unlike Koreans, always got along fine with African Americans in the past.[7] "Suddenly," admitted another Chinese American, "I am scared to be Asian. More specifically, I am afraid to be mistaken for Korean."[8] I was enraged when I overheard European Americans discussing the conflicts as if they were watching a dogfight or a boxing match. The situation reminded me of the Chinese film "Raise the Red Lantern," in which we never see the husband's face. We only hear his mellifluous voice as he benignly admonishes his four wives not to fight among themselves. He can afford to be kind and pleasant because the structure that pits his wives against each other is so firmly in place that he need never sully his hands or even raise his voice.

Battleground legacy.   Korean Americans are squeezed between black and white   8
and also between U.S. and South Korean political agendas. Opportunistic American and South Korean presidential candidates toured the burnt ruins, posing for the television cameras but delivering nothing of substance to the victims. Like their U.S. counterparts, South Korean news media seized upon *sa-i-ku,* featuring sensational stories that depicted the problem as that of savage African Americans attacking innocent Koreans for no reason.[9] To give the appearance of authenticity, Seoul newspapers even published articles using the names of Korean Americans who did not in fact write them.[10]

Those of us who chafe at being asked whether we are Chinese or Japanese as if there   9
were no other possibilities or who were angered when the news media sought Chinese and Japanese but not Korean American views during *sa-i-ku* are sensitive to an invisibility that seems particular to us. To many Americans, Korea is but the gateway to or the bridge between China and Japan, or a crossroads of major Asian conflicts.[11]

It can certainly be said that, although little known or cared about in the Western   10
world, Korea has been a perennial battleground. Besides the Mongols and the Manchus, there were the *Yŏjin* (Jurched), the *Koran* (Khitan), and the *Waegu* (Wäkö) invaders. In relatively recent years, there was the war between China and Japan that ended in 1895 and the war between Japan and Russia in 1905, both of which were fought on Korean soil and resulted in extreme suffering for the Korean people. Japan's 36 years of brutal colonial rule ended with the U.S. and what was then the Soviet Union dividing the country in half at the 38th parallel. Thus, Korea was turned into a Cold War territory that ultimately became a battleground for world superpowers during the conflict of 1950–53.

Becoming American.   One of the consequences of war, colonization, national di-   11
vision, and superpower economic and cultural domination has been the migration of Koreans to places like Los Angeles, where they believed their human rights would be protected by law. After all, they had received U.S.-influenced political educations. They started learning English in the seventh grade. They all knew the story of the poor boy from Illinois who became president. They all learned that the U.S. Constitution and Bill of Rights protected the common people from violence and injustice. But they who grew up in Korea watching "Gunsmoke," "Night Rider," and "McGyver" dubbed in Korean were not prepared for the black, brown, red, and yellow America they encountered when they disembarked at the Los Angeles International Airport.[12] They hadn't heard that there is no equal justice in the U.S. They had to learn

about American racial hierarchies. They did not realize that, as immigrants of color, they would never attain political voice or visibility but would instead be used to uphold the inequality and the racial hierarchy they had no part in creating.

Most of the newcomers had underestimated the communication barriers they would face. Like the Turkish workers in Germany described in John Berger and Jean Mohr's *A Seventh Man*,[13] their toil amounted to only a pile of gestures and the English they tried to speak changed and turned against them as they spoke it. Working 14 hours a day, six or seven days a week, they rarely came into sustained contact with English-speaking Americans and almost never had time to study English. Not feeling at ease with English, they did not engage in informal conversations easily with non-Koreans and were hated for being curt and rude. They did not attend churches or do business in banks or other enterprises where English was required. Typically, the immigrant, small-business owners utilized unpaid family labor instead of hiring people from local communities. Thanks to Eurocentric American cultural practices, they knew little or nothing good about African Americans or Latinos, who in turn and for similar reasons knew little or nothing good about them. At the same time, Korean shopowners in South Central and Koreatown were affluent compared with the impoverished residents, whom they often exploited as laborers or looked down upon as fools with an aversion to hard work.[14] Most Korean immigrants did not even know that they were among the many direct beneficiaries of the African American–led civil rights movement, which helped pave the way for the 1965 immigration reforms that made their immigration possible.

Korean-immigrant views, shaped as they were by U.S. cultural influences and official, anticommunist, South Korean education,[15] differed radically from those of many poor people in the communities Korean immigrants served: unaware of the shameful history of oppression of nonwhite immigrants and other people of color in the U.S., they regarded themselves as having arrived in a meritocratic "land of opportunity" where a person's chances for success are limited only by individual lack of ability or diligence. Having left a homeland where they foresaw their talents and hard work going unrecognized and unrewarded, they were desperate to believe that the "American dream" of social and economic mobility through hard work was within their reach.

Sa-i-ku.   What they experienced on 29 and 30 April was a baptism into what it really means for a Korean to "become American" in the 1990s.[16] In South Korea, there is no 911, and no one really expects a fire engine or police car if there is trouble. Instead, people make arrangements with friends and family for emergencies. At the same time, guns are not part of Korean daily life. No civilian in South Korea can own a gun. Guns are the exclusive accoutrement of the military and police who enforce order for those who rule the society. When the Korean Americans in South Central and Koreatown dialed 911, nothing happened. When their stores and homes were being looted and burned to the ground, they were left completely alone for three horrifying days. How betrayed they must have felt by what they had believed was a democratic system that protects its people from violence. Those who trusted the government to protect them lost everything; those who took up arms after waiting for help for two days were able to defend themselves. It was as simple as that. What they had to learn was that, as in South Korea, protection in the U.S. is by and large for the rich and powerful. If there were a choice between Westwood and Koreatown, it is clear that Koreatown would have to be sacrificed. The familiar concept of privilege for the rich and powerful would have been easy for the Korean immigrant to grasp if only those exhortations about democracy and equality had not obfuscated the picture. Perhaps they should have relied even more on whatever they brought with them from Korea instead of fretting over trying to understand what was going on around them here. That Koreatown became a battleground does seem like the further playing out of a tragic legacy that has followed them across oceans and continents. The difference is that this was a battle between the poor and disenfranchised and the invisible rich, who were being protected by a layer of clearly visible Korean American human shields in a battle on the buffer zone.

This difference is crucial. Perhaps the legacy is not one carried across oceans and continents but one assumed immediately upon arrival, not the curse of being Korean but the initiation into becoming American, which requires that Korean Americans take on this country's legacy of five centuries of racial violence and inequality, of divide and rule, of privilege for the rich and oppression of the poor. Within this legacy, they have been assigned a place on the front lines. Silenced by those who possess the power to characterize and represent, they are permitted to speak only to reiterate their acceptance of this role.

Silencing the Korean American voice. Twelve years ago, in Kwangju, South Korea, hundreds of civilians demonstrating for constitutional reform and free elections were murdered by U.S.-supported and -equipped South Korean elite paratroopers. Because I recorded it and played it over and over again, searching for a sign or a clue, I remember clearly how what were to me heartrendingly tragic events were represented in the U.S. news media. For a few fleeting moments, images of unruly crowds of alien-looking Asians shouting unintelligible words and phrases and wearing white headbands inscribed with unintelligible characters flickered across the screen. The Koreans were made to seem like insane people from another planet. The voice in the background stated simply that there were massive demonstrations but did not explain what the protests were about. Nor was a single Korean ever given an opportunity to speak to the camera.

The next news story was about demonstrations for democracy in Poland. The camera settled on individuals' faces which one by one filled the screen as each man or woman was asked to explain how he or she felt. Each Polish person's words were translated in a voice-over or subtitle. Solidarity leader Lech Walesa, who was allowed to speak often, was characterized as a heroic human being with whom all Americans could surely identify personally. Polish Americans from New York and Chicago to San Francisco, asked in man-on-the-street interviews about their reactions, described the canned hams and blankets they were sending to Warsaw.

This was for me a lesson in media representation, race, and power politics. It is a given that Americans are encouraged by our ideological apparatuses to side with our allies (here, the Polish resisters and the anti-communist South Korean government) against our enemies (here, the communist Soviet Union and protesters against the South Korean government). But visual-media racism helps craft and reinforce our identification with Europeans and whites while distancing us from fearsome and alien Asiatic hordes.

In March of last year, when two delegates from North Korea visited the Bay Area to participate in community-sponsored talks on Korean reunification, about 800 people from the Korean American community attended. The meeting was consummately newsworthy, since it was the first time in history that anyone from North

Korea had ever been in California for more than 24 hours just passing through. The event was discussed for months in the Korean-language media—television, radio, and newspapers. Almost every Korean-speaking person in California knew about it. Although we sent press releases to all the commercial and public radio and television stations and to all the Bay Area newspapers, not a single mainstream media outfit covered the event. However, whenever there was an African American boycott of a Korean store or whenever conflict surfaced between Korean and African Americans, community leaders found a dozen microphones from all the main news media shoved into their faces, as if they were the president's press secretary making an official public pronouncement. Fascination with interethnic conflicts is rooted in the desire to excuse or minimize white racism by buttressing the mistaken notion that all human beings are "naturally" racist, and when Korean and African Americans allow themselves to be distracted by these interests, their attention is deflected from the social hierarchies that give racism its destructive power.

Without a doubt, the U.S. news media played a major role in exacerbating the   20
damage and ill will toward Korean Americans, first by spotlighting tensions between African Americans and Koreans above all efforts to work together and as opposed to many other newsworthy events in these two communities, and second by exploiting racist stereotypes of Koreans as unfathomable aliens, this time wielding guns on rooftops and allegedly firing wildly into crowds.[17] In news programs and on talk shows, African and Korean American tensions were discussed by blacks and whites, who pointed to these tensions as the main cause of the uprising. I heard some European Americans railing against rude and exploitative Korean merchants for ruining peaceful race relations for everyone else. Thus, Korean Americans were used to deflect attention from the racism they inherited and the economic injustice and poverty that had been already well woven into the fabric of American life, as evidenced by a judicial system that could allow not only the Korean store owner who killed Latasha Harlins but also the white men who killed Vincent Chin and the white police who beat Rodney King to go free, while Leonard Peltier still languishes in prison.

As far as I know, neither the commercial nor the public news media has men-   21
tioned the many Korean and African American attempts to improve relations, such as joint church services, joint musical performances and poetry readings, Korean merchant donations to African American community and youth programs, African American volunteer teachers in classes for Korean immigrants studying for citizenship examinations, or Korean translations of African American history materials.

While Korean immigrants were preoccupied with the mantra of day-to-day sur-   22
vival, Korean Americans had no voice, no political presence whatsoever in American life. When they became the targets of violence in Los Angeles, their opinions and views were hardly solicited except as they could be used in the already-constructed mainstream discourse on race relations, which is a sorry combination of blaming the African American and Latino victims for their poverty and scapegoating the Korean Americans as robotic aliens who have no "real" right to be here in the first place and therefore deserve whatever happens to them.

The Newsweek *experience.*   In this situation, I felt compelled to respond when   23
an editor from the "My Turn" section of *Newsweek* magazine asked for 1000-word personal essay.[18] Hesitant because I was given only a day and a half to write the piece, not enough time in light of the vastness of American ignorance about Kore-

ans and Korean Americans, I decided to do it because I thought I could not be made into a sound bite or a quote contextualized for someone else's agenda.

I wrote an essay accusing the news media of using Korean Americans and ten- 24
sions between African and Korean Americans to divert attention from the roots of racial violence in the U.S. I asserted that these lie not in the Korean-immigrant-owned corner store situated in a community ravaged by poverty and police violence, but reach far back into the corridors of corporate and government offices in Los Angeles, Sacramento, and Washington, D.C. I suggested that Koreans and African Americans were kept ignorant about each other by educational and media institutions that erase or distort their experiences and perspectives. I tried to explain how racism had kept my parents from ever really becoming Americans, but that having been born here, I considered myself American and wanted to believe in the possibility of an American dream.

The editor of "My Turn" did everything he could to frame my words with his 25
own viewpoint. He faxed his own introductory and concluding paragraphs that equated Korean merchants with cowboys in the Wild West and alluded to Korean/African American hatred. When I objected, he told me that my writing style was not crisp enough and that as an experienced journalist, he could help me out. My confidence wavered, but ultimately I rejected his editing. Then he accused me of being overly sensitive, confiding that I had no need to be defensive—because his wife was a Chinese American. Only after I had decided to withdraw the piece did he agree to accept it as I wrote it.

Before I could finish congratulating myself on being able to resist silencing and the 26
kind of decontextualization I was trying to describe in the piece, I started receiving hate mail. Some of it was addressed directly to me, since I had been identified as a University of California faculty member, but most of it arrived in bundles, forwarded by *Newsweek*. Hundreds of letters came from all over the country, from Florida to Washington state and from Massachusetts to Arizona. I was unprepared for the hostility expressed in most of the letters. Some people sent the article, torn from the magazine and covered with angry, red-inked obscenities scratched across my picture. "You should see a good doctor," wrote someone from Southern California, "you have severe problems in thinking, reasoning, and adjusting to your environment."

A significant proportion of the writers, especially those who identified them- 27
selves as descendants of immigrants from Eastern Europe, wrote *Newsweek* that they were outraged, sickened, disgusted, appalled, annoyed, and angry at the magazine for providing an arena for the paranoid, absurd, hypocritical, racist, and childish views of a spoiled, ungrateful, whining, bitching, un-American bogus faculty member who should be fired or die when the next California earthquake dumps all of the "so-called people of color" into the Pacific Ocean.

I was shocked by the profound ignorance of many writers' assumptions about 28
the experiences and perspectives of American people of color in general and Korean and other Asian Americans in particular. Even though my essay revealed that I was born in the U.S. and that my parents had lived in the U.S. for more than six decades, I was viewed as a foreigner without the right to say anything except words of gratitude and praise about America. The letters also provided some evidence of the dilemma Korean Americans are placed in by those who assume that we are aliens who should "go back" and at the same time berate us for not rejecting "Korean-American identity" for "American identity."

How many Americans migrate to Korea? If you are so disenchanted, Korea is still there. Why did you ever leave it? Sayonara.

Ms. Kim appears to have a personal axe to grind with this country that has given her so much freedom and opportunity. . . . I should suggest that she move to Korea, where her children will learn all they ever wanted about that country's history.

[Her] whining about the supposedly racist U.S. society is just a mask for her own acute inferiority complex. If she is so dissatisfied with the United States why doesn't she vote with her feet and leave? She can get the hell out and return to her beloved Korea—her tribal afinity [*sic*] where her true loyalty and consciousness lies [*sic*].

You refer to yourself as a Korean American and yet you have lived all your life in the United States . . . you write about racism in this country and yet you are the biggest racist by your own written words. If you cannot accept the fact that you are an American, maybe you should be living your life in Korea.

My stepfather and cousin risked their lives in the country where your father is buried to ensure the ideals of our country would remain. So don't expect to find a sympathetic ear for your pathetic whining.

Many of the letter writers assumed that my family had been the "scum" of Asia   29
and that I was a college teacher only because of American justice and largesse. They were furious that I did not express gratitude for being saved from starvation in Asia and given the opportunity to flourish, no doubt beyond my wildest dreams, in America.

Where would she be if her parents had not migrated to the United States? For a professor at Berkeley University [*sic*] to say the American dream is only an empty promise is ludicrous. Shame, shame, shame on Elaine!

[Her father and his family] made enough money in the USA to ship his corpse home to Korea for burial. Ms. Kim herself no doubt has a guaranteed life income as a professor paid by California taxpayers. Wouldn't you think that she might say kind things about the USA instead of whining about racism?

At the same time some letters blamed me for expecting "freedom and opportu-   30
nity":

It is wondrous that folks such as you find truth in your paranoia. No one ever promised anything to you or your parents.

Besides providing indications of how Korean Americans are regarded, the letters   31
revealed a great deal about how American identity is thought of. One California woman explained that although her grandparents were Irish immigrants, she was not an Irish American, because "if you are not with us, you are against us." A Missouri woman did not seem to realize that she was conflating race and nationality and confusing "nonethnic" and "nonracial," by which she seems to have meant

"white," with "American." And, although she insists that it is impossible to be both "black" and "American," she identifies herself at the outset as a "white American."

> I am a white American. I am proud to be an American. You cannot be black, white, Korean, Chinese, Mexican, German, French, or English or any other and still be an American. Of course the culture taught in schools is strictly American. That's where we are and if you choose to learn another [culture] you have the freedom to settle there. You cannot be a Korean American which assumes you are not ready to be an AMERICAN. Do you get my gist?

The suggestion that more should be taught in U.S. schools about America's many immigrant groups and people of color prompted many letters in defense of Western civilization against non-Western barbarism: 32

> You are dissatisfied with current school curricula that excludes Korea. Could it possibly be because Korea and Asia for that matter has [sic] not had . . . a noticeable impact on the shaping of Western culture, and Korea has had unfortunately little culture of its own?
>
> Who cares about Korea, Ms. Kim? . . . And what enduring contributions has the Black culture, both here in the US and on the continent contributed to the world, and mankind? I'm from a culture, Ms. Kim, who put a man on the moon 23 years ago, who established medical schools to train doctors to perform open heart surgery, and . . . who created a language of music so that musicians, from Beethoven to the Beatles, could easily touch the world with their brilliance forever and ever and ever. Perhaps the dominant culture, whites obviously, "swept aside Chicanos . . . Latinos . . . African-Americans . . . Koreans," because they haven't contributed anything that made—be mindful of the cliche—a world of difference?
>
> Koreans' favorite means of execution is decapitation . . . Ms. Kim, and others like her, came here to escape such injustice. Then they whine at riots to which they have contributed by their own fanning of flames of discontent. . . . Yes! Let us all study more about Oriental culture! Let us put matters into proper perspective.
>
> Fanatical multiculturalists like you expect a country whose dominant culture has been formed and influenced by Europe . . . , nearly 80% of her population consisting of persons whose ancestry is European, to include the history of every ethnic group who has ever lived here. I truly feel sorry for you. You and your bunch need to realize that white Americans are not racists. . . . We would love to get along, but not at the expense of our own culture and heritage.
>
> Kim's axe-to-grind confirms the utter futility of race-relations—the races were never meant to live together. We don't get along and never will. . . . Whats [sic] needed is to divide the United States up along racial lines so that life here can finally become livable.

What seemed to anger some people the most was their idea that, although they worked hard, people of color were seeking handouts and privileges because of their race, and the thought of an ungrateful Asian American siding with African Americans, presumably against whites, was infuriating. How dare I "bite the hand that 33 feeds" me by siding with the champion "whiners who cry 'racism'" because to do so is the last refuge of the "terminally incompetent"?

> The racial health in this country won't improve until minorities stop erecting "me first" barriers and strive to be Americans, not African-Americans or Asian-Americans expecting privileges.
>
> Ms. Kim wants preferential treatment that immigrants from Greece-to-Sweden have not enjoyed. . . . Even the Chinese . . . have not created any special problems for themselves or other Americans. Soon those folk are going to express their own resentments to the insatiable demands of the Blacks and other colored peoples, including the wetbacks from Mexico who sneak into this country then pilfer it for all they can.
>
> The Afroderived citizens of Los Angeles and the Asiatic derivatives were not suffering a common imposition. . . . The Asiatics are trying to build their success. The Africans are sucking at the teats of entitlement.

As is usual with racists, most of the writers of these hate letters saw only themselves in their notions about Korea, America, Korean Americans, African Americans. They felt that their own sense of American identity was being threatened and that they were being blamed as individuals for U.S. racism. One man, adept at manipulating various fonts on his word processor, imposed his preconceptions on my words: 34

> Let me read between the lines of your little hate message:
>
> . . . "The roots . . . stretch far back into the corridors of corporate and government offices in Los Angeles, Sacramento, and Washington, D.C."
>
> **All white America and all American institutions are to blame for racism.**
>
> . . . "I still want to believe the promise is real."
>
> **I have the savvy to know that the American ideals of freedom and justice are a joke but if you want to give me what I want I'm willing to make concessions.**
>
> Ms. Kim, . . . if you want to embody the ignorant, the insecure, and the emotionally immature, that's your right! Just stop preaching hate and please, please, quit whining.
>
> Sincerely, A proud White-American teaching
my children not to be prejudicial

Especially since my essay had been subdued and intensely personal, I had not anticipated the fury it would provoke. I never thought that readers would write over my words with their own. The very fact that I used words, and English words at that, particularly incensed some: one letter writer complained about my use of words and phrases like "manifestation" and "zero-sum game," and "suzerain relationship," which is the only way to describe Korea's relationship with China during the T'ang Dynasty. "Not more than ten people in the USA know what [these words] mean," he wrote. "You are on an ego trip." I wondered if it made him particularly angry that an Asian American had used those English words, or if he would make such a comment to George Will or Jane Bryant Quinn.   35

Clearly I had encountered part of America's legacy, the legacy that insists on si-   36
lencing certain voices and erasing certain presences, even if it means deportation,
internment, and outright murder. I should not have been surprised by what happened in Koreatown or by the ignorance and hatred expressed in the letters to
Newsweek, any more than African Americans should have been surprised by the
Rodney King verdict. Perhaps the news media, which constituted *sa-i-ku* as news, as
an extraordinary event in no way continuous with our everyday lives, made us forget for a moment that as people of color many of us simultaneously inhabit two
Americas: the America of our dreams and the America of our experience.

Who among us does not cling stubbornly to the America of our dreams, the   37
promise of a multicultural democracy where our cultures and our differences might
be affirmed instead of distorted in an effort to destroy us?

After *sa-i-ku,* I was able to catch glimpses of this America of my dreams because   38
I received other letters that expressed another American legacy. Some people iden-
tified themselves as Norwegian or Irish Americans interested in combating racism.
Significantly, while most of the angry mail had been sent not to me but to
Newsweek, almost all of the sympathetic mail, particularly the letters from African
Americans, came directly to me. Many came from Korean Americans who were glad
that one of their number had found a vehicle for self-expression. Others were from
Chinese and Japanese Americans who wrote that they had had similar experiences
and feelings. Several were written in shaky longhand by women fervently wishing
for peace and understanding among people of all races. A Native American from
Nashville wrote a long description of cases of racism against African, Asian, and Native Americans in the U.S. criminal-justice system. A large number of letters came
from African Americans, all of them supportive and sympathetic—from judges and
professors who wanted better understanding between Africans and Koreans to
poets and laborers who scribbled their notes in pencil while on breaks at work. One
man identified himself as a Los Angeles African American whose uncle had married
a Korean woman. He stated that as a black man in America, he knew what other
people feel when they face injustice. He ended his letter apologizing for his spelling
and grammar mistakes and asking for materials to read on Asian Americans. The
most touching letter I received was written by a prison inmate who had served
twelve years of a 35-to-70-year sentence for armed robbery during which no physical injuries occurred. He wrote:

> I've been locked in these prisons going on 12 years now . . . and since being
> here I have studied fully the struggles of not just blacks, but all people of color.
> I am a true believer of helping "your" people "first," but also the helping of all
> people no matter where there at or the color of there skin. But I must be
> truthful, my struggle and assistance is truly on the side of people of color like
> ourselves. But just a few years ago I didn't think like this.
>
> I thought that if you wasn't black, then you was the enemy, but . . . many
> years of this prison madness and much study and research changed all of
> this. . . . [I]t's not with each other, blacks against Koreans or Koreans against
> blacks. No, this is not what it's about. Our struggle(s) are truly one in the
> same. What happened in L.A. during the riot really hurt me, because it was no
> way that blacks was suppose to do the things to your people, my people (Kore-
> ans) that they did. You're my sister, our people are my people. Even though

our culture may be somewhat different, and even though we may worship our God(s) different . . . white-Amerikkka [doesn't] separate us. They look at us all the same. Either you're white, or you're wrong. . . . I'm just writing you to let you know that, you're my sister, your people's struggle are my people's struggle.

This is the ground I need to claim now for Korean American resistance and re-   39
covery, so that we can become American without dying of *han*.

Although the sentiments expressed in these letters seemed to break down   40
roughly along racial lines—that is, all writers who were identifiably people of color wrote in support—and one might become alarmed at the depth of the divisions they imply, I like to think that I have experienced the desire of many Americans, especially Americans of color, to do as Rodney King pleaded on the second day of *sa-i-ku:* "We're all stuck here for awhile. . . . Let's try to work it out."

In my view, it's important for us to think about *all* of what Rodney King said and   41
not just the words "we all can get along," which have been depoliticized and transformed into a Disneyesque catchphrase for Pat Boone songs and roadside billboards in Los Angeles. It seems to me the emphasis is on the being "stuck here for awhile" together as we await "our day in court."[19]

Like the African American man who wrote from prison, the African American   42
man who had been brutally beaten by white police might have felt the desire to "love everybody," but he had to amend—or rectify—that wish. He had to speak last about loving "people of color." The impulse to "love everybody" was there, but the conditions were not right. For now, the most practical and progressive agenda may be people of color trying to "work it out."

Finding community through national consciousness.   The place where Korean   43
and American legacies converge for Korean Americans is the exhortation to "go home to where you belong."

One of the letters I received was from a Korean American living in Chicago. He   44
had read a translation of my essay in a Korean language newspaper. "Although you were born in the U.S.A.," he wrote, noticing what none of the white men who ordered me to go back to "my" country had, "your ethnical background and your complexion belong to Korea. It is time to give up your U.S. citizenship and go to Korea."

Some ruined merchants are claiming that they will pull up stakes and return to   45
Korea, but I know that this is not possible for most of them. Even if their stores had not been destroyed, even if they were able to sell their businesses and take the proceeds to Korea, most of them would not have enough to buy a home or business there, since both require total cash up front. Neither would they be able to find work in the society they left behind because it is plagued by recession, repression, and fierce economic competition.

Going back to Korea. The dream of going back to Korea fed the spirit of my fa-   46
ther, who came to Chicago in 1926 and lived in the United States for 63 years, during which time he never became a U.S. citizen, at first because the law did not allow it and later because he did not want to. He kept himself going by believing that he would return to Korea in triumph one day. Instead, he died in Oakland at 88. Only his remains returned to Korea, where we buried him in accordance with his wishes.

Hasn't the dream of going back home to where you belong sustained most of   47
America's unwanted at one time or another, giving meaning to lives of toil and mak-

ing it possible to endure other people's hatred and rejection? Isn't the attempt to find community through national consciousness natural for people refused an American identity because racism does not give them that choice?

Korean national consciousness, the resolve to resist and fight back when threatened with extermination, was all that could be called upon when the Korean Americans in Los Angeles found themselves abandoned. They joined together to guard each other's means of livelihood with guns, relying on Korean-language radio and newspapers to communicate with and help each other. On the third day after the outbreak of violence, more than 30,000 Korean Americans gathered for a peace march in downtown L.A. in what was perhaps the largest and most quickly organized mass mobilization in Asian American history. Musicians in white, the color of mourning, beat traditional Korean drums in sorrow, anger, and celebration of community, a call to arms like a collective heartbeat.[20] I believe that the mother of Edward Song Lee, the Los Angeles–born college student mistaken for a looter and shot to death in the streets, has been able to persevere in great part because of the massive outpouring of sympathy expressed by the Korean-American community that shared and understood her *han*.

I have been critical lately of cultural nationalism as detrimental to Korean Americans, especially Korean American women, because it operates on exclusions and fosters intolerance and uniformity of thought while stifling self-criticism and encouraging sacrifice, even to the point of suicide. But *sa-i-ku* makes me think again: what remains for those who are left to stand alone? If Korean Americans refuse to be victims or political pawns in the U.S. while rejecting the exhortation that we go back to Korea where we belong, what will be our weapons of choice?

In the darkest days of Japanese colonial rule, even after being stripped of land and of all economic means of survival, Koreans were threatened with total erasure when the colonizers rewrote Korean history, outlawed the Korean language, forced the subjugated people to worship the Japanese emperor, and demanded that they adopt Japanese names. One of the results of these cultural-annihilation policies was Koreans' fierce insistence on the sanctity of Korean national identity that persists to this day. In this context, it is not difficult to understand why nationalism has been the main refuge of Koreans and Korean Americans.

While recognizing the potential dangers of nationalism as a weapon, I for one am not ready to respond to the antiessentialists' call to relinquish my Korean American identity. It is easy enough for the French and Germans to call for a common European identity and an end to nationalisms, but what of the peoples suppressed and submerged while France and Germany exercised their national prerogatives? I am mindful of the argument that the resurgence of nationalism in Europe is rooted in historical and contemporary political and economic inequality among the nations of Europe. Likewise, I have noticed that many white Americans do not like to think of themselves as belonging to a race, even while thinking of people of color almost exclusively in terms of race. In the same way, many men think of themselves as "human beings" and of women as the ones having a gender. Thus crime, small businesses, and all Korean–African American interactions are seen and interpreted through the lens of race in the same dominant culture that angrily rejects the use of the racial lens for viewing yellow/white or black/white interactions and insists suddenly that we are all "American" whenever we attempt to assert our identity as people of color. It is far easier for Anglo Americans to call for an end to cultural nationalisms than for Korean Americans to give up national consciousness, which makes it possible to survive the vicious racism that would deny our existence as either Korean Americans or Americans.

Is there anything of use to us in Korean nationalism? During one thousand years   52
of Chinese suzerainty, the Korean ruling elite developed a philosophy called *sadaejui,* or reliance of the weak on the strong. In direct opposition to this way of thought is what is called *jaju* or *juche sasang,* or self-determination.[21] Both *sadaejui* and *juche sasang* are ways of dealing with unequal power relationships and resisting the transformation of one's homeland into a battlefield for others, but *sadaejui* has never worked any better for Koreans than it has for any minority group in America. *Juche sasang,* on the other hand, has the kind of oppositional potential needed in the struggle against silence and invisibility. From Korean national consciousness, we can recover this fierce refusal to accept subjugation, which is the first step in the effort to build community, so that we can work with others to challenge the forces that would have us annihilate each other instead of our mutual oppression.

What is clear is that we cannot "become American" without dying of *han* unless   53
we think about community in new ways. Self-determination does not mean living alone. At least for now, that may mean mining the rich and haunted lode of Korean national consciousness while we struggle to understand how our fate is entwined with the fate of others lying prostrate before the triumphal procession of the winners of History.[22] During the past fifteen years or so, many young Korean nationalists have been studying the legacies of colonialism and imperialism that they share with peoples in many Asian, African, and Latin American nations. At the same time that we take note of this work, we can also try to understand how nationalism and feminism can be worked together to demystify the limitations and reductiveness of each as a weapon of empowerment. If Korean national consciousness is ever to be such a weapon for us, we must use it to create a new kind of nationalism-in-internationalism to help us call forth a culture of survival and recovery, so that our *han* might be released and we might be freed to dream fiercely of different possibilities.

NOTES

1. According to a September 1992 Dun and Bradstreet survey of 560 business owners in Koreatown in South Central Los Angeles, an estimated 40 percent of the businesses damaged during *sa-i-ku* have closed their doors permanently. Moreover, almost 40 percent had no insurance or were insured for 50 percent or less of their total losses ("L.A. Riot Took Heavy Toll on Businesses," *San Francisco Chronicle,* 12 September 1992).

2. Following quota changes in U.S. immigration laws in 1965, the Korean population in America increased more than eightfold to almost one million. Between 1970 and 1990, Los Angeles Koreatown grew from a few blocks of stores and businesses into a community base for all sorts of economic and cultural activities.

3. Pretense, of course, because I was only passing for Chinese. The temporary comfort I experienced would come to an end whenever it was discovered that I could speak no Chinese and that I had no organic links to Chinese Americans, who frequently underscored both our commonalities and our differences by telling me that everything Korean—even *kimchi,* that quintessentially Korean vegetable eaten at every Korean meal—was originally Chinese.

4. The Black-Korean Alliance (BKA) was formed, with the assistance of the Los Angeles County Human Relations Commission, to improve relations between the Korean and African American communities after four Korean merchants were killed in robberies during the month of April 1986. The BKA sponsored activities and events, such as joint church ser-

vices, education forums, joint cultural events, and seminars on crime prevention and community economic development. The BKA never received political or financial support from the public or private sectors. The organization had neither its own meeting place nor a telephone. Grass-roots participation was not extensive, and despite the good intentions of the individuals involved, the BKA was unable to prevent the killing of a dozen more Korean merchants in southern California between 1990 and *sa-i-ku,* or to stop the escalation of tensions between the two communities after the shooting of 15-year-old Latasha Harlins by Korean merchant Soon Ja Du in March, 1991. By June of that year, after police declared the killing of an African American man by a Korean liquor-store owner "justifiable homicide," African American groups began boycotting the store, and the BKA failed to convince African American boycotters and Korean merchants to meet together to negotiate an end to the conflict. Nor were the members of the BKA successful in obtaining the help of members of the Los Angeles City Council or the California State Legislature, who might have been instrumental in preventing the destructive violence of *sa-i-ku* if they had had the integrity and farsightedness to address the intensifying hostilities before it was too late. After *sa-i-ku,* the BKA was in disarray, and as of this writing, its members are planning to dissolve the group.

5. According to John Murray, founder of the southern California chapter of Cal-Pac, the black beverage and grocers' association, African American liquor-store owners "sold stores they had bought in the mid-1960s for two times monthly gross sales—roughly $80,000 at the time, depending on the store—for five times monthly gross, or about $300,000." After the Jews fled in the wake of the Watts riots, African Americans were enabled by civil rights legislative mandates to obtain for the first time credit from government-backed banks to start a number of small businesses. But operating liquor stores, although profitable, was grueling, dangerous, and not something fathers wanted their sons to do, according to interviews with African American owners and former owners of liquor stores in African American communities. Former liquor merchant Ed Piert exclaimed: "Seven days a week, 20 hours a day, no vacations, people stealing. That's slave labor. I wouldn't buy another liquor store." When liquor prices were deregulated in 1978 and profit margins shrank in the face of competition from volume buyers, many African American owners sold out to Korean immigrants carrying cash collected in rotating credit clubs called *kye* (Susan Moffat, "Shopkeepers Fight Back: Blacks Join with Koreans in a Battle to Rebuild Their Liquor Stores," *Los Angeles Times,* 15 May 1992).

6. In a newspaper interview, Alberto Machon, an 18-year-old junior at Washington Preparatory High School who had moved to South Central Los Angeles with his family from El Salvador ten years ago, said that he was laughing as he watched every Korean store looted or burned down because "I felt that they deserved it for the way they was treatin' people . . . the money that we are giving to the stores they're taking it to their community, Koreatown." Thirty-two-year-old Arnulfo Nunez Barrajas served four days in the Los Angeles County jail for curfew violation. He was arrested while going from Santa Ana to Los Angeles to see his aunt, whose son had been killed during the upheavals. According to Nunez, "[T]he ones they've caught are only from the black race and the Latin race. I haven't seen any Koreans or Chinese. Why not them? Or white? Why only the black race and the Latinos? Well, it's racism" (*Los Angeles Times,* 13 May 1992).

7. L. A. Chung, "Tensions Divide Blacks, Asians," *San Francisco Chronicle,* 4 May 1992.

8. *Los Angeles Times,* 5 May 1992.

9. They were also given to gloating over the inability of American authorities to maintain social order as well as the South Korean government can. In an interview, a South Korean diplomat in Los Angeles remarked to me that he was astonished at how ill-prepared the Los Angeles police and the National Guard were for "mass disturbances." They did not react quickly enough, they were very inefficient, they had no emergency plan, and even their communications network broke down, he observed. He could not imagine "riots" getting out of

control in South Korea, which was ruled by the military from 1961 to 1987; there, he com-mented, "the police are very effective. They work closely with the military."

10. For example, a story about the "black riots" in the 6 May 1992 *Central Daily News* in Seoul listed the writer as Korean-American sociologist Edward T'ae-han Chang, who was as-tonished when he saw it because he hadn't written it (personal communication).

11. In 1913, a group of Korean-American laborers was run out of Hemet Valley, California by a mob of anti-Japanese whites. The Koreans responded by insisting that they were Korean, not Japanese. What might seem a ludicrous response to racist expulsion has to be viewed in light of the fact that the U.S. sanctioned Japan's 1909 annexation of Korea, closing all Korean delegations and placing Korean immigrants under the authority of Japanese consulates. Since they were classified as Japanese, Korean Americans were subject to the Alien Land Acts that targeted Japanese by denying them the right afforded all others regardless of race, nativity, or citizenship: the right to own land in California and nine other states. Also, foreign-born Ko-reans were able to become naturalized U.S. citizens only after the McCarran-Walter Act of 1952 permitted naturalization of Japanese. I have heard some Asian Americans equate the Chinese- and Japanese-American use of signs and buttons reading "I Am Not Korean" dur-ing *sa-i-ku* with the Korean American (and, not coincidentally, Chinese American) practice of wearing buttons saying "I Am Not Japanese" during World War II. But, in light of the speci-ficities of Korean and Korean American history, this cannot be a one-to-one comparison.

12. In a 23 July 1992 interview, a 50-year-old Korean immigrant woman whose South Central Los Angeles corner grocery store had been completely destroyed during *sa-i-ku* told me, "The America I imagined [before I arrived here] was like what I saw in the movies—clean, wide streets, flowers everywhere. I imagined Americans would be all big, tall . . . with white faces and blond hair. . . . But the America here is not like that. When I got up to walk around the neighborhood the morning after we arrived in Los Angeles from Korea, it was as if we had come to Mexico."

13. John Berger and Jean Mohr, *A Seventh Man: A Book of Images and Words about the Ex-periences of Migrant Workers in Europe* (New York: Penguin Books, 1975). I want to thank Barry Maxwell for bringing this work to my attention.

14. I am not grappling directly with social class issues here because, although I am cog-nizant of their crucial importance, I am simply not qualified to address them at the present time. The exploited "guest workers" in Europe described by Berger and Mohr, unlike the Korean immigrants to the U.S., brought with them their laboring bodies but not capital to start small businesses. Because they are merchants, the class interests of Korean American shopowners in Los Angeles differ clearly from the interests of poor African American and Latino customers. But working with simple dyads is impossible, since Korean American shopowners are also of color and mostly immigrants from a country colonized by the United States. At the same time, it seems to me that class factors have been more important than race factors in shaping Korean-American immigrants' attitudes toward African American and Latino populations. Perhaps because of the devastation caused by Japanese colonization and the Korean War, many Koreans exhibit intensely negative attitudes toward the poor and in-deed desperately fear being associated with them. I have often marveled at the importance placed on conspicuous consumer items, especially clothing, in South Korean society, where a shabbily dressed person can expect only shabby treatment. In the 1960s, a middle-class Amer-ican could make a social statement against materialistic values by dressing in tattered clothing without being mistaken for a homeless person. Now that this is no longer true, it seems to me that middle-class Americans exhibit some of the fears and aversions that I witnessed in South Korea. Ironically, in the society where blackness and brownness have historically been almost tantamount to a condemnation to poverty, prejudice against the poor brought from Korea is combined with home-grown U.S. racism, and the results have been explosive.

At the same time, I have also noticed among Korean merchants profound empathy with the poor, whose situation many older immigrants know from first-hand past experiences. I personally witnessed many encounters between Korean merchants who lost their stores and African American neighbors in South Central during July 1992, when I accompanied the merchants as they visited their burned-out sites. None of the encounters were hostile. On the contrary, most of the African American neighbors embraced the Korean shopowners and expressed concern for them, while the merchants in turn asked warmly after the welfare of their neighbors' children. Although Korean–African American interaction has been racialized in the dominant culture, the quality of these relationships, like the quality of all human relationships, proved far more individual than that racial schematizing allows for.

15. Every South Korean middle school, high-school, and college student is required to take a course in "National Ethics," formerly called "Anticommunism." This course, which loosely resembles a civics class on Western civilization, government, constitutionalism, and political ideology, emphasizes the superiority of capitalism over communism and the importance of the national identity and the modern capitalist state. From the early 1960s through the 1970s, when most of the Los Angeles Korean immigrant merchants studied "Anticommunism" or "National Ethics," they were taught that "capitalism" and "democracy" are the same, and that both are antithetical to "communism" or "socialism." According to this logic, criticisms of the U.S., a "democracy," are tantamount to praise of "communism." Such a view left little room for acknowledgment of racism and other social problems in American society. Indeed, the South Korean National Security Law formerly prosecuted and jailed writers who depicted Americans negatively and film makers who portrayed North Koreans as good-looking or capable of falling in love. Today, however, the interpretation of what constitutes antistate activity is far narrower than in former decades, and although the South Korean government maintains that "pro–North Korea" activities are against the law, anti-U.S. sentiments have been common in South Korea since the mid-1980s.

16. I cannot help thinking that these violent baptisms are an Asian American legacy of sorts, for in some sense it was the internment that forced the Japanese Americans to "become American" half a century ago.

17. Many Korean Americans have criticized the *Los Angeles Times* and local television news, and the ABC network in particular, for repeatedly running stories about Soon Ja Du shooting Latasha Harlins (the tape was the second-most-played video during the week of the riots, according to the media-watch section of *A Magazine: An Asian American Quarterly* 1, no. 3, 4). They complained that the Los Angeles ABC affiliate aired the store videotape in tandem with the King footage. ABC even inserted the Du-Harlins tape segment into its reportage of the height of the *sa-i-ku* upheavals. Korean Americans have also protested the media focus on armed Korean American merchants. In particular, they objected to the repeated use of the image of a Korean merchant pointing a gun at an unseen, off-camera target. They knew that he was being shot at and that he was firing only at the ground, but they felt that the image was used to depict Korean immigrants as violent and lawless. They argued that by blocking out the context, the news media harmed Korean Americans, about whom little positive was known by the American public. Tong S. Suhr wrote in a Korean American newspaper:

> The Harlins killing is a tragic but isolated case. . . . This is not to condone the Harlins killing; nor is it to justify the death by countering with how many merchants in turn have been killed. Our complaint is directed to the constant refrain of "the Korean-born grocer killing a black teen-ager," which couldn't help but sow the seeds of racial hatred . . . [and make me wonder]: Was there any conspiracy among the . . . white-dominated media to pit one ethnic group against another and sit back and watch them destroy one another? . . . Why were the Korean American merchants portrayed as gun-toting vigilantes shooting indiscriminately when they decided to protect their lives and businesses by arming themselves because no po-

lice protection was available? Why wasn't there any mention of the fact that they were fired upon first? Why such biased reporting? ("Time for Soul Searching by Media," *Korea Times*, 29 June 1992).

I would challenge representatives of the news media who argue that visual images of beatings and shootings, especially when they are racialized or sexualized, are "exciting" and "interesting," even when they are aired hundreds or thousands of times, when compared with "boring" images of the everyday. Three months after *sa-i-ku*, I visited a videotape brokerage company in search of generic footage that could be used in a documentary about the Korean immigrant experience of losing their means of livelihood. Almost every inch of the stringers' footage contained images of police cars, fire engines, and uniformed men heroically wiping their brows as they courageously prepared to meet the challenges before them. Since there were neither police nor firemen anywhere in sight in South Central or Koreatown during the first three days of *sa-i-ku*, none of this footage was of use to me. No doubt the men who shot these scenes chose what seemed to them the most "interesting" and "exciting" images. But if I, a woman and a Korean American, had had a camera in my hands, I would have chosen quite different ones.

18. *Newsweek*, 18 May 1992.

19. The text of King's statement was printed in the *Los Angeles Times* (2 May 1992) as follows:

> People I just want to say . . . can we all get along? Can we get along? Can we stop making it horrible for the older people and the kids? . . . We've got enough smog here in Los Angeles, let alone to deal with the setting of those fires and things. It's just not right. It's not right, and it's not going to change anything.
>
> We'll get our justice. They've won the battle but they haven't won the war. We will have our day in court and that's all we want. . . . I'm neutral. I love everybody. I love people of color. . . . I'm not like they're . . . making me out to be.
>
> We've got to quit. We've got to quit. . . . I can understand the first upset in the first two hours after the verdict, but to go on, to keep going on like this, and to see a security guard shot on the ground, it's just not right. It's just not right because those people will never go home to their families again. And I mean, please, we can get along here. We all can get along. We've just got to, just got to. We're all stuck here for awhile. . . . Let's try to work it out. Let's try to work it out.

20. The news media that did cover this massive demonstration invariably focused on the Korean musicians because they looked and sounded alien and exotic. Ironically, most of them were young, American-born or at least American-educated Korean Americans who learned traditional music as a way to recover their cultural heritage. They perform at many events: I remember them in the demonstrations against the 1991 Gulf War.

21. *Juche sasang*, the concept of self-determination, was attractive to Koreans before the division of the country after the defeat of Japan in World War II. However, since the term *juche* is central to the official political ideology in communist North Korea, the synonym *jaju* is used in South Korean officialdom.

22. I borrow this image from Walter Benjamin, "Theses on the Philosophy of History," *Illuminations* (New York: Schocken Books, 1969), 256. I would like to thank Shelly Sunn Wong for helping me see its relevance to Korean Americans in the 1990s.

Working with the Text

1. Kim states as the core of her essay her desire to "explore the questions of whether or not recovery is possible for Korean Americans, and what will become of [their] attempts to 'become American' without dying of *han*." Why is it so hard for Korean Americans to "become American"? How do various

people portrayed in the essay see the process of Koreans and Korean Americans "becoming American" differently?

2. How does Kim characterize the Korean immigrant experience? How is it similar to or different from other immigrant experiences? How does she describe Korean Americans' relationship to Korea? How does the history of Korea help shape Korean immigrants' relationship to America?

3. One of the premises of Kim's essay is that interracial relations in America are very dependent on the images of race and racial conflict that are depicted in the news media. How does she describe the media as creating and perpetuating certain images and attitudes about Korean Americans in particular and interracial conflict generally? Do you agree with her that these images perpetuate and even create racist attitudes? Do you think that media images help construct views of certain minorities as alien and difficult to assimilate into U.S. society?

 4. Near the end of the essay, Kim asks, "Isn't the attempt to find community through national consciousness natural for people refused an American identity because racism does not give them that choice?" Her assertion is contrary to some popular opinion (of which she gives many examples) that groups like Korean Americans encounter "racist" responses because they refuse to accept an American identity. Does her essay imply that there are any possible routes out of these contrary perspectives of cause and effect? How would you argue one way or the other about whether racist attitudes give rise to "national consciousness" and "cultural nationalisms" (as she calls them) or vice versa? Do you think that this central tension can also be applied to other groups in the United States?

 5. In his essay earlier in this chapter, Guillermo Gómez-Peña refers to the city of Los Angeles as the "epicenter" and "capital city" of "America's racial and social crisis." How do Kim's accounts of the Los Angeles upheavals, Korean/African American conflict, and the responses to her essay in *Newsweek* support Gómez-Peña's claim? To what extent do her claims about race and ethnicity apply to America's race problem in general? Do you think that Kim overstates the case? Do you agree with Gómez-Peña's assertion that America has a "race crisis"?

UNDERSTANDING AFROCENTRISM: WHY BLACKS DREAM OF A WORLD WITHOUT WHITES

GERALD EARLY

■ Born in 1952, Gerald Early attended the University of Pennsylvania and received his master's and doctoral degrees from Cornell. Currently a professor of English and African American studies at Washington University in St. Louis, Early also lectures widely on literary, cultural, and racial topics. His books include *Tuxedo Junction: Essays on American Culture* (1990), *The Culture of Bruising: Essays on*

Literature, Prizefighting, and Modern American Culture (1991), and *One Nation Under a Groove: Motown and American Culture* (1995). He has also published a volume of poems and a memoir. In the following 1996 essay, Early, though not an Afrocentrist himself, attempts to explain the appeal of this movement among the black middle and working classes today.

The White man will never admit his real references. He will steal everything you have and still call you those names.

—Ishmael Reed, *Mumbo Jumbo* (1972)

Furthermore, no one can be thoroughly educated until he learns as much about the Negro as he knows about other people.

—Carter G. Woodson, *The Mis-Education of the Negro* (1933)

[Alexander] Crummell's black nationalism was marked by certain inconsistencies, but they derived from the inconsistencies and hypocrisy of American racism, rather than from any intellectual shortcomings on his part. It was impossible to create an ideology that responded rationally to an irrational system.

—Wilson Jeremiah Moses, *Alexander Crummell: A Study of Civilization and Discontent* (1989)

I n a span of three weeks during the early spring semester of 1995, Angela Davis   1
and bell hooks, two notable black leftist, feminist thinkers, visited the campus of Washington University in St. Louis, invited by different student groups. They were generally well received, indeed, enthusiastically so. But there was, for each of them during these visits, something of a jarring note, both involving black students.

Professor Davis, entertaining questions during a panel session after having spo-   2
ken earlier on the subject of prison reform, was asked by a black woman student what she had to offer black people as a solution to their problems. The student went on to explain that she did not consider herself an African American. She was simply an African, wishing to have nothing to do with being an American or with America itself. She wanted black people to separate themselves entirely from "Europeans," as she called white Americans, and wanted to know what Davis could suggest to further that aim.

Davis answered that she was not inclined to such stringent race separation. She   3
was proud of being of African descent but wished to be around a variety of people, not just people like herself. Davis felt further that blacks should not isolate themselves but accept in partnership anyone who was sincerely interested in the cause of overthrowing capitalism, a standard and reasonable Marxist response to the "essentializing" of race in a way that would divert true political engagement "against the system." The student was visibly annoyed with the answer, which presumably smacked of "white" intellectualism.

Professor bell hooks, after her address on ending racism and sexism in Amer-   4
ica—love, I think, was the answer—was asked by a black woman student how feminism was relevant to black women. Hooks explained that feminism was not only for white women, that black women needed to read more feminist texts, even if

some of them were racist. After all, Karl Marx was racist, but he did give the world a brilliant analysis of capitalism. She had said in her speech how disappointed she was that her black women students at City College of New York were not inclined to embrace feminism, rejecting it as something white. She felt that these black women were unduly influenced by black male rappers who bashed feminism. The answer did not persuade or please the student.

Later that day, I heard many black undergraduates dismiss hooks's talk as not addressing the needs of black people, as being too geared to the white feminists in the audience. Some were disturbed that hooks would feel that they formed their opinions on the basis of listening to rap records. None of this was said, necessarily, with hostility, but rather with regret and a shade of condescension that only the young can so keenly and innocently express when speaking about the foolishness of their elders. 5

I recall a fairly recent incident where a black student, a very bright young woman, asked if, when doing research, one had to acknowledge racist books. I told her that a certain amount of objectivity was part of the discipline of being a scholar. Anger at unjust or inaccurate statements and assessments was understandable, but personalizing everything often caused a kind of tunnel vision where crude self-affirmation seemed to be the only fit end of scholarship. She responded that she would refuse to acknowledge racist sources, that if the book was racist, then everything it said was tainted and should be disregarded. 6

The attitudes of these students have been shaped by Afrocentrism, an insistence by a growing number of black Americans on seeing the world from an "African-centered" perspective in response to the dominant "European-centered" perspective, to which they feel they have been subjected throughout their lives. Afrocentrism is many things and has many degrees of advocacy. It can range from the commercialism and pretense of the shallow holiday called Kwanza (no shallower, it should be said, than the commercialized celebration of Christmas) to the kente-cloth ads and nationalist talk that one finds in most black publications these days; from talk about racist European scholarship to a view that world culture is essentially African in origin and that Europeans are usurpers, thieves, and generally inferior. On the one hand, we have the recent cover story "Is Jesus Black?" in *Emerge,* an Afrocentric-tinged news magazine for the black middle class. The answer in this instance, of course, is clearly yes. (Obviously, this is grounds for competing claims between blacks and Jews; whatever can be said about Jesus' skin color or the religious movement that bears his name, there is no question that he was a Jew.) On the other hand, we have the first explicitly Afrocentric Hollywood western in Mario Van Peebles's 1993 film *Posse,* a jumbled multicultural critique of white fin-de-siècle imperialism and the myth of how the West was won. 7

No doubt, Afrocentrists specifically and black folk generally found it to be a signal victory that in the recent television dramatization of the love affair between Solomon and Sheba, Sheba was played by a black actress and Solomon by a swarthy Hispanic. In the 1959 Hollywood film version of *Solomon and Sheba,* directed by King Vidor—who, incidentally, made the first all-black Hollywood film—Solomon was played by Yul Brynner and Sheba by Gina Lollobrigida. It is safe to say that the real Solomon and the real Sheba, if they ever existed, did not look remotely like any of the actors who ever played them. But whom we want them to look like is very im- 8 portant. The Afrocentrists will feel their triumph to be complete when black actors portray Beethoven, Joseph Haydn, Warren G. Harding, Alexander Hamilton, Hannibal, Abraham Lincoln, Dwight Eisenhower, Cleopatra, Moses, Jesus Christ, and Saint Augustine. Many African Americans are inclined to believe that any noted white with ambiguous ancestry must be black. They are also inclined to believe that any white with dark skin tones, one who hangs around blacks or who "acts black" in some way is truly black. At various times in my life, I have heard blacks argue vehemently that Madonna, Phoebe Snow, Keith Jarrett, Mae West, Ava Gardner, and Dorothy Parker were black, even though they did not have a shred of evidence to support the claims. Blacks have always been fascinated by "passing," by the possibility that some whites are really black—"fooling old massa," so to speak.

Afrocentrism is an intellectual movement, a political view, a historically traceable 9 evolution, a religious orthodoxy. It derives in part from Negritude and Pan-Africanism, which stressed the culture and achievements of Africans. Both movements were started by Africans, West Indians, and African Americans in response to European colonialism and the worldwide oppression of African-descended people. But Afrocentrism is also a direct offshoot of earlier forms of black nationalism, in which blacks around the world believed they had a special destiny to fulfill and a special consciousness to redeem. More important, Afrocentrism is a mood that has largely erupted in the past ten to fifteen years in response to integration, or, perhaps more precisely, to the failure of integration. Many blacks who have succeeded in the white world tend to feel most Afrocentric, although I think it would be a mistake to see Afrocentrism purely as middle class, since significant numbers of working-class blacks are attracted to some elements of it. The bourgeois, "midcult" element of Afrocentrism, nonetheless, is very strong. "Integrated" middle-class blacks see it as a demonstration of their race loyalty and solidarity with their brothers and sisters throughout the world, whether in American cities or on African farms. (It is worth noting the economic clout of the black middle class, which can be seen in the growing number of black Hollywood films and filmmakers, in new black magazines ranging from *Body and Soul* to *The Source* to *Upscale,* and in the larger audience for black books. It is the market power of this class that has given Afrocentrism its force as a consumer ideology.)

So the middle-class black, having had more contact with whites and their insti- 10 tutions, is expected to speak for and to other blacks. Afrocentrism, like Negritude and Pan-Africanism, is meant to be an ideological glue to bring black people together, not just on the basis of color but as the expression of a cultural and spiritual will that crosses class and geographical lines. As W.E.B. Du Bois wrote in 1940: "Since the fifteenth century these ancestors of mine and their other descendants have had a common history; have suffered a common disaster and have one long memory. . . . The real essence of this kinship is its social heritage of slavery; the discrimination and insults; and this heritage binds together not simply the children of Africa, but extends through yellow Asia and into the South Seas. It is this unity that draws me to Africa."

Louis H. Farrakhan, the head of the Nation of Islam, is probably the most famil- 11 iar figure associated with Afrocentrism. (Muhammad Ali introduced Islamic conversion to an even bigger public, suffering greatly for his religious and political beliefs and becoming the most noted and charismatic dissident of his era. Ali's prodigious athletic abilities and his genial temperament succeeded in endearing him to the American public despite his religion. He never became a member of Farrakhan's sect.) Farrakhan is a fiery preacher, prone to making extreme statements, with a militant flair and a racist edge, that have the conviction of truth among some blacks. He especially exploits the idea that he is a heroic black man at grave risk for daring to tell the truth about the white man. (Malcolm X used this device effectively, too.) He is also a master demagogue who exploits the paranoia of his audience. But then, as a friend once said to me, "What black person isn't justified in being at least half paranoid?"

Farrakhan has found three effective lines of entry among blacks, particularly young blacks, that draw on the Afrocentric impulse: First, that Islam is the true religion of black people. (This has led to a move among black Christian leaders to point out with great vehemence the African origins of Christianity, to make it, in effect, a black religion.) Second, that black people need business enterprise in their community in order to liberate themselves (an old belief among blacks, going back to at least the early part of the nineteenth century). And third, that Jews of European descent (whom he calls "false Jews") are not to be trusted, a charge that exploits the current tension between blacks and Jews—and that Farrakhan has used to move into the black civil rights establishment. All three positions enjoy remarkable support within the black middle class, a situation that has helped Farrakhan tap people's insecurities for his own purposes. The Nation of Islam may be famous for converting addicts and criminals, but above all, it wants, as all religions do, to win over the middle class, with its money, its respectability, and its organizational know-how.

Whatever might be said of Farrakhan's importance as a political figure in the black community or in the United States, he is a minor figure in the development of Afrocentrism. His position in the history of Afrocentrism is similar to that of, say, Rush Limbaugh in the development of American conservatism. He is, like Limbaugh, a figure the media can use to give a sellable face and voice to a unique temper among a group of people. For both Limbaugh and Farrakhan represent an intense sentimentality in American life, a yearning for a fantasized, idealized past of racial grandeur and simplicity. This sentimentality appeals powerfully to the black middle class, which yearns for a usable, untainted past. This partly explains why Farrakhan and the Muslims can often be found speaking to black college students.

In thinking about the connection between class and nationalistic feelings, it should be recalled that in Harriet Beecher Stowe's 1852 novel *Uncle Tom's Cabin*, the most light-complexioned blacks, the ones with the greatest skills, George, Eliza, and Cassy, return to Africa at the novel's end to retrieve their degraded patrimony. It might be said that this is purely Stowe's own perverse vision, since some of the fiercest advocates for returning to Africa have been Martin Delany, Alexander Crummell, and Marcus Garvey, all very dark men. Yet there is more than a little truth to the idea that class, caste, and race consciousness are closely interwoven. Nationalism of whatever sort has almost always been an affair of a disaffected middle class. And until the 1920s, the black middle class in America was disproportionately made up of light-skinned people.

The paradox of the bourgeois aspect of Afrocentrism is that it rejects cosmopolitanism as being "white" or "Eurocentric." Yet Afrocentrism has no other way of seeing cosmopolitanism except on the "Eurocentric" model, so it tries to make Africa for black Americans the equivalent of what Europe is for white Americans: the source of civilization. Indeed, by trying to argue that Africa is the source of Western civilization, the Afrocentric sees the African, symbolically, as the mother of white Europe (just as the black mother, the mammy, is the mythic progenitor of the white South, or so Langston Hughes seemed to believe, in his famous short story "Father and Son," which became his even more famous play *Mulatto*). The African becomes, in this view, the most deeply cultured person on the planet, which matches his status as the oldest person on the planet, with the longest and deepest genetic history. In short, Afrocentrism becomes another form of the American apologizing for being American to people he imagines are his cultural superiors. Afrocentrism tries to mask a quest for American filiopiety behind a facade of African ancestor and culture worship.

It would be easy, on one level, to dismiss Afrocentrism as an expression, in white workplaces and white colleges, of intimidated black folk who are desperately trying to find a space for themselves in what they feel to be alien, unsympathetic environments. Seen this way, Afrocentrism becomes an expression of the low self-esteem and inferiority that blacks feel most intensely when they are around whites; their response is to become more "black," estranged from the environment that they find so unaccepting of them. The greatest psychic burden of the African American is that he must not only think constantly about being different but about what his difference means. And it might be suggested that Afrocentrism does not solve this problem but merely reflects it in a different mirror. There is a certain amount of truth to this, especially at a time when affirmative action, which promotes group identification and group difference, tends to intensify black self-consciousness. And black people, through no fault of their own, are afflicted with a debilitating sense of self-consciousness when around whites. When whites are in the rare situation of being a minority in a sea of blacks, they often exhibit an abject self-consciousness as well, but the source of that self-consciousness is quite different. The white is used to traveling anywhere in the world and having his cultural inclinations accommodated. The black is neither used to this nor does he realistically expect it. The European exults in his culture, while the African is utterly degraded by his. That blacks should want to free themselves from the white gaze seems not merely normal but essential to the project of reconstructing themselves as a people on their own terms. And the history of blacks in the United States has been an ongoing project—tragic, pathetic, noble, heroic, misguided, sublime—of self-reconstruction.

16

> When it comes to black folk in America, the white man wants to say that if you have a ½₂ portion of black blood, a mere drop of black blood, then you are black, no matter what your skin color. But when it comes to the ancient Egyptians, it doesn't matter if they have a drop of black blood—and we know that they had at least a ½₂ portion of African blood. It doesn't matter how much African blood they have, they are still white. The white man wants to have his cake and eat it too. When it's convenient he wants you to be black, and when it's convenient he wants you to be white. Either you're a nigger, because he thinks you're nothing. Or you're white, if you have done anything he's bound to respect. The white man wants to control all the definitions of blackness.

—A conversation with an Afrocentric friend

... There are several texts that might be considered the literary and intellectual 17
cornerstones of the Afrocentrism movement. Molefi K. Asante, professor and chair
of African American studies at Temple University in Philadelphia, is credited with
inventing the name "Afrocentrism" or "Afrocentricity" (although currently the term
"Africentrism" is on the rise in certain quarters, probably because there is a group of
black folk who, for some reason, despise the prefix "Afro," as if the word "Africa" itself were created by the people of the continent rather than by Europeans). Asante's
very short books, including *The Afrocentric Idea,* published in 1987, and *Afrocentricity: The Theory of Social Change,* published in 1980, are frequently the starting
points for people seeking a basic explanation of this ideology. As defined by Asante,
Afrocentrism seems to take the terms and values of Eurocentrism—intense individualism, crass greed, lack of spirituality, warlike inclinations, dominance and racism,
dishonesty and hypocrisy—and color their opposites black, giving us a view of
black people not terribly different from the romantic racism of Harriet Beecher
Stowe and other whites like her in the nineteenth and twentieth centuries. I cannot
recount the number of "race sensitivity" meetings I have attended where blacks
begin to describe themselves (or those they perceive to be Africans) as more spiritual, more family-oriented, more community-oriented, more rhythmic, more natural, and less combative than whites. All of which is, of course, a crock of nonsense,
largely the expression of wishes for qualities that blacks see as absent from their
community life now. But, thanks to Asante, this has become the profile of the
African in the Afrocentric vision.

Martin Bernal's massively researched two-volume *Black Athena* (published in 18
1987 and 1991) is a popular title in Afrocentric circles, in large measure because
Bernal, a professor at Cornell, is one of the few white scholars to take Afrocentrism
seriously—William Piersen, Robert Farris Thompson, and Andrew Hacker, in de-
cidedly different ways, are others—and one of the few to write an academic treatise
in its defense that forces whites to take it seriously too. (The irony that blacks still
need whites, in some measure, to sell their ideas and themselves to other whites is
not entirely lost on those who have thought about this.)

Black Athena supports three major contentions of the Afrocentrists: 1) ancient 19
Egypt was a black civilization; 2) the Greeks derived a good deal, if not all, of their
philosophy and religion from the Egyptians; 3) European historiography has tried
strenuously and with clear political objectives to deny both. Bernal's book provoked
a scathing attack by Mary R. Lefkowitz, a professor at Wellesley, who characterizes
Afrocentrism as a perversion of the historiography of antiquity and a degradation
of academic standards for political ends. Lefkowitz has also battled with Tony Martin, a cultural historian, barrister, and Marcus Garvey specialist, who began using
and endorsing the Nation of Islam's anti-Semitic *The Secret Relationship Between
Blacks and Jews* (Volume 1) in his classes on slavery at Wellesley. Martin responded
in 1993 with his own account of the dispute, *The Jewish Onslaught: Despatches from
the Wellesley Battlefront,* which elaborates his claims of Jewish racism and the
hypocrisy of academic freedom. ...

Perhaps the most popular Afrocentric text is Chancellor Williams's *The Destruc-* 20
tion of Black Civilization: Great Issues of a Race from 4500 B.C. to 2000 A.D. (published
in 1987), an account of his exhaustive research trips to Africa. Although not directly
trained in the study of African history, Williams studied under William Leo Hans-

berry, a history professor at Howard University and probably the leading black American authority on Africa during the 1930s, 1940s, and 1950s. Hansberry did path-breaking work in an utterly neglected field, eventually becoming known as "the father of African studies" in the United States. (Scholars, until recently, did not think Africa had a "history." The continent, especially its sub-Saharan regions, had an "anthropology" and an "archaeology," folkways to be discovered and remains to be unearthed, but never a record of institutions, traditions, political ideologies, and complex societies.) Williams also did research on African history at Oxford and at the University of London, where, because of colonialism, interest in the nature of African societies was far keener than in the United States. His book *The Re-Birth of African Civilization,* an account of his 1953–1957 research project investigating the nature of education in Europe and Africa, calls for Pan-African education of blacks in Africa and around the world. Williams concluded that "European" and "Euro-centric" education was antithetical, both politically and intellectually, to African in-terests, a common refrain in Afrocentrist thought. . . .

In some ways, the rise of Afrocentrism is related to the rise of "black psychology" as a discipline. The Association of Black Psychologists was organized in 1968, a time when a number of black professional offshoots were formed in political and ideo-logical protest against the mainstream, white-dominated versions of their organiza-tions. Somewhat later came the *Journal of Black Psychology,* given impetus by the initial assaults against black intelligence or pointed suggestions of black genetic in-feriority by Richard Herrnstein, Arthur Jensen, and others in the early 1970s; this was also the time of the first wave of court challenges against affirmative action. The black psychology movement argued for new modes of treatment for black mental illness, the medical efficacy of using black history to repair a collectively damaged black psyche, and the destruction of "Eurocentrism" and the values it spawned—from the idealization of white standards of beauty to the scientific measurement of intelligence—as totally inimical to the political and psychological interests of black people. Rationality, order, individualism, dominance, sexual repression as well as sexual license, aggression, warmaking, moneymaking, capitalism itself—all soon became "white values." [21]

That all of this happened during the era of Vietnam War protests, when white Western civilization was coming under withering intellectual attack from the radi-cal left, is not without significance. Radical white intellectuals, who otherwise had no more use for a black epic history than a white one, found the black version use-ful as a weapon against "Eurocentrism," which, as a result of the Vietnam War, they held in utter contempt. In short, Jean-Paul Sartre and Susan Sontag were as instru-mental, albeit indirectly, in the formation of Afrocentrism as, say, the Black Power movement of the late 1960s or the writings of African psychiatrist Frantz Fanon, whose *The Wretched of the Earth* became the revolutionary psychological profile of the oppressed black diaspora. Also occurring at this time was the movement on white college campuses to establish black studies programs, which provided a black intellectual wedge into the white academy. These programs, largely multidisciplinary, required an ideological purpose and mission to bind together the various dis-ciplines, which is why many began to articulate some kind of Afrocentrism or, as it was called in the 1970s, "black aesthetic"—in other words, an ideological frame-work to give black studies a reason for being. When used to challenge the domi- [22]

nance of Western thought, Afrocentrism becomes part of a multicultural wave of complaint and resentment against the white man by a number of groups that feel they have been oppressed.

In an age of dysfunction and psychotherapy, no one can have greater claim to having been made dysfunctional by political oppression than the African American, who was literally a slave; and no one can have a greater need for recourse to psychotherapy in the form of Afrocentrism. But what made the black psychology movement possible was the rise of the Nation of Islam, particularly the rise of Malcolm X. 23

The charismatic Muslim minister did two things. First, he forced the white mainstream press to take notice of black nationalism, Pan-Africanism, and the concept of African unity. Previously these ideas had been marginalized as ridiculous or even comic expressions of black nationalism, to be read by blacks in black barbershops and beauty salons as they thumbed through the Ripley's-Believe-It-or-Not-type work of the self-taught black historian J. A. Rogers (*One Hundred Amazing Facts about the Negro, Five Negro Presidents,* and the like). Malcolm X revitalized the ideas of Marcus Garvey, the great black nationalist leader of the 1910s and 1920s, whose Universal Negro Improvement Association became, for a time, one of the most popular black political groups in America. Malcolm, like Garvey, felt that the Negro still needed to be "improved," but unlike Garveyites, the Muslims did not offer costumes and parades but sober suits, puritanical religion, dietary discipline, and nononsense business practices. Malcolm himself was also, by his physical appearance alone, a figure who would not be dismissed as a buffoon, as Garvey often was by both blacks and whites. According to Malcolm's *Autobiography,* his father had been a Garveyite as well as a wife beater who favored his lighter-skinned children. Malcolm's Islamic-based black nationalism, his sexual abstinence, which lasted from his religious conversion until his marriage a decade later, and his triumph over his own preference for lighter-skinned blacks and whites were all meant to demonstrate vividly how he superseded his father as a nationalist and how the Nation of Islam had superseded Garveyism. 24

Malcolm enlisted a body of enforcers, the feared Fruit of Islam, grim-faced men who, one imagines, were supposed to personify the essence of an unbowed yet disciplined black manhood. In this way, he dramatically associated black nationalism with a new type of regenerated black male. It was said in the black community, and may still be, that no one bothers a Muslim for fear of retribution from the Fruit of Islam. Certainly, there was a point in the development of the Fruit of Islam and the Nation itself in the 1960s and early 1970s (Malcolm was assassinated in 1965) when both were closely associated with racketeering and gangster activity. During this period, many East Coast mosques were among the most terrifying organizations in the black community. 25

Second, Malcolm, in his *Autobiography,* also managed to link the psychological redemption of the Negro with his reacquaintance with his history. The prison chapters of the *Autobiography* have become nearly mythic as a paradigm of black reawakening. Malcolm's religious conversion became, in a sense, the redemption of the black male and the rehabilitation of black masculinity itself. Lately, we have seen two major black male public figures who were incarcerated for serious crimes, Marion Barry and Mike Tyson, use the Malcolm paradigm to resuscitate their standing 26 with the black public. The martyrdom of Malcolm gave this paradigm a blood-endorsed political heroism that has virtually foreclosed any serious criticism of either its origins or its meaning.

It is extraordinary to contemplate how highly regarded Malcolm X is in the black community today, especially in comparison with Martin Luther King. (When I wrote an article for *Harper's Magazine* that was critical of Malcolm X, I received three death threats.) Despite the fact that King's achievements were enormous—and that Malcolm left really nothing behind other than a book—King's association with integration, with nonviolence, even with Christianity has reduced him in the eyes of many blacks. When blacks in major cities, inspired by figures like Malcolm X and the romanticization of Africa that Malcolm's nationalism wrought, began to organize African-oriented celebrations, such as my aunts did in Philadelphia with the creation of the Yoruba-inspired Odunde festival in 1975, then Afrocentrism has succeeded not only in intellectual spheres but on the grassroots level as well. Its triumph as the legitimation of the black mind and the black aesthetic vision was complete. 27

Afrocentrism may eventually wane in the black community, but probably not very soon. Moreover, a certain type of nationalistic mood, a kind of racial preoccupation, will always exist among blacks. It always has, in varying degrees. Homesickness is strong among black Americans, although it is difficult to point to a homeland. What Afrocentrism reflects is the inability of a large number of black people to deal with the reality of being American and with the meaning of their American experience. 28

Stanley Crouch is right in pointing out that the Afrocentrist is similar to the white Southerner after the Civil War. To black nationalists, the lost war was the "war of liberation" led by black "revolutionaries" in the late 1960s, which in their imagination was modeled on the struggles against colonialism then taking place around the world. (The enslavement of the Africans, of course, was an earlier lost war, and it also weighs heavily on the Afrocentrist. He, like the white Southerner, hates the idea of belonging to a defeated people.) This imaginative vision of a restored and indomitable ethnicity is not to be taken lightly. In a culture as driven by the idea of redemption and as corrupted by racism as this one, race war is our Armageddon. It can be seen in works as various as Thomas Jefferson's *Notes on the State of Virginia*, David Walker's *Appeal to the Colored Citizens of the World*, Joseph Smith's *Book of Mormon*, D. W. Griffith's *Birth of a Nation*, and Mario Van Peebles's *Posse*. 29

Today, Afrocentrism is not a mature political movement but rather a cultural style and a moral stance. There is a deep, almost lyrical poignancy in the fantasy of the Afrocentrist, as there is in the white Southerner's. What would I have been had I not lost the war? The Afrocentrist is devoted to his ancestry and his blood, fixated on the set of traditions that define his nobility, preoccupied with an imagined lost way of life. What drives the Afrocentrist and the white Southerner is not the expression of a group self-interest but concern with pride and honor. One group's myth is built on the surfeit of honor and pride, the other on the total absence of them. 30

Like the white Southerner, the Afrocentrist is in revolt against liberalism itself, against the idea of individual liberty. In a way, the Afrocentrist is right to rage against it, because liberalism set free the individual but did not encourage the development of a community within which the individual could flower. This is what 31 the Afrocentrist wishes to retrieve, a place for himself in his own community. Wilson Jeremiah Moses, a black historian, is right: Afrocentrism is a historiography of decline, like the mythic epic of the South. The tragedy is that black people fail to see their "Americanization" as one of the great human triumphs of the past five hundred years. The United States is virtually the only country where the ex-masters and the ex-slaves try to live together as equals, not only by consent of the ex-masters but by the demand of the ex-slaves. Ironically, what the Afrocentrist can best hope for is precisely what multiculturalism offers: the idea that American culture is a blend of many white and nonwhite cultures. In the end, although many Afrocentrists claim they want this blending, multiculturalism will not satisfy. For if the Euro-American is reminded through this that he is not European or wholly white, the African American will surely be reminded that he is not African or wholly black. The Afrocentrist does not wish to be a mongrel. He wants, like the Southerner, to be pure.

Afrocentrism is intense now because blacks are in a special period of social development in a nation going through a period of fearsome transition. Social development, by its nature, is ambivalent, characterized by a sense of exchange, of gaining and losing. Afrocentrism, in its conservatism, is opposed to this ambivalence and to this sense of exchange. What blacks desire during these turbulent times is exactly what whites want: the security of a golden past that never existed. A significant number of both blacks and whites want, strangely, to go back to an era of segregation, a fantasy time between 1920 and 1955, when whites felt secure in a stable culture and when blacks felt unified and strong because black people were forced to live together. Afrocentrism wants social change without having to pay the psychic price for it. Perhaps many black folk feel that they have paid too much already, and who is to say they are not right. 32

The issue raised by Afrocentrism is the meaning and formation of identity, which is the major fixation of the American, especially the black American. In a country that relentlessly promotes the myth of self-reliance because it is unable to provide any sense of security in a cauldron of capitalistic change, identity struggle is so acute because so much is at stake. Afrocentrism may be wrong in many respects, and it certainly can be stifling and restrictive, but some of its impulses are right. In a culture where information and resources of knowledge are the main levers for social and economic advancement, psychological well-being has become increasingly important as, in the words of one scholar, "a social resource," just as "social networks of care and community support [have become] central features of a dynamic economy." Black folk know, and rightly so, that their individual identities are tied to the strength of their community. The struggle over black identity in the United States has been the struggle over the creation of a true black community here. What integration has done to the individual black mind in the United States is directly related to what it has done to the black community. This is the first lesson we must learn. The second is that perhaps many black folk cling to Afrocentrism because the black *American* experience still costs more, requires more courage, than white Americans—and black Americans—are willing to admit. 33

Working with the Text

1. Obviously, Afrocentrism is a response to Eurocentrism, but what kind? How does Early characterize the relationship between Eurocentrism and

Afrocentrism? How are they alike? How are they different? At one point he implies that while Eurocentrism is built on the idea of cultural progress, Afrocentrism is built on the idea of decline. Do you see this position throughout his essay? Does Early imply that these differences are based on reality and historical fact—or are they more a matter of wish fulfillment and emotion?

2. Throughout the essay, Early describes Afrocentrism as many different things: political ideology, consumer ideology, even psychotherapy. Clearly, he is not a proponent of Afrocentrism, but is he sympathetic? Of the various ways that he characterizes Afrocentrism, which view of it do you think he most closely shares?

3. Why is the black middle class so important to Afrocentrism? Early argues that "nationalism has always been an affair of the disaffected middle class." Do you think that situation is generally true in the United States?

4. Late in the essay, Early says: "The imaginative vision of a restored and indomitable ethnicity is not to be taken lightly. In a culture as driven by the idea of redemption and as corrupted by racism as this one, race war is our Armageddon." What does he mean by that statement? How is the dream of "racial purity" (as held by either white Southerners or Afrocentrists) somehow at the heart of American ideals, even if it also seems at odds with them? How might Afrocentrism be a direct outgrowth of American ideals or—if not of American ideals alone—of American ideals in conjunction with American realities?

5. Early concludes that the integration that was the goal and, to a limited extent, the result of the civil rights movement of the 1960s has done damage to "the black community" in the United States, and that Afrocentrism in some ways is the result of those gains and damage. That irony is related, then, to the conflict between what he calls "liberalism" or the "idea of individual liberty" and group identity. How does Afrocentrism represent a conflict between individual liberty and group self-determination (or communal unity)? If this is a conflict at the heart of black nationalism, can the same be said for *nationalism,* in the sense that we traditionally think of it?

THE MULTICULTURAL MISTAKE

K. ANTHONY APPIAH

■ Anthony Appiah was born in London in 1954. His father was a Ghanian diplomat while his mother was an English artist, thus he spent his childhood in both England and Ghana. Educated at Cambridge University, Appiah taught in Ghana as well as at Yale, Cornell, and Duke Universities. He is currently professor of African American studies at Harvard. His books include *Necessary Questions: An Introduction to Philosophy* (1989) and *In My Father's House: Africa in the Philosophy of Culture* (1992) as well as *Avenging Angel* (1990), a novel. He has also coedited *Color Conscious: A Political Morality of Race* (1995) and a series of critical studies of African American writers. He has said, " . . . most of my publications have grown

out of my philosophical training, my upbringing in Europe and Africa, my explorations of African American culture and history, and my love of reading." In the
following essay, Appiah suggests that he finds "the broad cultural homogeneity of
America much more striking than its much-vaunted variety."

Have you noticed that *culture*—the word—has been getting a heavy workout   1
recently? Anthropologists, of course, have used it zealously for over a century, though the term's active life in literature and politics began long before that. But some current ways in which the concept of culture has been put to use
would have surprised even midcentury readers, especially the idea that everything
from anorexia to zydeco is illuminated by being displayed as the product of some
group's culture.

Culture's main competitor in its kudzu-like proliferation is *diversity,* a favorite   2
now of corporate and educational CEOs, politicians, and pundits. And *cultural diversity* brings the two together. Is it not, indeed, one of the most pious of the pieties
of our age that the United States is a society of enormous cultural diversity? And
isn't Nathan Glazer right to say, in his new book, *We Are All Multiculturalists Now*
(Harvard, 1997), that "multiculturalism is just the latest in [a] sequence of terms describing how American society, particularly American education, should respond to
its diversity"?

Well, yes, American diversity is easily granted, and so is the need for a response to   3
that diversity. But what isn't so clear is that it's our *cultural* diversity that deserves
attention.

When Jews from the *shtetl* and Italians from the *villaggio* arrived at Ellis Island,   4
they brought with them a rich mixture of what we call culture. That is, they brought
a language and stories and songs and sayings; they transplanted a religion with
specific rituals, beliefs, and traditions, a cuisine of a certain hearty peasant quality, and distinctive modes of dress; and they came with particular ideas about
family life. It was often reasonable for their new neighbors to ask what these first-
generation immigrants were doing, and why; and a sensible answer would frequently have been, "It's an Italian thing" or "a Jewish thing," or, simply, "It's their
culture."

It's striking how much of this form of difference has disappeared. There are still   5
seders and nuptial masses, still gefilte fish and spaghetti, but how much does an Italian name tell you these days about church attendance, or knowledge of Italian, or
taste in food or spouses? Even Jews, whose status as a small non-Christian group in
an overwhelmingly Christian society might have been expected to keep their "difference" in focus, are getting harder to identify as a cultural group. (At the seder I go
to every Passover, nearly half of those in attendance are gentiles.)

One way—the old way—of describing what has happened would be to say that   6
the families that arrived during the turn-of-the-century wave of immigration have
assimilated, become American. But, from another perspective, we might say that
they became white. When the Italians and the Jews of Eastern Europe arrived, they
were thought of as racially different both from African Americans and from the
white Protestant majority. Now hardly anybody thinks of their descendants this
way. They are Americans, but unless their ancestors include people from Africa or

Asia, they are also white. And nobody, except perhaps a few oddballs in the Aryan Nation, thinks white people share a culture different from everybody else's.

The contrast between blacks and whites seems very evident, of course. White 7 people rarely think of anything in their culture as white: normal, no doubt, middle-class, maybe, and even, sometimes, American; but not white. Black Americans, by contrast, do think of much in their lives in racial terms; they may speak black English (which some respectfully call Ebonics), go to black churches, listen and dance to black music. (And this isn't just how black people think; other people think that way about them.)

Yet to contrast black and white stories is to neglect much that they have in com- 8 mon. There are, indeed, forms of English speech that are black, even if there are also large regional and class variations in black, as in white, speech. But these are all forms of English we're talking about. Indeed, despite the vast waves of immigration of the past few decades, something like 97 percent of adult Americans, whatever their color, speak English "like a native"; and, with the occasional adjustment for an accent here and there, those 97 percent can all understand one another. Leave out recent immigrants and the number gets close to 100 percent.

Language is only one of many things most Americans share. This is, for example, 9 a country where almost every citizen knows something about baseball and basket-ball. Americans also share a familiarity with the consumer culture. They shop American style and know a good deal about the same consumer goods: Coca-Cola, Nike, Levi's, Ford, Nissan, GE. They have seen Hollywood movies and know the names of some stars; and even the few who watch little or no television can proba-bly tell you the names of some of its personalities. Even the supposedly persisting differences of religion turn out to be shallower than you might think. American Ju-daism is, as is often observed, extraordinarily American. Catholics in this country are a nuisance for Rome just because they are . . . well, so Protestant.

Coming as I do from Ghana, I find the broad cultural homogeneity of America 10 more striking than its much-vaunted variety. So why, in this society, which has less diversity of culture than most others, are we so preoccupied with diversity and so inclined to conceive of it as cultural?

Let me offer a name—not an explanation, just a piece of terminology for our 11 much-vaunted diversity. Let's say that we are creatures of *diverse social identities.* The cozy truism that we are a diverse society reflects the fact that many people now insist that they are profoundly shaped by the groups to which they belong, that their social identity—their membership in these groups—is central to who they are. Moreover, they go on to pursue what the Canadian philosopher Charles Taylor calls a "politics of recognition"; they ask the rest of us to acknowledge publicly their "au-thentic" identities.

The identities that demand recognition are multifarious. Some groups have the 12 names of the earlier ethnic cultures: Italian, Jewish, Polish. Some correspond to the old races (black, Asian, Indian) or to religions (Baptist, Catholic, Jewish). Some are basically regional (Southern, Western, Puerto Rican). Yet others are new groups modeled on the old ethnicities (Hispanic, Asian American) or are social categories (woman, gay, bisexual, disabled, deaf) that are none of these.

Nowadays, we are not the slightest bit surprised when someone remarks upon a 13 feature of the "culture" of groups like these. Gay culture, deaf culture, Chicano culture, Jewish culture—see how these phrases trip off the tongue. But if you ask what distinctively marks off gay people or deaf people or Jews from others, it is not obviously the fact that to each identity there corresponds a distinct culture. *Hispanic* sounds like the name of a cultural group defined by sharing the cultural trait of speaking Spanish, but half the second-generation Hispanics in California don't speak Spanish fluently, and in the next generation the proportion will fall even further.

You may wonder, in fact, whether there isn't a connection between the thinning   14
of the cultural content of identities and the rising stridency of their claims. Those European immigrants who lived in their rich ethnic cultures were busy demanding the linguistic Americanization of their children, making sure they learned America's official culture. One suspects that they didn't need to insist on the public recognition of their culture, because—whether or not they were happy with it—they simply took it for granted. Their middle-class descendants, whose domestic lives are conducted in English and extend eclectically from *Seinfeld* to Chinese takeout, are discomfited by a sense that their identities are shallow by comparison with those of their grandparents; some of them fear that unless the rest of us acknowledge the importance of their difference, there soon won't be anything worth acknowledging.

For many middle-class Americans, families have changed. Grandparents have   15
moved into retirement communities, cousins no longer live down the street, parents have separated. In sum, many of the social preconditions of that extended intergenerational family life have disappeared, and, for many Americans, the will to live that way has vanished too. Given the connection between the old family life and the old cultural identities, it is not surprising that the loss of the former has produced nostalgia for the latter.

The trouble with appealing to cultural difference is that it obscures rather than   16
illuminates this situation. It's not black culture that the racist disdains, but blacks. No amount of knowledge of the architectural achievements of Nubia or Kush guarantees respect for African Americans. No African American is entitled to greater concern because he is descended from a people who created jazz or produced Toni Morrison. Culture is not the problem, and it is not the solution.

So maybe we should conduct our discussions of education and citizenship, tol-   17
eration and social peace, without the talk of cultures. Long ago, in the mists of prehistory, our ancestors learned that it is sometimes good to let a field lie fallow.

Working with the Text

1. What is the definition of *culture* that Appiah is applying in this essay? How does it compare to other uses of *culture* in this reader or that you have explored during the course of the semester? Would you define *culture* differently? More broadly? More narrowly?

2. How do you respond, based on your own experience, to this statement: "I find the broad cultural homogeneity of America more striking than its much-vaunted variety"?

3. Write a paper in which you explore the meanings of and differences between the two main phrases at the heart of Appiah's essay: *cultural diversity* and *diverse social identities*. What is the difference between the two? Which do

you think is most applicable to America? What are the consequences of paying attention to one more than the other?

La conciencia de la mestiza/ Towards a New Consciousness

GLORIA ANZALDÚA

■ Gloria Anzaldúa was born in Southwest Texas in 1942 into a farmworking family that had been U.S. citizens for generations. A *mestiza* (that is, a person of mixed Mexican, Indian, and Anglo ancestry), Anzaldúa early in life rebelled against the limited role assigned to females in Chicano culture. As a writer and lecturer, she has explored issues of feminism and lesbianism, as well as Mexican and Mexican American culture. In 1983, she coedited with Cherríe Moraga a groundbreaking collection, *The Bridge Called My Back: Writings by Radical Women of Color.* She also edited *Haciendo Caras: Making Face, Making Soul: Creative and Critical Perspectives by Feminists of Color* (1990). In addition, she has written two children's books, *Amigos del otro lado/Friends from the Other Side* (1994) and *Prietia y la Llorena/Prietia and the Ghost Woman* (1996). The following is an excerpt from *Borderlands/La frontera* (1987), a sort of cultural and political autobiography that mixes genres—narrative, poetry, critical analysis—as well as languages—English, Castilian Spanish, and various Spanish-influenced and Native American dialects. In it, Anzaldúa argues that, by straddling contradictory cultures, the "new *mestiza*" must achieve a new consciousness that tolerates ambiguity and "includes rather than excludes."

> *Por la mujer de mi raza*
> *hablará el espíritu.*[1]

Jose Vascocelos, Mexican philosopher, envisaged *una raza mestiza, una mezcla de razas afines, una raza de color—la primera raza síntesis del globo.* He called it a cosmic race, *la raza cósmica,* a fifth race embracing the four major races of the world.[2] Opposite to the theory of the pure Aryan, and to the policy of racial purity that white America practices, his theory is one of inclusivity. At the confluence of two or more genetic streams, with chromosomes constantly "crossing over," this mixture of races, rather than resulting in an inferior being, provides hybrid progeny, a mutable, more malleable species with a rich gene pool. From this racial, ideological, cultural and biological cross-pollination, an "alien" consciousness is presently in the making—a new *mestiza* consciousness, *una conciencia de mujer.* It is a consciousness of the Borderlands.

UNA LUCHA DE FRONTERAS / A STRUGGLE OF BORDERS

> Because I, a *mestiza,*
> continually walk out of one culture

and into another,
because I am in all cultures at the same time,
alma entre dos mundos, tres, cuatro,
me zumba la cabeza con lo contradictorio.
Estoy norteada por todas las voces que me hablan
simultáneamente.

The ambivalence from the clash of voices results in mental and emotional states   2
of perplexity. Internal strife results in insecurity and indecisiveness. The mestiza's
dual or multiple personality is plagued by psychic restlessness.

In a constant state of mental nepantilism, an Aztec word meaning torn between   3
ways, *la mestiza* is a product of the transfer of the cultural and spiritual values of one
group to another. Being tricultural, monolingual, bilingual, or multilingual, speaking
a patois, and in a state of perpetual transition, the *mestiza* faces the dilemma of the
mixed breed: which collectivity does the daughter of a darkskinned mother listen to?

El choque de un alma atrapado entre el mundo del espíritu y el mundo de la técnica   4
a veces la deja entullada. Cradled in one culture, sandwiched between two cultures,
straddling all three cultures and their value systems, *la mestiza* undergoes a struggle
of flesh, a struggle of borders, an inner war. Like all people, we perceive the version
of reality that our culture communicates. Like others having or living in more than
one culture, we get multiple, often opposing messages. The coming together of two
self-consistent but habitually incompatible frames of reference[3] causes *un choque,* a
cultural collision.

Within us and within *la cultura chicana,* commonly held beliefs of the white cul-   5
ture attack commonly held beliefs of the Mexican culture, and both attack commonly held beliefs of the indigenous culture. Subconsciously, we see an attack on
ourselves and our beliefs as a threat and we attempt to block with a counterstance.

But it is not enough to stand on the opposite river bank, shouting questions,   6
challenging patriarchal, white conventions. A counterstance locks one into a duel of
oppressor and oppressed; locked in mortal combat, like the cop and the criminal,
both are reduced to a common denominator of violence. The counterstance refutes
the dominant culture's views and beliefs, and, for this, it is proudly defiant. All reaction is limited by, and dependent on, what it is reacting against. Because the counterstance stems from a problem with authority—outer as well as inner—it's a step
towards liberation from cultural domination. But it is not a way of life. At some
point, on our way to a new consciousness, we will have to leave the opposite bank,
the split between the two mortal combatants somehow healed so that we are on
both shores at once and, at once, see through serpent and eagle eyes. Or perhaps we
will decide to disengage from the dominant culture, write it off altogether as a lost
cause, and cross the border into a wholly new and separate territory. Or we might go
another route. The possibilities are numerous once we decide to act and not react.

A TOLERANCE FOR AMBIGUITY

These numerous possibilities leave *la mestiza* floundering in uncharted seas. In per-   7
ceiving conflicting information and points of view, she is subjected to a swamping
of her psychological borders. She has discovered that she can't hold concepts or
ideas in rigid boundaries. The borders and walls that are supposed to keep the un-
desirable ideas out are entrenched habits and patterns of behavior; these habits and

patterns are the enemy within. Rigidity means death. Only by remaining flexible is she able to stretch the psyche horizontally and vertically. *La mestiza* constantly has to shift out of habitual formations; from convergent thinking, analytical reasoning that tends to use rationality to move toward a single goal (a Western mode), to divergent thinking,[4] characterized by movement away from set patterns and goals and toward a more whole perspective, one that includes rather than excludes.

The new *mestiza* copes by developing a tolerance for contradictions, a tolerance   8
for ambiguity. She learns to be an Indian in Mexican culture, to be Mexican from an Anglo point of view. She learns to juggle cultures. She has a plural personality, she operates in a pluralistic mode—nothing is thrust out, the good, the bad and the ugly, nothing rejected, nothing abandoned. Not only does she sustain contradictions, she turns the ambivalence into something else.

She can be jarred out of ambivalence by an intense, and often painful, emotional   9
event which inverts or resolves the ambivalence. I'm not sure exactly how. The work takes place underground—subconsciously. It is work that the soul performs. That focal point or fulcrum, that juncture where the mestiza stands, is where phenomena tend to collide. It is where the possibility of uniting all that is separate occurs. This assembly is not one where severed or separated pieces merely come together. Nor is it a balancing of opposing powers. In attempting to work out a synthesis, the self has added a third element which is greater than the sum of its severed parts. That third element is a new consciousness—a mestiza consciousness—and though it is a source of intense pain, its energy comes from continual creative motion that keeps breaking down the unitary aspect of each new paradigm.

En unas pocas centurias, the future will belong to the mestiza. Because the future   10
depends on the breaking down of paradigms, it depends on the straddling of two or more cultures. By creating a new mythos—that is, a change in the way we perceive reality, the way we see ourselves, and the ways we behave—*la mestiza* creates a new consciousness.

The work of *mestiza* consciousness is to break down the subject-object duality   11
that keeps her a prisoner and to show in the flesh and through the images in her work how duality is transcended. The answer to the problem between the white race and the colored, between males and females, lies in healing the split that originates in the very foundation of our lives, our culture, our languages, our thoughts. A massive uprooting of dualistic thinking in the individual and collective consciousness is the beginning of a long struggle, but one that could, in our best hopes, bring us to the end of rape, of violence, of war.

LA ENCRUCIJADA / THE CROSSROADS

A chicken is being sacrificed
     at a crossroads, a simple mound of earth
a mud shrine for *Eshu,*
          Yoruba god of indeterminacy,
     who blesses her choice of path.
          She begins her journey.

Su cuerpo es una bocacalle. La mestiza has gone from being the sacrificial goat to   12
becoming the officiating priestess at the crossroads.

As a *mestiza* I have no country, my homeland cast me out; yet all countries are 13 mine because I am every woman's sister or potential lover. (As a lesbian I have no race, my own people disclaim me; but I am all races because there is the queer of me in all races.) I am cultureless because, as a feminist, I challenge the collective cultural/religious male-derived beliefs of Indo-Hispanics and Anglos; yet I am cultured because I am participating in the creation of yet another culture, a new story to explain the world and our participation in it, a new value system with images and symbols that connect us to each other and to the planet. *Soy un amasamiento,* I am an act of kneading, of uniting and joining that not only has produced both a creature of darkness and a creature of light, but also a creature that questions the definitions of light and dark and gives them new meanings.

We are the people who leap in the dark, we are the people on the knees of the 14 gods. In our very flesh, (r)evolution works out the clash of cultures. It makes us crazy constantly, but if the center holds, we've made some kind of evolutionary step forward. *Nuestra alma el trabajo,* the opus, the great alchemical work; spiritual *mestizaje,* a "morphogenesis,"[5] an inevitable unfolding. We have become the quickening serpent movement.

Indigenous like corn, like corn, the *mestiza* is a product of crossbreeding, de- 15 signed for preservation under a variety of conditions. Like an ear of corn—a female seed-bearing organ—the *mestiza* is tenacious, tightly wrapped in the husks of her culture. Like kernels she clings to the cob; with thick stalks and strong brace roots, she holds tight to the earth—she will survive the crossroads.

Lavando y remojando el maíz en agua de cal, despojando el pellejo. Moliendo, mix- 16 *teando, amasando, haciendo tortillas de masa.*[6] She steeps the corn in lime, it swells, softens. With stone roller on *metate,* she grinds the corn, then grinds again. She kneads and moulds the dough, pats the round balls into *tortillas.*

> We are the porous rock in the stone *metate*
> squatting on the ground.
> We are the rolling pin, *el maíz y agua,*
> *la masa harina. Somos el amasijo.*
> *Somos lo molido en el metate.*
> We are the *comal* sizzling hot,
> the hot *tortilla,* the hungry mouth.
> We are the coarse rock.
> We are the grinding motion,
> the mixed potion, *somos el molcajete.*
> We are the pestle, the *comino, ajo, pimienta,*
> We are the *chile colorado,*
> the green shoot that cracks the rock.
> We will abide.

EL CAMINO DE LA MESTIZA / THE MESTIZA WAY

Caught between the sudden contraction, the breath sucked in and the endless space, the brown woman stands still, looks at the sky. She decides to go down, digging her way along the roots of trees. Sifting through the bones, she shakes them to see if there is any marrow in them. Then, touching the dirt to her fore-head, to her tongue, she takes a few bones, leaves the rest in their burial place.

She goes through her backpack, keeps her journal and address book, throws away the muni-bart metromaps. The coins are heavy and they go next, then the greenbacks flutter through the air. She keeps her knife, can opener and eyebrow pencil. She puts bones, pieces of bark, *hierbas,* eagle feather, snakeskin, tape recorder, the rattle and drum in her pack and she sets out to become the complete *tolteca.*[7]

Her first step is to take inventory. *Despojando, desgranando, quitando paja.* Just what did she inherit from her ancestors? This weight on her back—which is the bag-gage from the Indian mother, which the baggage from the Spanish father, which the baggage from the Anglo?   17

Pero es difícil differentiating between *lo heredado, lo adquirido, lo impuesto.* She puts history through a sieve, winnows out the lies, looks at the forces that we as a race, as women, have been a part of. *Luego bota lo que no vale, los desmientos, los desen-cuentos, el embrutecimiento. Aguarda el juicio, hondo y enraízado, de la gente antigua.* This step is a conscious rupture with all oppressive traditions of all cultures and reli-gions. She communicates that rupture, documents the struggle. She reinterprets his-tory and, using new symbols, she shapes new myths. She adopts new perspectives toward the darkskinned, women and queers. She strengthens her tolerance (and in-tolerance) for ambiguity. She is willing to share, to make herself vulnerable to foreign ways of seeing and thinking. She surrenders all notions of safety, of the familiar. De-construct, construct. She becomes a *nahual,* able to transform herself into a tree, a coyote, into another person. She learns to transform the small "I" into the total Self. *Se hace moldeadora de su alma. Según la concepción que tiene de sí misma, así será.*   18

QUE NO SE NOS OLVIDE LOS HOMBRES

"Tú no sirves pa' nada—
you're good for nothing.
Eres pura vieja."

"You're nothing but a woman" means you are defective. Its opposite is to be *un macho.* The modern meaning of the word "machismo," as well as the concept, is ac-tually an Anglo invention. For men like my father, being "macho" meant being strong enough to protect and support my mother and us, yet being able to show love. Today's macho has doubts about his ability to feed and protect his family. His "machismo" is an adaptation to oppression and poverty and low self-esteem. It is the result of hierarchical male dominance. The Anglo, feeling inadequate and infe-rior and powerless, displaces or transfers these feelings to the Chicano by shaming him. In the Gringo world, the Chicano suffers from excessive humility and self-effacement, shame of self and self-deprecation. Around Latinos he suffers from a sense of language inadequacy and its accompanying discomfort; with Native Amer-icans he suffers from a racial amnesia which ignores our common blood, and from guilt because the Spanish part of him took their land and oppressed them. He has an excessive compensatory hubris when around Mexicans from the other side. It overlays a deep sense of racial shame.   19

The loss of a sense of dignity and respect in the macho breeds a false machismo   20 which leads him to put down women and even to brutalize them. Coexisting with his sexist behavior is a love for the mother which takes precedence over that of all others. Devoted son, macho pig. To wash down the shame of his acts, of his very being, and to handle the brute in the mirror, he takes to the bottle, the snort, the needle, and the fist.

Though we "understand" the root causes of male hatred and fear, and the subse- 21 quent wounding of women, we do not excuse, we do not condone, and we will no longer put up with it. From the men of our race, we demand the admission/acknowledgment/disclosure/testimony that they wound us, violate us, are afraid of us and of our power. We need them to say they will begin to eliminate their hurtful put-down ways. But more than the words, we demand acts. We say to them: We will develop equal power with you and those who have shamed us.

It is imperative that mestizas support each other in changing the sexist elements 22 in the Mexican-Indian culture. As long as woman is put down, the Indian and the Black in all of us is put down. The struggle of the mestiza is above all a feminist one. As long as *los hombres* think they have to *chingar mujeres* and each other to be men, as long as men are taught that they are superior and therefore culturally favored over *la mujer,* as long as to be a *vieja* is a thing of derision, there can be no real healing of our psyches. We're halfway there—we have such love of the Mother, the good mother. The first step is to unlearn the *puta/virgen* dichotomy and to see *Coatlapopeuh-Coatlicue* in the Mother, *Guadalupe.*

Tenderness, a sign of vulnerability, is so feared that it is showered on women with 23 verbal abuse and blows. Men, even more than women, are fettered to gender roles. Women at least have had the guts to break out of bondage. Only gay men have had the courage to expose themselves to the woman inside them and to challenge the current masculinity. I've encountered a few scattered and isolated gentle straight men, the beginnings of a new breed, but they are confused, and entangled with sexist behaviors that they have not been able to eradicate. We need a new masculinity and the new man needs a movement.

Lumping the males who deviate from the general norm with man, the oppressor, 24 is a gross injustice. *Asombra pensar que nos hemos quedado en ese pozo oscuro donde el mundo encierra a las lesbianas. Asombra pensar que hemos, como femenistas y lesbianas, cerrado nuestros corazónes a los hombres, a nuestros hermanos los jotos, desheredados y marginales como nosotros.* Being the supreme crossers of cultures, homosexuals have strong bonds with the queer white, Black, Asian, Native American, Latino, and with the queer in Italy, Australia and the rest of the planet. We come from all colors, all classes, all races, all time periods. Our role is to link people with each other—the Blacks with Jews with Indians with Asians with whites with extraterrestrials. It is to transfer ideas and information from one culture to another. Colored homosexuals have more knowledge of other cultures; have always been at the forefront (although sometimes in the closet) of all liberation struggles in this country; have suffered more injustices and have survived them despite all odds. Chicanos need to acknowledge the political and artistic contributions of their queer. People, listen to what your *jotería* is saying.

The mestizo and the queer exist at this time and point on the evolutionary con- 25 tinuum for a purpose. We are a blending that proves that all blood is intricately woven together, and that we are spawned out of similar souls.

SOMOS UNA GENTE

Hay tantísimas fronteras
que dividen a la gente,
pero por cada frontera
existe también un puente.
   —Gina Valdés[8]

Divided Loyalties. Many women and men of color do not want to have any dealings with white people. It takes too much time and energy to explain to the downwardly mobile, white middle-class women that it's okay for us to want to own "possessions," never having had any nice furniture on our dirt floors or "luxuries" like washing machines. Many feel that whites should help their own people rid themselves of race hatred and fear first. I, for one, choose to use some of my energy to serve as mediator. I think we need to allow whites to be our allies. Through our literature, art, *corridos,* and folktales we must share our history with them so when they set up committees to help Big Mountain Navajos or the Chicano farmworkers or *los Nicaragüenses* they won't turn people away because of their racial fears and ignorances. They will come to see that they are not helping us but following our lead.   26

Individually, but also as a racial entity, we need to voice our needs. We need to say to white society: We need you to accept the fact that Chicanos are different, to acknowledge your rejection and negation of us. We need you to own the fact that you looked upon us as less than human, that you stole our lands, our personhood, our self-respect. We need you to make public restitution: to say that, to compensate for your own sense of defectiveness, you strive for power over us, you erase our history and our experience because it makes you feel guilty—you'd rather forget your brutish acts. To say you've split yourself from minority groups, that you disown us, that your dual consciousness splits off parts of yourself, transferring the "negative" parts onto us. (Where there is persecution of minorities, there is shadow projection. Where there is violence and war, there is repression of shadow.) To say that you are afraid of us, that to put distance between us, you wear the mask of contempt. Admit that Mexico is your double, that she exists in the shadow of this country, that we are irrevocably tied to her. Gringo, accept the doppelganger in your psyche. By taking back your collective shadow the intracultural split will heal. And finally, tell us what you need from us.   27

BY YOUR TRUE FACES WE WILL KNOW YOU

I am visible—see this Indian face—yet I am invisible. I both blind them with my beak nose and am their blind spot. But I exist, we exist. They'd like to think I have melted in the pot. But I haven't, we haven't.   28

The dominant white culture is killing us slowly with its ignorance. By taking away our self-determination, it has made us weak and empty. As a people we have resisted and we have taken expedient positions, but we have never been allowed to   29 develop unencumbered—we have never been allowed to be fully ourselves. The whites in power want us people of color to barricade ourselves behind our separate tribal walls so they can pick us off one at a time with their hidden weapons; so they can whitewash and distort history. Ignorance splits people, creates prejudices. A misinformed people is a subjugated people.

Before the Chicano and the undocumented worker and the Mexican from the 30 other side can come together, before the Chicano can have unity with Native Americans and other groups, we need to know the history of their struggle and they need to know ours. Our mothers, our sisters and brothers, the guys who hang out on street corners, the children in the playgrounds, each of us must know our Indian lineage, our afro-*mestisaje,* our history of resistance.

To the immigrant *mexicano* and the recent arrivals we must teach our history. 31 The 80 million *mexicanos* and the Latinos from Central and South America must know of our struggles. Each one of us must know basic facts about Nicaragua, Chile and the rest of Latin America. The Latinoist movement (Chicanos, Puerto Ricans, Cubans and other Spanish-speaking people working together to combat racial discrimination in the market place) is good but it is not enough. Other than a common culture we will have nothing to hold us together. We need to meet on a broader communal ground.

The struggle is inner: Chicano, *indio,* American Indian, *mojado, mexicano,* immi- 32 grant Latino, Anglo in power, working class Anglo, Black, Asian—our psyches resemble the border-towns and are populated by the same people. The struggle has always been inner, and is played out in the outer terrains. Awareness of our situation must come before inner changes, which in turn come before changes in society. Nothing happens in the "real" world unless it first happens in the images in our heads.

EL DÍA DE LA CHICANA

I will not be shamed again
Nor will I shame myself.

I am possessed by a vision: that we Chicanas and Chicanos have taken back or 33 uncovered our true faces, our dignity and self-respect. It's a validation vision.

Seeing the Chicana anew in light of her history. I seek an exoneration, a seeing 34 through the fictions of white supremacy, a seeing of ourselves in our true guises and not as the false racial personality that has been given to us and that we have given to ourselves. I seek our woman's face, our true features, the positive and the negative seen clearly, free of the tainted biases of male dominance. I seek new images of identity, new beliefs about ourselves, our humanity and worth no longer in question.

Estamos viviendo en la noche de la Raza, un tiempo cuando el trabajo se hace a lo 35 *quieto, en el oscuro. El día cuando aceptamos tal y como somos y para en donde vamos y porque—ese día será el día de la Raza. Yo tengo el conpromiso de expresar mi visión, mi sensibilidad, mi percepción de la revalidación de la gente mexicana, su mérito, estimación, honra, aprecio, y validez.*

On December 2nd when my sun goes into my first house, I celebrate *el día de la* 36
Chicana y el Chicano. On that day I clean my altars, light my *Coatlalopeuh* candle,
burn sage and copal, take *el baño para espantar basura,* sweep my house. On that day
I bare my soul, make myself vulnerable to friends and family by expressing my feelings. On that day I affirm who we are.

On that day I look inside our conflicts and our basic introverted racial tempera- 37
ment. I identify our needs, voice them. I acknowledge that the self and the race have
been wounded. I recognize the need to take care of our personhood, of our racial
self. On that day I gather the splintered and disowned parts of *la gente mexicana* and
hold them in my arms. *Todas las partes de nosotros valen.*

On that day I say, "Yes, all you people wound us when you reject us. Rejection 38
strips us of self-worth; our vulnerability exposes us to shame. It is our innate identity you find wanting. We are ashamed that we need your good opinion, that we
need your acceptance. We can no longer camouflage our needs, can no longer let de-
fenses and fences sprout around us. We can no longer withdraw. To rage and look
upon you with contempt is to rage and be contemptuous of ourselves. We can no
longer blame you, nor disown the white parts, the male parts, the pathological parts,
the queer parts, the vulnerable parts. Here we are weaponless with open arms, with
only our magic. Let's try it our way, the mestiza way, the Chicana way, the woman
way.

On that day, I search for our essential dignity as a people, a people with a sense 39
of purpose—to belong and contribute to something greater than our *pueblo.* On
that day I seek to recover and reshape my spiritual identity. *¡Anímate! Raza, a cele-
brar el día de la Chicana.*

EL RETORNO

All movements are accomplished in six stages,
and the seventh brings return.
—I Ching[9]

Tanto tiempo sin verte casa mía,
mi cuna, mi hondo nido de la huerta.
—"Soledad"[10]

I stand at the river, watch the curving, twisting serpent, a serpent nailed to the 40
fence where the mouth of the Rio Grande empties into the Gulf.

I have come back. *Tanto dolor me costó el alejamiento.* I shade my eyes and look 41
up. The bone beak of a hawk slowly circling over me, checking me out as potential
carrion. In its wake a little bird flickering its wings, swimming sporadically like a
fish. In the distance the expressway and the slough of traffic like an irritated sow.
The sudden pull in my gut, *la tierra, los aguaceros.* My land, *el viento soplando la
arena, el lagartijo debajo de un nopalito. Me acuerdo como era antes. Una región desér-
tica de vasta llanuras, costeras de baja altura, de escasa lluvia, de chaparrales formados
por mesquites y huizaches.* If I look real hard I can almost see the Spanish fathers who
were called "the cavalry of Christ" enter this valley riding their burros, see the clash
of cultures commence.

Tierra natal. This is home, the small towns in the Valley, *los pueblitos* with chicken pens and goats picketed to mesquite shrubs. *En las colonias* on the other side of the tracks, junk cars line the front yards of hot pink and lavender-trimmed houses—Chicano architecture we call it, self-consciously. I have missed the TV shows where hosts speak in half and half, and where awards are given in the category of Tex-Mex music. I have missed the Mexican cemeteries blooming with artificial flowers, the fields of aloe vera and red pepper, rows of sugar cane, of corn hanging on the stalks, the cloud of *polvareda* in the dirt roads behind a speeding pickup truck, *el sabor de tamales de rez y venado.* I have missed *la yegua colorada* gnawing the wooden gate of her stall, the smell of horse flesh from Carito's corrals. *He hecho menos las noches calientes sin aire, noches de linternas y lechuzas* making holes in the night. 42

I still feel the old despair when I look at the unpainted, dilapidated, scrap lumber houses consisting mostly of corrugated aluminum. Some of the poorest people in the U.S. live in the Lower Rio Grande Valley, an arid and semi-arid land of irrigated farming, intense sunlight and heat, citrus groves next to chaparral and cactus. I walk through the elementary school I attended so long ago, that remained segregated until recently. I remember how the white teachers used to punish us for being Mexican. 43

How I love this tragic valley of South Texas, as Ricardo Sánchez calls it; this borderland between the Nueces and the Rio Grande. This land has survived possession and ill-use by five countries: Spain, Mexico, the Republic of Texas, the U.S., the Confederacy, and the U.S. again. It has survived Anglo-Mexican blood feuds, lynchings, burnings, rapes, pillage. 44

Today I see the Valley still struggling to survive. Whether it does or not, it will never be as I remember it. The borderlands depression that was set off by the 1982 peso devaluation in Mexico resulted in the closure of hundreds of Valley businesses. Many people lost their homes, cars, land. Prior to 1982, U.S. store owners thrived on retail sales to Mexicans who came across the border for groceries and clothes and appliances. While goods on the U.S. side have become 10, 100, 1000 times more expensive for Mexican buyers, goods on the Mexican side have become 10, 100, 1000 times cheaper for Americans. Because the Valley is heavily dependent on agriculture and Mexican retail trade, it has the highest unemployment rates along the entire border region; it is the Valley that has been hardest hit.[11] 45

"It's been a bad year for corn," my brother, Nune, says. As he talks, I remember my father scanning the sky for a rain that would end the drought, looking up into the sky, day after day, while the corn withered on its stalk. My father has been dead for 29 years, having worked himself to death. The life span of a Mexican farm laborer is 56—he lived to be 38. It shocks me that I am older than he. I, too, search the sky for rain. Like the ancients, I worship the rain god and the maize goddess, but unlike my father I have recovered their names. Now for rain (irrigation) one offers not a sacrifice of blood, but of money. 46

"Farming is in a bad way," my brother says. "Two or three thousand small and big farmers went bankrupt in this country last year. Six years ago the price of corn was $8.00 per hundred pounds," he goes on. "This year it is $3.90 per hundred pounds." And, I think to myself, after taking inflation into account, not planting anything puts you ahead. 47

I walk out to the back yard, stare at *los rosales de mamá*. She wants me to help her   48
prune the rose bushes, dig out the carpet grass that is choking them. *Mamagrande
Ramona también tenía rosales.* Here every Mexican grows flowers. If they don't have
a piece of dirt, they use car tires, jars, cans, shoe boxes. Roses are the Mexican's favorite flower. I think, how symbolic—thorns and all.

Yes, the Chicano and Chicana have always taken care of growing things and the   49
land. Again I see the four of us kids getting off the school bus, changing into our
work clothes, walking into the field with Papí and Mamí, all six of us bending to the
ground. Below our feet, under the earth lie the watermelon seeds. We cover them
with paper plates, putting *terremotes* on top of the plates to keep them from being
blown away by the wind. The paper plates keep the freeze away. Next day or the next,
we remove the plates, bare the tiny green shoots to the elements. They survive and
grow, give fruit hundreds of times the size of the seed. We water them and hoe them.
We harvest them. The vines dry, rot, are plowed under. Growth, death, decay, birth.
The soil prepared again and again, impregnated, worked on. A constant changing of
forms, *renacimientos de la tierra madre.*

> This land was Mexican once
> was Indian always
> and is.
> And will be again.

NOTES

1. This is my own "take off" on Jose Vasconcelos' idea. Jose Vasconcelos, *La Raza Cósmica: Misión de la Raza Ibero-Americana* (México: Aguilar S.A. de Ediciones, 1961).

2. Vasconcelos.

3. Arthur Koestler termed this "bisociation." Albert Rothenberg, *The Creative Process in
Art, Science, and Other Fields* (Chicago, IL: University of Chicago Press, 1979), 12.

4. In part, I derive my definitions for "convergent" and "divergent" thinking from
Rothenberg, 12–13.

5. To borrow chemist Ilya Prigogine's theory of "dissipative structures." Prigogine discovered that substances interact not in predictable ways as it was taught in science, but in different and fluctuating ways to produce new and more complex structures, a kind of birth he
called "morphogenesis," which created unpredictable innovations. Harold Gilliam, "Searching for a New World View," *This World* (January, 1981), 23.

6. *Tortillas de masa harina:* corn tortillas are of two types, the smooth uniform ones
made in a tortilla press and usually bought at a tortilla factory or supermarket, and *gorditas,*
made by mixing *masa* with lard or shortening or butter (my mother sometimes puts in bits
of bacon or *chicharrones*).

7., 8. Gina Valdés, *Puentes y Fronteras: Coplas Chicanas* (Los Angeles, CA: Castle Litho-
graph, 1982), 2.

9. Richard Wilhelm, *The I Ching or Book of Changes,* trans. Cary F. Baynes (Princeton, NJ:
Princeton University Press, 1950), 98.

10. "*Soledad*" is sung by the group, Haciendo Punto en Otro Son.

11. Out of the twenty-two border counties in the four border states, Hidalgo County
(named for Father Hidalgo who was shot in 1810 after instigating Mexico's revolt against Spanish rule under the banner of *la Virgen de Guadalupe*) is the most poverty-stricken county in the
nation as well as the largest home base (along with Imperial in California) for migrant farmworkers. It was here that I was born and raised. I am amazed that both it and I have survived.

CHAPTER SEVEN

Working with the Text

1. What is "*mestiza* consciousness"? What characterizes it? How is it different from being from either Mexico or the United States?

2. Throughout her essay Anzaldúa engages in what she calls "code switching" between English and Spanish. How does her use of language contribute to her argument about cultural hybridization? In what ways is language integral to the new *mestiza* consciousness? How did you feel as you read an essay written in two languages? Do you read enough Spanish to be able to follow both? Was the use of Spanish alienating to you? If so, how do you analyze that response?

3. Clearly, an important part of Anzaldúa's argument is based on issues of gender and sexuality. What are some of the connections among sexuality, gender, and culture? To what, for example, does she attribute the prevailing attitudes of machismo in Mexican culture? How are current constructions of masculinity important to the future of the new race consciousness? How does homosexuality fit into her argument? How does her position as a lesbian woman of color shape her vision of the new *mestiza* consciousness?

4. Near the end of the essay, Anzaldúa describes a vision she has of the first Christian missionaries entering the Rio Grande Valley. What does she see in this vision of the valley? What conflicts does she foresee? In the subsequent paragraph she shifts to a series of memories of her own childhood in this same valley. What does she remember about her upbringing? How do these memories influence her vision of the "borderlands" as a cultural crossroads?

5. In what way is her essay about "tribal" consciousness? Does it emphasize *tribalism* over *nationalism*? She calls the new *mestiza* consciousness a new "race" consciousness. Is this concept racial consciousness as you understand it? Does her essay uphold traditional racial constructions or try to reconstruct them? In a paper, address the idea of a new *mestiza* consciousness. Begin by defining some of these terms as you understand their usage by Anzaldúa and others; then take a position on whether you think a "new consciousness" is necessary or possible for the future. What difference would it make?

DISINFORMOCRACY

HOWARD RHEINGOLD

■ Howard Rheingold, an author of books on science and technology as well as science fiction novels, has been praised for his ability to translate scientific and technological concepts into language that lay readers can understand. His *Talking Tech: A Conversational Guide to Science and Technology* (1982, coauthored with Howard Levine) defines seventy scientific terms currently in popular usage and explains each in a brief, accessible, scientifically accurate essay. An early writer on computer technology, Rheingold has also published *Tools for Thought: The Peo-*

ple and Ideas behind the Next Computer Revolution (1985), *The Cognitive Connection: Thought and Language in Man and Machine* (1987), *Virtual Reality* (1991), and *The Virtual Community: Homesteading on the Electronic Frontier* (1993). His science fiction includes the "Sisterhood Trilogy" and the "Savage Report" series. In the following essay from *The Virtual Community*, Rheingold discusses some critics' fears that computer mediated communication (CMC) could ultimately stifle public discourse both nationally and internationally.

V irtual communities could help citizens revitalize democracy, or they could   1
be luring us into an attractively packaged substitute for democratic discourse. A few true believers in electronic democracy have had their say. It's
time to hear from the other side. We owe it to ourselves and future generations to
look closely at what the enthusiasts fail to tell us, and to listen attentively to what the
skeptics fear. . . .

Three different kinds of social criticisms of technology are relevant to claims of   2
CMC as a means of enhancing democracy. One school of criticism emerges from the
longer-term history of communications media, and focuses on the way electronic
communications media already have preempted public discussions by turning more
and more of the content of the media into advertisements for various commodities—a process these critics call commodification. Even the political process, according to this school of critics, has been turned into a commodity. The formal
name for this criticism is "the commodification of the public sphere." The public
sphere is what these social critics claim we used to have as citizens of a democracy,
but have lost to the tide of commodization. The public sphere is also the focus of the
hopes of online activists, who see CMC as a way of revitalizing the open and widespread discussions among citizens that feed the roots of democratic societies.

The second school of criticism focuses on the fact that high-bandwidth interac-   3
tive networks could be used in conjunction with other technologies as a means of
surveillance, control, and disinformation as well as a conduit for useful information. This direct assault on personal liberty is compounded by a more diffuse erosion
of old social values due to the capabilities of new technologies; the most problematic example is the way traditional notions of privacy are challenged on several
fronts by the ease of collecting and disseminating detailed information about individuals via cyberspace technologies. When people use the convenience of electronic
communication or transaction, we leave invisible digital trails; now that technologies for tracking those trails are maturing, there is cause to worry. The spreading use
of computer matching to piece together the digital trails we all leave in cyberspace is
one indication of privacy problems to come.

Along with all the person-to-person communications exchanged on the world's   4
telecommunications networks are vast flows of other kinds of personal information—credit information, transaction processing, health information. Most people
take it for granted that no one can search through all the electronic transactions that
move through the world's networks in order to pin down an individual for marketing—or political—motives. Remember the "knowbots" that would act as personal
servants, swimming in the info-tides, fishing for information to suit your interests?
What if people could turn loose knowbots to collect all the information digitally

linked to *you*? What if the Net and cheap, powerful computers give that power not only to governments and large corporations but to everyone?

Every time we travel or shop or communicate, citizens of the credit-card society contribute to streams of information that travel between point of purchase, remote credit bureaus, municipal and federal information systems, crime information databases, central transaction databases. And all these other forms of cyberspace interaction take place via the same packet-switched, high-bandwidth network technology—those packets can contain transactions as well as video clips and text files. When these streams of information begin to connect together, the unscrupulous or would-be tyrants can use the Net to catch citizens in a more ominous kind of net.

The same channels of communication that enable citizens around the world to communicate with one another also allow government and private interests to gather information about them. This school of criticism is known as Panoptic in reference to the perfect prison proposed in the eighteenth century by Jeremy Bentham—a theoretical model that happens to fit the real capabilities of today's technologies.

Another category of critical claim deserves mention, despite the rather bizarre and incredible imagery used by its most well known spokesmen—the hyper-realist school. These critics believe that information technologies have already changed what used to pass for reality into a slicked-up electronic simulation. Twenty years before the United States elected a Hollywood actor as president, the first hyper-realists pointed out how politics had become a movie, a spectacle that raised the old Roman tactic of bread and circuses to the level of mass hypnotism. We live in a hyper-reality that was carefully constructed to mimic the real world and extract money from the pockets of consumers: the forests around the Matterhorn might be dying, but the Disneyland version continues to rake in the dollars. The television programs, movie stars, and theme parks work together to create global industry devoted to maintaining a web of illusion that grows more lifelike as more people buy into it and as technologies grow more powerful.

Many other social scientists have intellectual suspicions of the hyper-realist critiques, because so many are abstract and theoretical, based on little or no direct knowledge of technology itself. Nevertheless, this perspective does capture something about the way the effects of communications technologies have changed our modes of thought. One good reason for paying attention to the claims of the hyper-realists is that the society they predicted decades ago bears a disturbingly closer resemblance to real life than do the forecasts of the rosier-visioned technological utopians. While McLuhan's image of the global village has taken on a certain irony in light of what has happened since his predictions of the 1960s, "the society of the spectacle"—another prediction from the 1960s, based on the advent of electronic media—offered a far less rosy and, as events have proved, more realistic portrayal of the way information technologies have changed social customs.

THE SELLING OF DEMOCRACY: COMMODIFICATION AND THE PUBLIC SPHERE

There is an intimate connection between informal conversations, the kind that take place in communities and virtual communities, in the coffee shops and computer conferences, and the ability of large social groups to govern themselves without monarchs or dictators. This social-political connection shares a metaphor with the idea of cyberspace, for it takes place in a kind of virtual space that has come to be known by specialists as the public sphere.

Here is what the preeminent contemporary writer about the public sphere, social critic and philosopher Jurgen Habermas, had to say about the meaning of this abstraction: 10

> By "public sphere," we mean first of all a domain of our social life in which such a thing as public opinion can be formed. Access to the public sphere is open in principle to all citizens. A portion of the public sphere is constituted in every conversation in which private persons come together to form a public. They are then acting neither as business or professional people conducting their private affairs, nor as legal consociates subject to the legal regulations of a state bureaucracy and obligated to obedience. Citizens act as a public when they deal with matters of general interest without being subject to coercion; thus with the guarantee that they may assemble and unite freely, and express and publicize their opinions freely.

In this definition, Habermas formalized what people in free societies mean when we say "The public wouldn't stand for that" or "It depends on public opinion." And he drew attention to the intimate connection between this web of free, informal, personal communications and the foundations of democratic society. People can govern themselves only if they communicate widely, freely, and in groups—publicly. The First Amendment of the U.S. Constitution's Bill of Rights protects citizens from government interference in their communications—the rights of speech, press, and assembly are communication rights. Without those rights, there is no public sphere. Ask any citizen of Prague, Budapest, or Moscow. 11

Because the public sphere depends on free communication and discussion of ideas, as soon as your political entity grows larger than the number of citizens you can fit into a modest town hall, this vital marketplace for political ideas can be powerfully influenced by changes in communications technology. According to Habermas, 12

> When the public is large, this kind of communication requires certain means of dissemination and influence; today, newspapers and periodicals, radio and television are the media of the public sphere. . . . The term "public opinion" refers to the functions of criticism and control or organized state authority that the public exercises informally, as well as formally during periodic elections. Regulations concerning the publicness (or publicity [Publizitat] in its original meaning) of state-related activities, as, for instance, the public accessibility required of legal proceedings, are also connected with this function of public opinion. To the public sphere as a sphere mediating between state and society, a sphere in which the public as the vehicle of publicness—the publicness that once had to win out against the secret politics of monarchs and that since then has permitted democratic control of state activity.

Ask anybody in China about the right to talk freely among friends and neighbors, to own a printing press, to call a meeting to protest government policy, or to 13 run a BBS. But brute totalitarian seizure of communications technology is not the only way that political powers can neutralize the ability of citizens to talk freely. It is also possible to alter the nature of discourse by inventing a kind of paid fake discourse. If a few people have control of what goes into the daily reporting of the news, and those people are in the business of selling advertising, all kinds of things become possible for those who can afford to pay.

Habermas had this to say about the corrupting influence of ersatz public opinion: 14

> Whereas at one time publicness was intended to subject persons or things to the public use of reason and to make political decisions subject to revision before the tribunal of public opinion, today it has often enough already been enlisted in the aid of the secret policies of interest groups; in the form of "publicity" it now acquires public prestige for persons or things and renders them capable of acclamation in a climate of nonpublic opinion. The term "public relations" itself indicates how a public sphere that formerly emerged from the structure of society must now be produced circumstantially on a case-by-case basis.

The idea that public opinion can be manufactured and the fact that electronic 15 spectacles can capture the attention of a majority of the citizenry damaged the foundations of democracy. According to Habermas,

> It is no accident that these concepts of the public sphere and public opinion were not formed until the eighteenth century. They derive their specific meaning from a concrete historical situation. It was then that one learned to distinguish between opinion and public opinion. . . . Public opinion, in terms of its very idea, can be formed only if a public that engages in rational discussion exists. Public discussions that are institutionally protected and that take, with critical intent, the exercise of political authority as their theme have not existed since time immemorial.

The public sphere and democracy were born at the same time, from the same sources. Now that the public sphere, cut off from its roots, seems to be dying, democracy is in danger, too.

The concept of the public sphere as discussed by Habermas and others includes 16 several requirements for authenticity that people who live in democratic societies would recognize: open access, voluntary participation, participation outside institutional roles, the generation of public opinion through assemblies of citizens who engage in rational argument, the freedom to express opinions, and the freedom to discuss matters of the state and criticize the way state power is organized. Acts of speech and publication that specifically discuss the state are perhaps the most important kind protected by the First Amendment of the U.S. Constitution and similar civil guarantees elsewhere in the world. Former Soviets and Eastern Europeans who regained it after decades of censorship offer testimony that the most important freedom of speech is the freedom to speak about freedoms.

In eighteenth-century America, the Committees of Correspondence were 17 one of the most important loci of the public sphere in the years of revolution and constitution-building. If you look closely at the roots of the American Revolution, it becomes evident that a text-based, horseback-transported version of networking was an old American tradition. In their book *Networking*, Jessica Lipnack and Jeffrey Stamps describe these committees as

> a communications forum where homespun political and economic thinkers hammered out their ideological differences, sculpting the form of a separate and independent country in North America. Writing to one another and sharing letters with neighbors, this revolutionary generation nurtured its adolescent ideas into a mature politics. Both men and women participated in the debate over independence from England and the desirable shape of the American future. . . .
>
> During the years in which the American Revolution was percolating, letters, news-sheets, and pamphlets carried from one village to another were the means by which ideas about democracy were refined. Eventually, the correspondents agreed that the next step in their idea exchange was to hold a face-to-face meeting. The ideas of independence and government had been debated, discussed, discarded, and reformulated literally hundreds of times by the time people in the revolutionary network met in Philadelphia.
>
> Thus, a network of correspondence and printed broadsides led to the formation of an organization after the writers met in a series of conferences and worked out a statement of purpose—which they called a "Declaration of Independence." Little did our early networking grandparents realize that the result of their youthful idealism, less than two centuries later, would be a global superpower with an unparalleled ability to influence the survival of life on the planet.

As the United States grew and technology changed, the ways in which these public discussions of "matters of general interest," as Habermas called them—slavery and the rights of the states versus the power of the federal government were two such matters that loomed large—began to change as well. The text-based media that served as the channel for discourse gained more and more power to reshape the nature of that discourse. The communications media of the nineteenth century were the newspapers, the penny press, the first generation of what has come to be known as the mass media. At the same time, the birth of advertising and the beginnings of the public-relations industry began to undermine the public sphere by inventing a kind of buyable and sellable phony discourse that displaced the genuine kind. 18

The simulation (and therefore destruction) of authentic discourse, first in the United States, and then spreading to the rest of the world, is what Guy Debord would call the first quantum leap into the "society of the spectacle" and what Jean Baudrillard would recognize as a milestone in the world's slide into hyper-reality. Mass media's colonization of civil society turned into a quasi-political campaign promoting technology itself when the image-making technology of television came along. ("Progress is our most important product," said General Electric spokesman Ronald Reagan, in the early years of television.) And in the twentieth century, as the telephone, radio, and television became vehicles for public discourse, the nature of political discussion has mutated into something quite different from anything the framers of the Constitution could have foreseen. 19

A politician is now a commodity, citizens are consumers, and issues are decided   20
via sound-bites and staged events. The television camera is the only spectator that
counts at a political demonstration or convention. According to Habermas and others, the way the new media have been commoditized through this evolutionary
process from hand-printed broadside to telegraph to penny press to mass media has
led to the radical deterioration of the public sphere. The consumer society has become the accepted model both for individual behavior and political decision making. Discourse degenerated into publicity, and publicity used the increasing power
of electronic media to alter perceptions and shape beliefs.

The consumer society, the most powerful vehicle for generating short-term   21
wealth ever invented, ensures economic growth by first promoting the idea that the
way to be is to buy. The engines of wealth depend on a fresh stream of tabloids sold
at convenience markets and television programs to tell us what we have to buy next
in order to justify our existence. What used to be a channel for authentic communication has become a channel for the updating of commercial desire.

Money plus politics plus network television equals an effective system. It works.   22
When the same packaging skills that were honed on automobile tail fins and fast
foods are applied to political ideas, the highest bidder can influence public policy to
great effect. What dies in the process is the rational discourse at the base of civil society. That death manifests itself in longings that aren't fulfilled by the right kind of
shoes in this month's color or the hot new prime-time candidate everybody is talking about. Some media scholars are claiming a direct causal connection between the
success of commercial television and the loss of citizen interest in the political
process.

Another media critic, Neal Postman, in his book *Amusing Ourselves to Death*,   23
pointed out that Tom Paine's *Common Sense* sold three hundred thousand copies in
five months in 1776. The most successful democratic revolution in history was
made possible by a citizenry that read and debated widely among themselves. Postman pointed out that the mass media, and television in particular, had changed the
mode of discourse itself, by substituting fast cuts, special effects, and sound-bites for
reasoned discussion or even genuine argument.

The various hypotheses about commodification and mode of discourse focus on   24
an area of apparent agreement among social observers who have a long history of
heated disagreements.

When people who have become fascinated by BBSs or networks start spreading   25
the idea that such networks are inherently democratic in some magical way, without
specifying the hard work that must be done in real life to harvest the fruits of that
democratizing power, they run the danger of becoming unwitting agents of commodification. First, it pays to understand how old the idea really is. Next, it is important to realize that the hopes of technophiles have often been used to sell
technology for commercial gain. In this sense, CMC enthusiasts run the risk of becoming unpaid, unwitting advertisers for those who stand to gain financially from
adoption of new technology.

The critics of the idea of electronic democracy have unearthed examples from a   26
long tradition of utopian rhetoric that James Carey has called "the rhetoric of the
'technological sublime.'" He put it this way:

Despite the manifest failure of technology to resolve pressing social issues over the last century, contemporary intellectuals continue to see revolutionary potential in the latest technological gadgets that are pictured as a force outside history and politics. . . . In modern futurism, it is the machines that possess teleological insight. Despite the shortcomings of town meetings, newspaper, telegraph, wireless, and television to create the conditions of a new Athens, contemporary advocates of technological liberation regularly describe a new postmodern age of instantaneous daily plebiscitory democracy through a computerized system of electronic voting and opinion polling.

Carey was prophetic in at least one regard—he wrote this years before Ross Perot   27
and William Clinton both started talking about their versions of electronic democracy during the 1992 U.S. presidential campaign. If the United States is on the road to a version of electronic democracy in which the president will have electronic town hall meetings, including instant voting-by-telephone to "go directly to the people" (and perhaps bypass Congress?) on key issues, it is important for American citizens to understand the potential pitfalls of decision making by plebiscite. Media-manipulated plebiscites as political tools go back to Joseph Goebbels, who used radio so effectively in the Third Reich. Previous experiments in instant home polling and voting had been carried out by Warners, with their Qube service, in the early 1980s. One critic, political scientist Jean Betheke Elshtain, called the television-voting model an

> interactive shell game [that] cons us into believing that we are participating when we are really simply performing as the responding "end" of a prefabri-cated system of external stimuli. . . . In a plebiscitary system, the views of the majority . . . swamp minority or unpopular views. Plebiscitism is compatible with authoritarian politics carried out under the guise of, or with the con-nivance of, majority views. That opinion can be registered by easily manipu-lated, ritualistic plebiscites, so there is no need for debate on substantive questions.

What does it mean that the same hopes, described in the same words, for a de-   28
centralization of power, a deeper and more widespread citizen involvement in mat-ters of state, a great equalizer for ordinary citizens to counter the forces of central control, have been voiced in the popular press for two centuries in reference to steam, electricity, and television? We've had enough time to live with steam, elec-tricity, and television to recognize that they did indeed change the world, and to rec-ognize that the utopia of technological millenarians has not yet materialized.

An entire worldview and sales job are packed into the word *progress,* which links   29
the notion of improvement with the notion of innovation, highlights the benefits of innovation while hiding the toxic side-effects of extractive and lucrative technolo-gies, and then sells more of it to people via television as a cure for the stress of living in a technology-dominated world. The hope that the next technology will solve the problems created by the way the last technology was used is a kind of millennial, even messianic, hope, apparently ever-latent in the breasts of the citizenry. The myth of technological progress emerged out of the same Age of Reason that gave us

the myth of representative democracy, a new organizing vision that still works pretty well, despite the decline in vigor of the old democratic institutions. It's hard to give up on one Enlightenment ideal while clinging to another.

I believe it is too early to judge which set of claims will prove to be accurate. I also believe that those who would prefer the more democratic vision of the future have an opportunity to influence the outcome, which is precisely why online activists should delve into the criticisms that have been leveled against them. If electronic democracy advocates can address these critiques successfully, their claims might have a chance. If they cannot, perhaps it would be better not to raise people's hopes. Those who are not aware of the history of dead ends are doomed to replay them, hopes high, again and again.

The idea that putting powerful computers in the hands of citizens will shield the citizenry against totalitarian authorities echoes similar, older beliefs about citizen-empowering technology. As Langdon Winner (an author every computer revolutionary ought to read) put it in his essay "Mythinformation,"

> Of all the computer enthusiasts' political ideas, there is none more poignant than the faith that the computer is destined to become a potent equalizer in modern society. . . . Presumably, ordinary citizens equipped with micro-computers will be able to counter the influence of large, computer-based organizations.
>
> Notions of this kind echo beliefs of eighteenth-century revolutionaries that placing fire arms in the hands of the people was crucial to overthrowing entrenched authority. In the American Revolution, French Revolution, Paris Commune, and Russian Revolution the role of "the people armed" was central to the revolutionary program. As the military defeat of the Paris Commune made clear, however, the fact that the popular forces have guns may not be decisive. In a contest of force against force, the larger, more sophisticated, more ruthless, better equipped competitor often has the upper hand. Hence, the availability of low-cost computing power may move the baseline that defines electronic dimensions of social influence, but it does not necessarily alter the relative balance of power. Using a personal computer makes one no more powerful vis-à-vis, say, the National Security Agency than flying a hang glider establishes a person as a match for the U.S. Air Force.

The great power of the idea of electronic democracy is that technical trends in communications technologies can help citizens break the monopoly on their attention that has been enjoyed by the powers behind the broadcast paradigm—the owners of television networks, newspaper syndicates, and publishing conglomerates. The great weakness of the idea of electronic democracy is that it can be more easily commodified than explained. . . .

What should those of us who believe in the democratizing potential of virtual communities do about the technological critics? I believe we should invite them to the table and help them see the flaws in our dreams, the bugs in our designs. I believe we should study what the historians and social scientists have to say about the illusions and power shifts that accompanied the diffusion of previous technologies. CMC and technology in general [have] real limits; it's best to continue to listen to those who understand the limits, even as we continue to explore the technologies' positive capabilities. Failing to fall under the spell of the "rhetoric of the techno-logical sublime," actively questioning and examining social assumptions about the effects of new technologies, [and] reminding ourselves that electronic communication has powerful illusory capabilities are all good steps to take to prevent disasters.

If electronic democracy is to succeed, however, in the face of all the obstacles, activists must do more than avoid mistakes. Those who would use computer networks as political tools must go forward and actively apply their theories to more and different kinds of communities. If there is a last good hope, a bulwark against the hyper-reality of Baudrillard or Forster, it will come from a new way of looking at technology. Instead of falling under the spell of a sales pitch, or rejecting new technologies as instruments of illusion, we need to look closely at new technologies and ask how they can help build stronger, more humane communities—and ask how they might be obstacles to that goal. The late 1990s may eventually be seen in retrospect as a narrow window of historical opportunity, when people either acted or failed to act effectively to regain control over communications technologies. Armed with knowledge, guided by a clear, human-centered vision, governed by a commitment to civil discourse, we the citizens hold the key levers at a pivotal time. What happens next is largely up to us.

34

Working with the Text

1. What do you think is the Internet's value for democracy? Can you find examples of participatory democracy online? Do you think that the Internet and online technologies will enhance democracy, civic participation, and the First Amendment?

2. Rheingold spends much time explaining the concept of the *public sphere* (which is not in itself an easy concept to comprehend). Based on his description and definitions, would you say that you have experienced a version of the public sphere while participating in politics, government, and democracy in the United States at either the national or local level? What, if anywhere, constitutes a public sphere in which you participate? What defines for you the "marketplace of political ideas"? Do you agree with those critics who see that public sphere as commodified and commercialized? Does the Internet seem like an extension of these tendencies or a possible opposition to them?

3. Rheingold quotes James Carey's use of the term *technological sublime.* Where do you see evidence of this concept in media images of new network technologies, such as in commercials for personal computers and the Internet? How do media images of new technologies invoke connections between individuals and cultures around the world? How do media images bring together ideals of participatory democracy, community values, and international networking and understanding?

4. What aspects of cyberspace (or CMC, Computer Mediated Communication) does Rheingold claim might enhance personal liberty and democracy, and which might inhibit it? What are the major arguments against the "democratizing" effects of the Net that Rheingold summarizes? Which do you find

most compelling? Which are supported by your experience of online communication?

ONE WORLD, READY OR NOT

WILLIAM GREIDER

■ A graduate of Princeton University, journalist William Greider (born 1936) worked as a reporter for the *Washington Post* from 1968 to 1982 and has since served as the Washington columnist and national affairs editor for *Rolling Stone* magazine. He has also written for periodicals such as *Ramparts, Esquire,* and the *Atlantic Monthly.* In addition, he has published a number of books on political issues, including *Who Will Tell the People?: The Betrayal of American Democracy* (1992), which is about America's decaying political process, and *One World, Ready or Not: The Manic Logic of Global Capitalism* (1997). In the following adaptation from that book, which originally appeared in *Rolling Stone,* Greider reports on working conditions in American-owned factories in Southeast Asia. In it, he poses "the gut question for any citizen of the new world": "Do you believe that every human being has a thirst for self-realization and is entitled . . . to the opportunity? Or are those others who make our products really lesser beings, incapable of an expanding self-awareness and larger ideas of themselves?"

1. MOTOROLA'S LADIES

In the industrial zone at Petaling Jaya, outside of Kuala Lumpur, Malaysia, the dingy blue buses drop off workers for the 2 P.M. shift at the Motorola plant. Though it is visible from the highway, Motorola's blue logo is not the only familiar sign in this compound of global commerce—Canon, Sanyo, Panasonic, and Minolta also maintain large manufacturing plants here. Motorola's factory, like many other U.S. semiconductor companies located nearby, looks like a low-slung office-type building. It faces an asphalt parking lot that is neatly bordered by palms and giant yews. The building's white façade is decorated with red paper lanterns and gilded banners in honor of the Chinese New Year. Above the front entrance, a billboard invites employees to enter the Motorola 10K Run. The winners will get a chance to compete in a marathon in Austin, Texas.

The building's glass entry leads to a long, gleaming corridor that takes Motorola's 2 P.M. shift, all of them young, delicate-looking women, past the company library, a health center and an automatic banking machine. The women dress in the modest garb of Islam: flowing ankle-length dresses, and silk scarves of pale blue, orange and brown that are called *tundjung.* A few of the women wear the more conservative black veils that shape their faces into pale brown hearts.

"Good afternoon, ladies," says Roger Bertelson, Motorola's national manager for Malaysia, who is showing me around. The two of us tower above the stream of women who pass by, eyes lowered, barely nodding. With his brush cut and sunny American forwardness, Bertelson comes off like a taller version of Ross Perot. He's explaining the I RECOMMEND board, a wall display covered with snapshots of employees who have made successful suggestions.

"We had to change the culture," Bertelson says, "because the Malay home does not encourage women to speak out. The daughter is supposed to have babies and take care of the husband. The idea was to break down the resistance to speaking out."

Here at what is one of Motorola's largest plants outside the U.S. (5,000 employees, 80 percent Malay, 3,900 of them "ladies," as they are called), the main hallway is decorated with a series of Norman Rockwell paintings—warm, nostalgic scenes of American life—each accompanied by an inspirational aphorism in English: PEOPLE WILL TAKE NOTE OF EXCELLENT WORK; YOU'LL BE PREPARED FOR ANYTHING WITH ENTHUSIASM; WHAT WE SAY IS AS IMPORTANT AS HOW WE SAY IT.

The women pass these paintings each day on their way to the changing room where they prepare for work. They remove their shoes and veils before proceeding to the "gowning room" across the hall. A few minutes later they emerge, cloaked in ghostly white jumpsuits, surgical masks and hooded bonnets. Dressed for their high-tech work, they appear even more chaste than they would in the most traditional Islamic garments. But there's one more step. The hooded, masked women step into an "air shower," which blasts away any remaining particles of dust. Only then are they ready to enter the sealed operations room, where rows of complex machines and monitors await their gloved touch.

Once inside, the 2 P.M. shift begins the exacting daily routine of manufacturing semiconductor chips. The women work in a realm of submicrons, attaching leads to components too small to see without the aid of electronic monitors. It is likely that the silicon wafers they bend over are designed and fabricated back in the United States (or in Scotland) and flown by 747 here (or to Singapore, the Philippines or elsewhere in Asia) for final assembly—sawed into individual boards, wired, tested and packaged. The finished chips are shipped back to North America, Asia and Europe, where they will function as the brains and memories—the functional guts—of cars, televisions, computers, portable phones, missile control systems and countless other products.

The one-world spectacle of Motorola's Petaling Jaya plant is quite routine—three shifts a day, seven days a week—but watching it up close conveyed to me something of the high human drama of intertwining cultures. Our partners in high technology are now shy young women from the *kampong,* the rural Malaysian villages where, not long ago, a girl's future was limited to helping her father or husband with the rice harvest. Now she stares at electronic monitors for hours at a time and must try to explain to the men back home how her pay comes out of an automatic teller machine in the hallway at the electronics plant.

This cultural exchange, as profound as it is, constitutes a single transaction in a great, unfolding economic story. To find out what else the increasingly global nature of finance and business might mean for us, I spent three months visiting factories, plants and communities on three continents. Among the contradictions and surprising juxtapositions I encountered, I also found out firsthand that people from the most unpromising circumstances are now producing the most highly advanced artifacts of our daily lives. The notion that only certain populations—specifically, white people from Europe or America—are capable of producing goods of world-class quality is simply wrong. A great leveling has begun, I've found, and the tools of advanced industrial civilization are being shared with other tribes. Ironically, it is the multinational corporations, imperious, aloof and powerful, that are the vehicles for this historical act of generosity.

At a small house in a working-class neighborhood in Kuala Lumpur, I spent time   10
talking to six young women who live together and work at Motorola and the other electronics factories of Petaling Jaya. Some had just arrived at this union-subsidized hostel after evening prayers at a mosque; others would depart later for the 11 P.M. shift. They spoke of the details of their lives, their modest ambitions, their mild complaints, the stories of how they had come to join the global work force.

"The company came to my *kampong* and approached my father, and he sug-   11
gested that I work," says Rosita. "The basic pay was 270 ringgit [$108 a month]; now it is 300."

A 24-year-old woman named Raziah says she changed jobs three times because   12
at each one, the salary was less than what she was promised. She says that the Japanese-owned factory was "not a happy place, and my supervisors were very rude and pressured me. . . . I want to better myself, but I've got no money for classes."

I ask what brought them here. Some of them answer that they were bored at   13
home. Others say that they are saving for something. Still others followed their friends. A 25-year-old named Rakimah says, "I have put away some savings. I might even start a small business—like a nursery for children. That is my plan. I love to cook, so if not a nursery, I will open a restaurant."

Dutiful daughters all, each woman sends some money home every month to her   14
father and mother. One girl is getting married and will soon quit the factory. Another talks about a friend who was overwhelmed by the fast life of Kuala Lumpur and returned home to her village. They discuss the relative merits of the foreign employers and agree that Koreans are the worst, Americans are the best, and Motorola is the best among the Americans.

The frank discussion, which could have taken place in any company cafeteria in the   15
States, reminds me of Roger Bertelson's I RECOMMEND board. "The government would like to maintain Islamic principles and protect people from Western values," he says, "but whether the government likes it or not, the people are becoming Westernized."

2. A VISIT TO BOEING'S ITCH

Boeing's assembly plant in Everett, Wash., is one of the great wonders of the indus-   16
trial world. The cavernous factory, located north of Seattle on the Puget Sound, encompasses 98 acres of manufacturing activity under a single roof and is said to be the largest building on earth. Ten stories above the factory floor, an intricate grid of pale green girders covers the ceiling like a steel spider web. Yellow cranes creep silently through this network, dangling pieces of a wing or tail section beneath them on long, slender threads. To orchestrate the construction of the wide-body aircraft known as the 747, 767 and 777, the Boeing plant keeps 40 such cranes in motion—so many that an air-traffic control center is required to coordinate their movements.

The dimensions of the place are overwhelming. From an observation loft near   17
the ceiling, the dangling, disconnected shells of fuselages, nose cones, tails and wings resemble pieces from a fabulous model-airplane kit fastidiously arranged by a precocious child. Every seven days these pieces are methodically, miraculously brought together by the yellow cranes, then fitted and fastened by the people down

below. Wings and center section are joined to fuselage, electronics wired in, jet engines attached, and every week a finished airplane, weighing as much as 400 tons, emerges from the Everett plant.

On the shop floor, the perspectives are reversed, and the workers are dwarfed by what they are making. People bicycle from one behemoth to another, carrying plans from the dozens of computerized design stations. The nose section of a 777, its delicate aluminum skin protected by an iridescent blue coating, floats down on cables. To the rear, a wing surface is being walked into place by four machinists, who gently coax it back and forth into a snug fit with its frame. An automatic riveting machine, two stories high and mounted on railed track, moves patiently along the wing, punching out precision stitches almost noiselessly. Not counting the millions of rivets that hold it together, the "Triple Seven" has 132,000 parts.

In some circumstances, a display of technology may approach the power of art in its ability to inspire. One could not observe the majesty of the Everett factory without experiencing such exultation—or, at the least, a momentary joy—at the beauty of things actually working. The making of one of these planes requires the fusing of sensitive touch and Gargantuan strength, computerized tolerances with the human gentleness of assembly workers.

The Everett plant likewise demonstrates, perhaps even more tangibly, the international character of advanced manufacturing. On the shop floor, wooden crates marked BELFAST, IRELAND contain nose landing-gear doors. Stacked on a metal rack are outboard wing flaps, their tags labeled ALENIA OF ITALY.

The 777's entire fuselage arrives in quarter sections from Japan, shipped by Mitsubishi from Nagoya to Washington's Puget Sound, where the pieces are barged from Tacoma to the port of Everett, then hauled by railcars up the steep grade to the factory. The wingtip assembly comes from Korea, rudders from Australia, dorsal fins from Brazil, main landing gear from Canada and France. Flight computers are made in the United Kingdom. And so on.

"I am scratching their itch," says Lawrence W. Clarkson, Boeing's senior vice president for planning and international development, of his many international vendors. Clarkson explains: "I have to create some jobs in those countries to get those markets. But what we're trying to do in the net equation is to protect the jobs here. I think I can show that happened with China or with Japan. But overall, it's a tougher problem as I look at the future. Will I have a lot of U.S. suppliers, or will I have more international suppliers? I don't know, but it's clear the U.S. suppliers don't bring me any market."

A few months later, I visit a small Chinese village that hopes to provide the answer to Clarkson's question. The village of Sanyuan, in the Shaanxi province, is a settlement of worn, brown-brick dwellings located in a narrow river valley. A steep ridge, gullied and desiccated by erosion, rises behind the village, and the pale walls in the center of town have the same tired, washed-out look. The houses here are small, with dark tile or thatched roofs, and for the most part are clustered together, though several newer ones stand apart, their doorways decorated with dramatic floral designs. Behind the courtyard wall of one home, a family's possessions are scattered about on the hard-baked ground: a two-wheeled farm cart, a bicycle and tools, jumbled rows of unused bricks, mounds of darkening cornstalks, a tethered cow for plowing and two white goats for milk.

I came to this place at the suggestion of a Boeing manager who thought I should see the other end of the global aircraft industry. Sanyuan is like 10,000 other villages in China—poor and primitive, removed from the rest of the world. But this farm village is also home to the Hongyuan Aviation Forging & Casting Industry Company, a state-owned enterprise that manufactures a titanium-alloy jet-engine mount for Boeing's world-class aircraft.

In Sanyuan there are no streetlights along the paved road that leads through the village. At night the blackness is broken only by the occasional glow of a TV set seen through an open doorway. People, bicycles, handcarts appear abruptly from the thick darkness, then seem to evaporate. The night strollers are indifferent to the speeding, honking trucks that flash through the village with loads of crushed stone or steel rods. 25

In the morning the peasant farmers open up their daily market at the center of the village. They squat back on their heels in the universal manner of plain country folk, behind abundant piles of produce—carrots, greens, cauliflower, scallions and cabbages spread out on white muslin. A young man in a blue sweater jabbers self-importantly through a bullhorn. He is selling lotus flour, a milky white powder that he has packaged in clear plastic bags and weighed on a crude, hand-held scale. 26

At the north end of town, the Hongyuan Forging plant sits behind high fences, its gates guarded by young soldiers wearing the olive-green jackets of the People's Liberation Army. Inside, the shop floors are soiled and pitted, and casually littered with scrap metal. The towering green Weingarten screw press from Germany and a few other advanced machine tools look out of place in the factory's gloom. I watch four workers wrestle with a large steel plate that elsewhere in the world might have been handled by a heavy crane. A row of solemn young machinists standing at their lathes looks like a sepia photograph from a bygone industrial era. 27

Hongyuan Forging is itself rising from the dead past, a surviving legacy of China's Cold War paranoia. In the 1960s, Mao Tse-tung became convinced that either Russia or the United States was about to launch a pre-emptive nuclear strike against China, so he ordered China's heavy industries to relocate to the country's interior—the so-called Third Front. Factories were hidden in obscure places like Sanyuan so that China might survive a nuclear first strike and fight on. It might have been a lunatic defense strategy, but it brought industrial development to some very poor places. 28

In Sanyuan, scores of caves were dug in the narrow ravines of the valley wall. These broad tunnels run several hundred feet into the mountainside, and within them the company placed its laboratories and most valuable technical equipment. Thirty years later, Hongyuan's technicians are still operating in these caves, running the high-tech machines that test alloys or monitor quality control in the forgings. The company officials who show me around seem slightly embarrassed by these primitive aspects of their enterprise. 29

In the village, some families still live in the man-made caves—quite comfortably, it seems. A farmer invited me to inspect one of them, a cool, cluttered dwelling lit by a single light bulb. Walls curve into ceilings and are whitewashed, decorated with colorful travel posters and his daughter's school certificates. We sat in the coolness and drank tea from glass jars. Times are good, he says. Soon he expects to build a new house, above ground. Prosperity, Chinese style. 30

It feels like an impossible distance from the dazzling factory of Puget Sound, yet Hongyuan Forging is a Boeing subcontractor in good standing—ambitious, in fact, to become a world-class producer of advanced industrial goods. The company al- 31 ready makes precision turbine blades for Siemens of Germany and ABB of Switzerland and is pursuing business deals with General Electric. Hongyuan Forging has opened sales offices on three continents. Its general manager, Kang Feng Xiao, a gray-haired engineer who came to the city 29 years earlier to build Mao's Third Front, seems confident of the new vision.

"Since we have business with Boeing," Kang says, "this makes us upgrade our forgings so our technology is very close to world standards. Also, we learned the quality-control system. Our purpose is to push into the world market, mainly aerospace, steam turbines, car forgings. We intend to develop our company as the biggest in China, the biggest in East Asia. I think in this way—the way of the market—it won't be long before China will have great changes."

In Hongyuan Forging's showroom are displayed the wheels, joints, rings, rods and axles that go out from this small village to customers in Germany, Japan, Korea and the United States. An honored place is reserved for the American aircraft company that has shared its precious knowledge. Displayed on a blue felt drape are five of the titanium-alloy support struts that Hongyuan Forging manufactures for the engine mounts of the Boeing 747.

3. A TOY-FACTORY FIRE IN THAILAND

On May 10, 1993, the worst industrial fire in the history of capitalism decimated a toy factory on the outskirts of Bangkok, Thailand. The news was reported on Page 25 of the *Washington Post*. The *Financial Times* of London, which styles itself as the daily newspaper of the global economy, ran a brief item on Page 5. The *Wall Street Journal* followed a day later with an account on Page 11. The *New York Times* also put the story inside but printed a dramatic photo on its front page: rows of small, shrouded bodies on bamboo pallets—dozens of them—lined along the damp pavement, while dazed rescue workers stood awkwardly among the corpses. In the background, one could see the collapsed, smoldering structure of the mammoth factory where the Kader Industrial toy company of Thailand had employed 3,000 workers, manufacturing stuffed toys and plastic dolls, playthings destined for American children.

The official count was 188 dead, 469 injured, but the actual toll was undoubtedly higher, since the four-story buildings had collapsed swiftly in the intense heat, and many bodies were incinerated. Some of the missing were never found; others fled home to their villages. All but 14 of the dead were women, most of them young, some as young as 13 years old. Hundreds of workers had been trapped on upper floors of the burning building and were forced to jump from third- and fourth-floor windows because the main exit doors were kept locked by the managers and the narrow stairways collapsed or became clotted with trampled bodies.

When I visit Bangkok about nine months later, physical evidence of the disaster is gone—the site was scraped clean by bulldozers—and Kader is already resuming production at a new toy factory, built far from the city in a rural province of northeastern Thailand. When I talk with Thai labor leaders and civic activists, the people who had rallied to the cause of the fire victims, some of them are under the impression that a worldwide boycott of Kader products is under way, organized by conscience-stricken Americans and Europeans. I have to inform them that the civilized world barely noticed their tragedy.

As news accounts pointed out, the Kader fire surpassed what was previously the worst industrial fire in history, the Triangle Shirtwaist Company fire of 1911, in which 146 young immigrant women died in similar circumstances at a garment factory in Lower Manhattan. The Triangle factory fire became a pivotal event in American politics. It was a public scandal that provoked citizen reform and energized the growth of the International Ladies' Garment Workers' Union. The fire in Thailand produced no such response or even a sign of shame among consumers. The indifference of the powerful newspapers merely reflects the tastes of their readers, who might be moved by human suffering in their own communities but are inured to news of recurring calamities in distant places. A fire in Bangkok was like a typhoon in Bangladesh or an earthquake in Turkey.

The Kader fire might have become more meaningful for Americans if they could   38 have seen the thousands of soot-stained dolls that spilled from the wreckage, the macabre litter scattered among the dead: Bugs Bunny, Bart Simpson, Big Bird and other *Sesame Street* dolls, Playskool Water Pets, Santa Claus dolls. What the initial news accounts did not mention was that Kader's Thai factory had produced most of its toys for American companies—Toys "R" Us, Fisher-Price, Hasbro, Tyco, Arco, Kenner, Gund and J.C. Penney.

Americans worry obsessively over the everyday safety of their children, and the   39 U.S. government's regulators diligently police the design of toys. Yet neither American citizens nor their government took any interest in the brutal and dangerous conditions imposed on the toy makers, many of whom were mere adolescents themselves.

The toy industry, not surprisingly, felt the same way. Hasbro Industries, maker of   40 Playskool, subsequently told the *Boston Globe* that it would no longer do business with Kader, but in general, the U.S. companies shrugged off responsibility. Kader, a major toy manufacturer based in Hong Kong, is "extremely reputable, not sleazebags," David Miller, president of the Toy Manufacturers of America, assured *USA Today*. "The responsibility for those factories," Miller told ABC News, "is in the hands of those who are there and managing the factory."

The grisly details of what occurred reveal the casual irresponsibility of both companies and governments. The Kader factory compound consisted of four interconnected, four-story industrial barns on a three-acre lot on Buddhamondhol VI Road in the Sampran district, west of Bangkok. It is only one among Thailand's many thriving new industrial zones for garments, textiles, electronics and toys. More than 50,000 people, most of them migrants from the Thai countryside, work in the Sampran district at 7,500 large and small firms. Thailand's economic boom is based on places such as this, and Bangkok is almost choking on its own fantastic growth, dizzily erecting luxury hotels and office towers.

The fire started late on a Monday afternoon on the ground floor in the first   42 building and spread rapidly upward, jumping to two adjoining buildings, all three of which swiftly collapsed. Investigators noted afterward that the structures had been cheaply built, without adequate reinforcement, so steel girders and stairways crumpled easily in the heat. Thai law requires that in such a large factory, fire-escape stairways must be 16 to 33 feet wide, but Kader's stairways measured only 4½ feet. The factory's main doors were locked, and many windows were barred to prevent pilfering by the employees. Flammable raw materials—fabric, stuffing, animal fibers—were stacked everywhere, on walkways and next to electrical boxes. Neither safety drills nor fire alarms and sprinkler systems had been provided.

A young woman named Lampan Taptim who survived the fire remembers "the   43
sound of yelling about a fire. I tried to leave the section, but my supervisor told me
to get back to work. My sister, who worked on the fourth floor with me, pulled me
away and insisted we try to get out. We tried to go down the stairs and go to the second floor; we found that the stairs had already caved in. There was a lot of yelling
and confusion. . . . In desperation, I went back up to the windows, and went back
and forth, looking down below. The smoke was thick, and I picked the best place to
jump in a pile of boxes. My sister jumped, too. She died."

Another young woman, a survivor named Cheng, recalls: "[People were shout-   44
ing], 'There is no way out. The security guard has locked the main door out!' It was
horrifying. I thought I would die. I took off my gold ring and kept it in my pocket,
and put on my name tag so that my body could be identifiable. I had to decide
[whether] to die in the fire or from jumping down from a three stories' height."

An older textile worker named Vilaiwa Satieti, who sewed shirts and pants at a   45
neighboring factory, describes to me the carnage she encountered: "I got off work
about 5 and passed by Kader, and saw many dead bodies lying around uncovered.
They had broken legs and broken arms and broken heads. We tried to keep them
alive until they got to the hospital—that's all you could do. Oh, they were teenagers,
15 to 20 years, no more than that, and so many of them, so many."

Similar tragedies, large and small, are now commonplace across developing Asia   46
and elsewhere. Two months after Kader, another fire at a Bangkok shirt factory
killed 10 women. Three months after Kader, a six-story hotel collapsed and killed
133 people, injuring 351. The embarrassed minister of industry ordered special inspections of 244 large factories in the Bangkok region and found that 60 percent of
them had basic violations similar to Kader's. Just as Thai industry is growing explo-
sively—12 to 15 percent a year—workplace injuries and illnesses are growing even
faster, from 37,000 victims in 1987 to more than 150,000 in 1992 and an estimated
200,000 in 1994.

Which brings up these questions: Why does global commerce, with its wondrous   47
technologies and sophisticated economics, restore barbaric conditions that were
long ago forbidden by law? If the Information Age has enabled corporations to become truly multinational—managing production and distribution spread across
continents—why are their managers unable or unwilling to manage such mundane
matters as fire prevention?

4. SHOES AND POWER IN INDONESIA

The young Indonesian factory workers gathered around the table steal glances at   48
one another and at me like embarrassed teenagers not sure they are dressed properly for the occasion. My questions in English draw them forward in their chairs.
When they hear the translation in Bahasa, they sink back, wearing nervous smiles.

"Why did you come here from your villages?" I ask.   49

"To earn money . . . to be independent," says a worker.   50

"Were your hopes fulfilled?"   51

"Not really."   52

"Why?"   53

"The costs are very big; the pay is very small." Each answer is accompanied by   54
scattered giggles and nodding heads.

It is a Sunday afternoon in the dim front room of a small house in the Tangerang   55
district, an hour or so outside Jakarta. The house is maintained by YAKOMA, a
church-supported social foundation that uses it as an informal training center. It is
a place for young workers to come on their days off for frank discussions about
working conditions in this industrial zone, where famous American brands like
Nike shoes, Arrow shirts and Levi's jeans are manufactured. The young men and
women in the room with me make the shoes and the jeans, though they work for
contractor concerns with less familiar names like Sung Hwa Dunia, Nasa and Hasi.

YAKOMA is prominent among the dozens of nongovernmental organizations   56
that have taken hold in Indonesia during the last 10 years as advocates for civil
rights, environmental issues and women. Inevitably, many of these groups con-
verged on the core issue of labor rights, since the outcome of that struggle would determine almost everything else—personal dignity and civic democracy, economic
justice and individual freedom.

"This is a paternalistic culture," explains Indera Nababan, the YAKOMA leader   57
who arranged the session for me. "It teaches the people that all that comes from
above is good, that you never raise your voice. Some do resist, but most of the workers are rural girls and unsure of themselves. It's only through experience that they
learn they must take their destiny in their own hands."

Their names are Sadisah, Cicih, Sugeng, Suprato, Hazimah, Eva, Enaf, among   58
others. Most of them are in their late teens or early 20s, but their hesitant manner
makes them seem much younger than their American counterparts. The young
women are unmarried—still girls in Indonesian social status. They have sweetly
beautiful Javanese faces with rich, loosely flowing black hair. They are simply
dressed in slacks and bright print blouses or striped cotton shirts. One of the boys,
Suprato, wears a crisp T-shirt that declares in English: FOLLOW THE FLAG.

What do you expect for the future, I want to know. A blank pause, then tentative   59
and unfocused answers: "We hope to improve ourselves," one of them says.

Can you do that? No. . . . Yes. . . . Possibly. . . . "If we struggle. . . ." There is   60
something painfully innocent in their mien. They seem so young and unequipped,
too frail and vulnerable to be caught up by such heavy questions. Still, they lean
earnestly into the conversation, chins up, trying to answer correctly, bravely.

"If we fight, things may be different," Eva Novitasari offers slowly at last. "I think   61
we will fight."

"We are hopeful," Suprato says. "Right now, we accept what we have, but we   62
would like to change that."

They are well aware of the risks of organizing against their companies, since a   63
new national heroine has arisen in Indonesia as a courageous symbol of their aspirations. Marsinah, a 23-year-old worker, tried to organize her fellow workers at a
watch factory in East Java. She was abducted, raped and murdered. The brutal details of her death have become a national scandal, and though the military itself was
implicated in her murder, President Suharto's regime has anointed Marsinah
posthumously as a "worker hero." Her story inspires these young workers in
Tangerang and also reminds them of the dangers of asserting themselves.

Cicih and Sadisah themselves organized a strike at one of Nike's contractor   64
plants, demanding the legal minimum wage and other improvements. They were
fired, along with 20 others (suspended, the company said, for damaging the plant.

Nike insists that it has since taken steps to ensure that contractors comply with prevailing labor legislation). "I was scared because we were fighting for our rights," Cicih says. What about losing your job? "No, I wasn't afraid of that," she says. "The pay is very poor."

"I expected much higher wages, but I was new," Sadisah says. "I expected to rise, then I found it was not true. It's no good going back home without success; you don't feel satisfied."

Sadisah signed on with YAKOMA as a community organizer, living in an impoverished settlement near the factories and trying to engage the workers in dialogue about their conditions. Progress is slow and difficult. "The community is too close; they won't take advice," she grumbles. "The women workers, I hope, will be independent and brave enough to fight for their rights. But, you know, in Indonesia, the women are the weak ones, not strong, not brave."

Beyond the question of courage, the young workers lack even the most basic knowledge about how the industrial world works and how they might cope with it. What is a union? What rights do they possess to complain? "We have a union at Hasi," Enaf says, "but it is not the union that told us to strike. [That was] the workers. The union is all from the company." Eva adds: "The company told us to choose our union leader from the company staff. We didn't know about the union or what it was."

Our meeting adjourns, and the kids rush out to find their friends, to stroll along the dusty streets or to hang out at shops for the few hours that remain of their day off. On the long ride back to Jakarta, I try to imagine what young Americans would say to the young people from Tangerang, what commonality they might discover if they were ever brought together in the same room.

Here in Indonesia, kids assemble the basketball shoes and brand-name jeans so valued back in the United States, the goods that are expensive symbols of style and grace for American youth. In their advertising messages, the most successful athletic-shoe manufacturers have concocted an artful fantasy of power that status-conscious young Americans eagerly consume: the idea of magical shoes that embody superhuman athletic prowess.

The young Indonesians who actually make the shoes are still trying to understand real power, even as it buffets their lives in the real world. They thought, perhaps naively, that if the American kids would stop buying Nike shoes, their own grievances might be heard, and some of them have signed a petition asking other young people around the world to boycott a company that the workers maintain collaborates in their oppression.

Though Americans seldom read about it, thousands of wildcat strikes are launched against the new factories of developing Asia, staged by brave young people like the ones I met. They want better pay and working conditions, but they also want a voice in their own destiny. An infant labor movement is struggling to be born in these countries and faces extraordinary obstacles. It is not simply the multinational companies standing in the way but, usually, the workers' own governments.

5. AN EMERGING DIGNITY

Several months after my visit to Indonesia, I meet with a group of community leaders in Texas. I recount some of what I have seen in Southeast Asia—the bewilderment of the young workers, the terrible conditions imposed on the powerless. One of the community leaders, a Mexican-American woman named Dora Olivo from the Rio Grande Valley, responds with her own story.

"When I was a kid and we used to pick cotton," Olivo says. "Our family lived in a barracks, all of us in one room, and we didn't have water or toilets or anything. We were very poor; we didn't know to expect anything else. Then Cesar Chavez came and told us we had dignity. And that started to change things. People began to recognize their dignity—that they have a right to dignity—and we began to expect something better for ourselves."   73

Olivo's eloquent comment sounds disarmingly simple, yet she is expressing the vital, universal core of human experience—the possibilities of self-realization. Across vastly disparate cultures, people in different places define the search in wildly various terms, from material accumulation to spiritual awareness, but the unifying thread of mortal existence is the search for self-discovery. Who am I? What is my purpose here on earth, my true potential? Where do I fit in the larger scheme of things? Part of the human struggle, in every time and place, among wealthy and poor, is to seek answers to those questions.   74

When all the economic complexities are set aside, the question before the world is really about that word—*dignity*—and the possibilities for individual self-realization. It cannot be only about money. It must begin from the understanding that the human potential is vast, unfathomable and largely unrealized. The unknown is what makes the future so interesting, so promising in every age, especially in this one.   75

Some Asian political leaders belittle the Western understanding of individualism and assure us that their cultures do not share in these assumptions. These smug politicians, I think, are in for a rude surprise. They may dismiss the concept of personal identity, but ultimately their prospering societies will be unable to hold back the tide of individualism that is carried in on the waves of capitalist enterprise.   76

Japanese culture has already been changed by Western-style capitalism's impact and wrestles now with the social and economic implications. In Malaysia, the young Muslim women working for Motorola gain personal control over their own wages for the first time by using ATMs. In Indonesia or China, it is self-realization that is present in the courage to aspire to make great products or even to contemplate a strike against powerful employers. Commerce invades with revolutionary ideas and challenges. Once the concepts are implanted, a regime will need enormous force to keep them down.   77

So the gut question for any citizen of the new world is: Do you believe that every human being has a thirst for self-realization and is entitled, in his or her own terms, to the opportunity? Or are those others who make our products really lesser beings, incapable of an expanding self-awareness and larger ideas of themselves? The human struggles and aspirations that I encountered around the world make the answer seem obvious to me.   78

Working with the Text

1. Greider says that watching the operation of the Motorola plant in Malaysia showed him something of the "high human drama of intertwining cultures."

What are some of the details of that drama that he describes in his article? Who are the players? What are the tensions? Why do you think he calls it "high human drama"?

2. What key issues are raised in the story about the toy-factory fire in Thailand? How does it reveal certain changing realities in relations between "First World" and "Third World" nations? How does it represent the continuation of values?

3. Greider compares the toy-factory fire in Thailand to the Triangle Shirtwaist Company fire in 1911, which he says was a pivotal event in American industrial history. There is a good site on the World Wide Web about the Triangle Shirtwaist Company fire. Read around the site and find at least one document that raises some of the issues that Greider does about the international work force. Are there similarities or differences in attitudes about women, work, and culture?

4. At the end of the essay, Greider says, "When all the economic complexities are set aside, the question before the world is really about that word—*dignity*—and the possibilities for individual self-realization." Later he says, "So the gut question for any citizen of the new world is: Do you believe that every human being has a thirst for self-realization and is entitled, in his or her own terms, to the opportunity?" How are the world's new borders, especially as they are shaped by new global economic realities, affecting individual quests for "dignity" and self-fulfillment? How can the new globalism advance the cause of individual rights and opportunities? In what ways might the course of individual rights be set back by the new globalism?

5. In discussing the Western world's lack of concern over the conditions that workers of developing countries experience to produce "First World" consumer products, Greider notes: "Americans worry obsessively over the everyday safety of their children, and the U.S. government's regulators diligently police the design of toys. Yet neither American citizens nor their government took any interest in the brutal and dangerous conditions imposed on the toy makers, many of whom were mere adolescents themselves." In a paper, explore the question of the responsibility that American consumers have for conditions that produce their products. How much should you know? What difference should it make?

JIHAD VS. MCWORLD

BENJAMIN BARBER

■ A professor of political science at Rutgers University, Benjamin Barber was born in New York City. He attended the London School of Economics and Grinnell College, receiving his master's and doctoral degrees from Harvard. His research and writing have focused on a wide variety of topics, and his books include *Liberating Feminism* (1975), *The Artist and Political Vision* (1982), *Strong*

Democracy: Participatory Politics for a New Age (1984), and *An Aristocracy of Every-one* (1992). The author of a novel as well as a number of plays, Barber also collaborated on the prize-winning television series and companion book *The Struggle for Democracy* (1988). The following essay is the introduction to his 1995 book, *Jihad vs. McWorld,* in which Barber focuses on two competing forces in global culture: "the one driven by parochial hatreds, the other by universalizing markets, the one re-creating ancient subnational and ethnic borders from within, the other making national borders porous from without."

H istory is not over. Nor are we arrived in the wondrous land of techné promised by the futurologists. The collapse of state communism has not delivered people to a safe democratic haven, and the past, fratricide and civil discord perduring, still clouds the horizon just behind us. Those who look back see all of the horrors of the ancient slaughterbench reenacted in disintegral nations like Bosnia, Sri Lanka, Ossetia, and Rwanda and they declare that nothing has changed. Those who look forward prophesize commercial and technological interdependence—a virtual paradise made possible by spreading markets and global technology—and they proclaim that everything is or soon will be different. The rival observers seem to consult different almanacs drawn from the libraries of contrarian planets.

Yet anyone who reads the daily papers carefully, taking in the front page accounts of civil carnage as well as the business page stories on the mechanics of the information superhighway and the economics of communication mergers, anyone who turns deliberately to take in the whole 360-degree horizon, knows that our world and our lives are caught between what William Butler Yeats called the two eternities of race and soul: that of race reflecting the tribal past, that of soul anticipating the cosmopolitan future. Our secular eternities are corrupted, however, race reduced to an insignia of resentment, and soul sized down to fit the demanding body by which it now measures its needs. Neither race nor soul offers us a future that is other than bleak, neither promises a polity that is remotely democratic.

The first scenario rooted in race holds out the grim prospect of a retribalization of large swaths of humankind by war and bloodshed: a threatened balkanization of nation-states in which culture is pitted against culture, people against people, tribe against tribe, a Jihad in the name of a hundred narrowly conceived faiths against every kind of interdependence, every kind of artificial social cooperation and mutuality: against technology, against pop culture, and against integrated markets; against modernity itself as well as the future in which modernity issues. The second paints that future in shimmering pastels, a busy portrait of onrushing economic, technological, and ecological forces that demand integration and uniformity and that mesmerize peoples everywhere with fast music, fast computers, and fast food—MTV, Macintosh, and McDonald's—pressing nations into one homogenous global theme park, one McWorld tied together by communications, information, entertainment, and commerce. Caught between Babel and Disneyland, the planet is falling precipitously apart and coming reluctantly together at the very same moment.

Some stunned observers notice only Babel, complaining about the thousand newly sundered "peoples" who prefer to address their neighbors with sniper rifles

1

2

3

4

and mortars; others—zealots in Disneyland—seize on futurological platitudes and the promise of virtuality, exclaiming "It's a small world after all!" Both are right, but how can that be?

We are compelled to choose between what passes as "the twilight of sovereignty" and an entropic end of all history; or a return to the past's most fractious and demoralizing discord; to "the menace of global anarchy," to Milton's capital of hell, Pandaemonium; to a world totally "out of control."

The apparent truth, which speaks to the paradox at the core of this book, is that the tendencies of both Jihad *and* McWorld are at work, both visible sometimes in the same country at the very same instant. Iranian zealots keep one ear tuned to the mullahs urging holy war and the other cocked to Rupert Murdoch's Star television beaming in *Dynasty, Donahue,* and *The Simpsons* from hovering satellites. Chinese entrepreneurs vie for the attention of party cadres in Beijing and simultaneously pursue KFC franchises in cities like Nanjing, Hangzhou, and Xian where twenty-eight outlets serve over 100,000 customers a day. The Russian Orthodox church, even as it struggles to renew the ancient faith, has entered a joint venture with California businessmen to bottle and sell natural waters under the rubric Saint Springs Water Company. Serbian assassins wear Adidas sneakers and listen to Madonna on Walkman headphones as they take aim through their gunscopes at scurrying Sarajevo civilians looking to fill family watercans. Orthodox Hasids and brooding neo-Nazis have both turned to rock music to get their traditional messages out to the new generation, while fundamentalists plot virtual conspiracies on the Internet.

Now neither Jihad nor McWorld is in itself novel. History ending in the triumph of science and reason or some monstrous perversion thereof (Mary Shelley's Doctor Frankenstein) has been the leitmotiv of every philosopher and poet who has regretted the Age of Reason since the Enlightenment. Yeats lamented "the center will not hold, mere anarchy is loosed upon the world," and observers of Jihad today have little but historical detail to add. The Christian parable of the Fall and of the possibilities of redemption that it makes possible captures the eighteenth-century ambivalence—and our own—about past and future. I want, however, to do more than dress up the central paradox of human history in modern clothes. It is not Jihad and McWorld but the relationship between them that most interests me. For, squeezed between their opposing forces, the world has been sent spinning out of control. Can it be that what Jihad and McWorld have in common is anarchy: the absence of common will and that conscious and collective human control under the guidance of law we call democracy?

Progress moves in steps that sometimes lurch backwards; in history's twisting maze, Jihad not only revolts against but abets McWorld, while McWorld not only imperils but re-creates and reinforces Jihad. They produce their contraries and need one another. My object here then is not simply to offer sequential portraits of McWorld and Jihad, but while examining McWorld, to keep Jihad in my field of vision, and while dissecting Jihad, never to forget the context of McWorld. Call it a dialectic of McWorld: a study in the cunning of reason that does honor to the radical differences that distinguish Jihad and McWorld yet that acknowledges their powerful and paradoxical interdependence.

There is a crucial difference, however, between my modest attempt at dialectic and that of the masters of the nineteenth century. Still seduced by the Enlightenment's faith in progress, both Hegel and Marx believed reason's cunning was on the side of progress. But it is harder to believe that the clash of Jihad and McWorld will issue in some overriding good. The outcome seems more likely to pervert than to nurture human liberty. The two may, in opposing each other, work to the same ends, work in apparent tension yet in covert harmony, but democracy is not their beneficiary. In East Berlin, tribal communism has yielded to capitalism. In Marx-Engelsplatz, the stolid, overbearing statues of Marx and Engels face east, as if seeking distant solace from Moscow: but now, circling them along the streets that surround the park that is their prison are chain eateries like T.G.I. Friday's, international hotels like the Radisson, and a circle of neon billboards mocking them with brand names like Panasonic, Coke, and GoldStar. New gods, yes, but more liberty?

What then does it mean in concrete terms to view Jihad and McWorld dialectically   10 when the tendencies of the two sets of forces initially appear so intractably antithetical? After all, Jihad and McWorld operate with equal strength in opposite directions, the one driven by parochial hatreds, the other by universalizing markets, the one re-creating ancient subnational and ethnic borders from within, the other making national borders porous from without. Yet Jihad and McWorld have this in common: they both make war on the sovereign nation-state and thus undermine the nation-state's democratic institutions. Each eschews civil society and belittles democratic citizenship, neither seeks alternative democratic institutions. Their common thread is indifference to civil liberty. Jihad forges communities of blood rooted in exclusion and hatred, communities that slight democracy in favor of tyrannical paternalism or consensual tribalism. McWorld forges global markets rooted in consumption and profit, leaving to an untrustworthy, if not altogether fictitious, invisible hand issues of public interest and common good that once might have been nurtured by democratic citizenries and their watchful governments. Such governments, intimidated by market ideology, are actually pulling back at the very moment they ought to be aggressively intervening. What was once understood as protecting the public interest is now excoriated as heavy-handed regulatory browbeating. Justice yields to markets, even though, as Felix Rohatyn has bluntly confessed, "there is a brutal Darwinian logic to these markets. They are nervous and greedy. They look for stability and transparency, but what they reward is not always our preferred form of democracy." If the traditional conservators of freedom were democratic constitutions and Bills of Rights, "the new temples to liberty," George Steiner suggests, "will be McDonald's and Kentucky Fried Chicken."

In being reduced to a choice between the market's universal church and a retrib-   11 alizing politics of particularist identities, peoples around the globe are threatened with an atavistic return to medieval politics where local tribes and ambitious emperors together ruled the world entire, women and men united by the universal abstraction of Christianity even as they lived out isolated lives in warring fiefdoms defined by involuntary (ascriptive) forms of identity. This was a world in which princes and kings had little real power until they conceived the ideology of nationalism. Nationalism established government on a scale greater than the tribe yet less cosmopolitan than the universal church and in time gave birth to those intermediate, gradually more democratic institutions that would come to constitute the nation-state. Today, at the far end of this history, we seem intent on re-creating a world in which our only choices are the secular universalism of the cosmopolitan market and the everyday particularism of the fractious tribe.

In the tumult of the confrontation between global commerce and parochial eth-   12
nicity, the virtues of the democratic nation are lost and the instrumentalities by which it permitted peoples to transform themselves into nations and seize sovereign power in the name of liberty and the commonweal are put at risk. Neither Jihad nor McWorld aspires to resecure the civic virtues undermined by its denationalizing practices; neither global markets nor blood communities service public goods or pursue equality and justice. Impartial judiciaries and deliberative assemblies play no role in the roving killer bands that speak on behalf of newly liberated "peoples," and such democratic institutions have at best only marginal influence on the roving multinational corporations that speak on behalf of newly liberated markets. Jihad pursues a bloody politics of identity, McWorld a bloodless economics of profit. Belonging by default to McWorld, everyone is a consumer; seeking a repository for identity, everyone belongs to some tribe. But no one is a citizen. Without citizens, how can there be democracy?

FROM SELF-DETERMINATION TO JIHAD

Not long ago, Daniel Patrick Moynihan predicted that the next half hundred states   13
likely to come into existence over the next fifty years will all be defined by ethnic conflict: that is to say, by civil war. The Soviet Union and Yugoslavia have together already produced twenty or more new (old) "nations" or national fragments. In the most egregious cases, the United Nations sends peacekeeping forces, although its member nations are increasingly loath to put their soldiers at risk. Currently, it has stationed troops in eighteen countries—in nearly every case, arrayed against forces of domestic insurrection and civil discord. The Carter Center in Atlanta has a still more nuanced and thus expansive list that is more or less mirrored in the forty-eight trouble spots charted by *The New York Times* at the beginning of 1993. Amnesty International reports political prisoners and political executions in more than sixty countries.

In this tumultuous world, the real players are not nations at all but tribes, many of   14
them at war with one another. Their aim is precisely to redraw boundaries in order to divide—say in Kurdish Iraq or Muslim Sudan or Serbian-populated sections of Croatia. Countries like Afghanistan, recently fighting a foreign invader in the name of its national independence, have been effectively dismembered: divided among Panthans, Hazaras, Uzbeks, and Tajiks. This is ethnic membership enhanced via national dismemberment—or by expulsion or expunction of unwanted contaminators, as has occurred in slaughter-happy Rwanda. Is this pandaemonium just an extension of benign efforts at multiculturalism? A natural consequence of a centuries-old impulse to self-determination? Or the appearance of a new disease that has corrupted integral nationalism and opened the way to ethnic and religious Jihad?

Jihad is, I recognize, a strong term. In its mildest form, it betokens religious   15
struggle on behalf of faith, a kind of Islamic zeal. In its strongest political manifestation, it means bloody holy war on behalf of partisan identity that is metaphysically defined and fanatically defended. Thus, while for many Muslims it may signify only

ardor in the name of a religion that can properly be regarded as universalizing (if not quite ecumenical), I borrow its meaning from those militants who make the slaughter of the "other" a higher duty. I use the term in its militant construction to suggest dogmatic and violent particularism of a kind known to Christians no less than Muslims, to Germans and Hindis as well as to Arabs. The phenomena to which I apply the phrase have innocent enough beginnings: identity politics and multi-cultural diversity can represent strategies of a free society trying to give expression to its diversity. What ends as Jihad may begin as a simple search for a local identity, some set of common personal attributes to hold out against the numbing and neuter-ing uniformities of industrial modernization and the colonizing culture of McWorld.

America is often taken as the model for this kind of benign multiculturalism, al-   16
though we too have our critics like Arthur Schlesinger, Jr., for whom multicultural-ism is never benign and for whom it signals the inaugural logic of a long-term disintegration. Indeed, I will have occasion below to write about an "American Jihad" being waged by the radical Right. The startling fact is that less than 10 per-cent (about twenty) of the modern world's states are truly homogenous and thus, like Denmark or the Netherlands, can't get smaller unless they fracture into tribes or clans. In only half is there a single ethnic group that comprises even 75 percent of the population. As in the United States, multiculturalism is the rule, homogeneity the exception. Nations like Japan or Spain that appear to the outside world as inte-gral turn out to be remarkably multicultural. And even if language alone, the na-tion's essential attribute, is made the condition for self-determination, a count of the number of languages spoken around the world suggests the community of na-tions could grow to over six thousand members.

The modern nation-state has actually acted as a cultural integrator and has   17
adapted well to pluralist ideals: civic ideologies and constitutional faiths around which their many clans and tribes can rally. It has not been too difficult to contrive a civil religion for Americans or French or Swiss, since these "peoples" actually con-tain multitudes of subnational factions and ethnic tribes earnestly seeking common ground. But for Basques and Normans? What need have they for anything but blood and memory? And what of Alsatians, Bavarians, and East Prussians? Kurds, Osse-tians, East Timorese, Quebecois, Abkhazians, Catalonians, Tamils, Inkatha Zulus, Kurile Islander Japanese—peoples without countries inhabiting nations they can-not call their own? Peoples trying to seal themselves off not just from others but from modernity? These are frightened tribes running not to but from civic faith in search of something more palpable and electrifying. How will peoples who define themselves by the slaughter of tribal neighbors be persuaded to subscribe to some flimsy artificial faith organized around abstract civic ideals or commercial markets? Can advertising divert warriors of blood from the genocide required by their an-cient grievances?

Like McWorld, Jihad can of course be painted in bright as well as dark colors. Just   18
as McWorld's sometimes rapacious markets have been advanced in the name of democratic free choice, so Jihad's combative interests can be touted in the name of self-determination. Indeed, the ideology of self-determination may be the source of more than a few of Jihad's pathologies. President Woodrow Wilson's own secre-tary of state, Robert L. Lansing, failed to share his chief's enthusiasm for the idea, asking would not self-determination "breed discontent, disorder and rebellion? The

phrase is simply loaded with dynamite. It will raise hopes which can never be realized. It will, I fear, cost thousands of lives. What a calamity that the phrase was ever
uttered! What misery it will cause!"

Lansing's anxieties seem well justified. In Wilson's own time, the politics of self-   19
determination balkanized Europe, fanned nationalist wildfires, and created instabilities that contributed to the rise of fascism. Today there is no tribe, no faction or
splinter group or neighborhood gang, that does not aspire to self-determination.
"Don't dis me!" shouts the gangsta rapper, "I gotta get some respect." The futile
Owen-Vance map for the partition of Bosnia, multiplying boundaries as it nar-
rowed the compass of ethnic communities, finally seemed to give respectability to a
gang logic, trying to write into law the absurdity of treating nearly each city block as
a nation, almost every housing unit a potential sovereign. In other times, this bankrupt political arrangement, sanctioned for a considerable time by a desperate
United Nations Security Council, would carry the name anarchy.

One cannot really blame the cartographers or peacemakers for Jihad's absurdity,   20
however. They do not rearrange the scene, they just take snapshots of it. Multiculturalism has in some places conjured anarchy. Self-determination has at times
amounted to little more than other-extermination. Colonial masters did still worse
in their time, drawing arbitrary lines across maps they could not read with consequences still being endured throughout the ex-colonial world, above all in Africa
and the Middle East. Jihad is then a rabid response to colonialism and imperialism
and their economic children, capitalism and modernity; it is diversity run amok,
multiculturalism turned cancerous so that the cells keep dividing long after their division has ceased to serve the healthy corpus.

Even traditionally homogenous integral nations have reason to feel anxious   21
about the prospect of Jihad. The rising economic and communications interdependence of the world means that such nations, however unified internally, must
nonetheless operate in an increasingly multicultural global environment. Ironically,
a world that is coming together pop culturally and commercially is a world whose
discrete subnational ethnic and religious and racial parts are also far more in evidence, in no small part as a reaction to McWorld. Forced into incessant contact,
postmodern nations cannot sequester their idiosyncrasies. Post-Maastricht Europe,
while it falls well short of earlier ambitions, has become integrated enough to force
a continent-wide multicultural awareness whose consequences have by no means
been happy, let alone unifying. The more "Europe" hoves into view, the more reluctant and self-aware its national constituents become. What Günter Grass said of
Germany—"unified, the Germans were more disunited than ever"—applies in
spades to Europe and the world beyond: integrated, it is more disintegral than ever.

Responding to McWorld, parochial forces defend and deny, reject and repel   22
modernity wherever they find it. But they also absorb and assimilate, utilizing the
native's strategy against every colonizer to have crossed a border since the Romans
came to Gaul. When the Hilton came to the Hills of Buda, a local architect grafted
the new structure onto a thirteenth-century monastery. When the French restored
the Champs Élysées to its former glory, they banished the arch from McDonald's.
When American music invaded the Caribbean, Orlando Patterson reminds us, the
Caribbean reacted with enormous music production of its own, of which reggae is
only one well-known example. Yet to think that indigenization and globalization are

entirely coequal forces that put Jihad and McWorld on an equal footing is to vastly underestimate the force of the new planetary markets. The Budapest Hilton's "monastery" houses a casino; Paris's McDonald's serves Big Macs and fries with or without the arch; reggae gets only a tiny percentage of MTV play time even in Latin markets. It's no contest.

A pattern of feudal relations does, however, persist. And so we are returned to the   23 metaphor of feudalism, that puzzling world of fragments knit together by the abstraction of Christianity. Today's abstraction is the consumers' market, no less universal for all its insistent materialist secularism. Following McDonald's golden arch from country to country, the market traces a trajectory of dollars and bonds and ads and yen and stocks and currency transactions that reaches right around the globe. Grass's observation works the other way around as well: disunited, pulled apart by Jihad, the world is more united than ever. And more interdependent as well.

THE SMALLING WORLD OF MCWORLD

Even the most developed, supposedly self-sufficient nations can no longer pretend   24 to genuine sovereignty. That is the meaning of *ecology,* a term that marks the final obsolescence of all man-made boundaries. When it comes to acid rain or oil spills or depleted fisheries or tainted groundwater or fluorocarbon propellants or radiation leaks or toxic wastes or sexually transmitted diseases, national frontiers are simply irrelevant. Toxins don't stop for customs inspections and microbes don't carry passports. North America became a water and air free-trade zone long before NAFTA loosened up the market in goods.

The environmental tocsin has been sounded, loudly and often, and there is little   25 to add here to the prodigious literature warning of a biospherical Armageddon. We have learned well enough how easily the German forests can be devastated by Swiss and Italians driving gas-guzzling roadsters fueled by leaded gas (the Europeans are far behind the Americans in controlling lead). We know that the planet can be asphyxiated by greenhouse gases because Brazilian farmers want to be part of the twentieth century and are burning down their tropical rain forests to clear a little land to plow, and because many Indonesians make a living out of converting their lush jungles into toothpicks for fastidious Japanese diners, upsetting the delicate oxygen balance and puncturing our global lungs.

Ecological interdependence is, however, reactive: a consequence of natural forces   26 we cannot predict or fully control. But McWorld's interdependence and the limits it places on sovereignty is more a matter of positive economic forces that have globalism as their conscious object. It is these economic and commercial forces—the latest round in capitalism's long-standing search for world markets and global consumers—that are the primary subject of this book.

Every demarcated national economy and every kind of public good is today vul-   27 nerable to the inroads of transnational commerce. Markets abhor frontiers as nature abhors a vacuum. Within their expansive and permeable domains, interests are private, trade is free, currencies are convertible, access to banking is open, contracts are enforceable (the state's sole legitimate economic function), and the laws of production and consumption are sovereign, trumping the laws of legislatures and courts. In Europe, Asia, and the Americas such markets have already eroded national sovereignty and given birth to a new class of institutions—international banks, trade associations, transnational lobbies like OPEC, world news services like CNN and the BBC, and multinational corporations—institutions that lack distinctive national identities and neither reflect nor respect nationhood as an organizing or a regulative principle. While mills and factories sit somewhere on sovereign territory under the eye and potential regulation of nation-states, currency markets and the Internet exist everywhere, but nowhere in particular. Without an address or a national affiliation, they are altogether beyond the devices of sovereignty. Even products are becoming anonymous: whose national workforce do you fault on a defective integrated circuit labeled:

> Made in one or more of the following countries: Korea, Hong Kong, Malaysia, Singapore, Taiwan, Mauritius, Thailand, Indonesia, Mexico, Philippines. The exact country of origin is unknown.

How are the social and political demands of responsibility preserved under such remarkable circumstances?

The market imperative has in fact reinforced the quest for international peace and stability, requisites of an efficient international economy, without improving the chances for civic responsibility, accountability, or democracy, which may or may not benefit from commerce and free markets and which, although it depends on peace, is not synonymous with it. The claim that democracy and markets are twins has become a commonplace of statesmanship, especially in light of the demise of state socialism, which has left capitalism's zealots free to regard themselves not only as victors in the Cold War but as the true champions of a democracy that (they are certain) markets alone make possible. Thus have they managed to parlay the already controversial claim that markets are free into the even more controversial claim that market freedom entails and even defines democracy. President Clinton employed the phrase *democratic markets* as a mantra during his historic visit to Eastern Europe and Russia at the beginning of 1994. His foreign policy aides have consistently done the same.

This stealth rhetoric that assumes capitalist interests are not only compatible with but actively advance democratic ideals, translated into policy, is difficult to reconcile with the international realities of the last fifty years. Market economies have shown a remarkable adaptability and have flourished in many tyrannical states from Chile to South Korea, from Panama to Singapore. Indeed, the state with one of the world's least democratic governments—the People's Republic of China—possesses one of the world's fastest-growing market economies. "Communist" Vietnam is not far behind, and was opened to American trade recently, presumably on the strength of the belief that markets ultimately defeat ideology. Capitalism requires consumers with access to markets and a stable political climate in order to succeed: such conditions may or may not be fostered by democracy, which can be disorderly and even anarchic, especially in its early stages, and which often pursues public goods costly to or at odds with private-market imperatives—environmentalism or full employment for example. On the level of the individual, capitalism seeks consumers susceptible to the shaping of their needs and the manipulation of their wants while democracy needs citizens autonomous in their thoughts and independent in their deliberative judgments. Aleksandr Solzhenitsyn wishes to "tame savage capitalism," but capitalism wishes to tame anarchic democracy and appears to have little problem tolerating tyranny as long as it secures stability.

Certainly the hurried pursuit of free markets regardless of social consequences has put democratic development in jeopardy in many nations recently liberated from communism. Social insecurity and rampant unemployment for peoples accustomed to the cradle-to-the-grave ministrations of paternalistic socialist bureaucracies are unlikely to convert them to a system of democracy for which they have otherwise had no preparation. This is perhaps why majorities in all but a handful of ex-Soviet lands have been busy reelecting former Communist officials (usually wearing new party labels and carrying new ideological doctrines) to their new democratic legislatures. In economist Robert McIntyre's blunt words: "Communists and former Communists are winning because the Western economic advice has led to pointless, dysfunctional pain, while failing to set the foundations for politically and socially viable future growth." The right to choose between nine VCR models or a dozen automobile brands does not necessarily feel like freedom to workers whose monthly salaries can hardly keep up with the rising price of bread, let alone to women and men with no jobs at all. Capitalists may be democrats but capitalism does not need or entail democracy. And capitalism certainly does not need the nation-state that has been democracy's most promising host.

This is not to criticize capitalism in and of itself: joint-stock, limited-liability corporations are quite properly interested primarily in profits and pursue civic liberty and social justice only where they do not interfere with the bottom line. Indeed, they have certain conspicuous virtues beyond their intrinsic economic utilities like efficiency, productivity, elasticity, profitability. They are enemies of parochialism, isolation, fractiousness, and war and are hostile to constraints on economic choice and social mobility, although this hardly makes them friends of justice. Market psychology also can attenuate the psychology of ideological and religious cleavages and nurture concord among producers and consumers, identities that ill-suit Jihad's narrowly conceived ethnic or religious cultures. But it also undermines the psychology of skeptical inquiry upon which autonomous judgment and resistance to manipulation are founded. In the world of McWorld, the alternative to dogmatic traditionalism may turn out to be materialist consumerism or relativistic secularism or merely a profitable corruption. Democracy's ties to McWorld are at best contingent. Shopping, it is true, has little tolerance for blue laws, whether dictated by pub-closing British paternalism, Sabbath-observing Jewish Orthodoxy, or no-Sunday-liquor-sales Massachusetts Puritanism; but intolerance for blue laws is hardly a condition for constitutional faith or a respect for due process. In the context of common markets, international law has largely ceased to be a vision of justice and has become a workaday framework for getting things done: enforcing contracts, certifying deals, regulating trade and currency relations, and supervising mergers or bankruptcies. Moralists used to complain that international law was impotent in curbing the injustices of nation-states, but it has shown even less capacity to rein in markets that, after all, do not even have an address to which subpoenas can be sent. As the product of a host of individual choices or singular corporate acts, markets offer no collective responsibility. Yet responsibility is the first obligation of both citizens and civic institutions.

While they produce neither common interests nor common law, common mar-   32
kets do demand, along with a common currency, a common language; moreover,
they produce common behaviors of the kind bred by cosmopolitan city life everywhere. Commercial pilots, computer programmers, film directors, international
bankers, media specialists, oil riggers, entertainment celebrities, ecology experts,
movie producers, demographers, accountants, professors, lawyers, athletes—these
compose a new breed of men and women for whom religion, culture, and ethnic nationality are marginal elements in a working identity. Although sociologists of
everyday life will continue to distinguish a Japanese from an American mode, shopping has a common signature throughout the world. Cynics might even suggest that
some of the recent revolutions in Eastern Europe had as their true goal not liberty
and the right to vote but well-paying jobs and the right to shop. Shopping means
consumption and consumption depends on the fabrication of needs as well as of
goods in what I will call the infotainment telesector of the service economy.

McWorld is a product of popular culture driven by expansionist commerce. Its   33
template is American, its form style. Its goods are as much images as matériel, an
aesthetic as well as a product line. It is about culture as commodity, apparel as ideology. Its symbols are Harley-Davidson motorcycles and Cadillac motorcars hoisted
from the roadways, where they once represented a mode of transportation, to the
marquees of global market cafés like Harley-Davidson's and the Hard Rock where
they become icons of lifestyle. You don't drive them, you feel their vibes and rock to
the images they conjure up from old movies and new celebrities, whose personal appearances are the key to the wildly popular international café chain Planet Hollywood. Music, video, theater, books, and theme parks—the new churches of a
commercial civilization in which malls are the public squares and suburbs the
neighborless neighborhoods—are all constructed as image exports creating a common world taste around common logos, advertising slogans, stars, songs, brand
names, jingles, and trademarks. Hard power yields to soft, while ideology is trans-
muted into a kind of videology that works through sound bites and film clips. Videology is fuzzier and less dogmatic than traditional political ideology: it may as a
consequence be far more successful in instilling the novel values required for global
markets to succeed.

McWorld's videology remains Jihad's most formidable rival, and in the long run   34
it may attenuate the force of Jihad's recidivist tribalisms. Yet the information revolution's instrumentalities are also Jihad's favored weapons. Hutu or Bosnian Serb
identity was less a matter of real historical memory than of media propaganda by a
leadership set on liquidating rival clans. In both Rwanda and Bosnia, radio broad-
casts whipped listeners into a killing frenzy. As *New York Times* rock critic Jon Pare-
les has noticed, "regionalism in pop music has become as trendy as microbrewery
beer and narrowcasting cable channels, and for the same reasons." The global culture is what gives the local culture its medium, its audience, and its aspirations. Fascist pop and Hasid rock are not oxymorons; rather they manifest the dialectics of
McWorld in particularly dramatic ways. Belgrade's radio includes stations that
broadcast Western pop music as a rebuke to hard-liner Milosevic's supernationalist
government and stations that broadcast native folk tunes laced with antiforeign and
anti-Semitic sentiments. Even the Internet has its neo-Nazi bulletin boards and

Turk-trashing Armenian "flamers" (who assail every use of the word *turkey,* fair and fowl alike, so to speak), so that the abstractions of cyberspace too are infected with a peculiar and rabid cultural territoriality all their own.

The dynamics of the Jihad-McWorld linkage are deeply dialectical. Japan has, for   35 example, become more culturally insistent on its own traditions in recent years even as its people seek an ever greater purchase on McWorld. In 1992, the number-one restaurant in Japan measured by volume of customers was McDonald's, followed in the number-two spot by the Colonel's Kentucky Fried Chicken. In France, where cultural purists complain bitterly of a looming Sixième République ("la République Américaine"), the government attacks "franglais" even as it funds EuroDisney park just outside of Paris. In the same spirit, the cinema industry makes war on American film imports while it bestows upon Sylvester Stallone one of France's highest honors, the Chevalier des arts et lettres. Ambivalence also stalks India. Just outside of Bombay, cheek by jowl with villages still immersed in poverty and notorious for the informal execution of unwanted female babies or, even, wives, can be found a new town known as SCEEPZ—the Santa Cruz Electronic Export Processing Zone—where Hindi-, Tamil-, and Mahratti-speaking computer programmers write software for Swissair, AT&T, and other labor-cost-conscious multinationals. India is thus at once a major exemplar of ancient ethnic and religious tensions and "an emerging power in the international software industry." To go to work at SCEEPZ, says an employee, is "like crossing an international border." Not into another country, but into the virtual nowhere-land of McWorld.

More dramatic even than in India, is the strange interplay of Jihad and McWorld   36 in the remnants of Yugoslavia. In an affecting *New Republic* report, Slavenka Drakulic recently told the brief tragic love story of Admira and Bosko, two young star-crossed lovers from Sarajevo: "They were born in the late 1960's," she writes. "They watched Spielberg movies; they listened to Iggy Pop; they read John le Carré; they went to a disco every Saturday night and fantasized about traveling to Paris or London." Longing for safety, it seems they finally negotiated with all sides for safe passage, and readied their departure from Sarajevo. Before they could cross the magical border that separates their impoverished land from the seeming sanctuary of McWorld, Jihad caught up to them. Their bodies lay along the riverbank, riddled with bullets from anonymous snipers for whom safe passage signaled an invitation to target practice. The murdered young lovers, as befits émigrés to McWorld, were clothed in jeans and sneakers. So too, one imagines, were their murderers.

Further east, tourists seeking a piece of old Russia that does not take them too far   37 from MTV can find traditional Matryoshka nesting dolls (that fit one inside the other) featuring the nontraditional visages of (from largest to smallest) Bruce Springsteen, Madonna, Boy George, Dave Stewart, and Annie Lennox.

In Russia, in India, in Bosnia, in Japan, and in France too, modern history then   38 leans both ways: toward the meretricious inevitability of McWorld, but also into Jihad's stiff winds, heaving to and fro and giving heart both to the Panglossians and the Pandoras, sometimes for the very same reasons. The Panglossians bank on EuroDisney and Microsoft, while the Pandoras await nihilism and a world in Pandaemonium. Yet McWorld and Jihad do not really force a choice between such polarized scenarios. Together, they are likely to produce some stifling amalgam of the two suspended in chaos. Antithetical in every detail, Jihad and McWorld nonetheless conspire to undermine our hard-won (if only half-won) civil liberties and the possibility of a global democratic future. In the short run the forces of Jihad, noisier and more obviously nihilistic than those of McWorld, are likely to dominate the near future, etching small stories of local tragedy and regional genocide on the face of our times and creating a climate of instability marked by multimicrowars inimical to global integration. But in the long run, the forces of McWorld are the forces underlying the slow certain thrust of Western civilization and as such may be unstoppable. Jihad's microwars will hold the headlines well into the next century, making predictions of the end of history look terminally dumb. But McWorld's homogenization is likely to establish a macropeace that favors the triumph of commerce and its markets and to give to those who control information, communication, and entertainment ultimate (if inadvertent) control over human destiny. Unless we can offer an alternative to the struggle between Jihad and McWorld, the epoch on whose threshold we stand—postcommunist, postindustrial, postnational, yet sectarian, fearful, and bigoted—is likely also to be terminally postdemocratic.

Working with the Text

1. The two basic forces about which Barber speaks—Jihad versus McWorld—are not separate or exclusive, but rather interdependent in many ways. What are at least two ways in which he talks about their interdependence? He talks about their relationship as a "dialectic" one. What does he mean by that term? Is it possible for one to exist without the other?

2. In a number of places, Barber focuses on distinctions between capitalism and democracy, critiquing the claims of "capitalism's zealots" that "market freedom entails and even defines democracy." For example, he discusses differing tendencies between capitalism and democracy by saying, "On the level of the individual, capitalism seeks consumers susceptible to the shaping of their needs and the manipulation of their wants while democracy needs citizens autonomous in their thoughts and independent in their deliberative judgments." Elsewhere he paraphrases some "cynics" who suggest that "freedom" and "democracy" are less about the "right to vote" than the "right to shop." What are the possible conflicts and alliances between democracy and capitalism as he describes them and as you see them? We tend to think of them as going hand in hand, but are there contradictions? How do the factors of capitalism and consumerism influence the two tendencies of Jihad and McWorld (tribalism and globalism)? McWorld, he claims, is all about "global markets." In what ways do these global markets enhance freedom, and in what ways do they not?

3. How do the two forces of Jihad and McWorld relate to the issues of freedom and rights? Barber argues that both tribal communities and global markets share an "indifference to civil liberty." He maintains that civil liberties, like citizenship, are the property of nations and that both Jihad and McWorld are hostile to nations and to nationalism. Yet both forces also seem to affect

individual liberties. Which of these two forces results in more or less liberty? What different kinds of freedoms or liberties are implied by his discussion? What is the relationship between group identity and self-determination or between individual liberty and freedom?

4. It is possible to see the Internet and the World Wide Web as embodying and facilitating both of these tendencies. That is, the network of the World Wide Web makes possible both global and tribal connections. In pairs, do some research on the Web and find one example for each tendency. What would you consider a "tribal" tendency or a "global" tendency on the Web? What about "national" interests (the cultural force left out in the tension between Jihad and McWorld)? Are there any ways that the WWW fosters national identity? Or are the identifications one finds on the Web either bigger or smaller than the "national"?

Thinking and Writing: *Critical Questions Revisited*

1. A Sense of Belonging, a Sense of Citizenship

One of the themes running throughout this chapter's readings concerns one's sense of belonging to a larger social, political, or cultural community. To whom or to what do you feel as if you belong? Where is your sense of loyalty and allegiance? Do you have a sense of belonging to your state? Your region of the country? Your country of citizenship? What about other groups? In a personal essay explore your own sense of belonging and citizenship and analyze why you feel the way you do. Are there potential conflicts in your loyalties? Do you have a hierarchy of belonging? That is, do you consider one of your attachments or allegiances as more important than another?

2. Group Identity Versus National Identity

In many ways throughout this chapter's readings, there are points of conflict between the phenomenon of *group identity* and what we traditionally think of as *national identity* in terms of the whole United States. Explore some of the ways that this potential conflict takes shape. Do you agree with Lewis Lapham that the tendency to qualify the noun *American* with adjectives like *gay, African,* or *Jewish* makes a "mockery of the democratic spirit"? What are some examples of growing group consciousness in the United States? Are these examples of *group consciousness* or *cultural nationalisms* a response to certain pressures to conform to a sense of national identity? Or, as Elaine Kim suggests in the case of Korean Americans, is group consciousness a response to being excluded from national identity? That is, does group consciousness give rise to racist responses in the name of national and cultural identity, or do racist and exclusionist responses increase group consciousness? Use at least two examples drawn from this chapter or from your own knowledge to elaborate further.

3. The United States and Global Culture

One of the key themes of this chapter is the relationship between the United States and the rest of the world. That relationship is getting increasingly complex and is characterized not only by the United States' increased involvement around the globe, but also by the ever-increasing global nature of the society inside the United States. Yet, of course, the United States has always been a "global crossroads," and from its very roots has been a "multicultural" nation. In an essay explore one or more aspects of the United States as a global crossroads and its involvement with global culture. Specifically, look at some conflict or tension that seems to exist at the root of that exchange between an American nation and its global character. How has America's multicultural character always defined its ideals, and vice versa? In what ways have American values and ideals been at odds with multiculturalism as much as consonant with it? How is America's multicultural character related to its multinational interests?

4. Economics and Culture

Many of the writers in this chapter focus on the interrelationship between economic concerns, on the one hand, and cultural concerns, on the other. When considering the United States and the countries along its border, writers like Anzaldúa and Gómez-Peña focus on the way that cultural mixing in the borderlands becomes an outward manifestation of the economic interdependence between the two countries. Similarly, the writers who focus on the new global economy, such as Greider and Barber, discuss a number of ways that global economic forces conflict with local customs and culture. At times economic and cultural values can be at odds, just as economic values about capitalism do not necessarily imply parallel support for the principles of democratic freedom. Write an essay in which you explore how economic values and cultural values are interdependent—either mutually reinforcing or in direct conflict. Find examples in the readings and, if you like, supplement these with examples from U.S. society that you've observed.

How do economic considerations drive cultural values and structures? When are they at odds? Does economic success for U.S. immigrants, for example, mean a certain level of cultural loss? Does economic success for so-called "Third World" countries in the new global economy mean a certain level of cultural loss, as you surmise from these readings? How would you pursue this question for further research? Do American attitudes about Third World cultures reflect the level of economic interdependence that American society shares with them?

5. Hybrid Culture and Cultural Purity

One central anxiety that runs through many of these readings is the tension between cultural mixing (or hybrid culture) and cultural purity. The writers in this chapter approach this issue in many different ways—whether from the standpoint of the hybrid culture that has developed along the United States–Mexico border, in Afrocentric beliefs in a unified cultural origin, or in the tensions between American national unity (and cultural conformity) and the apparent resistance to it by some immigrant groups. At the heart of these tensions are often the ideas that "culture" is something homogenous and that a society that is heterogeneous could only be threatening to cultural identity. Traditionally, racial and ethnic mixing is often seen as degraded and dangerous. Yet on the other hand, many writers look for an alternative interpretation by trying to imagine culture as something "plural" rather than "singular," or as something that can be both coherent and diverse. In an essay write about this very central conflict between cultural hybridity and cultural purity. How central is this conflict to American values and ideals? Is it part of the American vision to have a "pure" culture? This needn't necessarily mean that it is not an ideal of American society to have diversity, but rather that such diversity is not imagined as being a kind with significant social differences. To what extent does American society value the ideas of a hybrid culture and cultural purity? Can you see these issues at work in various current events, such as the California immigration legislation of recent years or the debates about English as the official national language?

6. Individual Liberty, Local Rights, and Community Values

Throughout this chapter's readings are many questions about the fate of individual liberty, civil rights, and local, community values. Although we might think of these concepts as all positive and going hand in hand, there are many examples presented throughout the readings about possible conflicts and contradictions. For example, some of the writers raise the possibility that individual rights, which are generally guaranteed as civil rights, come from one's relationship to national government, and that group self-determination tends to value the rights of the group over the liberty of the individual. Thinking about international situations, we can see that there are different kinds of potential conflicts between individual freedom to improve oneself and the values of the local community. In an essay explore the idea of individual rights in a changing world.

How are individual rights increasing or decreasing within American society as group consciousness and identity politics define much of that society? Do you think individualism and individual rights matter less and less? What about the Internet? How are new online technologies advancing the role of individuals and democracy? Do online technologies give a stronger voice to individuals over groups? In what ways are integration and assimilation at odds with the power of communities?

CREDITS

TEXT

Sherman Alexie. "Family Portrait" from *The Lone Ranger and Tonto Fistfight in Heaven* by Sherman Alexie. Copyright © 1993 by Sherman Alexie. Used by permission of Grove/Atlantic, Inc.

Benedict Andersen. From "Imagined Communities" by Benedict Andersen from *Imagined Communities: Reflections on the Origins and Spread of Nationalism,* Verso, 1983. Reprinted by permission of Verso.

Gloria Anzaldúa. From *Borderlands/La Frontera: The New Mestiza,* © 1987 by Gloria Anzaldúa. Reprinted with permission from aunt lute books.

K. Anthony Appiah. "The Multicultural Mistake" by K. Anthony Appiah from *New York Review of Books* (October 9, 1997). Reprinted with permission from *The New York Review of Books.* Copyright © 1997 NYREV, Inc.

Toni Cade Bambara. From *Gorilla, My Love* by Toni Cade Bambara. Copyright © 1972 by Toni Cade Bambara. Reprinted by permission of Random House, Inc.

Russell Banks. "The Visitor" by Russell Banks found in *Disorderly Conduct: The VLS [Voice Literary Supplement] Fiction Reader,* New York: Serpent's Tail, 1991. Reprinted by permission of Ellen Levine Literary Agency, Inc. Copyright © 1988 by Russell Banks.

Benjamin R. Barber. From *Jihad vs. McWorld* by Benjamin R. Barber. Copyright © 1995 by Benjamin R. Barber. Reprinted by permission of Times Books, a division of Random House, Inc.

Robert F. Berkhofer, Jr. From *The White Man's Indian* by Robert F. Berkhofer, Jr. Copyright © 1978 by Robert F. Berkhofer, Jr. Reprinted by permission of Alfred A. Knopf Inc.

Elizabeth Bishop. "In the Waiting Room" from *The Complete Poems 1927–1979* by Elizabeth Bishop. Copyright © 1979, 1983 by Alice Helen Methfessel. Reprinted by permission of Farrar, Straus & Giroux, Inc.

Clark Blaise. "Border as Fiction" by Clark Blaise from *The Thinking Heart: Best Canadian Essays,* ed. George Galt. Reprinted by permission of Clark Blaise.

Robert Blauner. "Talking Past Each Other: Black and White Languages About Race" by Robert Blauner, reprinted with permission from *The American Prospect* 10 Summer. Copyright 1992 The American Prospect, P. O. Box 383080, Cambridge, MA 02138. All rights reserved.

Marianne Boruch. "The Quiet House" by Marianne Boruch has appeared in *Townships,* edited by Michael Martone, University of Iowa Press, 1992, and *Poetry's Old Air,* University of Michigan Press, 1995. Reprinted by permission of the author.

Ivette Chavarria. "Cooking Culture—The Tamale" by Ivette Chavarria. Reprinted by permission.

Chrystos. "I Have Not Signed a Treaty with the United States" by Chrystos first published in *Not Vanishing,* Press Gang: Vancouver, B.C., 1988. Reprinted by permission of the poet.

Michelle Cliff. "Screen Memory" from *Bodies of Water* by Michelle Cliff. Copyright © 1990 by Michelle Cliff. Used by permission of Dutton, a division of Penguin Putnam Inc.

IMAGE PORTFOLIO

Plate 1: *Turnabout Map,* Jesse Levine/Laguna Sales.

Plate 2: *La Fruta del Diablo,* mural by Professor Patricia Rodriguez and her students: Salvador Chavarin, Brock Essick, Patricia Fernandez, Diana Ferreira, Maria Jacobo, Wesley Maas, Pedro Mejinez, Tamora Schoenberg, and Mariela Vargas.

Plate 3: *Studio City, California,* June 1982 by Joel Sternfeld. Copyright Joel Sternfeld, courtesy PaceWildensteinMacGill.

Plate 4: *Familiar Names and Not-so-Familiar Faces,* 1985 by Lynette Molnar.

Plate 5: *The Bronx, New York,* sculpture by John Ahearn and Rigoberto Torres, November, 1982. Copyright Joel Sternfeld, courtesy PaceWildensteinMacGill.

Plate 6: *Mr. Lee's House,* by Margaret Morton.

Plate 7: *Tom, Manhattan,* 1988 by Eugene Richards.

Plate 8: *Sewer Grate,* 1989 by Mario Lamont.

Plate 9: *Street Arabs in the Area of Mulberry Street,* c. 1889 by Jacob A. Riis (Jacob A. Riis Collection, Museum of the City of New York), Accession No. Riis 123.

Plate 10: *Bird,* 1990 by Charlene Williams.

Plate 12: *Defining Moments #4: Kwang Ju Massacre,* by Yong Soon Min.

Plate 13: *American Progress,* 1872 by John Gast (Library of Congress).

Plate 14: IBM ad, courtesy, IBM Corporation.

Plate 15: *Biblical Times, New York City, 1987/93,* by Pedro Meyer.

Plate 16: *Biblical Times* [annotated] from *Truths and Fictions: A Journal from Documentary to Digital Photography* by Pedro Meyer.

INDEX